Annual Update

INTRODUCTION

One of the problems that textbook authors face is that events in the real world move more rapidly than textbook revision cycles. Most textbooks are revised on a three-year cycle, and yet new research arrives in a continuous stream. One of the goals that we have always strived to meet for this book has been to make it as up-to-date and relevant as possible. Accordingly, we have decided to write a postscript that will be included in new printings of each edition. The objective of the postscript is to alert the reader to significant new research that has implications for how we should be thinking about strategy.

NEW RESEARCH STREAMS AND THEIR IMPLICATIONS FOR STRATEGY

In this section of the Annual Update, we review four streams of research in the strategy literature that have received increasing attention over the last two years and are having an important influence on management practice. The first stream of research, which we will consider under the heading "The Innovator's Dilemma," is based on the work of Clayton Christensen, among others. This work deals with the manner in which technological innovations can revolutionize industry structure and present incumbent enterprises with difficult strategic challenges while giving new ventures that pursue the correct strategy the opportunity to rise to market dominance. This is a relevant topic for review given the rapid rate of technological change that now confronts modern businesses. New technologies, including Internet-based commerce, optical communications equipment, hand-held computers, wireless technologies, biotechnology, and genomics, are upsetting the status quo in many industries. The work of Christensen and others can help us understand the implications of these events and hence make better strategic decisions.

The second stream of research we will review looks at how companies faced with uncertainty about the future can maintain their strategic flexibility by taking a real options approach to strategic decision making. It is linked to the first stream of research, for rapid technological change is a major producer of uncertainty in the real world. The exploration of real options is a topic that initially was confined to the academic literature. However, in recent years companies like Merck and Microsoft have embraced a real options methodology and are using it to evaluate their strategic decisions and maintain flexibility in the face of the uncertainty generated by technological change.

The third stream of research looks at the strategies that companies need to pursue to win a format war. A **format war** occurs when two competing and incompatible technologies vie for market acceptance and different companies are backing different technologies. A classic example was the format war between Sony and Matsushita to establish their rival formats for videocassette recorders as the dominant design in the marketplace. Sony championed the Betamax format and Matsushita the VHS format. In the end, Matsushita won this format war, and Sony was left with zero market share. Format wars are an increasingly important aspect of competition in many high-technology industries, including consumer electronics, computers, and telecommunications. In this Annual Update, we draw on recent research to discuss the strategies companies can adopt to win a format war.

Finally, we explore some specific ways in which new information technologies affect strategy formulation and implementation. We focus on how new computer software and hardware are changing the way organizations operate and the nature of the value chain they confront. Recent developments both inside and among organizations are reviewed.

These four streams of research cover material that assumes knowledge of many of the topics covered in the first half of the book. To get the most out of this new material, we suggest that you read this update after you have worked your way through at least the first six chapters of the text.

The Innovator's Dilemma

Clayton Christensen explores how new technologies cause great firms to fail.[1] Christensen's approach is historical; he has carefully documented the development of a number of industries over long periods of time. The patterns he has uncovered are quite alarming and have important implications for strategy.

Innovation as the Engine of Change Christensen's starting point is the widely accepted observation that technological innovations can revolutionize industry structure and may lead to the decline of incumbent firms. A well-known example is the computer industry. The arrival of the personal computer in the late 1970s triggered a number of changes in the industry that ultimately led to the demise of incumbents such as IBM, Digital Equipment Corporation (DEC), and Wang Computers, and the rise of new entrants such as Microsoft, Intel, Seagate, Micron Technology, Apple, Dell, and Compaq. Prior to the arrival of the personal computer, the industry was dominated by vertically integrated enterprises such as IBM that sold mainframe or mid-range computers, to corporate or government buyers. These enterprises manufactured many of the hardware components that went into the computers, including central processing units, memory chips, and storage devices such as disk drives. They also developed proprietary operating systems and applications software to go with those computers, and sold the machines directly to customers using their own sales force.

The PC changed all of this. Because it was based on "open standards," the PC led to the fragmentation (de-integration) of the industry, with different companies focusing on different segments of the industry value chain. Thus, Microsoft produced the operating system and applications software, Seagate produced storage devices (disk drives), Intel manufactured microprocessors, Micron manufactured memory chips, and Dell and Compaq assembled the personal computers and also the servers that sat at the hubs of networks. The PC was initially sold through a new distribution channel (retail stores) to a new customer group (individuals or departments in businesses rather than centralized corporate buyers). The PC subsequently grew up to become an indispensable business tool and a mass market consumer appliance that was connected with other PCs and servers through networks based on Internet protocols. As this process unfolded, the incumbent firms of the pre-PC era went into decline, while new entrants rose to dominance with the growth of the new technology.

The Decline of Incumbents One question Christensen focuses on is "Why do incumbent firms often decline following the introduction of radical new technology?" The answer uncovered through his research is that such incumbent firms listen closely to their customers, and their customers do not want the new technology, at least not initially. Thus, the incumbents decide not to invest in the new technology, or to make it a low priority. Subsequently, the new technology often increases rapidly in functionality so that ultimately the firms' customers change their minds and decide they do want it. By this point, however, it is not the incumbent firms that lead in the development and commercialization of the new technology, but the new entrants. At this juncture, the long-established customers of the incumbents turn to the new entrants, leaving the incumbents to play catch-up.

The mechanical excavator industry provides a good example of this process. Excavators are used to dig out foundations for large buildings, create trenches to lay large pipes for sewers and the like, and dig out foundations and trenches for residential construction and small trenches for farm work. Prior to the 1940s, the dominant technology used to manipulate the bucket on a mechanical excavator was based on a system of cables and pulleys. Although these mechanical systems could lift large buckets of earth, the excavators themselves were quite large, cumbersome, and expensive. Thus, they were rarely used to dig small trenches for house foundations, irrigation ditches for farmers, and the like. In most cases, these small trenches were dug by hand.

In the 1940s a new technology made its appearance—hydraulics. In theory, hydraulic systems had certain advantages over the established cable-and-pulley systems. Most important, their energy efficiency was higher. This meant that for a given bucket size, a smaller engine would be required using a hydraulic system. However, the initial hydraulic systems also had drawbacks. The seals on hydraulic cylinders were prone to leak under high pressure, effectively limiting the size of bucket that could be lifted using hydraulics. Notwithstanding this drawback, when hydraulics first appeared many incumbent firms in the mechanical excavation industry took the technology seriously enough to ask their primary customers whether they would be interested in products based on hydraulics. Since the primary customers of incumbents needed excavators with large buckets to dig out the foundations for buildings and large trenches, their reply was negative. For this customer set, the hydraulic systems of the 1940s were not reliable enough or powerful enough. Consequently, after consulting their customers, incumbent firms took the strategic decision not to invest in hydraulics. Instead, they continued to produce excavation equipment based on the dominant cable-and-pulley technology.

It was left to a number of new entrants to pioneer hydraulic excavation equipment. Because of the limits on bucket size imposed by the "seal problem," these companies initially focused on a poorly served niche in the market that could make use of small buckets—residential contractors and farmers. These new entrants included J. I. Case, John Deere, and Caterpillar. Over time, these new entrants were able to solve the engineering problems associated with weak hydraulic seals. As they did so, they manufactured excavators with larger buckets. Ultimately, these companies invaded the market niches served by the old-line incumbents—general contractors who dug the foundations for large buildings, sewers, and so on. At this point, Case, Deere, Caterpillar, and their kin rose to dominance in the industry, while the majority of incumbents from the prior era lost share. Most ultimately went out of business.

The message of this story is that the incumbent manufacturers of mechanical excavation equipment went out of business partly because they listened to their customers too closely! Neither they nor their customers appreciated the fact that like all new technologies, the efficacy of hydraulics would improve over time, allowing the technology to be used for applications that initially were out of reach. Thus, it was left to new entrants to commercialize the new technology. Over time, these new entrants moved into the market segments once dominated by incumbents.

Disruptive Technology The story of the mechanical excavation industry is not unique. Christensen has documented similar developments in a number of other industries, including the computer and steel industries. Christensen uses the term **disruptive technology** to refer to a technology that gets its start outside the mainstream of a market and then, as its functionality improves over time, invades the main market. Such a technology is disruptive because it revolutionizes industry structure, reshaping the industry value chain and leading to the decline of incumbent firms.

Generalizing from industry studies, Christensen makes a number of points. First, he notes that initially, the functionality of new technologies is often very limited. Thus, the early hydraulic excavators could lift only small buckets. Similarly, the limited power of the early personal computers reduced their appeal to information system professionals in large corporations. However, as in the case of hydraulics and the personal computer, the performance of new technologies typically improves rapidly over time as basic engineering problems are solved.

Richard Foster has formalized the relationship between the performance of a technology and time in terms of what he calls the *technology S-curve* (see Figure 1).[2] This curve shows the relationship over time of *cumulative* investments in R&D and the performance (or functionality) of a given technology. Early in its evolution, R&D investments in the new technology tend to yield rapid improvements in performance as basic engineering problems are solved. After a time, however, diminishing returns to R&D begin to set in, the rate of performance improvement slows down, and the technology starts to approach its natural limit where further advances are not possible. For example, one can argue that there was more improvement in the first fifty years of the commercial aerospace business following the pioneering flight by the Wright Brothers than there was in the second fifty years. Indeed, the world's largest commercial jet aircraft, the Boeing 747, is based on a 1960s design, as is the world's fastest commercial jet aircraft, the Concorde.

Christensen argues that initially, many incumbents tend to ignore or underinvest in new technologies. One reason is negative feedback from established customers, who themselves

FIGURE 1:

The Technology S-Curve

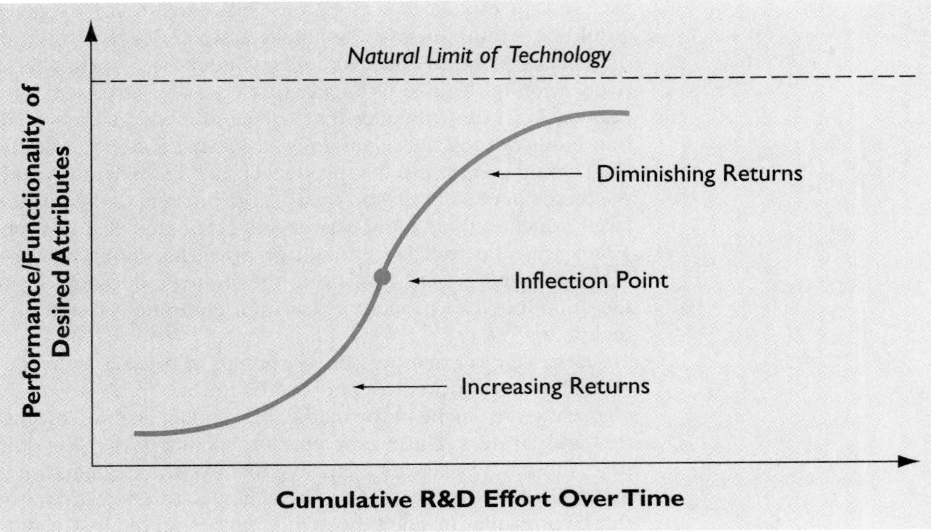

cannot see a need for the new technology given its limited functionality. In terms of the technology S-curve, the new technology initially delivers fewer of the desired performance benefits than the established technology (see Figure 2) and thus is not favored by established customers. Because the new technology initially has limited appeal to established customers, the revenue stream from products incorporating that technology is projected to be very small and, consequently, not worth going after. The dominant attitude of incumbents seems to be: "It's a small market, it's not worth our bother."

As a consequence, it is often left to new entrants to commercialize new technologies. New entrants typically do so by focusing on small, out-of-the-way niches that are poorly served by incumbent enterprises and where customers are looking for different attributes. Thus, Caterpillar, now the dominant firm in the market for excavation equipment, got its start by focusing on the needs of farmers, a niche that the incumbent firms of the time generally ignored. Similarly, Microsoft got its start in 1975 by writing computer-programming software for hobbyists to run on the early personal computers, which again was a market of no interest to dominant enterprises of the mainframe era such as IBM. However, as the functionality of a technology improves over time, its performance attributes improve, its applications

FIGURE 2:

Technology S-Curves

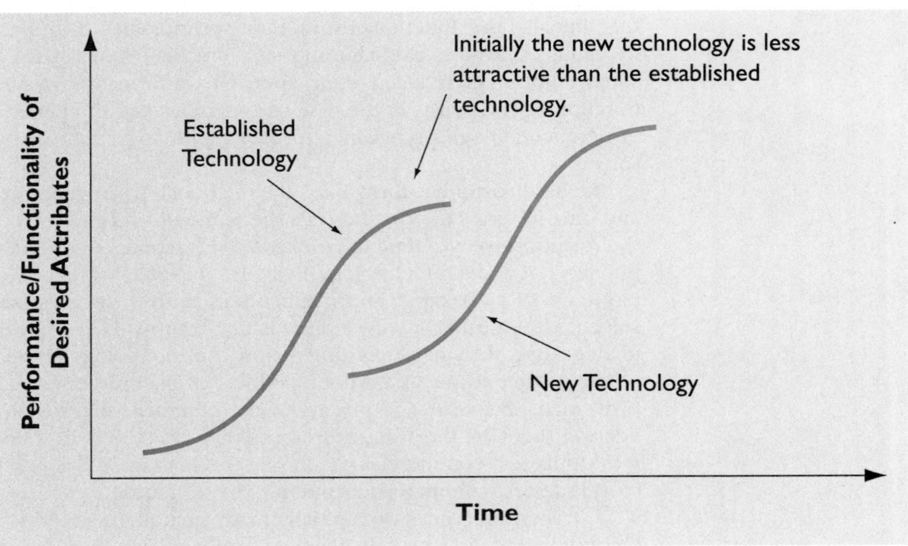

broaden, and it begins to attract the attention of the customer set that originally ignored it. Thus, by the 1960s general contractors were suddenly expressing interest in hydraulic excavators, and by the early 1990s chief information officers had as their major priority the establishment of companywide computer networks based on the personal computer and servers that used PC technology. At this point, it is the new entrants that are best positioned to serve the needs of this long-established customer set, not the old incumbents that failed to invest in the new technology.

Christensen takes this argument one step further, however. He notes that a new network of suppliers and distributors—a new value chain—typically grows up around the new entrants. Just as incumbent firms often initially ignore disruptive technology, so do their suppliers and distributors. This creates an opportunity for new suppliers and distributors to enter the market to serve the new entrants. As the new entrants grow, so does the associated network. Ultimately, Christensen suggests, the new entrants and their network may replace not only established enterprises, but also the entire value chain associated with incumbent enterprises. So, for example, as the PC grew in importance in the computer industry, not only did the primary PC manufacturers grow with the market; so did their network of component part suppliers, distributors, and providers of complementary products such as application software, printers, and modems. Taken to its logical extreme, this view suggests that disruptive technologies may result in the demise of the entire industry value chain associated with incumbent enterprises and the emergence of a new value chain associated with the new entrants.

Strategic Implications for Incumbents What are the strategic implications of this story for incumbents? First, it is important to recognize that while Christensen has uncovered an important tendency, it is by no means written in stone that all incumbents are doomed to fail when faced with disruptive technologies. After all, although IBM was the dominant firm in the pre-PC era, it was also one of the early movers in the PC market. True, despite its entry into the PC marketplace, IBM remained focused on mainframes, and true, as Christensen's arguments would lead us to expect, the company went through several years of severe financial turmoil. However, IBM was able to cross the abyss created by the emergence of the PC and today has reinvented itself as a provider of e-business software, hardware, and consulting services.

If incumbents are not doomed to failure, what can they do to meet the challenges created by the emergence of disruptive technologies? First, knowledge about how disruptive technologies can revolutionize markets is itself a valuable strategic asset. Many of the incumbents Christensen examined failed because they took a myopic view of the new technology and because they asked their customers the wrong question. Instead of asking, "Are you interested in this new technology?" they should have recognized that the new technology was likely to improve rapidly over time and asked their customers, "Would you be interested in this new technology if it improves its functionality over time?" If they had done this, they might have made very different strategic decisions.

Second, following on from this, it is clearly important for incumbent enterprises to invest in newly emerging technologies that may ultimately become disruptive technologies. Companies have to hedge their bets about new technology. At any given point in time, there may be a swarm of emerging technologies, any one of which might ultimately become a disruptive technology (see Figure 3). Large incumbent companies that are generating significant cash flows can, and often should, establish and fund central R&D operations to invest in and develop such technologies. In addition, they may wish to acquire newly emerging companies that are pioneering potentially disruptive technologies. Cisco Systems, a dominant provider of Internet network equipment, is famous for pursuing this strategy. At the heart of this strategy must lie a recognition by the incumbent enterprise that it is better for the company to develop a disruptive technology, and then cannibalize its established sales base, than to have that sales base taken away by new entrants.

However, Christensen makes the very valid point that even when incumbents do undertake R&D investments in potentially disruptive technologies, they often fail to commercialize those technologies because of internal inertia forces. Christensen argues that in many cases, because the new technology initially promises only incremental revenues, when internal capital resources are constrained, R&D investments aimed at developing the new technology are limited by a lack of capital. While the company may intend to invest in the new technology, in practice those parts of the business that are currently generating the most cash may also

FIGURE 3:

New Technology Swarms

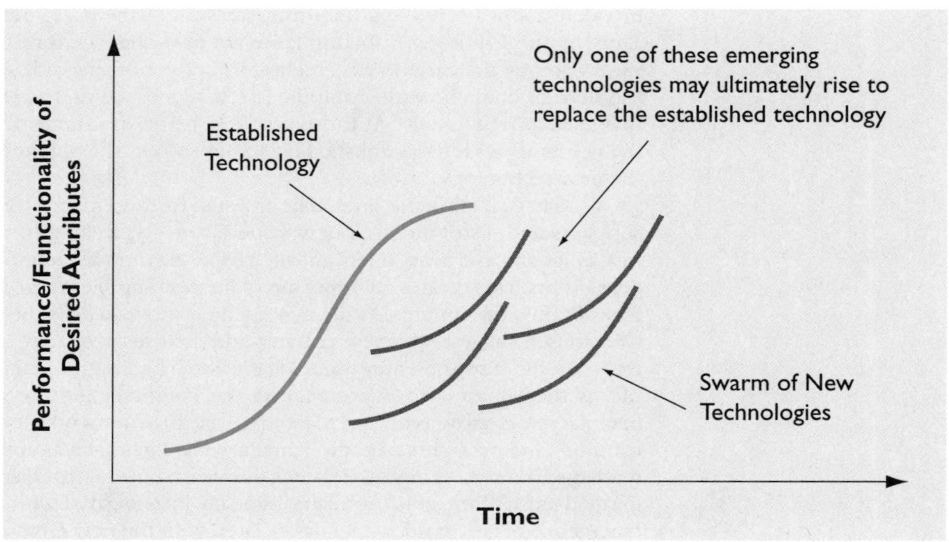

claim that they need the greatest R&D investment to maintain their market position. Particularly early on in the development of a new technology, when it is very unclear what its long-term prospects may be, this can be a powerful argument. The consequence, however, may be that the incumbent fails to build a sufficient competence in the new technology and, if and when the technology emerges as a disruptive technology, the incumbent is successfully challenged by new entrants.

In addition, Christensen states that the commercialization of a new disruptive technology typically requires a radically different value chain with a completely different cost structure. In effect, he is saying that a new disruptive technology requires a new business model. It may require a different manufacturing system, and a different distribution system, a different price structure, and involve very different gross margins and operating margins. Christensen argues that it is almost impossible for two distinct business models to co-exist within the same organization. When companies try to do that, almost inevitably the established business model will suffocate the business model associated with the disruptive technology.

The solution to this problem: Separate out the disruptive technology and place it in its own autonomous operating division. For example, during the early 1980s, Hewlett-Packard (HP) built a very successful laser jet printer business. Then along came ink jet technology. Some in the company believed that ink jet printers would cannibalize sales of laser jets, and consequently argued that HP should not produce ink jets. Fortunately for HP, senior management at the time saw ink jet technology for what it was—a potentially disruptive technology. Far from not investing in this technology, they allocated significant R&D funds toward the commercialization of ink jets. Furthermore, when the technology was ready for market introduction, they established an autonomous ink jet division at a different geographical location with its own manufacturing, marketing, and distribution activities. They accepted that the ink jets division might take sales away from the laser jet division. They decided that it was better to have an HP division cannibalize the sales of another HP division than have those sales cannibalized by another company. Happily for HP, it turns out that ink jets cannibalize only sales of laser jets on the margin, and both have profitable market niches. This happy outcome, however, does not detract from the message of the story: If your company is developing a potentially disruptive technology, the chances of success will be enhanced if it is placed in a stand-alone product division and given its own mandate.

Strategic Implications for New Entrants This stream of work also holds implications for new entrants. The new entrants, or attackers, have several advantages over incumbent enterprises. Internal inertia forces do not hamstring the new entrants. They do not have to worry about product cannibalization issues. They do not have to worry about their established customer base or existing value network. Instead, they can focus like a laser beam on the opportunities offered by the new disruptive technology, ride the S-curve of technology improvement, and grow rapidly with the market for that technology. But this does not mean the new entrants are without problems. They may be constrained by a lack of capital; they have to manage the organizational problems associated with rapid growth; and, perhaps most important, they need to find a way to take their technology from an out-of-the-way niche into the mass market.

Geoffrey Moore has referred to this problem as one of *crossing the chasm*.[3] Moore's point is that a chasm exists between the resources and capabilities required to succeed in a small, emerging market, where disruptive technologies typically take root, and the resources and capabilities required to succeed in the mass market that disruptive technologies invade once they start to mature. A major reason for this is that customers in the mass market are very different from the early adopters typically found in small, emerging markets. They have different needs, look for different things in the product, are often reached by different distribution channels, require different selling techniques and different marketing messages, and demand a different level of after-sales service and support. Again, a good example of this is the development of the market for personal computers. MITS, Southwest Technical Products, Digital Microsystems, and IMSAI dominated the early market for personal computers.[4] If you haven't heard of these companies, that is not surprising. All of them failed to cross the chasm to the mass market and instead went out of business. The reason is that they all produced personal computers that were designed to be used by individuals who could write programming languages. The mass market wanted personal computers that were easy to use, and the early personal computers were anything but that. It was left to Apple Computer to cross the chasm and market the first personal computer designed for the nontechnical user, the Apple II. Subsequently, Compaq, Dell Computer Corporation, and IBM, all of which focused on the mass business and consumer market, dominated the industry.

The message here is that if they are to succeed, new entrants need to focus not just on the niche where the disruptive technology first takes root, but also on the needs of the future mass market. Geoffrey Moore recommends that new entrants try to identify "beachheads" into the mass market. For example, Apple's beachhead into the mass market for personal computers was the educational market, where many of the first adopters of user-friendly personal computers were to be found. At the same time, new entrants need to be careful not to become locked into that beachhead. Again, Apple became so attuned to the needs of the educational market that it failed to build the resources and capabilities—such as a direct corporate sales force—required to succeed in the mass business market. New entrants, therefore, need to pay great attention to the resources and capabilities they are building, and must make sure they are able to serve the needs not only of small, out-of-the-way niches, but also of the emerging mass market. Paradoxically, just as incumbents may be hamstrung by internal inertia forces, so may new entrants be handicapped if they focus myopically on the very early adopters of their technology and fail to recognize the different needs of the mass market as it emerges.

Strategic Flexibility and Real Options

In Chapter 1 of this book, we note that one reason strategic planning often fails to deliver good results is that the real world is characterized by significant uncertainty and complexity. The future, by definition, cannot be known, it can only be guessed at; and even the best-laid strategic plans can run aground on the rocks of unforeseen changes in industry conditions. Uncertainty about the future is always there; it cannot be eradicated. One main source of uncertainty in the modern world, of course, is the rapid rate of technological progress. As should be clear from the last section, rapid technological change can give rise to disruptive technologies that revolutionize industry structure and threaten the very existence of incumbent enterprises. Other common sources of uncertainty are unanticipated moves by competitors, changing political conditions, changing regulatory regimes, or unanticipated macroeconomic shocks, such as the 1997–1998 Asian currency crises and the 2000 oil price shock. The question we will explore in this section is: What can companies do to manage uncertainty and improve their odds of pursuing viable strategies? As we will see, a technique called *real options* can be used to help manage uncertainty.[5]

Uncertainty, Commitments, and Opportunity Costs Uncertainty significantly complicates the process of strategic decision making. The essence of the problem is that pursuing a course of action—a strategy—may require significant *irreversible* commitments, both financial and nonfinancial, before the uncertainty is resolved or reduced to acceptable levels. For example, Airbus is currently evaluating whether to build a super-jumbo jet, the A3XX.[6] If built, this aircraft, the largest commercial jet ever, will carry between 550 and 650 people and compete against Boeing's 747, which can carry a maximum of 520 people. The plane will cost $12 billion to develop. To generate a decent economic return, Airbus will have to sell some 600 A3XX planes by 2020. Airbus estimates worldwide demand for aircraft of more than 400 seats to be 1,200 between 2000 and 2020. On the basis of this estimate, it believes it can sell at least 600 A3XXs. Boeing estimates total worldwide demand for aircraft of more than 400 seats to be about 400 over the same period. Clearly there is a significant difference between the two estimates of market size. This difference is due to uncertainties about a number of variables, including future economic growth rates, fuel prices, and future travel patterns. Boeing assumes that in the future, more people will fly point to point, which reduces demand for very large aircraft; Airbus assumes that a significant number of flights will still be routed through hubs, which increases demand for very large aircraft.

It is also worth noting that Airbus is currently slated to receive $4 billion in European Union subsidies to help build the A3XX. Uncertainties exist here too. The legality of the subsidies may be challenged by the United States at the World Trade Organization. If the subsidies are reduced, Airbus will have to sell significantly more aircraft to make a profit, making the future of the subsidies another source of uncertainty.

At this point in time, these various uncertainties are irreducible. It will be several years before we know whether Boeing or Airbus is right. Thus, Airbus faces the prospect of making a major irreversible commitment now—one that totals $12 billion—long before it knows whether its assumptions are correct! If Airbus is right, the current managers will no doubt be lauded twenty years from now for betting the farm on the A3XX, just as Boeing management is now lauded for betting the company on the 747 in the 1960s. But if Airbus is wrong, the consequence could be financially disastrous. And sometimes companies are wrong.

In the early 1990s, Motorola made a similar bet in the face of uncertainty when it launched the Iridium project.[7] Billed as the world's first global wireless telephone service, Iridium was based on a network of seventy-seven satellites placed in low earth orbit. Motorola believed that the service could be sold to globetrotting business executives. Equipped with a suitable satellite telephone, they would be able to place and receive calls anywhere in the world, whether in the heart of New York City or deep in the Amazon jungle. In November 1998, Iridium switched on the service. By this time, the Iridium project had consumed $5.5 billion in investment and Iridium itself had been spun out of Motorola as an independent company in which Motorola held an 18 percent stake. Iridium's business plan called for 100,000 customers to be signed on by the end of 1998 and 500,000 by late 1999. However, customers were scarce from the outset. By the summer of 1999, Iridium had only 20,000 customers, well short of the half-million it needed to break even. On August 17 1999, Iridium filed for Chapter 11 bankruptcy protection after it defaulted on scheduled payments for $3 billion in bank loans and bonds.

Why did Iridium fail? One problem was that unlike wireless phones, Iridium phones did not work well among high buildings. Another problem was the design of the telephones themselves. The Iridium phones were cumbersome and difficult to use, and came with several attachments whose functions were not immediately obvious. The comparison with miniature wireless phones was not favorable. Then there was the cost of the service. The phones went for $3,000 apiece, and call time was billed at $4 to $9 per minute. Again, the comparison with wireless phones was unfavorable. Most important, in the decade since Iridium was originally conceived, wireless phones had become an attractive, inexpensive, and ubiquitous alternative technology. By 1999, wireless phone service was available in more than 60 countries and there were 300 million cell phone users worldwide. Why did anyone need a cumbersome, expensive, and inefficient Iridium phone when a wireless phone would suffice? As it turned out, nobody did.

As these two examples illustrate, future uncertainties about technology, demand conditions, and the like can scuttle expensive strategic initiatives. Worse still, one must consider the opportunities that a company must forgo once it makes an irreversible commitment to a course of action. Any strategy has associated opportunity costs. If Airbus does decide to invest $12 billion in the A3XX, the investment will obviously limit the firm's ability to pursue other projects. Similarly, Motorola's investment in Iridium limited its ability to invest in other technologies. In a world of limited resources, whenever a company pursues one course of action, it constrains or shuts off other possible courses of action; that is the opportunity cost. Yet, faced with uncertainty, it may be impossible to know which course of action will ultimately turn out to be the best.

Look again at Figure 3, and what do you see? A swarm of emerging technologies. It is quite possible that only one of these technologies will succeed and replace the dominant technology in the industry. This places a company deciding which technology to pursue in a difficult conundrum: In which of the four technologies shown in Figure 3 should it invest? There is no easy answer. At the time the decision must be made, the fog of uncertainty inevitably clouds the decision. So is there a way out of such a conundrum? Is there a way that Airbus can reduce the uncertainty associated with investing in the A3XX? Is there a way that Motorola might have reduced the uncertainty it confronted in 1991 when it initiated the Iridium project? Well, uncertainty cannot be eliminated, but it can be managed. Real options are a tool for managing uncertainty and reducing opportunity costs, thereby maintaining strategic flexibility.

Real Options In financial terms, an **option** is simply the right to purchase an asset at some future date and at a predetermined price. The most familiar use of options is in stock options. For example, imagine the current price of Microsoft stock is $60 a share. Suppose I want to buy 1,000 shares of Microsoft, but I won't have the $60,000 in cash for three months until I receive my royalties from the sale of this book. Imagine also that I think the price of Microsoft stock will be a lot higher in three months; in fact, I think it might be trading at $100 a share in three months. Ideally, I'd like to lock in today's low price and then pay for the stock in three months when I get my next book royalty check. Can I do that? Yes! All I have to do is purchase an option to buy 1,000 shares of Microsoft at $60 a share in three months. Of course, I will have to pay for this option. Let's say it costs $6 a share for a total of $6,000. So it will cost me $66 a share to buy the 1,000 shares in three months, for a grand total of $66,000. If I'm correct about the stock going up to $100, this is a great deal. In effect, it will cost me $66,000 to purchase something worth $100,000.

Of course, the world is full of uncertainties, and I might be wrong. The stock might go a lot higher, in which case I will look really smart! But it could also go a lot lower. Let's say it goes to $30 a share. What then? Do I still have to buy the stock? No, I don't! And here is the important point: *The option gives me the right, but not the obligation, to buy the stock*. Obviously, if the stock falls, I will have lost the $6,000 I paid for the options, but I won't have to pay $60 for a $30 stock. In effect, the purchase of the option allows me to participate in the upside potential of the stock while limiting my downside risk to the cost of the option. The option buys me time—in this case, three months—before I have to make a purchase decision. With time comes flexibility, for if things don't turn out the way I planned due to some uncertain event that would have been hard to predict, I can put my $60,000 elsewhere. If Microsoft stock declines, I don't have to buy it. Or perhaps I can find a better use for my $60,000 in three months, in which case, even if Microsoft goes up somewhat, I may still not want to buy the stock, but instead invest the $60,000 in another company. The option allows me to wait for more information before making my investment decision. It gives me time during which some of the key uncertainties surrounding the future of the company may be resolved due to the unfolding of events. It puts off for three months the opportunity cost associated with sinking $60,000 into Microsoft, as opposed to some other, possibly better investment. The option allows me to keep my options open! It gives me flexibility. Of course, I have to pay for this luxury, but few things in life are free.

Real Options and Strategy So what has all of this to do with strategy? As it turns out, quite a lot. The principal reason is that many strategic investment decisions have characteristics that are similar to an investment in a financial asset, such as a stock, and it might pay to take an options approach toward such a strategic investment.[8] To illustrate this issue, let's consider a pharmaceutical company such as Merck. Let's imagine that Merck has identified a small biotechnology company, BioHope, that is developing a promising drug that might eventually be used to cure Alzheimer's disease. The drug, which is given the name Recall, is just entering phase I clinical trials in human patients. (There are three phases in human clinical trials: phase I, II, and III. Each subsequent phase is bigger and more expensive to undertake. A drug must show beneficial effects in a phase III trial and a favorable safety profile for the Food and Drug Administration to approve its sale.)

Alzheimer's disease is a terrible affliction with no known cure. A treatment for Alzheimer's disease would probably generate sales of several billion dollars a year and profits approaching $1 billion. Merck knows it can purchase BioHope for $600 million. Sounds like a bargain, right? Well, hang on a minute. First, we need to ask: What are the unknowns here? It turns out there are several huge uncertainties. For one thing, history tells us that only one in ten drugs that enters human clinical trials actually makes it through the clinical process and is approved by the Food and Drug Administration (FDA) and marketed (this is the true figure). The hard fact is that when tested in humans, most promising drugs turn out to either not work very well or have nasty side effects. So there is a 90 percent chance that Recall may never see the light of day. Moreover, history also tells us that on average, taking a drug from early clinical trials to market approval can take ten years and cost $500 million in investment (these figures are true too).

Now let's rethink this decision. If Merck purchases BioHope for $600 million, it will then have to pay another $500 million to take the drug through clinical trials and the FDA approval process, and the probability that Recall will actually work is only about 10 percent! Suddenly this does not seem like such a great investment. Paying $1.1 billion and waiting ten years to get a 10 percent chance of something paying off doesn't look like very good odds. Of course, the $500 million will be spread out over ten years, but even so, the total investment is large. Also, we have to think about the opportunity cost here. What else might Merck have done with that $1.1 billion while waiting to see if Recall actually works? Ten years is a long time; all sorts of other opportunities might arise. Does Merck really want to sink $1.1 billion into Recall? That's one heck of an opportunity cost to bear! But wait a minute—let's not forget the upside here. Recall may not work—in fact, it probably won't if history is any guide—but if it does, this will be a huge financial boon to Merck worth billions of dollars. Can we afford to pass on this investment?

At this point, the smart people at Merck are probably asking themselves if there is a better way to deal with this problem. The answer is that there is: real options. In reality, under the leadership of its CFO, Judy Lewent, Merck was one of the very first companies to apply a real options perspective to evaluate decisions like this.[9] The people at Merck realized that investment decisions such as the one about BioHope have characteristics that are analogous to those of straight financial options, such as stock options. Specifically, the upside potential is large, the uncertainties are significant, and making an irreversible commitment to this venture today involves significant opportunity costs. In such cases, rather than making an irreversible commitment today, the company might try to structure a series of sequential investments over time that allow it to participate in the potential upside while minimizing short-term commitments. The idea is to gain more information, thereby reducing uncertainty, and make subsequent investment decisions on the basis of that information.

So here is what Merck could do with BioHope. Rather than purchase BioHope outright, Merck might go to the company and offer an options contract. This contract might be structured as follows. Merck commits to paying $10 million up front to BioHope and a further $290 million in milestone payments spread out over ten years. Then, Merck requests the exclusive right to manufacture, market, and sell Recall if the FDA approves the drug and commit to paying a 20 percent royalty on all sales of Recall to BioHope. The milestone payments might be associated with major events such as the successful completion of phase II clinical trials, the initiation of phase III trials, the successful completion of phase III trials, filing a new-drug application with the FDA, and marketing approval for Recall by the FDA. The milestone payments will get larger as Recall moves through this process and gets closer to the market—that is, as the uncertainty about the eventual outcome is reduced. Merck will reserve the right to terminate the contract if Recall does not successfully pass through any of these milestones (that is, if it fails to show efficacy in one of the trials).

This is an option contract because Merck has to invest only a relatively small amount (initially just $10 million) to get the right to participate in the upside for Recall while hedging against the uncertainty associated with the drug's development. The downside risk is limited to the size of the milestone (option) payments made at any one point in time. Because the contract is structured as an option contract, Merck is able to wait for more information before deciding whether to invest more, thereby maintaining Merck's strategic flexibility and allowing the company to pursue other ventures in the future if a more attractive opportunity comes along. In fact, because Merck does not have to invest too much initially in this venture, it can better leverage its available R&D resources, investing them in a number of different biotech companies that are pursuing different product opportunities.

Of course, just as with a financial option contract, there is a price to be paid here. In this example, Merck will ultimately bear three-fifths of all development costs for Recall, incur all manufacturing, sales, and marketing costs, and be required to pay a 20 percent royalty to BioHope on sales of Recall. Despite these costs, the deal still will bear major benefits for Merck if Recall ultimately makes it to market. The contract also represents a good deal for BioHope, since Merck picks up the majority of the development costs and all the manufacturing, sales, and marketing costs while still giving BioHope a substantial share in the potential upside from Recall.

Although beyond the scope of this book, it should be noted that in practice, sophisticated financial models can be and are used to work out a fair value for real options contracts such as our example.[10] What is important to note here is that a real options perspective can lead management to structure their strategic decisions and investments in a very different way. The perspective forces management to think about the uncertainties associated with a strategic investment (which is always a useful exercise), focuses attention on the opportunity costs of pursuing a strategy, places a premium on gathering more information to reduce uncertainty, and encourages managers to think of different ways to structure strategic investments so that additional commitments are made only after new information reduces uncertainty. Thus, a real options perspective encourages Merck to think about alternatives to purchasing BioHope outright. In fact, like Merck, many pharmaceutical companies now use a real options perspective to structure their investments in biotechnology firms, which helps explain why strategic alliances are so prevalent in this sector of the economy. Many of these "alliances" are based on option contracts that have as their central element a mix of upfront payments and successive milestone payments that are made only if additional information shows that further investment may bear fruit.

Nor is this approach confined to the pharmaceutical and biotechnology sectors of the industry. It is in fact being used by an increasing number of companies in a wide variety of sectors, from oil drilling to computer software. For example, Microsoft now trains all of its financial analysts in real options techniques. To return to the earlier examples of Airbus and Motorola, both of these companies have taken an options perspective. Airbus, for example, will not commit to building the A3XX until it has sixty firm orders for the aircraft. In other words, so far Airbus has only taken an option on producing the A3XX. The cost of that option is the price of all the development work done to date, which runs to about $1 billion. Airbus will commit to spending the other $11 billion only if it gets additional information—in the form of sixty orders—that reduces some of the uncertainties associated with the project. Similarly, Motorola reduced the costs associated with Iridium by spinning out the venture as an independent entity in which Motorola held an 18 percent stake and other investors held the rest. This strategy allowed Motorola to participate in the potential upside associated with Iridium while hedging against the downside risk, which turned out to be substantial.

One final point worth emphasizing here is that a real options perspective encourages companies to not shut down potential investment opportunities too early. It encourages companies to keep their options open until they can collect more information and resolve the uncertainty. Thus, if you look one more time at Figure 3, you will see that four alternative technologies are depicted as vying to replace the established technology. What if only one of these technologies ultimately wins out while the remainder fall by the wayside? A real options perspective would tell us that due to uncertainty, we cannot know early in the game which technology will win out. Therefore, we should try to buy an option on each technology, winnowing down the options only when more information becomes available. What we should not do, according to this perspective, is commit entirely to a single technology too early in the game. Doing so involves a double jeopardy, for not only might our choice be wrong, but by committing to one technology we risk failing to build a capability in the other emerging technologies that might ultimately win. We may be at a distinct disadvantage if our preferred choice fails to come through. Thus, at its core, a real options perspective is about how best to hedge bets among alternative courses of action when confronted with substantial uncertainty about the future. This makes it a very useful technique for evaluating real-world strategic decisions.

Competitive Strategy in Format Wars

As noted earlier, a *format war* occurs when two or more competing and incompatible technological formats vie for market acceptance and different companies back different technologies. Format wars are becoming increasingly common in technology-driven industries where technological standards (that is, formats) are required to ensure a product works seamlessly with its complements. This is the case in the personal computer industry, where it is important for a computer to work well with complements such as software, printers, and modems. In the PC industry, we currently have two formats; a dominant one based on an Intel microprocessor and a Windows operating system, which accounts for about 90 percent of the installed base (the so-called "Wintel" standard or format), and a niche format based on the Macintosh operating system, which accounts for much of the remainder. As most people realize, the two formats are incompatible: Software written for the Mac will not run on a Windows machine, and vice versa. We see the same phenomenon in the video game industry, where games for the Sony PlayStation will not run on a Nintendo game player (again, vice versa). Similarly, a wireless telephone that works in one region of the country may not work in another because of different technological standards.

In Chapter 3 of this book, we explored the topic of network economics. There we noted that in industries where standards are required to ensure that a product works well with its complements, positive feedback loops tend to operate. Specifically, the greater the installed base of a format (such as Wintel PCs), the greater the supply of complementary products, such as application software to run on that format, and the greater the value of that format to consumers, which tends to reinforce demand for the format. Thus, demand begets further demand (see Figure 3.7 in Chapter 3 and the related discussion for further details). Such positive feedback loops reinforce the dominance of the format with the greater installed base and can lead to concentrated market structures. Many argue that it is because of the positive feedback loop at work in the personal computer industry that Microsoft and Intel currently enjoy dominant positions in the markets for PC software and microprocessors, respectively.

More generally, in industries where standards are important and positive feedback loops operate, the market will often "lock in" to a single format or a limited number of formats. If a single company owns the technological format or key aspects of the format, as Microsoft does with the Windows operating system, that company alone can achieve market dominance. In other cases, several companies may jointly develop the format. This occurred with DVD players: Several companies collaborated in an industry association called the DVD Forum to establish a technological standard for DVD equipment.

Winning a Format War From the perspective of a company pioneering a new technological format in a marketplace where positive feedback loops operate, the key question becomes "What strategy should we pursue to establish our format as the dominant one?" Potential competitors to the Wintel standard in computers, such as companies producing PCs and computer servers based on the Linux operating system, must grapple with this question. So must video game producers when they introduce a new format, such as Sony with the PlayStation II, Sega with the Dreamcast, and Microsoft with its X Box. Telecommunications equipment companies have to grapple with this issue when deciding to promote a certain format, such as Qualcomm, which is trying to get a technological format it developed, CDMA, adopted as a global standard for next-generation wireless telephones. Companies selling hand-held computers must grapple with this question; Palm, for example, is trying to establish its Palm operating system for hand-held computers, like the popular Palm series, as the dominant global format against stiff competition from Microsoft with its rival Windows CE format.

At the core, winning a format war requires a company to build the installed base for its format as rapidly as possible, thereby leveraging the positive feedback loop and locking customers into its design. Put differently, it requires the company to somehow jump-start and then accelerate demand for its format to establish it as the industry standard quickly as possible, thereby locking out competing formats. How can a company do this? A number of key strategies and tactics can be adopted to try to achieve this.[11]

Ensure a Supply of Complements It is important for the company to make sure that in addition to the product itself, there is an adequate supply of complements. For example, no one will buy the Sony PlayStation II unless there is an adequate supply of games to run on that machine. Similarly, no one will purchase a Palm VII hand-held computer unless there are enough software applications to run on the Palm VII. Companies normally take two steps to ensure an adequate supply of complements.

First, they may diversify into the production of complements and seed the market with sufficient supply to help jump-start demand for their format. For example, before Sony produced the original PlayStation in the early 1990s, it established its own in-house unit to produce video games for the PlayStation. Then, when it launched the PlayStation, Sony also simultaneously issued sixteen games to run on the machine, giving consumers a reason to purchase the format.

Second, companies may create incentives or make it easy for independent companies to produce complements. Again, consider Sony's tactics with the original PlayStation. Sony licensed the right to produce games to a number of independent game developers, charged game developers a lower royalty than they had to pay to competitors such as Nintendo and Sega, and provided developers with software tools that made it easier for them to develop the games. Thus, the launch of the Sony PlayStation was accompanied by the simultaneous launch of thirty or so games, which quickly helped to stimulate demand for the machine.

Aggressive Pricing and Marketing A common tactic is to adopt a razor-and-razor-blades pricing strategy. This involves pricing the product low to stimulate demand and grow installed base, and then trying to make large profits on the sale of complements, which are priced relatively high. For example, consider Hewlett-Packard's popular ink jet printers. To operate these printers, you must use Hewlett-Packard's ink jet cartridges. Hewlett-Packard typically sells its printers at cost, but it makes significant unit profits on the subsequent sale of replacement cartridges. In this case, the printer is the "razor," which is priced low to stimulate demand, while the cartridges are the "blades," which are priced high to make profits. It is important to realize that the ink jet printer represents a proprietary technological format because only Hewlett-Packard cartridges can be used with the printers and not cartridges designed for competing ink jet printers, such as those sold by Canon. A similar strategy is used in the video game industry, where manufacturers price video game consoles at cost, making profits on the royalties they receive from the sales of games that run on their systems.

With regard to marketing, again the trick is to try to jump-start demand to get an early lead in installed base. Substantial upfront marketing and point-of-sales promotion techniques are often used to try to get potential early adopters to buy a format and set the ball rolling with regard to a positive feedback loop. Again, the Sony PlayStation provides a good example, for Sony co-linked the introduction of the PlayStation with nationwide television advertising aimed at its primary demographic (eighteen- to thirty-four-year-olds) and in-store displays that allowed potential buyers to play games on the machine before making a purchase.

Cooperation with Competitors In several cases, a number of companies have come close to simultaneously introducing competing and incompatible technological formats. A good example is the compact disk. Initially three companies—Sony, Philips, and Telefunken—were developing CD players using different variations of the underlying laser technology. If this situation had persisted, the three companies might have ultimately introduced incompatible technologies into the marketplace. In such a scenario, a CD made for a Philips CD player would not play on a Sony CD player. The near simultaneous introduction of such incompatible technologies can create significant confusion among consumers, and often leads them to delay their purchases. When this happens, the technologies may not take in the marketplace. Recognizing this problem, Sony and Philips decided to join forces and cooperate on development of the technology. Sony contributed its error correction technology, while Philips contributed its laser technology. The result of this cooperation was that momentum among other players in the industry value chain shifted toward the Sony/Philips alliances, and Telefunken was left with little support. Most important, record labels announced that they would support the Sony/Philips format but not the Telefunken format. Telefunken subsequently decided to abandon its efforts to develop CD technology. The cooperation was important because it reduced confusion in the industry and allowed a single format to rise to the fore, which in turn reduced confusion among consumers and speeded up adoption of the technology. The cooperation was a win-win for both Philips and Sony, which eliminated the third competitor (Telefunken) and were able to share in the success of the format.

Licensing of the Format Another often-adopted strategy is to license the format to other enterprises so that they can produce products based on the format. The company that pioneered the format gains from the licensing fees that flow back to it and from the enlarged supply of the product, which in turn can stimulate demand and help accelerate market adoption. This was the strategy that Matsushita adopted with its VHS format for the videocassette recorder. In addition to producing VCRs at its own factory in Osaka, Matsushita let a number of other companies produce VHS format players under license. In direct contrast, Sony decided not to license its competing Betamax format, and produced all Betamax format players itself. One effect of this very different strategy was that VHS players became more widely available. This meant that more people purchased VHS players, which created an incentive for film companies to issue more films on VHS tapes (as opposed to Betamax tapes), which in turn further increased demand for VHS players and hence helped Matsushita to lock in VHS as the dominant format in the marketplace. Meanwhile, Sony, which ironically was first to market, saw its position marginalized by the reduced supply of the critical complement, prerecorded films, and ultimately withdrew Betamax players from the consumer marketplace.

Summary In summary, the correct strategy to pursue in a particular scenario requires that the company consider all of these different strategies and tactics, and pursue those that seem most appropriate given the competitive circumstances prevailing in the industry. While there is no one best mix of strategies and tactics to pursue, it is critical for the company to keep the goal of rapidly growing installed base at the front of its mind. What matters is that the company pick strategies that help to jump-start demand for its format and leverage any positive feedback process that may exist. It is also important for the company not to pursue strategies that have the opposite effect. For example, pricing high to capture profits from early adopters, who tend to be less price sensitive than later adopters, can have the unfortunate effect of slowing down demand growth and letting a more aggressive competitor pick up share and establish its format as the dominant design.

Strategy and Information Technology (IT)

While we have discussed the effects of new information technology on organizations in many of our book's chapters, the rate at which changes in information systems and technologies are affecting organizational strategy and structure deserves more consideration. Total spending on computers and related services doubled from approximately $80 billion in 1984 to more than $160 billion in 1998, and continues to soar. Much of the increase in corporate profits and soaring stock prices in the 1990s has been attributed to its effects.[12] Information systems include many varieties of software platforms and databases. These encompass enterprisewide systems designed to manage all major functions of the organization, provided by companies such as SAP, PeopleSoft, JD Edwards, and so on, to more general-purpose database products targeted toward specific uses, such as the products offered by Oracle, Microsoft, and many others. Information technologies encompass a broad array of communication media and devices that link information systems and people, including voice mail, e-mail, voice conferencing, videoconferencing, the Internet, groupware and corporate intranets, car phones, fax machines, personal digital assistants, and so on. Information systems and information technologies are often inextricably linked and, since it has become conventional to do so, for the rest of this update we will refer to them jointly as information technology (IT).

Information technology affects all aspects of an organization's competitive strategy. First, IT is instrumental in both shaping core capabilities and integrating capabilities into the organization context, making them apparent at all organizational levels. Moreover, IT capabilities can be difficult to imitate since they are present not just in physical information systems but in the organization-specific information technologies developed inside the organization over time. Hence, Wal-Mart's ability to protect what it regards as a core competency in IT by legally blocking the movement of some of its key programmers to dot.coms like Amazon.com.

Second, competitive strategy and the ability to pursue a low-cost and/or differentiation strategy ultimately depends on a firm's ability to increase efficiency, quality, innovation, and customer responsiveness[13]—and IT has a major impact on these sources of competitive advantage. For example, one advantage of IT is knowledge leveraging, which involves sharing and integrating cross-functional expertise through appropriate forms of technology.[14] Benefits from knowledge leveraging include the development of synergies and delivery to customers of value-added services and products, which in turn may result in competitive advantage in the form of product or service differentiation. The way in which Citibank implemented an organizationwide IT to increase responsiveness to customers is instructive. In 2000, Citibank set its goal to be the premier global international financial company. Studying its business processes, it was clear that the main customer complaint was the amount of time customers had to wait for a response to their request, so Citibank set out to solve this problem. Teams of managers examined the way Citibank's current IT worked and then redesigned it to empower employees and reduce the "handoffs" between people and functions. Employees were then given extensive training in operating the new IT system. Citibank has been able to document significant time and cost savings as well as an increase in the level of personalized service it is able to offer its clients, which has led to a significant increase in the number of global customers.[15]

At the corporate level, IT, by reducing the bureaucratic costs associated with managing the relationships between corporate headquarters and divisions and among divisions, has allowed organizations to grow in the sense that the number of decision-making units has increased. IT also facilitates the sharing of knowledge and information not just inside divisions but also among divisions, which may lead to a broader product range for single-business firms and the ability to reap synergies or "product opportunities" for firms engaged in related diversification, such as AOL–Time Warner or Sony.

IT has very important effects on an organization's ability to innovate, an ability that is very important today, as discussed earlier. IT improves the base of knowledge that employees draw on when they engage in problem solving and decision making; it provides a mechanism to promote collaboration and information sharing both inside and across functions and divisions. However, knowledge or information availability alone will not lead to innovation; it is the ability to creatively use knowledge that is the key to promoting innovation and creating competitive advantage. Prahalad and Hamel, for example, suggest that it is not the absolute level of knowledge a firm possesses that leads to competitive advantage, but the speed with which it circulates in the firm.[16] IT produces information synergies and reallocates knowledge resources to the place where they can add the highest value to the organization.

Project-based work provides a vivid example of this process. As a project progresses, the need for particular team members waxes and wanes. Some employees will be part of a project from beginning to end, and others will be asked to participate only at key times when their expertise is required. IT provides management with the real-time capability to monitor project progress and needs and allocates knowledge resources accordingly in an effort to optimize the overall value added of each employee. Traditionally, product design has involved sequential processing across functions, with handoffs as each stage of the process is completed (see Chapter 4). This linear process is being replaced by parallel, concurrent engineering made possible through the application of IT, allowing employees to work simultaneously with continual interaction through electronic communication, which can promote innovation.

At the level of organizational structure, IT is changing organizational forms and promoting innovation inside virtual organizational forms. The real power of IT-enabled virtual organizations emerges when relationships among electronically connected people or firms produce new and/or qualitatively different communication that yields product or process innovation. For example, one type of IT-enabled interorganizational relationship noted by Venkatraman is knowledge leveraging, the sharing and integrating of expertise within a team or partnership through real-time, interconnected IT.[17] Some benefits from these arrangements include the development of cross-functional synergies that may result in competitive advantage in the form of product or service differentiation. Unlike more rigid bureaucratic organizational forms, new IT-enabled forms are viewed as more innovatively responsive to varied environmental pressures such as heightened market volatility or the globalization of business.

IT's effects on interorganizational relations such as joint ventures or strategic alliances is becoming an increasingly important topic given the promise that business-to-business networks hold for increasing organizational efficiency and innovation. For example, four categories of IT-enabled interorganizational relationships are transaction processing (such as EDI), inventory movement (use of IT to move materials or information about inventories across organizational boundaries), process links (connection of interdependent processes such as design and engineering across organizational boundaries), and knowledge leveraging (focuses on sharing and leveraging expertise within a partnership).[18] Similar to the situation inside an organization, one of the most obvious benefits from IT is the cost savings that stem from the ease with which information can be transmitted and utilized between organizations. Interorganizational electronic networks reduce the information costs associated with the search, evaluation, and monitoring of competing suppliers, often making strategic alliances more attractive than vertical integration. In addition, firms that use electronic networks not only reduce costs but, because they increase the pool of potential suppliers, reduce their exposure to opportunism.

It also affects strategic alliances in other ways. For instance, aside from electronically linking backward with suppliers, firms may use IT to link forward in the value chain to connect their operations with those of customers, which reduces their costs and creates a disincentive for customers to seek other suppliers. Increasingly, IT is being used in strategic alliances to break down barriers between industries and to link divergent value chains.[19] An additional perspective on how IT can enhance the effects of interorganizational relationships can be seen in how firms manage various structural parameters of partnerships. Also, specialization between organizations can be facilitated through IT that allows firms to transfer technical knowledge and other resource exchanges.[20]

A final important factor concerns the way IT is implemented in the strategy-making process. The appropriateness of the IT system chosen (and firms do make mistakes), the time needed to implement a technology, the supporting training and other learning processes that facilitate the technology, and so on affect IT's impact on efficiency and innovation. For example, an organization's ability to effectively train its work force to use a given IT will vary widely with its complexity, something many firms have failed to consider.

Thus, in conclusion, the implications of IT for strategy formulation and implementation are still evolving and will continue to do so as new software and hardware reshape competitive strategy. IT is changing the nature of value chain activities both inside and between organizations, affecting all four building blocks of competitive advantage—efficiency, quality, innovation, and responsiveness to customers.

Endnotes

1. See C. M. Christensen, *The Innovator's Dilemma* (Boston: Harvard Business School Press, 1997); C. M.Christensen and M. Overdorf, "Meeting the Challenge of Disruptive Change," *Harvard Business Review* (March–April 2000), 66–77.
2. R. N. Foster, *Innovation: The Attacker's Advantage* (New York: Summit Books, 1986).
3. G. A. Moore; *Crossing the Chasm* (New York: HarperCollins, 1991); G. A. Moore, *Living on the Fault Line* (New York: HarperBusiness, 2000).
4. P. Freiberger and M. Swaine, *Fire in the Valley* (New York: McGraw-Hill, 2000).
5. See T. A. Luehrman, "Strategy as a Portfolio of Real Options," *Harvard Business Review* (September–October, 1998), 89–99; E. D. Beinhocker, "Robust Adaptive Strategies," *Sloan Management Review,* 40 (1999). R. G. McGrath and I. C. MacMillan. "Assessing Technology Projects Using Real Options Reasoning," *Research Technology Management,* 43 (July–August 2000); F. P. Boer, "Valuation of Technology Using 'Real options,'" *Research Technology Management,* 43 (July–August 2000). T. Copland and V. Antikarov, *Real Options: A Practitioner's Guide* (Monitor Books, 2001).
6. "Super-Jumbo Trade War Ahead," *Economist,* May 6, 2000, pp. 63–64.
7. J. N. Sheth and R. Sisodia, "Why Cell Phones Succeeded Where Iridium Failed," *Wall Street Journal,* August 23, 1999, p. A14.
8. See Luehrman, "Strategy as a Portfolio"; Beinhocker. "Robust Adaptive Strategies". McGrath and MacMillan, Assessing Technology Projects"; Boer, "Valuation of Technology"; Copland and Antikarov, "Real Options."
9. N. A. Nichols, "Scientific Management at Merck: An Interview with Judy Lewent," *Harvard Business Review* (January–February 1994) 89–95.
10. For details, see Copland and Antikarov, "Real Options"; Nichols, "Scientific Management at Merck."
11. See C. Shapiro and H. R. Varian, *Information Rules* (Boston: Harvard Business School Press, 1999); Charles W. L. Hill, Establishing a Standard: Competitive Strategy and Technological Standards in Winner Take All Industries," *Academy of Management Executive,* 11 (1997) 7–25, M. A. Shilling, "Technological Lockout: An Integrative Model of the Economic and Strategic Factors Driving Technology Success and Failure," *Academy of Management Review* 23 (1998), 267–285.
12. G. H. Taylor, "Knowledge Companies," In W. E. Halal, ed., *The Infinite Resource* 97–109.
13. M. E. Porter, "What Is Strategy?" *Harvard Business Review* 74 (November–December, 1996); 61–78. C. K. Prahalad, & G. Hamel, "The Core Competence of the Corporation," *Harvard Business Review,* 68 (May-June 1990) 43–59.
14. N. Venkatraman, N. "IT-Enabled Business Transformation: From Automation to Business Scope Redefinition," *Sloan Management Review,* 35 (Winter 1994), 73–87.
15. R. Rucker, "*Citibank Increases Customer Loyalty with Defect-Free Processes," Journal for Quality and Participation* (Fall 2000), 32–36.
16. Prahalad and Hamel, "Core Competence."
17. Venkatraman, "IT-Enabled Business Transformation."
18. Ibid.
19. J. Fulk and G. DeSanctis, "Electronic Communication and Changing Organizational Forms," *Organization Science,* 6 (1996), 337–349.
20. N. Nohria and R. Eccles, Face-to-Face: Making Network Organizations Work," N. Nohria and R. G. Eccles, eds., *Networks and Organizations: Structure, Form, and Action* (Boston: Harvard Business School Press, 1992), 28–908.

Strategic Management Theory

AN INTEGRATED APPROACH

Fifth Edition

Charles W. L. Hill
University of Washington

Gareth R. Jones
Texas A&M University

HOUGHTON MIFFLIN COMPANY
Boston New York

For Alexandra, Elizabeth, Charlotte, and Michelle

C.W.L.H.

For Jennifer, Nicholas, and Julia

G.R.J.

Sponsoring Editor: *George Hoffman*
Senior Associate Editor: *Susan M. Kahn*
Senior Project Editor: *Maria Morelli*
Editorial Assistants: *Cecilia Molinari, Tanius Stamper*
Production/Design Coordinator: *Jennifer Meyer Dare*
Manufacturing Coordinator: *Sally Culler*
Marketing Manager: *Melissa Russell*

Cover image and design: Harold Burch, Harold Burch Design, New York City

Printed in the U.S.A.

Library of Congress Catalog Card number: 00-104963

ISBN: 0-618-14721-7

3456789-QWV-05 04 03 02

Contents

Preface

In its fourth edition, *Strategic Management Theory: An Integrated Approach* became the most widely used strategic management textbook on the market. In every edition we have attracted new users who share with us the concern for currency in text and examples to ensure that cutting edge issues and theories in strategic management are addressed. The increased support for and acceptance of our integrated approach to strategic management has led us to revise the fifth edition of our book to explore the most important current new development affecting strategic management: the effects of the growing use of the Internet and new information technologies on all aspects of strategic management. In addition, the enthusiasm that greeted our interactive approach to involving students in strategic management has also led us to refine our hands-on approach in the section at the end of each chapter called Practicing Strategic Management.

We are grateful to the many instructors using our text, and we have continued to use feedback from them as well as from instructors not using our text to increase the value of *Strategic Management Theory*. We have continued to update our coverage of all the flourishing strategic management literature while keeping the text readable. We have also broadened the offerings in our supplements package for both students and instructors. We believe that together, the text, interactive teaching approach in our Practicing Strategic Management sections, and supplements package provides students and instructors with a learning and teaching experience that is second to none.

COMPREHENSIVE AND UP-TO-DATE COVERAGE

Significant Content Changes

The overall organization of this edition, as noted in Figure 1.1 on page 6, reflects that of previous editions and is designed so that the concepts build upon one another, with early chapters providing a strong foundation for later ones. Though the organization remains familiar, nearly every chapter in the fifth edition has been significantly revised to include coverage of issues related to the effects of new information technologies on company strategy and structure. This theme of the ***new economy***—the information technology complex in all of its facets, including computing, communications, and most obviously, the Internet—is emphasized throughout the text. The ongoing revolution in computing and communications technology, as embodied most vividly by the emergence of the Internet, has major strategic implications for the strategy of enterprises in a wide range of industries, from computers and communications, through financial services, to manufacturing and retailing. The Internet in particular represents a competitive paradigm shift of major proportions.

In this edition we draw on recent contributions to the academic literature to explain the implications of the new economy for competitive strategy. In addition, we have used numerous examples throughout the text to illustrate how the Internet affects businesses in a wide range of industries. For examples of the changes made in this edition to reflect the new economy theme, consider the following.

- The chapter-opening cases and Strategy in Action features in many of the chapters look at enterprises competing in the Internet space and highlight the way new information technologies and the Internet are changing the way companies compete and do business today. For example, Chapter 1 opens with a review of the strategy pursued by Yahoo!; Chapter 3 opens with a discussion of how the Internet is revolutionizing the stockbrokerage industry; and Chapter 4 opens with a discussion of how Cisco Systems has used the Internet to automate much of its customer and service interface, in the process taking hundreds of millions of dollars annually out of its cost structure.
- Within the text, we discuss the changes taking place in the information technology environment. For example, in Chapter 3, which deals with the environment, we now analyze the effects of market externalities on the competitive environment and how these externalities influence business- and corporate-level strategy. We also analyze how externalities affect the ***sources of competitive advantage***—efficiency, quality, innovation, and customer responsiveness—and have continued to revise our explanation of how organizations build strengths in these areas through functional-, business-, and corporate-level strategy. In this chapter, we have also added a section on ***network economics.*** We explain how network effects, positive feedback loops, and switching costs can result in a market being dominated by a single enterprise. A good example is Microsoft's domination of the market for desktop computer operating systems.
- In Chapter 5, which deals with operations, we look at how companies are using Internet-based information systems to dramatically increase their productivity and customer responsiveness.
- In Chapter 7, we look at the strategies that firms can adopt to exploit network effects and establish themselves as market leaders.
- Chapter 10, "Corporate Development," continues to provide students with a clear picture of the major changes that have been taking place in contemporary corporate strategy.
- The chapters on strategy implementation now analyze how new information technologies influence organizational design and build competitive advantage.

This new focus on the Internet and new information technologies brings our integrated picture of the strategic management process up to date.

Although we have included a large amount of theoretical and anecdotal material that relates to the new economy, it is also important to stress that we have continued to update other sections of the book to include recent advances in the literature and to use recent examples. For example:

- In Chapter 1 we have drawn on the work of Daniel Goldman in the new section on ***emotional intelligence*** and its relevance to strategic leadership.
- Also in Chapter 1, we have added a section on the role of ***serendipity and strategy***. We explore the way serendipitous events can drive the strategy of an enterprise.

- In Chapter 3 we have expanded Porter's famous five-forces model to include a sixth force now recognized to be extremely important in many technology-driven industries: the power and vigor of enterprises that supply products that are ***complements*** to those produced by the industry. Porter focuses on substitutes, but ignores complements. See the section on **A Sixth Force: Complementors.**

- In Chapter 5 we have expanded the section on innovation in recognition of the important role that ***continuous innovation*** plays in sustaining a competitive advantage in the modern economy.

- Almost all of the opening cases for each chapter and many of the Strategy in Action features are either completely new or significantly revised.

Throughout the revision, we have been careful to preserve the ***balanced and integrated*** nature of our account of the strategic management process. Moreover, as we added new material, we deleted less current or less important concepts and information to ensure that students would concentrate on the core concepts and issues in the field. We have also paid close attention to retaining the book's readability.

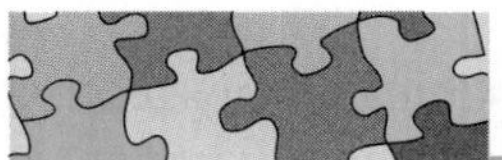

PRACTICING STRATEGIC MANAGEMENT: AN INTERACTIVE APPROACH

We hope you are excited by the hands-on learning possibilities provided by the exercises and assignments in the end-of-chapter ***Practicing Strategic Management*** sections. Following the Chapter Summary and Discussion Questions, each chapter contains the following assignments/exercises:

Small Group Exercise This short (twenty-minute) experiential exercise asks students to divide into groups and discuss a scenario concerning some aspect of strategic management. For example, the scenario in Chapter 11 asks students to discuss how they would reengineer the structure of a greeting cards company to increase the speed of product innovation.

Exploring the Web The Internet exercise requires students to explore a particular web site and answer chapter-related questions. For example, the Chapter 8 assignment requires students to go IBM's web site and analyze its strategy for competing in the global marketplace. This section also asks students to explore the web for relevant sites of their own choosing and answer questions.

Article File As in the last edition, this exercise requires students to research business magazines to identify a company that is facing a particular strategic management problem. For instance, students are asked to locate and research a company pursuing a low-cost or a differentiation strategy, and to describe this company's strategy, its advantages and disadvantages, and the core competencies required to pursue it. Students' presentations of their findings lead to lively class discussions.

Strategic Management Project Students in small groups choose a company to study for the whole semester and then analyze the company using the series of questions provided at the end of every chapter. For example, students might select Ford Motor Co. and, using the series of chapter questions, they will collect information on Ford's top managers, mission, ethical position, domestic and global strategy and structure, and so on. Eventually, students write a case study of their company and present it to the class at the end of the semester. We typically had students present one or more cases early in the semester, but now in our classes we tend to treat the students' own projects as the major class assignment and their case presentations as the climax of the semester's learning experience.

Closing Case Study A short closing case provides an opportunity for a short class discussion on a chapter-related theme.

In creating these exercises it is not our intention to suggest that they should *all* be used for *every* chapter. For example, over a semester an instructor might combine a group strategic management project with five to six article file assignments and five to six exploring the web exercises, while doing eight to ten small group experiential exercises in class.

Another tool we provide in *Strategic Management Theory* is a special section that helps students learn how to effectively analyze and write a case study. This section includes a checklist and explanation of areas to consider, suggested research tools, tips on financial analysis, and guidelines for using the Strategic Management Project.

We have found that our interactive approach to teaching strategic management appeals to students. It also greatly improves the quality of their learning experience. Our approach is more fully discussed in the *Instructor's Resource Manual*.

TEACHING AND LEARNING AIDS

Taken together, the teaching and learning features of *Strategic Management Theory* provide a package that is unsurpassed in its coverage and that supports the integrated approach, which we have taken throughout the book.

For the Instructor

- The **Instructor's Resource Manual**, which users liked so much in the first four editions of *Strategic Management*, has been completely revised. For each chapter we provide a *synopsis*, a list of *teaching objectives*, a *comprehensive lecture outline*, and *answers to discussion questions*. Each of the chapter opening cases also has a corresponding *teaching note* to help guide class discussion. Furthermore, the lecture outlines include summaries of the material in the *Strategy in Action* boxes. Finally, the manual includes comments on the Practicing Strategic Management sections and suggested answers to the Closing Case Discussion Questions.
- The **Test Bank** (in the *Instructor's Resource Manual*) has been revised and offers a set of comprehensive true/false and multiple-choice questions, and the answers to them, for each chapter in the book. The **Computerized Test Bank** allows instructors to generate and change tests easily on the computer. Instructors can edit or add questions, select questions, or generate randomly selected tests. The program will print an answer key appropriate to each version created, and it lets instructors customize the printed appearance of the text. A

call-in test service is also available through Faculty Services. The program also includes the Online Testing System and Gradebook. This feature allows instructors to administer tests via a network system, modem, or personal computer. It also includes a grading function that lets instructors set up a new class; record grades; analyze grades; and produce class and individual statistics.

- A package of **color transparencies** accompanies the book. These include nearly all the figures found in the chapters.
- Accompanying this edition is a set of **PowerPoint® slides**. This lecture tool combines clear, concise text and art to create a total presentation package that follows the concepts found in the text. Instructors with PowerPoint can edit slides and customize them to fit their own course needs; a viewer is included for those without. Slides can also be printed for lecture notes and class distribution.
- **Videos** pertaining to several of the examples and concepts in the text are available to instructors. They help highlight many issues of interest and can be used to spark class discussion.
- An extensive **Web site** contains many features to aid instructors including downloadable files from the *Instructor's Resource Manual*, the downloadable PowerPoint slides, the Video Guide, and sample syllabi. Additional materials on the student Web site may also be of use to instructors.

For the Student

- A student **Web site** provides help for students as they make their way through the course. The Web site features links to the companies highlighted in the boxes and opening and closing cases, links to other sites of general interest while studying strategic management, the Exploring the Web exercises with any updates as necessary to account for the inevitable changes that occur to the relevant sites, and ACE self-tests related to each chapter.
- The Real Deal UpGrade **CD-ROM** includes a glossary of key terms, chapter learning objectives to guide student study, and quizzes to test their understanding of the major concepts.

ACKNOWLEDGMENTS

This book is the product of far more than two authors. We are grateful to George Hoffman, our executive editor, and Melissa Russell, our marketing manager, for their help in promoting and developing the book and for providing us with timely feedback and information from professors and reviewers that have allowed us to shape the book to meet the needs of its intended market. We are also grateful to Susan Kahn, senior development editor, for ably coordinating the planning of our book and for managing the creation of the ancillary materials, and to Maria Morelli for her adept handling of production. We also want to thank the departments of management at the University of Washington and Texas A&M University for providing the setting and atmosphere in which the book could be written, and the students of these universities who reacted to and provided input for many of our ideas. In addition, the following reviewers of this and earlier editions gave us valuable suggestions for improving the manuscript from its original version to its current form:

Ken Armstrong
Anderson University
Kunal Banerji
West Virginia University
Glenn Bassett
University of Bridgeport
Thomas H. Berliner
The University of Texas at Dallas
Richard G. Brandenburg
University of Vermont
Steven Braund
University of Hull
Philip Bromiley
University of Minnesota
Geoffrey Brooks
Western Oregon State College
Lowell Busenitz
University of Houston
Gene R. Conaster
Golden State University
Steven W. Congden
University of Hartford
Catherine M. Daily
Ohio State University
Robert DeFillippi
Suffolk University Sawyer School of Management
Helen Deresky
SUNY—Plattsburgh
Gerald E. Evans
The University of Montana
John Fahy
Trinity College, Dublin
Patricia Feltes
Southwest Missouri State University
Mark Fiegener
Oregon State University
Isaac Fox
Washington State University
Craig Galbraith
University of North Carolina at Wilmington
Scott R. Gallagher
Rutgers University
Eliezer Geisler
Northeastern Illinois University
Gretchen Gemeinhardt
University of Houston
Lynn Godkin
Lamar University
Robert L. Goldberg
Northeastern University
Graham L. Hubbard
University of Minnesota
Tammy G. Hunt
University of North Carolina at Wilmington
James Gaius Ibe
Morris College
W. Grahm Irwin
Miami University
Jonathan L. Johnson
University of Arkansas Walton College of Business Administration
Marios Katsioloudes
University of South Carolina Coastal Carolina College
Robert Keating
University of North Carolina at Wilmington
Geoffrey King
California State University—Fullerton
Rico Lam
University of Oregon
Robert J. Litschert
Virginia Polytechnic Institute and State University
Franz T. Lohrke
Louisiana State University
Lance A. Masters
California State University—San Bernardino
Robert N. McGrath
Embry-Riddle Aeronautical University
Charles Mercer
Drury College
Van Miller
University of Dayton
Joanna Mulholland
West Chester University of Pennsylvania
Francine Newth
Providence College
Paul R. Reed
Sam Houston State University
Rhonda K. Reger
Arizona State University
Malika Richards
Indiana University
Ronald Sanchez
University of Illinois
Joseph A. Schenk
University of Dayton
Brian Shaffer
University of Kentucky
Pradip K. Shukla
Chapman University
Dennis L. Smart
University of Nebraska at Omaha
Barbara Spencer
Clemson University
Lawrence Steenberg
University of Evansville
Kim A. Stewart
University of Denver
Ted Takamura
Warner Pacific College
Bobby Vaught
Southwest Missouri State
Robert P. Vichas
Florida Atlantic University
Daniel L. White
Drexel University
Edgar L. Williams, Jr.
Norfolk State University

Finally, thanks are due to our families for their patience and support during the revision process. We especially thank our wives, Alexandra Hill and Jennifer George, for their ever increasing support and affection.

Charles W. L. Hill
Gareth R. Jones

PART ONE

Introduction to Strategic Management

1. The Strategic Management Process
2. Stakeholders and the Corporate Mission

1 The Strategic Management Process

OPENING CASE

Strategy at Yahoo!

BACK in 1993, Jerry Yang and David Filo were two graduate engineering students at Stanford University. Instead of writing their dissertations, which they probably should have been doing, the two were spending a lot of time surfing the World Wide Web and building lists of their favorite sites. On a whim, they decided to post their list on the Web. They dubbed the site "Jerry's Guide to the World Wide Web." Almost by accident, they had created one of the first Web directories. In doing so, they had solved a pressing need: how to find things on the Web. In 1994, they changed the name of the directory to Yahoo! (http://www.yahoo.com), which is supposed to stand for "Yet Another Hierarchical Officious Oracle," although Filo and Yang insist they selected the name because they considered themselves "yahoos."

By late 1994, Yahoo! was drawing more than 100,000 people a day. The directory had outgrown the limited capacity of the Stanford site, and Yahoo! was borrowing server space from nearby Netscape. Yang and Filo had decided to put their graduate studies on hold while they turned their attention to building Yahoo! into a business. One of their first hires, Srinija Srinivasan, or "ontological yahoo" as she is known within the company, refined and developed the classification scheme that has become the hallmark of Yahoo!'s Web directory. Yang and Filo's business model was to derive revenues from renting advertising space on the pages of the fast-growing directory.

To grow the business, however, they needed capital to fund investments in servers, software development, and classification personnel. A solution came in the form of an investment from Sequoia Capital, a Silicon Valley venture capital firm. As part of the investment package, Sequoia required Yang and Filo to hire an experienced chief executive officer (CEO). The man chosen for the job was Andrew

Koogle, a forty-five-year-old engineer with fifteen years experience in the management of high technology firms, including a stint as president of InterMec, a Seattle-based manufacturer of bar code scanning equipment.

By mid 1996, Koogle was heading a publicly traded company that listed 200,000 Web sites under 20,000 different categories and was being used by 800,000 people per day. This, however, was just the beginning. In conjunction with Yang, Filo, and another "gray-haired" hire—the chief operating officer, Jeffrel Mallett—Koogle crafted a vision of Yahoo! as a global media company whose principal asset would be a major Internet gateway, or portal, that would enable anyone to connect with anything or anybody. Koogle's ambition was to transform Yahoo!'s simple directory service into a conduit for bringing together buyers and sellers, thereby facilitating commercial transactions over the Web (e-commerce). In this vision, Yahoo! would continue to generate revenues from the sale of advertising space on its directory pages, but it would also garner significant revenues from e-commerce transactions by taking a small slice of each transaction executed over its service. The service, Yahoo! Store (http://store.yahoo.com), enables businesses to quickly create, publish and manage secure on-line stores to market and sell goods and services. After launching their store, merchants are included in searches on Yahoo! Shopping (http://shopping.yahoo.com), Yahoo!'s Internet shopping service.

To make this vision a reality, Yahoo! had to become one of the most useful and well-known locations on the Web—in short, it had to become a megabrand. A directory alone would not suffice, no matter how useful. So in order to increase traffic, Yahoo! began to add features that enhanced its appeal to Web users. One aspect of this was to supplement the directory with compelling content. Another was to allow registered users to customize Yahoo! pages to best match their needs. For example, registered Yahoo! users can customize a page in Yahoo!'s financial area so that they can track the value of their personal stock portfolio. The page provides links to message boards, where individual investors can discuss a company's prospects. Other links connect investors to valuable content pertaining to the companies in their stock portfolio, including news reports and commentary, research reports, detailed financial data and each company's Web site.

To build brand awareness, Yahoo! spent heavily on advertising, using radio and television ads targeted at mainstream America. To expand the reach of the service, Yahoo! embarked on a strategy of opening up Yahoo! services around the world. Yahoo! also began to work with content providers and merchants to build their on-line presence, and by extension, to increase the value of Yahoo!'s site to users who could access the content and merchants through Yahoo! Moreover, Yahoo! increased its value to advertisers by enabling them to better target their advertising message to certain demographics. For example, the on-line broker E*Trade advertises heavily on Yahoo!'s financial pages. Such targeted advertising increases the conversion rate or yield associated with advertisements.

The results of this strategy have been quite spectacular. By 1998, the company had 50 million unique users, up from 26 million in the prior year. Some 35 million of these were registered with Yahoo! These users were accessing 167 million Yahoo! pages per day in December 1998. By the end of 1998, 3,800 companies were advertising on Yahoo!'s pages, up from 2,600 in 1997 and 700 in 1996. As of May 1999, some 5,000 merchants were selling products over Yahoo! Shopping, up from 3,500 in December 1998. At the same time, there were eighteen Yahoo!s outside the United States, and Yahoo! could be accessed in twelve languages. The company's revenues had grown from $21.5 million in 1996 to $203 million in 1998. Meanwhile, Yahoo!'s stock price soared from $5 a share in 1996 to a high of $244 a share in early 1999, effectively valuing Yahoo! at a staggering $45 billion and making Yang and Filo billionaires.

Going forward, Yahoo!'s strategy has been characterized by Koogle as "Yahoo! everywhere." To facilitate this, Yahoo! has been developing technology that will enable users to access Yahoo! over a wide range of digital devices, from conventional personal computers to hand-held personal assistants, smart cellular phones, television equipment with set top boxes, and hand-held Web tablets. Yahoo! has also continued to enhance the value of its service and brand by acquiring valuable Web properties. For example, in March 1999, Yahoo! acquired GeoCities, a popular Web service that allows individuals to publish their own home pages and related material on the Web. This was followed in April by the acquisition of Broadcast.com inc, the Web's leading aggregator and broadcaster of streaming audio and video programming. The Broadcast.com acquisition should allow Yahoo! to broadcast audio and video content over the Web, in addition to text, making Yahoo!'s network even more valuable to users.[1]

OVERVIEW

Why do some organizations succeed while others fail? In the fast-evolving world of the Internet, for example, how is it that companies like Yahoo! and AOL have managed to build a strong presence, whereas others, such as Prodigy, Excite, and Compuserve, have not had the same degree of success? In the retail industry, what distinguishes successes such as Wal-Mart from failures such as rival American discount retailer Kmart? Why has Wal-Mart consistently outperformed the industry, even in difficult years, whereas Kmart found itself facing the possibility of bankruptcy in the mid 1990s? In the personal computer industry, what are the factors that differentiate successful firms, such as Dell and Gateway 2000, from the failures, such as AST and Packard Bell, both of which saw their market share slump during the late 1990s? In the market for database software, why have Oracle and Microsoft managed to build strong market positions, whereas rivals such as Informix and Sybase have lost significant market share? In the airline industry, how is it that Southwest Airlines has managed to keep growing its revenues and profits through both good times and bad, whereas TWA has repeatedly flirted with bankruptcy? In the toy industry, what differentiates the successful firms such as Mattel and Hasbro from failures such as Coleco, which rode to fame with the Cabbage Patch Kids only to see sales slump as its brand lost appeal among America's young? How did Sony come to dominate the market for video games with its highly successful PlayStation, whereas former industry leader Sega saw its market share slump from 60 percent in the early 1990s to the low single digits by the end of the decade?

This book argues that the strategies an organization pursues have a major impact on its performance relative to its peers. A **strategy** is an action a company takes to attain one or more of its goals. For most if not all organizations, an overriding goal is to achieve superior performance. Thus, a strategy can often be defined more precisely as *an action a company takes to attain superior performance*. The overriding goal of Yahoo!, for example, is to achieve significant revenue and earnings growth. Yahoo!'s strategies for attaining this goal include maximizing the value of its service to individual Web users, thereby attracting a large volume of Web traffic, which in turn allows the company to garner significant revenues from renting advertising space to merchants and facilitating e-commerce transactions. The company has taken various actions that are consistent with maximizing the value of its service. These include building the best directory on the Web, enabling Yahoo! users to customize their Yahoo! service and post their own home page on the service (hence the acquisition of GeoCities) and providing valuable text, audio, and video content. Yahoo! has been more successful than its peers because it has a well-thought-out and well-executed strategy.

Much of this book is devoted to identifying and describing the pros and cons of the various strategies a company can pursue. Many of these strategies are generic—that is, they apply to all organizations, large or small, manufacturing or service, and profit-seeking or not-for-profit. The aim is to give you a thorough understanding of the analytical techniques and skills necessary to identify and exploit strategies successfully. The first step toward achieving this objective is to give you an overview of the **strategic management process,** that is, the process by which managers choose a set of strategies for the enterprise. By the end of this chapter, you will understand the processes managers use to select strategies for their company, and you will have an appreciation of these processes' strengths and weaknesses.

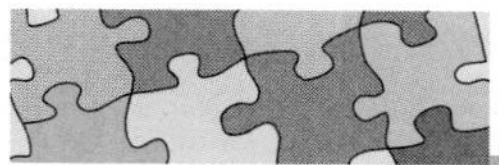

STRATEGIC PLANNING

Ask the average person in the street how an organization chooses its strategy, and the answer will probably be that the strategy is the result of a *rational planning* process orchestrated, if not dominated, by the *top management* of the organization. To a certain extent, this emphasis on a rational planning process dominated by top management reflects the military roots of strategy, with its imagery of generals clustered around a map table with their staff plotting out a strategy for defeating the enemy. This imagery has been propagated in the business literature by a number of writers, who have emphasized that strategy is the outcome of a formal planning process and that top management plays the most important role in this process.[2] The story of Yahoo!, discussed in the Opening Case, provides us with an example of the role of top management in strategy formulation. Koogle, Yahoo!'s CEO, seems to have been the principal strategic architect behind Yahoo!'s transformation from a Web directory into a compelling on-line destination that will connect anyone to anybody or anything.

Although the view of strategy as the product of a rational planning process driven by top management has some basis in reality, it is not the whole story. As we shall see later in the chapter, not all of an organization's strategies result from formal strategic planning exercises. Valuable strategies often emerge from deep within the organization without prior planning. Nevertheless, a consideration of planning is a useful starting point for our journey into the world of strategy. Accordingly, in this section we consider what might be described as a stereotypical strategic planning model.

A Basic Planning Model

The strategic planning process can be broken down into five main steps illustrated in Figure 1.1. You might want to think of Figure 1.1 as a plan of the book, for it also shows how the different chapters relate to the different steps of the strategic planning process. The five steps are (1) selection of the corporate mission and major corporate goals; (2) analysis of the organization's external competitive environment to identify **opportunities** and **threats**; (3) analysis of the organization's internal operating environment to identify the organization's **strengths** and **weaknesses**; (4) selection of strategies that build on the organization's strengths and correct its weaknesses in order to take advantage of external opportunities and counter external threats; and (5) strategy implementation. The task of analyzing the organization's external and internal environment and then selecting an appropriate strategy is normally referred to as **strategy formulation**. In contrast, **strategy implementation** typically involves designing appropriate organizational structures and control systems to put the organization's chosen strategy into action.

Each component illustrated in Figure 1.1 constitutes a *sequential* step in the strategic planning process. Each *cycle* of the planning process begins with a statement of the corporate mission and major corporate goals. The mission statement is followed by external analysis, internal analysis, and strategic choice. The process ends with the design of the organizational structure and control systems necessary to implement the organization's chosen strategy.

Some organizations go through this kind of process every year, although this should not be taken to imply that the organization chooses a new strategy each

FIGURE 1.1

The Main Components of the Strategic Planning Process

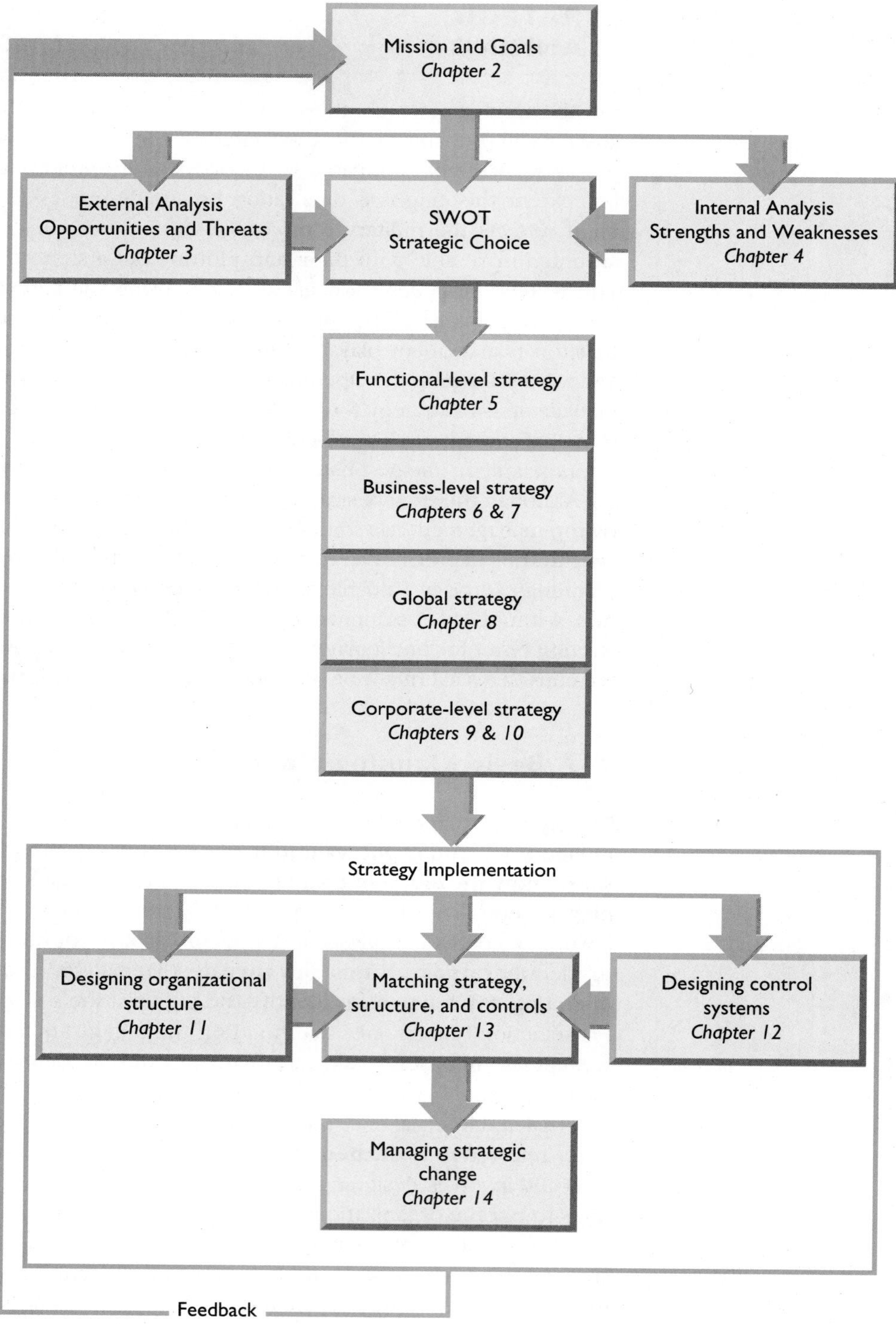

year. In many instances, the result is simply to reaffirm a strategy and structure that is already in place. The strategic plans generated by this kind of process generally cover a one-to-five-year period, with the plan being updated, or "rolled forward," every year. In many organizations, the results of the annual strategic planning process are used as input into the budget process for the coming year. Thus, strategic planning shapes resource allocation within the organization.

Mission and Major Goals

The first component of the strategic management process is defining the mission and major goals of the organization. This topic is covered in depth in Chapter 2. The mission and major goals of an organization provide the context within which strategies are formulated.

The **mission** sets out why the organization exists and what it should be doing. For example, the mission of a national airline might be defined as satisfying the needs of individual and business travelers for high-speed transportation at a reasonable price to all the major population centers of North America. Similarly, the mission of Yahoo! might be defined as "connecting anyone to anybody or anything."

Major goals specify what the organization hopes to fulfill in the medium to long term. Most profit-seeking organizations operate with a hierarchy of goals, in which attaining superior performance is placed at or near the top. Secondary goals are objectives judged necessary by the company if it is to attain superior performance. For example, under the leadership of Jack Welch, General Electric has operated with a secondary goal of being first or second in every major market in which it competes. This secondary goal reflects Welch's belief that building market share is the best way to achieve superior performance. Similarly, a major goal of Coca-Cola has been to put a Coke within an arm's reach of every consumer in the world. If Coca-Cola achieves this goal, superior performance is likely to follow. Not-for-profit organizations typically have a more diverse set of goals.

External Analysis

The second component of the strategic management process is the analysis of the organization's external operating environment. This topic is covered in detail in Chapter 3. The objective of external analysis is to identify strategic *opportunities* and *threats* in the organization's operating environment. Three interrelated environments should be examined at this stage: the immediate, or industry, environment in which the organization operates, the national environment, and the wider macroenvironment.

Analyzing the industry environment requires an assessment of the competitive structure of the organization's industry, including the competitive position of the focal organization and its major rivals, as well as the stage of industry development. Since many markets are now global markets, analyzing the industry environment also means assessing the impact of globalization on competition within an industry. Analyzing the national environment requires an assessment of whether the national context within which a company operates facilitates the attainment of a competitive advantage in the global marketplace. If it does not, then the company might have to consider shifting a significant part of its operations to countries where the national context does facilitate the attainment of a competitive advantage. Analyzing the macroenvironment consists of examining macroeconomic, social, government, legal, international, and technological factors that may affect the organization.

Internal Analysis

Internal analysis, the third component of the strategic management process, serves to pinpoint the *strengths* and *weaknesses* of the organization. Such issues as identifying the quantity and quality of resources available to the organization are considered in Chapter 4, where we probe the sources of competitive advantage. We look at how companies attain a competitive advantage, and we discuss the role of distinctive competencies (unique company strengths), resources, and capabilities in building and sustaining a company's competitive advantage. One conclusion that we reach in Chapter 4 is that building and maintaining a competitive advantage requires a company to achieve superior efficiency, quality, innovation, and customer responsiveness. Company strengths lead to superiority in these areas, whereas company weaknesses translate into inferior performance.

SWOT and Strategic Choice

The next component requires generating a series of strategic alternatives, given the company's internal strengths and weaknesses and its external opportunities and threats. The comparison of **s**trengths, **w**eaknesses, **o**pportunities, and **t**hreats is normally referred to as a **SWOT** analysis.[3] The central purpose of the SWOT analysis is to identify strategies that *align, fit*, or *match* a company's resources and capabilities to the demands of the environment in which the company operates. To put it another way, the purpose of the strategic alternatives generated by a SWOT analysis should be to build on company strengths in order to exploit opportunities and counter threats and to correct company weaknesses.

Strategic choice is the process of choosing among the alternatives generated by a SWOT analysis. The organization has to evaluate various alternatives against each other with respect to their ability to achieve major goals. The strategic alternatives generated can encompass business-level, functional-level, corporate-level, and global strategies. The process of strategic choice requires the organization to identify the set of business-level, functional-level, corporate-level, and global strategies that would best enable it to survive and prosper in the fast-changing and globally competitive environment that characterizes most modern industries.

Business-Level Strategy The business-level strategy of a company encompasses the overall competitive theme that a company chooses to stress, the way it positions itself in the marketplace to gain a competitive advantage, and the different positioning strategies that can be used in different industry settings. The various strategic options available are first introduced in Chapter 4 and then discussed in more detail in Chapter 6. In Chapter 6, we review the pros and cons of three generic business-level strategies: a strategy of **cost leadership**, a strategy of **differentiation**, and a strategy of **focusing** on a particular market niche. Yahoo! pursues a differentiation strategy: the overall competitive theme the company has chosen is to stress differentiating its brand from those of competitors through a combination of marketing and product offering.

In Chapter 7, we build on Chapter 6 to consider the relationship between business-level strategy and industry structure. We concentrate on the different strategic options confronting companies in radically different industry settings, such as the benefits and drawbacks of establishing a first-mover advantage in a newly formed or embryonic industry. We also discuss the role of market signaling, price leadership, and product differentiation for sustaining a competitive advantage in mature industries, and we explore the different strategic options that a company can choose from in a declining industry.

Functional-Level Strategy Competitive advantage stems from a company's ability to attain superior efficiency, quality, innovation, and customer responsiveness—a point made in Chapter 4. In Chapter 5, we examine the different functional-level (operations) strategies that can be employed to achieve these four crucial aims. By functional-level strategies, we mean strategies directed at improving the effectiveness of *operations* within a company, such as manufacturing, marketing, materials management, product development, and customer service.

Global Strategy In today's world of global markets and global competition, achieving a competitive advantage and maximizing company performance increasingly require a company to expand its operations outside its home country. Accordingly, a company must consider the various global strategies it can pursue. In Chapter 8, we assess the benefits and costs of global expansion and examine four different strategies—multidomestic, international, global, and transnational—that a company can adopt to compete in the global marketplace. In addition, that chapter explores the benefits and costs of strategic alliances between global competitors, the different entry modes that can be used to penetrate a foreign market, and the role of host-government policies in influencing a company's choice of global strategy.

Corporate-Level Strategy We deal with the issue of corporate-level strategy in Chapters 9 and 10. An organization's corporate-level strategy must answer this question: What businesses should we be in to maximize the long-run profitability of the organization? For many organizations, competing successfully often means **vertical integration**—integrating its operations either backward into the production of inputs for the company's main operation or forward into the disposal of outputs from the operation. Beyond this, companies that succeed in establishing a sustainable competitive advantage may find that they are generating resources *in excess* of their investment requirements within their primary industry. For such organizations, maximizing long-run profitability may entail **diversification** into new business areas. Accordingly, in Chapter 9, we look closely at the costs and benefits of different diversification strategies. In addition, we examine the role of **strategic alliances** as alternatives to diversification and vertical integration. In Chapter 10, we review the different vehicles that companies use to achieve vertical integration and diversification, including **acquisitions** and **new ventures**. We also consider how diversified companies can **restructure** their portfolio of businesses in order to improve company performance.

Strategy Implementation

Once a company has chosen a strategy to achieve its goals, that strategy then has to be put into action. In this book, we break down the topic of strategy implementation into four main components: (1) designing appropriate organizational structures; (2) designing control systems; (3) matching strategy, structure, and controls; and (4) managing conflict, politics, and change.

Designing Organizational Structure Implementing a strategy requires the allocation of roles and responsibilities for different aspects of that strategy to different managers and subunits within the company. A company's organizational structure maps out roles and responsibilities, along with reporting relationships. In this sense, strategy is implemented through structure. At the toy company Mattel, for example, under CEO Jill Barad, there is a product group for each of Mattel's major brands: Barbie, Hot Wheels, Fisher Price, and Disney license products. Each of these subunits is headed by a vice president, who reports directly to Barad, and each vice president is responsible for ensuring that his or her product group successfully implements the company's brand extension strategy for that particular brand. If an organization's existing structure is not appropriate, given the company's strategy, a new structure may have to be designed. In Chapter 11, we discuss the different kinds of organizational structures that managers can use to implement strategy.

Designing Control Systems Besides choosing a structure, an organization must also establish appropriate organizational control systems. It must decide how best to assess the performance and control the actions of subunits. The options range from market and output controls to bureaucratic controls and control through organizational culture, all of which we tackle in Chapter 12. An organization also needs to decide what kind of reward and incentive systems to set up for employees. Chapter 12 reviews those options as well.

Matching Strategy, Structure, and Controls If it wants to succeed, a company must achieve a *fit,* or *congruence,* among its strategy, structure, and controls.[4] Chapter 13 focuses on the various means toward this end. Since different strategies and environments place different demands on an organization, they call for different structural responses and control systems. For example, a strategy of cost leadership demands that an organization be kept simple (so as to reduce costs) and that operations and controls stress productive efficiency. On the other hand, a strategy of differentiating a company's product by unique technological characteristics generates a need for integrating the company's activities around its technological core and establishing control systems that reward technical creativity.

Managing Strategic Change We live in a world in which the only constant is change. Much of this change is the result of technological progress. In recent years, the way in which technological change can impact established markets has been vividly illustrated by the rise of the Internet and the associated World Wide Web. Web-based commerce is providing a host of new opportunities, while simultaneously threatening to make established business models obsolete. In the stockbrokerage industry, for example, the ability to use the Internet as a conduit for individuals to directly buy and sell stocks without the aid of a stockbroker has propelled the growth of companies such as E*Trade and Charles Schwab. Simultaneously, this change has threatened the established business model of "full-service" stockbrokerage companies such as Merrill Lynch, which have traditionally employed stockbrokers to buy and sell stocks for individuals. Because change is so pervasive, companies that succeed in the long run are those that are able to adapt their strategy and structure to a changing world. In 1999, for example, Merrill Lynch embraced an on-line strategy, even though this will effectively reduce the need for its vast network of stockbrokers. In Chapter 14, we take a close look at the process of managing strategic change and discuss the different tactics that managers can utilize to successfully implement such change.

The Feedback Loop

The feedback loop in Figure 1.1 indicates that strategic planning is an ongoing process. Once a strategy has been implemented, its execution must be monitored to determine the extent to which strategic objectives are actually being achieved. This information passes back to the corporate level through feedback loops. At the corporate level, it is fed into the next round of strategy formulation and implementation. It serves either to reaffirm existing corporate goals and strategies or to suggest changes. For example, when put into practice, a strategic objective may prove to be too optimistic, and so the next time more conservative objectives are set. Alternatively, feedback may reveal that strategic objectives were attainable but implementation was poor. In that case, the next round in strategic management may concentrate more on implementation. Because feedback is an aspect of organizational control, it is considered in detail in Chapter 12.

STRATEGIC MANAGERS

We have already alluded to the fact that, within the context of the traditional strategic planning model, the major responsibility for orchestrating the planning process rests on the shoulders of top managers. But who are these top managers, and what precisely is their strategic role? What about lower-level managers within the organization? What is their role in the strategic management process? In this section, we look at the strategic role of managers at different levels in the organization *through the lens of traditional strategic management theory*. Later in the chapter, we shall modify this view somewhat, but for now it constitutes a useful starting point.

In most modern organizations, there are two types of managers: **general managers** and **operations managers**. General managers are individuals who bear responsibility for the overall performance of the organization or of one of its major self-contained divisions. Their overriding concern is for the health of the *total* organization under their direction. This responsibility puts them in the unique position of directing the total organization in a strategic sense. Operations managers, on the other hand, bear responsibility for specific business functions or operations, such as human resources, purchasing, production, sales, marketing, product development, customer service, accounts, and so on. Their sphere of authority is normally confined to one organizational activity.

A typical multibusiness company has three main levels of management: the corporate level, the business level, and the operational level (see Figure 1.2). General managers are found at the first two of these levels, but their strategic roles differ depending on their sphere of responsibility. Operations managers, too, have a strategic role, though of a different kind. We now examine each of the three levels and the strategic roles assigned to managers within them.

Corporate-Level Managers

The corporate level of management consists of the chief executive officer (CEO), other senior executives, the board of directors, and corporate staff. These individuals occupy the apex of decision making within the organization. The CEO is the main general manager at this level. In consultation with other senior executives, he or she has the strategic role *to oversee* the development of strategies for the total organization. This role includes defining the mission and goals of the organization, determining what businesses it should be in, allocating resources among the different businesses, formulating and implementing strategies that span individual businesses, and providing leadership for the organization.

Consider General Electric. The company is active in a wide range of businesses, including lighting equipment, major appliances, motor and transportation equipment, turbine generators, construction and engineering services, industrial electronics, medical systems, aerospace, and aircraft engines. The main strategic responsibilities of its CEO, Jack Welch, include setting overall strategic objectives, allocating resources among the different business areas, deciding whether the firm should divest itself of any of its businesses, and determining whether it should

FIGURE 1.2

Levels of Strategic Management

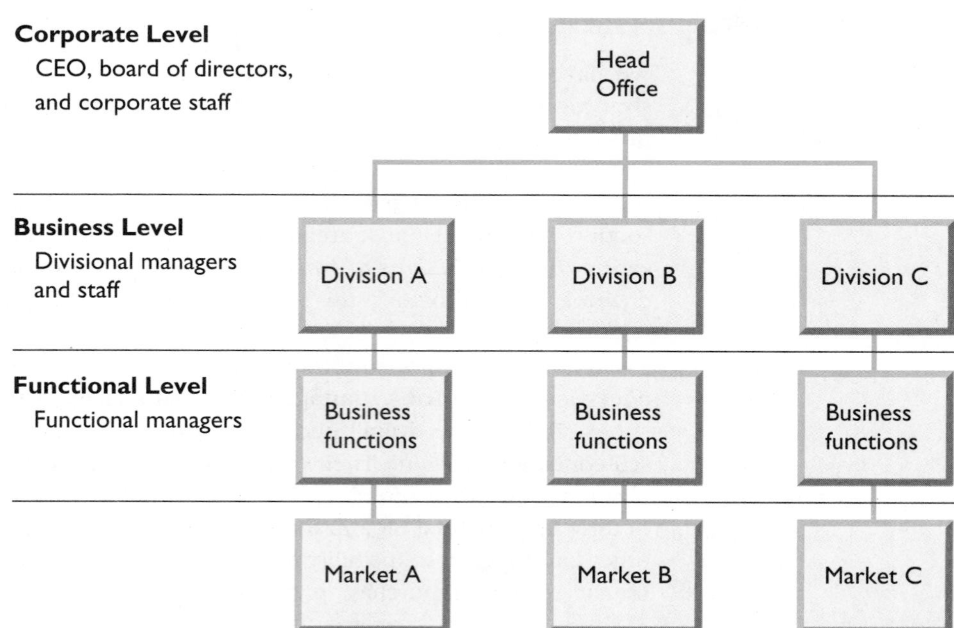

acquire any new ones. In other words, it is up to Welch to develop strategies that span individual businesses. He is concerned with building and managing the corporate portfolio of businesses. It is not his specific responsibility, however, to develop strategies for competing in the individual business areas, such as aeroengines or financial services. The development of such strategies is the responsibility of business-level strategic managers.

Besides overseeing resource allocation and managing the divestment and acquisition processes, corporate-level general managers also provide a link between the people who oversee the strategic development of a firm and those who own it (stockholders). Corporate-level general managers, and particularly the CEO, can be viewed as the guardians of stockholder welfare. It is their responsibility to ensure that corporate strategies pursued by the company are consistent with maximizing stockholder wealth. If they are not, then the CEO is likely to be called to account by the stockholders.

For another look at the roles and responsibilities of a general manager, see Strategy in Action 1.1, which discusses Larry Bossidy, the hard-driving hard-nosed CEO of AlliedSignal. Bossidy sets the overall goals and strategic direction for AlliedSignal, but because the company is a diversified one, with more than twenty different business units, he leaves it up to individual business managers to decide the best strategy for their particular operation. Bossidy's involvement is limited to vigorously probing managers with questions to test the logic underlying their strategic decisions.

Business-Level Managers

In a multibusiness company, such as General Electric or AlliedSignal, the business level consists of the heads of individual business units within the organization and their support staff. In a single-industry company, the business and corporate levels are the same. A business unit is an organizational entity that operates in a distinct business area. Typically, it is self-contained and has its own functional departments (for example, its own finance, buying, production, and marketing departments). Within most companies, business units are referred to as **divisions**.

The main strategic managers at the business level are the heads of the divisions. Their strategic role is to translate general statements of direction and intent from the corporate level into concrete strategies for individual businesses. Thus, while corporate-level general managers are concerned with strategies that span individual businesses, business-level managers concentrate on strategies that are specific to a particular business. At General Electric, Jack Welch has committed the company to the objective of being first or second in every business in which the corporation competes. However, it is up to the general managers who head each division to work out for their business the details of a strategy that is consistent with this objective. Similarly, at AlliedSignal it is up to the heads of each division to work out how they are going to meet Bossidy's demanding goals of 15 percent earnings growth, 8 percent sales growth, and 6 percent productivity growth "forever" (see Strategy in Action 1.1).

Operations Managers

Operations managers bear responsibility for specific business functions or processes, such as human resources, manufacturing, materials management, marketing, research

1.1 STRATEGY in ACTION

Larry Bossidy, CEO

Larry Bossidy, the CEO of the diversified engineering company AlliedSignal, is reputed to be one of the most sought-after CEOs in corporate America. Since leaving the number two spot at General Electric in 1991 to join AlliedSignal, Bossidy has been approached by IBM, Merck, Kodak, and Westinghouse, all of which were looking for a new CEO. The reasons for so much attention are not hard to find. When Bossidy joined AlliedSignal, the company was widely perceived as a poorly performing enterprise based in a number of dull businesses in aerospace, auto parts, and engineered materials. At around $3.50 per share, the stock price was no higher than it had been in 1984, while the 1991 net profit of $342 million was well below the peak profit of $559 million earned in 1986. Under Bossidy's leadership, however, earnings surged to over $1.33 billion in 1998, while the stock price climbed to $60 per share by early 1999.

How has Bossidy done it? He has articulated a handful of challenging goals that he wants AlliedSignal to attain and then relentlessly pushed the managers of each of AlliedSignal's twenty-odd businesses, or divisions, to find ways of meeting those goals. The primary goal of AlliedSignal under Bossidy has been profitable growth. Bossidy wants to increase earnings per share by 15 percent annually. To achieve that, he reckons that AlliedSignal must grow sales of existing businesses by 8 percent per annum, increase productivity at an annual rate of 6 percent "forever," and achieve operating profit margins of at least 15 percent. These are challenging "stretch" goals for a company such as AlliedSignal, which is based in mature low-growth industries. To reach these goals, Bossidy has been pushing his managers to do four things: (1) enter foreign markets, particularly in Asia; (2) make selected niche acquisitions that can help to round out the product line of a business; (3) focus effort on improving efficiencies by driving waste and defects out of the manufacturing process; and (4) develop new products that can boost earnings growth, a particularly difficult challenge in a company that was once known for its aversion to new ideas.

Technically, Bossidy "negotiates" goals with the head of each of AlliedSignal's twenty businesses, but the reality is that he pushes them to accept goals that require a significant improvement in the performance of their businesses. He then tirelessly monitors his managers to make sure they follow through. Nearly every week, Bossidy visits at least one of AlliedSignal's businesses. He is known for vigorously probing managers in all-day meetings to find out what strategies they are adopting to meet the goals he has set for them. And if they fail? Well, they had better not. Bossidy bestows an award on business units that do not meet their cost of capital—it is called the "leaky bucket" award. More significantly, when people fail to meet his stretch targets, he fires them. In the automotive division, which makes brake parts and where profits are below par, Bossidy fired or transferred six of the top ten executives in the course of a year. Bossidy admits that he is demanding, relentless, and tough, but in his view this management style offers the only way forward for companies such as AlliedSignal that have to compete with aggressive low-cost foreign enterprises.[5]

and development (R&D), customer satisfaction, and product development. While they are not responsible for the overall performance of the organization, they do have a major strategic role. Their responsibility is to develop functional strategies in manufacturing, marketing, R&D, and so on, that help fulfill the strategic objectives set by business- and corporate-level general managers. In the case of General Electric's financial services business, for instance, manufacturing managers are responsible for developing manufacturing strategies consistent with the corporate objective of being first or second in that industry. Moreover, operations managers provide most of the information that makes it possible for business- and corporate-level general managers to formulate realistic and attainable strategies. Indeed, because they are closer to the customer than the typical general manager, operations managers may themselves generate important strategic ideas, which subsequently become major strategies for the company. Thus, it is important for general managers to listen closely to the ideas of their operations managers. An equally great responsibility for managers at the operational level is strategy implementation—the execution of corporate- and business-level decisions.

STRATEGIC LEADERSHIP

One of the key strategic roles of managers, whether they are general or operations managers, is to provide strategic leadership for their subordinates. **Strategic leadership** refers to the ability to articulate a strategic vision for the company, or a part of the company, and to motivate others to buy into that vision. An enormous amount has been written about leadership, and it is beyond the scope of this book to review this complex topic in detail. However, a few key characteristics of good leaders have been identified by several authors, and we discuss them here.[6] These characteristics are (1) vision, eloquence, and consistency; (2) commitment; (3) being well informed; (4) willingness to delegate and empower; (5) astute use of power; and (6) emotional intelligence.

Vision, Eloquence, and Consistency

One of the key tasks of leadership is to give the organization a sense of direction. Strong leaders seem to have a vision of where the organization should go. Moreover, they are eloquent enough to communicate this vision to others within the organization in terms that can energize people, and they consistently articulate their vision until it becomes part of the culture of the organization.[7] John F. Kennedy, Martin Luther King, Jr., and Margaret Thatcher have all been held up as examples of visionary leaders. All three had their own clear vision of the society they would like to see, and all were able to communicate it eloquently to people using evocative language that energized the audience. Think of the impact of Kennedy's challenge, "Ask not what your country can do for you; ask what you can do for your country" and of King's "I Have a Dream" speech. Kennedy and Thatcher were also able to use their political office to push for governmental actions that were consistent with their vision, whereas King was able to pressure the government from outside to make changes in society. In the world of business, examples of strong business leaders include Microsoft's Bill Gates, Jack Welch of General Electric, Herb Kelleher of Southwest Airlines, and Larry Bossidy of AlliedSignal, who is profiled in Strategy in Action 1.1.

Commitment

A strong leader is someone who demonstrates commitment to his or her particular vision, often leading by example. Consider the case of Nucor's recently retired CEO, Ken Iverson. Nucor is a very efficient steel maker, with perhaps the lowest cost structure in the steel industry. The company has turned in twenty-five years of profitable performance in an industry where most companies have lost money. It has done so by relentlessly focusing on cost minimization. In his tenure as CEO, it was

Iverson who set the example here. Iverson answered his own phone, employed only one secretary, drove an old car, flew coach class, and was proud of being one of the lowest-paid CEOs in the *Fortune* 500. This kind of commitment was a powerful signal to employees within Nucor that Iverson was serious about doing everything possible to minimize costs. It earned him the respect of Nucor employees, which in turn made them more willing to work hard. Although Iverson has retired, his legacy lives in the cost-conscious organizational culture that has been built at Nucor. Like all great leaders, Iverson has had an impact that goes beyond his tenure as a leader.

Being Well Informed

Good leaders do not operate in a vacuum. Rather, they develop a network of formal and informal sources that keep them well informed about what is going on within their company. They develop back-channel ways of finding out what is going on within the organization so that they do not have to rely on formal information channels. Herb Kelleher at Southwest Airlines, for example, was able to find out a lot about the health of his company by dropping in unannounced on aircraft maintenance facilities and helping workers there perform their tasks. Using informal and unconventional ways to gather information is wise, since formal channels can be captured by special interests within the organization or by gatekeepers, who may misrepresent the true state of affairs within the company to the leader. People like Kelleher, who are constantly interacting with their employees at all levels within the organization, are better able to build informal information networks than leaders who closet themselves in remote corporate headquarters and never interact with lower-level employees.

Willingness to Delegate and Empower

Good leaders are skilled delegators. They recognize that unless they do delegate they can quickly become overloaded with responsibilities. They also recognize that empowering subordinates to make decisions is a good motivational tool. Delegating also makes sense when it results in decisions being made by those who must implement them. At the same time, good leaders recognize that they need to maintain control over certain key decisions. Thus, although they will delegate many decisions to lower-level employees, they will not delegate those that they judge to be critical to the future success of the organization under their leadership.

Astute Use of Power

In a now classic article on leadership, Edward Wrapp notes that good leaders tend to be very astute in their use of power.[8] By this he means three things. First, good leaders play the power game with skill, preferring to build consensus for their ideas rather than use their authority to force ideas through. They act as members or democratic leaders of a coalition, rather than as dictators. Second, good leaders often hesitate to commit themselves publicly to detailed strategic plans or precise objectives, since in all probability the emergence of unexpected contingencies will require adaptation. Thus, a successful leader might commit the organization to a particular vision, such as minimizing costs or boosting product quality, without stating precisely how or when this will be achieved. It is important to note that good leaders often have precise private objectives and strategies that they would like to see the organization pursue. However, they recognize the futility of public commitment, given the likelihood of change and the difficulties of implementation. Third, Wrapp claims that good leaders possess the ability to push through programs in a piecemeal fashion. They recognize that, on occasion, it may be futile to try and push total packages or strategic programs through an organization, since significant objections to at least part of such programs are likely to arise. Instead, the successful leader may be willing to take less than total acceptance in order to achieve modest progress toward a goal. The successful leader tries to push through his or her ideas one piece at a time, so that they appear as incidental to other ideas, though in fact they are part of a larger program or hidden agenda that moves the organization in the direction of the manager's objectives.

Jeffery Pfeffer has articulated a similar vision of the politically astute manager who gets things done in organizations by intelligent use of power.[9] In Pfeffer's view, power comes from control over resources—including budgets, positions, information, and knowledge that is important to the organization. Politically astute managers use these resources to acquire another critical resource: allies. Allies can then help the managers attain their strategic objectives. Pfeffer stresses that one does not need to be a CEO to assemble power in an organization. Sometimes quite junior operations managers can build a surprisingly effective power base and use it to influence organizational outcomes.

Emotional Intelligence

Emotional intelligence is a term coined by Daniel Goleman to describe a bundle of psychological attributes that many strong leaders exhibit.[10] They include self-awareness, self-regulation, motivation, empathy, and social skills. Self-awareness refers to the ability to understand one's moods, emotions, and drives, as well as their effect on others. Self-regulation is the ability to control or redirect disruptive impulses or moods—to think before acting. Motivation refers to a passion for work that goes beyond money or status and a propensity to pursue goals with energy and persistence. Empathy means understanding the feelings and viewpoints of subordinates and taking those into account when making decisions. Goleman defines social skills as "friendliness with a purpose."

According to Goleman, leaders who possess these attributes—who exhibit a high degree of emotional intelligence—tend to be more effective than those who lack them. Their self-awareness and self-regulation help elicit the trust and confidence of subordinates. In Goleman's view, people respect leaders who, through self-awareness, recognize their own limitations and, because of self-regulation, don't shoot from the hip but consider decisions carefully. Goleman also argues that self-aware and self-regulating individuals tend to be more self-confident and therefore better able to cope with ambiguity and more open to change. A strong motivation exhibited in a passion for work can also be infectious, persuading others to join together in pursuit of a common goal or organizational mission. Finally, strong empathy and social skills can help leaders earn the loyalty of subordinates. Empathetic and socially adept individuals tend to be skilled at managing disputes between managers, better able to find common ground and purpose among diverse constituencies, and more likely to move people in a desired direction than leaders who lack these qualities. In short, Goleman argues that the psychological makeup of a leader matters.

STRATEGY AS AN EMERGENT PROCESS

The planning model we reviewed earlier in the chapter suggests that an organization's strategies are the result of a plan, that the strategic planning process itself is rational and highly structured, and that the process is orchestrated, and indeed dominated, by top management. In recent years, several scholars have advocated an alternative view of strategy making, which has called into question the traditional view centered on planning.[11] These scholars have three main criticisms of the planning model: one focuses on the unpredictability of the real world; the second emphasizes the role lower-level managers can play in the strategic management process; and the third points out that many successful strategies are often the result of serendipity, not rational strategizing.

Strategy Making in an Unpredictable World

Critics of formal planning systems argue that we live in a world in which uncertainty, complexity, and ambiguity dominate and in which small chance events can have a large and unpredictable impact on outcomes.[12] In such circumstances, they claim, even the most carefully thought-out strategic plans are prone to being rendered useless by rapid and unforeseen change in the environment. This is something that military historians and thinkers have long recognized. Carl von Clausewitz, the famous Prussian military strategist of the early 1800s, once noted that "the principles, rules, or even systems of strategy must always fall short, undermined by the world's endless complexities . . . in strategy most things are uncertain and variable."[13] Although von Clausewitz was talking about military strategy, his observations are just as relevant to business strategy. Witness, for example, how Microsoft was caught off guard by the rapid rise of the Internet and the sudden emergence of companies such as Netscape and Sun Microsystems as potential competitors (see Strategy in Action 1.2 for details).

In an unpredictable world, there is a premium on being able to respond quickly to changing circumstances, altering the strategies of the organization accordingly (as Microsoft did in response to the threat posed by Netscape—see Strategy in Action 1.2). According to critics, such a flexible approach to strategy making is not possible within the framework of the traditional strategic planning process, with its implicit assumption that an organization's strategies need to be reviewed only during the annual strategic planning exercise.

Strategy Making by Lower-Level Managers

Another criticism leveled at the rational planning model of strategy is that too much importance is attached to the role of top management.[15] An alternative view now gaining wide acceptance is that individual managers deep within an organization can and often do exert a profound influence on the evolution of strategy.[16] Writing with Robert Burgelman of Stanford University, Andy Grove, the CEO of Intel, has recently described how many important strategic decisions at Intel were initiated not by top managers, but by the autonomous action of mid-level managers deep within Intel.[17] These strategic decisions included the decision to exit an important market (the DRAM memory chip market) and the decision to develop a certain class of microprocessors (RISC-based microprocessors) in direct contrast to the stated strategy of Intel's top managers.

Another famous example of autonomous action occurred at 3M corporation back in the 1920s. At that time, 3M was primarily a manufacturer of sandpaper. Richard Drew, who was then a young laboratory assistant, came up with what he thought would be a great new product, a glue-covered paper. Drew saw applications for the product in the automobile industry, where it could be used to mask parts of a vehicle during painting. He presented the idea to the company's president, William McKnight. An unimpressed McKnight suggested that Drew drop the research. Drew didn't; instead, he developed the paper and then went out and got endorsements from potential customers in the auto industry. Armed with this information, he approached McKnight again. A chastened McKnight reversed his original position and gave Drew the go-ahead to start developing what was to become one of 3M's main product lines—sticky tape, a business it dominates to this day.[18] The point of this story, of course, is that it illustrates how autonomous action by a lower-level employee can shape the strategic destiny of a company.

Serendipity and Strategy

Business history is replete with examples of accidental events that helped push companies in new and profitable directions. What these examples suggest is that many successful strategies are not the result of well-thought-out plans, but of serendipity. One such example occurred at 3M during the 1960s. At that time, 3M was producing fluorocarbons for sale as coolant liquid in air conditioning equipment. One day, quite by accident, a researcher working with fluorocarbons in a 3M lab spilled some of the liquid on her shoes. Later that day, the same researcher spilled coffee over her shoes. She watched with interest as the coffee formed into little beads of liquid and then ran off her shoes without leaving a stain. Reflecting on this phenomenon, she realized that a fluorocarbon-based liquid might turn out to be useful for protecting fabrics from liquid stains—and so the idea for Scotch Guard was born. Subsequently, Scotch Guard became one of 3M's most profitable products and took the company into the fabric protection business, an area it had never planned to participate in.[19]

A similar example of serendipitous discovery occurred at the Seattle-based biotechnology company ICOS. During the mid 1990s, ICOS was testing a potential drug candidate for the treatment of hypertension on a sample of males in their fifties. The drug candidate, code-named IC351, was a small molecule product that could be taken orally. Early on, ICOS researchers noted an unusual aspect of the trial: there was a very high compliance rate among the patient sample. Patients were not dropping out of the trials, as often happens in these studies. After some months of testing, the company reviewed the clinical data and concluded that the drug had no effect on hypertension. They decided to halt the trials and asked the patients to return their unused pills. It was at this point that they encountered a highly unusual reaction: some of the patients protested at having to give the surplus pills back to ICOS. Curious to discover why, the ICOS researchers held a series of interviews with the patients. What soon became apparent was that several of the patients who had been taking IC351, as opposed to a placebo, were reporting a dramatic improvement in their sex life. It turned out that these patients has been suffering from male erectile dysfunction (MED), or impotence, as it is commonly called. By inhibiting the production of a selected enzyme, IC351 appeared to relax blood vessels, allowing increased blood flow to tissues and resulting in an improved sexual

1.2 **STRATEGY *in* ACTION**

A Strategic Shift at Microsoft

In the early 1990s, Microsoft emerged as the dominant software company in the desktop computing market. By 1995, Microsoft's Windows operating system was to be found on 90 percent of all personal computers, while the company enjoyed a market share in excess of 50 percent for a large number of popular desktop computing applications, including word processing, presentation software, and spreadsheets. So complete was Microsoft's dominance, that in 1993 several of its competitors filed complaints with the U. S. Department of Justice, alleging that Microsoft engaged in unfair trade practices—a charge that Microsoft vigorously denies. Meanwhile, the business press hailed the company's founder and CEO, Bill Gates, as one of the greatest strategic thinkers in the computer industry. The linchpin of Gates's strategy was to ensure the continued dominance of Microsoft's Windows operating system as the standard of choice in the personal computer environment.

In mid 1995, however, Microsoft suddenly began to look vulnerable when it was blind-sided by two related and unexpected developments. The first of these was the explosive growth of the global network of interlinked computers known as the Internet and the associated World Wide Web, or WWW, that sits on top of the Internet. In the late 1980s, Tim Bernes Lee, a physicist at the CERN research institute for particle physics in Switzerland, developed a method for encoding, displaying, and transmitting text and graphics over the Internet using HTML (hypertext markup language). In effect, Bernes Lee had invented the World Wide Web. In 1993, a young computer programmer at the University of Illinois, Mark Andreessen, masterminded the development of a "browser" that could be used to travel the Internet, read HTML documents, and display them on a personal computer screen. In 1994, he left Illinois to help found Netscape, a software company that produced an improved version of the HTML browser, Netscape Navigator, along with "Web server software," which could be placed on the computer servers that were the nodes of the rapidly developing WWW to manage Web files and handle Web traffic. The growth of the WWW was nothing short of stunning. In 1990, fewer than 1 million users were connected to the Internet. By late 1995, largely as a result of the popularity of the WWW, the figure was approaching 80 million, and Netscape, not Microsoft, had supplied more than 70 percent of all Web browsers and Web server software.

The second development was the invention of the Java computer programming language at Sun Microsystems, one of the leading suppliers of computer workstations and servers. A program written in Java can be stored anywhere on the WWW and accessed by anyone with a Web browser that contains a Java interpreter—and by 1995, versions of Netscape Navigator did. Java is indifferent to

response. ICOS had stumbled on a powerful potential treatment for MED, a serious condition that affects approximately 20 million males in the United States alone. By 1999, ICOS had entered into a joint venture with Eli Lilly to develop the product and was close to initiating final clinical trials. In late 1998, Pfizer introduced a similar product, Viagra, and was experiencing rapid sales growth. Many analysts thought that the ICOS product was even more effective than Viagra and were predicting rapid market acceptance if it successfully cleared regulatory hurdles and made it to the market.[20]

As suggested by the 3M and ICOS examples, serendipitous discoveries are often the unintended consequence of scientific endeavor. This is not always the case, however. In the mid 1980s, for example, an employee at a small software company, WRQ, wanted to access the company's Hewlett-Packard computer from home by turning his personal computer into an HP terminal. Since no software existed to perform this task, he wrote a program for his personal use that enabled his personal computer to emulate a Hewlett-Packard terminal. Some of his colleagues thought that other companies might want to buy this software, so WRQ tried to sell it as a

the operating system of the personal computer on which a Web browser resides. So in theory, users of a current version of Netscape Navigator can access a word-processing program placed somewhere on the Web as and when they need it. Instead of purchasing the program outright for hundreds of dollars, all they need do is pay a few cents for the "run time" during which they use the program.

This development represented a potential body blow to Microsoft. It raised the possibility that people would no longer need to purchase expensive software applications from Microsoft and store them on their computers. Nor would they need a machine that utilized Microsoft's operating system. All they needed was a simple and inexpensive machine that was able to run a Netscape browser with a Java interpreter. They could then use this machine to access programs on the Web whenever they wanted, using the computing power of a remote server. As Scott McNealy, the CEO of Sun Microsystems, was fond of saying at the time, in this vision of the future "the network is the computer," while the standard is based not on Microsoft's Windows, but on Netscape and Java.

Microsoft's initial response to this unanticipated threat was to dismiss it. Bill Gates called Netscape's browser technology trivial. But by late 1995, it was clear that Microsoft had decided to respond to the unexpected threat posed by Netscape and Java by shifting its own strategic focus toward the WWW. Microsoft was to continue focusing on being the dominant software player in the desktop computing business, but its strategy for attaining this objective would start to change. In an all-day Internet conference, Microsoft stated that it would give away its own Web browser—Internet Explorer—and Web server software for free. Furthermore, the company promised that future software applications produced by Microsoft would contain "browser functions," which would enable users to roam the Web for information, and that new versions of its popular word-processing program would enable users to convert their documents into HTML format, which could be transmitted over the Web. Microsoft also declared that it would license Java from Sun and incorporate Java interpreters into some of its own products. In subsequent weeks, Microsoft announced an alliance with America Online (AOL), the world's largest on-line service, which would allow AOL's 5 million subscribers to use Microsoft's browser. This was followed by a deal with Intel to develop technology that would make video, voice, and data conferencing via the WWW as commonplace as placing a telephone call. By quickly abandoning its prior strategy and developing a new Internet strategy on the fly in response to an unanticipated threat, Microsoft suddenly positioned itself as a viable alternative to Netscape. The shift turned out to be remarkably successful. By late 1998, Microsoft's Internet Explorer was enjoying wide market acceptance while Netscape, facing shrinking demand for its products, agreed to be acquired by America Online.[14]

product. To its surprise, the company found that the demand was strong. Personal computers were starting to make their way onto the desks of many people in business, but these people still wanted to access data stored on mainframe computers, so they needed software that would transform their personal computers into mainframe terminals. For the next fifteen years, the company found it was generating sales of over $100 million from terminal emulation software.

The point is that serendipitous discoveries and events are commonplace and can open up all sorts of profitable avenues for a company. As a result, the strategy of many profitable firms is the product not of planning, but of the exploitation of serendipity. By the same token, some companies have missed out on profitable opportunities because serendipitous discoveries or events were inconsistent with their prior (planned) conception of what their strategy should be. In one of the classic examples of such myopia, a century ago the telegraph company Western Union turned down an opportunity to purchase the rights to an invention made by Alexander Graham Bell. The invention was the telephone, a technology that subsequently made the telegraph obsolete.

Intended and Emergent Strategies

Henry Mintzberg has incorporated the ideas discussed above into a model of strategy development that provides us with a more encompassing view of what strategy actually is. According to this model, which is illustrated in Figure 1.3, a company's **realized strategy** is the product of whatever planned, or **intended, strategies,** are actually put into action *and* of any unplanned, or **emergent, strategies.** In Mintzberg's view, emergent strategies are the unplanned responses to unforeseen circumstances. They often arise from autonomous action by individual managers deep within the organization (such as Richard Drew at 3M), or from serendipitous discoveries or events (such as those discussed at 3M, ICOS, and WRQ). They are *not* the product of formal top-down planning mechanisms.

Mintzberg maintains that emergent strategies are often successful and may be more appropriate than intended strategies. Richard Pascale has described how this was the case for the entry of Honda Motor into the U.S. motorcycle market.[21] When a number of Honda executives arrived in Los Angeles from Japan in 1959 to establish a U.S. subsidiary, their original aim (intended strategy) was to focus on selling 250-cc and 350-cc machines to confirmed motorcycle enthusiasts, rather than 50-cc Honda Cubs, which were a big hit in Japan. Their instinct told them that the Honda 50s were not suitable for the U.S. market, where everything was bigger and more luxurious than in Japan.

However, sales of the 250-cc and 350-cc bikes were sluggish, and the bikes themselves were plagued by mechanical failure. It looked as if Honda's strategy was going to fail. At the same time, the Japanese executives were using the Honda 50s to run errands around Los Angeles, attracting a lot of attention. One day they got a call from a Sears, Roebuck buyer who wanted to sell the 50-cc bikes to a broad market of Americans who were not necessarily already motorcycle enthusiasts. The Honda executives were hesitant to sell the small bikes for fear of alienating serious bikers, who might then associate Honda with "wimpy" machines. In the end, they were pushed into doing so by the failure of the 250-cc and 350-cc models. The rest is history. Honda had stumbled onto a previously untouched market segment that was to prove huge: the average American who had never owned a motorbike. Honda had also found an untried channel of distribution: general retailers rather than specialty motorbike stores. By 1964, nearly one out of every two motorcycles sold in the United States was a Honda.

The conventional explanation of Honda's success is that the company redefined the U.S. motorcycle industry with a brilliantly conceived *intended* strategy. The fact was that Honda's intended strategy was a near disaster. The strategy that *emerged* did so not through planning, but through unplanned action taken in response to unforeseen circumstances. Nevertheless, credit should be given to the Japanese management for recognizing the strength of the emergent strategy and for pursuing it with vigor.

The critical point demonstrated by the Honda example is that—in contrast to the view that all strategies are planned—successful strategies can emerge within an organization without prior planning, often in response to unforeseen circumstances. As Mintzberg has noted, strategies can take root in all kinds of strange places, virtually wherever people have the capacity to learn and the resources to support that capacity.

In practice, the strategies of most organizations are probably a combination of the intended (planned) and the emergent. The message for management is that it needs to recognize the process of emergence and to intervene when appropriate, killing off bad emergent strategies but nurturing potentially good ones.[22] To make

FIGURE 1.3

Emergent and Deliberate Strategies

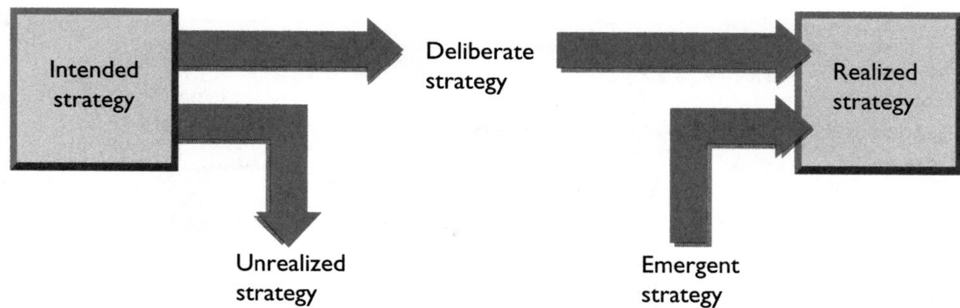

Source: Reprinted from "Strategy Formation in an Adhocracy," by Henry Mintzberg and Alexandra McGugh, published in *Administrative Science Quarterly,* Vol. 30, No. 2, June 1985, by permission of *Administrative Science Quarterly.*

such decisions, however, managers must be able to judge the worth of emergent strategies. They must be able to think strategically. Even though emergent strategies arise from within the organization without prior planning—that is, without going through the steps illustrated in Figure 1.1 in a *sequential* fashion—top management still has to evaluate emergent strategies. Such evaluation involves comparing each emergent strategy with the organization's goals, external environmental opportunities and threats, and the organization's internal strengths and weaknesses. The objective is to assess whether the emergent strategy fits the organization's needs and capabilities. In addition, Mintzberg stresses that an organization's capability to produce emergent strategies is a function of the kind of corporate culture fostered by the organization's structure and control systems.

In other words, the different components of the strategic management process are just as important from the perspective of emergent strategies as they are from the perspective of intended strategies. The essential differences between the strategic management process for intended and for emergent strategies are illustrated in Figure 1.4. The formulation of intended strategies is basically a top-down, planning-driven process, whereas the formulation of emergent strategies is a bottom-up process. In successful organizations, both processes are often at work.[23]

STRATEGIC PLANNING IN PRACTICE

Even the most vocal critics of formal strategic planning concede that it has a role. For example, Mintzberg's model of the strategy-making process, as illustrated in Figure 1.4, maintains a role for formal strategic planning, while simultaneously pointing to the importance of unplanned emergent strategies. Given that formal strategic planning is still widely practiced, and rightly so, it is pertinent to ask whether formal planning systems do actually help an organization attain superior performance.

On balance, the research evidence seems to indicate that formal planning systems do help companies make better strategic decisions. For example, a recent study analyzed in detail the results of twenty-six previously published studies of the relationship between strategic planning and company performance.[24] The study came to the conclusion that, on average, strategic planning does indeed have a positive impact on company performance, suggesting that strategic planning is a valuable activity.

Despite such results, many informed observers have increasingly questioned the use of formal planning systems as an aid to strategic decision making. Thomas J.

FIGURE 1.4

The Strategic Management Process for Intended and Emergent Strategies

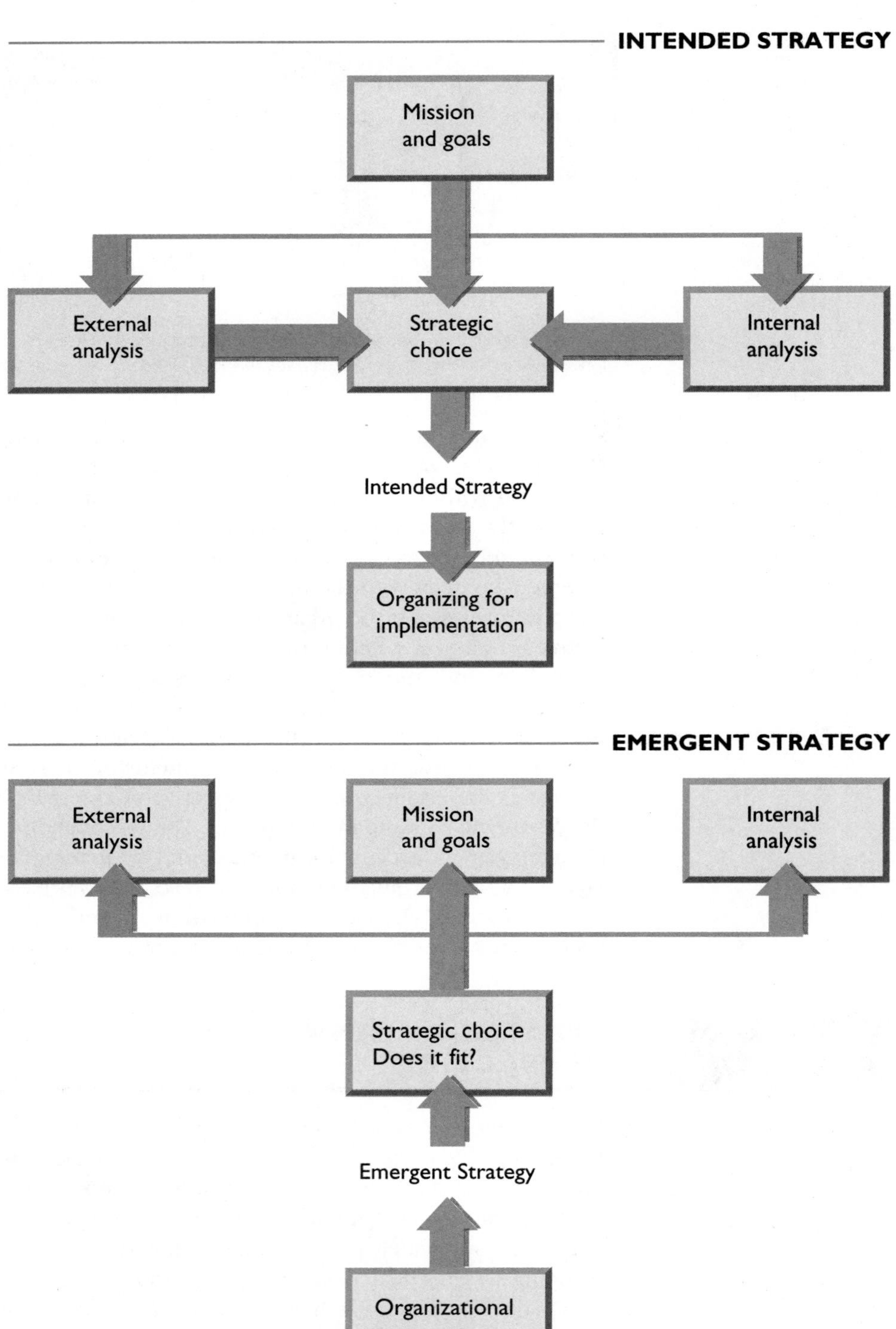

Peters and Robert H. Waterman, authors of the bestseller *In Search of Excellence*, were among the first to call into question the usefulness of formal planning systems, and the antiplanning rhetoric continues to be a theme in the more recent works of Peters.[25] Similarly, Mintzberg argues that business history is filled with examples of companies that have made poor decisions on the basis of supposedly comprehensive strategic planning.[26] For instance, Exxon's decisions to diversify into electrical equipment and office automation and to offset shrinking U.S. oil reserves by investing in shale oil and synthetic fuels resulted from a 1970s planning exercise that was overly pessimistic about the demand for oil-based products. Exxon foresaw ever higher prices for oil and predicted sharp falls in demand as a result. But oil prices actually tumbled during the 1980s, invalidating one of the basic assumptions of Exxon's plan. In addition, Exxon's diversification failed because of poor acquisitions and management problems in office automation.

Four explanations can be offered as to why formal strategic planning systems do not always produce the desired results. We consider three of them here and offer ways of dealing with them. We take up the fourth explanation, which focuses on decision-making biases among managers, in the next section. The three explanations are as follows: (1) planning under uncertainty; (2) top-down ivory tower planning; and (3) planning for the present, as opposed to the future.

Planning Under Uncertainty

One reason for the poor reputation of strategic planning is that many executives, in their initial enthusiasm for planning techniques, forgot that the future is inherently unpredictable. As at Exxon, a common problem was that executives often assumed it was possible to forecast the future accurately. But in the real world, the only constant is change. Even the best-laid plans can fall apart if unforeseen contingencies occur, and, as we noted earlier, in the real world unforeseen contingencies occur all the time.

Scenario Planning The recognition that in an uncertain world the future cannot be forecast with sufficient accuracy led Royal Dutch/Shell to pioneer the scenario approach to planning discussed in the Strategy in Action 1.3. Rather than try to forecast the future, Shell's planners attempt to model the company's environment and use that model to predict a range of possible scenarios. Executives are then asked to devise strategies to cope with the different scenarios. The objective is to get managers to understand the dynamic and complex nature of their environment, to think through problems in a strategic fashion, and to generate a range of strategic options that might be pursued under different circumstances.[27]

The scenario approach to planning seems to have spread quite rapidly among large companies. According to one survey, more than 50 percent of the *Fortune* 500 companies use some form of scenario-planning methods.[28] Although a detailed evaluation of the pros and cons of scenario planning has yet to appear, work by Paul Schoemaker of the University of Chicago seems to suggest that scenario planning does expand people's thinking, and as such it may lead to better plans, as seems to have occurred at Royal Dutch/Shell. However, Schoemaker cautions that forcing planners to consider extreme scenarios that are unbelievable can discredit the approach and cause resistance on the planners' part.

1.3 STRATEGY *in* ACTION

Strategic Planning at Royal Dutch/Shell

Royal Dutch/Shell, the world's largest oil company, is well known for its addiction to strategic planning. Despite the fact that many management gurus and CEOs now consider strategic planning an anachronism, Shell is convinced that long-term strategic planning has served the company well. Part of the reason for this success is that at Shell planning does not take the form of complex and inflexible ten-year plans generated by a team of corporate strategists far removed from operating realities. Rather, the planning process generates a series of "what if" scenarios, whose function is to try to get general managers at all levels of the corporation to think strategically about the environment in which they do business.

The strength of Shell's scenario-based planning system was perhaps most evident during the early 1980s. At that time, the price of a barrel of oil was hovering around $30. With exploration and development costs running at an industry average of around $11 per barrel, most oil companies were making record profits. Moreover, industry analysts were generally bullish; many were predicting that oil prices would increase to around $50 per barrel by 1990. Shell, however, was mulling over a handful of future scenarios, one of which included the possibility of a breakdown of the OPEC oil cartel's agreement to restrict supply, an oil glut, and a drop in oil prices to $15 per barrel. In 1984, Shell instructed the managers of its operating companies to indicate how they would respond to a $15-per-barrel world. This "game" set off some serious work at Shell to explore the question, "What will we do if it happens?"

By early 1986, the consequences of the "game" included efforts to cut exploration costs by pioneering advanced exploration technologies, massive investments in cost-efficient refining facilities, and a process of weeding out the least-profitable service stations. All this planning occurred at a time when most oil companies were busy diversifying outside the oil business rather than trying to improve the efficiency of their core operations. As it turned out, the price of oil was still $27 per barrel in early January 1986. But the failure of the OPEC cartel to set new production ceilings in 1985, new production from the North Sea and Alaska, and declining demand due to increased conservation efforts had created a growing oil glut. In late January, the dam burst. By February 1, oil was priced at $17 per barrel, and by April, the price was $10 per barrel.

Because Shell had already visited the $15 per barrel world, it had gained a head start over its rivals in its cost-cutting efforts. As a result, by 1989 the company's average oil and gas exploration costs were less than $2 per barrel, compared with an industry average of $4 per barrel. Moreover, in the crucial refining and marketing sector, Shell made a net return on assets of 8.4 percent in 1988, more than double the 3.8 percent average of the other oil majors: Exxon, BP, Chevron, Mobil, and Texaco.[29]

Ivory Tower Planning

A serious mistake made by many companies in their initial enthusiasm for planning has been to treat planning as an exclusively top-management function. This *ivory tower* approach can result in strategic plans formulated in a vacuum by planning executives who have little understanding or appreciation of operating realities. As a consequence, they formulate strategies that do more harm than good. For example, when demographic data indicated that houses and families were shrinking, planners at General Electric's appliance group concluded that smaller appliances were the wave of the future. Because the planners had little contact with home builders and retailers, they did not realize that kitchens and bathrooms were the two rooms that were not shrinking. Nor did they appreciate that working women wanted big refrigerators to cut down on trips to the supermarket. The result was that General Electric wasted a lot of time designing small appliances for which there was only limited demand.

The ivory tower concept of planning can also lead to tensions between planners and operating personnel. The experience of General Electric's appliance group is again illuminating. Many of the planners in this group were recruited from consulting firms or from topflight business schools. Many of the operating managers took this pattern of recruitment to mean that corporate executives did not deem them smart enough to think through strategic problems for themselves. They felt shut out from the decision-making process, which they believed to be unfairly constituted. Out of this perceived lack of procedural justice grew an us-versus-them state of mind, which quickly escalated into hostility. As a result, even when the planners were right, operating managers would not listen to them. In the early 1980s, the planners correctly recognized the importance of the globalization of the appliance market and the emerging Japanese threat. However, operating managers, who then saw Sears, Roebuck as the competition, paid them little heed.

Involving Operating Managers Correcting the ivory tower approach to planning requires recognizing that, to succeed, strategic planning must encompass managers at *all* levels of the corporation. It is important to understand that much of the best planning can and should be done by operating managers. They are the ones closest to the facts. The role of corporate-level planners should be that of facilitators, who help operating managers do the planning both by setting the broad strategic goals of the organization and by providing operating managers with the resources required to identify the strategies that might be necessary to attain those goals.

Procedural Justice It is not enough just to involve lower-level managers in the strategic planning process. They also need to perceive that the decision-making process is just. Chan Kim and Renee Mauborgne have written extensively about the importance of procedural justice in strategic decision making.[30] They define **procedural justice** as the extent to which the dynamics of a decision-making process are judged to be fair. If people perceive the decision-making process to be unjust, they are less likely to be committed to any resulting decisions and less likely to voluntarily cooperate in activities designed to implement those decisions. Consequently, their performance is likely to be below par. In short, a strategy chosen on the basis of a decision-making process that was perceived to be procedurally unjust might fail for lack of support among those who must implement it at the operating level.

Three criteria have been found to influence the extent to which strategic decisions are seen as just: engagement, explanation, and clarity of expectations.[31] *Engagement* means involving individuals in the decision-making process, both by asking them for their input and by allowing them to refute the merits of one another's ideas and assumptions. *Explanation* means that everyone involved and affected should be told the underlying rationale for strategic decisions, and explanations should be given as to why the ideas and inputs of individuals may have been overridden in reaching a decision. *Clarity of expectations* requires that before, during, and after strategic decisions are made managers have a solid understanding of what is expected of them and what the new "rules of the game" are. By paying close attention to engagement, explanation, and clarity of expectations, managers can greatly increase the likelihood that the strategic decision-making process is perceived as just, even when individuals have had their ideas and input overridden. In turn, this increases the probability that individuals will cooperate as fully as possible in the process of implementing those decisions. Consequently, company performance is likely to be higher than would have otherwise been the case.

Planning for the Present: Strategic Intent

The traditional strategic planning model we reviewed earlier has been characterized as the *fit model* of strategy making because it tries to achieve a fit between the internal resources and capabilities of an organization, and external environmental opportunities and threats. Gary Hamel and C. K. Prahalad have attacked the fit model as being too static and limiting.[32] They argue that adopting the fit model to strategy formulation leads to a mindset in which management focuses too much on the degree of fit between the *existing* resources of a company and *current* environmental opportunities, and not enough on building *new* resources and capabilities to create and exploit *future* opportunities. Strategies based on the fit model, say Hamel and Prahalad, tend to be more concerned with today's problems than with tomorrow's opportunities. As a result, companies that rely exclusively on the fit approach to strategy formulation are unlikely to be able to build and maintain a competitive advantage. This is particularly true in a dynamic competitive environment, where new competitors are continually arising and new ways of doing business are constantly being invented.

As Hamel and Prahalad note again and again, U.S. companies using the fit approach have been surprised by the ascent of foreign competitors that initially seemed to lack the resources and capabilities needed to make them a real threat. This happened to Xerox, which ignored the rise of Canon and Ricoh in the photocopier market until they had become serious global competitors; to General Motors, which initially overlooked the threat posed by Toyota and Honda in the 1970s; and to Caterpillar, which ignored the danger Komatsu posed to its heavy earthmoving business until it was almost too late to respond.

Strategic Intent The secret of the success of companies such as Toyota, Canon, and Komatsu, according to Hamel and Prahalad, is that they all had bold ambitions that outstripped their existing resources and capabilities. All wanted to achieve global leadership, and they set out to build the resources and capabilities that would enable them to attain this goal. Consequently, the top management of these companies created an obsession with winning at all levels of the organization and then sustained that obsession over a ten- to twenty-year quest for global leadership. It is this obsession that Hamel and Prahalad refer to as **strategic intent**. At the same time, they stress that strategic intent is more than simply unfettered ambition. They argue that strategic intent also encompasses an active management process, which includes "focusing the organization's attention on the essence of winning; motivating people by communicating the value of the target; leaving room for individual and team contributions; sustaining enthusiasm by providing new operational definitions as circumstances change; and using intent consistently to guide resource allocations."[33] Thus, underlying the concept of strategic intent is the notion that strategy formulation should involve setting ambitious goals, which stretch a company, and then finding ways to build the resources and capabilities necessary to attain those goals.

Although Hamel and Prahalad aptly criticize the fit model, they note that in practice the two approaches to strategy formulation are not mutually exclusive. All the components of the strategic management process that we discussed earlier, and that are summarized in Figure 1.1, are important. Managers do have to analyze the external environment to identify opportunities and threats. They do have to analyze the company's resources and capabilities to identify strengths and weaknesses. They need to be familiar with the range of functional-level, business-level, corporate-level, and global strategies that are available to them. And they need to have an appreciation for the structures required to implement different strategies. What Hamel and Prahalad seem to be saying is that the strategic management process should begin with challenging goals—such as attaining global leadership—that stretch the organization. Then, throughout the process the emphasis should be on finding ways (strategies) to develop the resources and capabilities necessary to achieve these goals, rather than on exploiting *existing* strengths to take advantage of *existing* opportunities. The difference between strategic fit and strategic intent, therefore, may just be one of emphasis. Strategic intent is more internally focused and is concerned with building new resources and capabilities. Strategic fit focuses more on matching existing resources and capabilities to the external environment.

IMPROVING STRATEGIC DECISION MAKING

Even the best-designed strategic planning systems will fail to produce the desired results if strategic decision makers do not use the information at their disposal effectively. There is in fact a good deal of evidence that many managers are poor strategic decision makers.[34] The reasons have to do with two related psychological phenomena: cognitive biases and groupthink. We discuss each of them in turn and then consider techniques for improving decision making.

Cognitive Biases and Strategic Decisions

The rationality of human decision makers is bounded by our own cognitive capabilities.[35] We are not supercomputers, and it is difficult for us to absorb and process large amounts of information effectively. As a result, we tend to fall back on certain rules of thumb, or heuristics, when making decisions. Many of these rules of thumb are actually quite useful, since they help us to make sense of a complex and uncertain world. However, sometimes they also lead to severe and systematic errors in the decision-making process.[36] Systematic errors are errors that appear time and time again. These systematic errors seem to arise from a series of **cognitive biases** in the way that human decision makers process information and reach decisions. Because of cognitive biases, many managers end up making poor strategic decisions.

Figure 1.5 presents five well-known cognitive biases. These biases have been verified repeatedly in laboratory settings, so we can be reasonably sure that they exist and that we are all prone to them.[37] The **prior hypothesis bias** refers to the fact

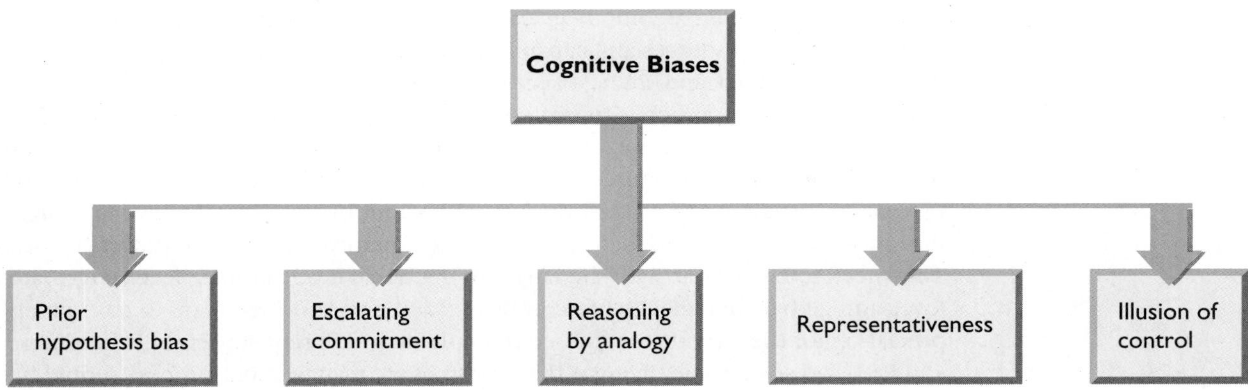

FIGURE 1.5

Five Well-Known Cognitive Biases

that decision makers who have strong prior beliefs about the relationship between two variables tend to make decisions on the basis of these beliefs, even when presented with evidence that their beliefs are wrong. Moreover, they tend to seek and use information that is consistent with their prior beliefs, while ignoring information that contradicts these beliefs. To put this bias in a strategic context, it suggests that a CEO who has a strong prior belief that a certain strategy makes sense might continue to pursue that strategy, despite evidence that it is inappropriate or failing.

Another well-known cognitive bias is referred to as **escalating commitment**.[38] Escalating commitment occurs when decision makers, having already committed significant resources to a project, commit even more resources if they receive feedback that the project is failing. This may be an irrational response; a more logical response would be to abandon the project and move on (that is, to cut your losses and run), rather than escalate commitment. Feelings of personal responsibility for a project apparently induce decision makers to stick with a project, despite evidence that it is failing. One of the most famous examples of escalating commitment is U.S. policy during the Vietnam War. President Lyndon B. Johnson's reaction to information that U.S. policy in Vietnam was failing was to commit ever more resources to the war.[39] To draw on a business example, during the 1960s and 1970s the response of large U.S. steel makers to cost-efficient competition from minimills and foreign steel makers was to increase their investments in the technologically obsolete steelmaking facilities they already possessed, rather than invest in new cutting-edge technology.[40] This was irrational; investments in such obsolete technology would never enable them to become cost efficient.

The bias of **reasoning by analogy** involves the use of simple analogies to make sense of complex problems. U.S. policy toward Vietnam in the 1960s, for example, was guided by the analogy of falling dominoes. U.S. policymakers believed that if Vietnam fell to the Communists the rest of Southeast Asia would also fall. The danger of using such analogies is that by oversimplifying a complex problem they can mislead. For example, several companies have relied on the analogy of a three-legged stool to justify diversifying into business areas of which they had little prior knowledge. The analogy suggests that a stool with fewer than three legs—and by extension, a company that is active in fewer than three different businesses—is unbalanced. Chrysler applied this analogy to justify its decision in the mid 1980s to diversify into the aerospace industry by acquiring Gulfstream, a manufacturer of executive jets. Five years later, Chrysler admitted that the diversification move had been a mistake and divested itself of this activity.

Representativeness is a bias rooted in the tendency to generalize from a small sample, or even a single vivid anecdote. This bias, however, violates the statistical law of large numbers, which says that it is inappropriate to generalize from a small sample, let alone from a single case. An interesting example of representativeness occurred after World War II, when Seawell Avery, the CEO of Montgomery Ward, shelved plans for national expansion to meet competition from Sears because he believed that a depression would follow the war. He based his belief on the fact that there had been a depression after World War I. As it turned out, there was no depression, and Sears went on to become a nationwide retailer, whereas Montgomery Ward did not. Avery's mistake was to generalize from one postwar experience and assume that depressions always follow wars.

The final cognitive bias is referred to as the **illusion of control**. It is the tendency to overestimate one's ability to control events. Top-level managers seem to be particularly prone to this bias. Having risen to the top of an organization, they tend to be overconfident about their ability to succeed. According to Richard Roll, such overconfidence leads to what he has termed the **hubris hypothesis** of takeovers.[41] Roll argues that senior managers are typically overconfident about their abilities to create value by acquiring another company. Hence, they end up making poor acquisition decisions, often paying far too much for the companies they acquire. Subsequently, servicing the debt taken on to finance such an acquisition makes it all but impossible to profit from the acquisition.

Groupthink and Strategic Decisions

The biases just discussed are individual biases. However, most strategic decisions are made by groups, not individuals. Thus, the group context within which decisions are made is clearly an important variable in determining whether cognitive biases will operate to adversely affect the strategic decision-making processes. The psychologist Irvin Janis has argued that many groups are characterized by a process known as groupthink and that as a result many groups do make poor strategic decisions.[42] **Groupthink** occurs when a group of decision makers embarks on a course of action without questioning underlying assumptions. Typically, a group coalesces around a person or policy. It ignores or filters out information that can be used to question the policy and develops after-the-fact rationalizations for its decision. Thus, commitment is based on an emotional, rather than an objective, assessment of the correct course of action. The consequences can be poor decisions.

This phenomenon may explain, at least in part, why companies often make poor strategic decisions in spite of sophisticated strategic management. Janis traced many historical fiascoes to defective policymaking by government leaders who received social support from their in-group of advisers. For example, he suggested that President John F. Kennedy's inner circle suffered from groupthink when the members of this group supported the decision to launch the Bay of Pigs invasion of Cuba, even though available information showed that it would be an unsuccessful venture and would damage U.S. relations with other countries.

Janis has observed that groupthink-dominated groups are characterized by strong pressures toward uniformity, which make their members avoid raising controversial

1.4 STRATEGY *in* ACTION

Groupthink at Imperial Tobacco

An example of groupthink concerns the 1979 acquisition of Howard Johnson by Britain's Imperial Group. In 1979, Imperial was the third largest tobacco company in the world, after British American Tobacco and Philip Morris. In the 1970s, Imperial began a diversification program designed to reduce its dependence on the declining tobacco market. Part of this program included a plan to acquire a major U.S. company. Imperial spent two years scanning the United States for a suitable acquisition opportunity. It was looking for an enterprise in a high-growth industry that had a high market share, a good track record, and good growth prospects and that could be acquired at a reasonable price. Imperial scanned more than 30 industries and 200 different companies before deciding on Howard Johnson.

When Imperial announced its plans to buy Howard Johnson for close to $500 million in 1979, the company's shareholders threatened rebellion. They were quick to point out that at $26 per share Imperial was paying double what Howard Johnson had been worth only six months previously, when share prices stood at $13. The acquisition hardly seemed to be at a reasonable price. Moreover, the motel industry was entering a low- rather than a high-growth phase, and growth prospects were poor. Besides, Howard Johnson did not have a good track record. Imperial ignored shareholder protests and bought the lodging chain. Five years later, after persistent losses, Imperial was trying to divest itself of Howard Johnson. The acquisition had been a complete failure.

What went wrong? Why, after a two-year planning exercise, did Imperial buy a company that so patently did not fit its own criteria? The answer would seem to lie not in the planning, but in the quality of strategic decision making. Imperial bought Howard Johnson in spite of its planning, not because of it. The CEO decided independently that Howard Johnson was a good buy. A rather authoritarian figure who was overconfident of his ability (a case of hubris), the CEO surrounded himself with subordinates who agreed with him. In a clear sign that groupthink was at work, once he had made his choice his advisers concurred with his judgment and shared in developing rationalizations for it. No one questioned the decision itself, even though information was available to show that it was flawed. Instead, strategic planning was used to justify a decision that in practice did not conform with strategic objectives.[43]

issues, questioning weak arguments, or calling a halt to softheaded thinking. An interesting example of groupthink in a business context, the acquisition of Howard Johnson by the Imperial Group, is highlighted in Strategy in Action 1.4. Note that in this case groupthink seemed to exacerbate a number of other cognitive biases, including the illusion of control and prior hypothesis bias.

Techniques for Improving Decision Making

The existence of cognitive biases and groupthink raises the issue of how to bring critical information to bear on the decision mechanism so that strategic decisions made by the company are realistic and based on thorough evaluation. Two techniques known to counteract groupthink and cognitive biases are devil's advocacy and dialectic inquiry.

Devil's advocacy and dialectic inquiry have been proposed as two means of improving decision making.[44] **Devil's advocacy** requires the generation of both a plan and a critical analysis of the plan. One member of the decision-making group acts as the devil's advocate, bringing out all the reasons that might make the proposal unacceptable. In this way, decision makers can become aware of the possible

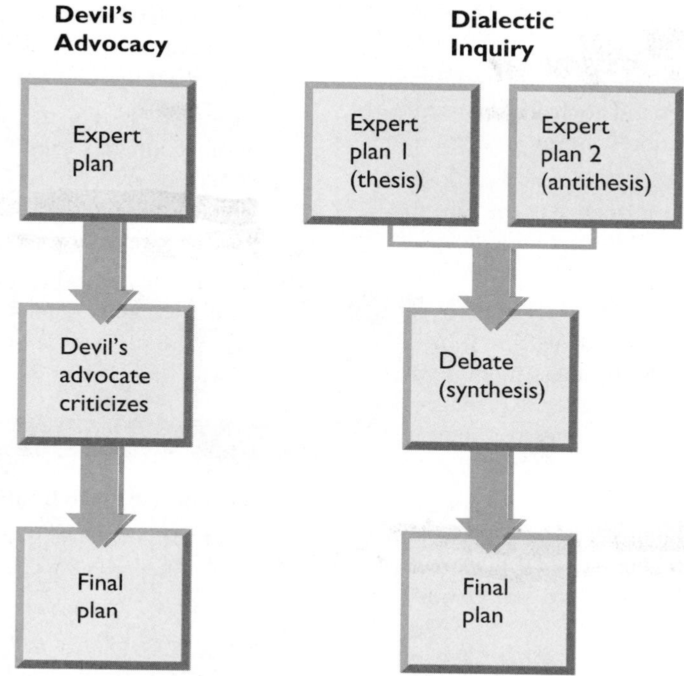

FIGURE 1.6

Two Decision-Making Processes That Cognitive Biases and Groupthink

perils of recommended courses of action. **Dialectic inquiry** is more complex, for it requires the generation of a plan (a thesis) and a counterplan (an antithesis). According to R. O. Mason, one of the early proponents of this method in strategic management, the plan and the counterplan should reflect plausible but conflicting courses of action.[45] Corporate decision makers consider a debate between advocates of the plan and counterplan. The purpose of the debate is to reveal problems with definitions, recommended courses of action, and assumptions. As a result, corporate decision makers and planners are able to form a new and more encompassing conceptualization of the problem, which becomes the final plan (a synthesis).

Both of these decision-making processes are illustrated in Figure 1.6. If either of them had been used in the Imperial case, very likely a different (and probably a better) decision would have been made. However, there is considerable dispute over which of the two methods is better.[46] Researchers have reached conflicting conclusions, and the jury is still out on this issue. From a practical point of view, however, devil's advocacy is probably the easier method to implement because it involves less commitment in terms of time than dialectic inquiry.

SUMMARY OF CHAPTER

- A strategy is an action that a company takes to attain one or more of its goals.
- A central objective of strategic management is to identify why some organizations succeed while others fail.
- Traditional definitions of strategy stress that an organization's strategy is the outcome of a rational planning process.
- The major components of the strategic management process include defining the mission and major goals of the organization; analyzing the external and internal environments of the organization;

choosing strategies that align, or *fit*, the organization's strengths and weaknesses with external environmental opportunities and threats; and adopting organizational structures and control systems to implement the organization's chosen strategy.

- General managers are individuals who bear responsibility for the overall performance of the organization or of one of its major self-contained divisions. Their overriding strategic concern is for the health of the total organization under their direction.
- Operating managers are individuals who bear responsibility for a particular business function or operation. Although they lack general management responsibilities, they do play a very important strategic role.
- The key characteristics of good leaders include vision, eloquence, and consistency; commitment; being well informed; a willingness to delegate and empower; astute use of power; and emotional intelligence.
- A revision of the concept suggests that strategy can emerge from deep within an organization in the absence of formal plans as lower-level managers respond to unpredicted situations.
- Strategic planning often fails because executives do not plan for uncertainty and because ivory tower planners lose touch with operating realities.
- Hamel and Prahalad have criticized the fit approach to strategy making on the ground that it focuses too much on the degree of fit between existing resources and current opportunities and not enough on building new resources and capabilities to create and exploit future opportunities.
- Strategic intent refers to an obsession with achieving an objective that stretches the company and requires it to build new resources and capabilities.
- In spite of systematic planning, companies may adopt poor strategies if their decision-making processes are vulnerable to groupthink and if individual cognitive biases are allowed to intrude into the decision-making process.
- Techniques for enhancing the effectiveness of strategic decision making include devil's advocacy and dialectic inquiry.

DISCUSSION QUESTIONS

1. What do we mean by *strategy?*
2. What are the strengths of formal strategic planning? What are its weaknesses?
3. The book "Barbarians at the Gate" by Bryan Burroughs and John Helyar (Harper & Row, 1990) contains a detailed description of the acqusition of RJR Nabisco by KKR. Using the book as your source, evaluate KKR's decision to acquire RJR Nabisco. Do you think cognitive biases were at work here, and would managers at KKR have reached a different decision if they had employed devil's advocacy? Was the acquisition of RJR an intended or an emergent strategy? (Note: Answering this question requires a fair amount of reading.)
4. Evaluate President Bill Clinton against the leadership characteristics discussed in the text. On the basis of this comparison, do you think that President Clinton is a good strategic leader?

Practicing Strategic Management

SMALL-GROUP EXERCISE
Designing a Planning System

Break up into groups of three to five people, and discuss the following scenario:

You are a group of senior managers working for a fast-growing computer software company. Your product allows users to engage in interactive role-playing games over the Internet (World Wide Web). In the last three years, your company has gone from being a start-up enterprise with 10 employees and no revenues to a company with 250 employees and revenues of $60 million. The company has been growing so rapidly that you have not had time to create a strategic plan, but now your board of directors tells you that it wants to see a plan and that it wants the plan to drive decision making and resource allocation at the company. The board wants you to design a planning process that will have the following attributes:

1. It will be democratic, involving as many key employees as possible in the process.
2. It will help build a sense of shared vision within the company about how to continue to grow rapidly.
3. It will lead to the generation of three to five key strategies for the company.
4. It will drive the formulation of detailed action plans, and these plans will be subsequently linked to the company's annual operating budget.

Design a planning process for presentation to your board of directors. Think carefully about who should be included in this process. Be sure to outline the strengths and weaknesses of the approach you choose, and be prepared to justify why your approach might be superior to alternative approaches.

ARTICLE FILE 1

At the end of every chapter in this book, you will find an Article File task. The task requires you to search newspapers or magazines in the library for an example of a real company that satisfies the task question or issue. Your first article file task is to find an example of a company that has recently changed its strategy. Identify whether this change was the outcome of a formal planning process or an emergent response to unforeseen events occurring in the company's environment.

STRATEGIC MANAGEMENT PROJECT
Module 1

To give you a practical insight into the strategic management process, we provide a series of strategic modules—one at the end of every chapter in this book. Each module asks you to collect and analyze information relating to the material discussed in that chapter. By completing these strategic modules, you will gain a clearer idea of the overall strategic management process. The first step in this project is to pick a company to study. We recommend that you focus on the same company throughout the book. Remember also that we will be asking you for information about the corporate and international strategy of your company, as well as its structure. We strongly recommend that you pick a company for which such information is likely to be available.

There are two approaches that can be used to select a company to study, and your instructor will tell you which one to follow. The first approach is to pick a well-known company that has a lot of information written about it. For example, large publicly held companies such as IBM, Microsoft, and Southwest Airlines are routinely covered in the business and financial press. By going to the library at your university, you should be able to track down a great deal of information on such companies. Many libraries now have electronic data search facilities such as *ABI/Inform*, *Wall Street Journal Index*, *F&S Index*, and *Nexis*. These enable you to identify any article that has been written in the business press on the company of your choice within the last few years. If you do not have electronic data search facilities at your university, we suggest that you ask your librarian about data sources. A number of nonelectronic data sources are available. For example, *F&S Predicasts* publishes an annual list of articles relating to major companies that appeared in the national and international business press. You will also want to collect full financial information on the company that you pick. Again, this can be accessed from electronic databases such as *Compact Disclosure*. Alternatively, your library might have the annual financial reports, 10-K filings, or proxy statements pertaining to the company you pick. Again, ask your librarians; they are the best source of information.

A second approach is to pick a smaller company in your city or town to study. Although small companies are not routinely covered in the national business press, they may be covered in the local press. More importantly, this approach can work well if the management of the company will agree to talk to you *at length* about the strategy and structure of the company. If you happen to know somebody in such a company or if you yourself have worked there at some point, this approach can be very worthwhile. However, we *do not* recommend this approach unless you can get a *substantial* amount of guaranteed access to the company of your choice. If in doubt, ask your instructor before making a decision. The key issue is to make sure that you have access to enough interesting information to complete the strategic modules.

Your assignment for Strategic Management Project, Module 1, is to choose a company to study and to obtain enough information about that company to carry out the following instructions and answer the questions asked.

1. Give a short account of the history of the company, and trace the evolution of its strategy over time. Try to determine whether the strategic evolution of your company is the product of intended strategies, emergent strategies, or some combination of the two.
2. Identify the mission and major goals of the company.
3. Do a preliminary analysis of the internal strengths and weaknesses of the company and of the opportunities and threats that it faces in its environment. On the basis of this analysis, identify the strategies that you think the company should pursue. (Note: You will need to perform a much more detailed analysis later in the book.)
4. Who is the CEO of the company? Evaluate the CEO's leadership capabilities.

EXPLORING THE WEB
Visiting Dell Computer

Go to the Web site of Dell Computer (http://www.dell.com) and find the section that describes Dell's history. Using the information contained there, map out the evolution of strategy at Dell from its establishment in the 1980s until the present day. To what degree do you think that the evolution of strategy at Dell was the result of detailed long-term strategic planning, and to what degree was it the result of unplanned actions taken in response to unpredictable circumstances?

Search the Web for a company site where there is sufficient information to map out the evolution of that company's strategy over a significant period of time. What drove the evolution of strategy at this company? To what degree was the evolution of strategy the result of detailed long-term strategic planning, and to what degree was it the result of unplanned actions taken in response to unpredictable circumstances?

CLOSING CASE

Jill Barad's Strategy for Mattel

On August 22, 1996, Jill Barad was named the next chief executive officer (CEO) of Mattel. At forty-five years of age, she had become one of the few women to head a major U.S. corporation. For Barad, the announcement was the fulfillment of a fifteen-year career at Mattel, during which she was best known for transforming Mattel's flagging line of Barbie dolls into the most profitable toy brand in the world. As product manager for Barbie, she had pioneered a brand extension strategy that had tripled Barbie sales to $1.4 billion between 1988 and 1995. In the process, she had gained a reputation for being a hard-driving manager and skilled marketing visionary. As CEO, one of Barad's first tasks was to decide on a strategy that would enable Mattel to grow earnings per share in line with the company's stated goal of 15 percent per annum compounded before the effects of any acquisitions.

Mattel is the world's largest toymaker, with 1995 revenues of $3.64 billion. Historically, the company's strengths have been in its Barbie brand, its Fisher-Price line of toys for young children (which generated 1995 revenues of more than $1 billion), the Hot Wheels brand, and its Disney licenses. Negotiated in 1988, the

Disney licenses give Mattel exclusive rights to make products based on Disney's movies for children. In 1995, Mattel earned revenues of $450 million from its Disney connection. Between 1988 and 1995 these four core product areas helped power Mattel to a compound annual growth rate of 20 percent for sales and 38 percent for operating income. By 1996, Mattel commanded about 16 percent of the market share for toys sold in the United States, although its share in Europe, the other great toy market, was less than 8 percent.

Despite Mattel's glittering past and Jill Barad's own starring role in it, many knowledgeable observers of the toy industry believed that the company's goal of 15 percent growth in earnings *before acquisitions* represented a difficult challenge for the new CEO. Barad took over the top spot at a time when Mattel's growth rate appeared to be slowing. In June 1996, Mattel reported that sales for its most recent quarter would be "approximately the same as last year," marking the first time quarterly results had been flat in eight years. To be sure, part of the slowdown was due to lackluster sales of its toys based on Disney's latest film, *The Hunchback of Notre Dame.* This shortfall could have easily been made up by a strong showing from toys linked to future Disney films. However, critics charged that the toy industry seemed to be suffering from a chronic lack of creativity. Of the fifteen top-selling toys in 1996, only three were toy company inventions that originated within the previous year. Mattel was very much a case in point. The Barbie brand had been around since 1959, Hot Wheels and Fisher-Price had been acquired rather than developed internally, and the creative impulse behind the Disney line of toys clearly came from that company, not Mattel.

Of course, it can be argued that given the fickle nature of the toy business, where last year's megahit can become this year's bust (remember Cabbage Patch Kids?), Mattel was right to focus on established and enduring brands. Nevertheless, by emphasizing established brands over innovations, Mattel ran the risk of missing successful new blockbusters. That is what happened with video games. Having given up after some early forays into video games, Mattel watched Japanese companies like Nintendo and Sega take that business from zero to $6 billion in sales.

As articulated in 1996, Barad's initial strategy for Mattel had four main elements. First, she made it clear that she would continue with the highly profitable practice of extending the company's existing brands. For example, she had plans to further develop a line of collectible Barbie dolls. Second, she would develop new product categories, particularly in boys' toys and board games, two areas where Mattel had traditionally been weak. That could be accomplished through internal product development or by acquiring an emerging company and then growing its business through further investments. Third, she would focus more effort on expanding overseas markets, where Mattel's presence was more limited than in the United States. Her stated goal was to increase overseas sales to more than 50 percent of Mattel's total—up from 40 percent in 1995. Finally, she would try to increase earnings by driving down costs. Cost reductions were to be achieved by outsourcing production to low-cost foreign factories in places such as China, a major shift for Mattel, which in 1995 manufactured two-thirds of its core product lines in its own plant.

Three years into her tenure, Barad's strategy for Mattel was increasingly being questioned by stockholders. After peaking at $44 a share in early 1998, the stock fell to $23 per share by June 1999 despite a record bull market in American stocks. The catalyst for the decline had been Barad's announcement that Mattel's profit growth would fall below the 15 percent goal during 1998 and 1999. The slowing growth was due to a number of problems that had stymied Barad's strategy. Parents were buying fewer toys and more computer software and video games for their children. Total U.S. toy sales were flat in 1998, while sales of video games increased by 20 percent and sales of software for children rose by 7 percent. Disney's most recent animated movies had been less successful than expected, and related toy sales had suffered accordingly. Moreover, most significantly, the popularity of the Barbie brand had declined, partly because of changing fashions. Parents were shifting their spending to computer software for girls and competing dolls, such as Pleasant Company's highly successful line of American Girl dolls. However, missteps by Mattel also contributed to the decline.

Throughout the 1990s, a big driver of Mattel's sales growth had been a line of Barbie collectibles known as Holiday Barbie—a line that Barad had introduced in 1988. Priced at $30 to $35 each, compared with less than $10 for a regular Barbie, by 1997 Holiday Barbie was generating $700 million of the total $1.7 billion in Barbie sales. In 1996, Barad had stated that she believed Holiday Barbie sales could exceed $1 billion. Accordingly, at Barad's insistence, in 1997 production of the Holiday Barbie line was set at 3 million dolls, a 1 million increase from 1996. However, much of the rise in demand during 1996 and 1997 stemmed from double ordering by retailers that had suffered from shortages in prior years. When

CLOSING CASE *(continued)*

the expected demand growth failed to materialize in 1998, retailers were left with excess stock of Holiday Barbie and started to discount, while putting new orders on hold. Consequently, after years of growth, Barbie sales fell by 15 percent in the first half of 1998. More significantly perhaps, overproduction had destroyed the collectible value of Holiday Barbie, and it was unclear whether Mattel could rebuild it.

To try to salvage her growth strategy, Barad took several actions in 1998 and 1999. In mid 1998, Mattel acquired the Pleasant Company for $700 million. By this point, the Pleasant Company was the number two doll maker in the United States. According to Barad, the Pleasant Company's highly successful American Girl brand was targeted at girls aged seven to twelve and was thus a perfect complement to Barbie, where the demographic was two- to seven-year-olds. This acquisition was followed in late 1998 by the acquisition of computer software maker The Learning Company for $3.5 billion. The Learning Company's software titles include the popular Reader Rabbit series, Carmen Sandiego, and Myst. In April 1999, after the announcement of a 2 percent decline in sales and a first-quarter loss of $18 million, Barad also laid out plans to cut 3,000 jobs in order to realize cost savings of $400 million over three years. Around the same time, she announced the formation of an on-line venture, www.mattelstore.com, to tap into the growing volume of on-line sales. Barad believed that this venture would generate revenues of $60 million in its first year alone. The company also stated that it had entered into an alliance with Intel to develop a generation of interactive toys.[47]

Case Discussion Questions

1. What was Jill Barad's primary goal for Mattel in 1996? What strategies did she choose in order to pursue these goals?
2. Why did Barad's strategies fail to generate the profit growth she had planned? Could better planning have helped Barad anticipate market trends?
3. Could better decision-making techniques have helped Barad avoid the decline in sales of Holiday Barbie?
4. How would you describe Mattel's strategy as of mid 1999? Does this strategy make sense, given changing conditions in the toy market? Would you describe this strategy as an emergent strategy or a planned strategy?

End Notes

1. S. G. Steinberg. "Seek and Ye Shall Find (Maybe)," *Wired*, release 4.05 (May 1996); L. Himelstein, H. Green, and R. Siklos, "Yahoo! The Company, The Strategy, The Stock," *Business Week*, September 7, 1998, p. 66; S. Moran, "For Yahoo, GeoCities May Only Be the Start," *Internet World*, March 15, 1999; Yahoo! 1998 Annual Report.
2. K. R. Andrews, *The Concept of Corporate Strategy* (Homewood, Ill.: Dow Jones Irwin, 1971); H. I. Ansoff, *Corporate Strategy* (New York: McGraw-Hill, 1965); C. W. Hofer and D. Schendel, *Strategy Formulation: Analytical Concepts* (St. Paul, Minn.: West, 1978).
3. Andrews, *The Concept of Corporate Strategy;* Ansoff, *Corporate Strategy;* Hofer and Schendel, *Strategy Formulation*.
4. M. E.Porter. "What Is Strategy?" *Harvard Business Review* (November–December 1996), 7, 61–90.
5. S. Tully, "So Mr. Bossidy, We Know You Can Cut. Now Show Us How to Grow," *Fortune*, August 21, 1995, pp. 70–80; E. G. Randall, "AlliedSignal," *Value Line*, February 9, 1999, p. 1353; "Chief Executive of the Year 1998: AlliedSignal's Larry Bossidy," *Chief Executive* (U.S.), November 1998, p. 32; J. P. Dolan, "The CEO's CEO," interview with Allied Signal CEO Larry Bossidy, *Chief Executive*, July 17, 1998, p. 28.
6. For a summary of research on strategic leadership, see D. C. Hambrick, "Putting Top Managers Back into the Picture," *Strategic Management Journal,* Special Issue, 10 (1989), 5–15. See also D. Goleman, "What Makes a Leader?" *Harvard Business Review* (November–December 1998), 92–105; and H. Mintzberg, "Covert Leadership," *Harvard Business Review* (November–December 1998), 140–148.
7. N. M. Tichy and D. O. Ulrich, "The Leadership Challenge: A Call for the Transformational Leader," *Sloan Management Review* (Fall 1984), 59–68; F. Westley and H. Mintzberg, "Visionary Leadership and Strategic Management," *Strategic Management Journal,* Special Issue, 10 (1989), 17–32.
8. E. Wrapp, "Good Managers Don't Make Policy Decisions," *Harvard Business Review* (September–October 1967), 91–99.
9. J. Pfeffer, *Managing with Power* (Boston: Harvard Business School Press, 1992).
10. Goleman. "What Makes a Leader?" pp. 92–105.
11. For details see R. A.Burgelman, "Intraorganizational Ecology of Strategy Making and Organizational Adaptation: Theory and Field Research," *Organization Science*, 2 (1991), 239–262; H. Mintzberg, "Patterns in Strategy Formulation," *Management Science*, 24 (1978), 934–948; S. L. Hart, "An Integrative Framework for Strategy Making Processes," *Academy of Management Review*, 17 (1992), 327–351; G. Hamel, "Strategy as Revolution," *Harvard Business Review* (July–August 1996), 74, 69–83.
12. This is the premise of those who advocate that chaos theory should be applied to strategic management. See R. Stacey and D. Parker, *Chaos, Management and Economics* (London: Institute for Economic Affairs, 1994); and H. Courtney, J. Kirkland, and P. Viguerie, "Strategy Under Uncertainty," *Harvard Business Review* (November–December 1997), 75, 66–79.
13. C. von Clausewitz, *On War*, translated and edited by M. Howard and P. Paret, (Princeton: 1976), pp. 134, 136.
14. "The Accidental Superhighway: A Survey of the Internet," *Economist,* July 1, 1995; G. Gilder, "The Coming Software Shift," *Forbes ASAP*, August 28, 1995, pp. 147–162; R. D. Hof, K. Rebello, and P. Burrows, "Scott McNealy's Rising Sun," *Business Week*, January 22, 1996, pp. 66–73. A. Cortese, J. Verity, K. Rebello, R. D. Hof, "The Software Revolution," *Business Week*, December 4, 1995, pp. 78–90; informal interviews by Charles Hill with key personnel at Microsoft.
15. Hart, "An Integrative Framework," pp. 327–351; Hamel, "Strategy as Revolution," pp. 74, 69–83.
16. See Burgelman, "Intraorganizational Ecology," pp. 239–262; Mintzberg, "Patterns in Strategy Formulation," pp. 934–948.
17. R. A. Burgelman and A. S. Grove, "Strategic Dissonance," *California Management Review* (Winter 1996), 8–28.
18. M. Dickson, "Back to the Future," *Financial Times*, May 30, 1994, p. 7.
19. Story was related to Charles Hill by George Rathmann, the head of 3M's research activities at the time.
20. Story related to the author by various employees of ICOS.
21. Richard T. Pascale, "Perspectives on Strategy: The Real Story Behind Honda's Success," *California Management Review*, 26 (1984), 47–72.
22. This viewpoint is strongly emphasized by Burgelman and Grove, "Strategic Dissonance," pp. 8–28.
23. Burgelman and Grove, "Strategic Dissonance," pp. 8–28.
24. C. C. Miller and L. B. Cardinal, "Strategic Planning and Firm Performance: A Synthesis of More than Two Decades of Research," *Academy of Management Journal*, 37, (1994), 1649–1665. See also see P. R. Rogers, A. Miller, and W. Q. Judge, "Using Information Processing Theory to Understand Planning/Performance Relationships in the Context of Strategy," *Strategic Management Journal*, 20 (1999), 567–577.
25. T. J. Peters and R. H. Waterman, *In Search of Excellence* (New York: Harper & Row, 1982); T. J. Peters, *Liberation Management: Necessary Disorganization for the Nanosecond Nineties* (New York: Knopf, 1992).
26. H. Mintzberg, "The Design School: Reconsidering the Basic Premises of Strategic Management," *Strategic Management Journal*, 11 (1990), 171–196; H. Mintzberg, *The Rise and Fall of Strategic Planning* (New York: Free Press, 1994).
27. Courtney, Kirkland, and Viguerie, "Strategy Under Uncertainty," pp. 66–79.
28. P. J. H. Schoemaker, "Multiple Scenario Development: Its Conceptual and Behavioral Foundation," *Strategic Management Journal*, 14 (1993), 193–213.
29. "According to Plan," *Economist,* July 22, 1989, pp. 60–63. A. P. de Geus, "Planning as Learning," *Harvard Business Review* (March–April 1988), 70–74; P. Wack, "Scenarios: Uncharted Waters Ahead," *Harvard Business Review* (September–October 1985), 73–89; T. Mack, "It's Time to Take Risks," *Forbes,* October 6, 1986, pp. 125–133.

30. W. C. Kim and R. Mauborgne, "Procedural Justice, Strategic Decision Making, and the Knowledge Economy," *Strategic Management Journal*, 19 (1998), 323–338; W. C. Kim and R. Mauborgne, "Fair Process: Managing in the Knowledge Economy," *Harvard Business Review*, July–August 1997), 75, 65–76.
31. Kim and Mauborgne, "Procedural Justice," pp. 323–338.
32. G. Hamel and C. K. Prahalad, *Competing for the Future* (New York: Free Press, 1994).
33. See G. Hamel and C. K. Prahalad, "Strategic Intent," *Harvard Business Review* (May–June 1989), p. 64.
34. For a review of the evidence, see C. R. Schwenk, "Cognitive Simplification Processes in Strategic Decision Making," *Strategic Management Journal*, 5 (1984), 111–128; and K. M. Eisenhardt and M. Zbaracki, "Strategic Decision Making," *Strategic Management Journal*, Special Issue, 13 (1992), 17–37.
35. H. Simon, *Administrative Behavior* (New York: McGraw Hill, 1957).
36. The original statement about this phenomenon was made by A. Tversky and D. Kahneman, "Judgment Under Uncertainty: Heuristics and Biases," *Science*, 185 (1974), 1124–1131.
37. Schwenk, "Cognitive Simplification Processes," pp. 111–128.
38. B. M. Staw, "The Escalation of Commitment to a Course of Action," *Academy of Management Review*, 6 (1981), 577–587.
39. Ibid.
40. M. J. Tang, "An Economic Perspective on Escalating Commitment," *Strategic Management Journal*, 9 (1988), 79–92.
41. R. Roll, "The Hubris Hypotheses of Corporate Takeovers," *Journal of Business*, 59 (1986), 197–216.
42. I. L. Janis, *Victims of Groupthink*, 2nd ed. (Boston: Houghton Mifflin, 1982). For an alternative view, see S. R. Fuller and R. J. Aldag, "Organizational Tonypandy: Lessons from a Quarter Century of the Groupthink Phenomenon," *Organizational Behavior and Human Decision Processes*, 73 (1998), 163–184.
43. The story ran on an almost daily basis in the *Financial Times* of London during the autumn of 1979.
44. See R. O. Mason, "A Dialectic Approach to Strategic Planning," *Management Science*, 13 (1969), 403–414; R. A. Cosier and J. C. Aplin, "A Critical View of Dialectic Inquiry in Strategic Planning," *Strategic Management Journal*, 1 (1980), 343–356; and I. I. Mintroff and R. O. Mason, "Structuring III—Structured Policy Issues: Further Explorations in a Methodology for Messy Problems," *Strategic Management Journal*, 1 (1980), 331–342.
45. Mason, "A Dialectic Approach," pp. 403–414.
46. D. M. Schweiger and P. A. Finger, "The Comparative Effectiveness of Dialectic Inquiry and Devil's Advocacy," *Strategic Management Journal* 5 (1984), 335–350.
47. Lisa Bannon, "Mattel Names Jill Barad Chief Executive," *Wall Street Journal*, August 23, 1996, p. B3; L. Sandler, "Mattel's Marriage to Disney Falters," *Wall Street Journal*, August 16, 1996, p. C2; "Mattel Growth Strategy to Pursue Acquisitions, Overseas Expansion," *Wall Street Journal*, June 15, 1996, p. B10; E. Schine, "Toys R Her," *Business Week*, September 2, 1996, p. 47; L. Bannon. "Mattel Tries to Adjust as Holiday Barbie Leaves Under a Cloud," *Wall Street Journal*, June 7, 1999, p. A1, A10; "Toys Were Us," *Financial Times*, December 19, 1998, p. 9.

2 Stakeholders and the Corporate Mission

OPENING CASE

Chainsaw Al Dunlap Gets the Ax

IN JULY 1996, Sunbeam, a troubled maker of small appliances, announced that it had hired Al Dunlap as its chief executive officer. Sunbeam's stock jumped 50 percent at the news, to $18 5/8 as investors eagerly anticipated the gains that the legendary "Chainsaw Al" would bring to Sunbeam. Dunlap's reputation was built on a highly successful career as a turnaround specialist. Before joining Sunbeam, Dunlap had engineered a tough turnaround at Scott Paper. There he had laid off 31 percent of the work force, including 70 percent of all upper-level managers. The stock market valuation of Scott tripled during his tenure. After only eighteen months at Scott, Dunlap walked away with $100 million in salary, bonus, stock gains, and perks. Dunlap claimed that this reward was richly deserved, given the gains that he engineered in the stock of Scott Paper. Now investors hoped that he would work the same magic at Sunbeam.

Upon arrival at Sunbeam, Dunlap quickly fired seven of Sunbeam's top executives. Then he spent three months formulating his strategy, which he unveiled at an analyst meeting in November 1996. It was classic Dunlap. He stated that Sunbeam's work force would be cut in half, to just 6,000, and that eighteen of the company's twenty-six factories would be closed, four divisions disposed of, and the number of products offered by Sunbeam reduced by 81 percent to 1,500. Together, these measures were projected to produce annual savings of $225 million. Dunlap also laid out ambitious growth goals for Sunbeam: doubling revenues to $2 billion (after divestitures), raising operating profit margins to 20 percent from 2.5 percent, launching at least 30 new products a year, and increasing international sales to $600 million. "Our growth mission," he proclaimed, "is to become the dominant and most profitable small household appliance and outdoor cooking company in North America, with a leading share of Latin American and Asian Pacific markets."

Right from the start there were questions about the feasibility of this strategy. Several securities analysts who followed Sunbeam wondered how the company could possibly grow revenues, given the depth of the cuts in employment and products, particularly since the North American market for small appliances was experiencing no growth. Initially, however, Sunbeam's results seemed to suggest that Dunlap could indeed pull off this trick. Sunbeam's revenues grew by 18 percent in 1997, while operating margins income rose to $109.4 million and the stock

OPENING CASE *(continued)*

price surged to around $50 a share. It looked like Dunlap was about to prove once again that tough guys finish first.

Under the surface, though, there were problems at Sunbeam. To grow revenues, Dunlap was urging Sunbeam's managers to engage in a "bill and hold" strategy with retailers. This arrangement allowed Sunbeam's products to be purchased at large discounts and then held at third-party warehouses for delivery later. In effect, Dunlap was shifting sales from future periods into the current period. Although the approach was not illegal, its ethics were questionable. Later, Dunlap defended the practice, claiming that it was an effort to extend the selling season and better meet surges in demand. Sunbeam's auditors, Arthur Anderson & Co., also insisted that the practice met accounting standards.

In early March 1998, Dunlap announced that Sunbeam would acquire three companies, including Coleman, the manufacturer of outdoor camping stoves. The market responded enthusiastically, and the stock hit an all-time high of $53. Some critics wondered, however, if this implied that Sunbeam could not reach its growth goals from internally generated sales. Shortly afterward, Dunlap announced that the company would book a first-quarter loss of $44.6 million. He blamed the loss on underlings who had offered "stupid, low-margin deals," and he insisted that it would "never happen again." To drive home his point, he fired a number of senior managers who, he claimed, were responsible for those deals. Among the dismissed was Donald Uzzi, Sunbeam's well-regarded executive vice president for worldwide consumer products. Around the same time, Dunlap announced that he would cut 5,100 more jobs at the acquired companies and at Sunbeam.

The layoff announcement did not stop the fall in Sunbeam's stock price, which had been declining ever since the announcement of a first-quarter loss and now stood under $20. The decline in the stock price accelerated in late May 1998, when the highly regarded financial newspaper *Barron's* published a scathing analysis of Sunbeam. In the article, *Barron's* alleged that Dunlap had employed $120 million of artificial profit boosters in 1997, without which Sunbeam would have recorded a loss.

Dunlap was so concerned about the *Barron's* article that he called a special meeting of the company's board of directors on June 9, 1998. The board had been supportive of Dunlap up to this point, and he could count several long-time friends among its members. What began as a straightforward meeting rebutting the *Barron's* article took a strange turn when one director asked Sunbeam's chief financial officer, Russ Kersh, if the company would make its next quarter's numbers. Kersh admitted that they were "challenging." At this point, Dunlap asked the outside advisers to step out and then told the board that he and the CFO would resign unless they got the right level of support from the board. "I have all of the necessary documents in my briefcase," Dunlap was reported to have said. Dunlap then stormed out of the room.

Over the next few days, the board members started to dig deeper into the Sunbeam situation. One director placed a call to several top executives. He quickly discovered that many of them had lost confidence in Dunlap, whom they characterized as abusive and unethical. He was also disturbed to hear that not only would Sunbeam miss its growth goals in the coming quarter, but that revenues would probably come in $60 million *below* the $290 million recorded in the same quarter a year earlier.

Armed with this information, the board convened a second meeting on June 13. At that meeting, the directors all agreed that Dunlap had to go. Most of the directors were Dunlap's friends, but they felt betrayed by him, misled about the company's financial condition, its second-quarter earnings, and its yearly numbers. That day they placed a call to Dunlap and told him that he had been dismissed. Three days later, the board also fired Russ Kersh, the CFO. Commenting on Dunlap's demise, the CEO of a Sunbeam competitor stated that Dunlap "is the logical extreme of an executive who has no values, no loyalty, no honor, no ethics. And yet he was held up as a corporate god in our culture. It greatly bothers me." A former plant manager fired by Dunlap remarked: "I guess the house of cards came tumbling down. When you reduce your work force by 50 percent, you lose your ability to manage. You can survive like that for months, not years." After the announcement that Dunlap had been fired, Sunbeam stock fell to under $8 a share, lower than it had been before Dunlap joined the company.[1]

OVERVIEW

The Opening Case tells the story of how Al Dunlap's career as a turnaround specialist came to an abrupt end at Sunbeam. Dunlap failed for a number of reasons. He lacked a strategic vision that went beyond cutting costs. He did not know how to pursue a growth strategy, and to disguise this fact, he pursued ethically suspect accounting policies. He also misled investors and the board of directors about the true financial condition of the company. Consequently, he lost the support of important constituencies in the company, most notably other senior managers and the board of directors. Ultimately, the board could no longer tolerate him as CEO and fired both him and his CFO, Russ Kersh. It should also be noted that long before Dunlap lost the support of the board and other senior managers, he had already lost the support of numerous employees, many of whom had seen their colleagues fired and plants shut down.

This chapter is concerned with how companies can maintain the support of key constituencies—or stakeholders. A company's **stakeholders** are individuals or groups that have an interest, claim, or stake in the company, in what it does, and in how well it performs.[2] We begin by looking at the relationship between stakeholders and a company. Then we move on to consider the corporate mission statement, which is the first key indicator of how an organization views the claims of its stakeholders. The purpose of the mission statement is to establish the guiding principles for strategic decision making. We then explore the issue of corporate governance. By **corporate governance**, we mean the mechanisms that are used to "govern" managers and ensure that the actions they take are consistent with the interests of key stakeholder groups. The board of directors is a very important corporate governance mechanism. As we saw in the Opening Case, the board has the power to remove a CEO who is not satisfying the interests of key stakeholders.

The chapter closes with a look at the ethical dimension of strategic decisions and at the relationship between ethics and stakeholders' welfare. The Opening Case offers a good illustration of the importance of ethics. Dunlap's questionable ethics allowed him to mislead investors about the true financial state of the company, which helped bring about his removal. By the end of this chapter you will have a good grasp of how stakeholders, corporate governance mechanisms, and ethical considerations all influence the strategies that managers choose for their organizations.

STAKEHOLDERS

A company's stakeholders can be divided into internal stakeholders and external stakeholders (see Figure 2.1). **Internal stakeholders** are stockholders and employees, including executive officers, other managers, and board members. **External stakeholders** are all other individuals and groups that have some claim on the company. Typically, this group comprises customers, suppliers, governments, unions, local communities, and the general public.

All stakeholders are in an exchange relationship with the company. Each of the stakeholder groups listed in Figure 2.1 supplies the organization with important resources (or contributions), and in exchange each expects its interests to be satisfied

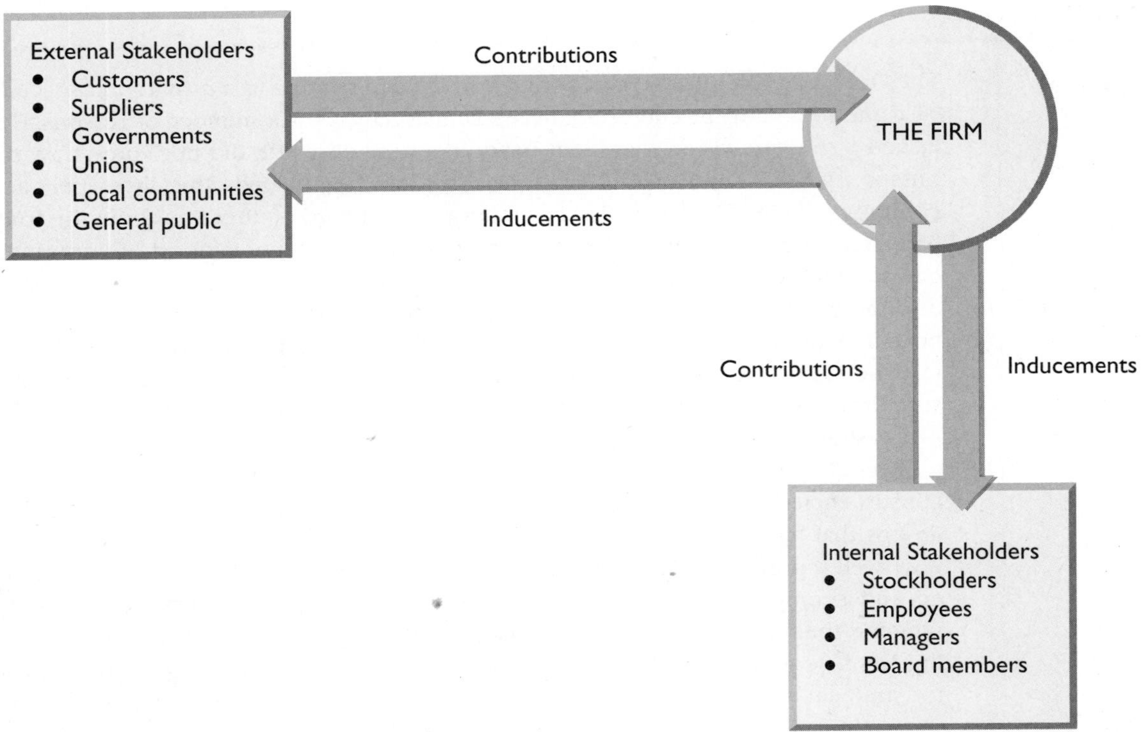

FIGURE 2.1

Stakeholders and the Enterprise

(by inducements).[3] Stockholders provide the enterprise with capital and in exchange expect an appropriate return on their investment. Employees provide labor and skills and in exchange expect commensurate income, job satisfaction, job security, and good working conditions. Customers provide a company with its revenues and in exchange they want high-quality, reliable products that represent value for money. Suppliers provide a company with inputs and in exchange seek revenues and dependable buyers. Governments provide a company with rules and regulations that govern business practices and maintain fair competition and in exchange want companies that adhere to these rules. Unions help to provide a company with productive employees and in exchange want benefits for their members in proportion to their contributions to the company. Local communities provide companies with local infrastructure and in exchange want companies that are responsible citizens. The general public provides companies with national infrastructure and in exchange seeks some assurance that the quality of life will be improved as a result of the company's existence.

A company must take these claims into account when formulating its strategies, or stakeholders may withdraw their support. For example, stockholders may sell their shares, employees leave their jobs, and customers buy elsewhere. Suppliers may seek more dependable buyers. Unions may engage in disruptive labor disputes. Communities may oppose the company's attempts to locate its facilities in their area, and the general public may form pressure groups, demanding action against companies that impair the quality of life. Any of these reactions can have a disastrous effect on an enterprise, as Strategy in Action 2.1 illustrates. It shows how Bill Agee, the former CEO of Morrison Knudsen, lost his job because he failed to satisfy the interests of two important stakeholder groups: the company's employees and its stockholders.

A company cannot always satisfy the claims of all stakeholders. The goals of different groups may conflict, and in practice few organizations have the resources to manage all stakeholders.[5] For example, union claims for higher wages can conflict with consumer demands for reasonable prices and stockholder demands for acceptable returns. Often the company must make choices. To do so, it must identify the most important stakeholders and give highest priority to pursuing strategies that satisfy their needs. Stakeholder impact analysis can provide such identification. Typically, stakeholder impact analysis follows these steps:

1. Identifying stakeholders
2. Identifying stakeholders' interests and concerns
3. As a result, identifying what claims stakeholders are likely to make on the organization
4. Identifying the stakeholders who are most important from the organization's perspective
5. Identifying the resulting strategic challenges[6]

Such an analysis enables a company to identify the stakeholders most critical to its survival and to make sure that the satisfaction of their needs is paramount. Most companies that go through this process quickly reach the conclusion that there are three stakeholder groups the company must satisfy if it is to survive and prosper: customers, employees, and stakeholders. Both Al Dunlap and Bill Agee lost their CEO positions because they failed to satisfy the demands of stockholders for a good return on their investment. Agee also failed to satisfy the demands of employees for income, job satisfaction, job security, and good working conditions (and one could argue that the same was true of Dunlap). More generally, any company that fails to satisfy the needs of its customers will soon see its revenues fall and will ultimately go out of business.

THE MISSION STATEMENT

As noted earlier, the corporate mission statement is a key indicator of how an organization views the claims of its stakeholders. It describes how a company intends to incorporate stakeholder claims into its strategic decision making and thereby reduce the risk of losing stakeholder support. Thus, in its mission statement, a company makes a formal commitment to its stakeholders, sending out the message that its strategies will be formulated with the claims of those stakeholders in mind.

Most corporate mission statements are built around three main elements: (1) a declaration of the overall vision, or mission, of the company; (2) a summing-up of the key philosophical values that managers are committed to and that influence the

2.1 STRATEGY *in* ACTION

Bill Agee at Morrison Knudsen

Bill Agee made his name as a whiz kid who became the chief financial officer of papermaker Boise Cascade during the 1970s while still in his early thirties. Agee left Boise Cascade after the company was forced to write down its profits by $250 million due to earlier overstatements of the value of timberland sales. At the time, the write-downs were the largest in corporate history, but this did not stop Agee from being appointed CEO of defense contractor Bendix in 1976, when he was only thirty-eight years old. At Bendix, Agee became involved in a famous corporate soap opera, which began when he promoted a young manager, Mary Cunningham, to a senior post, over the heads of other, more experienced, executives. At the time, many felt the promotion came about because the two were romantically involved. Both denied this, but in 1982 Agee divorced his wife and married Cunningham, who by this time had left Bendix.

In 1988, Agee became CEO of Idaho-based Morrison Knudsen (MK—a seventy-five-year-old construction company, which had made its name as the prime contractor on a number of large western construction projects, including the Hoover Dam and the trans-Alaska pipeline. By the time Agee joined MK, it was perceived as a venerable institution that wasn't quite living up to its performance potential. Agee's strategy for improving performance was to sell off some of MK's assets and invest the proceeds in the securities of other companies. He also pushed MK to aggressively pursue large construction projects and to grow its railcar manufacturing business. At one time, the railcar manufacturing business had been a major success at MK, but in recent years it had fallen on hard times, unable to hold its own against Japanese competition.

On the surface, MK appeared to be prospering under Agee's leadership. In 1993, the company earned $35.8 million, and Agee proclaimed it a "banner year" and a "watershed period" for MK's drive into railroad and mass-transit industries. Beneath the surface, however, things were unraveling for Agee. For one thing, 62 percent of MK's profits in 1993 came from Agee's financial plays in securities trading and capital gains on asset sales. Strip out these one-time gains, and it was clear that MK's operating performance was poor. The prime reason seems to have been Agee's insistence that in order to win new business MK should be the low bidder on large contracts. For instance, when MK bid on a contract to build eighty transit cars for the Bay Area Rapid Transit District (BART) in Oakland, California, Agee knocked down the bid to $142 million. According to one insider, the result was that "we were looking at a $14 million loss on the contract the day we won it." In the second quarter of 1994, MK announced a $40.5 million loss after taking a $59.4 million charge for underbidding various transit-car contracts. In the third quarter of 1994, MK took a $9.2 million charge against profits for underbidding on a $100 million contract to rebuild locomotives for Southern Pacific.

decisions they make; and (3) the articulation of key goals that management believes must be adhered to in order to attain the vision, or mission, and that are consistent with the values to which managers are committed.[7]

Vision, or Mission

The **vision,** or **mission,** of a company is what the company is trying to achieve over the medium to long term as formally declared in its mission statement. In practice, the terms *vision* and *mission* are often used interchangeably, and some companies use the term *purpose* instead. Boeing states that its mission is "to be the number one aerospace company in the world and among the premier industrial

To compound these problems, Agee's leadership had sparked significant employee opposition. In an anonymous letter sent to MK's board in November 1994, a group of MK executives calling themselves the MK Committee for Excellence leveled a slew of charges at Agee. Right off, they claimed, Agee had irked subordinates by removing the portrait of MK's founder from the headquarters and replacing it with a nearly life-sized portrait of himself and his wife, Mary Cunningham, paid for by the company. Agee further estranged insiders by quietly moving the CEO's office to his Pebble Beach estate in California and by scoffing at the company's engineering-oriented culture. Several old-hand MK engineering executives—people who had top reputations in their field—were fired, usually after crossing swords with Agee over his policies.

There was also the matter of Agee's pay and perks. At $2.4 million, Agee's 1993 compensation was equal to 6.8 percent of MK's net income, more than that of any other CEO of a company with earnings in the same range, according to a *Forbes* magazine list. According to insiders, MK paid $4 million a year for a corporate jet for Agee, equal to 13 percent of the company's general and administrative budget. The company also paid for landscaping services at Agee's Pebble Beach estate.

Things came to a head on February 1, 1995, when MK's board announced that the company would record a large loss for 1994. The board also announced that Agee would be stepping down as CEO, although initial indications were that he would stay on as chairman of the board. Preliminary figures suggested that MK would have to take a $179.6 million pretax charge in its 1994 fourth quarter, which would result in a net loss of $141 million for the quarter. At the same time, Standard & Poor's downgraded MK's long-term debt to junk bond rating, signaling that a significant risk of default existed.

The announcement gave rise to a blizzard of shareholder lawsuits and criticism, not only of Agee, but also of MK's board for acting so slowly. Many commentators wondered why it took a huge loss and an anonymous letter from MK executives to prod the board to action. Privately, several board members—most of whom were Agee's appointees and long-time friends—indicated that they were led astray by Agee, who repeatedly urged them not to worry about poor results. Still, many felt that the audit committee of the board of directors had not done a good job of vetting MK's financial accounts under Agee's leadership. Stung by this criticism, by the growing evidence of financial mismanagement under Agee's leadership, and by the Standard & Poor's downgrading of MK's debt, the board reversed its earlier position and decided to strip Agee of all posts at MK.

The shareholders' lawsuits were settled in September 1995. The settlement required MK to pay out $63 million in cash and stock to shareholders and to strengthen its board by adding seven new directors over the next two years. As part of the settlement, Agee agreed to relinquish rights to about $3 million in severance pay and to a cut in his MK pension from $303,000 a year for life to $99,750 a year for life.[4]

concerns in terms of quality, profitability, and growth."[8] The vision set forth by Weyerhaeuser, the world's largest forest products company, is to simply be "the best forest products company in the world."[9] Pfizer, one of the world's premier pharmaceutical companies, defines its mission as "helping humanity and delivering exceptional financial performance by discovering, developing and providing innovative health care products that lead to healthier and more productive lives."[10] The vision enunciated by Intel, the world's largest manufacturer of microprocessors, is "to get to a billion connected computers worldwide. . . .by providing the building blocks of the Internet.[11] Applied Materials, which manufactures the machines that make semiconductor chips, has as its mission to be "the leading supplier of semiconductor wafer processing systems and services worldwide through product innovation and enhancement of customer productivity."[12]

2.2 STRATEGY in ACTION

Engineering a Strategic Vision at AT&T

When Michael Armstrong was appointed CEO of AT&T in late 1997, he took over the reins of a company that seemed to be letting the rapid development of communications in the Internet age pass it by. The company still generated 90 percent of its revenues from its core long-distance phone business, but the growth in the communication market was in the wireless and Internet access arenas. Moreover, AT&T's core long-distance business was under threat. New entrants into this market, such as the Baby Bells, and aggressive newcomers, such as Qwest Communications, were driving down prices in an attempt to gain market share. Analysts predicted that prices for long-distance phone service could fall from an average of 15 cents per minute in 1998, to 5 cents per minute by 2002. As a result of new entry, some believed that AT&T's market share could decline from 50 percent to under 30 percent over the same period.

Surveying the competitive landscape, Armstrong was struck by the speed of the revolution sweeping the communications industry. He noted that it took radio thirty years to reach 50 million people. It took thirteen years for television to do the same. But the World Wide Web reached twice as many users in half the time. By 1998, more than 100 million people had logged on to the Internet. Projections suggested that there would be 250 million Internet users around the world by 2002. Commerce on the Internet, barely a blip a few years previously, was projected to surpass $300 billion by 2002. Wireless phones, once a novelty, were rapidly becoming a necessity, with 1 million Americans signing up for wireless service every month.

The conclusion that Armstrong drew from this analysis was that AT&T needed to shift rapidly from being a long-distance phone company to a company that could deliver high-speed and capacity (broadband) communications to business and residential consumers around the world, and do so profitably. Going forward, Armstrong stated, AT&T's strategic vision would be "to enrich our customers' personal lives and to make their businesses more successful by bringing to market exciting and useful communications services, building shareowner value in the process." By articulating this vision, Armstrong was signaling that AT&T intended to move aggressively into new communications markets. In January 1998, Armstrong announced that AT&T would move beyond the

What you may notice about these statements is that they all commit the corporation to an ambitious goal. To "be number one," "the best," to deliver "exceptional financial performance," "to get to a billion connected computers worldwide," and to be "the leading supplier." All these mission statements are examples of **strategic intent**.

Strategic Intent We encountered the concept of strategic intent in Chapter 1. As you recall, underlying it is the notion that managers should set an overarching ambitious goal that stretches a company.[13] Often, the vision, or mission, statement articulates the company's strategic intent. Thus, Boeing's strategic intent is to remain the number one aerospace company in the world, while that of Applied Materials is to become the leading supplier of specific product and services. The argument for setting an overarching stretch goal is that (1) it gives a sense of direction and purpose to those within the company; (2) it helps drive strategic decision making and resource allocation; and (3) it forces managers within the company to look for significant improvements in the way they run the business, since that is the only way to attain stretch goals. Put differently, as Jack Welch, the CEO of General Electric, has observed:

> If you don't demand something out of the ordinary, you won't get anything but ordinary results. . . . We used to say nudge the peanut along, moving from, say, 4.73 inventory turns to 4.91. Now we want big stretch results like ten turns or fifteen turns.[14]

long-distance phone business and make major investments in local wireless and Internet-based phone services. He also stated that AT&T would take $1.6 billion out of its cost structure that year. Fine words indeed, but skeptical investors had heard this kind of rhetoric before and wanted to see action.

They didn't have to wait long. By the end of 1998, AT&T had reduced its work force by 18,000 and reached its cost-reduction goals. The employment cuts came from voluntary buyouts, a hiring freeze, and normal attrition. Soon after, AT&T announced its Digital One Rate for wireless customers. This rate carries no long-distance or roaming charge for cellular telephone customers. Although per minute charges have declined as a result, increased usage has more than made up for this. By early 1999, the average subscriber bill was up to $60 per month, an increase of $10 from six months earlier.

However, AT&T's biggest strategic moves under Armstrong have been aimed at acquiring cable television networks. In June 1988, Armstrong announced that AT&T would purchase TCI, America's largest cable television provider, in a $48 billion stock swap. The goal was to offer local phone service and high-speed Internet access over cable TV networks. With the TCI purchase came a recently acquired TCI subsidiary, @Home Corp, which specializes in providing high-speed Internet access over cable TV networks. AT&T announced that it would use the cable network to begin delivering local phone service over the Internet by the end of 1999. To do this, AT&T stated that it would be using Internet Protocol switching, rather than the traditional circuit switch approach.

In May 1999, these developments were followed by the purchase for $58 billion of MediaOne Group, another large cable group. Simultaneously, AT&T announced that Microsoft would invest $5 billion in AT&T in return for a 3.9 percent ownership stake. For its part, AT&T agreed to use Microsoft's Windows CE as the operating system for set-top boxes.

From these deals it is now clear that AT&T's goal is to provide both local phone service and a broad array of Internet and multimedia services over its newly acquired cable network. Moreover, many of these services will be bundled together, with AT&T charging consumers a single rate for access to the entire range of services. The combination of TCI and MediaOne should enable AT&T to deliver these services to some 26 million homes in the United States. By acting on its vision, AT&T is in the process of evolving from a provider of long-distance phone service to a broad-based provider of communications services.[15]

However, managers must also make sure that the vision does not become so grandiose that it cannot be realized and thus loses credibility among employees. A stretch goal has to be attainable, even though it may require managers to strive for extraordinary performance improvements.

Strategy in Action 2.2 offers a detailed example of a vision that has driven the subsequent development of strategy. It examines CEO Michael Armstrong's process of selecting a strategic vision for AT&T, which is now guiding the repositioning of AT&T. The example illustrates how a new vision—a new articulation of strategic intent—can drive the strategic development of a company, even one as large as AT&T.

Customer Orientation and Business Definition An important first step in the process of formulating a mission statement is to define the organization's business. Essentially, the definition should answer these questions: "What is our business? What will it be? What should it be?"[16] The responses guide the formulation of a mission statement.

To answer the first question—"What is our business?"—Derek F. Abell has suggested that a company should define its business in terms of three dimensions: who is being satisfied (what customer groups), what is being satisfied (what customer

FIGURE 2.2

Abell's Framework for Defining the Business

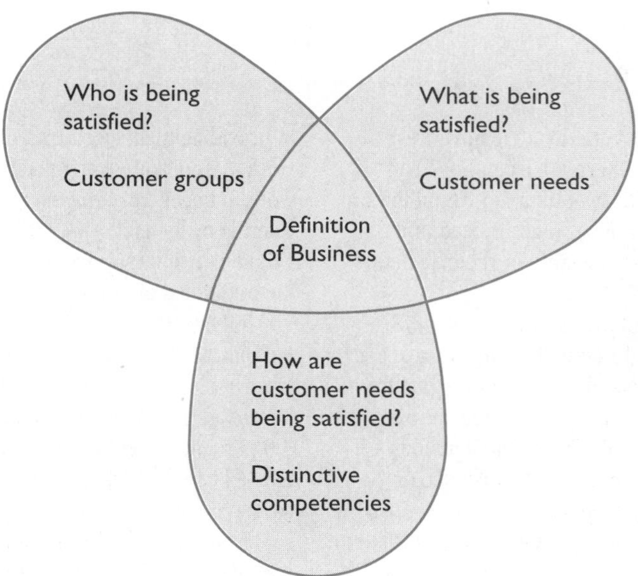

Source: Derek F. Abell, *Defining the Business: The Starting Point of Strategic Planning* (Englewood Cliffs, N.J.: Prentice-Hall, 1980), p. 17.

needs), and how are customer needs being satisfied (by what skills or distinctive competencies)?[17] Figure 2.2 illustrates these three dimensions.

Abell's approach stresses the need for a **consumer-oriented,** rather than a **product-oriented,** business definition. A product-oriented business definition focuses just on the products sold and the markets served. Abell maintains that such an approach obscures the company's function, which is to satisfy consumer needs. A product is only the physical manifestation of applying a particular skill to satisfy a particular need for a particular consumer group. In practice, that need can be served in different ways. A broad consumer-oriented business definition that identifies these ways can safeguard companies from being caught unaware by major shifts in demand. Indeed, by helping anticipate demand shifts, Abell's framework can assist companies in capitalizing on the changes in their environment. It can help answer the second question: "What will our business be?"

However, the need to take a customer-oriented view of a company's business has often been ignored. Consequently, history is littered with the wreckage of once great corporations that did not define their business or that defined it incorrectly. These firms failed to see what their business would become, and ultimately they declined. Theodore Levitt described the fall of the once mighty U.S. railroads in terms of their failure to define their business correctly:

> The railroads did not stop growing because the need for passenger and freight transportation declined. That grew. The railroads are in trouble today not because the need was filled by others (cars, trucks, airplanes, even telephones), but because it was not filled by the railroads themselves. They let others take customers away from them because they assumed themselves to be in the railroad business rather than in the transportation business. The reason they defined their industry wrong was because they were railroad oriented instead of transport oriented; they were product oriented instead of customer oriented.[18]

If the railroads had used Abell's framework, they might have anticipated the impact of technological change and decided that their business was transportation. In that case, they might have transferred their early strength in rail into dominance in today's diversified transport industry. But most railroads stuck to a product-oriented definition of their business and went bankrupt.

In contrast, for a long time IBM correctly foresaw what its business would be. Originally, IBM was a leader in the manufacture of typewriters and mechanical tabulating equipment using punch-card technology. However, IBM defined its business as providing a means for information processing and storage, rather than just supplying mechanical tabulating equipment and typewriters.[19] Given this definition, the company's subsequent moves into computers, software systems, office systems, and printers seem logical. It might also be argued that IBM's problems in the late 1980s and early 1990s arose because the company lost sight of the fact that increasingly consumer needs for information processing and storage were being satisfied by low-cost personal computers, and not by the mainframe computers produced by its core business.

The third question—"What should our business be?"—can also be answered using Abell's framework. Thus, IBM decided that its business should be information processing—that was its vision—and this vision drove its development of computers and office systems, all extensions of its original mechanical tabulating punch-card business. A similar kind of consumer-oriented thinking about "What our business should be" underlies AT&T's recent strategic moves (see Strategy in Action 2.2 for details). AT&T has clearly decided that it is in the communications services business, not the long-distance phone service business. Moreover, AT&T has recognized that changing technology—and particularly the rise of digital wireless networks and the Internet—is altering the way in which communications services will be delivered, including long-distance phone service. Hence AT&T's acquisition of cable TV networks and the introduction of its Digital One Rate for wireless customers.

Another company that has redefined its mission after taking a close look at the needs of its customers is Kodak, which used to see itself as a supplier of photographic equipment. More recently, Kodak has decided that it is in the "imaging business"—the business of providing any technology that allows customers to capture, process, manipulate, and display images. Thus the business includes not just photographic technology based on silver halide applications, which has been Kodak's mainstay, but also new digital imaging technology. Building on this new customer-oriented view of its business and having asked itself "What should our business be?" Kodak has articulated a new corporate vision, which is to be *the world leader in imaging*.[20]

Values

The values of a company state how managers intend to conduct themselves, how they intend to do business, and what kind of organization they want to build. Insofar as they direct behavior within a company, values are seen as the bedrock of a company's organizational culture and a driver of its competitive advantage.[21] Chapter 12 deals in depth with the issue of organizational culture.) For example, at General Electric, CEO Jack Welch has in recent years repeatedly articulated a set of values that includes "boundaryless behavior." He stressed its importance in a letter to shareholders:

> Boundaryless behavior, an odd awkward phrase just a few years ago, is increasingly a way of life at GE. It has led to an obsession for finding a better way—a better idea—be its source a colleague, another GE business, or another company across the street or on the other side of the globe that will share its ideas and practices with us.[22]

Stated in this manner, boundaryless behavior is the antithesis of the "not invented here" syndrome, which causes managers to ignore ideas from outside the organization. It is a value that encourages managers to look outside their own particular function, business, or organization for ideas and solutions to problems. According to Welch, the institutionalization of boundaryless behavior within GE has shaped the culture of GE and helped improve the competitive position of the enterprise. He gives an example in his letter to shareholders:

> Yokogawa, our partner in the Medical Systems business, has been using "Bullet Train Thinking" to take 30–50 percent out of product costs over a two-year period. This technique, which employs "out-of-the-box" thinking and cross-functional teams dedicated to removing obstacles to cost reduction, is now fully operational in our Aircraft Engines business. This effort should lead this business to double digit profitability growth in 1995, despite less than robust market conditions.[23]

Like GE, many companies articulate a set of values to emphasize their own distinctive outlook on business. The values of Lincoln Electric, for instance, emphasize that productivity increases should be shared with customers and employees through lower prices and higher wages. This belief distinguishes Lincoln Electric from many other enterprises and affects its goals and strategies.[24]

Another company whose values are famous is health care giant Johnson & Johnson. Its credo—a statement of its values—is reproduced in Figure 2.3. This credo expresses Johnson & Johnson's belief that the company's first responsibility is to the doctors, nurses, and patients who use J&J products. Next come its employees, the communities in which these employees live and work, and finally the stockholders. The credo is prominently displayed in every manager's office, and according to the Johnson & Johnson managers, it guides all important decisions. Strong evidence of the credo's influence was apparent in the company's response to the 1982 Tylenol crisis. Seven people in the Chicago area died after taking Tylenol capsules that had been laced with cyanide. Johnson & Johnson immediately withdrew all Tylenol capsules from the U.S. market, at an estimated cost to the company of $100 million. At the same time, the company embarked on a comprehensive communication effort targeted at the pharmaceutical and medical communities. By such means, Johnson & Johnson successfully presented itself to the public as a company that was willing to do what was right, regardless of the cost. Consequently, the Tylenol crisis enhanced rather than tarnished Johnson & Johnson's image. Indeed, because of its actions, the company was able to regain its status as a market leader in painkillers in a matter of months.[25]

In one study of organizational values, researchers identified a set of values associated with "high performing organizations" that, through their impact on employee behavior, help companies achieve superior financial performance.[26] Not surprisingly, these values include respect for the interest of key organizational stakeholders—particularly customers, employees, suppliers, and stockholders. They also include respect and encouragement of the assumption of leadership and entrepreneurial

FIGURE 2.3

Johnson & Johnson's Credo

Our Credo

We believe our first responsibility is to the doctors, nurses and patients,
to mothers and fathers and all others who use our products and services.
In meeting their needs everything we do must be of high quality.
We must constantly strive to reduce our costs
in order to maintain reasonable prices.
Customers' orders must be serviced promptly and accurately.
Our suppliers and distributors must have an opportunity
to make a fair profit.

We are responsible to our employees,
the men and women who work with us throughout the world.
Everyone must be considered as an individual.
We must respect their dignity and recognize their merit.
They must have a sense of security in their jobs.
Compensation must be fair and adequate,
and working conditions clean, orderly and safe.
We must be mindful of ways to help our employees fulfill
their family responsibilities.
Employees must feel free to make suggestions and complaints.
There must be equal opportunity for employment, development
and advancement for those qualified.
We must provide competent management,
and their actions must be just and ethical.

We are responsible to the communities in which we live and work
and to the world community as well.
We must be good citizens — support good works and charities
and bear our fair share of taxes.
We must encourage civic improvements and better health and education.
We must maintain in good order
the property we are privileged to use,
protecting the environment and natural resources.

Our final responsibility is to our stockholders.
Business must make a sound profit.
We must experiment with new ideas.
Research must be carried on, innovative programs developed
and mistakes paid for.
New equipment must be purchased, new facilities provided
and new products launched.
Reserves must be created to provide for adverse times.
When we operate according to these principles,
the stockholders should realize a fair return.

Johnson & Johnson

Source: Courtesy of Johnson & Johnson.

behavior by mid- and lower-level managers, and respect for and a willingness to support efforts at change within the organization. According to the authors of such studies, Hewlett-Packard, Wal-Mart, and PepsiCo are among the companies that apparently emphasize such values consistently throughout their organization.

The study mentioned above also identified the values of poorly performing companies. These values, as might be expected, are *not* articulated in company mission statements. They include arrogance, particularly in regard to ideas from outside the company; a lack of respect for key stakeholders such as customers, employees, suppliers, and stockholders; and a history of resisting efforts at change and "punishing" mid- and lower-level managers who showed "too much leadership." The authors depict General Motors as one such organization, noting that mid- and lower-level managers there who showed too much leadership and initiative were not promoted.

Goals

Having stated a vision founded on a consumer-orientated definition of the company's business and having articulated some key values, the company can take the next step in the formulation of a mission statement: establishing major goals. A **goal** is a desired future state that a company attempts to realize. In this context, the purpose of setting goals is to specify with precision what must be done if the company is to attain its mission. For example, consistent with its mission of remaining the number one aerospace company in the world, the Commercial Aerospace Group of the Boeing Corporation set itself a number of goals in 1992. The first goal was to maintain a global market share of at least 60 percent in the large commercial jet aircraft business. The second was to cut in half by 1997 the time it took to build an aircraft, and the third was to bring down the cost of building an aircraft by 30 percent by the same year.

Goal Characteristics To be meaningful, goals should have four main characteristics.[27] First, well-constructed goals are *precise and measurable*. If a goal cannot be stated precisely and measured, the company will be unable to assess its progress toward attaining that goal. Measurable goals give managers a yardstick for judging their performance.

Second, well-constructed goals *address important issues*. To maintain focus, an organization should operate with a limited number of major goals. Thus, the goals that are selected should all be important ones. In Boeing's case, the goals of reducing costs and "build time" focus managerial attention on two issues that are of critical significance if Boeing is to establish a competitive advantage in the commercial aircraft business: costs and customer responsiveness. The goal of attaining a minimum market share of 60 percent defines explicitly what it means to be an industry leader in commercial aircraft.

Third, well-constructed goals should be *challenging but realistic*. Challenging goals give managers an incentive to look for ways of improving the operations of an organization. However, if a goal is unrealistic in the challenges it poses, employees may give up, whereas a goal that is too easy may fail to motivate managers and other employees.[28] Again, Boeing can serve as an example. Reducing unit costs by 30 percent will require significant improvements in the efficiency of Boeing's operations, and this goal is challenging. Furthermore, experience at other companies has shown that it is possible to achieve 30 percent unit cost reductions over a six-year period; therefore, the goal is not unrealistic.[29]

Fourth, well-constructed goals should, when appropriate, *specify a time period* in which they ought to be achieved. Boeing committed itself to achieving its goals of cost and build-time reduction by 1997. Time constraints are important because they tell employees that success requires a goal to be attained by a given date, not after that date. Deadlines can inject a sense of urgency into the pursuit of a goal and act as a motivator. However, not all goals require time constraints. Boeing's goal of having a market share of at least 60 percent has no time period attached to it because Boeing already has around 60 percent of the market. By articulating this goal, management is saying that Boeing must not let its share slip below this critical level.

A final point worth emphasizing here is that well-constructed goals provide a means of evaluating the performance of managers. Again, the Boeing example is useful here, for the company *did not* attain its goals for build-time and cost reduction. Because of poor management of a production increase during 1997 and 1998, Boeing's unit costs *increased*, not decreased. This led to unanticipated financial losses and the removal of several key managers at Boeing's Commercial Airplane Group, including its head. These managers were dismissed because they failed to attain the goals that were set out in 1992. Goals, thus, are a very important element of a company's internal control systems. (This issue is condsidered further in Chapters 11 and 12.)

Maximizing Stockholder Returns Although most profit-seeking organizations operate with a variety of corporate goals, within a *public* corporation—at least in theory—many of these goals are directed toward maximizing stockholder returns. A company's stockholders are its legal owners. Consequently, an overriding goal of most corporations is to maximize stockholder returns, which means increasing the long-run returns earned by stockholders from owning shares in the corporation.

Stockholders receive returns in two ways: from dividend payments and from capital appreciation in the market value of a share (that is, by increases in stock market prices). A company can best maximize stockholder returns by pursuing strategies that maximize its own profitability, as measured by the rate of return that the company achieves on its investments in plant, equipment, R&D, and the like—that is, its rate of return on investment (ROI). In general, the more efficient a company becomes, the higher will be its ROI; moreover, its future prospects will look better to stockholders, and it will have a greater ability to pay dividends. Furthermore, higher ROI leads to greater demand for a company's shares. Demand bids up the share price and leads to capital appreciation.

The Short-Term Problem There is an important danger associated with overemphasizing a return on investment goal.[30] The overzealous pursuit of ROI can encourage managers to maximize short-run rather than long-run returns. A short-run orientation may encourage such misguided managerial action as cutting expenditures that are judged to be nonessential in the short run—for instance, expenditures for research and development, marketing, and new capital investments—but are vital in the long run. Although cutting current expenditures increases current ROI, the resulting underinvestment, lack of innovation, and poor market awareness jeopardize long-run ROI. Despite these negative consequences, managers may make such decisions because the adverse effects of a short-run orientation may not materialize and become apparent to stockholders for several years, or because they are under extreme pressure to achieve short-term ROI goals.

In a now famous *Harvard Business Review* article, Robert H. Hayes and William J. Abernathy argue that, historically, the widespread focus on short-run ROI was a major contributing factor in the loss of international competitiveness by U.S. companies.[31] Massachusetts Institute of Technology economist Lester Thurow likewise faulted the short-run orientation of many U.S. businesses for some of their problems. Thurow claims that many U.S. companies are unwilling to make long-run investments for fear of depressing their short-run ROI. He cites declining expenditures for research and development and reduced innovative activity within U.S. enterprises as evidence of this orientation.[32] Similarly, after a detailed study of productivity problems in U.S. industry, the MIT Commission on Industrial Productivity concluded that the short time horizons of many corporations placed them at a competitive disadvantage vis-à-vis their foreign rivals.[33] One of the consequences of short-term horizons, according to the MIT Commission, was the loss of U.S. leadership to Japanese companies in the videocassette recorder industry. The videocassette recorder was pioneered in the 1950s by the U.S.-based Ampex Corporation, primarily for use in the broadcasting industry. Ampex did try to produce a consumer variant of the product for a mass market but pulled out in 1970, when it decided it could not afford the R&D investment. Similarly, RCA, which also tried to develop a consumer videocassette recorder, pulled out in 1975 in the face of high development costs and manufacturing problems. This left the field open for Sony and Matsushita, both of which had been investing heavily during the 1970s to develop their own technology. Today the videocassette market is a multibillion-dollar market dominated by Matsushita. No U.S. company competes in this market.

As recounted in Strategy in Action 2.3, a similar story of short-term behavior seems to have hurt U.S. companies in the rapidly expanding market for active matrix liquid crystal displays (AM-LCDs). The AM-LCD technology, too, was originally developed in the United States, but the market is now dominated by Japanese companies.

Long-Term Goals To guard against short-run behavior, managers need to ensure that they adopt goals whose attainment will increase the long-run performance and competitiveness of their enterprise. Long-term goals are related to such issues as customer satisfaction, employee productivity and efficiency, product quality, and innovation. The thinking here is that in order to attain such goals companies have to make long-term investments in plant, equipment, R&D, people, and processes. Only by doing so can a company improve its customer satisfaction, productivity, product quality, and innovation. Moreover, insofar as the attainment of such goals enhances a company's competitive position and boosts its *long-term* profitability, attaining such goals will help the company maximize the returns to be had from holding its stock.

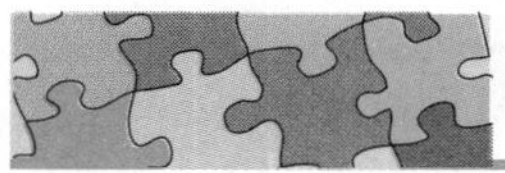

CORPORATE GOVERNANCE AND STRATEGY

We noted that one of a company's major goals is to give its stockholders a good rate of return on their investment. In most publicly held corporations, however, stockholders delegate the job of controlling the company and selecting its strategies to corporate managers, who become the agents of the stockholders.[35] As the agents of stockholders, managers should pursue strategies that maximize *long-run* returns for stockholders. Although most managers are diligent about doing so, not all act in this fashion, and this failure gives rise to the corporate governance problem: managers pursuing strategies that are not in the interest of stockholders.

2.3 STRATEGY *in* ACTION

A Short-Term Emphasis Costs U.S. Companies the Lead in Flat Panel Displays

Active matrix liquid crystal displays (AM-LCDs) are the flat-top color displays used in laptop and notebook personal computers. In addition to computer displays, the screens are also critical components in camcorders, medical instruments, high-definition television, auto dashboards, aerospace instruments, factory control devices and instrumentation for the military. Global sales of AM-LCDs increased from $250 million in 1990 to around $8 billion in 1998, and projections suggest the market will grow by 20 percent per annum compounded for the foreseeable future.

The AM-LCD technology was pioneered during the 1960s at two U.S. companies, RCA and Westinghouse. However, neither company succeeded in commercializing the technology. One reason for this was that corporate management at both companies balked at the development costs and long pay-back periods and so they cut funding. The principal Westinghouse researcher, Jim Fergason, subsequently left the company and set up a venture to manufacture AM-LCDs. However, few U.S. companies were willing to utilize the technology, and Fergason found it difficult to raise sufficient capital. Ultimately, his venture failed.

With no large U.S. company undertaking primary AM-LCD research, it was left to the Japanese to emerge as the major producers. Sharp, NEC, and Toshiba now dominate the market; in 1998, they were responsible for 80 percent of worldwide production. Unlike their major U.S. competitors, these firms made massive investments in AM-LCD research and production facilities in that period. Sharp alone reportedly spent more than $1 billion on developing the technology during the 1980s. Although a number of small U.S. companies are in this business, they tend to focus on highly specialized niches (such as supplying the Defense Department) and have made investments to support only limited production. With the exception of IBM, which has a joint venture with Toshiba in Japan to manufacture AM-LCDs, no major U.S. company has a presence in this industry, and no U.S. company is capable of mass production.[34]

The Corporate Governance Problem

Why should managers want to pursue other strategies than those consistent with maximizing stockholder returns? Some writers have argued that, like many other people, managers are motivated by the desire for status, power, job security, and income.[36] By virtue of their position within the company, certain managers, such as the CEO, can use their authority and control over corporate funds to satisfy this desire. For example, CEOs might use their position to invest corporate funds in various perks that enhance their status—executive jets, lavish offices, and expense-paid trips to Hawaii—instead of investing those funds in ways that increase stockholder returns. Economists have termed such behavior **on-the-job consumption**.[37] Bill Agee is an example of a CEO who appeared to engage in excessive on-the-job consumption (see Strategy in Action 2.1).

Besides engaging in on-the-job-consumption, CEOs, along with other senior managers, might satisfy their desire for greater income by awarding themselves excessive pay increases. Critics of U.S. industry claim that extraordinary pay has now become an endemic problem. They point out that CEO pay has been increasing far more rapidly than the pay of average workers, primarily due to very liberal stock option grants, which enable a CEO to earn huge pay bonuses in a rising stock market, even if his company under-performs the market and competitors.[38] For example, in 1980 the average CEO earned 42 times what the average blue-collar worker earned. In 1990, this figure had increased to 85 times. By 1998, the average CEO earned 419 times the pay of the average blue-collar worker.[39] In 1987, the average compensation of the CEOs in the largest 200 companies on the list compiled by *Fortune* magazine increased to $8.7 million.[40] According to a study by the compensation consultants, Towers Perrin, in 1998 CEOs in the United States, as a group, earned 185 times the average pay of *all* employees in their enterprises, including managers.[41]

What rankles critics is the size of some CEO pay packages and their apparent lack of relationship to company performance.[42] In 1998, for example, Disney CEO Michael Eisner earned $575 million, mostly in the form of stock options, despite the fact that Disney did not do particularly well that year and the stock price fell 10 percent. Stanford Weill, CEO of Citigroup, earned $166 million. Jack Welch, CEO of General Electric, earned $83 million. The critics felt that the size of these pay awards was out of all proportion to the CEOs' achievement.[43]

A further concern is that in trying to satisfy the desire for status, security, power, and income, a CEO might engage in "empire building"—buying many new businesses in an attempt to increase the size of the company through diversification.[44] Although such growth may do little to enhance the company's profitability, and thus stockholder returns, it increases the size of the empire under the CEO's control, and by extension, the CEO's status, power, security, and income (there is a strong relationship between company size and CEO pay). To quote Carl Icahn, a famous corporate raider of the 1980s:

> Make no mistake, a strongly knit corporate aristocracy exists in America. The top man, what's more, usually finds expanding his power more important than rewarding owners (stockholders). When Mobil and USX had excess cash, did they enrich shareholders? Of course not. They bought Marcor and Marathon—disastrous investments, but major increases in the size of the manor.[45]

Thus, instead of maximizing stockholder returns, some senior managers may trade long-run profitability for greater company growth by buying new businesses. Figure 2.4 graphs profitability against a company's growth rate. A company that does not grow is probably missing out on some profitable opportunities.[46] A growth rate of G_0 in Figure 2.4 is not consistent with maximizing profitability ($P_1 < P_{max}$). A moderate growth rate of G_1, on the other hand, does allow a company to maximize profits, producing profits equal to P_{max}. Achieving a growth rate in excess of G_1, however, requires diversification into areas that the company knows little about. Consequently, it can be achieved only by sacrificing profitability (that is, past G_1, the investment required to finance further growth does not produce an adequate return, and the company's profitability declines). Yet G_2 may be the growth rate favored by an empire-building CEO, for it will increase his or her power, status, and income. At this growth rate, profits are equal only to P_2. Because $P_{max} > P_2$, a company growing at this rate is clearly not maximizing its profitability, nor the wealth of its stockholders. However, a growth rate of G_2 may be consistent with attaining managerial goals of power, status, and income.

FIGURE 2.4

The Tradeoff Between Profitability and Growth Rate

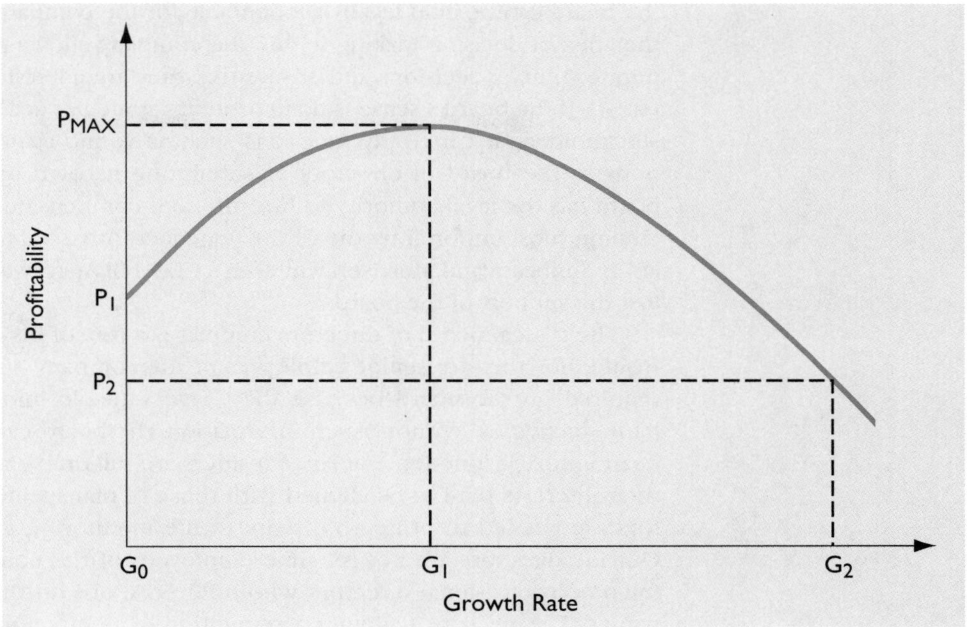

Corporate Governance Mechanisms

It must be stressed that by no means do all managers behave in the way just outlined. The vast majority are good stewards who consciously act to increase stockholder returns. Moreover, while some critics charge that CEOs are overpaid, one can argue that many deserve their high pay and rich bonuses from stock options. At Disney, for example, Michael Eisner has been responsible for transforming that company from an entertainment has-been into one of the most dynamic entertainment companies in the world. During his tenure, the stock price increased from $3 a share in 1985 to over $30 in 1998. Viewed this way, his 1998 earnings of $575 million, mostly from the exercise of stock options, were his just reward for the creation of billions of dollars in shareholder value. Similarly, the $83 million earned by Jack Welch in 1998 can be seen as the reward for the extraordinary increases in GE's share price over Welch's tenure; the price rose from $1 in 1980 when Welch started to $100 by 1998.

Nevertheless, given that some managers put their own interests first, the problem facing stockholders is how to govern the corporation so that managerial desire for on-the-job consumption, excessive salaries, or empire-building diversification is held in check. There is also a need for mechanisms that let stockholders remove incompetent or ineffective managers. A number of **governance mechanisms** allow stockholders to exert some control over managers. They include the board of directors, stock-based compensation schemes, corporate takeovers, and the exchange of equity for debt in leveraged buyouts.

Board of Directors Stockholders' interests are looked after within a company by the board of directors. Board members are directly elected by stockholders, and, under corporate law, they represent the stockholders' interests in the company. Thus, the board can be held legally accountable for the company's actions. Its position at the apex of decision making within the company allows the board to monitor corporate strategy decisions and ensure that they are consistent with stockholders' interests. If the board's sense is that corporate strategies are not in the best interest of stockholders, it can apply sanctions such as voting against management nominations to the board of directors or submitting its own nominees. In addition, the board has the legal authority to hire, fire, and compensate corporate employees, including, most importantly, the CEO.[47] One factor that led to the dismissal of Al Dunlap at Sunbeam and Morrison Knudsen's CEO, Bill Agee, was that their strategies had lost the support of the board.

The typical board of directors comprises a mix of inside and outside directors. Inside directors are senior employees of the company, such as the CEO. They are required on the board because they have valuable information about the company's activities. Without such information, the board cannot adequately perform its monitoring function. But since insiders are full-time employees of the company, their interests tend to be aligned with those of management. Hence, outside directors are needed to bring objectivity to the monitoring and evaluation processes. Outside directors are not full-time employees of the company. Many of them are full-time professional directors who hold positions on the boards of several companies. The need to maintain a reputation as competent outside directors gives them an incentive to perform their tasks as objectively and effectively as possible.[48]

Critics charge, however, that inside directors may be able to dominate the outsiders on the board. Insiders can use their position within the management hierarchy to exercise control over what kind of company-specific information the board receives. Consequently, insiders can present information in a way that puts them in a favorable light. In addition, insiders have the advantage of intimate knowledge of the company's operations. Because superior knowledge and control over information are sources of power (see Chapter 12), insiders may be better positioned to influence boardroom decision making than outsiders. The board may become the captive of insiders and merely rubber-stamp management decisions, instead of guarding stockholders' interests.

Some observers contend that many boards are dominated by the company CEO, particularly in those cases where the CEO is also the chairman of the board.[49] To support this view, they point out that both inside and outside directors are often the personal nominees of the CEO. The typical inside director is subordinate to the CEO in the company's hierarchy and therefore unlikely to criticize the boss. Since outside directors are frequently the CEO's nominees as well, they can hardly be expected to evaluate the CEO objectively. Thus, the loyalty of the board may be biased toward the CEO and not the stockholders. Moreover, when the CEO is also chairman of the board, he or she may be able to control the agenda of board discussions in such a manner as to deflect any criticisms of his or her leadership. That was a problem in the case of Bill Agee, who was both CEO and chairman of the board at Morrison Knudsen.

Today, there are clear signs that many corporate boards are moving away from merely rubber-stamping top-management decisions and are beginning to play a much more active role in corporate governance. One catalyst has been an increase in the number of lawsuits filed by stockholders against board members. The trend started in 1985, when a Delaware court ruled that the directors of Trans Union Corporation had been too quick to accept a takeover bid. The court held the directors personally liable for the difference between the offer they accepted and the price the company might have fetched in a sale. The directors then agreed to make up the $23.5 million difference. Since that ruling, a number of major lawsuits have been filed by stockholders against board members. These include suits directed against board members at Holly Farms, Northrup, Lincoln Savings & Loan, Lotus Development, and RJR Nabisco.[50]

Another catalyst has been the growing willingness of some institutional investors, such as the managers of large pension funds or index-linked mutual funds, to use their stockholding in a company, and the voting power it gives them, to gain seats on the board of directors, in order to pressure managers to adopt policies that improve the performance of the company's stock and to pressure the board to replace the CEOs of poorly performing companies. For example, in late 1995, officials of New York City's five major pension funds stated that they would nominate three candidates for seats on the board of Ethyl, a maker of petroleum additives that has performed poorly in recent years. Their objective was to use these board seats to push management harder to improve Ethyl's performance, and hence the value of their stock in Ethyl.[51]

Spurred on by the threat of legal action and pressures from powerful institutional shareholders, an increasing number of boards have started to assert their independence from company management in general and from corporate CEOs in particular. During the 1990s, boards of directors have engineered the removal or resignation of CEOs at a number of major companies, including American Express, Compaq Computer, Digital Equipment, General Motors, IBM, and Sunbeam. Another trend of some significance is the increasing tendency for an outside director to be made chairman of the board. In 1997, according to estimates from the National Association of Corporate Directors, 40 to 50 percent of big companies had an outside director as chairman, up from less than half that figure in 1990.[52] Such appointments limit the ability of corporate insiders, and particularly of the CEO, to exercise control over the board. It is notable that the removal of Robert Stempel as the CEO of General Motors followed the appointment of an outside director, John Smale, as chairman of the GM board.

Stock-Based Compensation As another way to align the interests of managers with those of stockholders, and thus solve the corporate governance problem, stockholders have urged many companies to introduce stock-based compensation schemes for their managers. In addition to their regular salary, managers are given stock options in the company. Stock options give managers the right to buy the company's shares at a predetermined (strike) price, which may often turn out to be less than the market price of the stock. The idea behind stock options is to motivate managers to adopt strategies that increase the share price of the company, for in doing so they will also increase the value of their own stock options.

As noted earlier, many top managers often earn huge bonuses by exercising stock options that were granted several years before. While not denying that these options do motivate managers to improve company performance, critics claim that they are often too generous. A particular cause for concern is that stock options are often granted at such low strike prices that CEOs can hardly fail to make a significant amount of money by exercising them, even if the companies they run underperform the stock market by a significant margin. Other critics, including the famous investor Warren Buffet, complain that huge stock option grants, by increasing the outstanding number of shares in a company, unjustifiably dilute the equity of stockholders and accordingly should be shown in company accounts as a charge against profits. Buffet has noted that when his investment company, Berkshire Hathaway, "acquires an option issuing company, we promptly substitute a cash compensation plan having an economic value equivalent to that of the previous option plan. The acquiree's true compensation cost is therefore brought out of the closet and charged, as it should be, against earnings."[53] Buffet's point is that stock options are accounted for incorrectly in company financial statements. They are not listed as a cost, and therefore result in an understating of true employee costs and a corresponding overstatement of net profits.

On the other hand, several academic studies suggest that stock-based compensation schemes for executives—such as stock options—can align management and stockholder interests. For instance, one study found that managers were more likely to consider the effects of their acquisition decisions on stockholder returns if they themselves were significant shareholders.[54] According to another study, managers who were significant stockholders were less likely to pursue strategies that would maximize the size of the company rather than its profitability.[55] More generally, it is difficult to argue with the proposition that the chance to get rich from exercising stock options is the primary reason for the fourteen-hour days and six-day workweeks that many employees of fast-growing high technology firms put in.

Corporate Takeovers If the board of directors is loyal to management rather than to stockholders, or if the company has not adopted stock-based compensation schemes, then a corporate governance problem may exist, and managers may pursue strategies that are inconsistent with maximizing stockholder wealth. However, stockholders still have some residual power, for they can always sell their shares. If they start doing so in large numbers, the price of the company's shares will decline. If the share price falls far enough, the company might be worth less on the stock market than the book value of its assets, at which point it may become an attractive acquisition target and runs the risk of being purchased by another enterprise, against the wishes of the target company's management.

The risk of being acquired by another company is known as the **takeover constraint**. The takeover constraint limits the extent to which managers can pursue strategies and take actions that put their own interests above those of stockholders. If they ignore stockholder interests and the company is acquired, senior managers typically lose their independence and probably their jobs as well. So the threat of takeover can constrain management action.

During the 1980s and early 1990s, the threat of takeover was often enforced by corporate raiders. **Corporate raiders** are individuals or corporations that buy up large blocks of shares in companies that they think are pursuing strategies inconsistent with maximizing stockholder wealth. Corporate raiders argue that if these underperforming companies pursued different strategies, they could create more wealth for stockholders. Raiders buy stock in a company either to take over the business and run it more efficiently, or to precipitate a change in the top management, replacing the existing team with one more likely to maximize stockholders' returns. Raiders, of course, are motivated not by altruism but by gain. If they succeed in their takeover bid, they can institute strategies that create value for stockholders—including themselves. Even if a takeover bid fails, raiders can still earn millions, for their stockholdings will typically be bought out by the defending company for a hefty premium. Called **greenmail**, this source of gain stirred much controversy and debate about its benefits. While some claim that the threat posed by raiders has had a salutary effect on enterprise performance by pushing corporate management to run their companies better, others claim there is little evidence of this.[56]

Leveraged Buyouts Whereas in a typical takeover attempt a raider buys enough stock to gain control of a company, in a leveraged buyout (LBO) a company's own managers are often among the buyers. The management group undertaking an LBO raises cash by issuing bonds and then uses that cash to buy the company's stock. In effect, the company replaces its stockholders with creditors (bondholders), transforming the corporation from a public into a private entity. However, often the same institutions that were major stockholders before an LBO are major bondholders afterward. The difference is that as stockholders they were not guaranteed a regular dividend payment from the company; as bondholders they do have such a guarantee.

During the 1980s, the number and value of LBOs undertaken in the United States increased dramatically. The value of the 76 LBOs undertaken in 1979 totaled $1.4 billion (in 1988 dollars). In comparison, the value of the 214 LBOs undertaken in 1988 exceeded $77 billion. Since then, however, the LBO business in the United States has slowed considerably, with only a handful of transactions being executed each year. In 1997, for example, the total value of all leveraged buyouts was $29 billion. The LBO's demise, though, may be only temporary. Takeovers tend to go in cycles, and it is quite possible that leveraged buyouts will return in the United States in the near future. On the other hand, the popularity of LBOs is increasing in Europe. In 1998, for example, LBO transactions completed within the European Union hit a record $38 billion, and European LBO funds reportedly have access to $100 billion of capital.[57]

Supporters of the LBO technique, most notably Michael Jensen, claim that the LBO should be viewed as yet another governance mechanism that keeps management discretion in check.[58] Jensen believes that LBOs solve many of the problems created by imperfect corporate governance mechanisms. According to Jensen, a major weakness and source of waste in the public corporation is the conflict between stockholders and managers over the payout of free cash flow (**free cash flow** is cash flow in excess of that required to fund all investment projects with positive net present values when discounted at the relevant cost of capital). Since free cash flow is cash that cannot be profitably reinvested within the company, Jensen argues that it should be distributed to stockholders, but he notes that managers resist such distributions of surplus cash. Instead, for reasons discussed earlier, they tend to invest such cash in empire-building strategies.

Jensen sees LBOs as a solution to this problem. Although management does not have to pay out dividends to stockholders, it must make regular debt payments to bondholders or face bankruptcy. Thus, according to Jensen, the debt used to finance an LBO helps limit the waste of free cash flow by compelling managers to pay out excess cash to service debt rather than spending it on empire-building projects with low or negative returns, excessive staff and perquisites, and other organizational inefficiencies. Furthermore, Jensen sees debt as a way of motivating managers to seek greater efficiencies; high debt payments can force managers to slash unsound investment programs, reduce overhead, and dispose of assets that are more valuable outside the company. The proceeds generated by these restructurings can then be used to reduce debt to more sustainable levels, creating a more competitive organization.

Not all commentators are as enthusiastic about the potential of LBOs as Jensen. The former secretary of labor in the Clinton administration, Robert Reich, is one of the most vocal critics of LBOs.[59] Reich sees two main problems with LBOs. First, he argues that the necessity of paying back large loans forces management to focus on the short term and cut back on long-term investments, particularly in R&D and new capital spending. The net effect is likely to be a decline in the competitiveness of LBOs. Second, Reich believes that the debt taken on to finance an LBO significantly increases the risk of bankruptcy.

The studies that have been done on this issue, although they are limited in number, suggest that LBOs do have some beneficial effects.[60] Companies that undergo an LBO do seem to be more diversified than their peers, suggesting that they had at one time been run by empire-building CEOs. After the LBO, they tend to divest business units and narrow the scope of the company's activities, thereby undoing the excessive diversification of the past. Moreover, there is some evidence that after an LBO, the productivity of the company increases, primarily because it sells off poorly performing business units and simplifies its management structures to reduce bureaucracy.

STRATEGY AND ETHICS

Any strategic action taken by a company inevitably affects the welfare of its stakeholders: employees, suppliers, customers, stockholders, the local communities in which it does business, and the general public. While a strategy may enhance the welfare of some stakeholder groups, it may harm others. For example, faced with falling demand and excess capacity, a steel producer may decide to close down a steel-making facility that is the major source of employment in a small town. Although this action might be consistent with maximizing stockholders' returns, it could also result in thousands of people losing employment and the death of a small town. Is such a decision ethical? Is it the right thing to do, considering the likely impact on employees and the community in which they live? Managers must balance these competing benefits and costs. They must decide whether to proceed with the proposed strategy in the light of their assessment not only of its economic benefits, but also of its ethical implications, given the potentially adverse effect on some stakeholder groups.[61]

The Purpose of Business Ethics

The purpose of business ethics is not so much to teach the difference between right and wrong as to give people the tools for dealing with moral complexity, tools that they can use to identify and think through the moral implications of strategic decisions.[62] Most of us already have a good sense of what is right and wrong. We already know that it is wrong to lie, cheat, and steal. We know that it is wrong to take actions that put the lives of others at risk. Such moral values are instilled in us at an early age through formal and informal socialization. The problem, however, is that although most managers rigorously adhere to such moral principles in their private life, some fail to apply them in their professional life, occasionally with disastrous consequences.

The sorry history of Manville Corporation illustrates such failure. (Strategy in Action 2.4 offers another example, that of Jack-in-the-Box). Two decades ago, Manville (then Johns-Manville) was solid enough to be included among the giants of U.S. industry. By 1989, however, 80 percent of the equity of Manville was owned by a trust representing people who had sued the company for liability in connection with one of its principal former products, asbestos. More than forty years ago, information began to reach the medical department of Johns-Manville—and through it the company's managers—suggesting that inhalation of asbestos particles was a major cause of asbestosis, a fatal lung disease. Manville's managers suppressed the research. Moreover, as a matter of company policy, they apparently decided to conceal the information from affected employees. The company's medical staff collaborated in the cover-up. Somehow, managers at Manville persuaded themselves that it was more important to cover up the situation than to take steps to improve working conditions and find safer ways to handle asbestos. They calculated that the cost of improving working conditions was greater than the cost of health insurance to cover those who became ill, and so the best "economic" decision was to conceal the information from employees.[63]

The key to understanding the Manville story is the realization that the men and women at Manville who participated in the cover-up were not amoral monsters, but just ordinary people. Most of them would probably never dream of breaking the law or of physically harming anyone. And yet they consciously made a decision that led directly to great human suffering and death. How could this happen? What seemed to have occurred was that the decision to suppress information was considered on purely economic grounds. Its moral dimension was ignored. Somehow, the managers involved at Manville were able to convince themselves that they were engaged in making a rational business decision, which should be subjected to an economic cost-benefit analysis. Ethical considerations never entered into this calculation. Such behavior is possible only in an environment where business decisions are viewed as having no ethical component. But as the Manville example shows, business decisions *do* have an ethical component.

The task of business ethics, therefore, is to make two central points: (1) that business decisions do have an ethical component and (2) that managers must weigh the ethical implications of strategic decisions before choosing a course of action. Had managers at Manville been trained to think through the ethical implications of their decision, it is unlikely that they would have chosen the same course of action.

Shaping the Ethical Climate of an Organization

To foster awareness that strategic decisions have an ethical dimension, a company must establish an organizational climate that emphasizes the importance of ethics. This requires at least three steps. First, top managers have to use their leadership position to incorporate an ethical dimension into the values they stress. At Hewlett-Packard, for example, Bill Hewlett and David Packard, the company's founders,

2.4 STRATEGY *in* ACTION

The Jack-in-the-Box Poisonings—Questionable Ethics?

In January 1993, several hospitals in Seattle started to notice a dramatic increase in the number of cases of E. coli bacterial infections. The E. coli bacteria are found in undercooked meat. The symptoms of infection include severe fever, diarrhea, and vomiting. In the case of young people, the infection can be life threatening. Most of the victims of this outbreak were young, and many were in very serious condition. Epidemiologists quickly found a common element: almost all of the victims had eaten hamburgers at local Jack-in-the-Box restaurants shortly before falling ill.

Foodmaker, the parent company of Jack-in-the-Box, was quick to issue a statement denying that the meat served in its restaurants was undercooked. At the same time, it blamed the outbreak on a batch of bad meat that had been delivered from a supplier. The supplier responded by placing blame on Jack-in-the-Box. While Foodmaker and its supplier traded insults, the number of those infected rose to 200, and several children became seriously ill. Then Washington State health inspectors revealed that local Jack-in-the-Box restaurants were cooking meat at 140 degrees Fahrenheit, 15 degrees below the 155-degree state standard that had been in force since March 1992. Foodmaker responded by claiming that it had never received notification of the increase in standards. When Health Department officials came up with a copy of the notification that had been sent to local Jack-in-the-Box restaurants, Foodmaker changed its position. According to Robert Nugent, president of Jack-in-the-Box, the company had received the notification but the vice president whose responsibility it was to notify local area restaurants hadn't done so. Jack-in-the-Box indicated that it would take disciplinary action against the vice president, whom it refused to name.

Meanwhile the number of children infected had soared to 450, one had died, several were in a coma, and a number of others were listed as being in critical condition. At this stage Jack-in-the-Box offered to pay the hospital costs for those infected. But there was a catch; in return for paying medical costs, the company's lawyers asked the parents of the infected children to sign forms waiving their rights to subsequently file a lawsuit against Jack-in-the-Box. This request was greeted with outrage, and Jack-in-the-Box once more had to shift its position. This time the company agreed to pay the full hospital costs without requiring a waiver.

By February 1993, the worst of the outbreak was over. However, for Foodmaker the impact was only just becoming apparent. Nationwide sales at Jack-in-the-Box restaurants had plunged 35 percent in the first two weeks of February, the company's stock price had lost 30 percent of its value, and the company announced that it had put on hold plans to open eighty-five new Jack-in-the-Box stores in 1993. In the next two years, Foodmaker recorded nine consecutive quarters of losses, totaling $167 million, while revenues dropped 18 percent. It cost the company a reported $44 million to settle lawsuits from angry franchisees, who blamed their falling sales on Foodmaker, and $4 million to settle a stockholder lawsuit. The company also reportedly ended up paying $90 million in damages to victims and their families.

What seems to have hurt Jack-in-the-Box most was not the outbreak itself, but the company's repeated attempts to shift responsibility for the outbreak onto others, and its cynical attempt to link the offer of financial help to victims with lawsuit waivers. As a result, Jack-in-the-Box came out of the crisis with its reputation tarnished and its sales slumping. Compare this to Johnson & Johnson, which came out of the Tylenol crisis with its reputation for ethical behavior enhanced. It should be noted, though, that the lesson was not lost on Foodmaker. The company has completely overhauled its food distribution and preparation system to make sure this kind of thing does not happen again. Now Foodmaker's system is reportedly the best in the industry. Moreover, the company has explicitly recognized that it responded inappropriately to the crisis and has vowed never to make the same mistake again.[64]

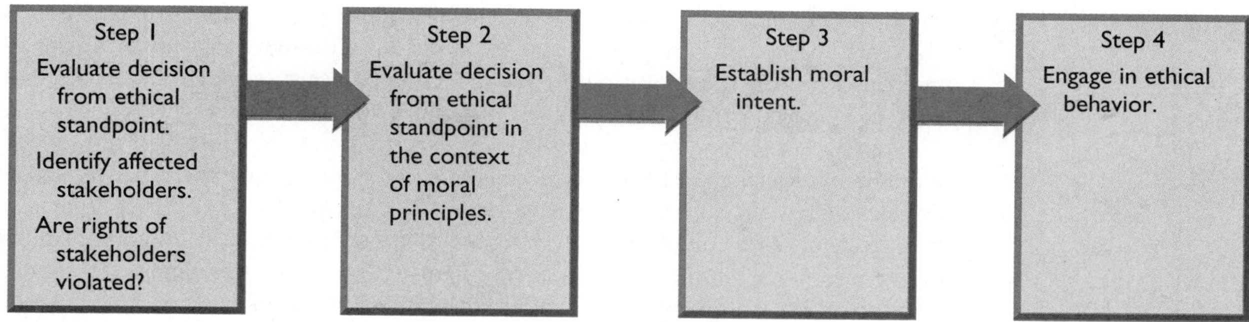

FIGURE 2.5

A Model of Ethical Decision Making

propagated a set of values known as The HP Way. These values, which shape the way business is conducted both within and by the corporation, have an important ethical component. Among other things, they stress the need for confidence in and respect for people, open communication, and concern for the individual employee. Had these values been operational at Manville, they would have helped managers there avoid their catastrophic mistake.

Second, ethical values must be incorporated into the company's mission statement. As noted earlier, Johnson & Johnson's credo helped the company respond to the Tylenol crisis in an ethical manner. Third, ethical values must be acted on. Top managers have to implement hiring, firing, and incentive systems that explicitly recognize the importance of adhering to ethical values in strategic decision making. At Hewlett-Packard, for example, it has been said that although it is difficult to lose your job (because of the concern for individual employees), nothing gets you fired more quickly than violating the ethical norms of the company as articulated in The HP Way.[65]

Thinking Through Ethical Problems

Besides establishing the right kind of ethical climate in an organization, managers must be able to think through the ethical implications of strategic decisions in a systematic way. A number of different frameworks have been suggested as aids to the decision-making process. The four-step model shown in Figure 2.5 is a compilation of the various approaches recommended by several authorities on this subject.[66]

Step 1—evaluating a proposed strategic decision from an ethical standpoint—requires managers to identify which stakeholders the decision would affect and in what ways. Most importantly, managers need to determine whether the proposed decision would violate the rights of any stakeholders. The term *rights* refers to the fundamental entitlements of a stakeholder. For example, we might argue that the right to information about health risks in the workplace is a fundamental entitlement of employees. It is also an entitlement that Manville ignored.

Step 2 involves judging the ethics of the proposed strategic decision, given the information gained in step 1. This judgment should be guided by various moral principles that should not be violated. The principles might be those articulated in a corporate mission statement or other company documents (such as Hewlett-Packard's The HP Way). In addition, certain moral principles that we have adopted as members of society—for instance, the prohibition on stealing—should not be violated. The judgment at this stage will also be guided by the decision rule that is chosen to assess the proposed strategic decision. Although long-run profit maximization is rightly the decision rule that most companies stress, it should be applied subject to the constraint that no moral principles are violated.

Step 3, establishing moral intent, means that the company must resolve to place moral concerns ahead of other concerns in cases where either the rights of stakeholders or key moral principles have been violated. At this stage, input from top management might be particularly valuable. Without the proactive encouragement of top managers, middle-level managers might tend to place the narrow economic interests of the company before the interests of stakeholders. They might do so in the (usually erroneous) belief that top managers favor such an approach.

Step 4 requires the company to engage in ethical behavior. Clearly, Johnson & Johnson fulfilled this requirement during the Tylenol poisoning scare by pulling all its product off retail store shelves at great cost to the company.

Corporate Social Responsibility

Corporate social responsibility is the sense of obligation on the part of companies to build certain social criteria into their strategic decision making. The concept implies that when companies evaluate decisions from an ethical perspective, there should be a presumption in favor of adopting courses of action that enhance the welfare of society at large. The goals selected might be quite specific: to enhance the welfare of communities in which a company is based, improve the environment, or empower employees to give them a sense of self-worth.

In its purest form, social responsibility can be supported for its own sake simply because it is the right way for a company to behave. Less pure but perhaps more practical are the arguments that socially responsible behavior is in a company's self-interest and can lead to better financial performance.[67] Economic actions have social consequences affecting a company's outside stakeholders. Therefore, to retain the support of these stakeholders, the company must take those social consequences into account when formulating strategies. Otherwise, it may generate ill will and opposition. For example, if a community perceives a company as having an adverse impact on the local environment, it may block the company's attempts to build new facilities in the area.

Still, there are those who argue that a company has no business pursuing social goals. Nobel laureate Milton Friedman, for one, insists that social responsibility considerations should not enter into the decision process:

> What does it mean to say that the corporate executive has a social responsibility in his capacity as a businessman? If this statement is not pure rhetoric, it must mean that he is to act in some way that is not in the interests of his employers. For example . . . that he is to make expenditures on reducing pollution beyond the amount that is in the best interests of the corporation or that is required by law in order to contribute to the social objective of improving the environment. . . . Insofar as his actions in accord with his social responsibility reduce returns to stockholders, he is spending their money. Insofar as his actions raise the price to customers, he is spending the customers' money. Insofar as the actions lower the wages of some employees, he is spending their money.[68]

Friedman's position is that a business has only one kind of responsibility: to use its resources for activities that increase its profits, so long as it stays within the rules of the game, which is to say, so long as it engages in open and free competition without deception or fraud.

On the other hand, Edward H. Bowman of the University of Pennsylvania's Wharton School argues that social responsibility is actually a sound investment strategy.[69] He maintains that a company's social behavior affects the price of its stock; thus socially responsible policy can also benefit a company's important inside claimants, the stockholders. According to Bowman, many investors see companies that are not socially responsible as riskier investments. Moreover, many institutional investors, such as churches, universities, cities, states, and mutual funds, pay attention to corporate social behavior and thus influence the market for a company's stock.

Evidence can certainly be found in favor of Bowman's arguments. For example, the withdrawal of U.S. assets from South Africa by companies such as IBM and General Motors in 1986 can at least in part be attributed to a desire to create a favorable impression with investors. At that time, for social or political reasons, many investors were selling any stock they held in companies that maintained a substantial presence in South Africa. Similarly, Union Carbide saw its market value plunge more than 37 percent in 1984, in the aftermath of the gas leak at its Bhopal plant in India (which killed 2,000 people and left 150,000 seriously injured) and subsequent revelations concerning poor safety procedures at many Union Carbide plants. For Union Carbide, the consequence was a takeover bid from GAF (which ultimately failed), extended litigation, and a negative image problem.

SUMMARY OF CHAPTER

The primary purpose of this chapter has been to identify the various factors that influence and shape the organizational context within which strategies are formulated. Normally, these factors are explicitly recognized through the corporate mission statement. The mission statement thus sets the boundaries within which strategies must be contained. Specifically, this chapter makes the following points:

- ✔ Stakeholders are individuals or groups, either within or outside an organization, that have some claim on the organization. They include customers, suppliers, employees, and stockholders. If an organization is to survive and prosper, it must pay attention to the interests of these different stakeholder groups.
- ✔ The mission statement describes how a company intends to incorporate stakeholder claims into its strategic decision making and thereby reduce the risk of losing stakeholder support.
- ✔ The mission statement contains three broad elements: (a) a declaration of the overall vision of the company; (b) a summing-up of the key philosophical values that managers are committed to; and (c) the articulation of key goals that management believes must be adhered to.
- ✔ An important step in the process of formulating a mission statement is to come up with a definition of the organization's business. Defining the business involves focusing on consumer groups to be served, consumer needs to be satisfied, and the technologies by which those needs can be satisfied.
- ✔ The values of a company state how managers intend to conduct themselves, how they intend to do business, and what kind of organization they want to build. Values can become the bedrock of a company's organization culture and a driver of its competitive advantage.
- ✔ The goals of a company specify what must be done if the company is to attain its mission.

Well-constructed goals are precise and measurable, address important issues, are challenging but realistic, and specify a time period within which they should be achieved.

✔ Stockholders are among a company's most important stakeholders. Maximizing stockholder wealth is one of the most important goals of a company. A corporate governance problem arises when managers pursue strategies that are not consistent with this goal.

✔ A number of governance mechanisms serve to limit the ability of managers to pursue strategies that are at variance with maximizing stockholder wealth. These include stockholder meetings, the board of directors, stock-based compensation schemes, and the threat of a takeover.

✔ Many strategic decisions have an ethical dimension. Any action by a company inevitably has an impact on the welfare of its stakeholders.

✔ The purpose of business ethics is not so much to teach the difference between right and wrong, as to give people the tools for dealing with moral complexity—for identifying and thinking through the moral implications of strategic decisions.

DISCUSSION QUESTIONS

1. Why is it important for a company to take a consumer-oriented view of its businesses? What are the possible shortcomings of such a view?
2. What are the strategic implications of a focus on short-run returns? Discuss these implications in terms of the impact on product innovation, marketing expenditure, manufacturing, and purchasing decisions.
3. Are corporate raiders a positive or negative influence on the U.S. economy? How can companies reduce the risk of a takeover?
4. "Companies should always behave in an ethical manner, whatever the economic cost." Discuss this statement.

Practicing Strategic Management

SMALL-GROUP EXERCISE
Constructing a Mission Statement

Break up into groups of three to five people, and perform the tasks listed:

1. Define the business of your educational institution.
2. Use this business definition to guide the construction of a mission statement for your educational institution. Be sure that the mission statement contains a long-term vision, a set of values, and a number of important precise and measurable goals. Be prepared to articulate the logic behind your choice of vision, values, and goals.
3. Try to identify a number of key strategies that your educational institution needs to pursue in order to attain the vision and goals outlined in your mission statement. Be sure that these strategies are consistent with the values you set down in the mission statement.

STRATEGIC MANAGEMENT PROJECT
Module 2

This module deals with the relationships your company has with its major stakeholder groups. With the information you have at your disposal, perform the tasks and answer the questions listed:

1. Find out whether your company has a formal mission statement. Does this statement define the business, identify major goals, and articulate the corporate philosophy?
2. If your company lacks a mission statement, what do you think its mission statement should be like?
3. If your company has a mission statement, do you see it as appropriate, given the material discussed in this chapter?
4. Identify the main stakeholder groups in your company. What claims do they place on the company? How is the company trying to satisfy those claims?
5. Evaluate the performance of the CEO of your company from the perspective of (a) stockholders, (b) employees, (c) customers, and (d) suppliers. What does this evaluation tell you about the ability of the CEO and the priorities that he or she is committed to?
6. Try to establish whether the governance mechanisms that operate in your company do a good job of aligning the interests of top managers with those of stockholders.
7. Pick a major strategic decision made by your company in recent years and consider the ethical implications of that decision. In the light of your review, do you think that the company acted correctly?

ARTICLE FILE 2

Find an example of a company that ran into trouble because it failed to take into account the rights of one of its stakeholder groups when making an important strategic decision.

EXPLORING THE WEB
Visiting Merck

Go to the Web site of Merck, the world's largest pharmaceutical company (http://www.merck.com/), and find the mission statement posted there.

1. Evaluate this mission statement in light of the material contained in this chapter. Does the mission state clearly what Merck's basic strategic goal is? Do the values listed provide a good guideline for managerial action at Merck?
2. Follow the hypertext link "benefits humanity." Read the section on corporate responsibility, and then answer the following question: How does Merck try to balance the goals of providing stockholders with an adequate rate of return on their investment, and at the same time developing medicines that benefit humanity and that can be acquired by people in need at an affordable price? Do you think that Merck does a good job of balancing these goals?

General Task. Using the World Wide Web, find an example of a company mission statement that you think exemplifies many of the issues discussed in this chapter.

CLOSING CASE

Body Shop International

THE BRITISH-BASED RETAILER, Body Shop International, is often viewed as a prime example of a company committed to being ethical and socially responsible in its business dealings. The company's founder and CEO, Anita Roddick, has become an energetic spokesperson for the importance of ethics and social responsibility. Body Shop competes in the international cosmetics and toiletries market but offers unique products derived from natural ingredients. The company has based its success on the claim that none of its products is tested on animals, contains artificial ingredients, or is elaborately packaged. The products appeal to consumers who are concerned about animal rights and the environment. Under a program called "Trade not Aid," Body Shop claims to purchase many of the ingredients for its products from Third World producers, and the company maintains that it pays its suppliers well. It also makes a point of plowing money back into the communities where its suppliers are based to support a variety of health and educational projects. This commitment to social responsibility helped propel Body Shop from a single store in 1976 to a global enterprise with 1,100 stores in forty-five countries and annual revenues of more than $700 million in 1995. According to Roddick,

> You can run a business differently from the way most businesses are run, you can share your prosperity with employees, and empower them without being in fear of them. You can rewrite the book in terms of how a company interacts with the community, on third world trade, global responsibility, and the role of educating customers and shareholders, and you can do all this and still play the game according to the City [the British version of Wall Street], still raise money, delight the Institutions and give shareholders a wondrous return on their investment.

Roddick's philosophy helped turn Body Shop into the darling of the business ethics community. However, the good feeling was rudely shattered in the fall of 1994 when a journalist, Jon Entine, published an article highly critical of Body Shop in the *Business Ethics* magazine. Among other things, Entine made the following claims:

- Body Shop uses many outdated, off-the-shelf product formulas filled with nonrenewable petrochemicals.
- Many of its products are contaminated and contain formaldehyde, an artificial ingredient.
- Body Shop has used ingredients in its products that have been tested on animals.
- Contrary to its claims, Body Shop sources only a tiny amount of ingredients through its Trade not Aid program. Moreover, Body Shop does not pay "first world wages for third world products," as it claims in its publicity.
- The company's charitable contributions and progressive environmental standards fall short of it's claims. Until 1994, the company never contributed more than 1.24 percent of its pretax profits to charitable organizations.
- The company invented stories about the exotic origins of some of its products.

Entine's article drew a vigorous response from Gordon Roddick, the chairman of Body Shop International. In a ten-page letter sent to all subscribers of *Business Ethics* magazine, Roddick claimed that Entine's article was filled with "many lies, distortions, and gross inaccuracies. . . . I am at a loss to find anything balanced or fair in this article." Roddick went on in the letter to give a detailed rebuttal of Entine's charges. For example, with regard to the Trade not Aid program, Roddick observed that Entine's article

> goes after our Trade not Aid program, building its attack around an utterly irrelevant statistic—the percentage of our ingredients that come from Trade not Aid projects. What is this number supposed to reveal? It certainly tells us nothing about the effectiveness of our efforts. Or the amount of time we have put into nurturing these projects. Or the obstacles we have had to overcome due to the lack of infrastructure in disenfranchised Third World communities. . . . One single ingredient, such as Brazil nut oil or cocoa butter, may take two years or more to source and develop. Believe me, there are much easier ways to do business than by taking on the problems of such projects. . . . We do it because we are asked to help by the disenfranchised communities themselves. The only significant measure of our success is the number of people who are directly beneficially affected by our activities. That is a number, I am proud to say, that runs into the thousands.

Body Shop followed up Entine's attack by commissioning an independent "ethics audit" by the New Economics Foundation, a London-based ethics business consultant. Issued in January 1996, the audit reported that

93 percent of Body Shop's employees feel the company lives up to its mission to be socially and environmentally responsible and that the purchases from suppliers in developing countries or poor communities increased by more than 30 percent during 1995. The audit also noted that less than 2 percent of the company's raw material inputs came from the Trade not Aid program in 1995, although about 17.8 percent of the accessories sold in Body Shop stores—such as brushes and sponges—came from the program. The company donated 2.3 percent of its pretax profits to charity in 1995.[70]

Case Discussion Questions

1. Is Anita Roddick correct when she claims that it is possible to run a business in a very ethical and socially responsible manner and still "give shareholders a wondrous return on their investment"?
2. Is the percentage of ingredients that come from Trade not Aid projects an irrelevant statistic, as Gordon Roddick claims?
3. In light of the ethics audit report, evaluate Body Shop's claims to be ethically responsible.

End Notes

1. J. Byrne, "How Al Dunlap Self-Destructed," *Business Week*, July 6, 1998, p. 58; G. DeGeorge, "Al Dunlap Revs Up His Chainsaw," *Business Week*, November 25, 1996, p. 37; "Exit Bad Guy," *Economist*, June 20, 1998, p. 70; E. Pollock and M. Brannigan, "Mixed Grill: The Sunbeam Shuffle," *Wall Street Journal,* August 19, 1998, p. A1.
2. E. Freeman, *Strategic Management: A Stakeholder Approach* (Boston: Pitman Press, 1984).
3. C. W. L. Hill and T. M. Jones, "Stakeholder-Agency Theory," *Journal of Management Studies*, 29 (1992) 131–154; J. G. March and H. A. Simon, *Organizations* (New York: Wiley, 1958).
4. J. E. Rigdon and J. S. Lubin, "Why Morrison Board Fired Agee," *Wall Street Journal*, February 13, 1995, p. B1; C. McCoy, "Worst 5 and 1 year Performer: Morrison Knudsen," *Wall Street Journal*, February 29, 1996, p. R2; "Morrison Knudsen Settles Most Shareholder Lawsuits," *Wall Street Journal*, September 21, 1995, p. B8; J. E. Rigdon, "William Agee to Leave Morrison Knudsen," *Wall Street Journal*, February 2, 1995, p. B1.
5. Hill and Jones, "Stakeholder-Agency Theory," pp. 131–154.
6. I. C. Macmillan and P. E. Jones, *Strategy Formulation: Power and Politics* (St. Paul, Minn.: West, 1986).
7. D. F. Abell, *Defining the Business: The Starting Point of Strategic Planning* (Englewood Cliffs, N.J.: Prentice-Hall, 1980); K. Andrews, *The Concept of Corporate Strategy* (Homewood, Ill.: Dow Jones Irwin, 1971); J. A. Pearce, "The Company Mission as a Strategic Tool," *Sloan Management Review* (Spring 1982), 15–24.
8. Boeing's World Wide Web home page (http://www.boeing.com).
9. Weyerhaeuser Annual Report, 1995.
10. Information from www.pfizer.com/pfizerinc/about/vision/visionfrm.html ( ).
11. Information from www.intel.com/intel/annual98/vision.html ( ).
12. Information from http://www.appliedmaterials.com/about/mission.html ( ).
13. G. Hamel and C. K. Prahalad, *Competing for the Future* (Boston: Harvard Business School Press, 1994). Also see J. C. Collins and J. I. Porras, "Building Your Company's Vision," *Harvard Business Review* (September–October, 1996), pp. 65–77.
14. Quoted in S. Tully, "Why Go for Stretch Targets," *Fortune*, November 14, 1995, pp. 145–158.
15. Speech given by Michael Armstrong to the Executives Club of Chicago, May 21, 1999, (archived at www.atl.com/speaches/99/990521_cma.html); P. Elstrom, "Mike Armstrong's Strong Showing," *Business Week*, January 25, 1999, p. 94; J. Rendleman, "The Morphing of a New AT&T," *PC Week*, May 10, 1999, p. 20; K. Kaplan, "AT&T Lays Out Bold Plan for Its Future," *Los Angeles Times,* January 27, 1998, p. D1.
16. These three questions were first proposed by P. F. Drucker. See P. F. Drucker, *Management—Tasks, Responsibilities, Practices* (New York: Harper & Row, 1974), pp. 74–94.
17. D. F. Abell, *Defining the Business.*
18. T. Levitt, "Marketing Myopia," *Harvard Business Review* (July–August 1960), 45–56.
19. P. A. Kidwell and P. E. Ceruzzi, *Landmarks in Digital Computing* (Washington D.C.: Smithsonian Institute, 1994).
20. Kodak's World Wide Web site (http://www.kodak.com) 1998.
21. Collins and Porras, "Building Your Company's Vision," pp. 65–77.
22. J. Welch, "To Our Share Owners." Letter in GE's 1994 Annual Report.
23. Ibid.
24. M. D. Richards, *Setting Strategic Goals and Objectives* (St. Paul, Minn.: West, 1986).
25. For details, see "Johnson & Johnson (A)," *Harvard Business School Case* No. 384-053, Harvard Business School.
26. See J. P. Kotter and J. L. Heskett, *Corporate Culture and Performance* (New York, Free Press, 1992). For similar work, see Collins and Porras, "Building your Company's Vision," pp. 65–77.
27. Richards, *Setting Strategic Goals.*
28. E. A. Locke, G. P. Latham, and M. Erez, "The Determinants of Goal Commitment," *Academy of Management Review*, 13 (1988), 23–39.
29. M. Hammer and J. Champy, *Reengineering the Corporation* (New York: Harper Business, 1993).
30. R. E. Hoskisson, M. A. Hitt, and C. W. L. Hill, "Managerial Incentives and Investment in R&D in Large Multiproduct Firms," *Organization Science*, 3 (1993), 325–341.
31. R. H. Hayes and W. J. Abernathy, "Managing Our Way to Economic Decline," *Harvard Business Review* (July–August 1980), 67–77.
32. L. C. Thurow, *The Zero Sum Solution* (New York: Simon & Schuster, 1985), 69–89.
33. M. L. Dertouzos, R. K. Lester, and R. M. Solow, *Made in America* (Cambridge, Mass.: MIT Press, 1989).
34. "Flat out in Japan," *Economist*, February 1, 1992, pp. 79–80; H. Nomura, "IBM, Apple Fight LCD Screen Tariffs: US Decision Forcing Assembly Offshore," *Nikkei Weekly*, October 26, 1992; A. Tanzer, "The New Improved Color Computer," *Forbes*, July 23, 1990, pp. 276–280; J. Ascierto, "A Death of a Dream?" *Electronic News*, April 5, 1999, p. 1.
35. M. C. Jensen and W. H. Meckling, "Theory of the Firm: Managerial Behavior, Agency Costs and Ownership Structure," *Journal of Financial Economics*, 3 (1976), 305–360.
36. For example, see R. Marris, *The Economic Theory of Managerial Capitalism* (London: Macmillan, 1964), and J. K. Galbraith, *The New Industrial State* (Boston: Houghton Mifflin, 1970).
37. E. F. Fama, "Agency Problems and the Theory of the Firm," *Journal of Political Economy*, 88 (1980), 375–390.
38. A. Rappaport, "New Thinking on How to Link Executive Pay with Performance," *Harvard Business Review* (March–April 1999) pp. 91–105.
39. E. Goodman, "CEO Pay Cap: Why Not Try It for Size?" *Houston Chronicle*, April 18, 1999, p. 6.

40. S. Tully, "Raising the Bar," *Fortune*, June 8, 1998, pp. 272–278.
41. A. Fisher, "CEO Pay," *Fortune,* June 8, 1998, p. 296.
42. For academic studies that look at the determinants of CEO pay, see M. C. Jensen and K. J. Murphy, "Performance Pay and Top Management Incentives," *Journal of Political Economy*, 98 (1990), 225–264; C. W. L. Hill and P. Phan, "CEO Tenure as a Determinant of CEO Pay," *Academy of Management Journal*, 34 (1991), 707–717; H. L. Tosi and L. R. Gomez-Mejia, "CEO Compensation Monitoring and Firm Performance," *Academy of Management Journal*, 37 (1994), 1002–1016; J. F. Porac, J. B. Wade, and T. G. Pollock, "Industry Categories and the Politics of the Comparable Firm in CEO Compensation," *Administrative Science Quarterly*, 44 (1999) 112–144.
43. Goodman, "CEO Pay Cap," p. 6.
44. For recent research on this issue, see P. J. Lane, A. A. Cannella, and M. H. Lubatkin, "Agency Problems as Antecedents to Unrelated Mergers and Diversification: Amihud and Lev Reconsidered," *Strategic Management Journal,* 19 (1998), 555–578.
45. C. Icahn, "What Ails Corporate America—and What Should Be Done?" *Business Week*, October 27, 1986, p. 101.
46. E. T. Penrose, *The Theory of the Growth of the Firm* (London: Macmillan, 1958).
47. O. E. Williamson, *The Economic Institutions of Capitalism* (New York: Free Press, 1985).
48. E. F. Fama, "Agency Problems and the Theory of the Firm," pp. 375–390.
49. S.Finkelstein and R. D'Aveni, "CEO Duality as a Double-Edged Sword," *Academy of Management Journal*, 37 (1994), 1079–1108; B. Ram Baliga and R.C.Moyer, "CEO Duality and Firm Performance," *Strategic Management Journal*, 17 (1996), 41–53; M. L. Mace, *Directors: Myth and Reality* (Cambridge, Mass.: Harvard University Press, 1971; S. C. Vance, *Corporate Leadership: Boards of Directors and Strategy* (New York: McGraw Hill, 1983).
50. M. Galen, "A Seat on the Board Is Getting Hotter," *Business Week*, July 3, 1989, pp. 72–73.
51. J. S. Lublin, "Irate Shareholders Target Ineffective Board Members," *Wall Street Journal*, November 6, 1995, p. B1.
52. G. Fuchsberg, "Chief Executives See Their Power Shrink," *Wall Street Journal*, March 15, 1993, pp. B1, B3.
53. Quoted in G. Morgenson, "Stock Options are Not a Free Lunch," *Forbes*, May 18, 1998, pp. 212–217.
54. W. G. Lewellen, C. Eoderer, and A. Rosenfeld, "Merger Decisions and Executive Stock Ownership in Acquiring Firms," *Journal of Accounting and Economics*, 7 (1985), 209–231.
55. C. W. L. Hill and S. A. Snell, "External Control, Corporate Strategy, and Firm Performance," *Strategic Management Journal*, 9 (1988), pp. 577–590.
56. J. P. Walsh and R. D. Kosnik, "Corporate Raiders and Their Disciplinary Role in the Market for Corporate Control," *Academy of Management Journal*, 36 (1993), 671–700.
57. S. Reed, "Buyout Fever," *Business Week*, June 14, 1999, p. 24.
58. See M. C. Jensen, "Agency Costs of Free Cash Flow, Corporate Finance, and Takeovers," *American Economic Review* (1986), 323–329; and M. C. Jensen, "The Eclipse of the Public Corporation," *Harvard Business Review* (September–October 1989), 61–74.
59. R. B. Reich, "Leveraged Buyouts: America Pays the Price," *New York Times Magazine*, January 29, 1989, pp. 32–40.
60. P. H. Pan and C. W. L. Hill, "Organizational Restructuring and Economic Performance in Leveraged Buyouts," *Academy of Management Journal*, 38 (1995), 704–739; M. F. Wiersema and J. P. Liebskind, "The Effects of Leveraged Buyouts on Corporate Growth and Diversification in Large Firms," *Strategic Management Journal*, 16 (1995), 447–460; J. P. Liebskind, M. F. Wiersema, and G. Hansen, "LBOs, Corporate Restructuring, and the Incentive Intensity Hypothesis," *Financial Management*, 21 (1992), 50–57.
61. R. E. Freeman and D. Gilbert, *Corporate Strategy and the Search for Ethics* (Englewood Cliffs, N.J.: Prentice-Hall, 1988).
62. R. C. Solomon, *Ethics and Excellence* (Oxford: Oxford University Press, 1992).
63. S. W. Gellerman, "Why Good Managers Make Bad Ethical Choices," *Ethics in Practice: Managing the Moral Corporation,* ed. Kenneth R. Andrews (Boston: Harvard Business School Press, 1989).
64. B. Holden, "Foodmaker Delays Expansion Plans in Wake of Food-Poisoning Outbreak," *Wall Street Journal*, February 16, 1993, p. B10; B. Holden, "Foodmaker, Struggling After Poisonings, Breaks with Its Public Relations Firm," *Wall Street Journal*, February 12, 1993, p. A4; R. Goff, "Coming Clean," *Forbes*, May 17, 1999, pp. 156–160.
65. K. O. Hanson and M. Velasquez, "Hewlett-Packard Company: Managing Ethics and Values," in *Corporate Ethics: A Prime Business Asset,* The Business Roundtable, February 1988.
66. For example, see Freeman and Gilbert, *Corporate Strategy and the Search for Ethics*; T. Jones, "Ethical Decision Making by Individuals in Organizations," *Academy of Management Review,* 16 (1991), 366–395; and J. R. Rest, *Moral Development: Advances in Research and Theory* (New York: Praeger, 1986).
67. S. A. Waddock and S. B. Graves, "The Corporate Social Performance–Financial Performance Link," *Strategic Management Journal,* 8 (1997), 303–319.
68. M. Friedman, "A Friedman Doctrine: The Social Responsibility of Business Is to Increase Its Profits," *New York Times Magazine,* September 13, 1970, p. 33.
69. E. D. Bowman, "Corporate Social Responsibility and the Investor," *Journal of Contemporary Business* (Winter 1973), 49–58.
70. T. P. Poe, "Body Shop Comes Clean About Audit of Its Operation," *Wall Street Journal*, January 26, 1996, p. B12; "Storm in a Bubble Bath," *Economist*, September 3, 1994, p. 56; J. Entine, "Shattered Image," *Business Ethics Magazine* (September–October 1994), 23–28; G. Roddick, letter to *Business Ethics* subscribers, September 22, 1994, Body Shop International.

PART TWO

The Nature of Competitive Advantage

3 External Analysis: The Identification of Industry Opportunities and Threats

OPENING CASE

On-line Firms Revolutionize the Stockbrokerage Industry

FOR YEARS, although trading on the stock market has been electronic, only professional stockbrokers with expensive computer hardware could trade on-line. If an individual investor wanted to buy or sell a stock, she had to call her stockbroker and place an order. The stockbroker would charge a commission for this service. At full-service stockbrokers such as Merrill Lynch—which offered their clients detailed research reports, stock recommendations, and financial planning services—these commissions could run to 2.5 percent of the value of the order. Thus, an order worth $10,000 could generate $250 in commissions.

The situation began to change in 1994 when a small discount broker, K. Aufhauser, took advantage of new technology to become the first to offer its clients the ability to trade on-line over the Internet, effectively bypassing stockbrokers. The offering allowed Aufhauser to operate with fewer personnel. The cost saving was passed on to consumers in the form of lower commissions. Initially, on-line trading was merely a curiosity, but several things changed this. First, the Internet started to make rapid inroads into the homes of individual Americans. Second, within a short space of time, a vast amount of investment information was being offered on the Internet. Individual investors soon found that they could go to sites such as the Motley Fool at America Online or Yahoo!'s finance site and get much of the information that they needed to make informed investment decisions. No longer did they have to call their stockbrokers to ask for information. Third, a number of small companies quickly followed Aufhauser's lead and took advantage of the Internet to offer their clients on-line trading for commissions that were significantly below those offered by full-service stockbrokers in the physical world. Finally, America's long bull market attracted ever more individuals to the stock market, particularly among America's large baby-boom generation, who were drawn to investing in order to build up funds for retirement. Increasingly, these newcomers set up on-line trading accounts.

The effects of these trends were dramatic. By 1999, there were 70 firms offering on-line trading via the Internet. Many of these companies did not even exist in 1994. The arrival of the Internet had lowered barriers to entry and allowed these companies to enter the stockbrokerage industry and compete against incumbents such as Merrill Lynch. As the competition for the business of on-line investors started to heat up, commissions started to fall. By early 1999, on-line brokerages such as E*Trade were charging deep discount fees of $14.95 per market order for trades of up to 5,000 shares. Thus, while an order for 1,000 shares of a stock trading at $20 a share could cost the client of a full-service broker as much as $500 in commission, the same trade could be executed vie E*Trade for $14.95! Attracted by such low prices, from little more than a trickle in 1994, the volume of on-line trades grew to account for 30–35 percent of all stock trades by individuals as of mid 1999.

At first, full-service brokers derided on-line trading as dangerous and justified their high commissions by claiming that they offered their clients sound financial advice and proprietary research reports. However, with as many as 40 percent of all stockbrokers lacking much in the way of experience, and with the rapid increase in the amount of investment information that could be accessed on-line, such arguments sounded increasingly shrill and self-serving. By early 1999, it was becoming apparent that full-service brokers need to adapt to the new technology or risk seeing their client base evaporate. The landmark event occurred in June 1999, when Merrill Lynch, the world's largest full-service broker, bowed to the inevitable and announced that it, too, would soon offer its clients the ability to trade on-line for a fee of $29.95 for trades of up to 1,000 shares. An internal Merrill report estimated that as a result its army of 14,800 well-paid stockbrokers, who were paid chiefly in commissions, might initially see their incomes decline by 18 percent as a result of this move. Merrill knew that it faced a potential rebellion from its stockbrokers, but it also knew that it had no choice, given the forecasts suggesting that more than 50 percent of stock trades by individuals would be on-line by 2001.[1]

OVERVIEW

The Opening Case illustrates the impact that changing market conditions can have on prices and strategies in an industry. The rise of a new technology, the Internet, has lowered barriers to entry into the stockbrokerage industry, allowing upstarts like E*Trade and Ameritrade to compete head-to-head with incumbents such as Merrill Lynch for the business of individual investors. As hordes of these new enterprises entered the industry, prices (fees and commissions) plunged and demand shifted from high-priced full-service stockbrokers toward discount on-line brokers. The revolutionary nature of this process was illustrated by Merrill Lynch's decision in June 1999 to offer its clients on-line trading for a flat fee of $29.95 per trade of 1,000 shares or less. In effect, Merrill substantially reduced the price it charged individual investors and altered the way it delivered its service so that it might maintain its revenues and profits in the face of a fundamental change in the environment of the stockbrokerage industry.

Consistent with the theme introduced in the Opening Case, in this chapter we consider the influence of the industry environment in which a company competes on its performance. First, we discuss a number of models that can assist managers in analyzing the environment. The models provide a framework for identifying environmental opportunities and threats. **Opportunities** arise when a company can take advantage of conditions in its external environment to formulate and implement strategies that enable it to earn higher profits. Thus, the advent of the Internet provided an opportunity for discount stockbrokers to capture business from full-service brokers by offering services on-line. **Threats** arise when conditions in the external environmental endanger the integrity and profitability of the company's business. On-line stock trading threatened incumbent full-service stockbrokers such as Merrill Lynch. Second, we consider the competitive implications that arise when groups of companies within an industry pursue similar strategies. Third, we examine the nature of industry evolution and discuss in detail how the globalization of the world economy is affecting the competitive forces at work in an industry environment. Finally, we assess the impact of conditions within a nation on competitive advantage. By the end of the chapter, you will understand that to succeed a company must either fit its strategy to the industry environment in which it operates or be able to reshape the industry environment to its advantage through its chosen strategy.

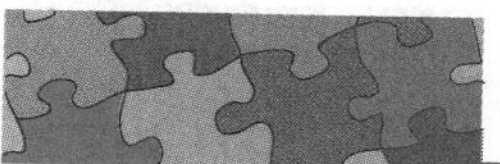

ANALYZING INDUSTRY STRUCTURE

An **industry** can be defined as a group of companies offering products or services that are close substitutes for each other. Close substitutes are products or services that satisfy the same basic consumer needs. For example, the metal and plastic body panels used in automobile construction are close substitutes for each other. Despite different production technologies, auto supply companies manufacturing metal body panels are in the same basic industry as companies manufacturing plastic body panels. They are serving the same consumer need, the need of auto assembly companies for body panels.

The task facing managers is to analyze competitive forces in an industry environment in order to identify the opportunities and threats confronting a company. Michael E. Porter of the Harvard School of Business Administration has developed a framework that helps managers in this analysis.[2] Porter's framework, known as the **five forces model,** appears in Figure 3.1. This model focuses on five forces that shape competition within an industry: (1) the risk of new entry by potential competitors; (2) the degree of rivalry among established companies within an industry; (3) the bargaining power of buyers; (4) the bargaining power of suppliers; and (5) the threat of substitute products.

Porter argues that the stronger each of these forces, the more limited is the ability of established companies to raise prices and earn greater profits. Within Porter's framework, a strong competitive force can be regarded as a threat since it depresses profits. A weak competitive force can be viewed as an opportunity, for it allows a company to earn greater profits. The strength of the five forces may change through time as industry conditions change, as illustrated by the Opening Case. The task facing managers is to recognize how changes in the five forces give rise to new opportunities and threats, and to formulate appropriate strategic responses. In addition, it is possible for a company, *through its choice of strategy*, to alter the strength of one

FIGURE 3.1

The Five Forces Model

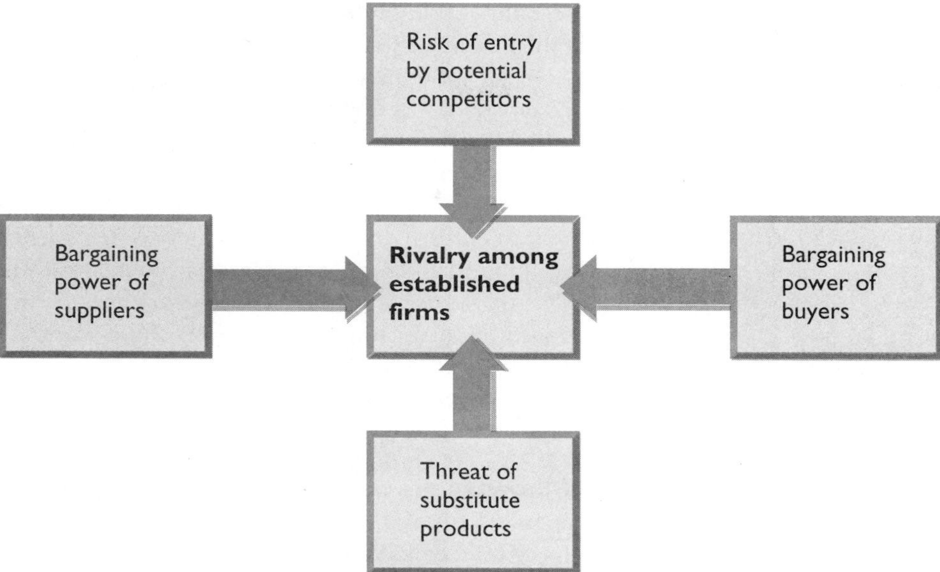

Source: Adapted and reprinted by permission of *Harvard Business Review.* An exhibit from "How Competence Forces Shape Strategy" by Michael E. Porter (March–April 1979). Copyright © 1979 by the President and Fellows of Harvard College; all rights reserved.

or more of the five forces to its advantage. This is discussed in the following chapters. In this section, we focus on understanding the impact that each of the five forces has on a company.

Potential Competitors

Companies that are not currently competing in an industry but have the capability to do so if they choose are **potential competitors**. For example, electric utilities are potential competitors to telecommunications companies in the markets for phone service and Internet access. In order to be able to deliver electricity to residential and commercial property, many electric utilities have been granted rights of way by state and local governments. They have laid electric cables down these rights of way, but there is nothing to stop them from putting in fiber-optic lines along these rights of way and offering high-bandwidth communication services to residential and commercial customers. In fact, a number of utilities have started to do this. For example, Tacoma City Light in Washington State has used its rights of way to run fiber-optic lines to several commercial buildings in the city of Tacoma and take away business from the dominant telecommunications service provider in the region, US West. Tacoma City Light is also laying coaxial cable to homes in its service region and offering a cable television service in direct competition with the local cable provider, TCI.[3]

Incumbent companies (those already operating in an industry) try to discourage potential competitors from entering the industry, since the more companies enter, the more difficult it becomes for established companies to hold their share of the market and to generate profits. For example, TCI's response to the potential entry of Tacoma City Light into the cable TV business in Tacoma was to threaten intense competition on both price and service offerings. Thus, a high risk of entry by potential competitors represents a threat to the profitability of established companies. On the other hand, if the risk of new entry is low, incumbent companies can take advantage of this opportunity to raise prices and earn greater returns.

The strength of the competitive force of potential rivals is largely a function of the height of barriers to entry. **Barriers to entry** are factors that make it costly for companies to enter an industry. The greater the costs that potential competitors must bear to enter an industry, the greater are the barriers to entry. High entry barriers keep potential competitors out of an industry even when industry returns are high. The classic work on barriers to entry was done by economist Joe Bain. He identified three main sources of barriers to new entry: brand loyalty, absolute cost advantages, and economies of scale.[4] To Bain's list we can add two more entry barriers of considerable significance in many situations: switching costs and government regulation.

Brand Loyalty Buyers' preference for the products of incumbent companies is termed **brand loyalty**. A company can create brand loyalty through continuous advertising of brand and company names, patent protection of products, product innovation achieved through company research and development programs, an emphasis on high product quality, and good after-sales service. Significant brand loyalty makes it difficult for new entrants to take market share away from established companies. Thus, it reduces the threat of entry by potential competitors since they may see the task of breaking down well-established consumer preferences as too costly.

Absolute Cost Advantages Sometimes incumbent companies have an absolute cost advantage relative to potential entrants. **Absolute cost advantages** seem to derive from three main sources. These are (a) superior production operations, due to past experience, patents, or secret processes; (b) control of particular inputs required for production, such as labor, materials, equipment, or management skills; and (c) access to cheaper funds because existing companies represent lower risks than companies that are not yet established. If incumbent companies have an absolute cost advantage, then the threat of entry decreases.

Economies of Scale The cost advantages associated with large company output are known as **economies of scale**. Sources of scale economies include cost reductions gained through mass-producing a standardized output, discounts on bulk purchases of raw-material inputs and component parts, the advantages gained by spreading of fixed costs over a large production volume, and economies of scale in advertising. If these cost advantages are significant, then a new entrant faces the dilemma of either entering on a small scale and suffering a significant cost disadvantage or taking a very large risk by entering on a large scale and bearing significant capital costs. A further risk of large-scale entry is that the increased supply of products will depress prices and result in vigorous retaliation by established companies. Thus, when established companies have economies of scale, the threat of entry is reduced.

Switching Costs When it costs a consumer to switch from the product offering of an incumbent company to the product offering of a new entrant, **switching costs** arise . When these costs are high, consumers can be **locked in** to the product offerings of incumbents, even if new entrants offer better products.[5] A familiar example of switching costs concerns the costs associated with switching from one computer operating system to another. If an individual currently uses Microsoft's Windows operating system, and has a library of related software applications (such as word-processing software, spreadsheet, games) and document files, it is expensive for that individual to switch to another computer operating system, such as the Macintosh OS produced by Apple Computer. The reason is simple; to effect the change the individual will have to buy a new set of software applications because applications written for Windows will not run on the Macintosh OS. Moreover, the individual will have to devote considerable time and effort to convert her document files so that they can be used by applications written for the Macintosh OS. Faced with such an expense of money and time, most people are unwilling to make the switch *unless* the competing operating system offers a *substantial* leap forward in performance (and arguably, the Mac OS does not). Thus, at this point one might argue that high switching costs have created barriers to entry into the market for a personal computer operating system and that competing operating systems have been locked out of the market. At the same time, it is important to understand that if a competitor offers an operating system that represents a substantial improvement over Windows, then users will switch to that operating system. In this regard, the Linux operating system, which is being sold by Red Hat Software, is viewed by some as a potential threat to Microsoft's market dominance.

Government Regulation Historically, government regulation has constituted a major entry barrier in many industries. For example, until recently in the United States, government regulation prohibited providers of long-distance telephone service, such as AT&T, MCI, and Sprint, from competing for local telephone service with the Regional Bell Operating Companies (RBOCs) such as US West and Bell Atlantic. Moreover, the RBOCs were prohibited from entering the long-distance telephone market. Other potential providers of telephone service, including cable television service companies such as TCI Communications and Viacom (which could in theory use their cables to carry telephone traffic as well as TV signals), were prohibited from entering the market altogether. These regulatory barriers to entry significantly reduced the level of competition in both the local and long-distance telephone markets, enabling telephone companies to earn higher profits than might otherwise have been the case. All this changed in January 1996 when the U.S. government deregulated the industry, removing all barriers to entry. In the months that followed this announcement, the RBOCs, long-distance companies, and cable TV companies all announced their intention to enter each other's markets. A significant increase in competitive intensity is to be expected. A similar move toward deregulating telephone service can be seen in many other countries. The member states of the European Union, for example, deregulated their telephone markets on January 1, 1998.

Entry Barriers and Competition If established companies have built brand loyalty for their products, have an absolute cost advantage with respect to potential competitors, have significant scale economies, are the beneficiaries of high switching costs, or enjoy regulatory protection, the risk of entry by potential competitors is greatly diminished. When this risk is low, established companies can charge higher prices and earn greater profits than would have been possible otherwise. Clearly, it is in the interest of companies to pursue strategies consistent with raising entry barriers. Indeed, empirical evidence suggests that the height of barriers to entry is one of the most important determinants of profit rates in an industry.[6] Examples of industries where entry barriers are considerable include pharmaceuticals, household detergents, and commercial jet aircraft. In the first two cases, product differentiation achieved through substantial expenditures for research and development and for advertising has built brand loyalty, making it difficult for new companies to enter these industries on a significant scale. So successful have the differentiation strategies of Procter & Gamble and Unilever been in household detergents that these two companies dominate the global industry. In the case of the commercial jet aircraft industry, the barriers to entry are primarily due to the enormous fixed costs of product development (it cost Boeing $5 billion to develop its new wide-bodied jetliner, the 777) and the scale economies enjoyed by the incumbent companies, which enable them to price below a potential entrant's costs of production and still make a significant profit. A more detailed example of entry barriers appears in Strategy in Action 3.1, which discusses the barriers to entry in the Japanese brewing industry.

Rivalry Among Established Companies

The second of Porter's five competitive forces is the extent of rivalry among established companies within an industry. If this rivalry is weak, companies have an opportunity to raise prices and earn greater profits. But if rivalry is strong, significant price competition, including price wars, may result. Price competition limits profitability by reducing the margins that can be earned on sales. Thus, intense rivalry among established companies constitutes a strong threat to profitability. The extent of rivalry among established companies within an industry is largely a function of three factors: (1) industry competitive structure, (2) demand conditions, and (3) the height of exit barriers in the industry.

Competitive Structure Competitive structure refers to the number and size distribution of companies in an industry. Structures vary from **fragmented** to **consolidated** and have different implications for rivalry. A fragmented industry contains a large number of small or medium-sized companies, none of which is in a position to dominate the industry. A consolidated industry may be dominated by a small number of large companies (in which case it is referred to as an oligopoly), or in extreme cases, by just one company (a monopoly). Fragmented industries range from agriculture, video rental, and health clubs to real estate brokerage and sun tanning parlors. Consolidated industries include aerospace, automobiles, and pharmaceuticals.

Many fragmented industries are characterized by low entry barriers and commodity-type products that are hard to differentiate. The combination of these traits tends to result in boom-and-bust cycles as industry profits rise and fall. Low entry barriers imply that whenever demand is strong and profits are high there will be a flood of new entrants hoping to cash in on the boom. The explosion in the number of video stores, health clubs, and sun tanning parlors during the 1980s exemplifies this situation.

Often the flood of new entrants into a booming fragmented industry creates excess capacity. Once excess capacity develops, companies start to cut prices in order to utilize their spare capacity. The difficulty companies face when trying to differentiate their products from those of competitors can worsen this tendency. The result is a price war, which depresses industry profits, forces some companies out of business, and deters potential new entrants. For example, after a decade of expansion and booming profits, many health clubs are now finding that they have to offer large discounts in order to hold on to their membership. In general, the more com-

3.1 STRATEGY *in* ACTION

Entry Barriers in the Japanese Brewing Industry

In 1565, an English visitor to Japan noted that the Japanese "feed moderately but they drink largely." This is still the case today; the Japanese have one of the highest levels of beer consumption per capita of any country in the world. In 1998, for example, fifty liters of beer were sold for every man, woman, and child in the country, making Japan's level of beer consumption per capita similar to that of big beer-drinking nations such as Australia, Britain, and Germany.

The Japanese market is dominated by four companies: Kirin, Asahi, Sapporo, and Suntory. In 1998, these four had a combined market share of around 97 percent. Collectively, these companies enjoy one of the highest profit rates of any industry in Japan. Despite this high level of profitability, however, there has been very little entry into this industry over the last three decades. Suntory has been the only successful new entrant in the last thirty years, and its market share stands at no more than 6 percent.

Normally, a lack of new entry into a profitable industry indicates the presence of high entry barriers, and that is certainly the case here. Like large brewers all over the world, Japan's big four spend heavily on advertising and promotions. Moreover, Japan's big brewers have been aggressive in the area of product development. During the 1990s, Asahi gained significant share from its competitors by pushing its "Super Dry" beer. The resulting product differentiation and brand identification have certainly helped to limit the potential for new entry. But some argue that there is more to it than this. Japan's big brewing companies have also benefited from significant regulatory barriers to entry. Brewers in Japan must have a license from the Ministry of Finance (MOF). Prior to 1994, the MOF would not issue a license to any brewer producing less than 2 million liters annually. This restriction represented an imposing hurdle to any potential new entrant. Interestingly enough, the reason for the licensing scheme was bureaucratic convenience rather than a desire to protect brewing companies from new entry; it is easier to collect tax from 4 companies than from 400.

Another significant barrier to entry has been Japan's distribution system. In Japan, there are often close ties between distributors and manufacturers, and this is the case in the brewing industry. Roughly half the beer consumed in Japan is sold in bars and restaurants. Their owners appear to be loyal to the big brewers and reluctant to take on competing brands that might alienate their main supplier. Small liquor stores are another main distribution outlet for beer, and they, too, have traditionally maintained close ties with the big brewers and are unwilling to sell the products of new entrants for fear that their main suppliers might "punish" them by denying them access to adequate supplies.

However, it now appears that some of the barriers to entering Japan's brewing industry are being lowered. As part of an economic liberalization plan, in 1994 the MOF reduced the production threshold required to gain a license from 2 million liters to 60,000 liters. This was low enough to allow the entry of microbreweries using the same technology that is now found in many brew pubs in the United States and Britain. Moreover, regulatory changes have also permitted the establishment of large new discount stores in Japan. (Until 1994, small retailers could effectively block the establishment of a large discount store in their region by appealing to the local authorities). Unlike traditional small retailers, large discount retailers are motivated more by price and profit than by loyalties to an established supplier and seem willing to sell the beer of foreign companies and microbreweries, in addition to that of Japan's big four.

Given the decline in barriers to entry associated with regulation and distribution channels, many observers thought that Japan's big four brewers would have to face new competitors in the years after 1994. So far, however, that has not happened. Instead, Japan's big four brewers continue to dominate the domestic market—a testament perhaps to the significance of advertising, promotions, and product differentiation as barriers to entry. On the other hand, Japan's brewers are facing indirect competition from an alternative alcoholic beverage, wine, which is starting to become fashionable among younger people.[7]

modity-like an industry's product, the more vicious will be the price war. This bust part of the cycle continues until overall industry capacity is brought into line with demand (through bankruptcies), at which point prices may stabilize again.

A fragmented industry structure, then, constitutes a threat rather than an opportunity. Most booms will be relatively short-lived because of the ease of new entry and will be followed by price wars and bankruptcies. Since it is often difficult to differentiate products in these industries, the best strategy for a company to pursue may be cost minimization. This strategy allows a company to rack up high returns in a boom and survive any subsequent bust.

The nature and intensity of rivalry in consolidated industries is much more difficult to predict. Because in consolidated industries companies are *interdependent*, the competitive actions of one company directly affect the profitability of others in the industry, and the impact on the market share of its rivals forces a response from them. The consequence of such competitive interdependence can be a dangerous competitive spiral, with rival companies trying to undercut each other's prices, pushing industry profits down in the process. The fare wars that have racked the airline industry in the early 1990s provide a good example. When demand for airline travel fell during 1990 as the U.S. economy slipped into a recession, airlines started cutting prices to try to maintain their passenger loads. When one airline serving a particular route cut its prices, its competitors would soon follow. The result was a particularly severe downward price spiral. So intense did price competition become that between 1990 and 1992 the industry lost a staggering $7.1 billion, more than had been made during its previous fifty years, and some long-established carriers, such as Pan American, disappeared into bankruptcy.

Clearly, high rivalry between companies in consolidated industries and the possibility of a price war constitute a major threat. Companies sometimes seek to reduce this threat by following the price lead set by a dominant company in the industry. However, they must be careful, for explicit price-fixing agreements are illegal, although tacit agreements are not. (A tacit agreement is one arrived at without direct communication). Instead, companies watch and interpret each other's behavior. Often tacit agreements involve following the price lead set by a dominant company.[8] However, tacit price-leadership agreements often break down under adverse economic conditions, as is beginning to occur in the beer industry. For most of the 1980s, Anheuser-Busch was the acknowledged price leader in this industry. The resulting absence of price competition helped keep industry profits high. However, slow growth in beer consumption during the late 1980s and early 1990s put pressure on the earnings of all beer majors and persuaded Miller Brewing—a division of Philip Morris—and Adolph Coors to break ranks and institute a policy of deep and continuous discounting for most of their beer brands. In 1990, market leader Anheuser-Busch announced that it would start offering similar discounts in order to protect its sales volume. Thus, after the breakdown of a tacit price-leadership agreement, the beer industry seemed to be sliding toward a price war.

More generally, when price wars are a threat, companies tend to compete on nonprice factors such as advertising and promotions, brand positioning, and product quality, functionality, and design. This type of competition constitutes an attempt to differentiate the company's product from those of competitors, thereby building brand loyalty and minimizing the likelihood of a price war. The effectiveness of this strategy, however, depends on how easy it is to differentiate the industry's product. Although some products (such as cars) are relatively easy to differentiate, others (such as airline travel) are difficult. Moreover, as Strategy in

Action 3.2 demonstrates, in practice nonprice competition in consolidated industries can often be as vigorous, expensive, and damaging as price competition.

Demand Conditions An industry's demand conditions are another determinant of the intensity of rivalry among established companies. Growing demand stemming from new customers or from additional purchases by existing customers, tends to moderate competition by providing greater room for expansion. Growing demand tends to reduce rivalry because all companies can sell more without taking market share away from other companies, and high profits are often the result. Conversely, declining demand results in more rivalry as companies fight to maintain revenues and market share. Demand declines when consumers are leaving the marketplace or when each consumer is buying less. In that situation, a company can grow only by taking market share away from other companies. Thus, declining demand constitutes a major threat, for it increases the extent of rivalry between established companies. Moreover, as we saw in the Opening Case, a slowdown in the rate of growth of demand can also create problems.

Exit Barriers Exit barriers are economic, strategic, and emotional factors that keep companies in an industry even when returns are low. If exit barriers are high, companies can become locked into an unprofitable industry where overall demand is static or declining. Excess productive capacity can result. In turn, excess capacity tends to lead to intensified price competition, with companies cutting prices in an attempt to obtain the orders needed to utilize their idle capacity.[10] Common exit barriers include the following:

1. Investments in plant and equipment that have no alternative uses and cannot be sold off. If the company wishes to leave the industry, it has to write off the book value of these assets.

2. High fixed costs of exit, such as severance pay to workers who are being made redundant.

3. Emotional attachments to an industry, as when a company is unwilling to exit from its original industry for sentimental reasons.

4. Economic dependence on the industry, as when a company is not diversified and so relies on the industry for its income.

The experience of the steel industry illustrates the adverse competitive effects of high exit barriers.[11] A combination of declining demand and new low-cost sources of supply created overcapacity in the global steel industry during the late 1980s. U.S. companies, with their high-cost structure, were on the sharp end of this decline. Demand for U.S. steel fell from a 1977 peak of 160 million tons to 70 million tons in 1986. The outcome was excess capacity amounting to an estimated 45 million tons in 1987, or 40 percent of total productive capacity. In order to try to utilize this capacity, many steel companies slashed their prices. As a consequence of the resulting price war, industry profits were low, and several of the majors, including LTV Steel and Bethlehem Steel, faced bankruptcy.

Since the steel industry was characterized by excess capacity for most of the 1980s, why did companies not reduce that capacity? The answer is that many tried to, but the costs of exit slowed this process and prolonged the associated price war. For example, in 1983 USX shut down 16 percent of its raw steel-making capacity at a cost of $1.2 billion. USX had to write off the book value of these assets; they could

3.2 **STRATEGY in ACTION**

The Great European Soap War

The European retail detergents market, like the global detergents market, is dominated by the products of just two companies, Unilever, the Anglo-Dutch concern, and the American consumer products giant, Procter & Gamble (P&G). Both companies sell a broad product line of detergents to consumers; both spend heavily on advertising, promotions, and brand positioning; and both de-emphasize price-based competition. The net result is that historically both companies have benefited from a relatively benign competitive environment, which has enabled them to earn higher profit margins than would be the case in a more price-competitive industry.

This cozy situation was rudely shattered in early 1994 after the Pan-European launch of a new detergent by Unilever. The product in question was Omo Power, which Unilever promoted as the biggest technical advance in fabric detergents in fifteen years. According to Unilever, Omo Power contained a powerful cleansing agent that washed clothes cleaner than any other product on the market. Consumers seemed to agree; sales of Omo Power surged in every country in which it was introduced during the first few months of 1994. P&G was alarmed by this development. The introduction of Omo Power seemed to violate a tacit understanding between the two companies that they would share technical information with each other. Moreover, Unilever was gaining market share at P&G's expense for the first time in two decades.

P&G's initial response was to try and discover what the secret ingredient in Omo Power might be. After extensive laboratory studies, P&G discovered that Unilever had used crystals of manganese. This surprised P&G, for although manganese could speed the bleaching process, P&G also knew from its own research that manganese attacked fabrics, which was why P&G had abandoned work on manganese ten years earlier. After submitting Omo Power to its own tests, P&G found that clothes washed repeatedly in the powder did indeed develop holes. Armed with this information, P&G decided to counterattack. Top executives from P&G visited top management at Unilever and stated bluntly that Omo Power was fundamentally flawed and should be pulled off the market. Unilever executives chose to discount this private warning. After two years of market testing with no complaints from consumers, Unilever saw no need to withdraw the product and believed P&G was overstating the problem because it was losing market share. It was at this point that P&G broke with the industry tradition of not criticizing the products of competitors and launched a ruthless public relations campaign pointing out the flaws of Omo Power. P&G gave the press a set of color pictures showing clothes purportedly suffering the ill effects of Omo Power—including shots of some tattered boxer shorts that were duly reproduced by the press all over Europe.

Unilever initially tried to dismiss P&G's claims, but a growing number of independent research institutes backed up P&G's findings. After several months of increasingly bitter public recriminations between the two companies, Unilever was eventually forced to concede that there was a problem. Unilever repositioned Omo Power in the market place from a product with broad applicability to a niche product for use with white fabrics and low water temperatures (conditions that minimized the damage problems).

In the end, Unilever was forced to admit that its $300 million investment in Omo had been a washout. By the end of 1994, Unilever's market share had fallen back to the level the company had attained prior to the launching of Omo Power. Moreover, executives from both companies admitted that the rules of the game in the industry had changed as a result of the dispute. Gone was the cozy agreement of sharing technical information and forbearing from directly attacking the products of a competitor. Nonprice competition in the industry would now be much more difficult than before. P&G fully expected Unilever to try and get its revenge by attacking any new product launch that it might try.[9]

not be sold. In addition, it had to cover pensions and insurance for 15,400 terminated workers. Given such high exit costs, companies such as USX have remained locked into this unprofitable industry. The effect of impeded exit has been more intense price competition than might otherwise have been the case. Thus, high exit barriers, by slowing the speed with which companies leave the industry, threaten the profitability of all companies within the steel industry.

The Bargaining Power of Buyers

The third of Porter's five competitive forces is the bargaining power of buyers. A company's buyers may be the customers who ultimately consume its products (its end users), but they may also be the companies that distribute its products to end users, such as retailers and wholesalers. For example, while Unilever sells its soap powder to end users, the major buyers of its products are supermarket chains, which then resell the product to the end users. Buyers can be viewed as a competitive threat when they are in a position to demand lower prices from the company, or when they demand better service (which can increase operating costs). On the other hand, when buyers are weak, a company can raise its prices and earn greater profits. Whether buyers are able to make demands on a company depends on their power relative to that of the company. According to Porter, buyers are most powerful in the following circumstances:

1. When the supply industry is composed of many small companies and the buyers are few in number and large. These circumstances allow the buyers to dominate supply companies.
2. When the buyers purchase in large quantities. In such circumstances, buyers can use their purchasing power as leverage to bargain for price reductions.
3. When the supply industry depends on the buyers for a large percentage of its total orders.
4. When the buyers can switch orders between supply companies at a low cost, thereby playing off companies against each other to force down prices.
5. When it is economically feasible for the buyers to purchase the input from several companies at once.
6. When the buyers can use the threat to supply their own needs through vertical integration as a device for forcing down prices.

An example of an industry whose buyers are powerful is the auto component supply industry. The buyers here are the large automobile companies, such as General Motors, Ford, and Chrysler. The suppliers of auto components are numerous and typically small in scale. Their buyers, the auto manufacturers, are large in size and few in number. Chrysler, for example, does business with nearly 2,000 different component suppliers and normally contracts with a number of different companies to supply the same part. The auto majors have used their powerful position to play off suppliers against each other, forcing down the price they have to pay for component parts and demanding better quality. If a component supplier objects, then the auto major uses the threat of switching to another supplier as a bargaining tool.

Additionally, to keep component prices down, both Ford and General Motors have used the threat of manufacturing a component themselves rather than buying it from auto component suppliers.

Another issue is that the relative power of buyers and suppliers tends to change over time in response to changing industry conditions. For example, because of changes now taking place in the pharmaceutical and health care industries, major buyers of pharmaceuticals (hospitals and health maintenance organizations) are gaining power over the suppliers of pharmaceuticals and have been able to demand lower prices.

The Bargaining Power of Suppliers

The fourth of Porter's competitive forces is the bargaining power of suppliers. Suppliers can be viewed as a threat when they are able to force up the price that a company must pay for its inputs or reduce the quality of the inputs they supply, thereby depressing the company's profitability. On the other hand, if suppliers are weak, this gives a company the opportunity to force down prices and demand higher input quality. As with buyers, the ability of suppliers to make demands on a company depends on their power relative to that of the company. According to Porter, suppliers are most powerful in these circumstances:

1. When the product that suppliers sell has few substitutes and is important to the company.
2. When the company's industry is not an important customer to the suppliers. In such instances, the suppliers' health does not depend on the company's industry, and suppliers have little incentive to reduce prices or improve quality.
3. When suppliers' respective products are differentiated to such an extent that it is costly for a company to switch from one supplier to another. In such cases, the company depends on its suppliers and cannot play them off against each other.
4. When, to raise prices, suppliers can use the threat of vertically integrating forward into the industry and competing directly with the company.
5. When buying companies cannot use the threat of vertically integrating backward and supplying their own needs as a means of reducing input prices.

Manufacturers of personal computers exemplify an industry that depends on a very powerful supplier. In this case, the supplier is Intel, the world's largest manufacturer of microprocessors for personal computers (PCs). The industry standard for personal computers runs on Intel's X86 microprocessor family, such as the Pentium series microprocessors currently sold in most PCs. So PC manufacturers have little choice but to use an Intel microprocessor as the brains for their machines. Although several companies have tried to produce clones of Intel's microprocessors, their success has been limited, leaving Intel with about 85 percent of the market. This puts Intel in a very powerful position with regard to the PC manufacturers. The product it supplies has few substitutes and switching costs facing the buyers are high, which enables Intel to raise prices above the level that would prevail in a more competitive supply market.[12]

Substitute Products

The final force in Porter's model is the threat of substitute products. Substitute products are the products of industries that serve similar consumer needs as the industry being analyzed. For example, companies in the coffee industry compete indirectly with those in the tea and soft-drink industries. All three industries serve consumer needs for drinks. The prices that companies in the coffee industry can charge are limited by the existence of substitutes such as tea and soft drinks. If the price of coffee rises too much relative to that of tea or soft drinks, then coffee drinkers will switch from coffee to those substitutes. This phenomenon occurred when unusually cold weather destroyed much of the Brazilian coffee crop in 1975–1976. The price of coffee rose to record highs, reflecting the shortage, and consumers began to switch to tea in large numbers.

The existence of close substitutes presents a strong competitive threat, limiting the price a company can charge and thus its profitability. However, if a company's products have few close substitutes (that is, if substitutes are a weak competitive force), then, other things being equal, the company has the opportunity to raise prices and earn additional profits. Consequently, its strategies should be designed to take advantage of this fact.

A Sixth Force: Complementors

Andrew Grove, the former CEO of Intel, and a part-time teacher at Stanford's Graduate School of Business, has argued that Porter's five forces model ignores a sixth force—the power, vigor, and competence of complementors.[13] **Complementors** are companies that sell complements to the enterprise's own product offerings. For example, the complementors to Sony's popular home video game system, the Play Station, are the companies that produce and sell games that run on the Play Station. Grove's point is that without an adequate supply of complementary products, demand in the industry will be weak, and revenues and profits will be low. No one would purchase the Play Station if there were not enough games to play on it. For another example, consider the early automobile industry. When the automobile was first introduced at the beginning of the twentieth century, demand for the product was very limited. One reason for this was the lack of important complementary products, such as a network of paved roads and gas stations. An automobile was of limited use when there were few paved roads to drive on, and when gas stations were few and far between. As the supply of complementary products increased—as roads and gas stations started to spring up—so did the attractiveness of owning a car. With roads to drive on and an adequate supply of gas stations, owning a car became more practical, and so demand started to pick up. In turn, this created a demand for more roads and gas stations, setting up a self-reinforcing positive feedback loop.

Grove's argument has a strong foundation in economic theory. Most economic textbooks have long argued that *both* substitutes and complements influenced demand in an industry.[14] Moreover, recent research has emphasized the importance of complementary products in determining demand and profitability in many high-technology industries, such as the computer industry, in which Grove made his mark.[15] The basic point, therefore, is that when complements are an important determinant of demand in an industry, the health of the industry depends critically on there being an adequate supply of complementary products produced by complementors. It follows that if complementors are weak and lack attractive product offerings, this can be a threat for the industry (the converse holds true as well).

The Role of the Macroenvironment

So far we have treated industries as self-contained entities. In practice, they are embedded in a wider **macroenvironment:** the broader economic, technological, social, demographic, and political and legal environment (see Figure 3.2). Changes in the macroenvironment can have a direct impact on any one of the forces in Porter's model, thereby altering the relative strength of these forces and with it, the attractiveness of an industry. We briefly consider how each aspect of these macroenvironmental forces can affect an industry's competitive structure.

The Macroeconomic Environment The state of the macroeconomic environment determines the general health and well-being of the economy. This in turn affects a company's ability to earn an adequate rate of return. The four most important factors in the macroeconomy are the growth rate of the economy, interest rates, currency exchange rates, and inflation rates.

Because it leads to an expansion in consumer expenditures, economic growth tends to produce a general easing of competitive pressures within an industry. This gives companies the opportunity to expand their operations and earn higher profits. Because economic decline leads to a reduction in consumer expenditures, it increases competitive pressures. Economic decline frequently causes price wars in mature industries.

FIGURE 3.2

The Role of the Macroenvironment

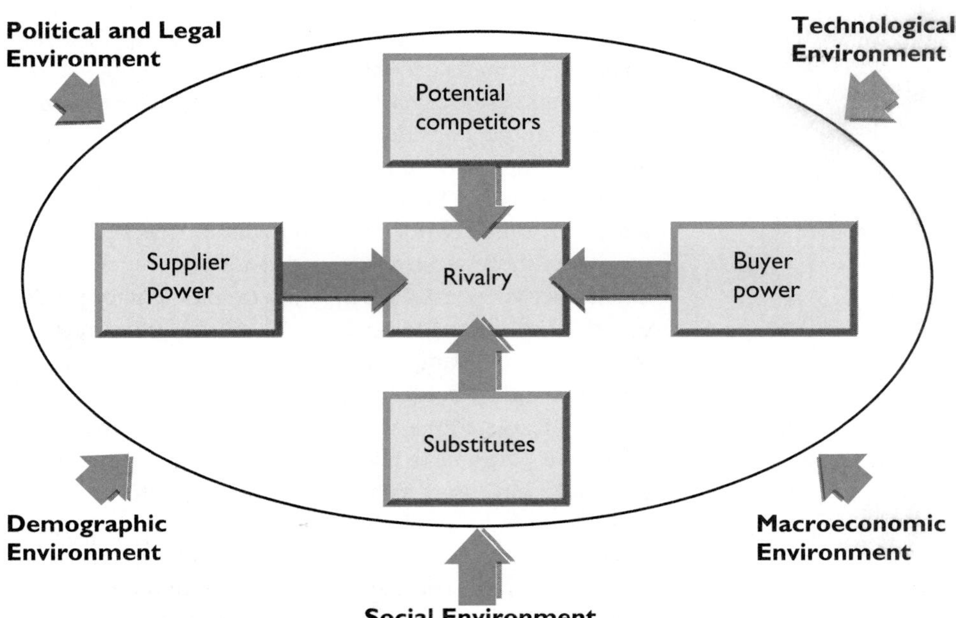

The level of interest rates can determine the level of demand for a company's products. Interest rates are important whenever consumers routinely borrow money to finance their purchase of these products. The most obvious example is the housing market, where the mortgage rate directly affects demand, but interest rates also have an impact on the sale of autos, appliances, and capital equipment, to give just a few examples. For companies in such industries, rising interest rates are a threat and falling rates an opportunity.

Currency exchange rates define the value of different national currencies against each other. Movement in currency exchange rates has a direct impact on the competitiveness of a company's products in the global marketplace. For example, when the value of the dollar is low compared with the value of other currencies, products made in the United States are relatively inexpensive and products made overseas are relatively expensive. A low or declining dollar reduces the threat from foreign competitors while creating opportunities for increased sales overseas. For example, the fall in the value of the dollar against the Japanese yen that occurred between 1985 and 1995, when the dollar/yen exchange rate declined from $1 = Y240 to $1 = Y85, sharply increased the price of imported Japanese cars, giving U.S. car manufacturers some degree of protection against the Japanese threat.

Inflation can destabilize the economy, producing slower economic growth, higher interest rates, and volatile currency movements. If inflation keeps increasing, investment planning becomes hazardous. The key characteristic of inflation is that it makes the future less predictable. In an inflationary environment, it may be impossible to predict with any accuracy the real value of returns that can be earned from a project five years hence. Such uncertainty makes companies less willing to invest. Their holding back in turn depresses economic activity and ultimately pushes the economy into a slump. Thus, high inflation is a threat to companies.

The Technological Environment Since World War II, the pace of technological change has accelerated,[16] unleashing a process that has been called a "perennial gale of creative destruction."[17] Technological change can make established products obsolete overnight, and at the same time it can create a host of new product possibilities. Thus, technological change is both creative and destructive—both an opportunity and a threat.

One of the most important impacts of technological change is that it can affect the height of barriers to entry and, as a result, radically reshape industry structure. This was clearly demonstrated in the Opening Case, when we saw how the spread of the Internet has lowered barriers to entry into the on-line stockbrokerage industry and produced a flood of new entrants and a more fragmented industry structure. In turn, these new entrants have driven down commission rates in the industry, just as theory would predict. In point of fact, the Internet represents a major technological change, and it appears to be in the process of unleashing a similar process of creative destruction across a wide range of industries. On-line retailers are springing up, selling everything from books and CDs to groceries and clothes, suggesting that the Internet has lowered entry barriers in the retail industry. The ability to buy airline tickets and book vacations on-line is a threat to established travel agents, while providing an opportunity for Internet-based start-ups that want to enter the travel industry. The rise of the Internet has also lowered barriers to entry into the news industry. For example, the providers of financial news now have to compete for advertising dollars and consumer attention with new Internet-based media organizations, which have sprung up in recent years, such as TheStreet.com, the Motley Fool, and Yahoo!'s financial section.

Another example of how technological change is reshaping an established industry can be found by considering the impact of biotechnology on the pharmaceutical industry. Although large companies such as Merck, Pfizer, and Eli Lilly have long dominated the pharmaceutical industry, a significant number of small biotechnology companies using recombinant DNA technology are threatening to change the competitive landscape. Between 1945 and 1990, only one new firm became a major player in the pharmaceutical industry, Syntex. Since 1990, a number of biotechnology companies have started to generate significant sales, including Amgen, Biogen, Genetech, Chiron, and Immunex. Moreover, there are now over 300 publicly traded companies in the United States developing novel medicines using biotechnology. The chance is that some of them will develop into significant companies in their own right, illustrating once again that technological change lowers entry barriers and allows new players to challenge the dominance of incumbents.

The Social Environment Like technological change, social change creates opportunities and threats. One of the major social movements of the 1970s and 1980s was the trend toward greater health consciousness. Its impact has been immense, and companies that recognized the opportunities early have often reaped significant gains. Philip Morris, for example, capitalized on the growing health-consciousness trend when it acquired Miller Brewing and then redefined competition in the beer industry with its introduction of low-calorie beer (Miller Lite). Similarly, PepsiCo was able to gain market share from its rival, Coca-Cola, by introducing diet colas and fruit-based soft drinks first. At the same time the health trend has created a threat for many industries. The tobacco industry, for example, is now in decline as a direct result of greater consumer awareness of the health implications of smoking. Similarly, the sugar industry has seen sales decrease as consumers have decided to switch to artificial sweeteners.

The Demographic Environment The changing composition of the population is another factor in the macroenvironment that can create both opportunities and threats. For example, as the baby-boom generation of the 1960s has aged, it has created a host of opportunities and threats. During the 1980s, many baby boomers were getting married and creating an upsurge in demand for the consumer appliances normally bought by couples marrying for the first time. Companies such as Whirlpool and General Electric capitalized on the resulting upsurge in demand for washing machines, dishwashers, spin dryers, and the like. The other side of the coin is that industries oriented toward the young, such as the toy industry, have seen their consumer base decline in recent years.

The Political and Legal Environment Political and legal factors also have a major effect on the level of opportunities and threats in the environment. One of the most significant trends in recent years has been the move toward deregulation. By eliminating many legal restrictions, deregulation has lowered barriers to entry and led to intense competition in a number of industries. The deregulation of the airline industry in 1979 created the opportunity to establish low-fare carriers—an opportunity that Southwest Airlines, Value Jet, and others tried to capitalize on. At the same time, the increased intensity of competition created many threats, including, most notably, the threat of prolonged fare wars, which have thrown the airline industry into turmoil several times since 1979. The global telecommunications industry is now beginning to experience the same kind of turmoil following the deregulation of that industry in both the United States and the European Union.

STRATEGIC GROUPS WITHIN INDUSTRIES

The Concept of Strategic Groups

So far we have said little about how companies in an industry might differ from each other and what implications these differences might have for the opportunities and threats they face. In practice, companies in an industry often differ from each other with respect to factors such as the distribution channels they use, the market segments they serve, the quality of their products, technological leadership, customer service, pricing policy, advertising policy, and promotions. As a result of these differences, within most industries, it is possible to observe groups of companies in which each member follows the same basic strategy as other companies in the group, but a strategy that is *different* from that followed by companies in other groups. These groups of companies are known as **strategic groups**.[18]

Normally, a limited number of groups captures the essence of strategic differences between companies within an industry. For example, in the pharmaceutical industry, two main strategic groups stand out (see Figure 3.3).[19] One group, which includes such companies as Merck, Pfizer, and Eli Lilly, is characterized by heavy R&D spending and a focus on developing new proprietary blockbuster drugs. The companies in this *proprietary group* are pursuing a high-risk/high-return strategy. It is a high-risk strategy because basic drug research is difficult and expensive. Bringing a new drug to market can cost $100 million to $300 million in R&D money and a decade of research and clinical trials. The strategy is also a high-return one because a single successful drug can be patented, giving the innovator a seventeen-year monopoly on its production and sale. This lets the innovator charge a very high price for the patented drug, allowing the company to earn millions, if not billions, of dollars, over the lifetime of the patent.

The second strategic group might be characterized as the *generic drug* group. This group of companies, which includes Marion Labs, Carter Wallace, and ICN Pharmaceuticals, focuses on the manufacture of generic drugs—low-cost copies of drugs pioneered by companies in the proprietary group whose patents have now expired. The companies in this group are characterized by low R&D spending and an emphasis on price competition. They are pursuing a low-risk, low-return strategy. It is low risk because they are not investing millions of dollars in R&D. It is low return because they cannot charge high prices.

Implications of Strategic Groups

The concept of strategic groups has a number of implications for identifying threats and opportunities within an industry. First, a company's closest competitors are those in its strategic group—not those in other strategic groups. Since all the companies in a strategic group are pursuing similar strategies, consumers tend to view

FIGURE 3.3

Strategic Groups in the Pharmaceutical Industry

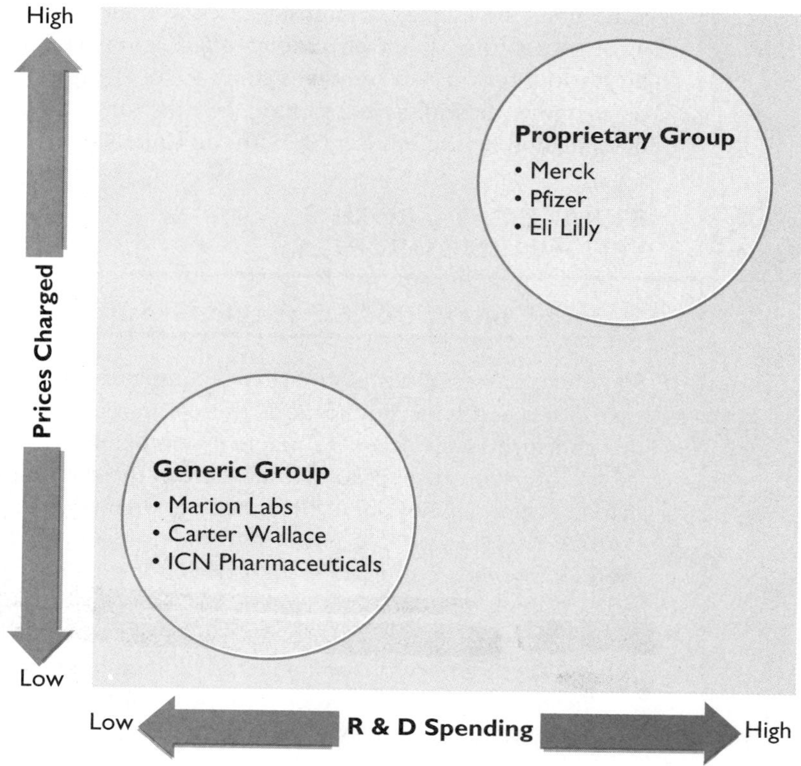

the products of such enterprises as direct substitutes for each other. Thus, a major threat to a company's profitability can come from within its own strategic group.

Second, different strategic groups can have a different standing with respect to each of the competitive forces. In other words, the risk of new entry by potential competitors, the degree of rivalry among companies within a group, the bargaining power of buyers, the bargaining power of suppliers, and the competitive force of substitute products can all vary in intensity among different strategic groups within the same industry.

For example, in the pharmaceutical industry, companies in the proprietary group have historically been in a very powerful position vis-à-vis buyers because their products are patented. Besides, rivalry within this group has been limited to competition to be the first to patent a new drug (so-called patent races). Price competition has been rare. Without price competition, companies in this group have been able to charge high prices and earn very high profits. In contrast, companies in the generic group have been in a much weaker position in regard to buyers since they lack patents for their products and since buyers can choose between very similar competing generic drugs. Moreover, price competition between the companies in this group has been quite intense, reflecting the lack of product differentiation. Thus, companies within this group have earned somewhat lower returns than companies in the proprietary group.

It follows that some strategic groups are more desirable than others, for they have a lower level of threats and greater opportunities. Managers must evaluate whether their company would be better off competing in a different strategic group. If the environment of another strategic group is more benign, then moving into that group can be regarded as an opportunity. Yet this opportunity is rarely without costs, mainly because of mobility barriers between groups. **Mobility barriers** are factors that inhibit the movement of companies between groups in an industry. They include both the barriers to entry into a group and the barriers to exit from a company's existing group. For example, Marion Labs would encounter mobility barriers if it attempted to enter the proprietary group in the pharmaceutical industry. These mobility barriers would arise from the fact that Marion lacks the R&D skills possessed by companies in the proprietary group, and building these skills would be an expensive proposition. Thus, a company contemplating entry into another strategic group must evaluate the height of mobility barriers before deciding whether the move is worthwhile.

Mobility barriers also imply that companies within a given group may be protected to a greater or lesser extent from the threat of entry by companies based in other strategic groups. If mobility barriers are low, the threat of entry from companies in other groups may be high, effectively limiting the prices companies can charge and the profits they can earn without attracting new competition. If mobility barriers are high, however, the threat of entry is low, and companies within the protected group have an opportunity to raise prices and earn higher returns without attracting entry.

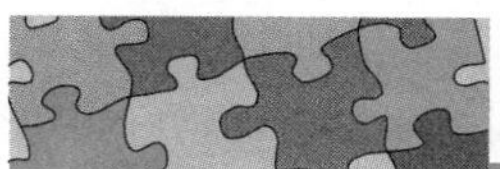

LIMITATIONS OF THE FIVE FORCES AND STRATEGIC GROUP MODELS

The five forces and strategic group models provide useful ways of thinking about and analyzing the nature of competition within an industry to identify opportunities and threats. However, managers need to be aware of their shortcomings, for both models (1) present a static picture of competition that slights the role of innovation and (2) de-emphasize the significance of individual company differences while overemphasizing the importance of industry and strategic group structure as determinants of company profit rates.

Innovation and Industry Structure

Over any reasonable length of time, in many industries competition can be viewed as a process driven by innovation.[20] Companies that pioneer new products, processes, or strategies can often earn enormous profits. This prospect gives companies a strong incentive to seek innovative products, processes, and strategies. Consider, for example, the explosive growth of Apple Computer, Dell Computer, Toys 'R' Us, or Wal-Mart. In one way or another, all these companies were innovators. Apple pioneered the personal computer, Dell pioneered a whole new way of selling personal computers (by mail order), Toys 'R' Us pioneered a new way of selling toys (through large discount warehouse-type stores), and Wal-Mart pioneered the low-price discount superstore concept.

Successful innovation can revolutionize industry structure. In recent decades one of the most common consequences of innovation has been to lower the fixed costs of production, thereby reducing barriers to entry and allowing new, and smaller, enterprises to compete with large established organizations. Take the steel industry as an example. Two decades ago the industry was populated by large integrated steel companies such as U.S. Steel, LTV, and Bethlehem Steel. Dominated by a small number of large producers, the industry was a typical oligopoly, in which tacit price collusion was practiced. Then along came a series of efficient minimill producers such as Nucor and Chaparral Steel, which utilized a new technology—electric arc furnaces. Over the last twenty years, they have revolutionized the structure of the industry. What was once a consolidated industry is now much more fragmented and price competitive. The successor company to U.S. Steel, USX, now has only a 15 percent market share, down from 55 percent in the mid 1960s, and both Bethlehem and LTV have been through Chapter 11 bankruptcy proceedings. In contrast, as a group, the minimills now hold more than 30 percent of the market, up from 5 percent twenty years ago. Thus, the minimill innovation has reshaped the nature of competition in the steel industry.[21] A five forces model applied to the industry in 1970 would look very different from a five forces model applied in 1995.

In his more recent work, Michael Porter, the originator of the five forces and strategic group concepts, has explicitly recognized the role of innovation in revolutionizing industry structure. Porter now talks of innovations as "unfreezing" and "reshaping" industry structure. He argues that after a period of turbulence triggered by innovation the structure of an industry once more settles down into a fairly stable pattern. When the industry stabilizes in its new configuration, the five forces and strategic group concepts can once more be applied.[22] This view of the evolution of industry structure is often referred to as *punctuated equilibrium*.[23] The punctuated equilibrium view holds that long periods of equilibrium, when an industry's structure is stable, are punctuated by periods of rapid change when industry structure is revolutionized by innovation; there is an unfreezing and refreezing process

Figure 3.4 shows what punctuated equilibrium might look like for one key dimension of industry structure—competitive structure. From time t_0 to t_1 the competitive structure of the industry is a stable oligopoly, with a few companies sharing the market. At time t_1 a major new innovation is pioneered by either an existing company or a new entrant. The result is a period of turbulence between t_1 and t_2. After a while, however, the industry settles down into a new state of equilibrium, but now the competitive structure is far more fragmented. Note that the opposite could have happened: the industry could have become more consolidated, although this seems to be less common. In general, innovations seem to lower barriers to entry, allow more companies into the industry, and as a result lead to fragmentation rather than consolidation.

It is important to understand that during periods of rapid change, when industry structure is being revolutionized by innovation, value typically migrates to new business models.[24] In stockbrokerage, which we discussed in the Opening Case, value is currently migrating from the full-service broker model toward the on-line trading model. In the steel industry, the introduction of electric arc technology led to a migration of value from large integrated enterprises toward small minimills. In the book-selling industry, value may be beginning to migrate from "brick and mortar" booksellers toward on-line bookstores such as amazon.com (although it is still too early to state definitively how successful the on-line retail model will eventually be).

Because the five forces and strategic group models are static, they cannot adequately capture what occurs during periods of rapid change in the industry environment when value is migrating, but they are useful tools for analyzing industry

FIGURE 3.4

Punctuated Equilibrium and Competitive Structure

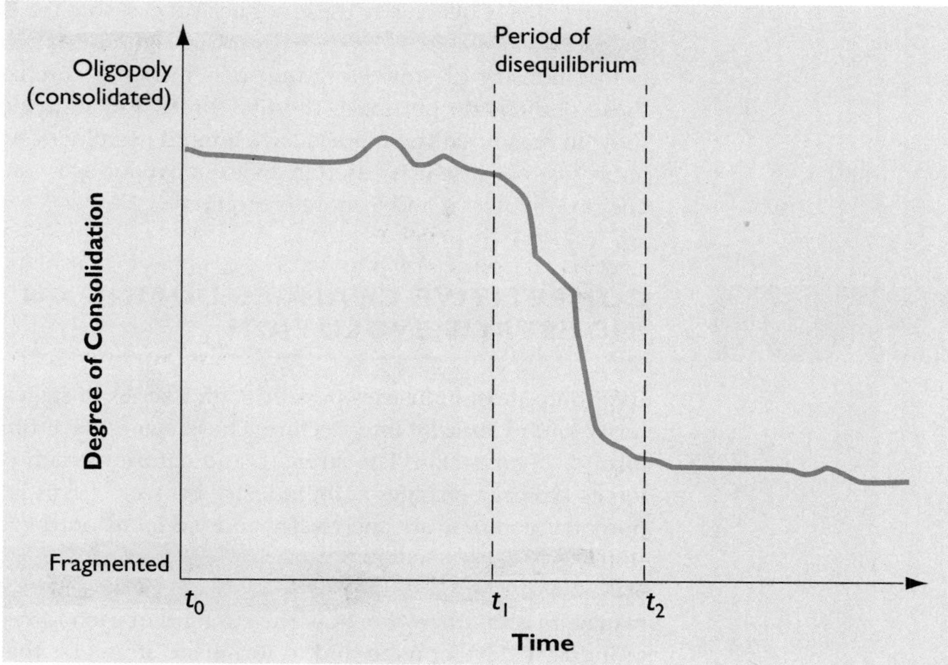

structure during periods of stability. Some scholars, though, question the validity of the punctuated equilibrium approach. Richard D'Avani has argued that many industries are **hypercompetitive**.[25] Hypercompetitive industries are characterized by permanent and ongoing innovation (the computer industry is often cited as an example of a hypercompetitive industry). The structure of such industries is constantly being revolutionized by innovation; there are no periods of equilibrium. When this is the case, some might argue that the five forces and strategic group models are of limited value since they represent no more than snapshots of a moving picture.

Industry Structure and Company Differences

The second criticism of the five forces and strategic group models is that they overemphasize the importance of industry structure as a determinant of company performance and underemphasize the importance of differences between companies within an industry or strategic group.[26] As we point out in the next chapter, there can be enormous variance in the profit rates of individual companies within an industry. Research by Richard Rumelt and others, for example, suggests that industry structure explains only about 10 percent of the variance in profit rates across companies.[27] The implication being that individual company differences explain much of the remainder. Other studies have put the explained variance closer to 20 percent, which is still not a large figure.[28] Similarly, a growing number of studies have found only very weak evidence of a link between strategic group membership and company profit rates, despite the fact that the strategic group model predicts a strong link.[29] Collectively, these studies suggest that the individual resources and capabilities of a company are far more important determinants of its profitability than is the industry or strategic group of which the company is a member. Although these findings do not make the five forces and strategic group models irrelevant, they do mean that the models have limited usefulness. A company will not be profitable just because it is based in an attractive industry or strategic group. As we discuss in Chapters 4 and 5, more is required.

COMPETITIVE CHANGES DURING AN INDUSTRY'S EVOLUTION

Over time, most industries pass through a series of stages, from growth through maturity and eventually into decline. These stages have different implications for the form of competition. The strength and nature of each of Porter's five competitive forces typically changes as an industry evolves.[30] This is particularly true regarding potential competitors and rivalry, and we focus on these two forces in our discussion. The changes in the strength and nature of these forces give rise to different opportunities and threats at each stage of an industry's evolution. The task facing managers is to *anticipate* how the strength of each force will change with the stage of industry development and to formulate strategies that take advantage of opportunities as they arise and that counter emerging threats.

The **industry life cycle model** is a useful tool for analyzing the effects of industry evolution on competitive forces. With it, we can identify five industry environments, each linked to a distinct stage of an industry's evolution: (1) an embryonic industry environment, (2) a growth industry environment, (3) a shakeout environment, (4) a mature industry environment, and (5) a declining industry environment (see Figure 3.5).

FIGURE 3.5

Stages of the Industry Life Cycle

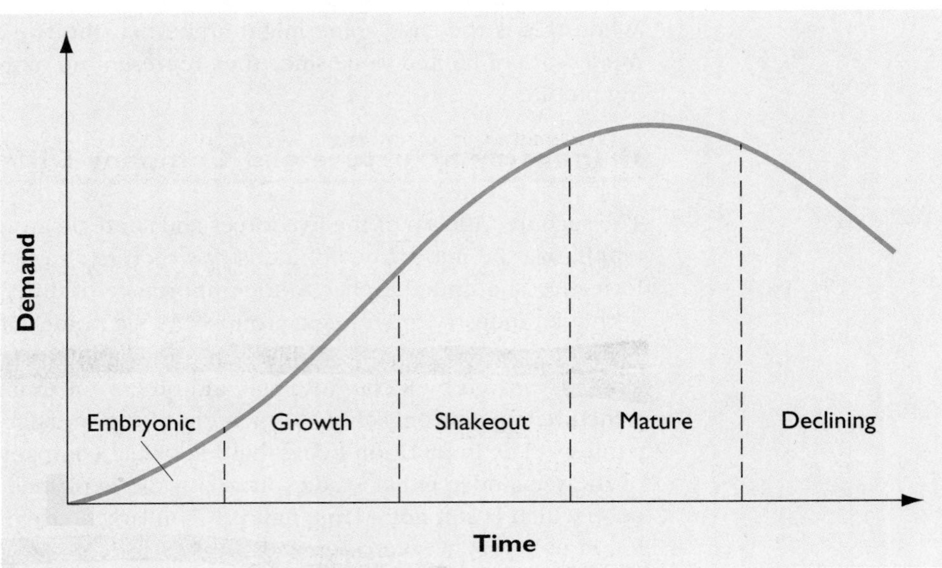

Embryonic Industries

An *embryonic* industry is one that is just beginning to develop (for example, personal computers in 1980). Growth at this stage is slow because of such factors as buyers' unfamiliarity with the industry's product, high prices due to the inability of companies to reap any significant scale economies, and poorly developed distribution channels. Barriers to entry at this stage in an industry's evolution tend to be based on access to key technological know-how rather than cost economies or brand loyalty. If the core know-how required to compete in the industry is complex and difficult to grasp, barriers to entry can be quite high and incumbent companies will be protected from potential competitors. Rivalry in embryonic industries is based not so much on price as on educating customers, opening up distribution channels, and perfecting the design of the product. Such rivalry can be intense, and the company that is the first to solve design problems often has the opportunity to develop a significant market position. An embryonic industry may also be the creation of one company's innovative efforts, as happened with personal computers (Apple), vacuum cleaners (Hoover), and photocopiers (Xerox). In such circumstances, the company has a major opportunity to capitalize on the lack of rivalry and build up a strong hold on the market.

Growth Industries

Once demand for the industry's product begins to take off, the industry develops the characteristics of a growth industry. In a *growth* industry, first-time demand is expanding rapidly as many new consumers enter the market. Typically, an industry grows when consumers become familiar with the product, when prices fall because experience and scale economies have been attained, and when distribution channels develop. The U.S. cellular telephone industry was in the growth stage for most of the 1990s. In 1990, there were only 5 million cellular subscribers in the nation. By 1998, however, this figure had increased to 70 million, and overall demand was still growing at a rate in excess of 25 percent per year. Similarly, in the United States the number of subscribers to on-line Internet services expanded from less than 1 million in 1990 to more than 60 million by the end of the decade.

Normally, the importance of control over technological knowledge as a barrier to entry has diminished by the time an industry enters its growth stage. Because few companies have yet achieved significant scale economies or differentiated their product sufficiently to guarantee brand loyalty, other entry barriers tend to be relatively low as well, particularly early in the growth stage. Thus, the threat from potential competitors is generally highest at this point. Paradoxically, however, high growth usually means that new entrants can be absorbed into an industry without a marked increase in competitive pressure.

During an industry's growth stage, rivalry tends to be relatively low. Rapid growth in demand enables companies to expand their revenues and profits without taking market share away from competitors. A company has the opportunity to expand its operations. In addition, a strategically aware company takes advantage of the relatively benign environment of the growth stage to prepare itself for the intense competition of the coming industry shakeout.

Industry Shakeout

Explosive growth of the type experienced by the cellular telephone or personal computer industries in the first half of the 1990s cannot be maintained indefinitely. Sooner or later the rate of growth slows, and the industry enters the shakeout stage. In the *shakeout* stage, demand approaches saturation levels. In a saturated market, there are few potential first-time buyers left. Most of the demand is limited to replacement demand.

As an industry enters the shakeout stage, rivalry between companies becomes intense. What typically happens is that companies that have become accustomed to rapid growth during an industry's growth phase continue to add capacity at rates consistent with past growth. Managers use historic growth rates to forecast future growth rates, and they plan expansions in productive capacity accordingly. As an industry approaches maturity, however, demand no longer grows at historic rates. The consequence is the emergence of excess productive capacity. This condition is illustrated in Figure 3.6, where the solid curve indicates the growth in demand over time and the broken curve indicates the growth in productive capacity over time. As you can see, past point t_1, demand growth becomes slower as the industry becomes mature. However, capacity continues to grow until time t_2. The gap between the solid and the broken lines signifies excess capacity. In an attempt to utilize this capacity, companies often cut prices. The result can be a price war, which drives many of the most inefficient companies into bankruptcy. This is itself enough to deter any new entry.

Mature Industries

The shakeout stage ends when the industry enters its *mature* stage. In a mature industry, the market is totally saturated and demand is limited to replacement de-

FIGURE 3.6

Growth in Demand and Capacity

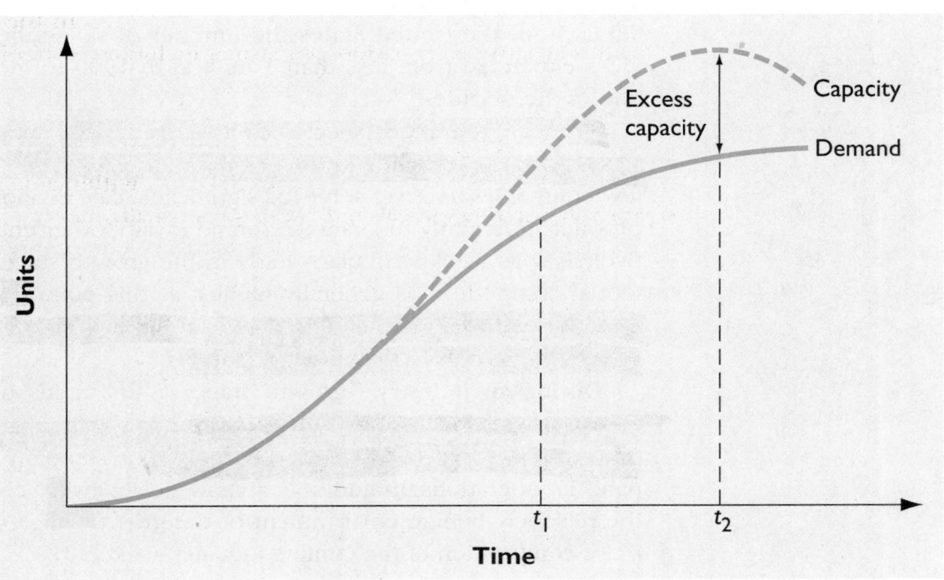

mand. During this stage, growth is low or zero. What little growth there is comes from population expansion bringing new consumers into the market.

As an industry enters maturity, barriers to entry increase and the threat of entry from potential competitors decreases. As growth slows during the shakeout, companies can no longer maintain historic growth rates merely by holding on to their market share. Competition for market share develops, driving down prices. Often the result is a price war, as happened in the airline industry during the 1988–1992 shakeout. To survive the shakeout, companies begin to focus both on cost minimization and on building brand loyalty. The airlines, for example, tried to cut operating costs by hiring nonunion labor and to build brand loyalty by introducing frequent-flyer programs. By the time an industry matures, the surviving companies are those that have brand loyalty and low-cost operations. Because both of these factors constitute a significant barrier to entry, the threat of entry by potential competitors is greatly diminished. High entry barriers in mature industries give companies the opportunity to increase prices and profits.

As a result of the shakeout, most industries in the maturity stage have consolidated and become oligopolies. In the airline industry, for example, because of the shakeout, the top five companies controlled 80 percent of the industry in 1995, up from only 50 percent in 1984. In mature industries, companies tend to recognize their interdependence and try to avoid price wars. Stable demand gives them the opportunity to enter into price-leadership agreements. The net effect is to reduce the threat of intense rivalry among established companies, thereby allowing greater profitability. However, as noted earlier, the stability of a mature industry is always threatened by further price wars. A general slump in economic activity can depress industry demand. As companies fight to maintain their revenues when demand flags, price-leadership agreements break down, rivalry increases, and prices and profits fall. The periodic price wars that occur in the airline industry seem to follow this pattern.

Declining Industries

Eventually, most industries enter a decline stage. In the *decline* stage, growth becomes negative for a variety of reasons, including technological substitution (for example, air travel for rail travel), social changes (greater health consciousness hitting tobacco sales), demographics (the declining birthrate hurting the market for baby and child products), and international competition (low-cost foreign competition pushing the U.S. steel industry into decline). Within a declining industry, the degree of rivalry among established companies usually increases. Depending on the speed of the decline and the height of exit barriers, competitive pressures can become as fierce as in the shakeout stage.[31] The main problem in a declining industry is that falling demand leads to the emergence of excess capacity. In trying to utilize this capacity, companies begin to cut prices, thus sparking a price war. As noted earlier, the U.S. steel industry experienced these problems because of the attempt of steel companies to utilize their excess capacity. The same problem occurred in the airline industry in the 1990–1992 period, as companies cut prices to ensure that they would not be flying with half-empty planes (that is, that they would not be operating with substantial excess capacity). Exit barriers play a part in adjusting excess capacity. The greater the exit barriers, the harder it is for companies to reduce capacity and the greater is the threat of severe price competition.

Variations on the Theme

It is important to remember that the industry life cycle model is a generalization. In practice, industry life cycles do not always follow the pattern illustrated in Figure 3.5. In some cases, growth is so rapid that the embryonic stage is skipped altogether. In other instances, industries fail to get past the embryonic stage. Industry growth can be revitalized after long periods of decline, either through innovations or through social changes. For example, the health boom brought the bicycle industry back to life after a long period of decline. The time span of the different stages can also vary significantly from industry to industry. Some industries can stay in maturity almost indefinitely if their products become basic necessities of life, as is the case for the automobile industry. Others skip the mature stage and go straight into decline. That is essentially what occurred in the vacuum tube industry. Vacuum tubes were replaced by transistors as a major component in electronic products while the industry was still in its growth stage. Still other industries may go through not one but several shakeouts before they enter full maturity.

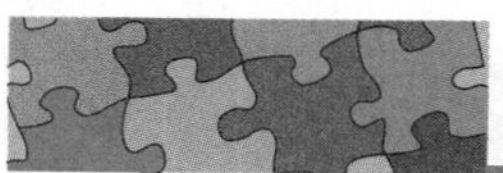

NETWORK ECONOMICS AS A DETERMINANT OF INDUSTRY CONDITIONS

In recent years, there has been a growing realization that network economics are a primary determinant of competitive conditions in many high-technology industries, including computer hardware and software, consumer electronics, home video games, telecommunications, and Internet service providers.[32] **Network economics** arise in industries where the size of the "network" of *complementary* products is a primary determinant of demand for the industry's product. As argued earlier, the demand for automobiles early in the twentieth century was an increasing function of the *network* of paved roads and gas stations. Similarly, the demand for telephones is an increasing function of the number of other numbers that can be called with that phone; in other words, of the size of the telephone network (that is, the telephone network is the complementary product). When the first telephone service was introduced in New York City, only a hundred numbers could be called. The network was very small. There was only a limited number of wires and telephone switches. Consequently, the telephone was a relatively useless piece of equipment, nothing more than a technological curiosity. However, as more and more people got telephones and as the network of wires and switches expanded, the value of a telephone connection increased. This led to an increase in demand for telephone lines, which further increased the value of owning a telephone, setting up a positive feedback loop.

The same type of positive feedback loop is now at work in the Internet. The value of an Internet connection to individual users is an increasing function of the supply of useful information that they can access over the Internet and of the opportunity for engaging in commercial transactions through the medium of the Internet. The number of people with Internet connections drives forward the supply of such information and commercial services. The larger the number of people who are connected to the Internet, the greater is the opportunity for making money by supplying information and commercial services over the Internet. Thus, as more people connect to the Internet, this produces an increase in the supply of information and commercial services offered over the Internet. This increase, in turn, enhances the value of an Internet connection, which drives forward the demand for Internet connections, which leads to a further increase in the supply of information and services, and so on.

Why do network economics affect industry conditions? Well, for a start, once established, a positive feedback loop can help generate rapid demand growth, as we are now seeing in the Internet arena. The demand for Internet on-line services has been expanding at an exponential pace, primarily because a positive feedback loop is at work. Of course, such exponential surges in demand cannot go on forever, but while they are at work they make for very attractive industry conditions. Second, the operation of positive feedback loops can result in an industry becoming very concentrated and potential competitors being locked out by high switching costs. To understand this process, consider the history of the personal computer industry.

The value of a personal computer is an increasing function of the amount of software that is used on that computer and of the number of other complementary products that can be used with that computer, including printers, modems, and Internet connections. In other words, the value of a PC is an increasing function of the "network" of complementary products. In the late 1970s, a large number of different personal computers were on the market, and they used different operating systems and different microprocessors. Now the market is dominated by just one offering, the so-called Windows-Intel (or Wintel) standard. The only other viable product offering is that sold by Apple Computer, which has a small share of the market (in recent years, its share has never been more than 10 percent). The markets for personal computer operating systems and for microprocessors have become very concentrated, with Microsoft and Intel, respectively, dominating them. Moreover, high switching costs have raised entry barriers, making it extremely difficult for new enterprises to enter these markets.

This situation developed because IBM picked a Microsoft operating system (MS-DOS) and an Intel microprocessor to power its first personal computer, which was introduced in 1981. The IBM brand name had a lot of clout among businesses at the time, and demand for IBM PCs took off. As the *installed base* of IBM PCs grew, independent software developers faced a choice: whether to first write applications for the IBM PC or for competing products, such as that sold by Apple Computer. They were forced into making this choice because software written to run on one operating system and microprocessor will not run on another. As the sales of IBM PCs expanded, increasingly software developers wrote applications to run on an MS-DOS operating system powered by an Intel microprocessor, before turning their attention to applications for other computers, such as Apple's offering. Consequently, from early on, there was always more software available to run on the MS-DOS/Intel computers than on Apple computers. This increased the value of MS-DOS/Intel computers, relative to the alternatives, which led to a further increase in demand, and in turn, a more rapid increase in the supply of software to run on MS-DOS/Intel machines. In other words, the early lead gained by MS-DOS/Intel-based machines set up a positive feedback loop which resulted in the installed base of MS-DOS/Intel machines growing much faster than the installed base of alternative product offerings. This lead was sustained when Apple introduced its Macintosh operating system, which was arguably superior to Microsoft's MS-DOS offering, and continued when Microsoft replaced MS-DOS with Windows to create the Wintel standard (see Figure 3.7).

As a result of network economics, the markets for personal computer operating systems and microprocessors have become very concentrated. Microsoft and Intel

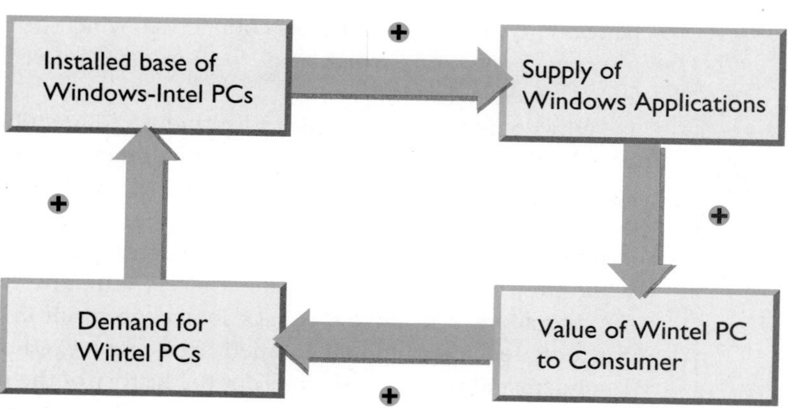

FIGURE 3.7

Positive Feedback in the Computer Industry

have tremendous bargaining power versus their suppliers and buyers, while switching costs have produced high barriers to entry. Because of these factors, as one might expect, Microsoft and Intel enjoy very high profit margins. Despite several attempts, new competitors have remained locked out of these profitable markets (see Strategy in Action 3.3 for an example). However, it would be wrong to assume that Microsoft and Intel are therefore immune to competition. If a new competitor should arise offering an operating system or microprocessor that is so superior that consumers are willing to bear switching costs, Microsoft and Intel could lose market share. The fact that this has not happened yet is partly a testament to the ability of Microsoft and Intel to improve continually the performance capabilities of the Windows operating systems and Intel's microprocessors.

In summary, a consideration of network economics leads to a number of important conclusions. First, in industries where network economics are important, positive feedback loops tend to operate. Once initiated, a positive feedback loop can lead to a rapid increase in demand. Second, markets where positive feedback loops operate tend to be winner-takes-all markets, with second- or third-string competitors being marginalized. This has occurred in the markets for computer operating systems and microprocessors. Third, enterprises that benefit from network economics tend to be in a powerful position relative to buyers and suppliers and tend to be protected from potential competitors by entry barriers arising from switching costs. From the perspective of an individual company, the trick is to find the right strategy that enables it to grow the installed base of its product rapidly in order to set up a positive feedback loop.

GLOBALIZATION AND INDUSTRY STRUCTURE

A fundamental change is occurring in the world economy.[34] We seem to be witnessing the globalization of production and of markets. With regard to the **globalization of production**, it has been observed that individual companies are increasingly dispersing parts of their production process to different locations around the globe to take advantage of national differences in the cost and quality of factors of production such as labor, energy, land, and capital. The objective is to lower costs and boost profits.

3.3 STRATEGY *in* ACTION

The Failure of Digital's Alpha Chip

In February 1992, Digital Equipment Corporation introduced the world's fastest microprocessor, the Alpha chip. Microprocessors are the brains of personal computers, workstations, and servers. The Alpha chip operated at more than twice the speed of Intel's best-selling microprocessors. Many at Digital had great hopes for the product, believing that it could ultimately grab a significant share of the booming market for microprocessors. By 1997, however, after Digital had spent $2.5 billion to develop the Alpha, the chip ranked dead last in market share, with an estimated 1 percent of the $18 billion microprocessor market. Intel's share stood at 92 percent.

The failure of the Alpha to gain market share despite its apparent performance advantage over existing microprocessors can be explained easily enough: there was never enough software to run on the Alpha. Hence, potential customers stayed away from investing in computers based on the Alpha chip. Digital was never able to get a positive feedback cycle going in which an increase in the supply of software configured to run on Alpha-based systems would have driven demand for Alpha-based computers, which would have meant that developers would have supplied more software for the Alpha, which would have further increased the demand for Alpha-based computers, and so on.

To be fair, Digital seemed to start off on the correct foot. In 1992, Microsoft agreed to adapt its next-generation operating system for corporate computers, Windows NT, so that it would run on the Alpha chip, in addition to Intel microprocessors. In return for this commitment from Microsoft, Digital agreed to make NT a central part of its own computer business. (Digital sold workstations, servers, and personal computers.) Following the agreement, Digital engineers devoted tremendous effort to fine-tuning the Alpha so that it would work with NT. However, when Digital engineers loaded tested versions of NT into their computers, it became clear that NT needed far too much computer memory to run on a typical PC, putting Alpha beyond the reach of the mass market Digital had been hoping for.

In the spring of 1995, Digital tried again to kick start demand for the Alpha. Under the terms of a revised agreement with Microsoft, Digital agreed to provide network installation services for Microsoft. For its part, Microsoft agreed to continue to write a version of NT for the Alpha chip and to pay Digital up to $100 million to help train Digital NT technicians. Moreover, in October of that year, Microsoft stopped writing versions of NT for the IBM Power PC chip and Motorola's MIPS microprocessor, leaving the Alpha and Intel's Pentium series as the only chips that could run Windows NT.

Despite these developments, sales of the Alpha chip were still slow to take off. The Intel-based system now had such a huge lead in the Windows NT business that few developers were willing to take the risk and customize their software applications to run on the Alpha version of Windows NT, as opposed to Intel-based machines. To make matters worse, Digital hurt its own prospects by continuing to attach a premium price to Alpha machines, which slowed demand growth. By late 1994, Digital engineers had found a way to deliver Alpha workstations for $4,995. However, some of Digital's senior management vetoed the move because they feared that it would damage the 50 percent gross margins that Digital enjoyed in the high-end computer markets, which at the time was one of the few bright spots in Digital's business. In the end, when Digital did introduce its Alpha-based workstations for Windows NT, they were priced at $7,995, significantly above the price of high-end Intel-based machines. For corporate customers, this made the decision to go with Intel machines for Windows NT obvious—they were cheaper and more software applications were available for the Intel versions.[33]

For example, Boeing's new commercial jet aircraft, the 777, involves 132,500 engineered parts, which are produced around the world by 545 different suppliers. Eight Japanese suppliers make parts of the fuselage, doors, and wings; a supplier in Singapore makes the doors for the nose landing gear; three suppliers in Italy manufacture wing flaps; and so on. Part of Boeing's rationale for outsourcing so much production to foreign suppliers is that these various suppliers are the best in the world at performing their particular activity. Therefore, the result of having foreign suppliers build specific parts is a better final product.[35]

As for the **globalization of markets**, it has been argued that we are moving away from an economic system in which national markets are distinct entities, isolated from each other by trade barriers and barriers of distance, time, and culture, and toward a system in which national markets are merging into one huge global marketplace. Increasingly, consumers around the world demand and use the same basic product offerings. Consequently, in many industries it is no longer meaningful to talk about the German market, the U.S. market, or the Japanese market—there is only the global market. The global acceptance of Coca-Cola, Citigroup credit cards, Levi's blue jeans, the Sony PlayStation, McDonald's hamburgers, Nokia wireless phones, and Microsoft's Windows operating system exemplifies this trend.[36]

The trend toward the globalization of production and markets has several important implications for competition within an industry. First, it is crucial for companies to recognize that an industry's boundaries do not stop at national borders. Because many industries are becoming global in scope, actual and potential competitors exist not only in a company's home market, but also in other national markets. Companies that scan just their home market can be caught unprepared by the entry of efficient foreign competitors. The globalization of markets and production all imply that companies around the globe are finding their home markets under attack from foreign competitors. To illustrate, in Japan, Merrill Lynch and Citicorp are making inroads against Japanese financial service institutions. In the United States, Fuji has been taking market share from Kodak and Finland's Nokia has taken the lead from Motorola in the market for wireless phone handsets (see Strategy in Action 3.4). In the European Union, the once dominant Dutch company, Philips, has seen its market share in the consumer electronics industry taken by Japan's JVC, Matsushita, and Sony.

Second, the shift from national to global markets during the last twenty years has intensified competitive rivalry in industry after industry. National markets that were once consolidated oligopolies, dominated by three or four companies and subjected to relatively little foreign competition, have been transformed into segments of fragmented global industries, where a large number of companies battle each other for market share in country after country. This rivalry has driven down profit rates and made it all the more critical for companies to maximize their efficiency, quality, customer responsiveness, and innovative ability. The painful restructuring and downsizing that has been going on at companies such as Motorola and Kodak is as much a response to the increased intensity of global competition as it is to anything else. However, not all global industries are fragmented. Many remain consolidated oligopolies, except that now they are consolidated global, rather than national, oligopolies.

Third, as competitive intensity has increased, so has the rate of innovation. Companies strive to gain an advantage over their competitors by pioneering new products, processes, and ways of doing business. The result has been to compress product life cycles and make it vital for companies to stay on the leading edge of technology. In regard to highly competitive global industries, where the rate of innovation is accelerating, the criticism that Porter's five forces model is too static may be particularly relevant.

Finally, even though globalization has increased both the threat of entry and the intensity of rivalry within many formerly protected national markets, it has also created enormous opportunities for companies based in those markets. The steady decline in trade barriers has opened up many once protected markets to companies based outside them. Thus, for example, in recent years, western European, Japanese, and U.S. companies have accelerated their investments in the nations of eastern Europe, Latin America, and Southeast Asia as they try to take advantage of growth opportunities in those areas.

THE NATION-STATE AND COMPETITIVE ADVANTAGE

Despite the globalization of production and markets, many of the most successful companies in certain industries are still clustered in a small number of countries. For example, many of the world's most successful biotechnology and computer companies are based in the United States, many of the world's most successful consumer electronics companies are based in Japan, and many of the world's most successful chemical and engineering companies are based in Germany. This suggests that the nation-state within which a company is based may have an important bearing on the competitive position of that company in the global marketplace.

Companies need to understand how national factors can affect competitive advantage, for then they will be able to identify (1) where their most significant competitors are likely to come from and (2) where they might want to locate certain productive activities. Thus, seeking to take advantage of U.S. expertise in biotechnology, many foreign companies have set up research facilities in U.S. locations such as San Diego, Boston, and Seattle, where U.S. biotechnology companies tend to be clustered. Similarly, in an attempt to take advantage of Japanese success in consumer electronics, many U.S. electronics companies have set up research and production facilities in Japan, often in conjunction with Japanese partners.

In a study of national competitive advantage, Porter identified four attributes of a nation-state that have an important impact on the global competitiveness of companies located within that nation:

- *Factor endowments:* a nation's position in factors of production such as skilled labor or the infrastructure necessary to compete in a given industry
- *Local demand conditions:* the nature of home demand for the industry's product or service
- *Competitiveness of related and supporting industries:* the presence or absence in a nation of supplier industries and related industries that are internationally competitive
- *Strategy, structure, and rivalry:* the conditions in the nation governing how companies are created, organized, and managed and the nature of domestic rivalry[37]

Porter speaks of these four attributes as constituting *the diamond* (see Figure 3.8). He argues that firms are most likely to succeed in industries or industry segments

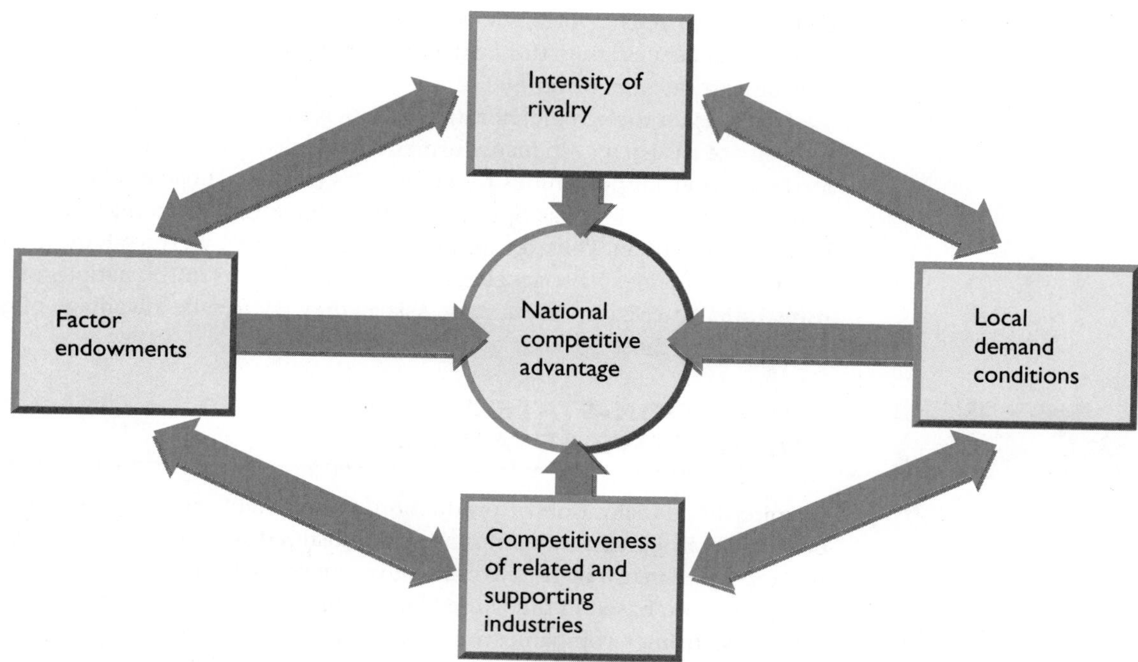

FIGURE 3.8

National Competitive Advantage

where conditions with regard to the four attributes are favorable. He also argues that the diamond's attributes form a mutually reinforcing system in which the effect of one attribute is dependent on the state of others.

Factor Endowments

Porter follows basic economic theory in stressing that **factor conditions**—the cost and quality of factors of production—are a prime determinant of the competitive advantage that certain countries might have in certain industries. Factors of production include **basic factors,** such as land, labor, capital, and raw materials, and **advanced factors** such as technological know-how, that is, managerial sophistication and physical infrastructure (such as, roads, railways, and ports). The competitive advantage that the United States enjoys in biotechnology might be explained by the presence of certain advanced factors of production—technological know-how, for instance—in combination with some basic factors, which might be a pool of relatively low-cost venture capital that can be used to fund risky start-ups in industries such as biotechnology.

Local Demand Conditions

Porter emphasizes the role home demand plays in providing the impetus for "upgrading" competitive advantage. Companies are typically most sensitive to the needs of their closest customers. Hence, the characteristics of home demand are particularly important in shaping the attributes of domestically made products and in creating pressures for innovation and quality. Porter argues that a nation's companies gain competitive advantage if their domestic consumers are sophisticated and demanding. Sophisticated and demanding consumers pressure local companies to meet high standards of product quality and to produce innovative products. Porter notes that Japan's sophisticated and knowledgeable buyers of cameras helped stimulate the Japanese camera industry to improve product quality and to introduce innovative models. A similar example can be found in the cellular phone equipment industry, where sophisticated and demanding local customers in Scandinavia helped push Nokia of Finland and Ericsson of Sweden to invest in cellular phone technology long before demand for cellular phones took off in other developed nations. As a result, Nokia and Ericsson, together with Motorola, are today dominant players in the global cellular telephone equipment industry. The case of Nokia is reviewed in more depth in Strategy in Action 3.4.

Competitiveness of Related and Supporting Industries

The third broad attribute of national advantage in an industry is the presence in a country of suppliers or related industries that are internationally competitive. The benefits of investments in advanced factors of production by related and supporting industries can spill over into an industry, thereby helping it achieve a strong competitive position internationally. Swedish strength in fabricated steel products (for instance, ball bearings and cutting tools) has drawn on strengths in Sweden's specialty steel industry. Technological leadership in the U.S. semiconductor industry during the period up to the mid 1980s provided the basis for U.S. success in personal computers and several other technically advanced electronic products. Similarly, Switzerland's success in pharmaceuticals is closely linked to its previous international success in the technologically related dye industry. One consequence of this process is that successful industries within a country tend to be grouped into "clusters" of related industries. Indeed, this was one of the most pervasive findings of Porter's study. One such cluster is the German textile and apparel sector, which includes high-quality cotton, wool, synthetic fibers, sewing machine needles, and a wide range of textile machinery.

Strategy, Structure, and Rivalry

The fourth broad attribute of national competitive advantage in Porter's model is the strategy, structure, and rivalry of companies within a nation. Porter makes two important points here. His first is that different nations are characterized by different "management ideologies," which either help them or do not help them build national competitive advantage. For example, he notes the predominance of engineers on the top-management teams of German and Japanese companies. He attributes this to the companies' emphasis on improving manufacturing processes and product design. In contrast, Porter notes a predominance of people with finance backgrounds on the top-management teams of many U.S. companies. He links this to the lack of attention paid in many U.S. companies to improving manufacturing processes and product design, particularly during the 1970s and 80s. He also argues that the dominance of finance has led to a corresponding overemphasis on maximizing short-term financial returns. According to Porter, one consequence of these different management ideologies has been a relative loss of U.S. competitiveness in

3.4 **STRATEGY in ACTION**

Finland's Nokia

The wireless phone market is one of the great growth stories of the 1990s. Starting from a very low base in 1990, annual global sales of wireless phones surged to 163 million units in 1998, representing an increase of 51 percent over the prior year. By 2000, some 300 million people worldwide will probably be using wireless phones. Four companies currently dominate the global market for wireless handsets: Motorola, Nokia, Ericsson, and Qualcomm. In 1998, the global market leader was Nokia, which had a 23 percent share, followed by Motorola with 20 percent and Ericsson with 15 percent. In the United States, the world's largest market, Nokia's dominance was even greater. The company had a 30 percent share of the U.S. market in 1998, compared with 23 percent for Motorola (which used to dominate the market), 11 percent for Ericsson, and 10 percent for Qualcomm.

Nokia's roots are in Finland, not normally a country that jumps to mind when we talk about leading-edge technology companies. Back in the 1980s, Nokia was a rambling Finnish conglomerate whose activities embraced tire manufacturing, paper production, consumer electronics and telecommunications equipment. How has this former conglomerate emerged to take a global leadership position in wireless handsets? Much of the answer lies in the history, geography, and political economy of Finland and its Nordic neighbors.

The story starts in 1981. It was then that the Nordic nations got together to create the world's first international wireless telephone network. Sparsely populated and inhospitably cold, they had good reason to become pioneers; it cost far too much to lay down a traditional wire line telephone service. Yet the very conditions causing the difficulty made telecommunications all the more valuable there; people driving through the Arctic winter and owners of remote northern houses needed a telephone to summon help if things went wrong. As a result, Sweden, Norway, and Finland became the first nations in the world to take wireless telecommunications seriously. They found, for example, that while it cost up to $800 per subscriber to bring a traditional wire line service to remote locations in the far north, the same locations could be linked by wireless cellular for only $500 per person. Consequently, 12 percent of people in Scandinavia owned cellular phones by 1994, compared with less than 6 percent in the United States, the world's second most developed market. This lead continued during the decade. It is estimated that by 2000 more than 50 percent of Finland's phone users will have a wireless phone, compared with 25 percent in the United States, and the figure may reach 100 percent by 2010.

Nokia, a long-time telecommunications equipment supplier, was well positioned to take advantage of this development from the start, but there were also other forces at work in Finland that helped Nokia gain a competitive edge. Unlike virtually every other developed country, Finland has never had a national telephone monopoly. Instead, telephone service has long been provided by fifty or so autonomous local telephone companies, whose elected boards set prices by referendum (which, naturally, results in low prices). This army of independent and cost-conscious telephone service providers prevented Nokia from taking anything for granted in its home country. With typical Finnish pragmatism, its customers were willing to buy from the lowest-cost supplier, whether that was Nokia, Ericsson, Motorola, or someone else. This situation contrasted sharply with that prevailing in most developed nations up until the late 1980s and early 1990s, where domestic telephone monopolies typically purchased equipment from a dominant local supplier or made it themselves. Nokia responded to this competitive pressure by doing everything possible to drive down its manufacturing costs while staying at the leading edge of wireless technology.

The consequences of these forces are clear: the once obscure Finnish firm is now a global leader in the wireless market. Moreover, Nokia has emerged as the leader in digital wireless technology, which is the wave of the future. In no small part, Nokia has the lead because Scandinavia started switching over to digital technology five years before the rest of the world. In addition, spurred on by its cost-conscious customers, Nokia now has the lowest cost structure of any wireless handset equipment manufacturer in the world, and as a result, it is a more profitable enterprise than its global competitors.[39]

those engineering-based industries where manufacturing processes and product design issues are all-important (such as automobiles).

Porter's second point is that there is a strong association between vigorous domestic rivalry and the creation and persistence of competitive advantage in an industry. Vigorous domestic rivalry induces companies to look for ways to improve efficiency, which in turn makes them better international competitors. Domestic rivalry creates pressures to innovate, to improve quality, to reduce costs, and to invest in upgrading advanced factors. All this helps create world-class competitors. As an illustration, Porter cites the case of Japan:

> Nowhere is the role of domestic rivalry more evident than in Japan, where it is all-out warfare in which many companies fail to achieve profitability. With goals that stress market share, Japanese companies engage in a continuing struggle to outdo each other. Shares fluctuate markedly. The process is prominently covered in the business press. Elaborate rankings measure which companies are most popular with university graduates. The rate of new product and process development is breathtaking.[38]

A similar point about the stimulating effects of strong domestic competition can be made with regard to the rise of Nokia of Finland to global preeminence in the market for cellular telephone equipment (see Strategy in Action 3.4).

In sum, Porter's argument is that the degree to which a nation is likely to achieve international success in a certain industry is a function of the combined impact of factor endowments, domestic demand conditions, related and supporting industries, and domestic rivalry. He argues that for this "diamond" to have a positive impact on competitive performance usually requires the presence of all four components (although there are some exceptions). Porter also contends that government can influence each of the four components of the diamond either positively or negatively. It can affect factor endowments through subsidies, policies toward capital markets, policies toward education, and the like, and it can shape domestic demand through local product standards or with regulations that mandate or influence buyer needs. Government policy can also influence supporting and related industries through regulation, and influence rivalry through such devices as capital market regulation, tax policy, and antitrust laws.

As an example of Porter's theory, consider the U.S. computer hardware industry (personal computers, workstations, minicomputers, and mainframes). The existence of a world-class industry in the United States can be explained by the presence of advanced factors of production in the form of technological know-how; an intense rivalry among myriad competing computer companies; a strong local demand for computers (more personal computers have been sold in the United States than in the rest of the world combined); and internationally competitive supporting industries, such as the computer software and microprocessor industries.

Perhaps the most important implication of Porter's framework is its message about the attractiveness of certain locations for performing certain productive activities. For instance, many Japanese computer companies have moved much of their R&D activity to the United States so that they can benefit from the international competitiveness of the United States in this industry. Most U.S. financial service companies have substantial operations in London so that they can take advantage of London's central position in the world financial services industry. And many international textile companies have design operations in Italy so that they can take advantage of Italian style and design know-how. In all these cases, companies are trying to build a competitive advantage by establishing critical productive activities in the optimal location, as defined by the various elements highlighted in Porter's framework. This is an issue we discuss in depth in Chapter 8.

SUMMARY OF CHAPTER

This chapter details a framework that managers can use to analyze the external environment of their company, enabling them to identify opportunities and threats. The following major points are made in the chapter:

- For a company to succeed, either its strategy must fit the environment in which the company operates, or the company must be able to reshape this environment to its advantage through its choice of strategy. Companies typically fail when their strategy no longer fits the environment in which they operate.
- The main technique used to analyze competition in the industry environment is the five forces model. The five forces are (1) the risk of new entry by potential competitors, (2) the extent of rivalry among established firms, (3) the bargaining power of buyers, (4) the bargaining power of suppliers, and (5) the threat of substitute products. The stronger each force, the more competitive is the industry and the lower is the rate of return that can be earned.
- The risk of entry by potential competitors is a function of the height of barriers to entry. The higher the barriers to entry, the lower is the risk of entry and the greater are the profits that can be earned in the industry.
- The extent of rivalry among established companies is a function of an industry's competitive structure, demand conditions, and barriers to exit. Strong demand conditions moderate the competition among established companies and create opportunities for expansion. When demand is weak, intensive competition can develop, particularly in consolidated industries with high exit barriers.
- Buyers are most powerful when a company depends on them for business, but they themselves are not dependent on the company. In such circumstances, buyers are a threat.
- Suppliers are most powerful when a company depends on them for business but they themselves are not dependent on the company. In such circumstances, suppliers are a threat.
- Substitute products are the products of companies serving consumer needs that are similar to the needs served by the industry being analyzed. The greater the similarity of the substitute products, the lower is the price that companies can charge without losing customers to the substitutes.
- Some argue that there is a sixth competitive force of some significance—the power, vigor and competence of complementors. Powerful and vigorous complementors may have a strong positive impact on demand in an industry.
- Most industries are composed of strategic groups. Strategic groups are groups of companies pursuing the same or a similar strategy. Companies in different strategic groups pursue different strategies.
- The members of a company's strategic group constitute its immediate competitors. Since different strategic groups are characterized by different opportunities and threats, it may pay a company to switch strategic groups. The feasibility of doing so is a function of the height of mobility barriers.
- The five forces and strategic group models have been criticized for presenting a static picture of competition that de-emphasizes the role of innovation. Innovation can revolutionize industry structure and completely change the strength of different competitive forces.
- The five forces and strategic group models have been criticized for de-emphasizing the importance of individual company differences. A company will not be profitable just because it is based in an

attractive industry or strategic group; much more is required.

- Industries go through a well-defined life cycle, from an embryonic stage, through growth, shakeout, and maturity, and eventually into decline. Each stage has different implications for the competitive structure of the industry, and each stage gives rise to its own set of opportunities and threats.
- In many high-technology industries, network economics are important and positive feedback loops tend to operate. Once initiated, a positive feedback loop can lead to a rapid increase in demand. Markets where positive feedback loops operate tend to be "winner takes all" markets. Enterprises that benefit from network economics tend to be in a powerful position relative to buyers and suppliers and tend to be protected from potential competitors by entry barriers arising from switching costs
- A fundamental change is occurring in the world economy: the globalization of production and of markets. The consequences of this change include more intense rivalry, more rapid innovation, and shorter product life cycles.
- There is a link between the national environment and the competitive advantage of a company in the global economy.

DISCUSSION QUESTIONS

1. Under what environmental conditions are price wars most likely to occur in an industry? What are the implications of price wars for a company? How should a company try to deal with the threat of a price war?
2. Discuss Porter's five forces model with reference to what you know about the U.S. airline industry. What does the model tell you about the level of competition in this industry?
3. Explain what impact network effects might have on demand and industry structure in the market for wireless handsets.
4. Identify a growth industry, a mature industry, and a declining industry. For each industry, identify the following: (a) the number and size distribution of companies; (b) the nature of barriers to entry; (c) the height of barriers to entry; and (d) the extent of product differentiation. What do these factors tell you about the nature of competition in each industry? What are the implications for the company in terms of opportunities and threats?
5. Assess the impact of macroenvironmental factors on the likely level of enrollment at your university over the next decade. What are the implications of these factors for the job security and salary level of your professors?

Practicing Strategic Management

SMALL-GROUP EXERCISE
Competing with Microsoft

Break up into groups of three to five people, and discuss the following scenario:

You are a group of managers and software engineers at a small start-up. You have developed a revolutionary new operating system for personal computers. This operating system offers distinct advantages over Microsoft's Windows operating system. It takes up less memory space on the hard drive of a personal computer. It takes full advantage of the power of the personal computer's microprocessor, and in theory can run software applications much faster than Windows. It is much easier to install and use than Windows. And it responds to voice instructions with an accuracy of 99.9 percent, in addition to input from a keyboard or mouse. The operating system is the only product offering that your company has produced.

1. Analyze the competitive structure of the market for personal computer operating systems. On the basis of this analysis, identify what factors might inhibit adoption of your operating system by consumers.
2. Can you think of a strategy that your company might pursue, either alone or in conjunction with other enterprises, in order to beat Microsoft? What will it take to successfully execute that strategy?

STRATEGIC MANAGEMENT PROJECT
Module 3

This module requires you to analyze the industry environment in which your company is based. Using the information you have at your disposal, perform the following tasks and answer the questions:

1. Apply the five forces model to the industry in which your company is based. What does this model tell you about the nature of competition in the industry?
2. Are there any changes taking place in the macroenvironment that might have an impact, either positive or negative, on the industry in which your company is based? If so, what are these changes and how will they affect the industry?
3. Identify any strategic groups that might exist in the industry. How does the intensity of competition differ across the strategic groups you have identified?
4. How dynamic is the industry in which your company is based? Is there any evidence that innovation is reshaping competition or has done so in the recent past?
5. In what stage of its life cycle is the industry in which your company is based? What are the implications of this for the intensity of competition, both now and in the future?
6. Is your company based in an industry that is becoming more global? If so, what are the implications of this change for competitive intensity?
7. Analyze the impact of national context as it pertains to the industry in which your company is based. Does national context help or hinder your company in achieving a competitive advantage in the global market place?

ARTICLE FILE 3

Find an example of an industry that has become more competitive in recent years. Identify the reasons for the increase in competitive pressure.

EXPLORING THE WEB
Visiting Boeing and Airbus

Visit the Web sites of Boeing (http://www.boeing.com) and of Airbus Industrie (http://www.airbus.com). Go to the news features of both sites and read through the press releases issued by both companies. Also look at the annual reports and company profile (or history features) contained on both sites. With this material as your guide, perform the following:

1. Use Porter's five forces model to analyze the nature of competition in the global commercial jet aircraft market.
2. Assess the likely outlook for competition during the next ten years in this market. Try to establish whether new entry into this industry is likely, whether demand will grow or shrink, how powerful buyers are likely to become, and what the impli-

cations of all this may be for the nature of competition ten years from now.

General Task Search the Web for information that allows you to assess the *current* state of competition in the market for personal computers. Use that information to perform an analysis of the structure of the market in the United States. (Hint: Try visiting the Web sites of personal computer companies. Also visit Electronic Business Today at http://www.ebtmag.com).

CLOSING CASE

Boom and Bust in the Market for DRAMs

FOR MUCH OF THE FIRST HALF OF THE 1990s, the semiconductor industry seemed like one of the most extraordinary moneymaking machines ever invented. In no case has this been more true than in the market for dynamic random access memories (DRAMs), the memory devices used in personal computers (PCs), which account for about one-third of all semiconductor sales. In 1993, the global market for DRAMs was valued at $13.6 billion. In 1994, it increased to $23.1 billion, and in 1995 it surged to $55 billion. This rapid increase in demand for DRAMs was due to the confluence of a number of favorable factors.

First, stimulated by price cutting in the PC market, worldwide sales of personal computers grew at an annual average compound rate of 30 percent over the 1990–1995 period. Second, as more and more users of PCs switched to graphics-based software, such as Microsoft's Windows 95 operating system, the memory component of PCs increased. (Running graphics programs on a PC requires a large amount of memory.) Between 1991 and 1995, the average amount of DRAM contained in each PC sold increased from 2 megabytes to 12 megabytes. Third, other applications for DRAMs—particularly in telecommunications equipment and cellular phone handsets—also grew rapidly. For example, global shipments of cellular phones increased from 5 million to 50 million between 1991 and 1995.

As demand for DRAMs was surging during the 1990–1995 period, the supply was constrained. One reason for the shortage was the reluctance of many semiconductor companies to invest in new semiconductor fabricating plants. By 1995, a new fabrication facility could cost anywhere from $1 billion to $2.5 billion and take eighteen months to construct. Such enormous fixed costs made many companies wary of investing in the plants, particularly since demand conditions could change significantly in the eighteen months required to bring the new facility on line. Managers in this industry still remember the 1985–1987 period when a combination of slowing demand and massive capacity expansions by Japanese semiconductor companies led to an excess supply of DRAMs, plunging prices, and significant financial losses for most of the world's DRAM manufacturers. Indeed, it was during this period that a number of U.S. companies exited the DRAM market, including Intel, the company that invented the DRAM.

The combination of surging global demand for DRAMs and the constrained supply caused DRAM prices to rise dramatically between 1993 and 1995. In 1993, the average selling price for DRAM was $8.89 per megabyte, in 1994 it was $11.69, and by the middle of 1995 it was $14. This situation, however, benefited Micron Technology of Boise, Idaho—one of only two U.S. firms that remained in the DRAM market after the debacle of 1985–1987 (the other was Texas Instruments). In 1990, Micron had sales of under $300 million and was barely breaking even. Riding the industry wave, by 1994 the company had revenues of $1.63 billion and net income of $400 million. In 1995, its revenues rose to $2.95 billion and the net income to $844 million. Micron's gross profit margin for 1995 was 55 percent—an almost unheard of figure for a DRAM company—compared with 23 percent in 1990. Nor was Micron alone in achieving such impressive profit performance. By 1995, almost every DRAM company in the world was making record profits.

The huge profits became a signal for incumbent companies to expand their capacity and for new companies to enter the semiconductor industry. Starting in late 1994, more and more companies announced their intentions to invest in semiconductor fabrication plants. Micron Technology, too, jumped on the capacity expansion bandwagon; in June 1995, it unveiled plans to invest $2.5 billion in a new fabrication facility in Lehi, Utah, which was scheduled to begin production at the end of 1996. When Micron made its announcement, almost 100 new semiconductor

CLOSING CASE *(continued)*

fabrication facilities were being constructed around the world, many of them scheduled to come on stream in 1995 and 1996. Moreover, by the end of 1995, plans to build another 100 facilities had been announced.

In the fall of 1995, the other shoe dropped. After four years of rapid growth, there was a sudden slowdown in the growth rate of personal computer sales, particularly in the huge North American market. This slowdown occurred just as the new DRAM capacity was becoming operational. To make matters worse, throughout 1995 manufacturers of personal computers had been building up their inventories of DRAMs, both as a hedge against future price increases and to ensure an adequate supply of DRAMs for what they thought would be a very busy Christmas season. When the expected surge in Christmas sales of PCs failed to materialize, PC manufacturers found themselves holding too much inventory. They responded by drastically cutting back on their orders for DRAMs. The result: DRAM sales volume and prices slumped. Between late 1995 and March 1996, DRAM prices fell from $14 to $7 per megabyte. The consequences included falling profit margins for DRAM companies.

Reflecting the widespread perception that excess demand and rising prices had been replaced in short order by excess supply and plunging prices, the Philadelphia Semi-Conductor Index, a measure of the share price of American semiconductor companies, fell by 45 percent between September 1995 and March 1996. In February 1996, Micron Technology responded to this situation by dramatically slowing down the construction schedule for its Lehi facility, pushing out the start date for volume manufacturing another two to five years. Nor was Micron alone. By the spring of 1996, companies around the world were also announcing that they had put their capacity expansion plans on hold.[40]

Case Discussion Questions

1. Analyze the competitive structure of the DRAM market.
2. Using this analysis, explain why the industry has been characterized by boom and bust cycles.
3. If you were a company such as Micron Technology, what strategy might you adopt to deal more effectively with the boom-and-bust nature of the industry?

End Notes

1. C. Gasparino and R. Buckman, "Horning In: Facing Internet Threat, Merrill to Offer Trading Online for Low Fee," *Wall Street Journal*, June 1, 1999, p. A1; "Bears or Bulls, More and More People Are Trading Shares Online," *Economist*, October 17, 1998; L. N. Spiro and E. C. Baig, "Who Needs a Broker?" *Business Week*, February 22, 1999, p. 113.
2. M. E. Porter, *Competitive Strategy* (New York: Free Press, 1980).
3. Charles W. L. Hill has acted as an outside consultant to Tacoma City Light and evaluated the strategy on its behalf.
4. J. E. Bain, *Barriers to New Competition* (Cambridge, Mass: Harvard University Press, 1956). For a review of the modern literature on barriers to entry, see R. J. Gilbert, "Mobility Barriers and the Value of Incumbency," in R. Schmalensee and R. D. Willig, *Handbook of Industrial Organization*, (Amsterdam: North Holland, 1989), I.
5. A detailed discussion of switching costs and lock-in can be found in C. Shapiro and H. R. Varian, *Information Rules: A Strategic Guide to the Network Economy* (Boston, Mass: Harvard Business School Press, 1999).
6. Most of this information on barriers to entry can be found in the industrial organization economics literature. See especially Bain, *Barriers to New Competition;* M. Mann, "Seller Concentration, Barriers to Entry and Rates of Return in 30 Industries," *Review of Economics and Statistics,* 48 (1966), 296–307; W. S. Comanor and T. A. Wilson, "Advertising, Market Structure and Performance," *Review of Economics and Statistics,* 49 (1967), 423–440; and Gilbert, "Mobility Barriers and The Value of Incumbency"; K. Cool, L. H. Roller, and B. Leleux, "The Relative Impact of Actual and Potential Rivalry on Firm Profitability in the Pharmaceutical Industry," *Strategic Management Journal*, 20 (1999), 1–14.
7. "Only Here for the Biru," *Economist*, May 14, 1994, pp. 69–71; T. Craig, "The Japanese Beer Industry," in C. W. L. Hill and G. R. Jones, *Strategic Management: An Integrated Approach* (Boston: Houghton Mifflin, 1995); "Japan's Beer Wars," *Economist*, February 28, 1998, p. 68; A. Harney, "Japan's Favorite Beer Could Face Losing Its Sparkle," *Financial Times*, March 24, 1999, p. 27.
8. For a discussion of tacit agreements, see T. C. Schelling, *The Strategy of Conflict* (Cambridge, Mass.: Harvard University Press, 1960).
9. R. Oram, "Washing Whiter Proves a Murky Business," *Financial Times*, December 21, 1994, p. 6.
10. P. Ghemawat, *Commitment: The Dynamics of Strategy* (Boston, Harvard Business School Press, 1991).
11. For details, see D. F. Barnett, and R. W. Crandall, 1986. "*Up from the Ashes*," (Washington D.C.: Brookings Institution, 1986); and F. Koelbel, "Strategies for Restructuring the Steel Industry," *Metal Producing, 33* (December 1986), pp. 28–33.
12. D. Kirkpatrick, "Why Compaq Is Mad at Intel," *Fortune*, October 31, 1994, pp. 171–178.
13. A.S.Grove, *Only the Paranoid Survive* (New York: Doubleday, 1996).
14. In standard microeconomic theory, the concept used for assessing the strength of substitutes and complements is the cross elasticity of demand.
15. For details and further references, see C. W. L. Hill, "Establishing a Standard: Competitive Strategy and Technology Standards in Winner Take All Industries," *Academy of Management Executive*, 11, (1997), 7–25; and C. Shapiro and H. R. Varian, *Information Rules: A Strategic Guide to the Network Economy* (Boston: Harvard Business School Press, 1999).
16. See M. Gort and J. Klepper, "Time Paths in the Diffusion of Product Innovations," *Economic Journal* (September 1982), 630–653. Looking at the history of forty-six different products, Gort and Klepper found that the length of time before other companies entered the markets created by a few inventive companies declined from an average of 14.4 years for products introduced before 1930 to 4.9 years for those introduced after 1949.
17. The phrase was originally coined by J. Schumpeter, *Capitalism, Socialism and Democracy* (London: Macmillan, 1950), p. 68.
18. The development of strategic-group theory has been a strong theme in the strategy literature. Important contributions include the following: R. E. Caves and M. E. Porter, "From Entry Barriers to Mobility Barriers," *Quarterly Journal of Economics* (May 1977), 241–262; K. R. Harrigan, "An Application of Clustering for Strategic Group Analysis," *Strategic Management Journal,* 6 (1985), 55–73; K. J. Hatten and D. E. Schendel, "Heterogeneity Within an Industry: Firm Conduct in the U.S. Brewing Industry, 1952–71," *Journal of Industrial Economics,* 26 (1977), 97–113; M. E. Porter, "The Structure Within Industries and Companies' Performance," *The Review of Economics and Statistics,* 61 (1979), 214–227. For an example of more recent work, see K. Cool and D. Schendel, "Performance Differences Among Strategic Group Members," *Strategic Management Journal*, 9 (1988), 207–233; and C. S. Galbraith, G. B. Merrill, and G. Morgan, "Bilateral Strategic Groups," *Strategic Management Journal*, 15 (1994), 613–626.
19. For details on the strategic group structure in the pharmaceutical industry, see K. Cool and I. Dierickx, "Rivalry, Strategic Groups, and Firm Profitability," *Strategic Management Journal*, 14 (1993), 47–59.
20. This perspective is associated with the Austrian school of economics. The perspective goes back to Schumpeter. For a recent summary of this school and its implications for strategy, see R. Jacobson, "The Austrian School of Strategy," *Academy of Management Review*, 17 (1992), 782–807; and C. W. L. Hill and D. Deeds, "The Importance of Industry Structure for the Determination of Industry Profitability, A Neo-Austrian Approach," *Journal of Management Studies*, 33 (1996), 429–451.
21. Barnett and Crandall, *Up from the Ashes*.
22. M. E. Porter, *The Competitive Advantage of Nations* (New York, Free Press, 1990).

23. The term *punctuated equilibrium* is borrowed from evolutionary biology. For a detailed explanation of the concept see M. L. Tushman, W. H. Newman, and E. Romanelli, "Convergence and Upheaval: Managing the Unsteady Pace of Organizational Evolution," *California Management Review*, 29 (1985), 29–44; and C. J. G. Gersick, "Revolutionary Change Theories: A Multilevel Exploration of the Punctuated Equilibrium Paradigm," *Academy of Management Review*, 16: (1991), 10–36.
24. A. J. Slywotzky, *Value Migration: How To Think Several Moves Ahead of the Competition* (Boston: Harvard Business School Press, 1996).
25. R. D'Avani, *Hypercompetition* (New York: Free Press, 1994).
26. Hill and Deeds, "The Importance of Industry Structure," 429–451.
27. R. P. Rumelt, "How Much Does Industry Matter?" *Strategic Management Journal*, 12 (1991), 167–185. See also A. J. Mauri and M. P. Michaels, "Firm and Industry Effects Within Strategic Management: An Empirical Examination," *Strategic Management Journal*, 19 (1998), 211–219.
28. See R. Schmalensee, "Inter-Industry Studies of Structure and Performance," in R. Schmalensee, and R. D. Willig, *Handbook of Industrial Organization*, Vol 1 (Amsterdam: North Holland, 1989). Similar results were found by A. N. McGahan and M. E. Porter, "How Much Does Industry Matter, Really?" *Strategic Management Journal*, 18 (1997), 15–30.
29. For example, see K. Cool and D. Schendel, "Strategic Group Formation and Performance: The Case of the U.S. Pharmaceutical Industry 1932–1992," *Management Science* (September 1987), 1102–1124.
30. C. W. Hofer has argued that life cycle considerations may be the most important contingency when formulating business strategy; see C. W. Hofer, "Toward a Contingency Theory of Business Strategy," *Academy of Management Journal*, 18 (1975), 784–810. There is also empirical evidence to support this view. See C. R. Anderson and C. P. Zeithaml, "Stages of the Product Life Cycle, Business Strategy, and Business Performance," *Academy of Management Journal*, 27 (1984), 5–24; and D. C. Hambrick and D. Lei, "Towards an Empirical Prioritization of Contingency Variables for Business Strategy," *Academy of Management Journal*, 28 (1985), 763–788. Also see G. Miles, C. C. Snow, and M. P. Sharfman, "Industry Variety and Performance," *Strategic Management Journal*, 14 (1993), 163–177.
31. The characteristics of declining industries have been summarized by K. R. Harrigan, "Strategy Formulation in Declining Industries," *Academy of Management Review*, 5 (1980), 599–604.
32. For details, see C. W. L. Hill, "Establishing a Standard," 7–25; Shapiro and Varian, *Information Rules*; B. Arthur, "Increasing Returns and the New World of Business," *Harvard Business Review* (July–August 1996), 100–109.
33. P. C. Judge and A. Reinhardt, "Why the Fastest Chip Didn't Win," *Business Week*, April 28, 1997, pp. 92–96.
34. P. Dicken, *Global Shift* (New York: Guilford Press, 1992).
35. I. Metthee, "Playing a Large Part," *Seattle-Post Intelligence*, April 9, 1994, p. 13.
36. T. Levitt, "The Globalization of Markets," *Harvard Business Review* (May–June 1983), 92–102.
37. M. E. Porter, *The Competitive Advantage of Nations* (New York: Free Press, 1990). See also R. Grant, "Porter's Competitive Advantage of Nations: An Assessment," *Strategic Management Journal*, 7 (1991), 535–548.
38. Porter, *The Competitive Advantage of Nations*, p. 121.
39. "Lessons from the Frozen North," *Economist*, October 8, 1994, pp. 76–77; G. Edmondson, "Grabbing Markets from the Giants," *Business Week*, Special Issue: 21st Century Capitalism, 1995, p. 156; Q. Hardy, "Bypassing the Bells—A Wireless World," *Wall Street Journal*, September 21, 1998, p. R16; Q. Hardy and G. Naik, "Nokia Takes the Lead as Wireless Makers Sell 162.9 Million Phones in 1998," *Wall Street Journal*, February 8, 1999, p. A1.
40. The World Wide Web page for Micron Technology (http://www.micron.com); "When the Chips Are Down," *Economist*, March 23, 1996, pp. 19–21; L. Kehoe, "U.S. Chip Makers Seek to Dispel the Gloom," *Financial Times*, April 20, 1996, p. 20; "Remind Me How to Make Money," *Economist*, August 26, 1995, pp. 55–56; Standard & Poor's Industry Surveys, *Electronics*, August 3, 1995.

4 Internal Analysis: Resources, Capabilities, Competencies, and Competitive Advantage

OPENING CASE STUDY

Cisco Systems

CISCO SYSTEMS is one of the great success stories of recent years. Two Stanford University computer scientists, Leonard Bosack and Sandra Lerner, founded the company in 1984. In the early 1980s, Stanford University had accumulated many separate computer networks—each using different machines and different electronic languages to communicate among themselves. The problem was that these networks could not talk to each other. Bosack and Lerner, who were married at the time, were the managers of separate networks. They worked on the problem of hooking these networks together, partly, so legend has it, in order to be able to send each other E-mail messages. Their solution was a specialized computer known as a router, which was able to connect different computer systems. Realizing that this device might have commercial value, they established Cisco and shipped their first product in 1987. The company went public in 1990, with annual sales of around $70 million. Soon afterward, Cisco's sales started to increase exponentially as routers became a critical component of the rapidly expanding Internet. By 2000, Cisco had evolved into the dominant supplier of network equipment for the Internet—including routers, switches, and hubs—with annual sales in excess of $14 billion, no debt, a return on equity of around 24 percent and a return on assets of around 20 percent.

Cisco's rapid sales growth and high profitability owe much to its product innovation, which has continued at a fast pace since the company went public, but they are also due to the company's aggressive adoption of an e-business infrastructure. Here, too, Cisco has been an innovator. This infrastructure has enabled the company to reap

OPENING CASE *(continued)*

major efficiency gains, while providing its customers with superior point-of-sales service and after-sales service and support. Cisco was one of the first companies to move much of its sales effort onto the Internet. The process began in 1996, when Cisco realized that its traditional sales infrastructure could not keep up with increasing demand. Rather than hire additional personnel to manage customer accounts, the company began to experiment with on-line sales. It developed a computer program to walk customers through the process of ordering equipment on-line. A critical feature of this program helps customers order exactly the right mix of equipment, thereby avoiding any ordering mistakes, such as the ordering of incompatible equipment. In 1997, the company sold $500 million worth of equipment on-line. By 1999, this figure had ballooned to $10 billion, or 80 percent of Cisco's total sales, making the company one of the most aggressive adopters of an on-line sales approach in the world.

Customers seem to love the automated order processing system, primarily because it minimizes ordering mistakes and allows quicker execution of orders. For example, at Sprint, which is a major customer, it used to take sixty days from the signing of a contract to complete a networking project. Now it takes thirty-five to forty-five days, primarily because of the efficiency of Cisco's on-line ordering system. Moreover, Sprint has been able to cut its order-processing staff from 21 to 6, significantly saving costs. As for Cisco, the company has just 300 service agents handling all of its customer accounts, compared with the 900 it would need if sales were not handled on-line. The difference represents an annual saving of $20 million.

Cisco has also placed its customer support functions on-line. All routine customer service functions are now handled on-line by a computer program that can translate a customer's fuzzy inquiry into a standard description of a familiar problem; then it provides the four most likely explanations on screen, so that the customer might avoid blind alleys and not waste time. Since the company implemented the system in 1996, its sales have quadrupled, while its engineering support staff has merely doubled to 800. Without automated sales support, Cisco calculates that it would need at least 1,000 additional service engineers, which would cost around $75 million. Cisco has also moved to distributing all support software over the Internet, rather than transferring it to disks and mailing it to customers. This has saved Cisco another $250 million per year in annual operating costs.[1]

OVERVIEW

In Chapter 3, we discuss the elements of the external environment that determine an industry's attractiveness, and we examine how industry structure explains why some industries are more profitable than others. However, industry structure is not the only force that affects company profits. Within any given industry some companies are more profitable than others. For example, in the global auto industry, Toyota has consistently outperformed General Motors for most of the last twenty years. In the steel industry, Nucor has consistently outperformed U.S. Steel. In the U.S. retail clothing industry, The Gap has consistently outperformed JC Penney's, while in the Internet network equipment market, Cisco Systems has consistently outperformed competitors such as Bay Networks and 3Com. The question, therefore, is why within a particular industry do some companies outperform others? What is the basis of their competitive advantage?

Cisco provides some clues as to the sources of **competitive advantage**, that is, a company's ability to outperform its competitors. In the Opening Case, we saw how Cisco's competitive advantage stems partly from product innovation—after all, the company invented the router, one of the key pieces of equipment required to make the Internet work. Moreover, although the Opening Case does not dwell on this fact, Cisco has continued to remain at the leading edge of product innovation in the market for networking equipment. But there is more to Cisco's success than its excellent track record with regard to product innovation. As explained in the Opening Case, Cisco's aggressive approach to moving sales and customer service on-line has yielded huge dividends in terms of efficiency gains and customer satisfaction. Put differently, Cisco's process innovations in the area of on-line sales and customer service have also had a positive impact on its competitive advantage.

As you will see in this chapter, *innovation*, *efficiency*, and *customer responsiveness* can be regarded as three of the main building blocks of competitive advantage. *Quality* is a fourth building block. Cisco has a competitive advantage because it has skills in product and process innovation, because it is efficient, and because its on-line, or e-business, infrastructure has made it more responsive to customer needs. It would also not be surprising to find that Cisco's product quality is excellent. It is not surprising, then, that Cisco has become one of the great success stories of recent years.

In this chapter and the next, we look inside an organization at the strengths and weaknesses that determine its efficiency, innovative capability, product quality, and customer responsiveness. We explore how the strengths of an organization are grounded in its resources, capabilities, and competencies, and we discuss how these help a company attain a competitive advantage based on superior efficiency, innovation, quality, and customer responsiveness. We also discuss three critical questions. First, once it is obtained, what factors influence the durability of competitive advantage? Second, why do successful companies lose their competitive advantage? Third, how can companies avoid competitive failure and sustain their competitive advantage over time? When you have finished this chapter, you will have a good understanding of the nature of competitive advantage. This understanding will help you make better strategic decisions as a manager.

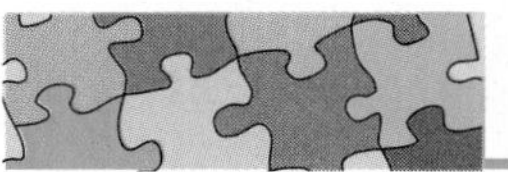

COMPETITIVE ADVANTAGE: VALUE CREATION, LOW COST, AND DIFFERENTIATION

We say that a company has a *competitive advantage* when its profit rate is higher than the average for its industry, and that it has a *sustained competitive advantage* when it is able to maintain this high profit rate over a number of years. In the U. S. department store industry, for example, Wal-Mart has had a sustained competitive advantage that has persisted for decades. This has been translated into a high profit rate (for details, see Strategy in Action 4.1). Two basic conditions determine a company's profit rate and hence whether it has a competitive advantage: the amount of value customers place on the company's goods or services, and the company's costs of production. In general, the more value customers place on a company's products, the higher the price the company can charge for those products. Note, however, that the price a company charges for a good or service is typically less than the value placed on that good or service by the customer because the customer captures some of that value in the form of what economists call a consumer surplus.[2] The customer gains this surplus because the company is competing with other companies for the customer's business, and so must charge a lower price than it

4.1 STRATEGY *in* ACTION

Competitive Advantage in the U.S. Department Store Industry

Figure 4.1 graphs the return on capital employed (ROK) earned by four companies active in the U.S. department stores industry between 1989 and 1998.[3] Their profitability is compared with the average profitability for the entire U.S. department store sector over the same time period. Figure 4.1 clearly illustrates that Wal-Mart and to a lesser degree, Nordstrom, had a sustained competitive advantage over the entire period. In contrast, the Hudson Bay company and Kmart were at a sustained competitive disadvantage most of the period. Among other things, the competitive advantage of Wal-Mart has been based on efficient logistics, high employee productivity, and excellent customer service. Moreover, Wal-Mart has led the industry in its *innovative* use of advanced information systems to manage everything, from its inventory and product mix to its pricing strategy. This process innovation has enabled Wal-Mart to reap substantial operating efficiencies while allowing the company to respond to differences in consumer demand across stores. Put differently, Wal-Mart excels on at least three of the building blocks of competitive advantage: innovation, efficiency, and customer responsiveness. Thus, it is not surprising that the company has consistently outperformed its peers.

Nordstrom too, has consistently outperformed its peers. This company's competitive advantage stems from the combination of a high-quality product offering linked with excellence in customer service, which has enabled the company to build a sustained competitive advantage on the basis of *quality* and *customer responsiveness.* In particular, Nordstrom is legendary for the attention that its salespeople devote to individual customers. For example, they will devote considerable time to assist "fashion-challenged" men to pick a stylish and matching combination of suit, shirts, shoes, and tie from the selection in a store. This differentiating factor has enabled Nordstrom to charge a high price for the products it sells.

In contrast, Kmart and Hudson Bay have been unable to build a strong competitive advantage, and both have underperformed the industry for years. Although Kmart has focused on the same discount niche that Wal-Mart has dominated, it lacks Wal-Mart's efficient operations and has a higher cost structure. Moreover, Kmart has generally followed Wal-Mart's lead in the adoption of information technology. Kmart has not been an innovator. As for Hudson Bay, this full-service department store chain has failed to build a significant differentiating feature that might enable it to mimic Nordstrom and charge a higher price for delivering excellent customer service. Indeed, both the product mix and customer service offered by Hudson Bay have left much to be desired, while operating margins have been further squeezed by operating inefficiencies and a high cost structure.

FIGURE 4.1

Return on Capital Employed for Selected U.S. Department Stores, 1989–1998

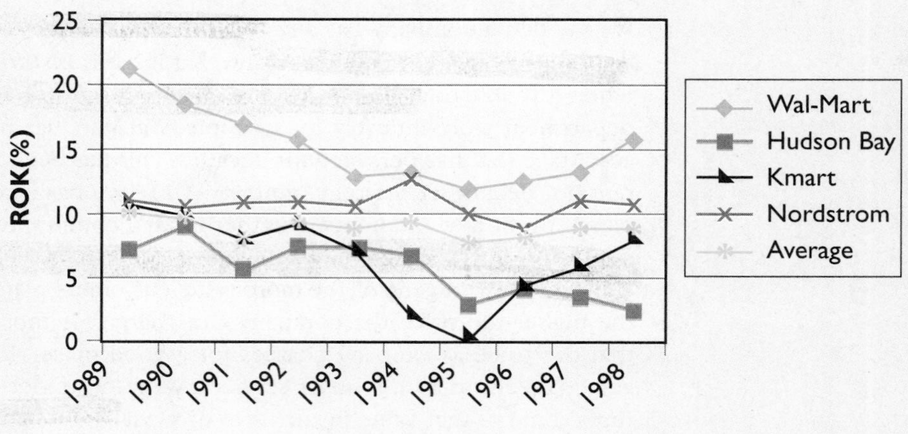

Source: Data from Value Line Investment Survey.

could as a monopoly supplier. Moreover, it is normally impossible to segment the market to such a degree that the company can charge each customer a price that reflects that individual's assessment of the value of a product—which economists refer to as a customer's reservation price. For these reasons, the price that gets charged tends to be less than the value placed on the product by many customers.

These concepts are illustrated in Figure 4.2. There you can see that the value of a product to a consumer may be V, the price that the company can charge for that product given competitive pressures may be P, and the costs of producing that product are C. The company's profit margin is equal to $P-C$, while the consumer surplus is equal to $V-P$. The company makes a profit so long as $P>C$, and its profit rate will be greater the lower C is *relative* to P. Bear in mind that the difference between V and P is in part determined by the intensity of competitive pressure in the marketplace. The lower the intensity of competitive pressure, the higher the price that can be charged relative to V.[4]

Note also that the value created by a company is measured by the difference between V and C $(V-C)$. A company creates value by converting inputs that cost C into a product on which consumers place a value of V. A company can create more value for its customers either by lowering C, or by making the product more attractive through superior design, functionality, quality, and the like, so that consumers place a greater value on it (V increases) and, consequently, are willing to pay a high price (P increases). This discussion suggests that a company has high profits, and thus a competitive advantage, when it creates more value for its customers than do rivals. Put differently, *the concept of value creation lies at the heart of competitive advantage.*[5]

For a more concrete example, consider the case of the personal computer industry. In the mid 1990s, Compaq Computer was selling its top-of-the-line personal computers for about $2,600 each ($P$), while all of the costs associated with producing these computers (C)—including material costs, administrative costs, manufacturing costs, marketing costs, R&D costs, and capital costs—amounted to $2,300 per computer, giving Compaq a net profit margin (net of all costs) of $300 per computer. In contrast, one of its competitors, AST, was able to charge only $2,300 for its equivalent personal computer, while the cost of producing these machines was $2,400, giving AST a net loss of $100 per computer.

This comparison shows how a company's profit rate is jointly determined by the price it can charge for its products and by its cost structure. Compaq made

FIGURE 4.2

Value Creation

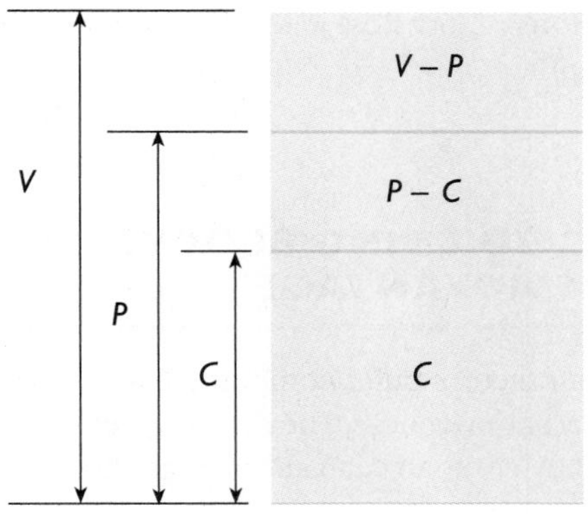

V = Value to consumer
P = Price
C = Costs of production
V – P = Consumer surplus
P – C = Profit margin

more profit per computer than AST in the mid 1990s because it could charge a higher price for its machines *and* because it had a lower cost structure. Compaq's lower cost structure came primarily from manufacturing efficiencies that AST lacked. As for its higher price, Compaq could command a higher price for its computers because consumers placed a higher value on a Compaq machine than on an AST machine, and therefore they were willing to pay more for a Compaq computer. Why did consumers place more value on Compaq machines? Primarily because they perceived Compaq products to be of a superior quality, functionality, and design relative to AST products. Put differently, Compaq had succeeded in differentiating its computers from those of AST (and various other producers) in the eyes of consumers. Thus, Compaq's competitive advantage in the mid 1990s came from a combination of low costs and differentiation. As a consequence of its superior cost and differentiation position, Compaq created more value for consumers than AST ($V - C$ was greater for Compaq than for AST). So one could say that Compaq's competitive advantage over AST was based on superior value creation.

We should note that superior value creation does not necessarily require a company to have the lowest cost structure in an industry or to create the most valuable product in the eyes of consumers, but it does require that the gap between perceived value (V) and costs of production (C) be greater than the gap attained by competitors. For example, as described in Strategy in Action 4.1, Nordstrom has had a sustained competitive advantage in the American department store industry. Although Nordstrom has a higher cost structure than many of its competitors, it was able to create more value because it successfully differentiated its service offering in the eyes of consumers so that consumers assigned a higher V to products purchased at Nordstrom. This perception of superior value was based on Nordstrom's obsession with customer service. It allowed Nordstrom to charge a higher price (P) for the products it sold than many competing full-service department stores. The higher price translated into a greater profit margin ($P - C$) for Nordstrom, as shown in Figure 4.1.

Michael Porter has argued that *low cost* and *differentiation* are two basic strategies for creating value and attaining a competitive advantage in an industry.[6] According to Porter, competitive advantage (along with higher profits) goes to those companies that can create superior value, and the way to create superior value is to drive down the cost structure of the business and/or differentiate the product in some way so that consumers value it more and are prepared to pay a premium price. But how can a company drive down its cost structure and differentiate its product offering from that of competitors so that it can create superior value? We tackle this question in both this chapter and the next one. In Chapter 6, we shall return to Porter's notions of low cost and differentiation strategies, when we examine his idea in more depth.

THE GENERIC BUILDING BLOCKS OF COMPETITIVE ADVANTAGE

As we have seen, four factors build competitive advantage: efficiency, quality, innovation, and customer responsiveness. They are the generic building blocks of competitive advantage that any company can adopt, regardless of its industry or the products

FIGURE 4.3

Generic Building Blocks of Competitive Advantage

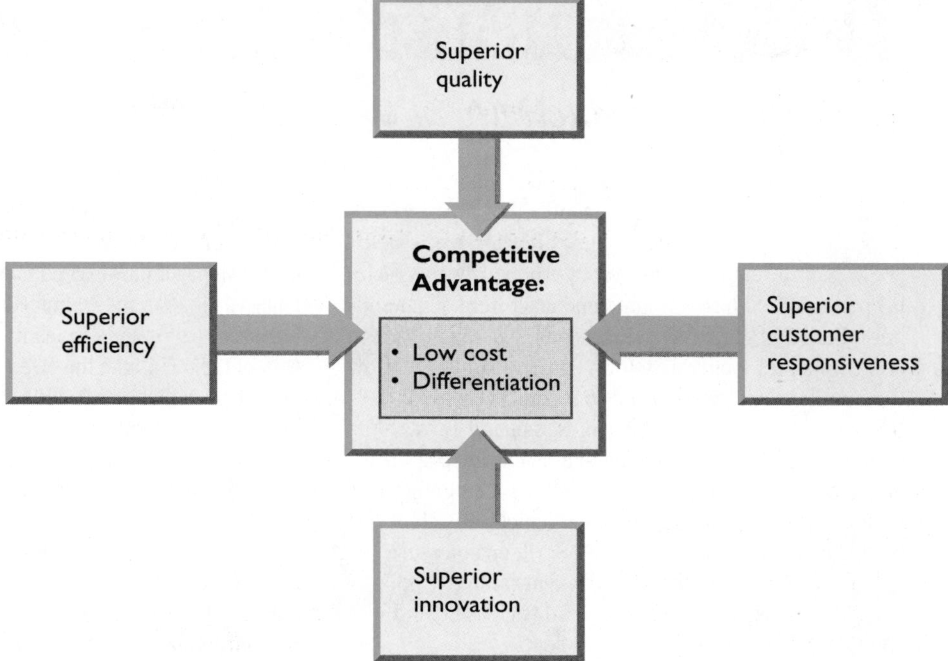

or services it produces (Figure 4.3). Although we discuss them separately below, they are highly interrelated. For example, superior quality can lead to superior efficiency, while innovation can enhance efficiency, quality, and customer responsiveness.

Efficiency

In one sense, a business is simply a device for transforming inputs into outputs. Inputs are basic factors of production such as labor, land, capital, management, and technological know-how. Outputs are the goods and services that the business produces. The simplest measure of efficiency is the quantity of inputs that it takes to produce a given output; that is, Efficiency = outputs/inputs. The more efficient a company, the fewer the inputs required to produce a given output. For example, if it takes General Motors thirty hours of employee time to assemble a car and it takes Ford twenty-five hours, we can say that Ford is more efficient than GM. Moreover, so long as other things are equal, such as wage rates, we can assume from these data that Ford will have a lower cost structure than GM. Thus, efficiency helps a company attain a low-cost competitive advantage. In the Opening Case, you saw how Cisco attained superior efficiency by pioneering the migration of sales and customer service functions to an on-line delivery model.

The most important component of efficiency for many companies is employee productivity, which is usually measured by output per employee. Holding all else constant, the company with the highest employee productivity in an industry will typically have the lowest costs of production. In other words, that company will have a cost-based competitive advantage. Strategy in Action 4.2 looks at the level of employee productivity attained by volume manufacturers of automobiles based in

4.2 STRATEGY in ACTION

Productivity in the Automobile Industry

Every year since 1980, Harbor Associates, a consulting company founded by former Chrysler executive James Harbor, has issued a report on the level of productivity in assembly plants of U.S.-based volume manufacturers of automobiles. Until 1993, the report focused on just the big three U.S. companies, General Motors, Ford, and Chrysler (now DaimlerChrysler), but now it also includes data on the U.S.-based assembly operations of Nissan and Toyota, both of which have a significant manufacturing presence in this country. The following table shows the number of hours of labor it took to assemble a vehicle at each of these companies from 1988 to 1998. On this measure, Nissan and Toyota are the most efficient volume producers in the United States, whereas Ford is close behind, and General Motors is the least efficient.

The higher labor productivity of Nissan, Toyota, and Ford is attributed to their lean production systems, which are based on a large number of productivity-enhancing management techniques. For example, all three companies make extensive use of self-managing work teams. Each team is given the responsibility for performing a major assembly task, and the teams are also set challenging productivity and quality goals. At the same time, the teams are empowered to find ways to improve their productivity and quality control and are rewarded through the use of incentive pay if they exceed their productivity or quality goals. While GM and DaimlerChrysler have also tried to introduce self-managing teams into the workplace, diffusion of the technique has been held back by a long history of adversarial labor relations at these companies, which has made it difficult for management and labor to cooperate to introduce new concepts.

However, DaimlerChrysler in particular claims that the data given above present an incomplete picture of productivity, primarily because it ignores that company's low product-development costs. According to DaimlerChrysler, these are a source of superior productivity not recognized in the Harbor Report. Until the early 1990s, it took DaimlerChrysler at least four years and 1,400 design engineers to design a new car, or 5,600 engineer years. The Chrysler Neon, however, was designed in just thirty-three months and required only 740 design engineers, which translates into 2,035 engineer years, a more than 50 percent improvement in productivity and a saving in design costs of $45 million. DaimlerChrysler estimates

the United States. These data suggest that in their assembly operations Japanese manufactures still enjoy a productivity-based competitive advantage relative to their U.S. counterparts but that the gap has closed significantly since the late 1980s. Moreover, it would seem that DaimlerChrysler in particular has realized huge productivity gains in its product design process, which, when added to its assembly process, may make the company the most efficient volume manufacturer in the United States.

The interesting issue, of course, is how to achieve superior productivity. Later chapters examine in detail how a company can achieve high productivity (and quality, innovation, and customer responsiveness). For now, we just note that to achieve high productivity a company must adopt the appropriate strategy, structure, and control systems.

Quality

Quality products are goods and services that are reliable in the sense that they do the job they were designed for and do it well. This concept applies whether we are talking about a Toyota automobile, clothes designed and sold by The Gap, the cus-

that the design for its next major car project can be completed in two years by just 540 design engineers. James Harbor, the author of the Harbor Report, agrees that DaimlerChrysler's superior design capabilities are an important source of superior productivity. In his 1995 report, he concluded that when design costs are added to assembly costs, Chrysler emerged as the most productive automobile company in the United States.

How has DaimlerChrysler done this? Primarily by forming teams of design engineers, component suppliers, manufacturing personnel, and marketing staff to oversee the design process. These teams make sure that there is very tight integration in the design process among suppliers, engineering, manufacturing, and marketing. Cars are now designed for ease of manufacturing, and with input up front from marketing, while suppliers are brought into the process early on to ensure that their design for component parts interfaces well with Chrysler's design for the finished car. As a result, the amount of redesign work required has been dramatically reduced, and the design cycle time of four to six years has been decreased to under three years.[7]

Hours of labor required to assemble a vehicle

Company	*1988*	*1994*	*1998*
General Motors	39.02	30.26	30.32
DaimlerChrysler	36.64	27.8	32.15
Ford	26.0	25.0	22.85
Toyota	Not Available	19.30	21.20
Nissan	Not Available	18.3	17.07

tomer service department of Citibank, or the ability of an airline to have its planes arrive on time. The impact of high product quality on competitive advantage is twofold.[8] First, providing high-quality products increases the value of those products in the eyes of consumers. In turn, this enhanced perception of value allows the company to charge a higher price for its products. In the automobile industry, for example, companies such as Toyota not only have had a productivity-based cost advantage, but they have also been able to charge a higher price for their cars because of the higher quality of their products. Thus, compared with a company like General Motors, Toyota has had both lower costs and the ability to charge higher prices. As a result, historically Toyota has operated with a bigger profit margin than GM.

The second impact of high quality on competitive advantage comes from the greater efficiency and the lower unit costs it brings. Less employee time is wasted making defective products or providing substandard services and less time has to be spent fixing mistakes, which translates into higher employee productivity and lower unit costs. Thus, high product quality not only lets a company charge higher prices for its product, but also lowers costs (see Figure 4.4).

The importance of quality in building competitive advantage has increased dramatically during the last decade. Indeed, so crucial is the emphasis placed on quality

FIGURE 4.4

The Impact of Quality on Profits

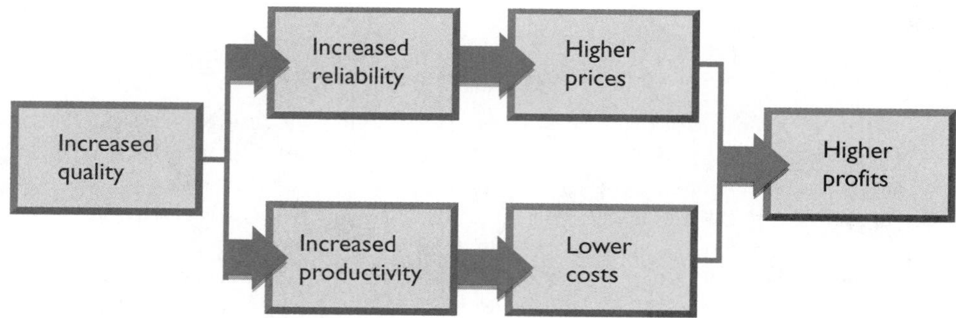

by many companies that achieving high product quality can no longer be viewed as just one way of gaining a competitive advantage. In many industries, it has become an absolute imperative for survival. Strategy in Action 4.3, which discusses the turnaround of Continental Airlines, illustrates the importance of quality in a service environment.

Innovation

Innovation can be defined as anything new or novel about the way a company operates or the products it produces. Innovation includes advances in the kinds of products, production processes, management systems, organizational structures, and strategies developed by a company. All of the following can be viewed as *innovations*: Intel's development of the microprocessor; the discounting strategy of Toys 'R' Us in the retail toy business; Toyota's lean production system for manufacturing automobiles; Cisco's development of the router and pioneering approach to on-line selling and customer service; and Wal-Mart's pioneering efforts to use information systems to manage its logistics, product mix, and product pricing. Successful innovation is about developing new products and/or managing the enterprise in a novel way that creates value for consumers.[10]

Innovation is perhaps the single most important building block of competitive advantage. In the long run, competition can be viewed as a process driven by innovation. Although not all innovations succeed, those that do can be a major source of competitive advantage because, by definition, they give a company something **unique**—something its competitors lack (until they imitate the innovation). Uniqueness lets a company differentiate itself from its rivals and charge a premium price for its product, or reduce its unit costs far below those of competitors.

As with efficiency and quality, we explore the issue of innovation more fully later in the book. A few examples can highlight the importance of innovation as the bedrock of competitive advantage. Consider Xerox's development of the photocopier, Cisco's development of the router, Intel's development of new microprocessors, Hewlett-Packard's development of the laser printer, Nike's development of high-tech athletic shoes, Bausch & Lomb's development of contact lenses, or Sony's development of the Walkman. All these product innovations helped build a competitive advantage for the pioneering companies. In each case, the company, by virtue of being the sole supplier of a new product, could charge a premium price. By the time competitors succeeded in imitating the innovator, the innovating com-

4.3 STRATEGY *in* ACTION

Continental Airlines Goes from Worst to First

When Gordon Bethune left Boeing to become the CEO of Continental Airlines in 1994, the company was the worst performing and least profitable of all major U.S. airlines. One of the main problems was the lack of reliability. In 1994, Continental planes arrived on time only 61 percent of the time, placing the company dead last in the influential Air Customer Satisfaction Study, produced by J.D. Power & Associates. To make matters worse, airline travelers ranked on-time performance as the most important factor when deciding which airline to fly on. Reliability was the primary metric passengers used to determine an airline's quality.

Bethune soon came to the conclusion that the prior management had cut costs so far that the service had suffered. In his words, "our service was lousy and nobody knew when a plane might land. We were unpredictable and unreliable, and when you are an airline, where does that leave you? It leaves you with a lot of empty planes. We had a lousy product, and nobody particularly wanted to buy it." Bethune's solution: he told Continental employees that if the airline's on-time performance improved, every employee would receive a $65 bonus. The total cost to the airline was $2.6 million. Bethune was proposing to improve performance by spending more money. It worked. When the program was launched in January 1995, 71 percent of the planes landed on time. By year-end, the figure was up to 80 percent, and Continental had risen to fifth in its on-time performance. For 1996, Bethune announced that the airline had to finish third or higher for employees to get the bonus, which he increased to $100. The airline finished second. It has not dropped out of the top three since then.

To support the drive toward greater reliability, Bethune also reorganized the way employees were managed. Out went the employee manual, to be replaced by a new set of guidelines, which gave front-line employees significant decision-making power to fix customer problems. For example, if a flight is canceled, a customer service agent might have to decide which passengers should receive priority to get on the next flight. Under the old system, the employee would have had to refer to the rule book, and if that did not provide an answer, ask a higher-level manager. This inflexible approach led to significant frustration among both passengers and employees. The new system allows customer service agents to fix problems as they see fit. According to Bethune, concentrating decision-making power in the hands of employees gave them the ability to solve customer problems in creative ways, which has had a dramatic impact on customers' perception of the quality of service they get at Continental.[9]

pany had built up such strong brand loyalty and supporting management processes that its position proved difficult for imitators to attack. Sony is still known for its Walkman, Hewlett-Packard for its laser printers, and Intel for its microprocessors.

Customer Responsiveness

To achieve superior customer responsiveness, a company must be able to do a better job than competitors of identifying and satisfying the needs of its customers. Consumers will then place more value on its products, creating a differentiation-based competitive advantage. Improving the quality of a company's product offering is consistent with achieving responsiveness, as is developing new products with features that existing products lack. In other words, achieving superior quality and innovation are an integral part of achieving superior customer responsiveness.

Another factor that stands out in any discussion of customer responsiveness is the need to customize goods and services to the unique demands of individual customers or customer groups. For example, the proliferation of different types of soft drinks and beers in recent years can be viewed partly as a response to this trend. Automobile companies, too, have become more adept at customizing cars to the demands of individual customers. For instance, following the lead of Toyota, the Saturn division of General Motors builds cars to order for individual customers, letting them choose from a wide range of colors and options.

An aspect of customer responsiveness that has drawn increasing attention is **customer response time,** which is the time that it takes for a good to be delivered or a service to be performed.[11] For a manufacturer of machinery, response time is the time it takes to fill customer orders. For a bank, it is the time it takes to process a loan or the time that a customer must stand in line to wait for a free teller. For a supermarket, it is the time that customers must stand in checkout lines. Customer survey after customer survey has shown slow response time to be a major source of customer dissatisfaction.[12]

Besides quality, customization, and response time, other sources of enhanced customer responsiveness are superior design, superior service, and superior after-sales service and support. All these factors enhance customer responsiveness and allow a company to differentiate itself from its less responsive competitors. In turn, differentiation enables a company to build brand loyalty and to charge a premium price for its products. For example, consider how much more people are prepared to pay for next-day delivery of Express Mail, as opposed to delivery in three to four days. In 1996, a two-page letter sent by overnight Express Mail within the United States cost about $10, compared with 32 cents for regular mail. Thus, the price premium for express delivery (reduced response time) was $9.68, or a premium of 3,025 percent over the regular price.

Summary

Efficiency, quality, customer responsiveness, and innovation are all important elements in obtaining a competitive advantage. Superior efficiency enables a company to lower its costs; superior quality lets it both charge a higher price and lower its costs; superior customer responsiveness allows it to charge a higher price; and superior innovation can lead to higher prices or lower unit costs (Figure 4.5). Together, these four factors help a company create more value by lowering costs or differentiating its products from those of competitors, which enables the company to outperform its competitors.

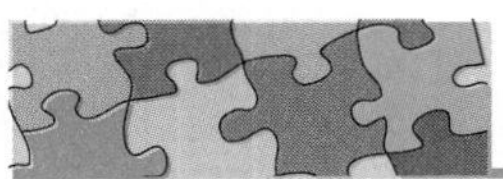

BUSINESS FUNCTIONS, THE VALUE CHAIN, AND VALUE CREATION

In this section, we consider the role played by the different functions of a company—such as production, marketing, R&D, service, information systems, materials management, and human resources—in the value creation process. Specifically, we briefly review how the different functions of a company can help in the process of driving down costs and increasing the perception of value through differentiation. As a first step, consider the concept of the value chain, which is illustrated in Figure

FIGURE 4.5

The Impact of Efficiency, Quality, Customer Responsiveness, and Innovation on Unit Costs and Prices

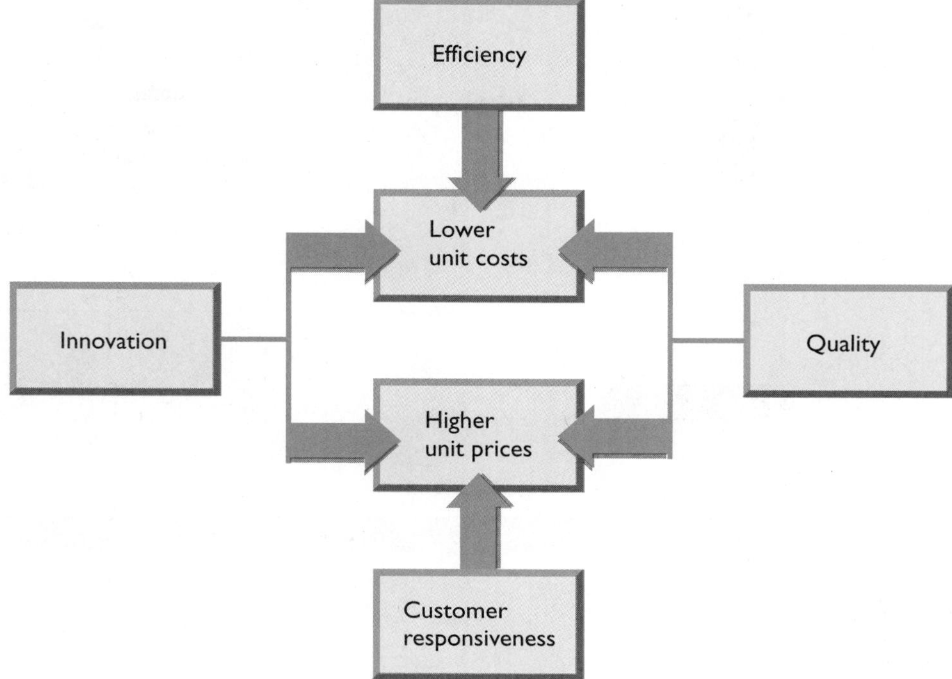

4.6. [13] The term ***value chain*** refers to the idea that a company is a chain of activities for transforming inputs into outputs that customers value. The process of transforming inputs into outputs comprises a number of primary and support activities. Each activity adds value to the product.

Primary Activities

Primary activities have to do with the design, creation, and delivery of the product, as well as its marketing and its support and after-sales service. In the value chain illustrated in Figure 4.6, the primary activities are broken down into four functions: research and development, production, marketing and sales, and service.

Research and development (R&D) is concerned with the design of products and production processes. Although we think of R&D as being associated with the design of physical products and production processes in manufacturing enterprises, many service companies also undertake R&D. For example, banks compete with each other by developing new financial products and new ways of delivering those products to customers. On-line banking and smart debit cards are two recent examples of the fruits of new product development in the banking industry. Earlier examples of innovation in the banking industry included ATM machines, credit cards, and debit cards.

By superior product design, R&D can increase the functionality of products, which makes them more attractive to consumers. Alternatively, the work of R&D may result in more efficient production processes, thereby lowering production

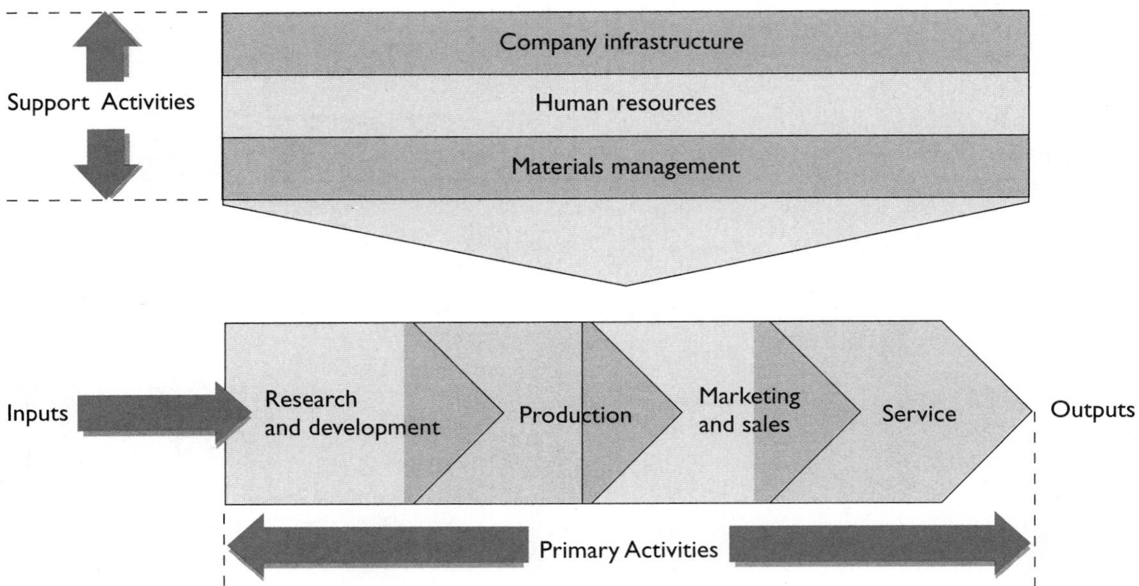

FIGURE 4.6
The Value Chain

costs. Either way, the R&D function of an enterprise can create value. At Intel, for example, R&D creates value both by developing ever more powerful microprocessors, and by helping to pioneer ever more efficient manufacturing processes (in conjunction with equipment suppliers).

Production is concerned with the creation of a good or service. For physical products, when we talk about production we generally mean manufacturing. For services such as banking or retail operations, production typically takes place when the service is actually delivered to the customer (for example, when a bank originates a loan for a customer, it is engaged in production of the loan). The production function of a company creates value by performing its activities efficiently so that lower costs result. Thus, as suggested by the data contained in Strategy in Action 4.2, the efficient production operations of Nissan, Ford, and Toyota are helping those automobile companies to create more value relative to competitors such as General Motors. Production can also create value by performing its activities in a way that is consistent with high product quality, which leads to differentiation and lower costs—both of which increase the value created by a company.

There are several ways in which the **marketing and sales** functions of a company can help create value. Through brand positioning and advertising, the marketing function can increase the value that consumers perceive to be contained in a company's product. Insofar as these activities help create a favorable impression of the company's product in the minds of consumers, they increase value. For example, in the 1980s the French company Perrier did a wonderful job of persuading U.S. consumers that slightly carbonated bottled water was worth $1.50 per bottle, rather than a price closer to the 50 cents that it cost to physically collect, bottle, and distribute the water. Perrier's marketing function increased the value that consumers ascribed to the product.

Marketing and sales can also create value by discovering consumer needs and communicating them back to the R&D function of the company, which can then design products that better match those needs. For another example of value creation by the marketing function of an enterprise, see Strategy in Action 4.4, which examines how the sales force of Pfizer increased the perception of the value associated with one of that company's main pharmaceuticals, Zoloft.

The role of the **service** function of an enterprise is to provide after-sales service and support. This function can create a perception of superior value in the minds of consumers by solving customer problems and supporting customers after they have purchased the product. For example, Caterpillar, the U.S.-based manufacturer

4.4 STRATEGY *in* ACTION

Value Creation at Pfizer

The antidepressant drug Prozac, introduced by Eli Lilly in 1988, has been one of the most lucrative mental health drugs in history. In 1995, U.S. consumers alone filled almost 19 million prescriptions for Prozac, hoping to mitigate the effects of a wide range of mental disorders including chronic depression, bulimia, and obsessive disorders. Worldwide sales of the drug topped $2 billion in 1995, making it a gold mine for Lilly.

But Prozac's market position is now under attack from an aggressive marketing and sales campaign by rival pharmaceutical company Pfizer. In 1992, Pfizer introduced its own antidepressant, Zoloft. According to medical experts, the differences between Prozac and Zoloft are slight at best. Both drugs function in the same basic manner, by boosting serotonin, a brain chemical believed to be in short supply in many depressed people. Both drugs also have a similar list of possible side effects: Prozac's label mentions nausea, nervousness, anxiety, insomnia, and drowsiness, and Zoloft's lists nausea and other stomach problems, diarrhea, sexual dysfunction, and sleepiness. As one expert noted, "these drugs are so similar that you have to be kidding yourself if you think one drug is going to be consistently superior to the other in treating patients."

Despite the similarity between the two products, however, Pfizer has been gaining share from Lilly in the antidepressant market. By 1998, Zoloft accounted for 40 percent of the market, up from little more than zero in 1992. The main reason for the success of Zoloft seems to be an aggressive marketing and sales campaign by Pfizer, which has given physicians the impression that Zoloft is a safer drug. Pfizer salespeople bill their product as a kind of Prozac Lite: just as effective but without Prozac's occasional downside, anxiety. The reference to anxiety seems carefully designed to remind doctors of a spate of failed lawsuits alleging that Prozac caused suicides and violent acts. Pfizer's sales force has also logged more "face time" with physicians than Lilly's. According to Scott-Levin and Associates, in 1995 Zoloft sales representatives made 660,000 sales visits to doctors—70,000 more than the Prozac sales force logged. About three-quarters of the visits by Zoloft representatives were not to psychiatrists but to primary care physicians, who increasingly prescribe antidepressants but presumably are less familiar with their more subtle properties. Doctors also claim that Pfizer salespeople play up Prozac's clinical reputation that it is more agitating than Zoloft. They also emphasize that unlike Zoloft, Prozac remains in the bloodstream for weeks after a patient stops taking it, raising the possibility of adverse drug interaction if a patient switches to other medications.

The important point here is that Pfizer's marketing and sales force is altering physicians' perceptions of the relative value of Prozac and Zoloft. For Pfizer, the payoff has come in terms of rapidly increasing revenues and market share and, of course, a greater return on the company's investment in developing Zoloft.[14]

of heavy earthmoving equipment, can get spare parts to any point in the world within twenty-four hours, thereby minimizing the amount of downtime its customers have to suffer if their Caterpillar equipment malfunctions. This is an extremely valuable support capability in an industry where downtime is very expensive. It has helped to increase the value that customers associate with Caterpillar products, and thus the price that Caterpillar can charge for them.

Support Activities

The **support activities** of the value chain provide inputs that allow the primary activities to take place (see Figure 4.6). The **materials management** (or logistics) function controls the transmission of physical materials through the value chain, from procurement through production and into distribution. The efficiency with which this is carried out can significantly lower costs, thereby creating more value. Wal-Mart, the U.S. retailing giant, reportedly has the most efficient materials management setup in the retail industry. By tightly controlling the flow of goods from its suppliers through its stores and into the hands of consumers, Wal-Mart has eliminated the need to hold large inventories of goods. Lower inventories mean lower costs, and hence greater value creation.

Similarly, there are a number of ways in which the **human resource** function can help an enterprise create more value. The human resource function ensures that the company has the right mix of skilled people to perform its value creation activities effectively. It is also the job of the human resource function to ensure that people are adequately trained, motivated, and compensated to perform their value creation tasks.

Information systems refer to the (largely) electronic systems for managing inventory, tracking sales, pricing products, selling products, dealing with customer service inquires, and so on. Information systems, when coupled with the communications features of the Internet, are holding out the promise of being able to alter the efficiency and effectiveness with which a company manages its other value creation activities. In the Opening Case, we saw how Cisco has used Internet-based information systems to profoundly alter the way its marketing, sales, and service functions are performed, realizing substantial efficiency gains in the process. Wal-Mart is another company that has used information systems to alter the way it does business. Wal-Mart's materials management function is able to track the sale of individual items very closely. This has enabled Wal-Mart to optimize its product mix and pricing strategy. Wal-Mart is rarely left with unwanted merchandise on its hands, which reduces costs, and the company is able to provide the right mix of goods to consumers, which increases the perception of value that consumers associate with Wal-Mart.

The final support activity is the **company infrastructure**. This has a somewhat different character from the other support activities. By infrastructure we mean the companywide context within which all the other value creation activities take place. The infrastructure includes the organizational structure, control systems, and culture of the company. Since top management can exert considerable influence on these aspects of a company, top management should also be viewed as part of a company's infrastructure. Indeed, through strong leadership, top management can consciously shape a company's infrastructure, and through it, the performance of all other value creation activities within the company.

Cross-Functional Goals

Achieving superior efficiency, quality, innovation, and customer responsiveness requires strategies that embrace several distinct value creation activities. Indeed, these goals can be regarded as *goals that cut across the different value creation functions of a company*; they are goals whose attainment requires substantial cross-functional integration. In Chapter 11, we consider in greater detail how to achieve cross-functional integration.

DISTINCTIVE COMPETENCIES, RESOURCES, AND CAPABILITIES

A **distinctive competency** is unique strength that allows a company to achieve superior efficiency, quality, innovation, or customer responsiveness and thereby to create superior value and attain a competitive advantage. A firm with a distinctive competency can differentiate its products or achieve substantially lower costs than its rivals. Consequently, it creates more value than its rivals and will earn a profit rate substantially above the industry average.

For example, it can be argued that Toyota has distinctive competencies in the development and operation of manufacturing processes. Toyota has pioneered a whole range of manufacturing techniques, such as just-in-time inventory systems, self-managing teams, and reduced setup times for complex equipment. These competencies have helped Toyota attain superior efficiency and product quality, which are the basis of its competitive advantage in the global automobile industry.[15]

Resources and Capabilities

The distinctive competencies of an organization arise from two complementary sources: its **resources** and **capabilities** (see Figure 4.7).[16] The financial, physical, human, technological, and organizational resources of the company can be divided into **tangible resources** (land, buildings, plant, and equipment) and **intangible resources** (brand names, reputation, patents, and technological or marketing know-how). To give rise to a distinctive competency, a company's resources must be both *unique* and *valuable*. A unique resource is one that no other company has. For example, Polaroid's distinctive competency in instant photography was based on a unique intangible resource: technological know-how in instant film processing protected from imitation by a thicket of patents. A resource is valuable if it in some way helps create strong demand for the company's products. Polaroid's technological know-how was valuable because it created strong demand for its photographic products.

Capabilities refer to a company's skills at coordinating its resources and putting them to productive use. These skills reside in an organization's routines; that is, in the way a company makes decisions and manages its internal processes in order to achieve organizational objectives. More generally, a company's capabilities are the product of its organizational structure and control systems. They specify how

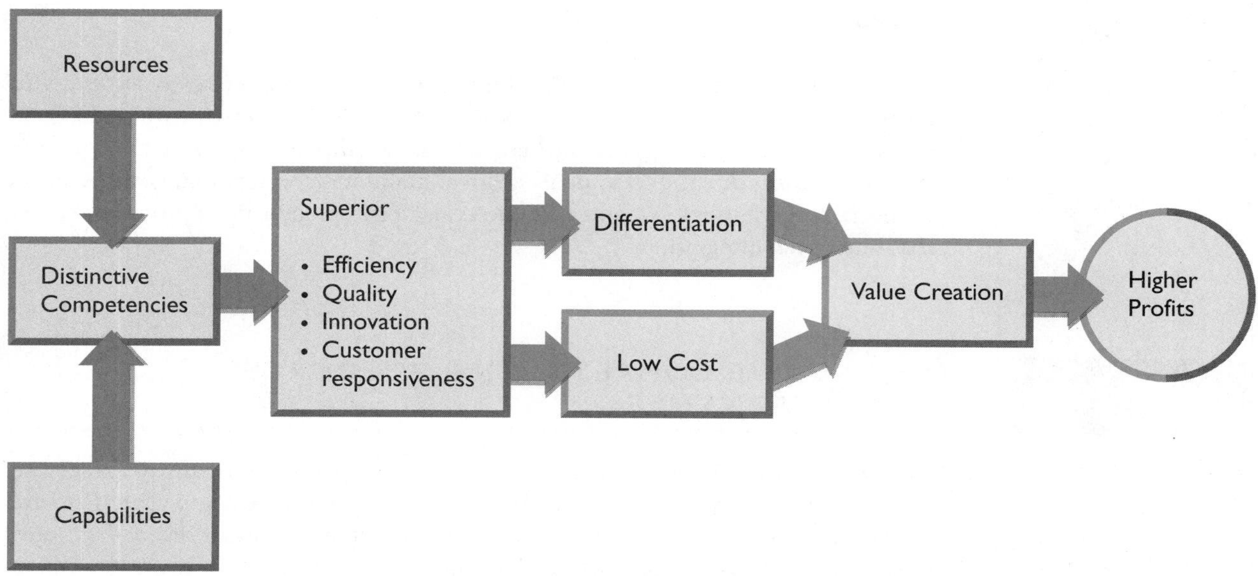

FIGURE 4.7

The Roots of Competitive Advantage

and where decisions are made within a company, the kind of behaviors the company rewards, and the company's cultural norms and values. (We discuss in Chapters 11 and 12 how organizational structure and control systems help a company obtain capabilities.) It is important to keep in mind that capabilities are, by definition, intangible. They reside not so much in individuals as in the way individuals interact, cooperate, and make decisions within the context of an organization.[17]

The distinction between resources and capabilities is critical to understanding what generates a distinctive competency. A company may have unique and valuable resources, but unless it has the capability to use those resources effectively, it may not be able to create or sustain a distinctive competency. It is also important to recognize that a company may not need unique and valuable resources to establish a distinctive competency so long as it has capabilities that no competitor possesses. For example, the steel minimill operator Nucor is widely acknowledged to be the most cost-efficient steel maker in the United States. But Nucor's distinctive competency in low-cost steel making does not come from any unique and valuable resources. Nucor has the same resources (plant, equipment, skilled employees, and know-how) as many other minimill operators. What distinguishes Nucor is its unique capability to manage its resources in a highly productive way. Specifically, Nucor's structure, control systems, and culture promote efficiency at all levels of the company.

In sum, for a company to have a distinctive competency, it must at a minimum have either (1) a unique and valuable resource and the capabilities (skills) necessary to exploit that resource (as illustrated by Polaroid) or (2) a unique capability to manage common resources (as exemplified by Nucor). A company's distinctive competency is strongest when it possesses *both* unique and valuable resources and unique capabilities to manage those resources.

Strategy and Competitive Advantage

The primary objective of strategy is to achieve a competitive advantage. Attaining this goal demands a two-pronged effort. A company needs to pursue strategies that build on its existing resources and capabilities (its competencies), as well as strategies that build additional resources and capabilities (that is, develop new competencies) and thus enhance the company's long-run competitive position.[18] Figure 4.8 illustrates the relationship between a firm's strategies and its resources and capabilities. It is important to note that by *strategies* we mean *all* types of strategy—functional-level strategies, business-level strategies, corporate-level strategies, international strategies, or, more typically, some combination of them. We discuss the various strategies available to a company in detail throughout the next six chapters. What needs stressing here is that successful strategies often either build on a company's existing distinctive competencies or help a company develop new ones.

The history of The Walt Disney Company during the 1980s exemplifies the need to pursue strategies that build on a firm's resources and capabilities. In the early 1980s, Disney suffered a string of poor financial years. This culminated in a 1984 management shakeup, when Michael Eisner was appointed CEO. Four years later, Disney's sales had increased from $1.66 billion to $3.75 billion, its net profits from $98 million to $570 million, and its stock market valuation from $1.8 billion to $10.3 billion. What brought about this transformation was the company's deliberate attempt to exploit its existing resources and capabilities more aggressively. These resources and capabilities included Disney's enormous film library, its brand name, and its in-house filmmaking skills, particularly in animation. Under Eisner, many old Disney classics were rereleased, first in movie theaters, and then on video, earning the company millions in the process. Disney also started a cable television channel, the Disney Channel, to utilize this library and capitalize on the firm's brand name. In addition, under Eisner, the filmmaking arm of Disney flourished, first with a string of low-budget box-office hits under the Touchstone label and then with the reintroduction of the product that had originally made Disney famous, the full-length animated feature. Putting together its brand name and in-house animation capabilities, Disney produced three major box-office hits in four years: *The Little Mermaid, Beauty and the Beast,* and *Aladdin*.[19] In sum, Disney's transformation was based primarily on strategies that exploited the company's existing resource base.

FIGURE 4.8

The Relationship Between Strategies and Resources and Capabilities

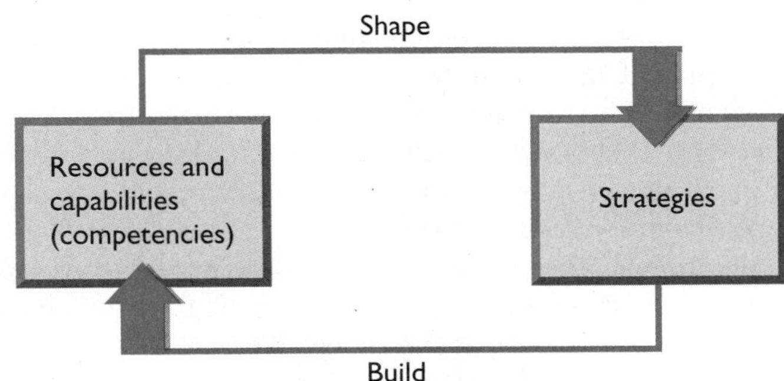

Other companies that have successfully exploited their resources and capabilities to create profitable opportunities include 3M and Honda. The former exploited its distinctive competency in sticky tape to create businesses as diverse as Post-it Notes, pressure-sensitive tapes, and coated abrasives. The latter exploited its distinctive competency in the design and manufacture of high-powered lightweight engines to move from motorcycles to cars, lawn mowers, and four-wheel off-road buggies. On the other hand, some of the most striking strategic failures have occurred at companies that have strayed too far from their distinctive competencies. For example, Exxon, which has distinctive competencies in oil exploration, extraction, and refining, spent much of the 1970s diversifying into areas such as office automation equipment, where it had no capabilities. The effort failed and Exxon sold off these diversified businesses during the 1980s.

As for the process of building resources and capabilities through strategies, consider Xerox. During the late 1970s, its market share in the photocopier business slumped by 50 percent because its main Japanese competitors, Canon and Ricoh, were paying close attention to their distinctive competencies, whereas Xerox was not. As a result, by the early 1980s, Canon and Ricoh were selling high-quality and technologically superior copiers at a price approximating that of Xerox. To recapture its lost market share, Xerox had to fundamentally rethink the way it did business. It launched a series of functional-level strategies designed to improve quality and product design, eliminate unnecessary inventory, and reduce new product development time (cycle time). The goal of these strategies was to develop the kind of resources and capabilities that had enabled Canon and Ricoh to take market share away from Xerox. Xerox was reasonably successful in this endeavor; its share of the U.S. copier market increased from a low of 10 percent in 1985 to 18 percent in 1991.[20] The company's renaissance stemmed from the successful implementation of functional-level strategies to build new distinctive competencies.

The Role of Luck

A number of scholars have argued that luck plays a critical role in determining competitive success and failure.[21] In its most extreme version, the luck argument devalues the importance of planned strategy. Instead, it states that in coping with uncertainty some companies just happened to stumble on the correct strategy. Put another way, they just happened to develop or possess the right kind of resources and capabilities by accident rather than by design.

Although luck may be the reason for a company's success in particular cases, it is an unconvincing explanation for the persistent success of a company. Recall our argument that the generic building blocks of competitive advantage are superior efficiency, quality, innovation, and customer responsiveness. Keep in mind also that competition is a process in which companies are continually trying to outdo each other in their ability to achieve high efficiency, quality, innovation, and customer responsiveness. It is possible to imagine a company getting lucky and coming into possession of resources that allow it to achieve excellence on one or more of these dimensions. However, it is difficult to imagine how *sustained* excellence on any of these four dimensions could be produced by anything other than conscious effort, that is, by strategy. Luck may indeed play a role in success, and Strategy in Action 4.5 discusses the role of luck in the early history of Microsoft. However, to argue that success is entirely a matter of luck is to strain credibility.

4.5 STRATEGY *in* ACTION

Microsoft's Luck

The product that launched Microsoft into its leadership position in the software industry was MS-DOS, the operating system for IBM and IBM-compatible PCs. The original DOS program, however, was not developed by Microsoft. Instead, it was developed by a company called Seattle Computer, where it was known as Q-DOS (which stood for "quick and dirty operating system"). When IBM was looking for an operating system to run its original PC, it made contact with a number of software companies, including Microsoft, asking them whether they could develop such a system. IBM did not, however, make contact with Seattle Computer. Bill Gates, a player in the emerging Seattle computer community, knew that Seattle Computer had already developed a disk operating system. Borrowing $50,000 from his father, a senior partner in a prominent Seattle law company, Gates went to see the CEO of Seattle Computer and offered to purchase the rights to the company's Q-DOS system. He did not, of course, reveal that IBM was looking for a disk operating system. Since Seattle Computer was short of cash, the CEO quickly agreed. Gates then renamed the system MS-DOS, upgraded it somewhat, and licensed it to IBM. The rest, as they say, is history.

So was Microsoft lucky? Of course it was. It was lucky that Seattle Computer had not heard about IBM's request. It was lucky that IBM approached Microsoft. It was lucky that Gates knew about Seattle Computer's operating system. And it was lucky that Gates had a father wealthy enough to lend him $50,000 on short notice. On the other hand, to attribute all of Microsoft's subsequent success to luck would be wrong. While MS-DOS gave Microsoft a tremendous head start in the industry, it did not guarantee Microsoft continued worldwide success. To achieve that, Microsoft had to build the appropriate set of resources and capabilities required to produce a continual stream of innovative software, which is precisely what the company did with the cash generated from MS-DOS.[22]

THE DURABILITY OF COMPETITIVE ADVANTAGE

The question that we now need to address is, How long will a competitive advantage last once it has been created? What is the durability of competitive advantage given that other companies are also seeking to develop distinctive competencies that will give them a competitive advantage? The answer depends on three factors: barriers to imitation, the capability of competitors, and the general dynamism of the industry environment.

Barriers to Imitation

A company with a competitive advantage will earn higher than average profits. These profits send a signal to rivals that the company is in possession of some valuable distinctive competency that allows it to create superior value. Naturally, its competitors will try to identify and imitate that competency. Insofar as they are successful, they may ultimately surpass the company's superior profits.[23] How quickly will rivals imitate a company's distinctive competencies? This is an important question, because the speed of imitation has a bearing upon the durability of a company's competitive advantage. Other things being equal, the more rapidly competitors imitate a company's distinctive competencies, the less durable will be its competitive advantage and the more urgent the need to continually improve its competencies in order to stay one step ahead of the imitators. It is important to stress at the outset that ultimately almost any distinctive competency can be imitated by a competitor. The critical issue is *time*. The longer it takes competitors to imitate a distinctive competency, the greater the opportunity the company has to build a strong market position and reputation with consumers, which is then more difficult for competitors to attack. Moreover, the longer it takes to achieve an imitation, the greater is the opportunity for the imitated company to enhance its competency, or build other competencies, that will keep it ahead of the competition.

Barriers to imitation are a primary determinant of the speed of imitation. **Barriers to imitation** are factors that make it difficult for a competitor to copy a company's distinctive competencies. The greater the barriers to such imitation, the more sustainable is a company's competitive advantage.[24]

Imitating Resources In general, the easiest distinctive competencies for prospective rivals to imitate tend to be those based on possession of unique and valuable tangible resources, such as buildings, plant, and equipment. Such resources are visible to competitors and can often be purchased on the open market. For example, if a company's competitive advantage is based on sole possession of efficient-scale manufacturing facilities, competitors may move fairly quickly to establish similar facilities. Although Ford gained a competitive advantage over General Motors in the 1920s by being the first to adopt an assembly line manufacturing technology to produce automobiles, General Motors quickly imitated that innovation. A similar process is occurring in the auto industry at present, as companies try to imitate Toyota's famous production system, which formed the basis for much of its competitive advantage during the 1970s and 1980s. GM's Saturn plant, for instance, is GM's attempt to replicate Toyota's production system.

Intangible resources can be more difficult to imitate. This is particularly true of brand names. Brand names are important because they symbolize a company's reputation. In the heavy earthmoving equipment industry, for example, the Caterpillar brand name is synonymous with high quality and superior after-sales service and support. Similarly, the St. Michael's brand name used by Marks & Spencer, Britain's largest retailer and one of the world's most profitable, symbolizes high-quality but reasonably priced clothing. Customers will often display a preference for the products of such companies because the brand name is an important guarantee of high quality. Although competitors might like to imitate well-established brand names, the law prohibits them from doing so.

Marketing and technological know-how are also important intangible resources. Unlike brand names, however, company-specific marketing and technological know-how can be relatively easy to imitate. In the case of marketing know-how, the movement of skilled marketing personnel between companies may facilitate the general dissemination of know-how. For example, in the 1970s, Ford was acknowledged as the best marketer among the big three U.S. auto companies. In 1979, it lost a lot of its marketing know-how to Chrysler when its most successful marketer, Lee Iacocca, joined Chrysler. Iacocca subsequently hired many of Ford's top marketing people to work with him at Chrysler. More generally, successful marketing strategies are relatively easy to imitate because they are so visible to competitors. Thus, Coca-Cola quickly imitated PepsiCo's Diet Pepsi brand with the introduction of its own brand, Diet Coke.

With regard to technological know-how, in theory the patent system should make technological know-how relatively immune to imitation. Patents give the inventor of a new product a twenty-year exclusive production agreement. Thus, for example, the biotechnology company Immunex discovered and patented a biological product that treats rheumatoid arthritis. Known as Enbrel, this product is capable of halting the disease-causing mechanism that leads to rheumatoid arthritis, whereas all prior treatments simply provided patients with some relief from the symptoms of the illness. Approved by the FDA in 1998, this product racked up sales of more than $400 million in its first year on the market and may ultimately generate revenues of $2 billion per year for Immunex. Despite the enormous market potential here, Immunex's patent stops potential competitors from introducing their own version of Enbrel. Many other inventions, however, are not as easily protected from imitation by the patent system as are biological products. In electrical and computer engineering, for instance, it is often possible to "invent around" patents. One study found that 60 percent of patented innovations were successfully invented around in four years.[26] This statistic suggests that, in general, distinctive competencies based on technological know-how can be relatively short-lived.

Imitating Capabilities Imitating a company's capabilities tends to be more difficult than imitating its tangible and intangible resources, chiefly because a company's capabilities are often invisible to outsiders. Since capabilities are based on the way decisions are made and processes managed deep within a company, by definition it is hard for outsiders to discern them. Thus, for example, outsiders may have trouble identifying precisely why 3M is so successful at developing new products, why Nucor is such an efficient steel producer, or why Cisco is able to stay at the cutting edge of the market for network equipment.

On its own, the invisible nature of capabilities would not be enough to halt imitation. In theory, competitors could still gain insights into how a company operates by hiring people away from that company. However, a company's capabilities rarely reside in a single individual. Rather, they are the product of how numerous individuals interact within a unique organizational setting. It is possible that no one individual within a company may be familiar with the totality of a company's internal operating routines and procedures. In such cases, hiring people away from a successful company in order to imitate its key capabilities may not be helpful.

Consider a football team. Its success is the product not of any one individual but of the way individuals work together as a team and the unwritten or tacit understanding between them. Therefore, the transfer of a star player from a winning to a losing team may not be enough to improve the performance of the losing team. However, suppose you buy the whole team. This is what almost happened in 1993 to the German subsidiary of General Motors. It had to obtain an injunction from the German government to prevent Ignacio Lopez de Arriortua, the former GM vice president of operations and the new CEO of Volkswagen, from poaching forty of GM's managers by offering them very high salaries. His intent was to take all the managers who were expert in low-cost production to Volkswagen, which is desperately trying to reduce its costs to compete with the Japanese. Clearly, he was trying to imitate GM's new-found competency in efficiency by buying GM's capabilities through buying its managers.

To sum up, since resources are easier to imitate than capabilities, a distinctive competency based on a company's unique capabilities is probably more durable (less imitable) than one based on its resources. It is more likely to form the foundation for a long-run competitive advantage.

Capability of Competitors

According to work by Pankaj Ghemawat, a major determinant of the capability of competitors to rapidly imitate a company's competitive advantage is the nature of the competitors' prior strategic commitments.[26] By **strategic commitment**, Ghemawat means a company's commitment to a particular way of doing business—that is, to developing a particular set of resources and capabilities. Ghemawat's point is that once a company has made a strategic commitment it will find it difficult to respond to new competition if doing so requires a break with this commitment. Therefore, when competitors already have long-established commitments to a particular way of doing business, they may be slow to imitate an innovating company's competitive advantage. Its competitive advantage will thus be relatively durable.

The U.S. automobile industry offers an example. From 1945 to 1975, the industry was dominated by the stable oligopoly of General Motors, Ford, and Chrysler, all of whom geared their operations to the production of large cars—which was what American consumers demanded at the time. When the market shifted from large cars to small, fuel-efficient ones during the late 1970s, U.S. companies lacked the resources and capabilities required to produce these cars. Their prior commitments had built the wrong kind of skills for this new environment. As a result, foreign producers, and particularly the Japanese, stepped into the market breach by providing compact, fuel-efficient, high-quality, and low-cost cars. The failure of U.S. auto manufacturers to react quickly to the distinctive competency of Japanese auto companies gave the latter time to build a strong market position and brand loyalty, which subsequently proved difficult to attack.

Another determinant of the ability of competitors to respond to a company's competitive advantage is their **absorptive capacity**[27]—that is, the ability of an enterprise to identify, value, assimilate and utilize new knowledge. For example, in the 1960s and 1970s, Toyota developed a competitive advantage based on its innovation of lean production systems. Competitors such as General Motors were slow to imitate this innovation, primarily because they lacked the necessary absorptive capacity. General Motors was such a bureaucratic and inward-looking organization that it was very difficult for the company to identify, value, assimilate, and utilize the knowledge underlying lean production systems. Indeed, long after General Motors had identified and understood the importance of lean production systems, the company was still struggling to assimilate and utilize that new knowledge. Put differently, internal inertia can make it difficult for established competitors to respond to a rival whose competitive advantage is based on new products or internal processes—that is, on innovation.

Taken together, factors such as existing strategic commitments and low absorptive capacity limit the ability of established competitors to imitate the competitive advantage of a rival, particularly when that competitive advantage derives from innovative products or processes. This is why, when innovations reshape the rules of competition in an industry, value often migrates away from established competitors and toward new enterprises that are operating with new business models.

Industry Dynamism

A dynamic industry environment is one that is changing rapidly. We examined the factors that determine the dynamism and intensity of competition in an industry in Chapter 3 when we discussed the external environment. The most dynamic industries tend to be those with a very high rate of product innovation—for instance, the consumer electronics industry and the personal computer industry. In dynamic industries, the rapid rate of innovation means that product life cycles are shortening and that competitive advantage can be very transitory. A company that has a competitive advantage today may find its market position outflanked tomorrow by a rival's innovation.

In the personal computer industry, for example, the rapid increase in computing power during the last two decades has contributed to a high degree of innovation and a turbulent environment. Reflecting the persistence of innovation, in the late 1970s and early 1980s Apple Computer had an industrywide competitive advantage due to its innovation. In 1981, IBM seized the advantage with its introduction of its first personal computer. By the mid 1980s, however, IBM had lost its competitive advantage to high-power "clone" manufacturers such as Compaq, which had beaten IBM in the race to introduce a computer based on Intel's 386 chip. In turn, in the 1990s Compaq subsequently lost its competitive advantage to companies such as Dell and Gateway, which pioneered new low-cost ways of delivering computers to consumers utilizing the Internet as a direct selling device.

Summary

The durability of a company's competitive advantage depends on three factors: the height of barriers to imitation, the capability of competitors to imitate its innovation, and the general level of dynamism in the industry environment. When barriers to imitation are low, capable competitors abound, and the environment is very dynamic, with innovations being developed all the time, then competitive advantage is likely to be transitory. On the other hand, even within such industries, companies can achieve a more enduring competitive advantage if they are able to make investments that build barriers to imitation. During the 1980s, Apple Computer built a competitive advantage based on the combination of a proprietary disk operating system and an intangible product image (as noted earlier, intangible resources are difficult to imitate). The resulting brand loyalty enabled Apple to carve out a fairly secure niche in an industry where competitive advantage has otherwise proved to be very fleeting. However, by the mid 1990s, its strategy had been imitated, primarily due to the introduction of Microsoft's Windows operating system, which imitated most of the features that had enabled Apple to build brand loyalty. As a result, by 1996 Apple was in financial trouble, providing yet another example that no competitive advantage lasts forever. Ultimately, anything can be imitated. (Interestingly enough, though, Apple has shown remarkable resilience. In the late 1990s, it clawed its way back from the brink of bankruptcy to once again establish a viable position within its niche).

WHY DO COMPANIES FAIL?

In this section, we take the issue of why a company might lose its competitive advantage one step further and ask, Why do companies fail? We define a failing company as one whose profit rate is substantially lower than the average profit rate of its competitors. A company can lose its competitive advantage but still not fail. It may just earn average profits. Failure implies something more drastic. Failing companies typically earn low or negative profits; in other words, they are at a competitive disadvantage.

The question is particularly pertinent since some of the most successful companies of the twentieth century have at times seen their competitive position deteriorate. Companies such as IBM, General Motors, American Express, Digital Equipment, and Compaq Computer, all at one time held up as examples of managerial excellence, have gone through periods of poor financial performance, when they clearly lacked any competitive advantage. We explore three related reasons for failure: inertia, prior strategic commitments, and the Icarus paradox.

Inertia

The inertia argument says that companies find it difficult to change their strategies and structures in order to adapt to changing competitive conditions.[28] IBM is a classic example of this problem. For thirty years, it was viewed as the world's most successful computer company. Then, in the space of a few short years, its success turned into a disaster, with a loss of $5 billion in 1992 leading to layoffs of more than 100,000 employees. IBM's troubles were caused by a dramatic decline in the cost of computing power as a result of innovations in microprocessors. With the advent of powerful low-cost microprocessors, the locus of the computer market shifted from mainframes to small, low-priced personal computers. This left IBM's huge mainframe operations with a diminished market. Even though IBM had, and still has, a significant presence in the personal computer market, it had failed to shift the focus of its efforts away from mainframes and toward personal computers. This failure meant deep trouble for one of the most successful companies of the twentieth century (although IBM has now executed a successful turnaround, primarily by repositioning the company as a provider of e-commerce infrastructure and solutions).

Why do companies find it so difficult to adapt to new environmental conditions? One factor that seems to stand out is the role of an organization's capabilities in causing inertia. Earlier in the chapter, we argue that organizational capabilities can be a source of competitive advantage; their downside, however, is that they are difficult to change. Recall that capabilities are the way a company makes decisions and manages its processes. IBM always emphasized close coordination between different operating units and favored decision processes that stressed consensus among interdependent operating units as a prerequisite for a decision to go forward.[29] This capability was a source of advantage for IBM during the 1970s, when coordination among its worldwide operating units was necessary in order to develop, manufacture, and sell complex mainframes. But the slow-moving bureaucracy that it had spawned was a source of failure in the 1990s, when organizations had to adapt readily to rapid environmental change.

Capabilities are difficult to change because a certain distribution of power and influence is embedded within the established decision-making and management processes of an organization. Those who play key roles in a decision-making process clearly have more power. It follows that changing the established capabilities of an organization means changing its existing distribution of power and influence, and those whose power and influence would diminish resist such change. Proposals for change trigger turf battles. The power struggle and the political resistance associated with trying to alter the way in which an organization makes decisions and manages its process—that is, trying to change its capabilities—bring on inertia. This is not to say that companies cannot change. However, because change is so often resisted by those who feel threatened by it, in most cases change has to be induced by a crisis. By then the company may already be failing, as happened at IBM.

Prior Strategic Commitments

Ghemawat has argued that a company's prior strategic commitments not only limit its ability to imitate rivals, but may also cause competitive disadvantage.[30] IBM, for instance, had made major investments in the mainframe computer business. As a result, when the market shifted, it was stuck with significant resources that were specialized to that particular business. The company had manufacturing facilities geared to the production of mainframes, research organizations that were similarly specialized, and a mainframe sales force. Since these resources were not well suited to the newly emerging personal computer business, IBM's difficulties in the early 1990s were in a sense inevitable. Its prior strategic commitments locked IBM into a business that was shrinking. Shedding these resources was bound to cause hardship for all organization stakeholders.

The Icarus Paradox

In his book, Danny Miller has postulated that the roots of competitive failure can be found in what he termed the Icarus paradox.[31] Icarus is a figure in Greek mythology who used a pair of wings—made for him by his father—to escape from an island where he was being held prisoner. He flew so well that he went higher and higher, ever closer to the sun, until the heat of the sun melted the wax that held his wings together and he plunged to his death in the Aegean Sea. The paradox is that his greatest asset, his ability to fly, caused his demise. Miller argues that the same paradox applies to many once successful companies. According to Miller, many companies become so dazzled by their early success that they believe more of the same type of effort is the way to future success. As a result, however, a company can become so specialized and inner-directed that it loses sight of market realities and the fundamental requirements for achieving a competitive advantage. Sooner or later this leads to failure.

Miller identifies four major categories among the rising and falling companies. The "craftsmen," such as Texas Instruments and Digital Equipment Corporation

4.6 STRATEGY *in* ACTION

The Road to Ruin at DEC

DEC's original success was founded on the minicomputer, a cheaper more flexible version of its mainframe cousins that Ken Olson and his brilliant team of engineers invented in the 1960s. Olson and his staff improved their original minis until they could not be surpassed in quality and reliability. In the 1970s, their VAX series of minicomputers was widely regarded as the most reliable computers ever produced. DEC was rewarded by high profit rates and rapid growth. By 1990, DEC was number twenty-seven on the *Fortune 500* list of the largest corporations in America.

However, buoyed up by its own success, DEC turned into an engineering monoculture. Its engineers became idols; its marketing and accounting staff were barely tolerated. Component specifications and design standards were all that senior managers understood. Technological fine-tuning became such an obsession that the needs of customers for smaller, more economical, user-friendly computers were ignored. For example, DEC's personal computers bombed because they were so out of touch with the needs of consumers. The company also failed to respond to the threat to its core market presented by the rise of computer workstations and client/server architecture. Indeed, Ken Olson was known for dismissing such new products. He once remarked, "We always say that customers are right, but they are not always right." That may be so, but DEC, blinded by its own early success, failed to remain responsive to its customers and to changing market conditions.

By the early 1990s, DEC was a company in deep trouble. Olson was forced out in July 1992, and the company lost billions of dollars between 1992 and 1995. It returned to profitability in 1996, primarily because of the success of a turnaround strategy aimed at re-orientating the company to serve precisely those areas that Olson had dismissed. In 1998, the company was acquired by Compaq Computer.[32]

(DEC) achieved early success through engineering excellence. But then the companies became so obsessed with engineering details that they lost sight of market realities. (The story of DEC's demise is summarized in Strategy in Action 4.6.) Then there are the "builders," for instance, Gulf & Western and ITT. Having built successful, moderately diversified companies, they then became so enchanted with diversification for its own sake that they continued to diversify far beyond the point at which it was profitable to do so. Miller's third group are the "pioneers," such as Wang Labs. Enamored of their own originally brilliant innovations they continued to search for additional brilliant innovations, but ended up producing novel but completely useless products. The final category comprises the "salesmen," exemplified by Procter & Gamble and Chrysler. They became so convinced of their ability to sell anything that they paid scant attention to product development and manufacturing excellence and as a result spawned a proliferation of bland, inferior products.

AVOIDING FAILURE AND SUSTAINING COMPETITIVE ADVANTAGE

How can a company avoid the traps that have snared so many once successful companies? How can it build a sustainable competitive advantage? We do not give a complete answer here as much of the remaining text deals with these issues. However, a number of key points can be made at this juncture.

Focus on the Building Blocks of Competitive Advantage

First, maintaining a competitive advantage requires a company to continue focusing on the four generic building blocks of competitive advantage—efficiency, quality, innovation, and customer responsiveness—and to develop distinctive competencies that contribute to superior performance in these areas. One of the messages of Miller's Icarus paradox is that many successful companies become unbalanced in their pursuit of distinctive competencies. DEC, for example, focused on engineering quality at the expense of almost everything else, including, most importantly, customer responsiveness. Other companies forget to focus on any distinctive competency. This was certainly the case at ITT, where an empire-building CEO, Harold Geneen, focused on diversification but lost sight of the need to focus on achieving excellence in efficiency, quality, innovation, and customer responsiveness at the level of business units within ITT.

Institute Continuous Improvement and Learning

The only constant in the world is change. Today's source of competitive advantage may soon be rapidly imitated by capable competitors, or it may be made obsolete by the innovations of a rival. In such a dynamic and fast-paced environment, the only way that a company can maintain a competitive advantage over time is to continually improve its efficiency, quality, innovation, and customer responsiveness. The way to do so is to recognize the importance of learning within the organization.[33] The most successful companies are not those that stand still, resting on their laurels. They are those that continually seek out ways of improving their operations and, in the process, are constantly upgrading the value of their distinctive competencies or creating new competencies. Companies such as General Electric and Toyota have a reputation for being learning organizations. What this means is that they are continually analyzing the processes that underlie their efficiency, quality, innovation, and customer responsiveness. Their objective is to learn from prior mistakes and to seek out ways to improve their processes over time. This has enabled Toyota, for example, to continually upgrade its employee productivity and product quality, allowing the company to stay one step ahead of imitators.

Track Best Industrial Practice and Use Benchmarking

One of the best ways to develop distinctive competencies that contribute to superior efficiency, quality, innovation, and customer responsiveness is to identify **best industrial practice** and to adopt it. Only by so doing will a company be able to build and maintain the resources and capabilities that underpin excellence in efficiency, quality, innovation, and customer responsiveness. What constitutes best industrial practice is an issue we discuss in some depth in Chapter 5. However, it requires tracking the practice of other companies, and perhaps the best way to do so is through **benchmarking**. This is the process of measuring the company against the products, practices, and services of some of its most efficient global competitors. For example, when Xerox was in trouble in the early 1980s, it decided to institute a policy of benchmarking as a means of identifying ways to improve the efficiency of its operations. Xerox benchmarked L.L. Bean for distribution procedures, Deere & Company for central computer operations, Procter & Gamble for marketing, and Florida Power & Light for total quality management processes. By the early 1990s, Xerox was benchmarking 240 functions against comparable areas in other companies. This process has been credited with helping Xerox dramatically improve the efficiency of its operations.[34]

Overcome Inertia

A further reason for failure is an inability to adapt to changing conditions because of organizational inertia. Overcoming the barriers to change within an organization is one of the key requirements for maintaining a competitive advantage, and we devote a whole chapter, Chapter 14, to this issue. Suffice it to say here that identifying barriers to change is an important first step. Once this step has been taken, implementing change requires good leadership, the judicious use of power, and appropriate changes in organizational structure and control systems. All these issues are discussed later in the book.

SUMMARY OF CHAPTER

The principal objective of this chapter is to identify the basis of competitive advantage by examining why, within a given industry, some companies outperform others. Competitive advantage is the product of at least one of the following: superior efficiency, superior quality, superior innovation, and superior customer responsiveness. Achieving superiority here requires that a company develop appropriate distinctive competencies, which in turn are a product of the kind of resources and capabilities that a company possesses. The chapter also examines issues related to the durability of competitive advantage. This durability is determined by the height of barriers to imitation, the capability of competitors to imitate a company's advantage, and the general level of environmental turbulence. Finally, the discussion of why companies fail and what they can do to avoid failure indicates that failure is due to factors such as organizational inertia, prior strategic commitments, and the Icarus paradox. Avoiding failure requires that a company constantly try to upgrade its distinctive competencies in accordance with best industrial practice and that it take steps to overcome organizational inertia. The main points made in this chapter can be summarized as follows:

- ✔ The source of a competitive advantage is superior value creation.
- ✔ To create superior value, a company must lower its costs, differentiate its product so that it can charge a higher price, or do both simultaneously.
- ✔ The four generic building blocks of competitive advantage are efficiency, quality, innovation, and customer responsiveness.
- ✔ Superior efficiency enables a company to lower its costs; superior quality allows it both to charge a higher price and to lower its costs; and superior customer service lets it charge a higher price. Superior innovation can lead to higher prices, particularly in the case of product innovations; or it can lead to lower unit costs, particularly in the case of process innovations.
- ✔ Distinctive competencies are the unique strengths of a company. Valuable distinctive competencies enable a company to earn a profit rate that is above the industry average.
- ✔ The distinctive competencies of an organization arise from its resources and capabilities.
- ✔ Resources refer to the financial, physical, human, technological, and organizational assets of a company.
- ✔ Capabilities refer to a company's skills at coordinating resources and putting them to productive use.
- ✔ In order to achieve a competitive advantage, companies need to pursue strategies that build on the existing resources and capabilities of an organization (its competencies), and they need to formu-

late strategies that build additional resources and capabilities (develop new competencies).

- The durability of a company's competitive advantage depends on the height of barriers to imitation, the capability of competitors, and environmental dynamism.
- Failing companies typically earn low or negative profits. Three factors seem to contribute to failure—organizational inertia in the face of environmental change, the nature of a company's prior strategic commitments, and the Icarus paradox.
- Avoiding failure requires a constant focus on the basic building blocks of competitive advantage, continuous improvement, identification and adoption of best industrial practice, and victory over inertia.

DISCUSSION QUESTIONS

1. What are the main implications of the material discussed in this chapter for strategy formulation?
2. When is a company's competitive advantage most likely to endure over time?
3. Which is more important in explaining the success and failure of companies, strategizing or luck?

Practicing Strategic Management

SMALL-GROUP EXERCISE
Analyzing Competitive Advantage

Break up into groups of three to five people. Drawing on the concepts introduced in this case, analyze the competitive position of your business school in the market for business education. Then answer the following questions:

1. Does your business school have a competitive advantage?
2. If so, on what is this advantage based and is this advantage sustainable?
3. If your school does not have a competitive advantage in the market for business education, identify the inhibiting factors that are holding it back.
4. How might the Internet change the way in which business education is delivered?
5. Does the Internet pose a threat to the competitive position of your school in the market for business education, or is it an opportunity for your school to enhance its competitive position? (Note: it can be both.)

ARTICLE FILE 4

Find an example of a company that has sustained its competitive advantage for more than ten years. Identify the source of the competitive advantage and describe why it has lasted so long.

STRATEGIC MANAGEMENT PROJECT
Module 4

This module deals with the competitive position of your company. With the information you have at your disposal, perform the tasks and answer the questions listed:

1. Identify whether your company has a competitive advantage or disadvantage in its primary industry. (Its primary industry is the one in which it has the most sales.)
2. Evaluate your company against the four generic building blocks of competitive advantage: efficiency, quality, innovation, and customer responsiveness. How does this exercise help you understand the performance of your company relative to its competitors?
3. What are the distinctive competencies of your company?
4. What role have prior strategies played in shaping the distinctive competencies of your company? What role has luck played?
5. Do the strategies currently pursued by your company build on its distinctive competencies? Are they an attempt to build new competencies?
6. What are the barriers to imitating the distinctive competencies of your company?
7. Is there any evidence that your company finds it difficult to adapt to changing industry conditions? If so, why do you think this is the case?

EXPLORING THE WEB
Visiting Johnson & Johnson

Visit the Web site of Johnson & Johnson (http://www.jnj.com). Read through the material contained on the site, paying particular attention to the features on the company's history, its credo, innovations, and company news. On the basis of this information, answer the following questions:

1. Do you think that Johnson & Johnson has a distinctive competency?
2. What is the nature of this competency? How does it help the company attain a competitive advantage?
3. What are the resources and capabilities that underlie this competency? Where do these resources and capabilities come from?
4. How imitable is Johnson & Johnson's distinctive competency?

Search the Web for a company site that goes into depth about the history, products, and competitive position of that company. On the basis of the information you collect, answer the following questions.

1. Does the company have a distinctive competency?
2. What is the nature of this competency? How does it help the company attain a competitive advantage?
3. What are the resources and capabilities that underlie this competency? Where do these resources and capabilities come from?
4. How imitable is the company's distinctive competency?

CLOSING CASE

Marks & Spencer

MARKS & SPENCER (M&S) is a British retailing institution. Founded in 1884 by Michael Marks, a Polish Jew who had emigrated to England, the company has been a national chain since the early 1900s. By 1926, the company had a branch in every major town in the country and had become Britain's largest retailer, a position it still holds in 2000. Primarily a supplier of clothing and foodstuffs, M&S is one of the world's most profitable retailers. In 1999, M&S's 300 United Kingdom stores had sales of over 7 billion pounds sterling, accounted for 15 percent of all retail clothing sales in the United Kingdom and 5 percent of all food sales. According to the *Guinness Book of Records,* in 1991 the company's flagship store at Marble Arch in London had a turnover of $3,700 per square foot—more than any other department store in the world.

M&S provides a selective range of clothing and food items aimed at rapid turnover. The firm sells all its products under its own St. Michael's label. M&S offers high-quality products at moderate rather than low prices. This combination of high quality and reasonable price encourages customers to associate M&S with value for money, and the firm's ability to deliver this combination consistently over the years has built up enormous customer goodwill in Britain. So strong is M&S's reputation among British consumers that the company does no advertising in that market.

To achieve the combination of moderate prices and high quality, M&S works very closely with its suppliers, many of whom have been selling a major portion of their output to M&S for generations. The focus on quality is reinforced by M&S's practice of having its technical people work closely with suppliers on product design. Suppliers are more than willing to respond to the firm's demands, for they know that M&S is loyal to its suppliers and as it grows so do they. The sales volume generated by M&S's strategy of providing only a selective range of clothing and food enables M&S's suppliers to realize substantial economies of scale from large production runs. These cost savings are then passed on to M&S in the form of lower prices. In turn, M&S passes on part of the savings to the consumer.

Crucial to M&S's effectiveness is a clear focus on the customer. The tone is set by top management. Each senior manager makes a habit of wearing M&S clothes and eating M&S food. Thus, managers develop an understanding of what it is that customers want and like about M&S products; by staying close to the customer, they can improve the quality and design of the products they offer. The customer focus is reinforced at the store level by store managers who monitor sales volume and quickly identify lines that are selling and those that are not. Then store managers can transmit this information to suppliers, which have the capacity to quickly modify their production, increasing the output of lines that are selling well and reducing the output of lines that are not moving.

Another central feature of M&S is its pioneering approach to human relations. Long before it became fashionable to do so, M&S had developed a commitment to the well-being of its employees. M&S has always viewed itself as a family business with a broad responsibility for the welfare of its employees. It offers employees medical and pension plans that provide benefits that are well above the industry average. The company pays its employees at a rate that is also well above the industry average, and it makes a practice of promoting employees from within, rather than hiring from outside. Furthermore, there are a series of in-store amenities for employees, including subsidized cafeterias, medical services, recreation rooms, and hairdressing salons. The reward for M&S is the trust and loyalty of its employees and, ultimately, high employee productivity.

Just as vital is the company's commitment to simplifying its operating structure and strategic control systems.

CLOSING CASE *(continued)*

M&S has a very flat hierarchy; there is little in the way of intervening management layers between store managers and top management. The firm utilizes just two profit margins, one for foodstuff and one for clothing. This practice reduces bureaucracy and frees its store managers from worrying about pricing issues. Instead, they are encouraged to focus on maximizing sales volume. A store's performance is assessed by its sales volume. Control is achieved partly through formal budgetary procedures and partly through an informal probing process, in which top management drops in unannounced at stores and quizzes managers there about the store. In a typical year, just about every store in Britain will receive at least one unannounced visit from top management. This keeps store managers on their toes and constantly alert to the need to provide the kind of value-for-money products that customers have come to associate with M&S.[35]

Case Discussion Questions

1. What do you think is the source of Marks & Spencer's competitive advantage?
2. Marks & Spencer has managed to maintain its competitive advantage in British retailing for more than fifty years. Why, do you think, have rival firms found Marks & Spencer's competitive position so difficult to attack?

End Notes

1. "Cisco @ speed," *Economist*, June 26, 1999, Special report: Business and the Internet, p. 12; S. Tully, "How Cisco Mastered the Net," *Fortune*, August 17, 1997, p. 207–210; C. Kano, The Real King of the Internet, *Fortune*, September 7, 1998, 82–93.
2. The concept of consumer surplus is an important one in economics. For a more detailed exposition, see D. Besanko, D. Dranove, and M. Shanley. *Economics of Strategy* (New York: John Wiley, 1996).
3. The data is taken from the Value Line Investment Survey. The average ROK is the average of all 17 department stores followed continuously by Value Line over this time period.
4. However, $P = V$ only in the special case where the company has a perfect monopoly and where it can charge each customer a unique price that reflects the value of the product to that customer (i.e., where perfect price discrimination is possible). More generally, except in the limiting case of perfect price discrimination, even a monopolist will see most consumers capture some of the value of a product in the form of a consumer surplus.
5. This point is central to the work of Michael Porter. See M. E. Porter, *Competitive Advantage* (New York: Free Press, 1985). See also Chapter 4 in P. Ghemawat, *Commitment: The Dynamic of Strategy* (New York: Free Press, 1991).
6. M. E. Porter, *Competitive Strategy* (New York: Free Press, 1980).
7. D. Lavin, "Chrysler Is Now Low-Cost Producer in the Automobile Industry," *Wall Street Journal*, June 23, 1994, p. B5; N. Templin, "The Auto Trade Fight," *Wall Street Journal*, May 18, 1995, p. A6; W. M. Bulkeley, "Pushing the Pace," *Wall Street Journal*, December 23, 1994, p. A1; D. Levin. "GM Would Have to Cut 20,000 Workers to Match Ford," *Wall Street Journal*, June 24, 1994, p. C22; The Harbor Report. Harbor & Associates, 1999.
8. See D. Garvin, "What Does Product Quality Really Mean," *Sloan Management Review*, 26 (Fall 1984), 25–44; P. B. Crosby, *Quality Is Free* (Mentor, 1980); and A. Gabor, *The Man Who Discovered Quality* (Times Books, 1990).
9. G. Bethune, "From Worst to First," *Fortune*, May 25, 1998, pp. 185–190.
10. W. Chan Kim and R. Mauborgne, "Value Innovation: The Strategic Logic of High Growth," *Harvard Business Review* (January-February 1997), 102–115.
11. G. Stalk and T. M. Hout, *Competing Against Time* (New York: Free Press, 1990).
12. Ibid
13. M. E. Porter, *Competitive Advantage*.
14. R. Langreth, "High Anxiety: Rivals Threaten Prozac's Reign," *Wall Street Journal*, May 9, 1996, pp. B1–B2.
15. M. Cusumano, *The Japanese Automobile Industry* (Cambridge, Mass.: Harvard University Press, 1989).
16. The material in this section relies on the so-called resource-based view of the firm. For summaries of this perspective, see J. B. Barney, "Firm Resources and Sustained Competitive Advantage," *Journal of Management*, 17 (1991), 99–120; J. T. Mahoney and J. R. Pandian, "The Resource-Based View Within the Conversation of Strategic Management," *Strategic Management Journal*, 13 (1992), 63–380; R. Amit and P. J. H. Schoemaker, "Strategic Assets and Organizational Rent," *Strategic Management Journal*, 14 (1993), 33–46; M. A. Peteraf, "The Cornerstones of Competitive Advantage: A Resource-Based View," *Strategic Management Journal*, 14 (1993), 179–191; and B. Wernerfelt, "A Resource Based View of the Firm," *Strategic Management Journal*, 5 (1994), 171–180.
17. For a discussion of organizational capabilities, see R. R. Nelson and S. Winter, *An Evolutionary Theory of Economic Change* (Cambridge, Mass.: Belknap Press, 1982).
18. R. M. Grant, *Contemporary Strategic Analysis* (Cambridge, Mass.: Blackwell, 1991). See also Chan Kim and Mauborgne, "Value Innovation," pp. 102–115.
19. "Disney's Magic," *Business Week*, March 9, 1987; "Michael Eisner's Hit Parade," *Business Week* , February 1, 1988.
20. D. Kearns, "Leadership Through Quality," *Academy of Management Executive*, 4 (1990), 86–89; J. Sheridan, "America's Best Plants," *Industry Week*, October 15, 1990, pp. 27–40.
21. The classic statement of this position was made by A. A. Alchain, "Uncertainty, Evolution, and Economic Theory," *Journal of Political Economy*, 84 (1950), 488–500.
22. S. Manes and P. Andrews, *Gates* (New York: Simon & Schuster, 1993).
23. This is the nature of the competitive process. For more details see C. W. L. Hill and D. Deeds, "The Importance of Industry Structure for the Determination of Firm Profitability: A Neo-Austrian Perspective," *Journal of Management Studies*, 33, 1996, p. 429–452.
24. Like resources and capabilities, the concept of barriers to imitation is also grounded in the resource-based view of the firm. For details, see R. Reed and R. J. DeFillippi, "Causal Ambiguity, Barriers to Imitation, and Sustainable Competitive Advantage," *Academy of Management Review*, 15 (1990), 88–102.
25. E. Mansfield, "How Economists See R&D," *Harvard Business Review* (November–December 1981), 98–106.
26. P. Ghemawat, *Commitment: The Dynamic of Strategy* (New York: Free Press, 1991).
27. W. M. Cohen and D. A. Levinthal, "Absorptive Capacity: a New Perspective on Learning and Innovation," *Administrative Science Quarterly*, 35 (1990), 128–152.
28. M. T. Hannah and J. Freeman, "Structural Inertia and Organizational Change," *American Sociological Review*, 49 (1984), 149–164.
29. See "IBM Corporation," *Harvard Business School Case* No. 180-034, 1985.
30. Ghemawat, *Commitment.*

31. D. Miller, *The Icarus Paradox* (New York: HarperBusiness, 1990).
32. Ibid. Also P. D. Llosa, "We Must Know What We Are Doing," *Fortune*, November 14, 1994, p. 68.
33. P. M. Senge, *The Fifth Discipline: The Art and Practice of the Learning Organization* (New York: Doubleday, 1990).
34. D. Kearns, "Leadership Through Quality," pp. 86–89.
35. J. Thornhill, "A European Spark for Marks," *Financial Times*, July 13, 1992, p. 8; Marks & Spencer, Ltd. (A)," *Harvard Business School Case* No. 91-392-089, 1991; J. Marcom, "Blue Blazers and Guacamole," *Forbes*, November 25, 1991, pp. 64–68; M. Evans, "Marks & Spencer Battles On," *Financial Post*, December 11, 1989, p. 32.

PART THREE

Strategies

5 Building Competitive Advantage Through Functional-Level Strategy

OPENING CASE

Levi's Original Spin

LEVI STRAUSS is an American icon. For two generations, it has dressed the world in its fabled blue jeans. In recent years, however, Levi's luster has begun to fade even more rapidly than the blue dye on an old pair of 501s. The fast-moving fashion world seems to be leaving Levi's behind. In 1998, for example, Levi's sales declined by 13 percent, to $6 billion, while its share of the domestic blue jeans market fell from 16.3 percent in 1997 to 14.8 percent. Levi's problems have two sources. First, a combination of good design and savvy marketing has helped competitors such as The Gap take share from Levi's. Second, Levi's jeans are just too expensive. Unlike most of its competitors, which have moved the bulk of their manufacturing to Asia or central America, Levi continues to have a significant manufacturing presence in the United States. But the high cost of labor in the United States means that Levi has to charge higher prices to recoup its costs, and consumers just don't seem willing to pay a premium price for Levi's jeans anymore.

Levi's solution to this problems has been twofold. First, the company announced that it would close eleven of its twenty-two U.S. plants, laying off 5,900 domestic employees, and move manufacturing to low-cost locations. Second, in an attempt to keep its remaining eleven U.S. plants humming, the company announced that it would step up its Original Spin program to supply jeans that are custom-made for individual consumers. Levi's thinking is that if it can customize its jeans for each individual's body shape—and no two people are identical—it will be able to charge a premium price and therefore cover the costs of continuing to have a substantial manufacturing presence in the United States.

At the core of the Original Spin program is an attempt to use Web-based technology and computer-controlled production equipment to implement a strategy of mass customization that has as its goal a desire to give each customer a better-fitting pair of jeans in the customer's preferred style. The idea is that, with the help of a sales associate, customers will create the jeans they want by picking from six colors, three basic models, five different leg openings, and two types of fly. Their waist, rear, and inseam will be measured, and then they will try on a pair of plain "test-drive" jeans to make sure that they like the fit. If they do, the order will be punched into a Web-based computer terminal linked to the stitching machines in a Levi Strauss factory. Customers can even give the jeans a name—for example, "Rebel" for a pair of black jeans. At the factory, computer-controlled tools precision-cut the jeans and stitch an individual bar code inside. The jeans are then sewn and washed, identified by the code, and shipped to the customer's home. The whole process takes no more than two to three weeks. The bar code tag stores the measurements for simple reordering.

Today, a fully stocked Levi's store carries approximately 130 pairs of ready-to-wear jeans. With the Original Spin program, the number of choices available will leap to 750. Sanjay Choudhuri, Levi's director of mass customization, feels that 750 is about the right number of choices. Unlimited choice would create inefficiencies at the manufacturing plant. Levi's strategy is to offer enough choice to give the customer the illusion of infinite variety, yet make it feasible to produce the jeans with little or no additional cost penalty. Levi hopes to charge a premium price—about 20 percent higher—for this service. However, in the company's view, the real benefit of the program is that it changes the nature of the relationship between Levi Strauss and its customers from an anonymous relationship in which the customer walks out of the store with a pair of off-the-shelf jeans, to one in which Levi Strauss aims to become each customer's personal jeans adviser. If the program works, Levi might extend it to embrace several other apparel offerings, such as its Dockers line of pants for men. It may also roll out the program in international markets.

Further down the road, Levi might use a device that will scan the entire body. The machine, developed by an independent company, projects 300,000 pinpoints of light from head to toe and then photographs the body from six angles to produce a kind of three-dimensional portrait. These data result in a custom pattern that can be transmitted to a production plant to manufacture jeans, shirts, or any other item of clothing. Within five years, body-scanning equipment may be available in Levi stores.[1]

OVERVIEW

In Chapter 4, we discuss the central role played by efficiency, quality, innovation, and customer responsiveness in building and maintaining a competitive advantage. In this chapter, we consider what managers can do at the level of functions, or operations, within a company to attain superior efficiency, quality, innovation, and customer responsiveness. Functional-level strategies are strategies directed at improving the effectiveness of basic operations within a company, such as production, marketing, materials management, research and development, and human resources. Even though these strategies may be focused on a given function, as often as not they embrace two or more functions and require close cooperation among functions to attain companywide efficiency, quality, innovation, and customer responsiveness goals.

For example, the Opening Case describes how Levi Strauss is utilizing Web-based technology and computer-controlled equipment to pursue a strategy of mass customization. If successful, this innovative program will change the nature of Levi's relationship with its customers. By customizing its basic product offering to the idiosyncratic body shapes and tastes of individual customers, Levi aims to build a reputation for customer responsiveness, to gain share from its competitors, and to charge a premium price for its products.

To explore the issue of functional-level strategies further, in this chapter we look at how companies can increase their efficiency, quality, innovation, and customer responsiveness. Although in some cases we will focus on the contribution of a given function—such as production or marketing—toward attaining these goals, we will also emphasize the importance of strategies and policies that cut across functions. By the time you have finished this chapter, you should have a much clearer understanding of the actions that managers can take at the operating level to attain superior efficiency, quality, innovation, and customer responsiveness.

ACHIEVING SUPERIOR EFFICIENCY

A company is a device for transforming inputs into outputs. Inputs are basic factors of production such as labor, land, capital, management, technological know-how, and so on. Outputs are the goods and services that a company produces. The simplest measure of efficiency is the quantity of inputs that it takes to produce a given output; that is, Efficiency = outputs/inputs. The more efficient a company is, the fewer the inputs required to produce a given output and, therefore, the lower its cost structure. Put another way, an efficient company has higher productivity than its rivals and, therefore, lower costs.

We review here the various steps that companies can take at the functional level to boost their efficiency and thus lower their unit costs. After considering the primary functions of production and marketing, we move on to examine the various support functions of the enterprise. We must stress, however, that achieving superior quality plays a major role in achieving superior efficiency. We delay discussion of how to achieve superior quality until the next section.

Production and Efficiency: Economies of Scale

Economies of scale are unit-cost reductions associated with a large scale of output. One source of economies of scale is the ability to spread fixed costs over a large production volume. Fixed costs are costs that must be incurred to produce a product regardless of the level of output; they include the costs of purchasing machinery, the costs of setting up machinery for individual production runs, the costs of facilities, and the costs of advertising and R&D. For example, it is costing Microsoft approximately $1 billion to develop the next version of its Windows operating system, Windows 2000. Microsoft can realize substantial scale economies by spreading the fixed costs associated with developing a new operating system over the enormous unit-sales volume it expects for this operating system (90 percent of the world's personal computers use a Microsoft operating system). In Microsoft's case, these scale economies are even more significant due to the trivial incremental (or marginal) cost of producing additional copies of Windows 2000 (once the master copy has been produced, additional CDs containing the operating system can be produced for just a few cents).

Many high-technology companies face a similar cost structure: high fixed costs and trivial marginal costs. It costs telecommunications companies billions of dollars in infrastructure to build out their networks, but almost nothing to transmit additional signals down those networks. It costs Intel approximately $5 billion to build a new fabrication facility to produce microprocessors, but only a few cents to produce each chip. It can cost pharmaceutical companies as much as $500 million to develop a new drug, but only a few cents to produce additional units of that drug. For all of these companies, the key to their efficiency and profitability is to increase sales rapidly enough so that fixed costs can be spread out over a large unit volume, and substantial scale economies can be realized.

Another source of scale economies is the ability of companies producing in large volumes to achieve a greater division of labor and specialization. Specialization, in turn, is said to have a favorable impact on productivity, mainly because it enables employees to become very skilled at performing a particular task. The classic example of such economies is Ford's Model T automobile. The world's first mass-produced car, the Model T Ford was introduced in 1923. Until then, Ford had made cars using an expensive hand-built "craft production" method. By introducing mass-production techniques, the company achieved greater division of labor (that is, it split assembly into small, repeatable tasks) and specialization, which boosted employee productivity. Ford was also able to spread the fixed costs of developing an automobile and setting up production machinery over a large volume of output. As a result of these economies, the cost of manufacturing a car at Ford fell from $3,000 to less than $900 (in 1958 dollars).

Nor are scale economies relevant just to manufacturing enterprises such as Ford and Du Pont. Many service companies also benefit from realizing substantial scale economies. An example is given in Strategy in Action 5.1, which looks at the economies of scale realized from the merger between two large New York banks, Chemical Bank and Chase Manhattan Bank.

Some experts argue that after a certain minimum efficient scale (MES) of output is reached there are few, if any, additional scale economies to be had from expanding volume.[3] (**Minimum efficient scale** is the minimum plant size necessary to gain significant economies of scale.) In other words, as shown in Figure 5.1, the long-run unit-cost curve of a company is L-shaped. At outputs beyond MES in Figure 5.1, additional cost reductions are hard to come by. Another point worth bearing in mind is that diseconomies of scale can arise when large enterprises build up a substantial corporate bureaucracy, which increases corporate overhead without reducing unit costs.

Production and Efficiency: Learning Effects

Learning effects are cost savings that come from learning by doing. Labor, for example, learns by repetition how best to carry out a task. In other words, labor productivity increases over time, and unit costs fall as individuals learn the most efficient way to perform a particular task. Equally important, in new manufacturing facilities management typically learns over time how best to run the new operation. Hence, production costs decline because of increasing labor productivity and management efficiency.

Learning effects tend to be more significant when a technologically complex task is repeated, since there is more to learn. Thus, learning effects will be more significant in an assembly process involving 1,000 complex steps than in an assembly process involving 100 simple steps. Although learning effects are normally associated with the manufacturing process, as with economies of scale there are reasons for believing that they are just as important in many service industries. For example, one famous study of learning in the context of the health care industry found that

5.1 STRATEGY *in* ACTION

Chemical and Chase Banks Merge to Realize Scale Economies

In August 1995, two of the world's largest banks, Chemical Bank and Chase Manhattan Bank, both of New York, announced their intention to merge. The merger was officially completed on March 31, 1996. The combined bank, which goes under the Chase name, has more than $300 billion in assets, making it the largest bank in the United States and the fourth largest in the world. The new Chase is capitalized at $20 billion and is number one or two in the United States in numerous segments of the banking business, including loan syndication, trading of derivatives, currency and securities trading, global custody services, luxury auto financing, New York City retail banking, and mortgaging services.

The prime reason given for the merger was anticipated cost savings of more than $1.7 billion per year, primarily through the realization of economies of scale. The newly merged bank had good reason for thinking that these kinds of cost savings were possible. In a 1991 merger between Chemical and Manufacturers Hanover, another New York–based bank, cost savings of $750 million per year were realized by eliminating duplicated assets, such as physical facilities, information systems, and personnel.

The cost savings in the Chase-Chemical combination had several sources. First, significant economies of scale were possible by combining the 600 retail branches of the original banks. Closing excess branches and consolidating its retail business into a smaller number of branches allowed the new bank to significantly increase the capacity utilization of its retail banking network. The combined bank was able to generate the same volume of retail business from fewer branches. The fixed costs associated with retail branches—including rents, personnel, equipment, and utility costs—dropped, which translated into a substantial reduction in the unit cost required to serve the average customer.

Another source of scale-based cost savings arose from the combination of a whole array of back-office functions. For example, the combined bank now has to operate only one computer network instead of two. By getting greater utilization out of a fixed computer infrastructure—mainframe computers, servers, and the associated software—the combined bank was able to further drive down its fixed cost structure. Combining management functions also brought substantial savings. For example, the new Chase bank has doubled the number of auto loans and mortgage originations it issues, but because of office automation it can manage the increased volume with less than twice the management staff. This saving implies a big reduction in fixed costs and a corresponding fall in the unit costs of servicing the average auto loan or mortgage customer.[2]

more experienced medical providers posted significantly lower mortality rates for a number of common surgical procedures, suggesting that learning effects are at work in surgery.[4] The authors of this study used the evidence to argue for the establishment of regional referral centers for the provision of highly specialized medical care. These centers would perform many specific surgical procedures (for instance, heart surgery), replacing local facilities with lower volumes and presumably higher mortality rates.

In terms of the long-run average cost curve of a company, while economies of scale imply a movement along the curve (say from A to B in Figure 5.2), the realization of learning effects implies a downward shift of the entire curve (B to C in Figure 5.2) as both labor and management become more efficient over time at performing their tasks at each and every level of output. No matter how complex the task, however, learning effects typically die out after a limited period of time. Indeed, it has been suggested that they are really important only during the start-up period of a new process and cease after two or three years.[5]

FIGURE 5.1

A Typical Long-Run Unit-Cost Curve

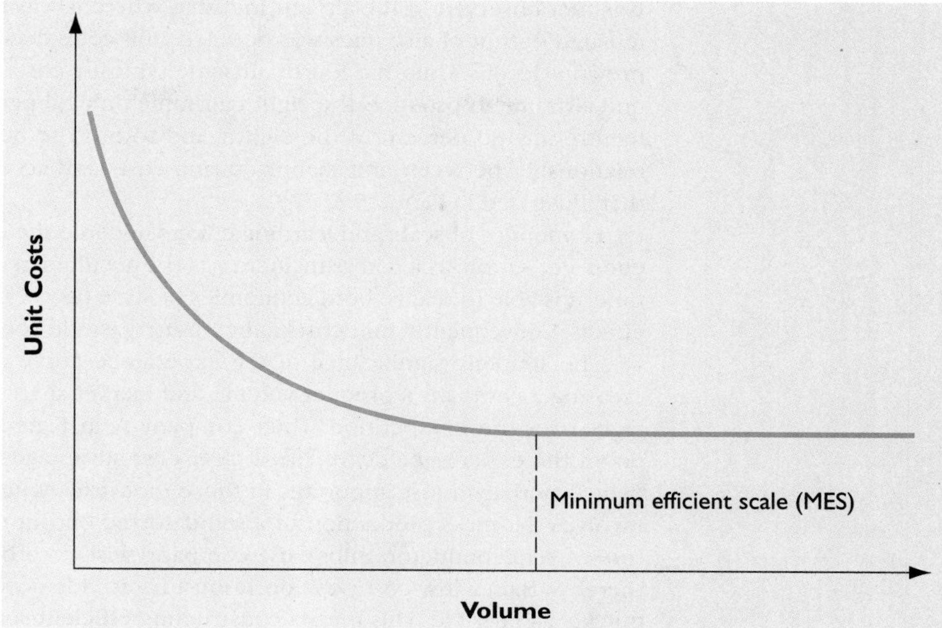

FIGURE 5.2

Economies of Scale and Learning Effects

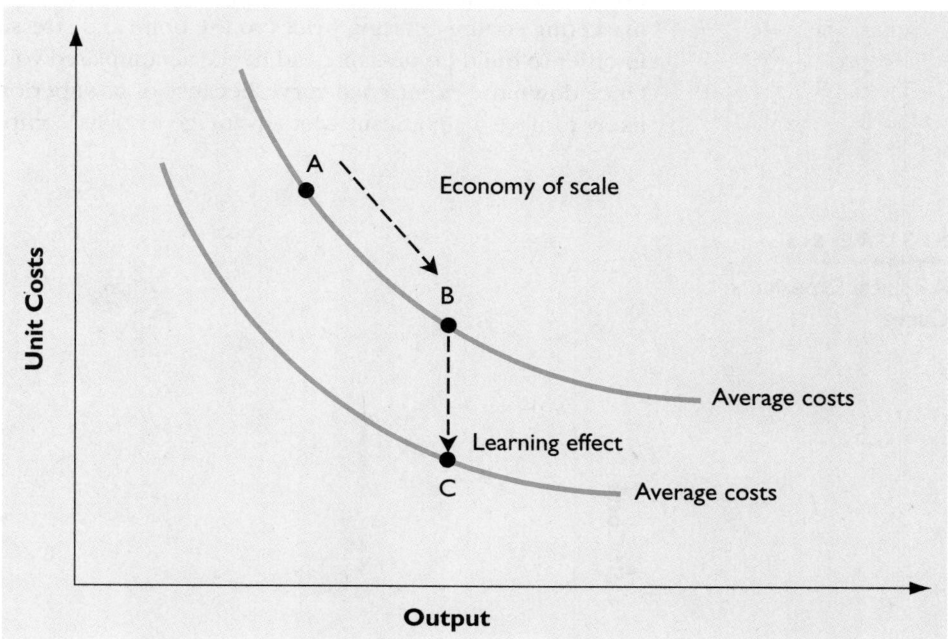

Production and Efficiency: The Experience Curve

The experience curve refers to the systematic unit-cost reductions that have been observed to occur over the life of a product.[6] According to the experience curve concept, unit manufacturing costs for a product typically decline by some characteristic amount each time accumulated output of the product is doubled (accumulated output is the total output of a product since its introduction). The relationship was first observed in the aircraft industry, where it was found that each time accumulated output of airframes was doubled, unit costs declined to 80 percent of their previous level.[7] Thus, the fourth airframe typically cost only 80 percent of the second airframe to produce, the eighth airframe only 80 percent of the fourth, the sixteenth only 80 percent of the eighth, and so on. The outcome of this process is a relationship between unit manufacturing costs and accumulated output similar to that illustrated in Figure 5.3.

Economies of scale and learning effects underlie the experience curve phenomenon. Put simply, as a company increases the accumulated volume of its output over time, it is able to realize both economies of scale (as volume increases) and learning effects. Consequently, unit costs fall with increases in accumulated output.

The strategic significance of the experience curve is clear. It suggests that increasing a company's product volume and market share will also bring cost advantages over the competition. Thus, company A in Figure 5.3, because it is further down the experience curve, has a clear cost advantage over company B. The concept is perhaps most important in those industries where the production process involves the mass production of a standardized output (for example, the manufacture of semiconductor chips). If a company wishes to become more efficient, and thereby attain a low-cost position, it must try to ride down the experience curve as quickly as possible. This means constructing efficient scale manufacturing facilities even before the company has the demand and aggressively pursuing cost reductions from learning effects. The company might also need to adopt an aggressive marketing strategy, cutting prices to the bone and stressing heavy sales promotions in order to build up demand, and hence accumulated volume, as quickly as possible. Once down the experience curve, because of its superior efficiency, the company is likely to have a significant cost advantage over its competitors. For example, it has

FIGURE 5.3

A Typical Experience Curve

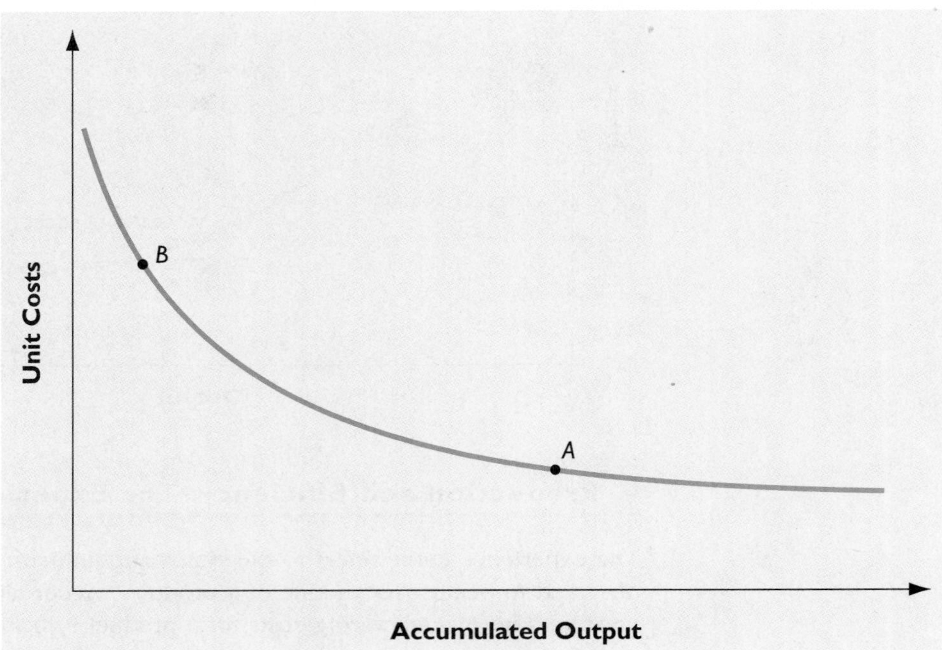

5.2 STRATEGY *in* ACTION

Too Much Experience at Texas Instruments

Texas Instruments (TI) was an early user of the experience curve concept. TI was a technological innovator, first in silicon transistors and then in semiconductors. The company discovered that with every doubling of accumulated production volume of a transistor or semiconductor, unit costs declined to 73 percent of their previous level. Building on this insight, whenever TI first produced a new transistor or semiconductor it would slash the price of the product to stimulate demand. The goal was to drive up the accumulated volume of production and so drive down costs through the realization of experience curve economies. As a result, during the 1960s and 1970s, TI hammered its competitors in transistors; then it moved on to prevail in semiconductors, and ultimately in hand-held calculators and digital watches. Indeed, for the twenty years up until 1982, TI enjoyed rapid growth, with sales quadrupling between 1977 and 1981 alone.

However, after 1982 things began to go wrong for TI. The company's single-minded focus on cost reductions, an outgrowth of its strategic reliance on the experience curve, left it with a poor understanding of consumer needs and market trends. Competitors such as Casio and Hewlett-Packard began to make major inroads into TI's hand-held calculator business by focusing on additional features that consumers demanded rather than on cost and price. TI was slow to react to this trend and lost substantial market share as a result. In the late 1970s, TI also decided to focus on semiconductors for watches and calculators, where it had gained substantial cost economies based on the experience curve, rather than develop metal-oxide semiconductors for computer memories and advanced semiconductors. As it turned out, however, with the growth in minicomputers and personal computers in the early 1980s, the market shifted toward high-power metal-oxide semiconductors. Consequently, TI soon found itself outflanked by Intel and Motorola. In sum, TI's focus on realizing experience curve economies initially benefited the company, but then it seems to have contributed toward a myopia that was to cost the company dearly.[9]

been argued that the early success of Texas Instruments was based on exploiting the experience curve (see Strategy in Action 5.2 for details); that Intel uses such tactics to ride down the experience curve and gain a competitive advantage over its rivals in the market for microprocessors; and that one reason Matsushita came to dominate the global market for VHS videotape recorders is that it based its strategy on the experience curve.[8]

However, the company farthest down the experience curve must not become complacent about its cost advantage. As Strategy in Action 5.2 points out, an obsession with the experience curve at Texas Instruments may have harmed the company. More generally, there are three reasons why companies should not become complacent about their efficiency-based cost advantages derived from experience effects. First, since neither learning effects nor economies of scale go on forever, the experience curve is likely to bottom out at some point; indeed, it must do so by definition. When this occurs, further unit-cost reductions from learning effects and economies of scale will be hard to come by. Thus, in time, other companies can catch up with the cost leader. Once this happens, a number of low-cost companies can have cost parity with each other. In such circumstances, a sustainable competitive advantage must rely on other strategic factors besides the minimization of production costs by utilizing existing technologies—factors such as better customer responsiveness, product quality, or innovation.

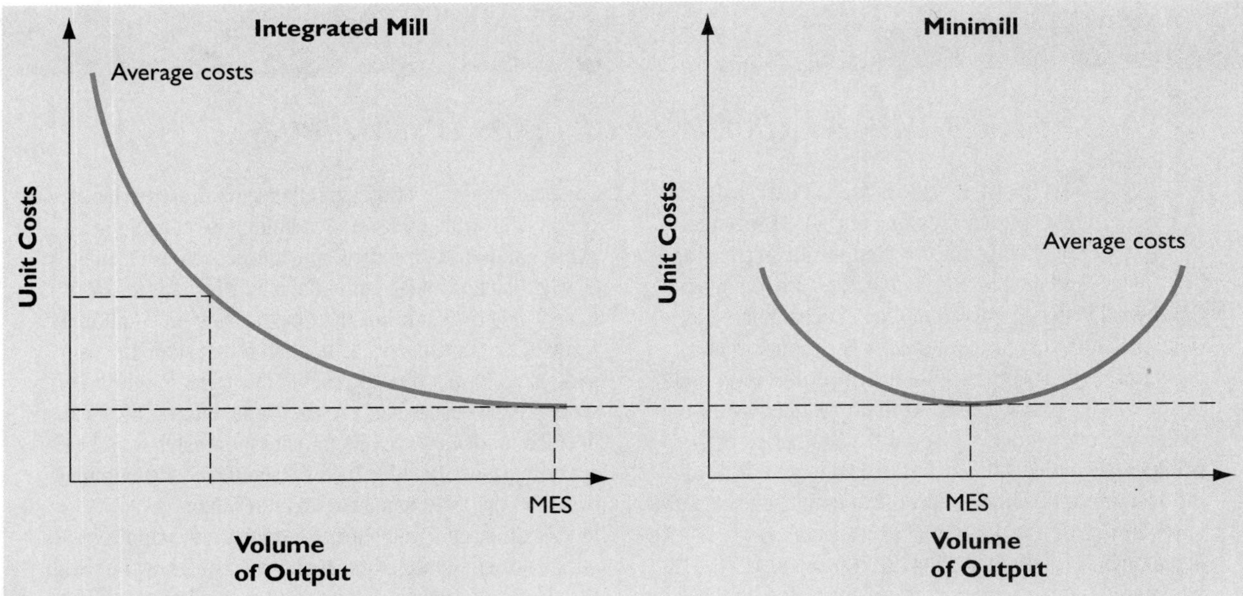

FIGURE 5.4

Unit Production Costs in an Integrated Steel Mill and a Minimill

Second, cost advantages gained from experience effects can be made obsolete by the development of new technologies. For example, the price of television picture tubes followed the experience curve pattern from the introduction of television in the late 1940s until 1963. The average unit price dropped from $34 to $8 (in 1958 dollars) in that time. The advent of color television interrupted the experience curve. Manufacturing picture tubes for color televisions required a new manufacturing technology, and the price for color TV tubes shot up to $51 by 1966. Then the experience curve reasserted itself. The price dropped to $48 in 1968, $37 in 1970, and $36 in 1972.[10] In short, technological change can alter the rules of the game, requiring that former low-cost companies take steps to reestablish their competitive edge.

A further reason for avoiding complacency is that high volume does not necessarily give a company a cost advantage. Some technologies have different cost functions. For example, the steel industry has two alternative manufacturing technologies: an integrated technology, which relies on the basic oxygen furnace, and a minimill technology, which depends on the electric arc furnace. As illustrated in Figure 5.4, the minimum efficient scale (MES) of the electric arc furnace is located at relatively low volumes, whereas the MES of the basic oxygen furnace is located at relatively high volumes. Even when both operations are producing at their most efficient output levels, steel companies with basic oxygen furnaces do not have a cost advantage over minimills.

Consequently, the pursuit of experience economies by an integrated company using basic oxygen technology may not bring the kind of cost advantages that a naive reading of the experience curve phenomenon would lead the company to expect. Indeed, there have been significant periods of time during which integrated companies have not been able to get enough orders to run at optimum capacity. Hence their production costs have been considerably higher than those of minimills.[11] More generally, as we discuss next, in many industries new flexible manufacturing technologies hold out the promise of allowing small manufacturers to produce at unit costs comparable to those of large assembly line operations.

Production and Efficiency: Flexible Manufacturing and Mass Customization

Central to the concept of economies of scale is the idea that the best way to achieve high efficiency, and hence low unit costs, is through the mass production of a standardized output. The tradeoff implicit in this idea is between unit costs and product variety. Producing greater product variety from a factory implies shorter production runs, which in turn imply an inability to realize economies of scale. That is, wide product variety makes it difficult for a company to increase its production efficiency and thus reduce its unit costs. According to this logic, the way to increase efficiency and drive down unit costs is to limit product variety and produce a standardized product in large volumes (see Figure 5.5a).

This view of production efficiency has been challenged by the rise of flexible manufacturing technologies. The term ***flexible manufacturing technology***—or ***lean production***, as it is often called—covers a range of manufacturing technologies designed to (1) reduce setup times for complex equipment, (2) increase the utilization of individual machines through better scheduling, and (3) improve quality control at all stages of the manufacturing process.[12] Flexible manufacturing technologies allow the company to produce a wider variety of end products at a unit cost that at one time could be achieved only through the mass production of a standardized output (see Figure 5.5b). Indeed, recent research suggests that the adoption of flexible manufacturing technologies may actually increase efficiency and lower unit costs relative to what can be achieved by the mass production of a standardized output, while at the same time enabling the company to customize its product offering to a much greater extent than was once thought possible. The term ***mass customization*** has been coined to describe the ability of companies to use flexible manufacturing technology to reconcile two goals that were once thought to be incompatible: low cost and product customization.[13]

Flexible manufacturing technologies vary in their sophistication and complexity. One of the most famous examples of a flexible manufacturing technology, Toyota's production system, is relatively unsophisticated, but it has been credited with making Toyota the most efficient auto company in the global industry. Toyota's flexible manufacturing system is profiled in Strategy in Action 5.3. **Flexible machine cells** are another common flexible manufacturing technology. A flexible machine cell is a grouping of various types of machinery, a common materials handler, and a centralized cell controller (computer). Each cell normally contains four to six machines capable of performing a variety of operations. The typical cell is dedicated to the production of a family of parts or products. The settings on machines are computer controlled, which allows each cell to switch quickly between the production of different parts or products.

Improved capacity utilization and reductions in work-in-progress (that is, stockpiles of partly finished products) and in waste are major efficiency benefits of flexible machine cells. Improved capacity utilization arises from the reduction in setup times and from the computer-controlled coordination of production flow between

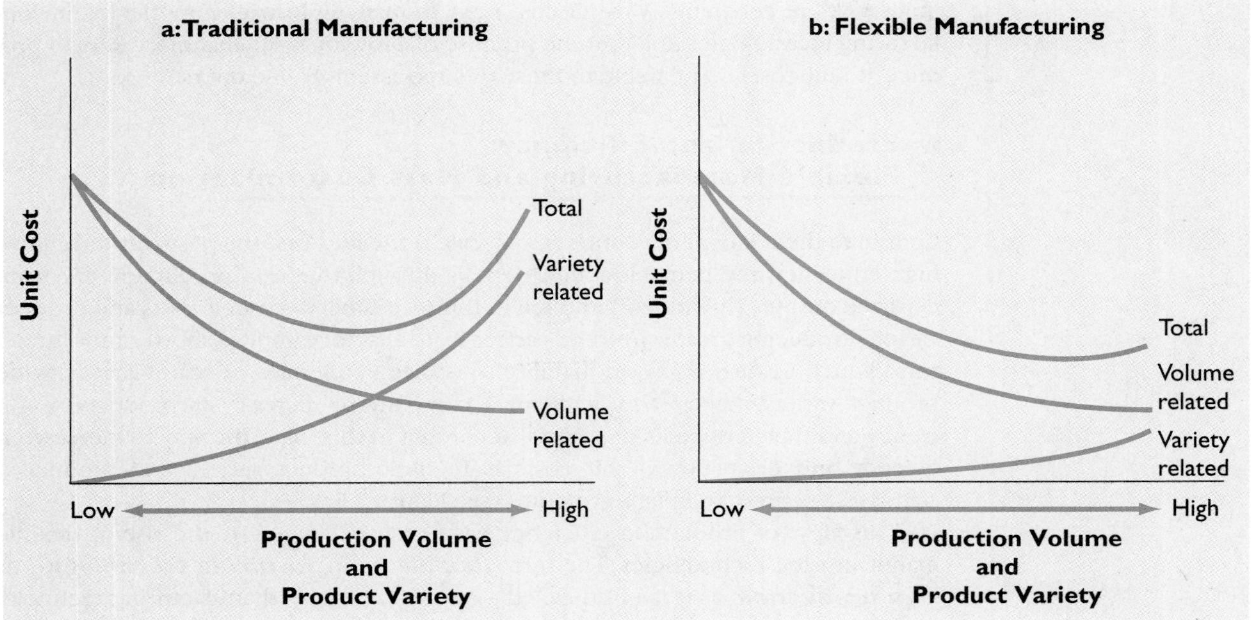

FIGURE 5.5

The Tradeoff Between Costs and Product Variety

machines, which eliminates bottlenecks. The tight coordination between machines also reduces work-in-progress. Reductions in waste are due to the ability of computer-controlled machinery to identify ways to transform inputs into outputs while producing a minimum of unusable waste material. Given all these factors, whereas free standing machines might be in use 50 percent of the time, the same machines when grouped into a cell can be used more than 80 percent of the time and produce the same end product with half the waste. This increases efficiency and results in lower costs.

The efficiency benefits of installing flexible manufacturing technology can be dramatic. W.L. Gore, a privately owned company that manufactures a wide range of products from high-tech computer cables to its famous Gore-Tex fabric, has adopted flexible cells in several of its forty-six factories. In its cable-making facilities, the effect has been to cut the time taken to make computer cables by 50 percent, to reduce stock by 33 percent, and to shrink the space taken up by the plant by 25 percent. Similarly, Compaq Computer, the manufacturer of personal computers, replaced three of the sixteen assembly lines in its Houston factory with twenty-one cells. As a result, employee productivity rose by 25 percent, and the cost of converting the three assembly lines to cells was recouped in six months. Lexmark, a producer of computer printers, has also converted 80 percent of its 2,700-employee factory in Lexington, Kentucky, to flexible manufacturing cells, and it too has seen productivity increase by around 25 percent.[14]

Besides improving efficiency and lowering costs, flexible manufacturing technologies also enable companies to customize products to the unique demands of small consumer groups—at a cost that at one time could be achieved only by mass-producing a standardized output. Thus, they help a company achieve mass cus-

5.3 **STRATEGY in ACTION**

Toyota's Lean Production System

Toyota's flexible manufacturing system was developed by one of the company's engineers, Ohno Taiichi. After working at Toyota for five years and visiting Ford's U.S. plants, Ohno became convinced that the mass-production philosophy for making cars was flawed. He saw numerous problems, including three major drawbacks. First, long production runs created massive inventories, which had to be stored in large warehouses. This was expensive, both because of the cost of warehousing, and because inventories tied up capital in unproductive uses. Second, if the initial machine settings were wrong, long production runs resulted in the production of a large number of defects (that is, waste). Third, the mass production system was unable to accommodate consumer preferences for product diversity.

Ohno looked for ways to make shorter production runs economical. He developed a number of techniques designed to reduce setup times for production equipment (a major source of fixed costs). By using a system of levers and pulleys, he was able to reduce the time required to change dies on stamping equipment from a full day in 1950 to three minutes by 1971. This made small production runs economical, which in turn allowed Toyota to respond better to consumer demands for product diversity. Small production runs also eliminated the need to hold large inventories, thereby reducing warehousing costs. Furthermore, small product runs and the lack of inventory meant that defective parts were produced only in small numbers and entered the assembly process immediately. This reduced waste and made it easier to trace defects to their source and fix the problem. In sum, Ohno's innovations enabled Toyota to produce a more diverse product range at a lower unit cost than was possible with conventional mass production.[15]

tomization, which increases its customer responsiveness. The Opening Case on Levi Strauss provides a good example of this. By linking flexible manufacturing technology with the power of the Web, Levi has been able to customize jeans to an individual's measurements and tastes.

Marketing and Efficiency

The marketing strategy that a company adopts can have a major impact upon the efficiency and cost structure of an enterprise. **Marketing strategy** refers to the position that a company takes with regard to pricing, promotion, advertising, product design, and distribution. It can play a major role in boosting a company's efficiency. Some of the steps leading to greater efficiency are fairly obvious. For example, we have already discussed how riding down the experience curve to gain a low-cost position can be facilitated by aggressive pricing, promotions, and advertising—all of which are the task of the marketing function. However, there are other aspects of marketing strategy that have a less obvious, though not less significant, impact on efficiency. One important aspect is the relationship between customer defection rates and unit costs.[16]

Customer defection rates are the percentage of a company's customers that defect every year to competitors. Defection rates are determined by customer loyalty, which in turn is a function of the ability of a company to satisfy its customers. Because acquiring a new customer entails certain one-time fixed costs for advertising, promotions, and the like, there is a direct relationship between defection rates and costs. The longer a company holds on to a customer, the greater is the volume of customer-generated unit sales that can be set against these fixed costs, and the lower the average unit cost of each sale. Thus, lowering customer defection rates allows a company to achieve substantial cost economies. This is illustrated in Figure 5.6, which shows that high defection rates imply high average unit costs (and vice versa).

One consequence of the relationship summarized in Figure 5.6 is a relationship, illustrated in Figure 5.7, between the length of time that a customer stays with the company and profit per customer. Because of the fixed costs of acquiring new customers, serving customers who stay with the company only for a short time before switching to competitors can often yield a negative profit. However, the longer a customer stays with the company, the more the fixed costs of acquiring that customer can be spread out over repeat purchases, which boosts the profit per customer. Thus, as shown in Figure 5.7, there is a positive relationship between the length of time that a customer stays with a company and profit per customer.

For an example of this phenomenon, consider the credit card business.[17] In 1990, most credit card companies spent an average of $51 to recruit a customer and set up a new account. These costs came from the advertising required to attract new customers, from credit checks required for each customer, and from the mechanics of setting up an account and issuing a card. These one-time fixed costs can be recouped only if a customer stays with the company for at least two years. Moreover, when customers stay a second year, they tend to increase their use of the credit card, which raises the volume of revenues generated by each customer over time. As a result, the average profit per customer in the credit card business increases from minus $51 in year 1 (that is, a loss of $51) to $44 in year 3 and $55 in year 6.

Another economic benefit of long-time customer loyalty is the free advertising that customers provide for a company. Loyal customers do a lot of talking, and they

FIGURE 5.6

The Relationship Between Average Unit Costs and Customer Defection Rates

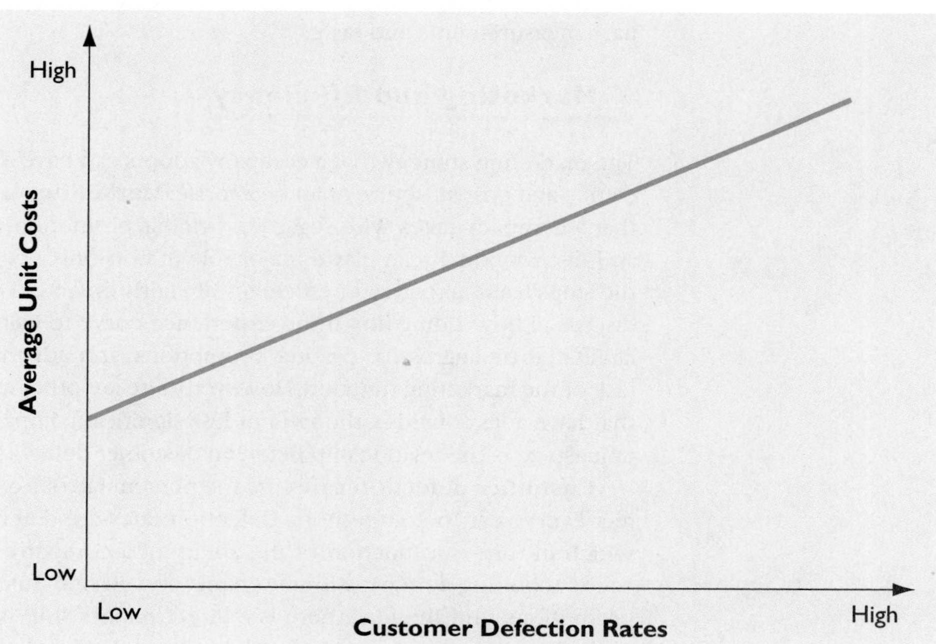

FIGURE 5.7

The Relationship Between Customer Loyalty and Profit per Customer

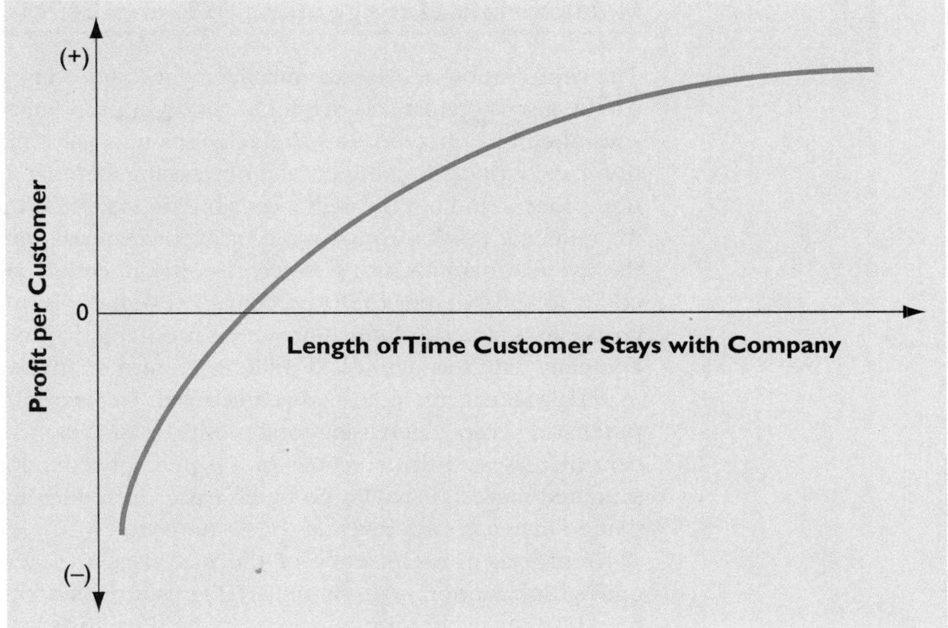

can dramatically increase the volume of business through referrals. A striking example of this is the clothing and food retailer Marks & Spencer, which is Britain's largest and most profitable retailer. Its success is built on a well-earned reputation for providing its customers with high-quality goods at a reasonable price. The company has generated such customer loyalty that it does not need to do much advertising in Britain—a major source of cost saving.

The key message, then, is that reducing customer defection rates and building customer loyalty can be a major source of cost saving. Because it leads to lower unit costs, reducing customer defection rates by just 5 percent can increase profits per customer anywhere from 25 percent to 85 percent, depending on the industry. For example, a 5 percent reduction in customer defection rates leads to the following increases in profits per customer over the average customer life: a 75 percent increase in profit per customer in the credit card business; a 50 percent increase in profit per customer in the insurance brokerage industry; a 45 percent increase in profit per customer in the industrial laundry business; and a 35 percent increase in profit per customer in the computer software industry.[18]

How can a company reduce customer defection rates? It can do so by building brand loyalty, which in turn requires that the company be responsive to the needs of its customers. We consider the issue of customer responsiveness later in the chapter. For now, note that a central component of developing a strategy to reduce defection rates is to spot customers who do defect, find out why they defected, and act on that information so that other customers do not defect for similar reasons in the future. To take these measures, the marketing function must have information systems capable of tracking customer defections.

Materials Management, JIT, and Efficiency

The contribution of materials management to boosting the efficiency of a company can be just as dramatic as the contribution of production and marketing. **Materials management** encompasses the activities necessary to get materials to a production facility (including the costs if purchasing material inputs), through the production process, and out through a distribution system to the end user.[19] The potential for reducing costs through more efficient materials management is enormous. In the average manufacturing enterprise, the materials and transportation costs account for 50 percent to 70 percent of revenues. Even a small reduction in these costs can have a substantial impact on profitability. According to one estimate, for a company with revenues of $1 million, a return on investment rate of 5 percent, and materials management costs that amount to 50 percent of sales revenues (including purchasing costs), increasing total profits by $15,000 would require either a 30 percent increase in sales revenues or a 3 percent reduction in materials costs.[20] In a saturated market, it would be much easier to reduce materials costs by 3 percent than to increase sales revenues by 30 percent.

Improving the efficiency of the materials management function typically requires the adoption of just-in-time (JIT) inventory systems. The basic philosophy behind JIT is to economize on inventory holding costs by having materials arrive at a manufacturing plant just in time to enter the production process, and not before. The major cost saving comes from increasing inventory turnover, which reduces inventory holding costs, such as warehousing and storage costs. For example, Wal-Mart uses JIT systems to replenish the stock in its stores at least twice a week. Many stores receive daily deliveries. The typical competitor—Kmart or Sears—replenishes its stock every two weeks. Compared with these competitors, Wal-Mart can maintain the same service levels with one-fourth the inventory investment, which is a major source of cost saving. Thus, faster inventory turnover has helped Wal-Mart achieve an efficiency-based competitive advantage in the retailing industry.[21]

The drawback of JIT systems is that they leave a firm without a buffer stock of inventory. Although buffer stocks of inventory are expensive to store, they can help tide a firm over shortages on inputs brought about by disruption among suppliers (for instance, a labor dispute at a key supplier). Buffer stocks can also help a firm respond quickly to increases in demand. However, there are ways around these limitations. For example, to reduce the risks linked to dependence on just one supplier for an important input, it might pay the firm to source inputs from multiple suppliers.

R&D Strategy and Efficiency

The role of superior research and development in helping a company achieve greater efficiency is twofold. First, the R&D function can boost efficiency by designing products that are easy to manufacture. By cutting down on the number of parts that make up a product, R&D can dramatically decrease the required assembly time, which translates into higher employee productivity and lower unit costs. For example, after Texas Instruments redesigned an infrared sighting mechanism that it supplies to the Pentagon, the company found that it had reduced the number of parts from 47 to 12, the number of assembly steps from 56 to 13, the time spent fabricating metal from 757 minutes per unit to 219 minutes per unit, and unit assembly time from 129 minutes to 20 minutes. The result was a substantial decline in production costs. Design for manufacturing requires close coordination between the production and R&D functions of the company, of course. Cross-functional teams that contain production and R&D personnel, so that they can work on the problem jointly, best achieve such coordination.

The second way in which the R&D function can help a company achieve greater efficiency is by pioneering process innovations. A process innovation is an innovation in the way production processes operate that improves their efficiency. Process innovations have often been a major source of competitive advantage. In the automobile industry, Toyota's competitive advantage is based partly on the company's invention of new flexible manufacturing processes, which dramatically reduced setup times. This process innovation enabled Toyota to obtain efficiency gains associated with flexible manufacturing systems years ahead of its competitors.

Human Resource Strategy and Efficiency

Employee productivity is one of the key determinants of an enterprise's efficiency and cost structure. The more productive the employees, the lower will be the unit costs. The challenge for a company's human resource function is to devise ways to increase employee productivity. It has three main choices: training employees, organizing the work force into self-managing teams, and linking pay to performance.

Employee Training Individuals are a major input into the production process. A company that employs individuals with higher skills is likely to be more efficient than one employing less skilled personnel. Individuals who are more skilled can perform tasks faster and more accurately and are more likely to learn the complex tasks associated with many modern production methods than individuals with lesser skills. Training can upgrade employee skill levels, bringing the firm productivity-related efficiency gains.[22]

Self-Managing Teams Self-managing teams are a relatively recent phenomenon. Few companies used them until the mid 1980s, but since then they have spread rapidly. The growth of flexible manufacturing cells, which group workers into teams, has undoubtedly facilitated the spread of self-managing teams among manufacturing enterprises. The typical team comprises five to fifteen employees who produce an entire product or undertake an entire task. Team members learn all team tasks and rotate from job to job. A more flexible work force is one result. Team members can fill in for absent coworkers. Teams also take over managerial duties such as work and vacation scheduling, ordering materials, and hiring new members. The greater responsibility thrust on team members and the empowerment it implies are seen as motivators. (Empowerment is the process of giving lower-level employees decision-making power.) People often respond well to being given greater autonomy and responsibility. Performance bonuses linked to team production and quality targets work as an additional motivator.

The net effect of introducing self-managing teams is reportedly an increase in productivity of 30 percent or more and a substantial increase in product quality. Further cost savings arise from eliminating supervisors and creating a flatter organizational hierarchy. In manufacturing enterprises, perhaps the most potent combination is that of self-managing teams and flexible manufacturing cells. The two seem designed for each other. For example, after the introduction of flexible manufacturing technology and work practices based on self-managing teams in 1988, a General

Electric plant in Salisbury, North Carolina, increased productivity by 250 percent compared with GE plants that produced the same products in 1984.[23] Still, teams are no panacea; in manufacturing enterprises, self-managing teams may fail to live up to their potential unless they are integrated with flexible manufacturing technology. More generally, teams thrust a lot of management responsibilities on team members, and helping the members to cope with these responsibilities often requires substantial training—a fact that many companies often forget in their rush to drive down costs, with the result that the teams don't work out as well as planned.[24]

Pay for Performance People work for money, so it is hardly surprising that linking pay to performance can help increase employee productivity. However, the issue is not quite so simple as just introducing incentive pay systems; it is also important to define what kind of performance is to be rewarded and how. Some of the most efficient companies in the world, mindful that cooperation among employees is necessary to realize productivity gains, do not link pay to individual performance. Instead they link pay to group or team performance. For example, at Nucor, which is widely viewed as one of the most efficient steel makers in the world, the work force is divided into teams of thirty or so. Bonus pay, which can amount to 30 percent of base pay, is linked to the ability of the team to meet productivity and quality goals. This link creates a strong incentive for individuals to cooperate with each other in pursuit of team goals; that is, it facilitates teamwork.

Information Systems, the Internet, and Efficiency

With the rapid spread of computers, the explosive growth of the Internet and corporate Intranets (internal corporate computer networks based on Internet standards), and the spread of high-bandwidth communication conduits from fiber optics to digital wireless technology, the information system functions of enterprises are moving to center stage in the quest for operating efficiencies.[25] The impact of information systems on productivity is wide ranging and potentially affects all other activities of an enterprise. For example, in the Opening Case of Chapter 4, we saw how Cisco Systems has been able to realize significant cost savings by moving its ordering and customer service functions on-line. The company has just 300 service agents handling all its customer accounts, compared with the 900 it would need if sales were not handled on-line. The difference represents an annual saving of $20 million. Moreover, without automated customer service functions, Cisco calculates that it would need at least 1,000 additional service engineers, which would cost around $75 million.[26]

Dell Computer is famous for having been the first to implement on-line selling in the personal computer industry and now sells some 40 percent of its computers on-line. Dell has also put much of its customer service functions on-line, replacing telephone calls to customer service representatives. Each week some 200,000 people access Dell's troubleshooting tips on-line. Each of these hits at Dell's Web site saves the company a potential $15, which is the average cost of a technical support call. If just 10 percent of these people were to call Dell using a telephone, it would cost the company $15.6 million per year.[27]

More generally, what companies like Cisco and Dell are doing is using Web-based information systems to reduce the costs of coordination between the company and its customers, and the company and its suppliers. By using Web-based programs to automate customer and supplier interactions, a company can substantially reduce the number of people required to manage these interfaces, thereby decreasing costs and increasing productivity. Nor is this trend limited to high-technology companies such as Cisco or Dell Computer. Banks and financial service companies are finding that they can substantially reduce costs by moving customer accounts and support functions on-line. Such a move reduces the need for customer service representatives, bank tellers, stockbrokers, insurance agents, and so on. For example, while the average cost of executing a transaction at a bank, such as shifting money from one account to another, is about $1.07, executing the same transaction over the Internet costs $0.01.[28] Similarly, the whole theory behind Internet-based retailers such as Amazon.com is that significant costs can be taken out of the retailing system by replacing physical stores and their supporting personnel with an on-line virtual store and automated ordering and checkout processes. Cost savings can also be realized by using Web-based information systems to automate many internal company activities, from managing expense reimbursements to benefits planning and hiring processes, thereby reducing the need for internal support personnel.

For many years, skeptics questioned the impact that computer-based information systems were having on productivity, but recent productivity data from America suggest that the productivity gains are starting to appear. For the 1996–1998 period, U.S. nonfarm productivity growth accelerated from a historic average of 1 percent per year to 2.2 percent a year. In late 1998 and early 1999, it accelerated again to over 3 percent per annum. The productivity growth was greatest in the computer industry itself, which is not surprising, given the efforts by companies like Cisco and Dell to implement Web-based sales and service functions.[29]

Infrastructure and Efficiency

The infrastructure sets the context within which all other value creation activities take place. It follows that the infrastructure can help in achieving efficiency goals. Above all, the infrastructure can foster a companywide commitment to efficiency and promote cooperation among different functions in pursuit of efficiency goals.

A companywide commitment to efficiency can be built through the leadership of top management. The leadership task is to articulate a vision that recognizes the need for all functions of the company to focus on improving their efficiency. It is not enough just to improve the efficiency of production, or marketing, or R&D. Achieving superior efficiency requires a companywide commitment to this goal, and this commitment can be articulated only by top management.

A further leadership task is to facilitate cross-functional cooperation needed to achieve superior efficiency. For example, designing products that are easy to manufacture requires that production and R&D personnel communicate; integrating JIT systems with production scheduling requires close communication between material management and production; designing self-managing teams to perform production tasks requires close cooperation between human resources and production; and so on.

TABLE 5.1

The Primary Roles of Different Value Creation Functions in Achieving Superior Efficiency

Value Creation Function	Primary Roles
Infrastructure (Leadership)	1. Provide companywide commitment to efficiency. 2. Facilitate cooperation among functions.
Production	1. Where appropriate, pursue economies of scale and learning economics. 2. Implement flexible manufacturing systems.
Marketing	1. Where appropriate, adopt aggressive marketing to ride down the experience curve. 2. Limit customer defection rates by building brand loyalty.
Materials Management	1. Implement JIT systems.
R&D	1. Design products for ease of manufacture. 2. Seek process innovations.
Information Systems	1. Use information systems to automate processes. 2. Use information systems to reduce costs of coordination.
Human Resources	1. Institute training programs to build skills. 2. Implement self-managing teams. 3. Implement pay for performance.

Summary: Achieving Superior Efficiency

Table 5.1 summarizes the primary roles that various functions must take in order to achieve superior efficiency. Bear in mind that achieving superior efficiency is not something that can be tackled on a function by function basis. It requires an organizationwide commitment and an ability to ensure close cooperation among functions. Top management, by exercising leadership and influencing the infrastructure, plays a major role in this process.

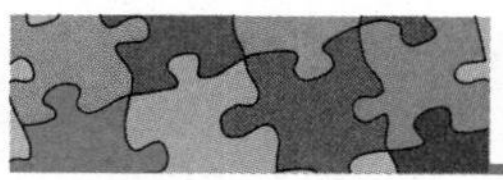

ACHIEVING SUPERIOR QUALITY

We note in Chapter 4 that superior quality gives a company two advantages. The enhanced reputation for quality lets the company charge a premium price for its product, and the elimination of defects from the production process increases efficiency and hence lowers costs. In this section, we examine the means a company can use to achieve superior quality. The main one is **total quality management** (TQM), a management philosophy that focuses on improving the quality of a company's products and services and stresses that all company operations should be oriented toward this goal.[30] A companywide philosophy, it requires the cooperation of all the different functions if it is to be successfully implemented. We first consider the total quality management concept and then discuss the various steps needed to implement TQM programs. Throughout, we highlight the roles that different functions must play in this process.

The TQM Concept

The total quality management concept was first developed by a number of U.S. consultants, including H. W. Edwards Deming, Joseph Juran, and A. V. Feigenbaum.[31] Originally, these consultants won few converts in the United States. In contrast, the Japanese embraced them enthusiastically and even named their premier annual prize for manufacturing excellence after Deming. The philosophy underlying TQM, as articulated by Deming, is based on the following five-step chain reaction:

1. Improved quality means that costs decrease because of less rework, fewer mistakes, fewer delays, and better use of time and materials.
2. As a result, productivity improves.
3. Better quality leads to higher market share and allows the company to raise prices.
4. This increases the company's profitability and allows it to stay in business.
5. Thus, the company creates more jobs.[32]

Deming identified fourteen steps that should be part of any TQM program; they are summarized in Table 5.2. (Deming continually changed these points in line with his belief in the importance of continuous quality improvement; those given here are the latest—1990—version.) In essence, Deming urged a company to have a definite strategic plan for where it is going and how it is going to get there. He argued that management should embrace the philosophy that mistakes, defects, and poor-quality materials are not acceptable and should be eliminated. Quality of supervision should be improved by allowing more time for supervisors to work with employees and giving them appropriate skills for the job. Furthermore, management should create an environment in which employees will not fear reporting problems or recommending improvements. Deming also believed that work standards should not only be defined as numbers or quotas, but should also include some notion of quality to promote the production of defect-free output. He argued that management has the responsibility to train employees in new skills to keep pace with changes in the workplace and that achieving better quality requires the commitment of everyone in the company.

It took the rise of Japan to the top rank of economic powers to alert western business to the importance of the TQM concept. Since the early 1980s, TQM practices have spread rapidly throughout western industry. Strategy in Action 5.4 describes one of the most successful implementations of a quality improvement process, General Electric's six sigma program. Despite such instances of spectacular success, TQM practices are still not universally accepted. A study by the American Quality Foundation found that only 20 percent of U.S. companies regularly review the consequences of quality performance, compared with 70 percent of Japanese companies.[33] Another study by Arthur D. Little of 500 American companies using TQM found that only 36 percent believed that TQM was increasing their competitiveness.[34] A prime reason for this, according to the study, was that many companies had not fully understood or embraced the TQM concept.

TABLE 5.2

Deming's Fourteen Points to Quality

1. Create constancy of purpose toward improvement of product and service, with the aim to become competitive and to stay in business, and to provide jobs.
2. Adopt the new philosophy. We are in a new economic age. Western management must awaken to the challenge, must learn their responsibilities, and take on leadership for change.
3. Cease dependence on inspection to achieve quality. Eliminate the need for inspection on a mass basis by building quality into the product in the first place.
4. End the practice of awarding business on the basis of price tag. Instead, minimize total cost.
5. Improve constantly and forever the system of production and service, to improve quality and productivity, and thus constantly decrease costs.
6. Institute training on the job.
7. Institute leadership. The aim of leadership should be to help people and machines and gadgets do a better job. Leadership of management is in need of an overhaul, as well as leadership of production workers.
8. Drive out fear, so that everyone may work effectively for the company.
9. Break down barriers between departments. People in research, design, sales, and production must work as a team, to foresee problems of production and in use that may be encountered with the product or service.
10. Eliminate slogans, exhortations, and targets for the work force asking for zero defects and new levels of productivity. Such exhortations only create adversarial relationships. The bulk of the causes of low quality and low productivity belong to the system and thus lie beyond the power of the work force.
11. (a) Eliminate work standards on the factory floor. Substitute leadership. (b) Eliminate management by objective. Eliminate management by numbers, numerical goals. Substitute leadership.
12. (a) Remove barriers that rob hourly workers of their right to pride of workmanship. The responsibility of supervisors must be changed from sheer numbers to quality. (b) Remove barriers that rob people in management and in engineering of their right to pride of workmanship.
13. Institute a vigorous program of education and self-improvement.
14. Put everybody in the company to work to accomplish the transformation. The transformation is everybody's job.

"Deming's 14 Points to Quality," from Gabor, Andrea, *The Man Who Discovered Quality: Howard W. Edwards Deming Brought the Quality Revolution to America—The Stories of Ford, Xerox, & GM* (New York: Random House, 1990).

Implementing TQM

Among companies that have successfully adopted TQM, certain imperatives stand out. We discuss them in the order in which they are usually tackled in companies implementing TQM programs, and we highlight the role that the various functions play in regard to each precept. What cannot be stressed enough, however, is that implementing TQM requires close cooperation among all functions in the pursuit of

5.4 **STRATEGY *in* ACTION**

General Electric's Six Sigma Quality Improvement Process

Six sigma is a quality and efficiency program that has been adopted by several major corporations, such as Motorola, General Electric, and Allied Signal. It is a philosophy that aims to reduce defects, boost productivity, eliminate waste and cut costs throughout a company. The term *sigma* comes from the Greek letter that statisticians use to represent a standard deviation from a mean. The higher the number of sigmas, the smaller the number of errors. At sigma, a production process would be 99.99966 percent accurate, creating just 3.4 defects per million units. While it is almost impossible for a company to achieve such perfection, six sigma quality is a goal that several strive toward.

General Electric is perhaps the most fervent adopter of six sigma programs. Under the direction of long-serving CEO, Jack Welch, GE spent nearly $1 billion between 1995 and 1998 to convert all its divisions to the six sigma faith. Welch credits the six sigma program with raising GE's operating profit margins to 16.6 percent in 1998, up from 14.4 percent three years earlier.

One of the first products designed from start to finish using six sigma processes was a $1.25 million diagnostic computer tomography, or CT, scanner called the Lightspeed, which produces three-dimensional images of the human body. Introducing it in 1998, GE spent $50 million to run 250 separate six sigma analyses designed to improve the reliability and lower the manufacturing cost of the Lightspeed scanner. The new scanner captures multiple images simultaneously, requiring only twenty seconds to do full body scans that once took three minutes—important because patients must remain perfectly still during the scan. Not only is the Lightspeed fast, but the first customers also noticed that it ran without downtime from the start, a testament to the reliability of the product.

Achieving that reliability took a lot of work. GE's engineers deconstructed the scanner into its basic components and tried to improve the reliability of each through a detailed step-by-step analysis. For example, the most important part of CT scanners is the vacuum tubes, which focus x-ray waves. The tubes that GE used in previous scanners, which cost $60,000 each, had low reliability. Hospitals and clinics wanted the tubes to operate twelve hours a day for at least six months, but typically they lasted only half that long. Moreover, GE was scrapping some $20 million in tubes each year because they failed preshipping performance tests, while a disturbing number of faulty tubes were slipping past inspection only to be pronounced dead on arrival.

To try and solve the reliability problem, the six sigma team took the tubes apart. They knew that one problem involves a petroleum-based oil used in the tube to prevent short circuits by isolating the anode, which has a positive charge, from the negatively charged cathode. The oil often deteriorated after a few months, leading to short circuits, but the team did not know why. By using statistical "what if" scenarios on all parts of the tube, however, the researchers learned that the lead-based paint on the inside of the tube was adulterating the oil. Acting on this information, the team developed a paint that would preserve the tube and protect the oil.

By pursuing this and other improvements, the six sigma team was able to extend the average life of a vacuum tube in the CT scanner from three months to over a year. Although the improvements increased the cost of the tube from $60,000 to $85,000, the increased cost was outweighed by the reduction in replacement costs, making it an attractive proposition for customers.[35]

the common goal of improving quality; it is a process that cuts across functions. The role played by the different functions in implementing TQM is summarized in Table 5.3. Strategy in Action 5.5 at the end of this section describes the efforts of a service company to put TQM into practice and the benefits it has gained.

Build Organizational Commitment to Quality There is evidence that TQM will do little to improve the performance of a company unless it is embraced by

TABLE 5.3

The Role Played by Different Functions in Implementing TQM

Value Creation Function	Primary Roles
Infrastructure (Leadership)	1. Provide leadership and commitment to quality. 2. Find ways to measure quality. 3. Set goals and create incentives. 4. Solicit input from employees. 5. Encourage cooperation among functions.
Production	1. Shorten production runs. 2. Trace defects back to source.
Marketing	1. Focus on the customer. 2. Provide customer feedback on quality.
Materials Management	1. Rationalize suppliers. 2. Help suppliers implement TQM. 3. Trace defects back to suppliers.
R&D	1. Design products that are easy to manufacture.
Information Systems	1. Use information systems to monitor defect rates.
Human Resources	1. Institute TQM training programs. 2. Organize employees into quality teams.

everyone in the organization.[36] For example, when Xerox launched its quality program in 1983, its first step was to educate its entire work force, from top management down, in the importance and operation of the TQM concept. It did so by forming groups, beginning with a group at the top of the organization that included the CEO. The top group was the first to receive basic TQM training. Each member of this group was then given the task of training a group at the next level in the hierarchy, and so on down throughout the organization until all 100,000 employees had received basic TQM training. Both top management and the human resource function of the company can play a major role in this process. Top management has the responsibility of exercising the leadership required to make a commitment to quality an organizationwide goal. The human resource function must take on responsibility for companywide training in TQM techniques.

Focus on the Customer TQM practitioners see a focus on the customer as the starting point, and indeed, the raison d'être, of the whole quality philosophy.[37] The marketing function, because it provides the primary point of contact with the customer, should play a major role here. It needs to identify what the customers want from the good or service that the company provides; what the company actually provides to customers; and the gap between what customers want and what they actually get, which could be called the quality gap. Then, together with the other functions of the company, it needs to formulate a plan for closing the quality gap.

5.5 STRATEGY *in* ACTION

Total Quality Management at Intermountain Health Care

Intermountain Health Care is a nonprofit chain of twenty-four hospitals operating in Idaho, Utah, and Wyoming. Intermountain first adopted TQM for certain sections of its system in the mid 1980s, and in 1990 it adopted TQM systemwide. The goal of TQM was to find and eliminate inappropriate variations in medical care—to provide the patient with better health care and, in the process, to reduce costs. The starting point was to identify variations in practice across physicians, particularly with regard to the cost and success rate of treatments. These data were then shared among physicians within the Intermountain system. The next step was for the physicians to take the data and use them to eliminate poor practices and to generally upgrade the quality of medical care.

The results have been quite striking. One early improvement was an attempt by Intermountain's hospital in Salt Lake City to lower the rate of postoperative wound infections. Before the effort began in 1985, the hospital's postoperative infection rate was 1.8 percent; this was 0.2 points below the national average, but still unacceptably high from a TQM perspective. By using a bedside computer system to make sure that antibiotics were given to patients two hours before surgery, the hospital dropped the infection rate in half, to 0.9 percent, within a year. Since then, the postoperative infection rate has dropped further still, to 0.4 percent compared with the national average of 2 percent. Given that the average postoperative infection adds $14,000 to a hospital bill, this constitutes a big cost saving.

Intermountain is now focusing on dozens of problems, including situations in which the wrong type or dose of medication is given, the top cause of poor medical care. Intermountain expects its efforts in this area to quickly eliminate at least 60 percent of such mistakes and to reduce medical related costs by up to $2 million a year per hospital.[40]

Find Ways to Measure Quality Another imperative of any TQM program is to create some metric that can be used to measure quality. This is relatively easy in manufacturing companies, where quality can be measured by criteria such as defects per million parts. It tends to be more difficult in service companies, but with a little creativity suitable metrics can be devised. For example, one of the metrics Florida Power & Light uses to measure quality is meter reading errors per month. Another is the frequency and duration of power outages. L.L. Bean, the Freeport, Maine, mail-order retailer of outdoor gear, uses the percentage of orders that are correctly filled as one of its quality measures. For some banks, the key measures are the number of customer defections per year and the number of statement errors per thousand customers. The common theme that runs through all these examples is identifying what quality means from a customer's perspective and devising a method to gauge this. Top management should take primary responsibility for formulating different metrics to measure quality, but to succeed in this effort, it must receive input from the various functions of the company.

Set Goals and Create Incentives Once a metric has been devised, the next step is to set a challenging quality goal and to create incentives for reaching that goal. Xerox again provides us with an example. When it introduced its TQM program, Xerox's initial goal was to reduce defective parts from 25,000 per million to 1,000 per million. One way of creating incentives to attain such a goal is to link rewards, such as bonus pay and opportunities for promotion, to the goal. Thus, within many companies that have adopted self-managing teams, the bonus pay of team members is determined in part by their ability to attain quality goals. The task of setting goals and creating incentives is one of the key tasks of top management.

Solicit Input from Employees Employees can be a vital source of information regarding the sources of poor quality. Therefore, some framework must be established for soliciting employee suggestions as to the improvements that can be made. Quality circles—which are meetings of groups of employees—have often been used to achieve this goal. Other companies have utilized self-managing teams as forums for discussing quality improvement ideas. Whatever the forum, soliciting input from lower-level employees requires that management be open to receiving, and acting on, bad news and criticism from employees. According to Deming, one problem with U.S. management is that it has grown used to "killing the bearer of bad tidings." But, he argues, managers who are committed to the quality concept must recognize that bad news is a gold mine of information.[38]

Identify Defects and Trace Them to the Source Product defects most often occur in the production process. TQM preaches the need to identify defects during the work process, trace them to their source, find out what caused them, and make corrections so that they do not recur. Production and materials management typically has primary responsibility for this task.

To uncover defects, Deming advocates the use of statistical procedures to pinpoint variations in the quality of goods or services. Deming views variation as the enemy of quality.[39] Once variations have been identified, they must be traced to their source and eliminated. One technique that helps greatly in tracing defects to their source is reducing lot sizes for manufactured products. With short production runs, defects show up immediately. Consequently, they can be quickly traced to the source and the problem can be fixed. Reducing lot sizes also means that when defective products are produced, their number will not be large, thus decreasing waste. Flexible manufacturing techniques, discussed earlier, can be used to reduce lot sizes without raising costs. Consequently, adopting flexible manufacturing techniques is an important aspect of a TQM program.

Just-in-time (JIT) inventory systems also play a part. Under a JIT system, defective parts enter the manufacturing process immediately; they are not warehoused for several months before use. Hence defective inputs can be quickly spotted. The problem can then be traced to the supply source and corrected before more defective parts are produced. Under a more traditional system, the practice of warehousing parts for months before they are used may mean that large numbers of defects are produced by a supplier before they enter the production process.

Build Relationship with Suppliers A major source of poor-quality finished goods is poor-quality component parts. To decrease product defects, a company has to work with its suppliers to improve the quality of the parts they supply. The primary responsibility in this area falls on the materials management function, since it is the function that interacts with suppliers.

To implement JIT systems with suppliers and to get suppliers to adopt their own TQM programs, two steps are necessary. First, the number of suppliers has to be reduced to manageable proportions. Second, the company must commit to building a cooperative long-term relationship with the suppliers that remain. Asking suppliers to invest in JIT and TQM systems is asking them to make major investments that tie them to the company. For example, in order to fully implement a JIT system, the company may ask a supplier to relocate its manufacturing plant so that it is next door to the company's assembly plant. Suppliers are likely to be hesitant about making such investments unless they feel that the company is committed to an enduring, long-term relationship with them.

Design for Ease of Manufacture The more assembly steps a product requires, the more opportunities there are for making mistakes. Designing products with fewer parts should make assembly easier and result in fewer defects. Both R&D and manufacturing need to be involved in designing products that are easy to manufacture.

Break Down Barriers Between Functions Implementing TQM requires organizationwide commitment and substantial cooperation among functions. R&D has to cooperate with production to design products that are easy to manufacture, marketing has to cooperate with production and R&D so that customer problems identified by marketing can be acted on, human resource management has to cooperate with all the other functions of the company in order to devise suitable quality-training programs, and so on. The issue of achieving cooperation among subunits within a company is explored in Chapter 11. What needs stressing at this point is that ultimately it is the responsibility of top management to ensure that such cooperation occurs.

ACHIEVING SUPERIOR INNOVATION

In many ways innovation is the single most important building block of competitive advantage. Successful innovation of products or processes gives a company something unique that its competitors lack. This uniqueness may allow a company to charge a premium price or lower its cost structure below that of its rivals. Competitors, however, will try to imitate successful innovations. Often they will succeed, although high barriers to imitation can slow down the speed of imitation. Therefore, maintaining a competitive advantage requires a continuing commitment to innovation.

Many companies have established a track record for successful innovation. Among them are Du Pont, which has produced a steady stream of successful innovations such as cellophane, nylon, Freon (used in all air conditioners), and Teflon (nonstick pans); Sony, whose successes include the Walkman and the compact disk; Merck, the drug company that during the 1980s produced seven major new drugs; 3M, which has applied its core competency in tapes and adhesives to developing a wide range of new products; and Intel, which has consistently managed to lead in the development of innovative new microprocessors to run personal computers.

The High Failure Rate of Innovation

Although innovation can be a source of competitive advantage, the failure rate of innovative new products is high. One study of product development in sixteen companies in the chemical, drug, petroleum, and electronics industries suggested that only about twenty percent of R&D projects ultimately result in a commercially successful product or process.[41] Another in-depth case study of product development in three companies (one in chemicals and two in drugs) reported that about 60 percent of R&D projects reached technical completion, 30 percent were commercialized, and only 12 percent earned an economic profit that exceeded the company's cost of capital.[42] Similarly, a famous study by the consulting division of Booz, Allen, & Hamilton found that over one-third of 13,000 new consumer and industrial products failed to meet company-specific financial and strategic performance criteria.[43] Another study found that 45 percent of new products introduced into the marketplace did not meet their profitability goals.[44] In sum, this evidence suggests that many R&D projects do not result in a commercial product and that between 33 percent and 60 percent of all new products that do reach the marketplace fail to generate an adequate economic return. Two well-publicized product failures have been Apple Computer's Newton, a personal digital assistant, and Sony's Betamax format in the video player and recorder market. Although many reasons have been advanced to explain why so many new products fail to generate an economic return, five explanations for failure appear on most lists: uncertainty, poor commercialization, poor positioning strategy, technological myopia, and a lack of speed in the development process.[45]

Uncertainty New product development is an inherently risky process. It requires testing a hypothesis whose answer is impossible to know prior to market introduction: namely, is there sufficient market demand for this new technology? Although good market research can minimize the uncertainty about likely future demand for a new technology, the uncertainty cannot be eradicated altogether. Therefore, a certain failure rate is to be expected.

We would expect that failure rate to be higher for quantum product innovations than for incremental innovations. A **quantum innovation** represents a radical departure from existing technology—the introduction of something that is new to the world. The development of the World Wide Web can be considered a quantum innovation in communications technology. Other quantum innovations include the development of the first photocopier by Xerox, the first videocassette recorder by AMPEX, and the first contact lenses by Bausch & Lomb. **Incremental innovation** refers to an extension of existing technology. For example, Intel's Pentium Pro microprocessor is an incremental product innovation because it builds on the existing microprocessor architecture of Intel's X86 series.

The uncertainty of future demand for a new product is much greater if that product represents a quantum innovation that is new to the world than if it is an incremental innovation designed to replace an established product whose demand profile is already well known. Consequently, the failure rate tends to be higher for quantum innovations.

Poor Commercialization A second reason frequently cited to explain the high failure rate of new product introductions is **poor commercialization**—a condition that occurs when there is an intrinsic demand for a new technology, but the technology is not well adapted to consumer needs because of factors such as poor design and poor quality. For instance, many of the early personal computers failed to sell because one needed to be a computer programmer to use them. It took Steve Jobs at Apple Computer to understand that if the technology could be made user-friendly (if it could be commercialized), there would be an enormous market for it.

Hence the original personal computers marketed by Apple incorporated little in the way of radically new technology, but they made existing technology accessible to the average person. The failure of Apple Computer to establish a market for the Newton—the personal digital assistant or hand-held computer that Apple introduced in the summer of 1993—can be traced to poor commercialization of a potentially attractive technology. Apple predicted a $1 billion market for the Newton, but sales failed to materialize when it became clear that the Newton's software could not adequately recognize messages written on the Newton's message pad. Despite this failure, many companies believe that there is an intrinsic demand for this kind of technology, but only if the product can be better commercialized.

Poor Positioning Strategy Poor positioning strategy arises when a company introduces an intrinsically attractive new product, but sales fail to materialize because it is poorly positioned in the market place. **Positioning strategy** is the position a company adopts for a product on four main dimensions of marketing: price, distribution, promotion and advertising, and product features. Apart from poor product quality, another reason for the failure of the Apple Newton was poor positioning strategy. The Newton was introduced at such a high initial price (close to $1,000) that probably there would have been few takers even if the technology had been adequately commercialized. Poor positioning strategy may have also affected the recent introduction of the digital compact cassette (DCC), discussed in Strategy in Action 5.6. The DCC suffered from high prices, poor promotion, and a failure by the innovating companies to produce products for the portable and car market.

Technological Myopia Another reason why many new product introductions fail is that companies often make the mistake of marketing a technology for which there is not enough consumer demand. **Technological myopia** occurs when a company gets blinded by the wizardry of a new technology and fails to consider whether there is consumer demand for the product. This problem may have been a factor in the failure of the desktop computer introduced by NeXT in the late 1980s. (NeXT was founded by Steve Jobs, the founder of Apple Computer.) Technologically, the NeXT machines were clearly ahead of their time, with advanced software and hardware features that would not be incorporated into most personal computers for another decade. However, consumer acceptance was very slow, primarily because of the complete lack of applications software such as spreadsheet and word-processing programs to run on the machines. Management at NeXT was so enthusiastic about the technology of their new computer that they ignored this basic market reality. After several years of slow sales, NeXT eventually withdrew the machines from the marketplace.

Slowness in Marketing Finally, companies fail when they are slow to get their products to market. The longer the time between initial development and final marketing—that is, the slower the "cycle time"—the more likely it is that someone else will beat the firm to market and gain a first-mover advantage.[47] By and large, slow innovators update their products less frequently than fast innovators. Consequently, they can be perceived as technical laggards relative to the fast innovators. In the automobile industry, General Motors has suffered from being a slow innovator. Its product development cycle has been about five years, compared with two to three years at Honda, Toyota, and Mazda, and three to four years at Ford. Because they are

5.6 STRATEGY *in* ACTION

Whatever Happened to the Digital Compact Cassette?

The Digital Compact Cassette (DCC) was developed by Philips, the Dutch consumer electronics company. The DCC is a recordable audio digital technology that offers sound qualities superior to those of analog cassette technology. The DCC was designed to replace analog cassette tapes in much the same way that digital compact disks have replaced analog long-playing records. An attractive feature of the technology was a design that allowed users to play their analog cassette tapes on the DCC, in addition to DCC digital tapes. The thinking at Philips was that this feature would make the product very attractive to users, who would not have to replace their existing collection of analog cassette tapes when they purchased a DCC player. To try and ensure initial acceptance of the technology, Philips lined up a number of recording companies—including MCA, Polygram, EMI, and Warner—all of whom agreed to issue prerecorded DCC tapes in conjunction with the launch by Philips of the tapes players.

Brought out in 1993, the DCC was hailed in the press as the biggest new product introduction in the consumer electronics industry since the introduction of the compact disk a decade earlier. However, as initial demand failed to materialize, retailers with unsold DCC tapes and decks on their hands refused to keep devoting valuable shelf space to DCC products, and recording companies soon stopped issuing prerecorded DCC tapes. It was obvious within a year that the product was stillborn in the marketplace.

Why did the DCC fail to gain market acceptance despite its apparently attractive features? Poor positioning strategy is probably part of the explanation. Philips introduced the technology at a very high price—around $1,000 for a basic home deck—out of the reach of most consumers. Moreover, Philips failed to introduce a portable model (to compete with Sony's Walkman) or a model for cars (most consumers still have analog tape players in their cars). To make matters worse, the original promotional advertising failed to mention one of the most attractive features of the technology—that DCC tape drives could play existing analog tapes. Finally, Philips implemented a very abstract advertising campaign, which left most consumers confused about the nature of the new technology.

Another reason for the poor market acceptance was the limited value placed on the technology by many consumers. Most consumers did not see the DCC as a big advance over CD players. True, CD technology did not have recording capability, but CD players were increasingly turning up in cars and Sony had marketed a very successful portable version of the CD (the Discman)—both market niches that were natural targets for the DCC. Consequently, few consumers valued the technology enough to pay $1,000 or so for a player. Whether Philips would have been able to build sales for the DCC had it entered the market at a lower price point, with better advertising and a broader range of models, remains an open question, but success would probably have been more likely.[46]

based on five-year-old technology and design concepts, GM cars are already out-of-date when they reach the market. Another example of the consequences of slow innovation, the demise of Apollo Computer at the hands of Sun Microsystems, is presented in Strategy in Action 5.7.

Building Competencies in Innovation

Companies can take a number of steps in order to build a competency in innovation and avoid failure. Three of the most important seem to be (1) building skills in basic and applied scientific research; (2) developing a good process for project selection and project management, and (3) integrating the different functions of the

5.7 **STRATEGY *in* ACTION**

Slow Cycle Time at Apollo Computer

In 1980, Apollo Computer created the market for engineering computer workstations. (Workstations are high-powered freestanding minicomputers.) Apollo was rewarded with rapid growth and a virtual monopoly position. Its first real competitor, Sun Microsystems, did not introduce a competing product until 1982. However, by 1988 Apollo had lost its lead in the workstation market to Sun. While Apollo was generating revenues of $600 million in 1988, Sun's revenues were more than $1 billion. Between 1984 and 1988, Sun's revenues from workstations grew at an annual rate of 100 percent, compared with Apollo's annual growth rate of 35 percent.

The cause of Apollo's slower growth was a slow cycle time. In the computer industry, innovations in microprocessor technology are proceeding at a furious pace. In order to stay abreast of new microprocessor technology, any manufacturer of computers must be continually updating their product. However, while Sun had succeeded in introducing a new product every twelve months and in doubling the power of its workstations every eighteen months on the average, Apollo's product development cycle had stretched out to more than two years. As a result, Apollo's products were regularly superseded by the more technologically advanced products introduced by Sun, and Apollo was falling further and further behind. Consequently, while Sun had increased its market share from 21 percent to 33 percent between 1985 and 1988, Apollo's fell from 41 percent to under 20 percent. In 1989, facing mounting problems, Apollo was acquired by Hewlett-Packard.[48]

company through cross-functional product development teams and partly parallel development processes.[49]

Building Skills in Basic and Applied Research Building skills in basic and applied research requires the employment of research scientists and engineers and the establishment of a work environment that fosters creativity. A number of top companies try to achieve this by setting up university-style research facilities, where scientists and engineers are given time to work on their own research projects, in addition to projects that are linked directly to ongoing company research. At Hewlett-Packard, for example, the company labs are open to engineers around the clock. Hewlett-Packard even encourages its corporate researchers to devote 10 percent of company time to exploring their own ideas—and does not penalize them if they fail. Similarly, at 3M there is a "15 percent rule," which allows researchers to spend 15 percent of the workweek researching any topic they want to investigate, as long as there is the potential of a payoff for the company. The most famous outcome of this policy is the ubiquitous yellow Post-it Notes. The idea for them evolved from a researcher's desire to find a way to keep the bookmark from falling out of his hymn book. Post-it Notes are now a major 3M consumer business, with revenues of around $300 million.

Project Selection and Management Project management is the overall management of the innovation process, from generation of the original concept, through development, and into final production and shipping. Project management requires three important skills: the ability to encourage as much generation of ideas as possible; the ability to select among competing projects at an early stage of development

FIGURE 5.8

The Development Funnel

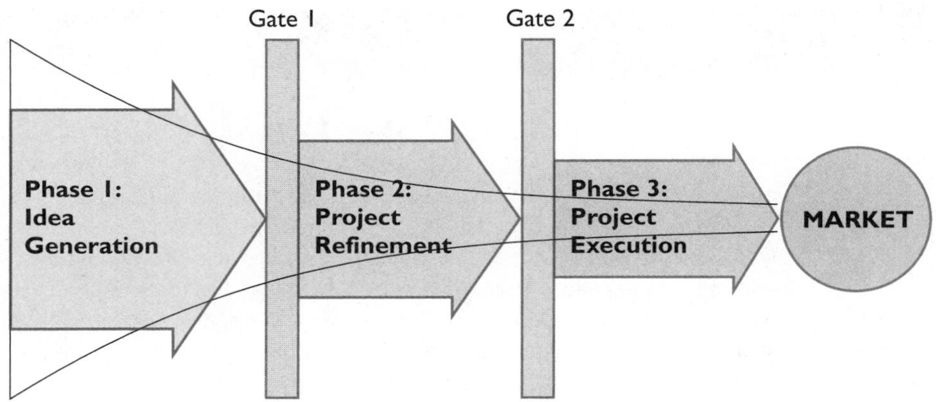

so that the most promising receive funding and potential costly failures are killed off; and the ability to minimize time to market. The concept of the development funnel, illustrated in Figure 5.8, summarizes what is required to build these skills.[50]

As Figure 5.8 shows, the development funnel is divided into three phases. The objective in phase 1 is to widen the mouth of the tunnel to encourage as much idea generation as possible. To this end, a company should solicit input from all its functions, as well as from customers, competitors, and suppliers.

At gate 1 the funnel narrows. Here ideas are reviewed by a cross-functional team of managers who were not involved in the original concept development. Those concepts that are ready to proceed then move on to phase 2 of the funnel, which is where the details of the project proposal are worked out. Note that gate 1 is not a go/no-go evaluation point. At this screen, ideas may be sent back for further concept development to be resubmitted for evaluation.

During phase 2, which typically lasts only one or two months, the data and information developed during phase 1 are put into a form that will enable senior management to evaluate proposed projects against competing projects. Normally, this requires the development of a careful project plan, complete with details of the proposed target market, attainable market share, likely revenues, development costs, production costs, key milestones, and the like. The next big selection point, gate 2, is a go/no-go evaluation point. Senior managers are brought in to review the various projects under consideration. Their task is to select those projects that seem likely winners and that make most sense from a strategic perspective, given the long-term goals of the enterprise. The overriding objective at this gate is to select projects whose successful completion will help maintain or build a competitive advantage for the company. A related objective is to ensure that the company does not spread its scarce capital and human resources too thinly over too many projects and that instead it concentrates resources on those projects where the probability of success and potential returns are most attractive. Any project selected to go forward at this stage will be funded and staffed, the expectation being that it will be carried through to market introduction. In phase 3, the project development proposal is executed by a cross-functional product development team.

Cross-Functional Integration Tight cross-functional integration between R&D, production, and marketing can help a company to ensure that

1. product development projects are driven by customer needs.
2. new products are designed for ease of manufacture.
3. development costs are kept in check.
4. time to market is minimized.

Close integration between R&D and marketing is required to ensure that product development projects are driven by the needs of customers. A company's customers can be one of its primary sources of new product ideas. Identification of customer needs, and particularly unmet needs, can set the context within which successful product innovation takes place. As the point of contact with customers, the marketing function of a company can provide valuable information in this regard. Moreover, integration of R&D and marketing is crucial if a new product is to be properly commercialized. Without integration of R&D and marketing, a company runs the risk of developing products for which there is little or no demand.

The case of Techsonic Industries illustrates the benefits of integrating R&D and marketing. This Alabama company manufactures depth finders—electronic devices used in fishing to measure the depth of water beneath a boat and to track the prey. Techsonic had weathered nine new-product failures in a row when the company decided to conduct interviews across the country with those engaged in the sport of fishing to identify what they needed. It discovered an unmet need for a depth finder with a gauge that could be read in bright sunlight, so that is what Techsonic developed. In the year after the $250 depth finder hit the market, Techsonic's sales tripled to $80 million and its market share surged to 40 percent.[51]

Integrating of R&D and production can help a company ensure that products are designed with manufacturing requirements in mind, which lowers manufacturing costs and leaves less room for mistakes, thus increasing product quality. Such integration can also reduce development costs and speed products to market. If a new product is not designed with manufacturing capabilities in mind, it may prove too difficult to build, given existing manufacturing technology. In that case, it will have to be redesigned, and both overall development costs and the time it takes to bring the product to market may increase significantly. For example, making design changes during product planning could raise overall development costs by 50 percent and add 25 percent to the time it takes to bring the product to market.[52] Moreover, many quantum product innovations require new processes to manufacture them. That makes it all the more important to integrate R&D and production, since minimizing time to market and development costs may require the simultaneous development of new products and new processes.[53]

Product Development Teams One of the best way to achieve cross-functional integration is to establish cross-functional product development teams. These are teams composed of representatives from R&D, marketing, and production. The objective of a team should be to take a product development project through from the initial concept development to market introduction. Certain attributes seem particularly important for a product development team to have if it is to function effectively and meet all its development milestones.[54]

First, the team should be led by a "heavyweight" project manager, who has both high status within the organization and the power and authority to obtain the financial and human resources that the team needs to succeed. This "heavyweight" leader should be dedicated primarily, if not entirely, to the project. The leader should be someone who believes in the project—that is, a champion of the project—and should also be skilled at integrating the perspectives of different functions and at helping personnel from different functions work together for a common goal. Moreover, the leader must also be able to act as the team's advocate to senior management.

Second, the team should include at least one member from each key function. The team members should have an ability to contribute functional expertise, high standing within their function, a willingness to share responsibility for team results, and an ability to put functional advocacy aside. Generally, it is preferable for core team members to be 100 percent dedicated to the project for its duration so that their focus is on the project, not on the ongoing work of their function.

Third, the team members should be physically colocated to create a sense of camaraderie and to facilitate communication.

Fourth, the team should have a clear plan and clear goals, particularly with regard to critical development milestones and development budgets. The team should have incentives to attain those goals—such as pay bonuses when major development milestones are hit.

Fifth, each team needs to develop its own processes for communication and conflict resolution. For example, one product development team at Quantum Corporation, a California-based manufacturer of disk drives for personal computers, instituted a rule that all major decisions would be made and conflicts resolved at meetings that were held every Monday afternoon. This simple rule helped the team to meet its development goals.[55]

Partly Parallel Development Processes One way in which a product development team can compress the time it takes to develop a product and bring it to market is to utilize a partly parallel development process. Traditionally, product development processes have been organized on a sequential basis, as illustrated in Figure 5.9a. A problem with this kind of process is that product development proceeds without consideration of manufacturing issues. Most significantly, since the basic design of a product is completed before the design of a manufacturing process and full-scale commercial production, there is no early warning system to indicate manufacturability. Consequently, the company may find that it cannot manufacture the product in a cost-efficient way and must send it back to the design stage for redesign. The result is that cycle time lengthens as the product iterates back and forth between stages.

To solve this problem, companies typically use a process similar to that illustrated in Figure 5.9b. In the partly parallel development process, development stages overlap so that, for example, work starts on the development of the production process before the product design is finalized. By reducing the need for expensive and time-consuming product redesigns, such a process can significantly reduce the time it takes to develop a new product and bring it to market.

What occurred after Intel introduced its 386 microprocessor in 1986 illustrates this point. A number of companies, including IBM and Compaq, were racing to be the first to introduce a 386-based personal computer. Compaq beat IBM by six months and gained a major share of the high-powered market, mainly because it used a cross-functional team and a partly parallel process to develop the product. The team included engineers (R&D) and marketing, production, and finance peo-

FIGURE 5.9

Sequential and Partly Parallel Development Processes

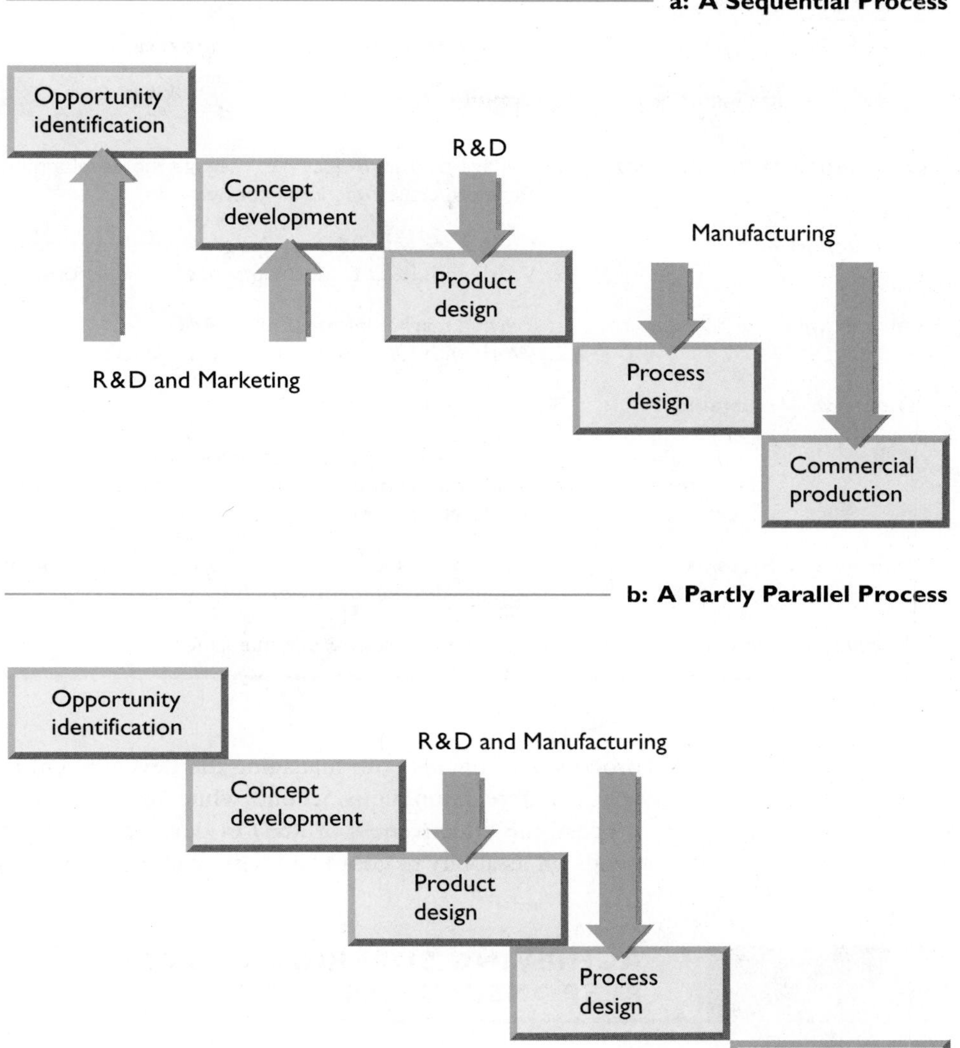

ple. Each function worked in parallel rather than sequentially. While the engineers were designing the product, the production people were setting up the manufacturing facilities, the marketing people were working on distribution and planning marketing campaigns, and the finance people were working on project funding.

Summary: Achieving Superior Innovation

The primary role that the various functions play in achieving superior innovation is summarized in Table 5.4. Two matters, especially, need noting. First, top management must bear primary responsibility for overseeing the whole development

TABLE 5.4

The Role Played by Various Functions in Achieving Superior Innovation

Value Creation Function	*Primary Roles*
Infrastructure (Leadership)	1. Manage overall project (i.e., manage the development function). 2. Facilitate cross-functional cooperation.
Production	1. Cooperate with R&D on designing products that are easy to manufacture. 2. Work with R&D to develop process innovations.
Marketing	1. Provide market information to R&D. 2. Work with R&D to develop new products.
Materials Management	No primary responsibility.
R&D	1. Develop new products and processes. 2. Cooperate with other functions, particularly marketing and manufacturing, in the development process.
Information Systems	1. Use information systems to coordinate cross-functional and cross-company product development work.
Human Resources	1. Hire talented scientists and engineers.

process. This entails both managing the development funnel and facilitating cooperation between functions. Second, while R&D plays a central role in the innovation process, the effectiveness of R&D in developing new products and processes depends on its ability to cooperate with marketing and production.

ACHIEVING SUPERIOR CUSTOMER RESPONSIVENESS

To achieve superior customer responsiveness, a company must give customers what they want when they want it—so long as the company's long-term profitability is not compromised in the process. The more responsive a company is to the needs of its customers, the greater the brand loyalty it can command. In turn, strong brand loyalty may allow a company to charge a premium price for its products or to sell more goods and services to customers. Either way, the company that is responsive to its customers' needs will have a competitive advantage.

Achieving superior customer responsiveness means giving customers value for money, and steps taken to improve the efficiency of a company's production process and the quality of its output should be consistent with this aim. In addition, giving customers what they want may require the development of new products with new features. In other words, achieving superior efficiency, quality, and innovation are all part of achieving superior customer responsiveness. There are two other prerequisites for attaining this goal. The first is to focus on the company's customers and their needs, and the second, to find ways to better satisfy those needs.

Customer Focus

A company cannot be responsive to its customers' needs unless it knows what those needs are. Thus, the first step in building superior customer responsiveness is to motivate the whole company to focus on the customer. The means to this end are demonstrating leadership, shaping employee attitudes, and using mechanisms for bringing customers into the company.

Leadership Customer focus must start at the top of the organization. A commitment to superior customer responsiveness brings attitudinal changes throughout a company that can ultimately be built only through strong leadership. A mission statement (see Chapter 2) that puts customers first is one way to send a clear message to employees about the desired focus. Another avenue is top management's own actions. For example, Tom Monaghan, the founder of Domino's Pizza, stays close to the customer by visiting as many stores as possible every week, running some deliveries himself, insisting that other top managers do the same, and eating Domino's pizza regularly.

Employee Attitudes Achieving a superior customer focus requires that all employees see the customer as the focus of their activity. Leadership alone is not enough to attain this goal. All employees must be trained to focus on the customer, whether their function is marketing, manufacturing, R&D, or accounting. The objective should be to make employees think of themselves as customers—to put themselves in the customers' shoes. At that point, employees will be better able to identify ways to improve the quality of a customer's experience with the company.

To reinforce this mindset, incentive systems within the company should reward employees for satisfying customers. For example, senior managers at the Four Seasons hotel chain, who pride themselves on their customer focus, like to tell the story of Roy Dyment, a doorman in Toronto who neglected to load a departing guest's briefcase into his taxi. The doorman called the guest, a lawyer, in Washington D.C., and found that he desperately needed the briefcase for a morning meeting. Dyment hopped on a plane to Washington and returned it—without first securing approval from his boss. Far from punishing Dyment for making a mistake and for not checking with management before going to Washington, the Four Seasons responded by naming him Employee of the Year.[57] This action sent a powerful message to Four Seasons employees about the importance of satisfying customer needs.

Bringing Customers into the Company "Know thy customer" is one of the keys to achieving superior customer responsiveness. Knowing the customer not only requires that employees think like customers themselves; it also demands that they listen to what their customers have to say, and, as much as possible, bring them into the company. While this may not involve physically bringing customers into the company, it does mean bringing in customers' opinions by soliciting feedback from customers on the company's goods and services and by building information systems that communicate the feedback to the relevant people.

For an example, consider mail-order clothing retailer Lands' End. Through its catalog and customer service telephone operators, Lands' End actively solicits comments from its customers about the quality of its clothing and the kind of merchandise they want Lands' End to supply. Indeed, it was customers' insistence that prompted the company to move into the clothing segment. Lands' End used to supply equipment for sailboats through mail-order catalogs. However, it received so many requests from customers to include outdoor clothing in its offering that it responded by expanding the catalog to fill this need. Soon clothing became the main business and Lands' End dropped the sailboat equipment. Today, the company still pays close attention to customer requests. Every month a computer printout of customer requests and comments is given to managers. This feedback helps the company to fine-tune the merchandise it sells. Indeed, frequently new lines of merchandise are introduced in response to customer requests.[58]

Satisfying Customer Needs

Once a focus on the customer has been achieved, the next task is to satisfy the customer needs that have been identified. As already noted, efficiency, quality, and innovation are all crucial to satisfying those needs. Beyond that, companies can provide a higher level of satisfaction if they customize the product, as much as possible, to the requirements of individual customers and if they minimize the time it takes to respond to customer demands.

Customization Varying the features of a good or service to tailor it to the unique needs of groups of customers or, in the extreme case, individual customers is known as **customization**. It used to be thought that customization raised costs. However, as noted earlier in this chapter, the development of flexible manufacturing technologies has made it feasible to produce a far greater variety of products than could previously be done without suffering a substantial cost penalty. Companies can now customize their products to a much greater extent than they could ten to fifteen years ago, particularly when flexible manufacturing technologies are linked with Web-based information systems. The Opening Case illustrates how Levi Strauss is using Web-based systems in conjunction with flexible manufacturing technology to customize its blue jeans for individual consumers. The same is true of service companies. For example, on-line retailers such as Amazon.com have used Web-based technologies to develop a home page for their stores that is customized for each individual user. When customers access Amazon.com, they are confronted with a list of recommendations for books or music to purchase that is based on an analysis of their prior buying history.

The trend toward customization has fragmented many markets, particularly consumer markets, into ever smaller niches. An example of this fragmentation occurred in Japan in the early 1980s, when Honda dominated the motorcycle market there. Second-place Yamaha decided to go after Honda's lead. In 1981, it announced the opening of a new factory, which, when operating at full capacity, would make Yamaha the world's largest manufacturer of motorcycles. Honda responded by proliferating its product line and stepping up its rate of new-product introduction. At the start of what became known as the "motorcycle wars," Honda had 60 motorcycles in its product line. Over the next eighteen months, Honda rapidly increased its range to 113 models, customizing them to ever smaller niches. Honda was able to accomplish this without bearing a significant cost penalty because it was a flexible manufacturer. The flood of Honda's customized models pushed Yamaha out of much of the market, effectively stalling its bid to overtake Honda.[59]

Response Time Giving customers what they want when they want it requires speed of response to customer demands. To gain a competitive advantage, a company must often respond to consumer demands very quickly, whether the transaction is a furniture manufacturer's delivery of a product once it has been ordered, a bank's processing of a loan application, an automobile manufacturer's delivery of a spare part for a car that broke down, or the wait in a supermarket checkout line. We live in a fast-paced society, where time is a valuable commodity. Companies that can satisfy customer demands for rapid response can build brand loyalty and set a higher price for the product or service.

Increased speed lets a company charge a significant premium, as the mail delivery industry illustrates. The air express niche of the mail delivery industry is based on the notion that customers are often willing to pay considerably more for overnight Express Mail, as opposed to regular mail. Another example of the value of rapid response is Caterpillar, the manufacturer of heavy earthmoving equipment, which can get a spare part to any point in the world within twenty-four hours. Since downtime for heavy construction equipment is very costly, Caterpillar's ability to respond quickly in the event of equipment malfunction is of prime importance to its customers. As a result, many of them have remained loyal to Caterpillar despite the aggressive low-price competition from Komatsu of Japan.

In general, reducing response time requires (1) a marketing function that can quickly communicate customer requests to production, (2) production and materials management functions that can quickly adjust production schedules in response to unanticipated customer demands, and (3) information systems that can help production and marketing in this process.

Summary: Achieving Superior Customer Responsiveness

Table 5.5 summarizes the steps different functions must take if a company is to achieve superior customer responsiveness. Although marketing plays the critical role in helping a company attain this goal, primarily because it represents the point

TABLE 5.5

The Primary Role of Different Functions in Achieving Superior Customer Responsiveness

Value Creation Function	*Primary Roles*
Infrastructure (Leadership)	1. Through leadership by example, build a companywide commitment to customer responsiveness.
Production	1. Achieve customization by implementing flexible manufacturing. 2. Achieve rapid response through flexible manufacturing.
Marketing	1. Know the customer. 2. Communicate customer feedback to appropriate functions.
Materials Management	1. Develop logistics systems capable of responding quickly to unanticipated customer demands (JIT).
R&D	1. Bring customers into the product development process.
Information Systems	1. Use Web-based information systems to increase customer responsiveness.
Human Resources	1. Develop training programs that get employees to think like customers.

of contact with the customer, Table 5.5 shows that the other functions also have major roles to perform. Moreover, like achieving superior efficiency, quality, and innovation, achieving superior customer responsiveness requires top management to lead in building a customer orientation within the company.

SUMMARY OF CHAPTER

This chapter discusses the role that functional-level strategies play in achieving efficiency, quality, innovation, and customer responsiveness. It examines in detail the different steps that lead to this end and makes the following main points:

- ✔ A company can increase efficiency through a number of steps. These include exploiting economies of scale and learning effects, adopting flexible manufacturing technologies, reducing customer defection rates, implementing just-in-time systems, getting the R&D function to design products that are easy to manufacture, upgrading the skills of employees through training, introducing self-managing teams, linking pay to performance, building a companywide commitment to efficiency through strong leadership, and designing structures that facilitate cooperation among different functions in pursuit of efficiency goals.
- ✔ Superior quality can help a company both to lower its costs and to differentiate its product and charge a premium price.
- ✔ Achieving superior quality demands an organizationwide commitment to quality and a clear focus on the customer. It also requires metrics to measure quality goals and incentives that emphasize quality; input from employees regarding ways in which quality can be improved; a methodology for tracing defects to their source and correcting the problems that produce them; rationalization of the company's supply base; cooperation with the suppliers that remain to implement TQM programs; products that are designed for ease of manufacturing; and substantial cooperation among functions.
- ✔ The failure rate of new-product introductions is high due to factors such as uncertainty, poor commercialization, poor positioning strategy, technological myopia, and slow cycle time.
- ✔ To achieve superior innovation, a company must build skills in basic and applied research; design good processes for managing development projects; and achieve close integration between the different functions of the enterprise, primarily through the adoption of cross-functional product development teams and partly parallel development processes.
- ✔ Achieving superior customer responsiveness often requires that the company achieve superior efficiency, quality, and innovation.
- ✔ To achieve superior customer responsiveness, a company needs to give customers what they want when they want it. It must ensure a strong customer focus, which can be attained through leadership; training employees to think like customers; bring customers into the company by means of superior market research; customizing the product to the unique needs of individual customers or customer groups; and responding quickly to customer demands.

DISCUSSION QUESTIONS

1. How are the four generic building blocks of competitive advantage related to each other?
2. What role can top management play in helping a company achieve superior efficiency, quality, innovation, and customer responsiveness?
3. In the long run, will adoption of TQM practices give a company a competitive advantage, or will it be required just to achieve parity with competitors?
4. In what sense might innovation be called the single most important building block of competitive advantage?

Practicing Strategic Management

SMALL-GROUP EXERCISE
Identifying Excellence

Break up into groups of three to five people, and discuss the following scenario:

You are the management team of a start-up company, which will produce disk drives for the personal computer industry. You will sell your product to manufacturers of personal computers (original equipment manufacturers). The disk drive market is characterized by rapid technological change, product life cycles of only six to nine months, intense price competition, high fixed costs for manufacturing equipment, and substantial manufacturing economies of scale. Your customers—the original equipment manufacturers—issue very demanding technological specifications that your product has to comply with. The original equipment manufacturers also pressure you to deliver your product on time so that it fits in with their own product introduction schedule. In this industry, what functional competencies are the most important for you to build? How will you design your internal processes to ensure that those competencies are built within the company?

STRATEGIC MANAGEMENT PROJECT
Module 5

This module deals with the ability of your company to achieve superior efficiency, quality, innovation, and customer responsiveness. With the information you have at your disposal, answer the questions and perform the tasks listed:

1. Is your company pursuing any of the efficiency-enhancing practices discussed in this chapter?
2. Is your company pursuing any of the quality-enhancing practices discussed in this chapter?
3. Is your company pursuing any of the practices designed to enhance innovation discussed in this chapter?
4. Is your company pursuing any of the practices designed to increase customer responsiveness discussed in this chapter?
5. Evaluate the competitive position of your company in the light of your answers to questions 1–4. Explain what, if anything, the company needs to do to improve its competitive position.

ARTICLE FILE 5

Find an example of a company that is widely regarded as excellent. Identify the source of its excellence and relate it to the material discussed in this chapter. Pay particular attention to the role played by the various functions in building excellence.

EXPLORING THE WEB
Visiting Applied Materials

Visit the Web site of Applied Materials, the world's largest manufacturer of semiconductor fabrication equipment at (http://www.appliedmaterials.com). Find and read the company's mission statement. What does this mission statement tell you about the kind of competitive advantage that Applied Materials is trying to build? How important are efficiency, quality, innovation, and customer responsiveness to this company?

Now go to the sections of Applied's Web site that detail the company's financial results, products, and press releases. Read through these sections and try to establish how successful Applied has been at meeting the objectives set down in its mission statement. What do you think the company has done at the functional level to increase its efficiency, customer responsiveness, innovative ability, and product quality?

Search the Web for a company whose home page describes in some detail its approach to achieving one of the following: superior productivity, product quality, customer service, or innovation. Using this information, document the company's functional-level strategy and assess whether the strategy makes sense, given what you have learned so far in this book.

CLOSING CASE

Reengineering Lloyds Bank

LLOYDS BANK is one of the largest banks in Britain, with 29,000 employees and 1,800 branches nationwide. It is also one of Britain's most profitable banks, with one of the lowest ratios of operating costs to income in the British banking industry. Lloyds' senior management gives much of the credit for the bank's recent performance to its Service Quality Improvement Program (SQIP), an exercise in business process reengineering. Business process reengineering is an attempt to reorganize companies around their core processes as opposed to their traditional functions, such as the production department, marketing department, or human resource department. The term *core processes* has been defined as "a collection of activities that takes one or more kinds of input and creates an output that is of value to the customer." Processes often include activities such as customer service, order fulfillment, and product development.

Lloyds Bank turned to process reengineering in September 1992 in an attempt to increase the quality of its service and drive down the cost structure of its retail branch banking network. The catalyst was the growing competition from Britain's building societies (which are similar to U.S. savings and loans). The building societies had aggressively pursued Lloyds' retail customers following the deregulation of the British financial services industry, which had allowed banks and building societies to enter each other's markets for the first time. The bank was also worried about the impact of service expansion on its cost structure. During the 1980s, each time the bank entered a new service market (for example, home mortgage financing), it simply added more staff to a retail branch. As a result, by the early 1990s, branch costs were beginning to spiral out of control.

Under the traditional system at Lloyds, staff were given narrowly defined functional responsibilities within the context of a rigid hierarchical structure. One set of people would be responsible for managing checking accounts, another for reviewing a customer's credit, and still another for issuing credit cards, and so on. One consequence was that countless people and bits of paper were involved in what, from the customers' point of view, was a single process. For example, under the old system for opening an account at a Lloyds branch, an application form could spend a month wandering from desk to desk as different staff ordered bank cards, reviewed credit details, ordered checkbooks, opened savings accounts, and so on. Under Lloyds' new system, a single person is now responsible for a largely paperless "quality welcome" process, which entails reviewing the customer's credit history, setting up an account, and issuing credit cards, ATM cards, and checkbooks. With this new process, it usually takes less than a week for a new account to be fully functional.

Besides the "quality welcome" process, Lloyds identified five other core processes within its branches, including "lending control," "periodic payments," and "customer retention."

Each process was assigned a process owner, whose job it was to make sure that the process was reengineered to achieve Lloyds' goals of driving down costs and increasing the quality of customer service. The processes were tested in a make-believe branch before being introduced across the bank's network of retail branches in a series of waves starting in July 1993. The indications are that SQIP is having the desired effect. Lloyds' managers claim that the reengineering project has comfortably cleared the 12 percent return on capital hurdle required of business ideas. For example, the number of faulty checkbook orders fell by 30 percent in the first two months of the program—producing savings large enough to pay for the computers that monitor this activity under the new process. There is also evidence that the bank is meeting its central aim of improving customer service. Lloyds' own measure of customer satisfaction rose from 73 percent in mid 1993, when the project began, to 80 percent by mid 1995, putting the bank comfortably ahead of its two largest British rivals. Having said that, however, a 7 percent improvement in customer satisfaction is less than stunning.

Also on the down side, Lloyds has had to deal with morale problems in many of its branches, where the reengineering process is often perceived to be a subtle way of cutting jobs and, in some cases, closing down branches altogether. The bank closed 300 branches between 1990 and 1995, although management claims that this effort was independent of the reengineering process, which focuses on what is happening within branches.

Management does not question the fact that 200 jobs have been lost as a result of the reengineering process but points out that all these losses were voluntary. Those hit hardest by the reengineering effort seem to be middle-level managers, as opposed to branch employees. Between mid 1993 and mid 1995, the bank reduced the number of area directors from 80 to 41, largely because the reengineering effort enabled the bank to do more with less. Whatever the true cause of the job losses, there are concerns that employee morale problems are inhibiting Lloyd's ability to realize the full benefits of its reengineering efforts.[60]

Case Discussion Questions

1. What are the goals of the reengineering project at Lloyds Bank? If successful, how will this project affect the efficiency, quality, and customer responsiveness of Lloyds Bank?
2. Is the kind of process reengineering described here consistent with Deming's approach to total quality management, as described in this chapter?
3. Can you see a down side to Lloyds' reengineering effort? What is it? How might the impact of this down side be limited?

End Notes

1. E. Schonfeld, "The Customized, Digitized, Have It Your Way Economy," *Fortune*, September 28, 1998, p. 117; M. Knight, "Levi's to Close 11 Plants in Shift to Offshore Manufacturing," *Business and Industry*, February 24, 1999, p. 6; "The View from the Outside, Levi's Needs More Than a Patch," *New York Times*, February 28, 1999, p. 4.
2. *Chase press release*, "Chase and Chemical Merger Creating Largest Banking Company in the United States," March 21, 1996, (http://www.chase.com); S. Lipin, "Joining Fortunes," *Wall Street Journal*, August 28, 1995, p. 1; G. B. Knecht, "Chemical Merger with Chase Echoes Earlier Alliance," *Wall Street Journal*, September 1, 1995, p. 4.
3. For example, see F. M. Scherer, A. Beckenstein, E. Kaufer, and R. D. Murphy, *The Economies of Multiplant Operations* (Cambridge, Mass.: Harvard University Press, 1975).
4. H. Luft, J. Bunker, and A. Enthoven, "Should Operations Be Regionalized?" *New England Journal of Medicine*, 301 (1979) 1364–1369.
5. G. Hall and S. Howell, "The Experience Curve from an Economist's Perspective," *Strategic Management Journal*, 6 (1985), 197–212; M. Lieberman, "The Learning Curve and Pricing in the Chemical Processing Industries," *RAND Journal of Economics*, 15 (1984), 213–228.
6. Boston Consulting Group, *Perspectives on Experience* (Boston: Boston Consulting Group, 1972); Hall and Howell, "The Experience Curve,"; W. B. Hirschmann, "Profit from the Learning Curve," *Harvard Business Review* (January–February 1964), 125–139.
7. A. A. Alchian, "Reliability of Progress Curves in Airframe Production," *Econometrica*, 31 (1963), 679–693.
8. M. Borrus, L. A. Tyson, and J. Zysman, "Creating Advantage: How Government Policies Create Trade in the Semi-Conductor Industry," *Strategic Trade Policy and the New International Economics*, ed. P. R. Krugman (Cambridge, Mass.: MIT Press, 1986); S. Ghoshal and C. A. Bartlett, "Matsushita Electrical Industrial (MEI) in 1987," *Harvard Business School Case* No. 388-144, 1988.
9. G. Stalk and T. M. Hout, *Competing Against Time* (New York: Free Press, 1990); D. Miller, *The Icarus Paradox* (New York: Harper Business, 1990).
10. Abernathy and Wayne, "Limits of the Learning Curve," *Harvard Business Review*, pp. 109–119, 1980.
11. D. F. Barnett and R. W. Crandall, *Up from the Ashes: The Rise of the Steel Minimill in the United States* (Washington, D.C.: Brookings Institution, 1986).
12. See P. Nemetz and L. Fry, "Flexible Manufacturing Organizations: Implications for Strategy Formulation," *Academy of Management Review*, 13 (1988), 627–638; N. Greenwood, *Implementing Flexible Manufacturing Systems* (New York: Halstead Press, 1986); J. P. Womack, D. T. Jones, and D. Roos, *The Machine That Changed the World* (New York: Rawson Associates, 1990); and R. Parthasarthy and S. P. Seith, "The Impact of Flexible Automation on Business Strategy and Organizational Structure," *Academy of Management Review*, 17 (1992), 86–111.
13. B. J. Pine, *Mass Customization: The New Frontier in Business Competition* (Boston: Harvard Business School Press, 1993); S. Kotha, "Mass Customization: Implementing the Emerging Paradigm for Competitive Advantage," *Strategic Management Journal*, 16 (1995), 21–42; J. H. Gilmore and B. J. Pine II, "The Four Faces of Mass Customization," *Harvard Business Review* (January–February, 1997), 91–101.
14. "The Celling Out of America," *Economist*, December 17, 1994, pp. 63–64.
15. M. A. Cusumano, *The Japanese Automobile Industry* (Cambridge, Mass.: Harvard University Press, 1989); Ohno Taiichi, *Toyota Production System* (Cambridge, Mass.: Productivity Press, 1990); Womack, Jones, and Roos, *The Machine That Changed the World.*
16. F. F. Reichheld and W. E. Sasser, "Zero Defections: Quality Comes to Service," *Harvard Business Review* (September–October 1990), 105–111.
17. The example comes from Reichheld and Sasser, "Zero Defections," 105–111.
18. Ibid.
19. R. Narasimhan and J. R. Carter, "Organization, Communication and Coordination of International Sourcing," *International Marketing Review*, 7 (1990) 6–20.
20. H. F. Busch, "Integrated Materials Management," *IJDP & MM*, 18 (1990) 28–39.
21. Stalk and Hout, *Competing Against Time.*
22. A. Sorge and M. Warner, "Manpower Training, Manufacturing Organization, and Work Place Relations in Great Britain and West Germany," *British Journal of Industrial Relations*, 18 (1980), 318–333; R. Jaikumar, "Postindustrial Manufacturing," *Harvard Business Review* (November-December 1986), 72–83.
23. J. Hoerr, "The Payoff from Teamwork," *Business Week*, July 10, 1989, pp. 56–62.
24. "The Trouble with Teams," *Economist*, January 14, 1995, p. 61.
25. T. C. Powell and A. Dent-Micallef, "Information Technology as Competitive Advantage: The Role of Human, Business, and Technology Resource," *Strategic Management Journal*, 18 (1997), 375–405; B. Gates, *Business @ the Speed of Thought* (New York: Warner Books, 1999).
26. "Cisco@Speed," *Economist*, Special Report: Business and the Internet, June 26, 1999, p. 12; S. Tully, "How Cisco Mastered the Net," *Fortune*, August 17, 1997, p. 207–210; C. Kano. "The Real King of the Internet," *Fortune*, September 7, 1998, pp. 82–93.
27. Gates, *Business@the Speed of Thought.*
28. Ibid.
29. "Work in Progress," *Economist*, July 24, 1999.
30. See the articles published in the special issue on total quality management, *Academy of Management Review*, 19 (1994). The following paper provides a good overview of many of the issues involved from an academic perspective: J. W. Dean and D. E. Bowen, "Management Theory and Total Quality," *Academy of Management Review*, 19 (1994),

392–418. Also see T.C.Powell, "Total Quality Management as Competitive Advantage," *Strategic Management Journal*, 16 (1995), 15–37.

31. For general background information, see "How to Build Quality," *Economist*, September 23, 1989, pp. 91–92; A. Gabor, *The Man Who Discovered Quality* (New York: Penguin, 1990); and P. B. Crosby, *Quality Is Free* (New York: Mentor, 1980).
32. W. E. Deming, "Improvement of Quality and Productivity Through Action by Management," *National Productivity Review*, 1 (Winter 1981–1982), 12–22.
33. J. Bowles, "Is American Management Really Committed to Quality?" *Management Review* (April 1992), 42–46.
34. O. Port and G. Smith, "Quality," *Business Week*, November 30, 1992, pp. 66–75. See also "The Straining of Quality," *Economist*, January 14, 1995, pp. 55–56.
35. C. H. Deutsch, "Six Sigma Enlightenment," *New York Times*, December 7, 1998, p. 1; J. J. Barshay, "The Six Sigma Story," *Star Tribune*, June 14, 1999, p. 1; D. D. Bak, "Rethinking Industrial Drives," *Electrical/Electronics Technology*, November 30, 1998, p. 58.
36. Bowles, "Is American Management Really Committed to Quality?"; "The Straining of Quality."
37. Gabor, *The Man Who Discovered Quality*.
38. Deming, "Improvement of Quality and Productivity."
39. W. E. Deming, *Out of the Crisis* (Cambridge, Mass.: MIT Center for Advanced Engineering Study, 1986).
40. J. F. Siler and S. Atchison, "The Rx at Work in Utah," *Business Week*, October 25, 1991, p. 113.
41. E. Mansfield. "How Economists See R&D," *Harvard Business Review* (November–December, 1981), 98–106.
42. Ibid.
43. Booz, Allen, & Hamilton, "New Products Management for the 1980's," privately published research report, 1982.
44. A. L. Page, "PDMA's New Product Development Practices Survey: Performance and Best Practices." PDMA 15th Annual International Conference, Boston, October 16, 1991.
45. See S. L. Brown and K. M. Eisenhardt, "Product Developlment: Past Research, Present Findings, and Future Directions," *Academy of Management Review*, 20 (1995), 343–378; M. B. Lieberman and D. B. Montgomery, "First Mover Advantages," *Strategic Management Journal* (Special Issue 9, Summer 1988), 41–58; D. J. Teece, "Profiting from Technological Innovation: Implications for Integration, Collaboration, Licensing and Public Policy," *Research Policy*, 15 (1987), 285–305; G. J. Tellis and P. N. Golder, "First to Market, First to Fail?" *Sloan Management Review* (Winter 1996), 65–75.
46. R. L. Hudson, "Philips Official Calls DCC Launch Flawed, Vows Division Comeback," *Wall Street Journal*, August 19, 1993, p. A7; (2) A. Kupfer, "The Next Wave in Cassette Tapes," *Fortune*, June 3, 1991, pp. 153–158; P. M. Reilly, "Sony's Digital Audio Format Pulls Ahead of Philips's, But Both Still Have Far to Go," *Wall Street Journal*, August 6, 1993, p. B1.
47. Stalk and Hout, *Competing Against Time*.
48. Ibid.; B. Buell and R.D. Hof, "Hewlett-Packard Rethinks Itself," *Business Week*, April 1, 1991, pp. 76–79.
49. Clark and Wheelwright, *Managing New Product and Process Development.*; M. A. Schilling and C. W. L. Hill. "Managing the New Product Development Process," *Academy of Management Executive*, 12, (August 1998), 67–81.
50. Clark and Wheelwright, *Managing New Product and Process Development*.
51. P. Sellers, "Getting Customers to Love You," *Fortune*, March 13, 1989, pp. 38–42.
52. O. Port, "Moving Past the Assembly Line," *Business Week*, Special Issue: Reinventing America, 1992, pp. 177–180.
53. G. P. Pisano and S. C. Wheelwright, "The New Logic of High Tech R&D," *Harvard Business Review*, September–October 1995, 93–105.
54. K. B. Clark and T. Fujimoto, "The Power of Product Integrity," *Harvard Business Review* (November–December 1990), 107–118; Clark and Wheelwright, *Managing New Product and Process;* Brown and Eisenhardt, "Product Development: Past Research, Present Findings, and Future Directions"; Stalk and Hout, *Competing Against Time*.
55. C. Christensen, "Quantum Corporation—Business and Product Teams," *Harvard Business School Case* No. 9-692-023.
56. S. Caminiti, "A Mail Order Romance: Lands' End Courts Unseen Customers," *Fortune*, March 13, 1989, pp. 43–44.
57. Sellers, "Getting Customers to Love You."
58. Caminiti, "A Mail Order Romance."
59. Stalk and Hout, *Competing Against Time*.
60. "The Black Horse Goes to the Vet," *Economist*, July 22, 1995, pp. 71–72; J. Kelley, "London Calling," *Journal of Business Strategy,* (March–April 1995), 22–26; K. Waterhouse and A. Morgan, "Using Research to Help Keep Good Customers," *Marketing and Research Today* (August 1994), 181–194; M. Hammer and J. Champy, *Reengineering the Corporation* (New York: Harper Business, 1993).

6 Business-Level Strategy

OPENING CASE

How E*Trade Uses the Internet to Gain a Low-Cost Advantage

As we saw in Chapter 3, in many industries new entrants have taken advantage of the opportunities opened up by the Internet to overcome barriers to entry and compete successfully against market leaders. Consider the situation of E*Trade, the on-line brokerage firm. As we discussed, for many years large established brokerages like Merrill Lynch had dominated the industry and used their protected positions to charge exorbitant brokerage fees. E*Trade's managers bought and developed software and hardware that allowed its customers to make their own trades, and to do so at a price as low as $19.95.[1]

However, the low-cost competition story in the brokerage industry did not end there. By 1999, E*Trade itself came under pressure from a new generation of on-line brokerage houses, such as Suretrade, Ameritrade and DLJ, which began offering customers trades for only $9.95 and even $7.95, undercutting E*Trade's prices by 100 percent. How could a company like E*Trade, which had made its reputation by being the low-cost leader in the industry, compete against companies that saw themselves as the new cost leaders?

The answer for E*Trade was to enhance its differentiated appeal to its customers by offering them a higher quality of service and a broader product line. E*Trade introduced a brand-new software package that made it even easier for customers to use the Internet to trade shares. What was very important, the new software was more reliable in that customers could make their trades when they wanted. Previously, E*Trade, like other brokerage firms, had experienced many problems when too many customers made trades at once; often the overloaded system simply crashed and customers were unable to buy or sell shares. E*Trade's new package also offered customers more financial research tools and gave them access to more information about specific companies to aid them in their investment decisions. In addition, E*Trade offered customers increased access to real-time stock quotes so that they could take advantage of second-to-second changes in stock prices to make money. Finally, it gave customers the opportunity to invest in Initial Public Offerings (IPOs) of shares from new companies where both potential risks and returns are high.

Furthermore, in 1999 E*Trade decided to merge with an on-line bank, Telebank, to provide its customers with a broad range of on-line banking services, such as paying bills on-line, and thus to become a one-stop on-line shopping site for all of a customer's financial needs.[2] It also took over a variety of other insurance and financial service companies to offer its customers a broad financial service product line.

The realization that it could not just be a low-cost company but also had to create a differentiation advantage in the quickly evolving on-line financial services industry has paid off for E*Trade. Its customers did not switch to the new low-cost leaders because customers perceived that for the $19.95 price they were receiving extra value for money in terms of service and reliability. E*Trade's customer accounts have increased steadily, and its stock price has soared as investors see that the company's competitive advantage is sustainable and that the company is likely to remain a dominant player in the changed industry environment. Indeed, E*Trade has shown the other firms in the industry that to remain viable they must all pursue a simultaneous low-cost and differentiation strategy—something that has become possible only because of the emergence of the Internet, which has created external economies that firms can exploit to increase their performance and competitive advantage.

OVERVIEW

As the E*Trade case suggests, this chapter examines how a company can compete effectively in a business or industry and scrutinizes the various strategies that it can adopt to maximize competitive advantage and profitability. Chapter 3, on the external industry environment, provides concepts for analyzing industry opportunities and threats. Chapters 4 and 5 discuss how a company develops functional-level strategies to build internal strengths and distinctive competencies to achieve a competitive advantage. The purpose of this chapter is to consider the business-level strategies that a company can use to exploit its competitive advantage and compete effectively in an industry. By the end of this chapter, you will be able to identify and distinguish between the principal kinds of business-level strategies that strategic managers can develop to give their companies a competitive advantage over their rivals.

WHAT IS BUSINESS-LEVEL STRATEGY?

Business-level strategy refers to the plan of action that strategic managers adopt for using a company's resources and distinctive competencies to gain a competitive advantage over its rivals in a market or industry. In Chapter 2, we discuss Derek F. Abell's view that the process of business definition entails decisions about (1) customers' needs, or *what* is to be satisfied; (2) customer groups, or *who* is to be satisfied; and (3) distinctive competencies, or *how* customer needs are to be satisfied.[3] These three decisions are the basis for choosing a business-level strategy because they determine how a company will compete in a business or industry. Consequently, we need to look at the ways in which a company makes these three decisions to gain a competitive advantage over its rivals.

Customers' Needs and Product Differentiation

Customers' needs are desires, wants, or cravings that can be satisfied by means of the characteristics of a product or service. For example, a person's craving for something sweet can be satisfied by a carton of Ben & Jerry's ice cream, a Snickers bar, or a spoonful of sugar. **Product differentiation** is the process of creating a competitive advantage by designing products—goods or services—to satisfy customers' needs. All companies must differentiate their products to a certain degree in order to attract customers and satisfy some minimal level of need. However, some companies differentiate their products to a much greater degree than others, and this difference can give them a competitive edge.

Some companies offer the customer a low-priced product without engaging in much product differentiation. Others seek to create something unique about their product so that they satisfy customers' needs in ways that other products cannot. The uniqueness may relate to the physical characteristics of the product, such as quality or reliability, or it may lie in the product's appeal to customers' psychological needs, such as the need for prestige or status.[4] Thus, a Japanese car may be differentiated by its reputation for reliability, and a Corvette or a Porsche may be differentiated by its ability to satisfy customers' needs for status.

Customer Groups and Market Segmentation

Market segmentation is the way a company decides to group customers, based on important differences in their needs or preferences, in order to gain a competitive advantage.[5] For example, General Motors groups its customers according to the amount of money they want and can afford to spend to buy a car, and for each group it builds different cars, which range from the low-priced GEO Metro to the high-priced Cadillac Seville.

In general, a company can adopt three alternative strategies toward market segmentation.[6] First, it can choose not to recognize that different groups of customers have different needs and instead adopt the approach of serving the average customer. Second, a company can choose to segment its market into different constituencies and develop a product to suit the needs of each. For example, in a recent catalog, Sony offered twenty-four different 19-inch color television sets, each targeted at a different market segment. Third, a company can choose to recognize that the market is segmented but concentrate on servicing only one market segment, or niche, such as the luxury-car niche pursued by Mercedes-Benz.

Why would a company want to make complex product/market choices and create a different product tailored to each market segment rather than create a single product for the whole market? The answer is that the decision to provide many products for many market niches allows a company to satisfy customers' needs better. As a result, customers' demand for the company's products rises and generates more revenue than would be the case if the company offered just one product for the whole market.[7] Sometimes, however, the nature of the product or the nature of the industry does not allow much differentiation, as is true, for instance, of bulk chemicals or cement.[8] These industries afford little opportunity for obtaining a competitive advantage through product differentiation and market segmentation because there is little opportunity for serving customers' needs and customer groups in different ways. Instead, price is the main criterion by which customers evaluate the product, and the competitive advantage lies with the company that has superior efficiency and can provide the lowest-priced product.

Distinctive Competencies

The third issue in business-level strategy is deciding which distinctive competencies to pursue to satisfy customers' needs and customer groups.[9] As we discuss in Chapter 4, there are four ways companies can obtain a competitive advantage: superior efficiency, quality, innovation, and responsiveness to customers. The Four Seasons hotel chain, for example, attempts to do all it can to provide its customers with the highest-quality accommodations and the best customer service possible. In making business strategy choices, a company must decide how to organize and combine its distinctive competencies to gain a competitive advantage. The source of these distinctive competencies is examined at length in Chapter 5.

CHOOSING A GENERIC BUSINESS-LEVEL STRATEGY

Companies pursue a business-level strategy to gain a competitive advantage that allows them to outperform rivals and achieve above-average returns. They can choose from three basic generic competitive approaches: cost leadership, differentiation, and focus, although, as we will see, these can be combined in different ways.[10] These strategies are called *generic* because all businesses or industries can pursue them regardless of whether they are manufacturing, service, or not-for-profit enterprises. Each of the generic strategies results from a company's making consistent choices on product, market, and distinctive competencies—choices that reinforce each other. Table 6.1 summarizes the choices appropriate for each of the three generic strategies.

Cost-Leadership Strategy

A company's goal in pursuing a **cost-leadership strategy** is to outperform competitors by doing everything it can to produce goods or services at a cost lower than theirs. Two advantages accrue from a cost-leadership strategy. First, because of its lower costs, the cost leader is able to charge a lower price than its competitors yet make the same level of profit. If companies in the industry charge similar prices for their products, the cost leader still makes a higher profit than its competitors because of its lower costs. Second, if rivalry within the industry increases and companies start to compete on price, the cost leader will be able to withstand competition

TABLE 6.1

Product/Market/Distinctive-Competency Choices and Generic Competitive Strategies

	Cost Leadership	*Differentiation*	*Focus*
Product Differentiation	Low (principally by price)	High (principally by uniqueness)	Low to high (price or uniqueness)
Market Segmentation	Low (mass market)	High (many market segments)	Low (one or a few segments)
Distinctive Competency	Manufacturing and materials management	Research and development, sales and marketing	Any kind of distinctive competency

better than the other companies because of its lower costs. For both these reasons, cost leaders are likely to earn above-average profits. How does a company become the cost leader? It achieves this position by means of the product/market/distinctive-competency choices that it makes to gain a low-cost competitive advantage (see Table 6.1).

Strategic Choices The cost leader chooses a low level of product differentiation. Differentiation is expensive; if the company expends resources to make its products unique, then its costs rise.[11] The cost leader aims for a level of differentiation not markedly inferior to that of the differentiator (a company that competes by spending resources on product development), but a level obtainable at low cost.[12] The cost leader does not try to be the industry leader in differentiation; it waits until customers want a feature or service before providing it. For example, a cost leader does not introduce stereo sound in television sets. It adds stereo sound only when it is obvious that consumers want it.

The cost leader also normally ignores the different market segments and positions its product to appeal to the average customer. The reason the cost leader makes this choice is, again, that developing a line of products tailored to the needs of different market segments is an expensive proposition. A cost leader normally engages in only a limited amount of market segmentation. Even though no customer may be totally happy with the product, the fact that the company normally charges a lower price than its competitors attracts customers to its products.

In developing distinctive competencies, the overriding goal of the cost leader must be to increase its efficiency and lower its costs compared with its rivals. The development of distinctive competencies in manufacturing and materials management is central to achieving this goal. Companies pursuing a low-cost strategy may attempt to ride down the experience curve so that they can lower their manufacturing costs.

Achieving a low-cost position may also require that the company develop skills in flexible manufacturing and adopt efficient materials-management techniques. (As you may recall, Table 5.1 outlines the ways in which a company's functions can be used to increase efficiency.) Consequently, the manufacturing and materials-management functions are the center of attention for a company pursuing a cost-leadership strategy; the other functions shape their distinctive competencies to meet the needs of manufacturing and materials management.[13] For example, the sales function may develop the competency of capturing large, stable sets of customers' orders. In turn, this allows manufacturing to make longer production runs and so achieve economies of scale and reduce costs. The human resource function may focus on instituting training programs and compensation systems that lower costs by enhancing employees' productivity, and the research and development function may specialize in process improvements to lower the manufacturing costs. We saw in the Opening Case, for example, how E*Trade took advantage of advances in information technology to lower the costs associated with exchanging goods between buyers and sellers. Similarly, Dell Computer uses the Internet to lower the cost of selling its computers—Internet sales now account for more than 30 percent of its sales.

Many cost leaders gear all their strategic product/market/distinctive-competency choices to the single goal of squeezing out every cent of costs to sustain their competitive advantage. A company such as H. J. Heinz is another excellent example of a cost leader. Because beans and canned vegetables do not permit much of a markup, the profit comes from the large volume of cans sold. Therefore, Heinz goes to extraordinary lengths to try to reduce costs—by even one-twentieth of a cent per can—because this will lead to large cost savings and thus bigger profits over the long run. As you will see in the chapters in Part Four on strategy implementation, another source of cost savings in pursuing cost leadership is the design of the organizational structure to match this strategy, since structure is a major source of a company's costs. As we discuss in Chapter 12, a low-cost strategy usually implies tight production controls and rigorous use of budgets to control the production process.

Advantages and Disadvantages The advantages of each generic strategy are best discussed in terms of Porter's five forces model, which is introduced in Chapter 3.[14] The five forces are threats from competitors, powerful suppliers, powerful buyers, substitute products, and new entrants. The cost leader is protected from *industry competitors* by its cost advantage. Its lower costs also mean that it will be less affected than its competitors by increases in the price of inputs if there are *powerful suppliers* and less affected by a fall in the price it can charge for its products if there are *powerful buyers*. Moreover, since cost leadership usually requires a big market share, the cost leader purchases in relatively large quantities, increasing its bargaining power over suppliers. If *substitute products* start to come into the market, the cost leader can reduce its price to compete with them and retain its market share. Finally, the leader's cost advantage constitutes a *barrier to entry*, since other companies are unable to enter the industry and match the leader's costs or prices. The cost leader is, therefore, relatively safe as long as it can maintain its cost advantage and price is the key for a significant number of buyers.

The principal dangers of the cost-leadership approach lurk in competitors' ability to find ways to produce at lower cost and beat the cost leader at its own game. For instance, if technological change makes experience-curve economies obsolete, new companies may apply lower-cost technologies that give them a cost advantage over the cost leader. The steel minimills discussed in Chapter 5 gained this advantage. Competitors may also draw a cost advantage from labor-cost savings. Foreign competitors in the Third World have very low labor costs; for example, wage costs in the United States are roughly 600 percent more than they are in Malaysia, China, or Mexico. Many U.S. companies now assemble their products abroad as part of their low-cost strategy; many are forced to do so simply to compete.

Competitors' ability to imitate easily the cost leader's methods is another threat to the cost-leadership strategy. For example, the ability of IBM-clone manufacturers to produce IBM-compatible products at costs similar to IBM's (but, of course, to sell them at a much lower price) was a major factor contributing to IBM's troubles.

Finally, the cost-leadership strategy carries a risk that the cost leader, in its single-minded desire to reduce costs, may lose sight of changes in customers' tastes. Thus, a company might make decisions that decrease costs but drastically affect demand for the product. For example, Joseph Schlitz Brewing lowered the quality of its beer's ingredients, substituting inferior grains to reduce costs. Consumers immediately caught on, with the result that demand for the product dropped dramatically. As mentioned earlier, the cost leader cannot abandon product differentiation, and even low-priced products, such as Timex watches, cannot be too inferior to the more expensive watches made by Seiko if the low-cost, low-price policy is to succeed.

Differentiation Strategy

The objective of the generic **differentiation strategy** is to achieve a competitive advantage by creating a product (good or service) that is perceived by customers to be *unique* in some important way. The differentiated company's ability to satisfy a customer's need in a way that its competitors cannot means that it can charge a *premium price* (a price considerably above the industry's average). The ability to increase revenues by charging premium prices (rather than by reducing costs as the cost leader does) allows the differentiator to outperform its competitors and gain above-average profits. The premium price is usually substantially above the price charged by the cost leader, and customers pay it because they believe the product's differentiated qualities are worth the difference. Consequently, the product is priced on the basis of what the market will bear.[15]

Thus, Mercedes-Benz cars are much more expensive in the United States than in Europe because they confer more status here. Similarly, a BMW is not a lot more expensive to produce than a Honda, but its price is determined by customers who perceive that the prestige of owning a BMW is something worth paying for. Similarly, Rolex watches do not cost much to produce; their design has not changed very much for years, and their gold content represents only a fraction of the price. Customers, however, buy a Rolex because of the unique quality they perceive in it: its ability to confer status on its wearer. In stereos, the name Bang & Olufsen of Denmark stands out; in jewelry, Tiffany; in airplanes, Learjets. All these products command premium prices because of their differentiated qualities.

Strategic Choices As Table 6.1 shows, a differentiator chooses a high level of product differentiation to gain a competitive advantage. Product differentiation can be achieved in three principal ways, which are discussed in detail in Chapter 4: quality, innovation, and responsiveness to customers. For example, Procter & Gamble claims that its product quality is high and that Ivory soap is 99.44 percent pure. Maytag stresses reliability and the best repair record of any washer on the market. IBM promotes the quality service provided by its well-trained sales force.

Innovation is very important for technologically complex products, for which new features are the source of differentiation, and many people pay a premium price for new and innovative products, such as a state-of-the-art computer, stereo, or car.

When differentiation is based on responsiveness to customers, a company offers comprehensive after-sales service and product repair. This is an especially important consideration for complex products such as cars and domestic appliances, which are likely to break down periodically. Companies such as Maytag, Dell Computer, and BMW all excel in responsiveness to customers. In service organizations, quality-of-service attributes are also very important. Why can Neiman Marcus, Nordstrom, and Federal Express charge premium prices? They offer an exceptionally high level of service. Similarly, firms of lawyers or accountants stress the service aspects of their operations to clients: their knowledge, professionalism, and reputation.

Finally, a product's appeal to customers' psychological desires can become a source of differentiation. The appeal can be to prestige or status, as it is with BMWs and Rolex watches; to patriotism, as with Chevrolet; to safety of home and family, as with Prudential Insurance; or to value for money, as with Sears and JC Penney. Differentiation can also be tailored to age groups and to socioeconomic groups. Indeed, the bases of differentiation are endless.

A company that pursues a differentiation strategy strives to differentiate itself along as many dimensions as possible. The less it resembles its rivals, the more it is protected from competition and the wider is its market appeal. Thus, BMWs do not offer only prestige. They also offer technological sophistication, luxury, and reliability, as well as good, although very expensive, repair service. All these bases of differentiation help increase sales.

Generally, a differentiator chooses to segment its market into many niches. Now and then a company offers a product designed for each market niche and decides to be a **broad differentiator**, but a company might choose to serve just those niches in which it has a specific differentiation advantage. For example, Sony produces twenty-four models of television, filling all the niches from mid-priced to high-priced sets. However, its lowest-priced model is always priced about $100 above that of its competitors, bringing into play the premium-price factor. You have to pay extra for a Sony. Similarly, although Mercedes-Benz has filled niches below its old high-priced models with its S and C series, until recently it made no attempt to produce a car for every market segment. In 1996, however, it announced that it was planning to introduce a new line of less expensive cars to appeal to a wider market, and analysts were at once concerned that this would affect its differentiated appeal.

Finally, in choosing which distinctive competency to pursue, a differentiated company concentrates on the organizational function that provides the sources of its differentiation advantage. Differentiation on the basis of innovation and technological competency depends on the R&D function, as discussed in Chapter 5. Efforts to improve service to customers depend on the quality of the sales function. A focus on a specific function does not mean, however, that the control of costs is not important for a differentiator. A differentiator does not want to increase costs unnecessarily and tries to keep them somewhere near those of the cost leader. However, since developing the distinctive competency needed to provide a differentiation advantage is often expensive, a differentiator usually has higher costs than the cost leader.

Still, it must control all costs that do not contribute to its differentiation advantage so that the price of the product does not exceed what customers are willing to pay. Since bigger profits are earned by controlling costs and by maximizing revenues, it pays to control costs, though not to minimize them to the point of losing the source of differentiation.[16] The owners of the famous Savoy Hotel in London faced just this problem in the 1990s. The Savoy's reputation has always been based on the incredibly high level of service it offers its customers. Three hotel employees attend to the needs of each guest, and in every room a guest can summon a waiter, maid, or valet by pressing a button at the bedside. The cost of offering this level of service has been so high that the hotel makes less than 1 percent net profit every year.[17] Its owners are trying to find ways to reduce costs to increase profits. However, their problem is that if they reduce the number of hotel staff (the main source of the Savoy's high costs), they may destroy the main source of its differentiated appeal.

Advantages and Disadvantages The advantages of the differentiation strategy can now be discussed in the context of the five forces model. Differentiation safeguards a company against competitors to the degree that customers develop *brand loyalty* for its products. Brand loyalty is a very valuable asset because it protects the company on all fronts. For example, powerful suppliers are rarely a problem because the differentiated company's strategy is geared more toward the price it can charge than toward the costs of production. Thus, a differentiator can tolerate moderate increases in the prices of its inputs better than the cost leader can. Differentiators are unlikely to experience problems with powerful buyers because the differentiator offers the buyer a unique product. Only it can supply the product, and it commands brand loyalty. Differentiators can pass on price increases to customers because customers are willing to pay the premium price. Differentiation and brand loyalty also create a barrier to entry for other companies seeking to enter the industry. New companies are forced to develop their own distinctive competency to be able to compete, and doing so is very expensive.

Finally, the threat of substitute products depends on the ability of competitors' products to meet the same customers' needs as the differentiator's products and to break customers' brand loyalty. This can happen, as when IBM-clone manufacturers captured a large share of the home computer market, but many people still want an IBM, even though there are many IBM clones available. The issue is, how much of a premium price a company can charge for uniqueness before customers switch products?

The main problems with a differentiation strategy center on the company's long-term ability to maintain its perceived uniqueness in customers' eyes. We have seen in the last ten years how quickly competitors move to imitate and copy successful differentiators. This has happened in many industries, such as computers, autos, and home electronics. Patents and first-mover advantages (the advantages of being the first to market a product or service) last only so long, and as the overall quality of products produced by all companies goes up, brand loyalty declines. The story of the way American Express lost its competitive advantage, told in Strategy in Action 6.1, highlights many of the threats that face a differentiator.

A strategy of differentiation, then, requires the firm to develop a competitive advantage by making choices about its product, market, and distinctive competency that reinforce each other and together increase the value of a good or service in the eyes of consumers. When a product has uniqueness in customers' eyes, differentiators can charge a premium price. However, the disadvantages of a differentiation strategy are the ease with which competitors can imitate a differentiator's product and the difficulty of maintaining a premium price. When differentiation stems from the design or physical features of the product, differentiators are at great risk because imitation is easy. The risk is that over time products such as VCRs or stereos become *commoditylike* products, for which the importance of differentiation diminishes as customers become more price sensitive. When differentiation stems from quality of service or reliability or from any *intangible source*, such as Federal Express's guarantee of fast delivery or the prestige of a Rolex, a company is much more secure. It is difficult to imitate intangibles, and the differentiator can reap the benefits of this strategy for a long time. Nevertheless, all differentiators must watch out for imitators and be careful that they do not charge a price higher than the market will bear.

Cost Leadership *and* Differentiation

Recently, changes in production techniques—in particular, the development of flexible manufacturing technologies (discussed in Chapter 5)—have made the choice between cost-leadership and differentiation strategies less clear-cut. With techno-

6.1 **STRATEGY *in* ACTION**

Who Wants an American Express Card?

American Express Company's green, gold, and platinum credit cards used to be closely linked with high status and prestige. Obtaining an American Express (AmEx) card required a high income, and obtaining a gold or platinum card required an even higher one. AmEx carefully differentiated its product by using famous people to advertise the virtues—exclusivity and uniqueness—of possessing its card. Consumers were willing to pay the high yearly fee to possess the card, even though every month they were required to pay off the debit balance they had accumulated. AmEx's cards were a premium product that allowed the company to charge both customers and merchants more because it offered quality service and conferred status on the user. For many years, its credit card operation was the money spinner of AmEx's Travel Related Services (TRS) Division, and the company's stock price soared as its profits surpassed $200 million by 1990.[18]

AmEx's differentiated strategy began to suffer in the 1990s, however. Rival companies such as MasterCard and Visa advertised that their cards can be used at locations where AmEx's are not accepted. Moreover, as these companies make clear, anybody can own a MasterCard or a Visa gold card; it is not just for the fortunate elite. In addition, various companies and banks have banded together to offer the consumer many other benefits of using their particular credit cards. For example, banks and airlines formed alliances that allow consumers to use a bank's credit card to accumulate miles toward the purchase of an airline's tickets. By 1995, thousands of other companies—among them, AT&T, General Motors, Yahoo!, Kroger's, and Dell—began issuing their own credit cards, which offer customers savings on their products, often without a yearly fee. The emergence of all these new credit cards broke the loyalty of AmEx customers and shattered the card's unique image. It lost its differentiated appeal and become one more credit card in an overcrowded market. More than 2 million of its users deserted Amex, and the firm lost hundreds of millions of dollars in the early 1990s.

However, Amex strove to fight back and restore profitability to its division. To reduce costs, it laid off more than 5,000 employees in the TRS division, started its own airline mileage program to entice its previous cardholders back, and made its card more available to potential users, such as college students. By lowering the fees it charges merchants, it also increased the number of outlets that accept the card. For example, the card can now be used at Kmart. Furthermore, in 1998, it spent $1.13 billion on marketing and promotion to rebuild its brand name.[19] Finally, in 1999, it announced that it was developing the "ultimate travel card," a new electronic smart card that it intended to make the global standard for travel and entertainment transactions. Among other things, this card permits electronic ticketing and boarding passes, automated car rental check-in, Internet identification and access, and payment functions, which include an electronic purse.[20] In this way, AMEX hopes to promote its differentiated image and once again become the credit card that everyone wants to use.

logical developments, companies have found it easier to obtain the benefits of both strategies. The reason is that the new flexible technologies allow firms to pursue a differentiation strategy at a low cost: that is, companies can combine these two generic strategies.

Traditionally, differentiation was obtainable only at high cost because the necessity of producing different models for different market segments meant that firms had to have short production runs, which raised manufacturing costs. In addition, the differentiated firm had to bear higher marketing costs than the cost leader because it was serving many market segments. As a result, differentiators had higher costs than cost leaders, which produced large batches of standardized products. However, flexible manufacturing may enable a firm pursuing differentiation to manufacture a range of products at a cost comparable to that of the cost leader. The use of robots and flexible manufacturing cells reduces the costs of retooling the production line and the costs associated with small production runs. Indeed, a factor promoting the current trend toward market fragmentation and niche marketing in many consumer goods industries, such as mobile phones, computers, and appliances, is the substantial reduction of the costs of differentiation by flexible manufacturing.

Another way that a differentiated producer may be able to realize significant economies of scale is by standardizing many of the component parts used in its end products. For example, in the 1990s Chrysler began to offer more than twenty different models of cars and minivans to different segments of the auto market. However, despite their different appearances, all twenty models were based on only three different platforms. Moreover, most of the cars used many of the same components, including axles, drive units, suspensions, and gear boxes. As a result, Chrysler was able to realize significant economies of scale in the manufacture and bulk purchase of standardized component parts.

A company can also reduce both production and marketing costs if it limits the number of models in the product line by offering packages of options rather than letting consumers decide exactly what options they require. It is increasingly common for auto manufacturers, for example, to offer an economy auto package, a luxury package, and a sports package to appeal to the principal market segments. Package offerings substantially lower manufacturing costs because long production runs of the various packages are possible. At the same time, the firm is able to focus its advertising and marketing efforts on particular market segments so that these costs are also decreased. Once again, the firm is getting gains from differentiation and from low cost at the same time.

Just-in-time inventory systems, too, can help reduce costs, as well as improve the quality and reliability of a company's products. This benefit is important to differentiated firms, for whom quality and reliability are essential ingredients of the product's appeal. Rolls-Royces, for instance, are never supposed to break down. Improved quality control enhances a company's reputation and thus allows it to charge a premium price, which is one object of TQM programs.

Taking advantage of the new production and marketing developments, some firms are managing to reap the gains from cost-leadership and differentiation strategies simultaneously. Since they can charge a premium price for their products compared with the price charged by the pure cost leader and since they have lower costs than the pure differentiator, they are obtaining at least an equal, and probably a higher, level of profit than firms pursuing only one of the generic strategies. Hence the combined strategy is the most profitable to pursue, and companies are quickly moving to take advantage of the new production, materials-management, and marketing techniques. Indeed, U.S. companies must take advantage of them if they are to regain a competitive advantage, for the Japanese pioneered many of these new developments. This explains why firms such as Toyota and Sony are currently much more profitable than their U.S. counterparts, General Motors and Zenith, respectively. However, American firms such as McDonald's, Motorola, and Ford, which is profiled in Strategy in Action 6.2, are pursuing both strategies simultaneously with great success.

6.2 **STRATEGY *in* ACTION**

Ford's Difficult Balancing Act

In the 1990s, Alex Trotman, Ford Motor's CEO at the time, faced the problem of how best to compete in an increasingly competitive car industry. On the one hand, Ford, like other large U.S. carmakers, had been forced to find ways to reduce costs to compete effectively against low-priced competitors from Japan and Europe. On the other, Ford had to differentiate its cars and make them stand out so that customers would be attracted to them and would buy them rather than the cars of its rivals.

To reduce costs, Ford forged ahead with a global cost-cutting plan called Ford 2000. The plan included producing very similar models of cars and trucks that could be sold globally to customers in all the countries of the world in which Ford does business. It also meant centralizing all car design activities at five global design centers to reduce costs. Finally, the plan reduced the number of different car platforms (the frames on which the car models are based) and the number of component parts, again to decrease costs. For example, instead of the more than thirty different kinds of car horns, Ford decided to use only three, which it bought in bigger volume from a few manufacturers. Ford projected a $1 billion saving in engineering costs and $11 billion in reduced plant investment costs from this plan.[21]

To make Ford's products unique, Trotman also authorized a radically new program of car styling. Throughout the 1970s and 1980s, Ford had been known for the big, boxy, plain look of its cars, a look that had changed little in decades. From the mid 1980s on, Ford began to restyle all its cars. Trotman's multibillion-dollar program culminated in the radical redesign of the best-selling car in the United States, the Ford Taurus, which Ford launched in the fall of 1995. The accentuated curves and oval shape of the Taurus reflected the redesign of Ford's other cars, such as the Lincoln Continental, the Mustang, and the Mondeo, Ford's first world car.

By 1996, however, it became clear to Trotman and other top Ford executives that the dual push to reduce costs on a global level while launching a whole new series of redesigned global cars was not working. The enormous development costs of the new cars had raised costs dramatically and forced up car prices. The typical well-equipped Taurus, for example, was retailing for more than $20,000, more than $3,000 above the old model, and customers were experiencing sticker shock. In essence, all the cost savings brought about by the Ford 2000 plan were being eaten up by the high costs associated with its push to produce a radically new, differentiated line of cars. By mid 1996 the Honda Accord had once again become the best-selling car in the United States, Ford's profits had plunged 58 percent, its stock price was flat, and many analysts were worried that Ford's new strategy was not working.[22]

In May 1996, Trotman announced a new plan to bring together the cost and differentiation sides of Ford's business-level strategy. He argued that Ford's basic strategy was correct and that all the benefits of the launch of new cars and the saving in costs would be reaped well into the next century. In the short term, however, to boost sales, Ford announced that it would bring out stripped-down models of the Taurus and other cars to reduce the price and attract more customers. In addition, recognizing that its new cars were costing too much to develop, Ford announced that it would close two of its global design centers and further consolidate its design program to reduce development costs. Trotman and his top management team continued to search for ways to align both the cost and differentiation sides of the business-strategy equation to provide Ford's customers with a well-designed car at a price they are willing to pay.

In 1999, a new CEO, Jacques Nasser, took control of the company and announced new moves to further the company's competitive advantage. First, he orchestrated Ford's purchase of Volvo to increase its product range. He also announced a new global push to reduce costs, including a new move to decentralize control to each of Ford's business units so that they might search out innovative ways to streamline their operations and increase efficiency.[23] By the end of the 1990s, Ford's strategy paid off as its sales and profits rose to record levels.

Focus Strategy

The third generic competitive strategy, the **focus strategy**, differs from the other two chiefly because it is directed toward serving the needs of a *limited customer group* or *segment*. A focus strategy concentrates on serving a particular market niche, which can be defined geographically, by type of customer, or by segment of the product line.[24] For example, a geographic niche can be defined by region or even by locality. Selecting a niche by type of customer might mean serving only the very rich, the very young, or the very adventurous. Concentrating only on a segment of the product line means focusing only on vegetarian foods, on very fast automobiles, on designer clothes, or on sunglasses. In following a focus strategy, a company is *specializing* in some way.

Once it has chosen its market segment, a company pursues a focus strategy through either a differentiation or a low-cost approach. Figure 6.1 shows these two different kinds of focused strategies and compares them with a pure cost-leadership or differentiation strategy.

In essence, a focused company is a specialized differentiator *or* a cost leader. If a company uses a focused low-cost approach, it competes against the cost leader in the market segments in which it has no cost disadvantage. For example, in local lumber or cement markets, the focuser has lower transportation costs than the low-cost national company. The focuser may also have a cost advantage because it is producing complex or custom-built products that do not lend themselves easily to economies of scale in production and, therefore, offer few experience-curve advantages. With a focus strategy, a company concentrates on small-volume custom products, for which it has a cost advantage, and leaves the large-volume standardized market to the cost leader.

If a company uses a focused differentiation approach, then all the means of differentiation that are open to the differentiator are available to the focused company. The point is that the focused company competes with the differentiator in only one or in just a few segments. For example, Porsche, a focused company, competes against General Motors in the sports car segment of the car market, not in other market segments. Focused companies are likely to develop differentiated product qualities successfully because of their knowledge of a small customer set (such as sports car buyers) or knowledge of a region.

FIGURE 6.1

Types of Business-Level Strategies

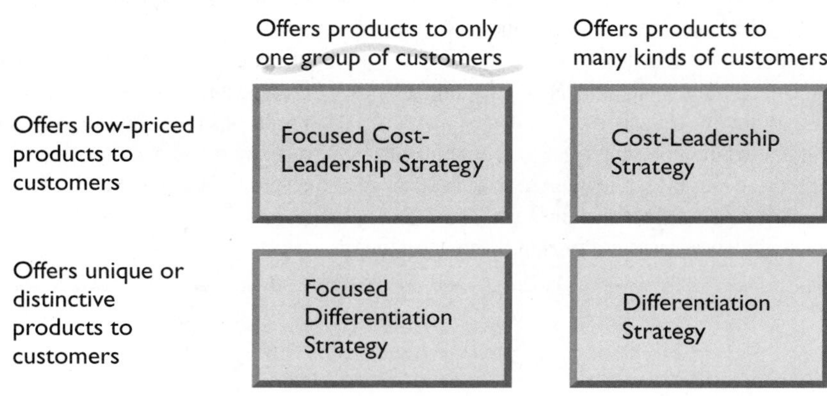

6.3 STRATEGY *in* ACTION

Finding a Niche in the Outsourcing Market

Outsourcing occurs when one company contracts with another to have it perform one of the value creation functions for it. Increasingly, many companies are finding it very difficult to keep up with the pace of technological change in the computer software industry and are outsourcing their data-processing needs to specialized software companies. For example, Electronic Data Systems (EDS), founded by Ross Perot, has grown into a $15 billion computer services giant that manages other companies' data-processing operations using its own proprietary software. IBM is another large company that has moved to exploit this developing market; in 1999, it signed many billion-dollar contracts with large computer makers such as Dell and Motorola to be their primary computer parts supplier.

As you can imagine, however, different kinds of organizations, such as universities, banks, insurance agencies, local governments, and utilities, have different kinds of data-processing needs and problems. Consequently, each kind of company requires a specialized kind of software system that can be customized to its specific needs. As a result, it is difficult for any one software company to serve the needs of a wide range of different companies, and the outsourcing market in data processing is very fragmented. Large companies such as EDS have only a small market share; for example, EDS had just 18 percent market share in 1996. Consequently, opportunities abound.

Increasingly, small, specialized software companies have been springing up to manage the needs of particular kinds of clients. An example is Systems & Computer Technology, based in Malvern, Pennsylvania, which went head-to-head with EDS to secure a seven-year $35 million outsourcing contract to serve the data-processing needs of Dallas County. The company has yearly revenues of only $200 million, compared with EDS's $15 billion, but it won the contract because it specializes in servicing the needs of local government and institutions of higher education.[25] It could show Dallas County its twelve ongoing contracts with municipal clients, whereas EDS could offer its experience with only one, a hospital. The focused company won out over the differentiator.

Other focused companies are also springing up—for instance, the Bisys Group and Systematics Company, which serves the needs of banks and universities. It appears that in the data-processing industry, small, focused companies are strong competitors because of their ability to provide specialized, personal service to specific clients in a way that large differentiators cannot.[26] Indeed, EDS has run into problems in the late 1990s because of the emergence of agile, Internet-based competitors that can provide e-commerce solutions at a price much lower than EDS's.[27] In 1999, EDS replaced its CEO and announced the appointment of a new e-business chief to catch up and get back in the game.[28] Only time will tell if it can regain its dominant position in the fast-changing Internet services industry environment.

Furthermore, concentration on a small range of products sometimes allows a focuser to develop innovations faster than a large differentiator can. However, the focuser does not attempt to serve all market segments, for doing so would bring it into direct competition with the differentiator. Instead, a focused company concentrates on building market share in one market segment and, if successful, may begin to serve more and more market segments, chipping away the differentiator's competitive advantage. The emergence of small software companies to take advantage of specialized niches in the outsourcing market, discussed in Strategy in Action 6.3, illustrates how focused companies can obtain a competitive advantage.

Strategic Choices Table 6.1 illustrates the specific product/market/distinctive-competency choices made by a focused company. Differentiation can be high or low because the company can pursue a low-cost or a differentiation approach. As for customer groups, a focused company chooses specific niches in which to compete rather than going for a whole market, as a cost leader does, or filling a large number of niches, as a broad differentiator does. The focused firm can pursue any distinctive competency because it can seek any kind of differentiation or low-cost advantage. Thus, it might find a cost advantage and develop a superior efficiency in low-cost manufacturing within a region. Alternatively, it might develop superior skills in responsiveness to customers, based on its ability to serve the needs of regional customers in ways that a national differentiator would find very expensive.

The many avenues a focused company can take to develop a competitive advantage explain why there are so many small companies in relation to large ones. A focused company has enormous opportunity to develop its own niche and compete against low-cost and differentiated enterprises, which tend to be larger. A focus strategy provides an opportunity for an entrepreneur to find and then exploit a gap in the market by developing an innovative product that customers cannot do without.[29] The steel minimills discussed in Chapter 5 are a good example of how focused companies specializing in one market can grow so efficient that they become the cost leaders. Many large companies started with a focus strategy, and, of course, one means by which companies can expand is to take over other focused companies. For example, Saatchi & Saatchi DFS Compton, a specialist marketing company, grew by taking over several companies that were also specialists in their own markets, such as Hay Associates, the management consultants.

Advantages and Disadvantages A focused company's competitive advantages stem from the source of its distinctive competency—efficiency, quality, innovation, or responsiveness to customers. The firm is protected from *rivals* to the extent that it can provide a product or service they cannot. This ability also gives the focuser power over its *buyers* because they cannot get the same thing from anyone else. With regard to *powerful suppliers*, however, a focused company is at a disadvantage, because it buys in small volume and thus is in the suppliers' power. However, as long as it can pass on price increases to loyal customers, this disadvantage may not be a significant problem. *Potential entrants* have to overcome the loyalty from customers the focuser has generated, and the development of customers' loyalty also lessens the threat from *substitute products.* This protection from the five forces allows the focuser to earn above-average returns on its investment. Another advantage of the focus strategy is that it permits a company to stay close to its customers and to respond to their changing needs. The difficulty a large differentiator sometimes experiences in managing a large number of market segments is not an issue for a focuser.

Since a focuser produces a small volume, its production costs often exceed those of a low-cost company. Higher costs can also reduce profitability if a focuser is forced to invest heavily in developing a distinctive competency—such as expensive product innovation—in order to compete with a differentiated firm. However, once again, flexible manufacturing systems are opening up new opportunities for focused firms because small production runs become possible at a lower cost. Increasingly, small specialized firms are competing with large companies in specific market segments in which their cost disadvantage is much reduced.

A second problem is that the focuser's niche can suddenly disappear because of technological change or changes in consumers' tastes. Unlike the more generalist differentiator, a focuser cannot move easily to new niches, given its concentration of resources and competency in one or a few niches. For example, a clothing manufacturer that focuses on heavy metal enthusiasts would find it difficult to shift to other segments if heavy metal loses its appeal, and a Mexican restaurant would find it difficult to move to Chinese food if customers' tastes change. The disappearance of niches is one reason that so many small companies fail.

Finally, there is the prospect that differentiators will compete for a focuser's niche by offering a product that can satisfy the demands of the focuser's customers; for example, GM's and Ford's new luxury cars are aimed at Lexus, BMW, and Mercedes-Benz buyers. A focuser is vulnerable to attack and, therefore, has to defend its niche constantly.

Stuck in the Middle

Each generic strategy requires a company to make consistent product/market/distinctive-competency choices to establish a competitive advantage. In other words, a company must achieve a fit among the three components of business-level strategy. Thus, for example, a low-cost company cannot strive for a high level of market segmentation, as a differentiator does, and provide a wide range of products because doing so would raise production costs too much and the company would lose its low-cost advantage. Similarly, a differentiator with a competency in innovation that tries to reduce its expenditures on research and development or one with a competency in responsiveness to customers through after-sales service that seeks to economize on its sales force to decrease costs is asking for trouble because it will lose its competitive advantage as its distinctive competency disappears.

Choosing a business-level strategy successfully means giving serious attention to all elements of the competitive plan. Many companies, through ignorance or through mistakes, do not do the planning necessary for success in their chosen strategy. Such companies are said to be **stuck in the middle** because they have made product/market choices in such a way that they have been unable to obtain or sustain a competitive advantage.[30] As a result, they have no consistent business-level strategy, experience below-average performance, and suffer when industry competition intensifies.

Some stuck-in-the-middle companies may have started out by pursuing one of the three generic strategies but then made wrong resource allocation decisions or experienced a hostile, changing environment. It is very easy to lose control of a generic strategy unless strategic managers keep close track of the business and its environment, constantly adjusting product/market choices to suit changing conditions within the industry. The experience of Holiday Inns in the 1980s, described in Strategy in Action 6.4, shows how a company can become stuck in the middle because of environmental changes.

As the experience of Holiday Inns suggests, there are many paths to being stuck in the middle. Quite commonly, a focuser can get stuck in the middle when it becomes overconfident and starts to act like a broad differentiator. People Express, the defunct airline, exemplified a company in this situation. It started out as a specialized air carrier serving a narrow market niche: low-priced travel on the eastern seaboard. In pursuing this focus strategy based on cost leadership, it was very successful, but when it tried to expand to other geographic regions and began taking over other airlines to gain a larger number of planes, it lost its niche. People Express became one more carrier in an increasingly competitive market, in which it had no special competitive advantage against the other national carriers. The result was financial troubles. People Express was swallowed up by Texas Air and incorporated into Continental Airlines. By contrast, Southwest Airlines, the focused low-cost company, has continued to focus on this strategy and has grown successfully.

6.4 STRATEGY *in* ACTION

Holiday Inns' Rough Ride

The history of the Holiday Inns motel chain is one of the great success stories in U.S. business. Its founder, Kemmons Wilson, vacationing in the early 1950s, found existing motels to be small, expensive, and of unpredictable quality. This discovery, along with the prospect of unprecedented highway travel that would come with the new interstate highway program, triggered a realization: There was an unmet customer need, a gap in the market for quality accommodations. Holiday Inns was founded to meet that need.

From the beginning, Holiday Inns set the standard for offering motel features such as air conditioning and icemakers while keeping room rates reasonable. These amenities enhanced the motels' popularity, and motel franchising, Wilson's invention, made rapid expansion possible. By 1960, Holiday Inns' motels dotted the U.S. landscape; they could be found in virtually every city and on every major highway. Before the 1960s ended, more than 1,000 of them were in full operation, and occupancy rates averaged 80 percent. The concept of mass accommodation had arrived.[31]

By the 1970s, however, the motel chain was in trouble. The service offered by Holiday Inns appealed to the average traveler, who wanted a standardized product (a room) at an average price. In essence, Holiday Inns had been targeting the middle of the hotel-room market. The problem was that travelers were beginning to make different demands on hotels and motels. Some wanted luxury and were willing to pay higher prices for better accommodations and service. Others sought low prices and accepted rock-bottom quality and service in exchange. Although the market had fragmented into different groups of customers with different needs, Holiday Inns was still offering an undifferentiated, average-cost, average-quality product.[32]

Holiday Inns missed the change in the market and thus failed to respond appropriately to it, but the competition did not. Companies such as Hyatt siphoned off the top end of the market, where quality and service sold rooms. Chains such as Motel 6 and Days Inns captured the basic-quality, low-price end of the market. In between were many specialty chains that appealed to business travelers, families, or self-caterers (people who want to be able to cook in their hotel rooms). Holiday Inns' position was attacked from all sides. The company's earnings declined as occupancy rates dropped drastically, and marginal Holiday Inns motels began to close as competition increased.

Wounded but not dead, Holiday Inns began a counterattack. The original chain was upgraded to suit quality-oriented travelers. At the same time, to meet the needs of different kinds of travelers, Holiday Inns created new hotel and motel chains, including the luxury Crowne Plazas; the Hampton Inns, which serve the low-priced end of the market; and the all-suite Embassy Suites. Holiday Inns tried to meet the demands of the many niches, or segments, of the hotel market that have emerged as customers' needs have changed over time.[33]

These moves were successful in the early 1990s, and Holiday Inns grew to become one of the largest suppliers of hotel rooms in the industry. However, by 1996, it became clear that Holiday Inns was once again losing its differentiated appeal as its revenues and profits fell. A new CEO, Thomas R. Oliver, was brought in to remake Holiday Inns. His solution? To upgrade the Holiday Inns flagship chain with new furniture, food, and a large new advertising budget.

While this worked, other moves to restore profitability created new problems. Oliver also wanted to open other budget chains aimed at the business traveler. However, he wanted to use the Holiday Inns name on them to give them instant name recognition. Many of the regular Holiday Inns franchisees objected, since this would reduce the differentiated appeal of their chain. For example, Oliver plans to open a chain called the Staybridge Suites by Holiday Inns which are tailored to long-term business customers. Whatever the outcome of these efforts, one thing is clear: Holiday Inns needs to remake its image in the highly competitive hotel room industry.

Differentiators, too, can fail in the market and end up stuck in the middle if competitors attack their markets with more specialized or low-cost products that blunt their competitive edge. This happened to IBM in the large-frame computer market as personal computers became more powerful and able to do the job of the much more expensive mainframes. The increasing movement toward flexible manufacturing systems aggravates the problems faced by cost leaders and differentiators. Many large firms will become stuck in the middle unless they make the investment needed to pursue both strategies simultaneously. No company is safe in the jungle of competition, and each must be constantly on the lookout to exploit competitive advantages as they arise and to defend the advantages it already has.

To sum up, successful management of a generic competitive strategy requires strategic managers to attend to two main matters. First, they need to ensure that the product/market/distinctive-competency decisions they make are oriented toward one specific competitive strategy. Second, they need to monitor the environment so that they can keep the firm's sources of competitive advantage in tune with changing opportunities and threats.

STRATEGIC GROUPS AND BUSINESS-LEVEL STRATEGY

As implied by the preceding discussion, companies in an industry can pursue many different kinds of business-level strategies that differ from each other with respect to factors such as the choice of market segments to serve, product quality, technological leadership, customer service, pricing policy, and advertising policy. As a result, within most industries, strategic groups emerge, each of which is composed of companies pursuing the same generic strategy.[34] Thus, for example, all the companies inside an industry pursuing a low-cost strategy form one strategic group; all those seeking to pursue a broad differentiation strategy constitute another strategic group; and all those pursing a focus-differentiation strategy or a focused low-cost strategy form yet other strategic groups.

For instance, in the pharmaceutical industry, which we discuss in Chapter 3, there are two main strategic groups.[35] One group includes such companies as Merck, Eli Lilly, and Pfizer (see Figure 3.5), which pursue a differentiation strategy characterized by heavy R&D spending and a focus on developing new proprietary blockbuster drugs. The other strategic group might be characterized as the *low-cost strategic group* because it focuses on the manufacture of low-priced generic drugs. Companies in this group are pursuing a low-cost strategy because they are not investing millions of dollars in R&D, and, as a result, they cannot expect to charge a premium price.

The concept of strategic groups has a number of implications for business-level strategy. First, a company's immediate competitors are those companies pursuing the same strategy in its strategic group. Consumers tend to view the products of such enterprises as being direct substitutes for each other. Thus, a major threat to a company's profitability may arise primarily from within its own strategic group, not necessarily from the other companies in the industry pursuing different generic business-level strategies. For example, the main competition for Toyota comes from Honda, Ford, and GM, not from Rolls-Royce.

Second, different strategic groups can have a different standing with respect to each of Porter's five competitive forces because, as already discussed, the five forces affect companies in different ways. In other words, the risk of new entry by potential competitors, the degree of rivalry among companies within a group, the bargaining power of buyers, the bargaining power of suppliers, and the competitive force of substitute products can all vary in intensity among different strategic groups within the same industry.

In the pharmaceutical industry, for example, companies in the differentiation strategic group have historically been in a very powerful position vis-à-vis buyers because their products are patented. Besides, rivalry within this group has been limited to competition to be the first to patent a new drug and achieve a **first-mover advantage**, the advantage that a company that is first to market a new product is said to possess. In contrast, companies in the low-cost group have been in a much weaker position, since they lack patents for their products and buyers can choose among very similar competing generic drugs. Moreover, price competition among the companies in this group has been quite intense, reflecting the lack of product differentiation. Thus, companies within this group have earned somewhat lower returns than companies in the proprietary group.

As discussed in Chapter 3, mobility barriers are factors that inhibit the movement of companies between groups in an industry. The relative height of mobility barriers determines how successfully companies in one group can compete with companies in another. For example, can a differentiation strategic group also pursue a low-cost strategy and thus achieve the low-cost/differentiation strategy previously discussed? To the degree that companies in one group can develop or obtain the functional and financial resources they need to either lower their costs or embark on a major R&D expansion, they may be able to compete successfully with companies in another strategic group. In effect, they have created yet another strategic group—a combined low-cost and differentiation strategic group, which, as we have seen, has the strongest competitive advantage and the greatest ability to earn above-average profits. In fact, the need to pursue a simultaneous global low-cost/differentiation strategy has been the major driving force behind the wave of merger activities that swept through the large drug companies in the 1990s. For example, the U.S. company Upjohn merged with the Swedish company Pharmacia to pursue a global low-cost/differentiation strategy. Thus, the strategic group map in the pharmaceutical industry is changing dramatically as firms fight to survive in the rapidly consolidating global pharmaceutical industry. So far, Pfizer, Merck, and Eli Lilly are still pursuing a pure differentiated strategy, but the other merged companies are moving quickly to reposition themselves as low-cost differentiators.

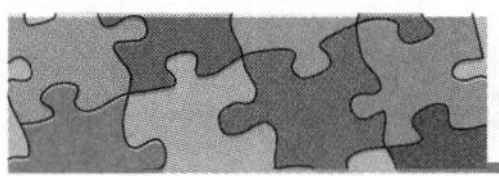

CHOOSING AN INVESTMENT STRATEGY AT THE BUSINESS LEVEL

We have been discussing business-level strategy in terms of making product/market/distinctive-competency choices to gain a competitive advantage. There is a second major choice to be made at the business level, however—the choice of which type of investment strategy to pursue in support of the competitive strategy.[36]

An **investment strategy** sets the amount and type of resources—human, functional, and financial—that must be invested to gain a competitive advantage.

Generic competitive strategies provide competitive advantages, but they are expensive to develop and maintain. A simultaneous differentiation/cost-leadership strategy is the most expensive, because it requires that a company invest resources not only in functions such as R&D, sales, and marketing to develop distinctive competencies, but also in functions such as manufacturing and materials management to find ways to reduce costs. Differentiation is the next most expensive generic strategy and then cost leadership, which is less expensive to maintain once the initial investment in a manufacturing plant and equipment has been made. Cost leadership does not require such sophisticated research and development or marketing efforts as a differentiation strategy. The focus strategy is cheapest because fewer resources are needed to serve one market segment than to serve the whole market.

In deciding on an investment strategy, a company must evaluate the potential returns from investing in a generic competitive strategy against the cost. In this way, it can determine whether it is likely to be profitable to pursue a certain strategy and how profitability will change as competition within the industry changes. Two factors are crucial in choosing an investment strategy: the strength of a company's position in an industry relative to its competitors and the stage of the industry's life cycle in which the company is competing.[37]

Competitive Position

Two attributes can be used to determine the strength of a company's relative competitive position. First, the larger a company's *market share*, the stronger is its competitive position and the greater are the potential returns from future investment. A large market share provides experience-curve economies and suggests that the company has earned brand loyalty. One of the main reasons a wave of mergers has taken place in the pharmaceutical industry, for example, is that the merging of two or more different companies creates a much larger customer base that can be more efficiently served by one global sales force rather than the two global sales forces that previously existed. Thus, large market share may help an organization to lower its costs on a global, as well as a national, basis.

The uniqueness, strength, and number of a company's *distinctive competencies* are the second measure of competitive position. If it is difficult to imitate a company's research and development expertise, its manufacturing and marketing skills, its knowledge of particular customer segments, and its unique reputation or brand name capital, the company's relative competitive position is strong and its returns from the generic strategy increase. Once again, an attempt to build new and improved distinctive competencies has been a principal reason for the merger of pharmaceutical companies. For example, Ciba-Geigy and Sandoz, two giant Swiss pharmaceutical companies, recently merged because they were developing complementary kinds of drugs for treating the same broad range of diseases. By pooling their skills and abilities, they have created the second largest pharmaceutical company in the world, and they hope to use their combined distinctive competencies to compete head-to-head with U.S. companies such as Pfizer and Merck.

In general, companies with the largest market share and the strongest distinctive competencies are in the best position to build and sustain their competitive advantage. A unique distinctive competency leads to increased demand for the company's products, and, as a result of the revenues obtained from larger market share, the company has more resources to invest in developing its distinctive competency.

These two attributes reinforce one another and explain why some companies get stronger and stronger over time. Companies with a smaller market share and little potential for developing a distinctive competency are in a much weaker competitive position.[38]

Life Cycle Effects

The second main factor influencing the investment attractiveness of a generic strategy is the *stage of the industry life cycle.* Each life cycle stage is accompanied by a particular industry environment, presenting different opportunities and threats. Each stage, therefore, has different implications for the investment of resources needed to obtain a competitive advantage. Competition is strongest in the shakeout stage of the life cycle and least important in the embryonic stage, for example. The risks of pursuing a strategy change over time. The difference in risk explains why the potential returns from investing in a competitive strategy depend on the life cycle stage.

Choosing an Investment Strategy

Table 6.2 summarizes the relationship among the stage of the life cycle, the competitive position, and the investment strategy at the business level.

Embryonic Strategy In the embryonic stage, all companies, weak and strong, emphasize the development of a distinctive competency and a product/market policy. During this stage, investment needs are great because a company has to establish a competitive advantage. Many fledgling companies in the industry are seeking resources to develop a distinctive competency. Thus, the appropriate business-level investment strategy is a **share-building strategy**. The aim is to build market share

TABLE 6.2

Choosing an Investment Strategy at the Business Level

	Strong Competitive Position	*Weak Competitive Position*
Stage of Industry Life Cycle		
Embryonic	Share building	Share building
Growth	Growth	Market concentration
Shakeout	Share increasing	Market concentration or harvest/liquidation
Maturity	Hold-and-maintain or profit	Harvest or liquidation/ divestiture
Decline	Market concentration or harvest (asset reduction)	Turnaround, liquidation, or divestiture

by developing a stable and unique competitive advantage to attract customers who have no knowledge of the company's products.

Companies require large amounts of capital to build research and development competencies or sales and service competencies. They cannot generate much of this capital internally. Thus, a company's success depends on its ability to demonstrate a unique competency to attract outside investors, or venture capitalists. If a company gains the resources to develop a distinctive competency, it will be in a relatively stronger competitive position. If it fails, its only option may be to exit the industry. In fact, companies in weak competitive positions at all stages in the life cycle may choose to exit the industry to cut their losses.

Growth Strategies At the growth stage, the task facing a company is to consolidate its position and provide the base it needs to survive the coming shakeout. Thus, the appropriate investment strategy is the **growth strategy**. The goal is to maintain a company's relative competitive position in a rapidly expanding market and, if possible, to increase it—in other words, to grow with the expanding market. However, other companies are entering the market and catching up with the industry's innovators. As a result, first movers require successive waves of capital infusion to sustain the momentum generated by their success in the embryonic stage. For example, differentiators need to engage in massive research and development to preserve their technological lead, and cost leaders need to invest in state-of-the-art machinery and computers to obtain new experience-curve economies. All this investment is very expensive.

The growth stage is also the time when companies try to consolidate existing market niches and enter new ones so that they can increase their market share. Increasing the level of market segmentation to become a broad differentiator is expensive as well. A company has to invest resources to develop a new sales and marketing competency. Consequently, at the growth stage, companies fine-tune their competitive strategy (which we discuss at length in the next chapter) and make business-level investment decisions about the relative advantages of a differentiation, low-cost, or focus strategy, given financial needs and relative competitive position. For instance, if one company has emerged as the cost leader, some companies may decide to compete head-to-head with it and enter this strategic group, whereas others will not. Instead, they will pursue a growth strategy using a differentiation or focus approach and invest resources in developing unique competencies. As a result, strategic groups start to develop in an industry as each company seeks the best way to invest its scarce resources to maximize its competitive advantage.

Companies must spend a lot of money just to keep up with growth in the market, and finding additional resources to develop new skills and competencies is a difficult task for strategic managers. Consequently, companies in a weak competitive position at this stage engage in a **market concentration strategy** to consolidate their position. They seek to specialize in some way and may adopt a focus strategy and move to a focused strategic group to reduce their investment needs. If very weak, they may choose to exit the industry and sell out to a stronger competitor.

Shakeout Strategies By the shakeout stage, demand increases slowly, and competition by price or product characteristics becomes intense. Companies in strong competitive positions need resources to invest in a **share-increasing strategy** to attract customers from weak companies that are exiting the market. In other words, companies attempt to maintain and increase market share despite fierce competition. The way companies invest their resources depends on their generic strategy.

For cost leaders, because of the price wars that can occur, investment in cost control is crucial if they are to survive the shakeout stage, and they must do all they can to reduce costs. Differentiators in a strong competitive position choose to forge ahead and become broad differentiators. Their investment is likely to be oriented toward marketing, and they are likely to develop a sophisticated after-sales service network. They also widen the product range to match the range of customers' needs. Differentiators in a weak position reduce their investment burden by withdrawing to a focused strategy—the **market concentration strategy**—to specialize in a particular niche or product. Weak companies exiting the industry engage in a **harvest** or **liquidation strategy**, both of which are discussed later in this chapter.

Maturity Strategies By the maturity stage, a relatively stable strategic group structure has emerged in the industry, and companies have learned how their competitors will react to their competitive moves. At this point, companies want to reap the rewards of their previous investments in developing a generic strategy. Until now, profits have been reinvested in the business, and dividends have been small. Investors in strong companies have obtained their rewards through the appreciation of the value of their stock, because the company has reinvested most of its capital to maintain and increase market share. As market growth slows in the maturity stage, a company's investment strategy depends on the level of competition in the industry and the source of the company's competitive advantage.

In environments where competition is high because technological change is occurring or where barriers to entry are low, companies need to defend their competitive position. Strategic managers need to continue to invest heavily in maintaining the company's competitive advantage. Both low-cost companies and differentiators adopt a **hold-and-maintain strategy** to support their generic strategies. They expend resources to develop their distinctive competency so as to remain the market leaders. For example, differentiated companies may invest in improved after-sales service, and low-cost companies may invest in the latest production technologies, such as robotics.

It is at this point, however, that companies realize they must begin to pursue both a low-cost and a differentiation strategy if they are to protect themselves from aggressive competitors (both at home and abroad) that are watching for any opportunity or perceived weakness to take the lead in the industry. Differentiators take advantage of their strong position to develop flexible manufacturing systems to reduce their production costs. Cost leaders move to start differentiating their products to expand their market share by serving more market segments. For example, Gallo moved from the bulk-wine segment and began marketing premium wines and wine coolers to take advantage of its low production costs. In 1996, Gallo's new premium brand, Falling Leaf, became the best-selling chardonnay in the United States. Similarly, in the fast-food industry in the 1990s, McDonald's experienced intense pressure to lower its costs after Taco Bell began to offer its $.99 tacos. To counter this competitive attack, McDonald's sought new ways to lower its costs and widen its menu.

Historically, however, many companies have felt protected from competition within the industry in the maturity stage. Consequently, they decide to exploit their competitive advantage to the fullest by engaging in a **profit strategy**. A company pursuing this strategy attempts to maximize the present returns from its previous investments. Typically, it reinvests proportionally less in improvement of its functional resources and increases returns to shareholders. The profit strategy works well only as long as competitive forces remain relatively constant, so that the company can maintain the profit margins developed by its competitive strategy. However, it must be alert to threats from the environment and must take care not to become complacent and unresponsive to environmental changes.

All too often market leaders fail to exercise vigilance in managing the environment, imagining that they are impervious to competition. Thus, General Motors felt secure against foreign-car manufacturers until changes in oil prices precipitated a crisis. Kodak, which had profited for so long from its strengths in film processing, was slow to respond to the threat of electronic imaging techniques. Paradoxically, the most successful companies often fail to sense changes in the market. As Strategy in Action 6.5 shows, Gucci is another example of a company that over time failed to pursue a hold-and-maintain strategy to manage the competitive environment.

6.5 STRATEGY *in* ACTION

Gucci Loses Its Grip

Gucci has one of the most readily recognized brand name of all luxury goods companies. Its leather products, such as shoes and handbags, and its clothes are global status symbols worn by the world's wealthiest people. However, the power of its brand name was put at great risk in the middle 1990s because its CEO, Maurizio Gucci, and its designers had lost track of its customers' desires and its industry environment. Unlike competitors such as Versace, Ferragamo, and Giorgio Armani, the company failed to innovate and offer styles that appealed to a new, more casual global audience. To save money as its losses mounted, Gucci reduced its advertising budget. This was a disastrous move, for it sharpened the perception that Gucci was outmoded and out of touch with the luxury market. The company became caught in a vicious cycle downward.

It was saved by a tragedy. Maurizio Gucci's wife arranged to have him gunned down in a Milan doorway in 1995; as a result Domenico De Sole became CEO, and he had a clear vision of what to do. Lacking money because of mounting losses, De Sole named a Texan, Thomas Ford, as Gucci's chief designer and invested all the company's resources in producing a revolutionary, new, Ford-designed line of clothes for both men and women to attract back Gucci's customers. An instant success, the clothes generated much attention and free advertising for Gucci. All of a sudden, customers flocked back to Gucci stores, and, as they bought clothes, they also bought Gucci's signature leather products, such as $500 shoes and handbags. The company's sales and profits increased, and De Sole invested the proceeds in advertising, tripling the advertising budget. He thus changed the vicious cycle downward into a virtuous cycle upward.

Gucci has gone from strength to strength under De Sole and Ford; it regained its status as one of the foremost brand names in the world. In fact, it became so successful that it attracted the attention of LVMH, the French luxury goods company that owns such brand names as Moet et Chandon, and Louis Vuitton. LVMH first bought a significant number of Gucci shares, and it looked like it might try to take over the company; however, De Sole fought back. In October 1999, it appeared that Gucci might take over Fendi, another Italian fashion house, as De Sole strove to keep Gucci under his control. No matter what happens, Gucci's global future looks bright indeed.

Decline Strategies The decline stage of an industry's life cycle begins when demand for the industry's product starts to fall. There are many possible reasons for decline, including foreign competition and the loss of a company's distinctive competency as its rivals enter with new or more efficient technologies. Thus, a company must decide what investment strategy to adopt in order to deal with new circumstances within its industry. Table 6.2 lists the strategies that companies can resort to when their competitive position is declining.[39]

The initial strategies that companies can adopt are market concentration and asset reduction.[40] With a **market concentration strategy**, a company attempts to consolidate its product and market choices. It narrows its product range and exits marginal niches in an attempt to redeploy its resources more effectively and improve its competitive position. Reducing customer groups served may also allow a company to pursue a focus strategy in order to survive the decline stage. (As noted earlier, weak companies in the growth stage tend to adopt this strategy.) That is what International Harvester did as the demand for farm machinery fell. It now produces only medium-sized trucks under the Navistar name.

An **asset reduction strategy** requires a company to limit or decrease its investment in a business and to extract, or milk, the investment as much as it can. This approach is sometimes called a **harvest strategy** because a company will exit the industry once it has harvested all the returns it can. It reduces to a minimum the assets it employs in the business and forgoes investment for the sake of immediate profits.[41] A market concentration strategy, on the other hand, generally indicates that a company is trying to turn around its business so that it can survive in the long run.

Low-cost companies are more likely to pursue a harvest strategy simply because a smaller market share means higher costs, and they are unable to move to a focus strategy. Differentiators, in contrast, have a competitive advantage in this stage if they can move to a focus strategy.

At any stage of the life cycle, companies that are in weak competitive positions may apply **turnaround strategies**.[42] The questions that a company has to answer are whether it has the resources available to develop a viable business-level strategy to compete in the industry and how much that will cost. If a company is stuck in the middle, for example, it must assess the investment costs of developing a low-cost or differentiation strategy. Perhaps a company pursuing a low-cost strategy has not made the right product or market choices, or perhaps a differentiator has been missing niche opportunities. In such cases, the company can redeploy resources and change its strategy.

Sometimes a company's loss of competitiveness may be due to poor strategy implementation. If so, the company must move to change its structure and control systems rather than its strategy. For example, Dan Schendel, a prominent management researcher, found that 74 percent of the turnaround situations he and his colleagues studied were due to inefficient strategy implementation. The strategy-structure fit at the business level is thus very important in determining competitive strength.[43] We discuss it in detail in Chapter 13.

If a company decides that turnaround is not possible, either for competitive or for life cycle reasons, then the two remaining investment alternatives are **liquidation** and **divestiture**. As the terms imply, the company moves to exit the industry either by liquidating its assets or by selling the whole business. Both can be regarded as radical forms of harvesting strategy, because the company is seeking to get back as much as it can from its investment in the business. Often, however, it can only exit at a loss and take a tax write-off. Timing is important, because the earlier a company senses that divestiture is necessary, the more it can get for its assets. There are many stories about companies that buy weak or declining companies, thinking they can turn them around, and then realize their mistake as the new acquisitions become a drain on their resources. Often the acquired companies have lost their competitive advantage, and the cost of regaining it is too great. However, there have also been spectacular successes, such as that achieved by Lee Iacocca, who engaged in a low-cost strategy at Chrysler that set the scene for its success in the 1990s.

SUMMARY OF CHAPTER

The purpose of this chapter is to discuss the factors that must be considered if a company is to develop a business-level strategy that allows it to compete effectively in the marketplace. The formulation of business-level strategy means matching the opportunities and threats in the environment to the company's strengths and weaknesses by making choices about products, markets, and distinctive competencies, as well as the investments necessary to pursue the choices. All companies, from one-person operations to the strategic business units of large corporations, must develop a business strategy if they are to compete effectively and maximize their long-term profitability. The chapter makes the following main points:

- ✔ Business-level strategy refers to the way strategic managers devise a plan of action for using a company's resources and distinctive competencies to gain a competitive advantage over rivals in a market or industry.
- ✔ At the heart of developing a generic business-level strategy are choices concerning product differentiation, market segmentation, and distinctive competency.
- ✔ The combination of those three choices results in the specific form of generic business-level strategy employed by a company.
- ✔ The three pure generic competitive strategies are cost leadership, differentiation, and focus. Each has advantages and disadvantages. A company must constantly manage its strategy; otherwise, it risks being stuck in the middle.
- ✔ Increasingly, developments in manufacturing technology are allowing firms to pursue both a cost-leadership and a differentiation strategy and thus obtain the economic benefits of both strategies simultaneously. Technical developments also allow small firms to compete with large firms on an equal footing in particular market segments and hence increase the number of firms pursuing a focus strategy.
- ✔ Companies can also adopt two forms of focus strategy: a focused low-cost strategy and a focused differentiation strategy.
- ✔ Most industries are composed of strategic groups. Strategic groups are groups of companies pursuing the same or a similar business-level strategy. The members of a strategic group constitute a company's immediate competitors.
- ✔ Since different strategic groups are characterized by different opportunities and threats, it may pay a company to switch strategic groups. The feasibility of doing so is a function of the height of mobility barriers.
- ✔ The second choice facing a company is an investment strategy for supporting the competitive strategy. The choice of investment strategy depends on two main factors: (1) the strength of a company's competitive position in the industry and (2) the stage of the industry's life cycle.
- ✔ The main types of investment strategy are share building, growth, share increasing, hold-and-maintain, profit, market concentration, asset reduction, harvest, turnaround, liquidation, and divestiture.

DISCUSSION QUESTIONS

1. Why does each generic competitive strategy require a different set of product/market/distinctive-competency choices? Give examples of pairs of companies in (a) the computer industry and (b) the auto industry that pursue different competitive strategies.
2. How can companies pursuing a cost-leadership, differentiation, or focus strategy become stuck in the

middle? In what ways can they regain their competitive advantage?

3. Over an industry's life cycle, what investment strategy choices should be made by (a) differentiators in a strong competitive position and (b) differentiators in a weak competitive position?

4. How do technical developments affect the generic strategies pursued by firms in an industry? How might they do so in the future?

5. Why is it difficult for a company in one strategic group to change to a different strategic group?

Practicing Strategic Management

SMALL-GROUP EXERCISE
Finding a Strategy for a Restaurant

Break up into groups of three to five people, and discuss the following scenario:

You are a group of partners contemplating opening a new restaurant in your city. You are trying to decide what business-level strategy would provide your restaurant with the best competitive advantage to make it as profitable as possible.

1. Create a strategic group of the restaurants in your city and define their generic strategies.
2. Identify which restaurants you think are the most profitable and why.
3. On the basis of this analysis, decide what kind of restaurant you want to open and why.

STRATEGIC MANAGEMENT PROJECT
Module 6

This part of the project focuses on the nature of your company's business-level strategy. If your company operates in more than one business, concentrate either on its core, or most central, business, or on its most important businesses. Using all the information you have collected on your company, answer the following questions:

1. How differentiated are the products/services of your company? What is the basis of their differentiated appeal?
2. What is your company's strategy toward market segmentation? If it segments its market, on what basis does it do so?
3. What distinctive competencies does your company have? (To answer this question, use the information from the module on functional-level strategy in the last chapter.) Is efficiency, quality, innovation, responsiveness to customers, or a combination of these factors the main driving force in your company?
4. Based on these product/market/distinctive-competency choices, what generic business-level strategy is your company pursuing?
5. What are the advantages and disadvantages associated with your company's choice of business-level strategy?
6. How could you improve its business-level strategy to strengthen its competitive advantage?
7. Is your company a member of a strategic group in an industry? If so, which group?
8. What investment strategy is your company pursuing to support its generic strategy? How does this match the strength of its competitive position and the stage of its industry's life cycle?

ARTICLE FILE 6

Find an example (or several examples) of a company pursuing one or more of the three generic business-level strategies. Which strategy is it? What product/market/distinctive-competency choices is it based on? What are its advantages and disadvantages?

EXPLORING THE WEB
Visiting the Luxury-Car Market

Enter the Web sites of three luxury-car makers such as Lexus (www.lexususa.com), BMW (www.bmwusa.com), or Cadillac (www.cadillac.com), all of which compete in the same strategic group. Scan the sites to determine the key features of each company's business-level strategy. In what ways are their strategies similar and different? Which of these companies do you think has a competitive advantage over the others? Why?

Search the Web for a company pursuing a low-cost strategy, a differentiation strategy, or both. What product/market/distinctive-competency choices has the company made to pursue this strategy? How successful has the company been in its industry using this strategy?

CLOSING CASE

Liz Claiborne, Inc.

DESIGNER LIZ CLAIBORNE founded her company in 1976 with the help of three partners. By 1990, the company had more than $2 billion in annual sales, and its stock had become a Wall Street favorite. The secret of the company's success was Liz Claiborne's decision to focus on the rapidly growing professional women's segment of the clothing market. By 1976, women were entering the work force in rapidly increasing numbers, but relatively few companies were producing clothes for this segment. Those that did cater to it were very high-priced firms such as Ellen Tracy, Donna Karan, and Anne Klein. Liz Claiborne decided to find out what kinds of clothing professional women wanted. Then she used her considerable talents to create a design team to focus on providing attractively designed clothing for professional women at reasonable prices. In doing so, she tapped an unmet customer need, and the result was dramatic as sales boomed.

To protect her firm's image, Liz Claiborne sold her clothing through established retailers, such as Macy's, Bloomingdale's, and Dillard's. Retailers were required to buy at least $50,000 worth of her collection, and the company controlled the way its suits and dresses were sold in each store—for example, the way clothes were hung and displayed. This attention to detail was part of her strategy of focusing on the upscale professional clothing niche. To promote its growth, the company then started to find new outlets for its clothes and opened a chain of Liz Claiborne boutiques and factory outlets. The Liz Claiborne team also used its design skills to produce a line of men's sportswear and to develop new products such as perfume, shoes, and accessories. By 1988, the Liz Claiborne name had become famous.

However, by 1990 the company's growth had slowed, and the company was in trouble. Competitors, recognizing the niche pioneered by Liz Claiborne, had begun to offer their own lines of professional women's clothing. Expensive designers such as Anne Klein and Donna Karan had new lines of cheaper clothing, priced to compete directly with Liz Claiborne. In addition, low-cost manufacturers had begun to produce clothing lines that undercut Liz Claiborne's prices, often using look-alike designs. This competition from both the top and the bottom end of the market took sales away from the company.

Another problem for Liz Claiborne came from the retail end. Many of the company's best customers, retailers such as Macy's, were in deep financial difficulty and were cutting back on purchases to reduce their debt. At the same time, cost-conscious consumers were buying more and more clothing from stores such as Casual Corner and JC Penney and even from discount stores such as Kmart and Wal-Mart, which do not sell the Liz Claiborne line but carry the low-priced lines of competitors. As customers switched to both cheaper stores and cheaper lines, Liz Claiborne's sales suffered.

Given this deteriorating situation, the company moved quickly to change its strategy. Jerry Chazen, who replaced Liz Claiborne as CEO of the company on her retirement, decided to broaden the company's product line and produce low-cost lines of clothing. To do so and at the same time protect the Liz Claiborne brand name, he bought Russ Togs, a clothing maker that produces three brands of women's clothing: Crazy Horse, The Villager, and Red Horse. As part of the company's new strategy, each of these clothing makers' lines was redesigned and targeted at a different price range in the women's clothing market. For example, Russ Togs, a sportswear line, was upgraded to sell a new line of clothing for 20 to 30 percent less than the Liz Claiborne line. Moreover, this clothing is sold through discount merchandisers such as Wal-Mart and in low-priced department stores such as Sears and JC Penney. In this way, the Liz Claiborne company began to serve the general women's clothing market, not just the professional women's clothing niche.[44]

Top management found that this new strategy bolstered the company's sagging sales and it led to a new period of growth and expansion in the late 1990s. In addition, they have taken the company's existing design skills and capabilities and applied them in other new market segments. Now, however, the company is going head-to-head with low-cost producers and has had to find new ways to reduce costs in order to compete. In 1999, the company reported record operating profits due to a growth in sales in its main product lines. Liz Claiborne has turned the corner and is once again a major player in the volatile women's clothing industry.[45]

Case Discussion Questions

1. What factors led to the success of Liz Claiborne, Inc.?
2. What changes has the company recently made in its strategy? Why?

End Notes

1. www.E*trade.com (1999).
2. Press releases, www.E*trade.com (1999).
3. D. F. Abell, *Defining the Business: The Starting Point of Strategic Planning* (Englewood Cliffs, N.J.: Prentice-Hall, 1980), p. 169.
4. R. Kotler, *Marketing Management*, 5th ed. (Englewood Cliffs, N.J.: Prentice-Hall, 1984); M. R. Darby and E. Karni, "Free Competition and the Optimal Amount of Fraud," *Journal of Law and Economics*, 16 (1973), 67–86.
5. Abell, *Defining the Business*, p. 8.
6. M. E. Porter, *Competitive Advantage: Creating and Sustaining Superior Performance* (New York: Free Press, 1985).
7. R. D. Buzzell and F. D. Wiersema, "Successful Share Building Strategies," *Harvard Business Review* (January–February 1981), 135–144; L. W. Phillips, D. R. Chang, and R. D. Buzzell, "Product Quality, Cost Position, and Business Performance: A Test of Some Key Hypotheses," *Journal of Marketing*, 47 (1983), 26–43.
8. M. E. Porter, *Competitive Strategy: Techniques for Analyzing Industries and Competitors* (New York: Free Press, 1980), p. 45.
9. Abell, *Defining the Business*, p. 15.
10. Although many other authors have discussed cost leadership and differentiation as basic competitive approaches—e.g., F. Scherer, *Industrial Market Structure and Economic Performance*, 2nd. ed. (Boston: Houghton Mifflin, 1980)—Porter's model (Porter, *Competitive Strategy*) has become the dominant approach. Consequently, this model is the one developed here and the discussion draws heavily on his definitions. The basic cost-leadership/differentiation dimension has received substantial empirical support; see, for instance, D. C. Hambrick, "High Profit Strategies in Mature Capital Goods Industries: A Contingency Approach," *Academy of Management Journal*, 26 (1983), 687–707.
11. Porter, *Competitive Advantage*, p. 37.
12. Ibid., pp. 13–14.
13. D. Miller, "Configurations of Strategy and Structure: Towards a Synthesis," *Strategic Management Journal*, 7 (1986), 217–231.
14. Porter, *Competitive Advantage*, pp. 44–46.
15. C. W. Hofer and D. Schendel, *Strategy Formulation: Analytical Concepts* (St. Paul, Minn.: West, 1978).
16. W. K. Hall, "Survival Strategies in a Hostile Environment," *Harvard Business Review*, 58 (1980), 75–85; Hambrick, "High Profit Strategies," pp. 687–707.
17. J. Guyon, "Can the Savoy Cut Costs and Be the Savoy?" *Wall Street Journal*, October 25, 1994, p. B1.
18. L. Nathans Spiro and M. Landler, "Less-Than-Fantastic Plastic," *Business Week*, November 9, 1992, pp. 100–101; Edward Baig, "Platinum Cards: Move over, Amex," *Business-Week*, August 19, 1996, p. 84; John N. Frank, "American Express's Attention Getter," *Credit Card Management* (August 1996), 36–37.
19. L. Beyer, "Breaking Tradition," *Credit Card Management*, 12, (1999) pp. 57–60.
20. R. Rolfe, "The Smart Centurion," *Credit Card Management*, 12 (1999), pp. 132–136.
21. D. McGinn, "For Ford, Making Wall Street Happy Is Job One," *Newsweek*, April 8, 1996, p. 48.
22. O. Suris, "Ford's Earnings Plunged 58% in 1st Quarter," *Wall Street Journal*, April 18, 1996, p. 7.
23. K. Kerwin and K. Naughton, "Remaking Ford," *Business Week*, 1999, October 11, pp. 68–75.
24. Porter, *Competitive Strategy*, p. 46.
25. J. W. Verity, "They Make a Killing Minding Other People's Business," *Business Week*, November 30, 1992, p. 96.
26. M. Willis, "Outsourcing Benefits Administration: A Disciplined Process for Conducting a Thorough Cost-Benefit Analysis," *Compensation & Benefits Management* (Winter 1996), 45–53; J. Gebhart, "Beyond the Information Systems Outsourcing Bandwagon: The Insourcing Response," *Sloan Business Review* (Winter 1996), 177.
27. B. Caldwell and J. Mateyaschuk, "Reviving EDS," *Informationweek*, 742 (1999), 18–19.
28. W. Zellner, "Can EDS Catch Up With the Net," *Business Week*, May 17, 1999, p.112.
29. P. F. Drucker, *The Practice of Management* (New York: Harper, 1954).
30. Porter, *Competitive Advantage*, pp. 44–46.
31. "The Holiday Inns Trip; A Breeze for Decades, Bumpy Ride in the 1980s," *Wall Street Journal*, February 11, 1987, p.1.
32. Holiday Inns, Annual Report, 1985.
33. Bureau of Labor Statistics, *U.S. Industrial Output* (Washington, D.C., 1986); M. Gleason and A. Salomon, "Fallon's Challenge: Make Holiday Inn More 'In'," *Advertising Age*, September 2, 1996, p. 14; J. Miller, "Amenities Range from Snacks to Technology," *Hotel and Motel Management*, July 3, 1996, pp. 38–40.
34. The development of strategic group theory has been a strong theme in the strategy literature. Important contributions include R. E. Caves and M. Porter, "From Entry Barriers to Mobility Barriers," *Quarterly Journal of Economics* (May 1977), 241–262; K. R. Harrigan, "An Application of Clustering for Strategic Group Analysis," *Strategic Management Journal*, 6 (1985), 55–73; K. J. Hatten and D. E. Schendel, "Heterogeneity Within an Industry: Firm Conduct in the U.S. Brewing Industry, 1952–1971," *Journal of Industrial Economics*, 26 (1976), 97–113; M. E. Porter, "The Structure Within Industries and Companies' Performance," *Review of Economics and Statistics*, 61 (1979), 214–227.
35. For details on strategic group structure in the pharmaceutical industry, see K. Cool and I. Dierickx, "Rivalry, Strategic Groups, and Firm Profitability," *Strategic Management Journal*, 14 (1993), 47–59.
36. Hofer and Schendel, *Strategy Formulation*, pp. 102–104.
37. Our discussion of the investment, or posturing, component of business-level strategy draws heavily on Hofer and Schendel's discussion in *Strategy Formulation*, especially Chapter 6.

38. Hofer and Schendel, *Strategy Formulation*, pp. 75–77.
39. K. R. Harrigan, "Strategy Formulation in Declining Industries," *Academy of Management Review*, 5 (1980), 599–604.
40. Hofer and Schendel, *Strategy Formulation*, pp. 169–172.
41. L. R. Feldman and A. L. Page, "Harvesting: The Misunderstood Market Exit Strategy," *Journal of Business Strategy*, 4 (1985), 79–85.
42. C. W. Hofer, "Turnaround Strategies," *Journal of Business Strategy*, 1 (1980), 19–31.
43. Hofer and Schendel, *Strategy Formulation*, p. 172.
44. N. Darnton, "The Joy of Polyester," *Newsweek*, August 3, 1992, p. 61.
45. C. Miller, "Liz Claiborne Throws a Curve with New Brand for Gen Xers," *Marketing News*, July 1, 1996, pp. 1, 10; E. Underwood, "Claiborne Back in Media," *Brandweek*, January 15, 1996, p. 2.

7 Competitive Strategy and the Industry Environment

OPENING CASE

How eBay Revolutionized the Auction Business

IN THE 1990S, many entrepreneurs have tried to use new information technologies, and particularly the Internet, to provide new or improved services to customers. Their goal in exploring the potential of the new technology was to find ways of gaining a competitive advantage over existing firms in a particular industry environment. Nowhere has this been more evident than in the auction industry.

Traditionally, auctions have been events bringing buyers and sellers face to face to determine the fair market value of a product. Auction houses range from the most prestigious ones, such as Sotheby's and Christie's, which sell fine art and antiques, to small local auction companies that sell the contents of someone's house.

In the early 1990s, Pierre Omidyar had an idea for a new kind of auction company, an on-line one, which he believed would revolutionize the selling of all kinds of products—not just fine arts and antiques; but any kind of collectible, from cars to Beanie Babies—by bringing buyers and sellers together through the Internet. He left his job at Microsoft and began to write the software that would provide the platform for an on-line auction service. The result was eBay, launched on Labor Day 1995.[1]

On the eBay Web site, sellers are able to electronically describe their product, post a photograph, and set an initial price, which buyers can then bid up. The highest bidder wins. The company charges a modest fee to list the product plus a low percentage of the final sales price. Sellers have the advantage that their product appears before buyers in every part of the United States, as well as abroad—wherever someone has a computer and can log on to eBay's on-line auction site. Buyers enjoy access to a huge array of merchandise, which can be quickly scanned by using the appropriate keywords on eBay's search engine.

OPENING CASE *(continued)*

Thus, eBay provides a low-cost forum where buyers and sellers can meet to buy and sell products. The company makes its money from the sheer volume of products that it sells. Every day, millions are listed, so that even with low fees eBay is able to generate high profits.

As you can imagine, eBay's low-cost approach has generated many imitators; after all, it is relatively easy to write a software program and develop an on-line auction site. However, eBay's early start has also given it another major competitive advantage. As the first in the on-line auction business, it has developed a loyal following of both buyers and sellers, who will not switch to other on-line auction companies even when they provide the service for free. By 1999, for instance, Yahoo! and MSN, and hundreds of small specialized companies, had developed their own on-line auction businesses and decided to charge users nothing for their services. Most of them, however, including Yahoo!'s auction site, have not attracted many buyers and sellers. The reason is simple. Sellers know that eBay's site attracts many more buyers than does Yahoo!'s and consequently that they are likely to obtain the highest price there; and eBay buyers know that they will find the greatest selection at that site and so focus their search there. Thus, besides achieving a low-cost competency, eBay has developed a substantial reputation, which has given it a differentiation advantage as well.

Other on-line companies, however, are not willing to give away the lucrative on-line auction market to eBay; they are searching for new ways to fight back. In June 1999, for example, bookseller Amazon.com announced that it was forming an alliance with Sotheby's to create an upmarket on-line auction service. Other companies have also been seeking partners. In October 1999, Yahoo!, Amazon.com, and others announced that they were banding together to combine their auction businesses and offer a credible alternative to eBay.[2]

After this announcement, eBay's price on the stock market fell. It had soared several thousand percent because investors thought that eBay's strategy had given it a sustainable competitive advantage over its rivals. Through his innovative use of new information technology, Omidyar had brought increased value for millions of buyers and sellers and in the meantime had created more than $1 billion of value for himself in his eBay stock. Now the question arises whether eBay can maintain this value.

OVERVIEW

Chapter 6 examines the different kinds of generic business-level strategies that companies can adopt to obtain a competitive advantage and outperform their rivals. If strategic managers do succeed in developing a successful generic business-level strategy, they face still another crucial task: choosing an appropriate competitive strategy to position their company so that it can sustain its competitive advantage over time in different kinds of industry environments. That is the issue we explore in this chapter.

First, we focus on how companies in *fragmented industries* try to develop competitive strategies that support their generic strategies. Second, we consider the challenges of developing a competitive advantage in *embryonic* and *growth industries.* Third, we probe the nature of competitive relations in *mature industries.* We concentrate here on how a set of companies that have been pursuing successful generic competitive strategies (such as the major burger chains) can use a variety of competitive tactics and gambits to manage the high level of competitive interdependence found in such industries. Finally, we assess the problems of managing a company's generic competitive strategy in *declining industries,* in which rivalry between competitors is high because market demand is slowing or falling. By the end of this chapter, you will understand how the successful pursuit of a generic strategy depends on the selection of the right competitive strategy to manage the industry environment.

STRATEGIES IN FRAGMENTED INDUSTRIES

A **fragmented industry** is one consisting of a large number of small and medium-sized companies. The video-rental industry, for example, is still very fragmented, as is the restaurant industry, the health-club industry, and the legal-services industry. There are several reasons why an industry may consist of many small companies rather than a few large ones.[3] Some industries offer few economies of scale, and so large companies do not have an advantage over smaller enterprises. Indeed, in some industries there are diseconomies of scale. For instance, many home buyers prefer to deal with local real estate agencies, which they perceive as having better local knowledge than national chains. Similarly, in the restaurant business, many customers prefer the unique style of a local restaurant. Because they lack economies of scale, fragmented industries are often characterized by low barriers to entry (and new entries keep the industry fragmented). That is the situation in the restaurant industry, since the costs of opening a restaurant are very moderate and can be borne by a single entrepreneur. High transportation costs, too, can keep an industry fragmented, for regional production may be the only efficient way to satisfy customers' needs, as in the cement business. Finally, an industry may be fragmented because customers' needs are so specialized that only small job lots of products are required, and thus there is no room for a large mass-production operation to satisfy the market.

For some fragmented industries, these factors dictate the competitive strategy to pursue, and the *focus strategy* stands out as the principal choice. Companies may specialize by customer group, customer need, or geographic region; consequently, many small specialty companies operate in local or regional market segments. All kinds of custom-made products—furniture, clothing, hats, boots, and so on—fall into this category, as do all small service operations that cater to particular customers' needs, such as laundries, restaurants, health clubs, and furniture-rental stores. Indeed, service companies make up a large proportion of the enterprises in fragmented industries because they provide personalized service to clients and, therefore, need to be responsive to their needs.

Strategic managers, however, are eager to gain the cost advantages of pursuing a low-cost strategy or the sales/revenue-enhancing advantages of differentiation by circumventing the problems of a fragmented industry. Because returns from consolidating a fragmented industry are often huge, during the last thirty years many companies have developed competitive strategies to achieve such consolidation. Among these companies are the large retailers Wal-Mart, Sears, and JC Penney; fast-food chains such as McDonald's and Burger King; video-rental chains such as Blockbuster Entertainment with its Blockbuster Video stores; and chains of health clubs, repair shops, and even lawyers and consultants. To grow, consolidate their industries, and become the industry leaders, these companies utilize three main competitive strategies: (1) chaining, (2) franchising, (3) horizontal merger and (4) using the Internet.

Chaining

Companies such as Wal-Mart and Midas International pursue a **chaining** strategy to obtain the advantages of cost leadership. They establish networks of linked merchandising outlets so interconnected that they function as one large business entity. The amazing buying power that these companies possess through their nationwide store chains allows them to negotiate large price reductions with their suppliers, which in turn promotes their competitive advantage. They overcome the barrier of high transportation costs by establishing sophisticated regional distribution centers, which can economize on inventory costs and maximize responsiveness to the needs of stores and customers. (This is Wal-Mart's specialty.) Last but not least, they realize economies of scale from sharing managerial skills across the chain and from advertising nationally rather than locally.

Franchising

For differentiated companies in fragmented industries, such as McDonald's or Century 21 Real Estate, the competitive advantage comes from a business strategy that employs franchise agreements. In **franchising** the franchisor (parent) grants the franchisee the right to use the parent's name, reputation, and business skills at a particular location or area. If the franchisee also acts as the manager, he or she is strongly motivated to control the business closely and make sure that quality and standards are consistently high so that customers' needs are always satisfied. Such motivation is particularly critical in a strategy of differentiation, for which a company's ability to maintain its uniqueness is very important. Indeed, one reason industries fragment is the difficulty of controlling the many small outlets that must be operated while at the same time retaining their uniqueness. Franchising solves this problem.[4] In addition, franchising lessens the financial burden of swift expansion and so permits rapid growth of the company. Finally, a differentiated large company can reap the advantages of large-scale advertising, as well as economies in purchasing, management, and distribution, as McDonald's does very efficiently. Indeed, McDonald's is able to pursue cost leadership and differentiation simultaneously only because franchising allows costs to be controlled locally and differentiation to be achieved by marketing on a national level.

Horizontal Merger

Companies such as Anheuser-Busch, Dillard Department Stores, and Blockbuster Entertainment have been choosing a business-level strategy of **horizontal merger** to consolidate their respective industries. For example, Dillard arranged the merger of regional store chains in order to form a national company. By pursuing horizontal merger, companies are able to obtain economies of scale or secure a national market for their product. As a result, they are able to pursue a cost-leadership or a differentiation strategy, or both.

Using the Internet

The latest means by which companies have been able to consolidate a fragmented industry is the Internet, and eBay, profiled in the Opening Case, is a good example of this approach. Before eBay, the auction business was extremely fragmented, and local auctions in cities were the usual way in which people could dispose of their antiques and collectibles. With the advent of eBay, sellers using it know that they are getting wide visibility for their collectibles, and therefore are likely to receive a higher price for their product. Amazon.com's success in the book market has led to the closing of many small bookstores, which simply cannot compete either by price or selection. The trend toward using the Internet seems likely to further consolidate even relatively oligopolistic industries.

The challenge in a fragmented industry is to choose the most appropriate means—franchising, chaining, horizontal merger, or Internet—of overcoming a fragmented market so that the competitive advantages associated with the different business-level strategies can be realized. It is difficult to think of any major service activities—from consulting and accounting firms to businesses satisfying the smallest consumer need, such as beauty parlors and car-repair shops—that have not been merged or consolidated by chaining, franchising, and now by the Internet.

STRATEGIES IN EMBRYONIC AND GROWTH INDUSTRIES

Embryonic industries are typically created by the innovations of pioneering companies that become the first movers in a new market. For example, Apple single-handedly created the market for personal computers, Xerox created the market for photocopiers, and McDonald's created the market for fast food. In most cases, the pioneering company can initially earn enormous profits from its innovation because it is the only company in the industry for a time. For example, before the entry of IBM into the personal computer market in 1981, Apple enjoyed a virtual monopoly. Similarly, during the seventeen years before its patents expired, Xerox enjoyed a monopoly in the market for photocopiers, earning enormous profits as a result.[5]

However, innovators' high profits also attract potential imitators and second movers, as the companies that enter the market later are known. Typically, second movers enter during the growth stage of an industry and may cause the pioneering, first-mover company to lose its commanding competitive position. Figure 7.1 shows how the profit rate enjoyed by the innovator in an embryonic industry can decline as imitators crowd into the market during its growth stage. Thus, Apple's onetime monopoly position was competed away as hordes of other personal computer makers entered the market in the early and mid 1980s, trying to share in Apple's success. Once its patents expired, Xerox, too, faced many imitators, and some of them, such as Canon and Ricoh, were ultimately very successful in the photocopier market. In the fast-food market, the early success of McDonald's drew imitators, including Burger King, Wendy's, and Foodmaker, with its Jack-in-the-Box restaurants.

Although their market share has declined since their early days, companies such as Apple, Xerox, and McDonald's are still major competitors. Other early innovators were not so lucky. For example, in the mid 1970s, EMI pioneered the development of the CAT scanner. Widely regarded as the most important advance in radiology since the x-ray, the CAT scanner takes three-dimensional x-ray pictures of the body. Despite being the pioneer, however, EMI soon saw imitators such as General Electric capture the market. EMI itself withdrew from the CAT market in the early 1980s. Similarly, Bowman invented the pocket calculator, only to see Texas Instruments reap the long-run rewards of the innovation, and Royal Crown Cola pioneered the introduction of diet colas, but it was Coca-Cola and PepsiCo that made

FIGURE 7.1

How an Innovator's Profits Can Be Competed Away

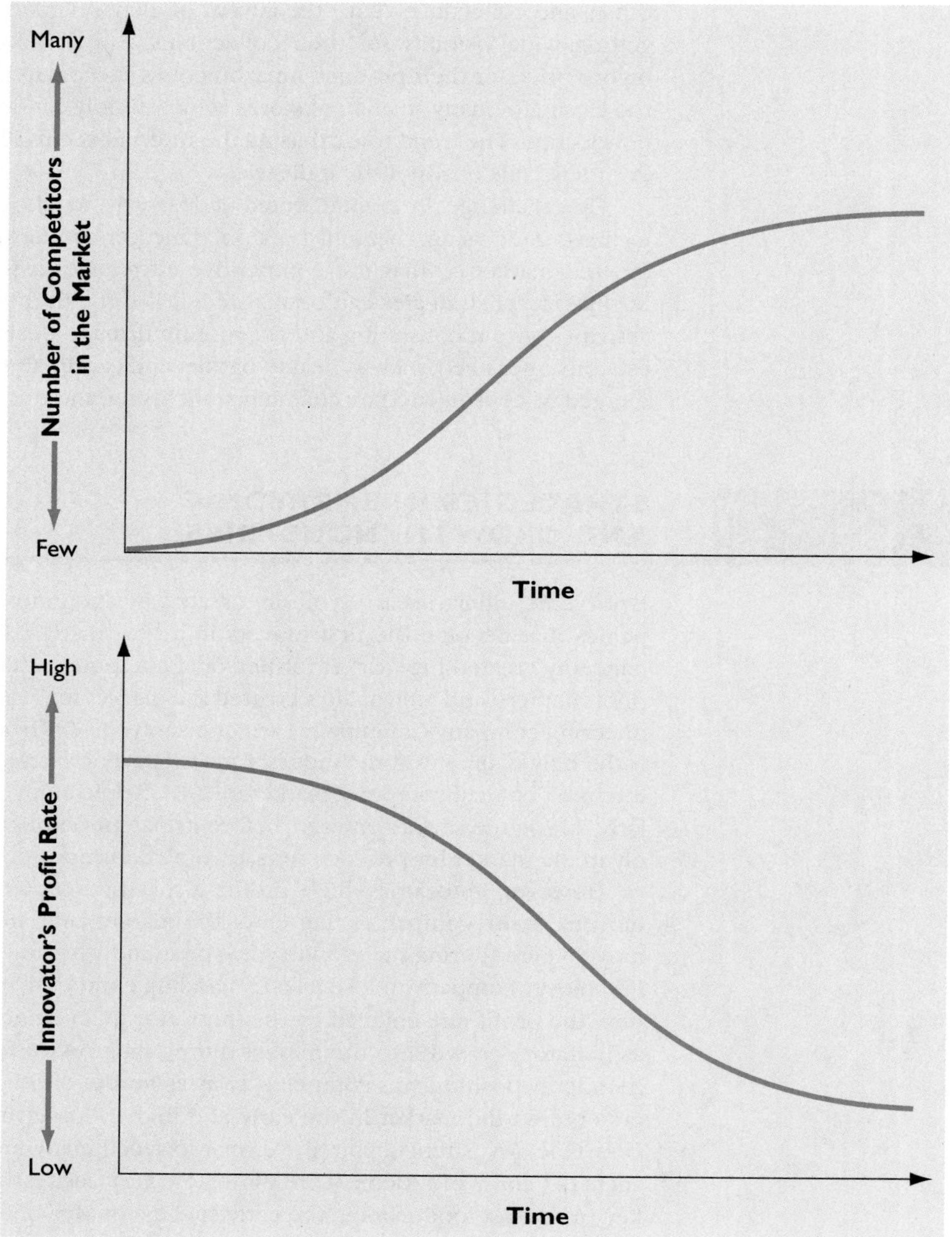

enormous profits from the concept. Thus, first movers often lose out to second movers as competition in an industry becomes intense.

Given the inevitability of imitation, the key issue for an innovating company in an embryonic industry is how to exploit its innovation and build an enduring long-run competitive advantage based on low cost or differentiation. Three strategies are available to the company: (1) to develop and market the innovation itself; (2) to develop and market the innovation jointly with other companies through a strategic alliance or joint venture; and (3) to license the innovation to others and let them develop the market.

The optimal choice of strategy depends on the answers to three questions. First, does the innovating company have the *complementary assets* to exploit its innovation and obtain a competitive advantage? Second, how difficult is it for imitators to copy the company's innovation—in other words, what is the *height of barriers to imitation?* And third, are there *capable competitors* that could rapidly imitate the innovation? Before we discuss the optimal choice of innovation strategy, we need to examine the answers to these three questions.

Complementary Assets

Complementary assets are those required to exploit a new innovation and gain a competitive advantage successfully.[6] Among the most important complementary assets are competitive manufacturing facilities capable of handling rapid growth in customers' demand while maintaining high product quality. State-of-the-art manufacturing facilities enable the innovator to move quickly down the experience curve without encountering production bottlenecks and/or problems with the quality of the product. The inability to satisfy demand because of these problems, however, creates the opportunity for imitators to enter the marketplace. For example, Compaq Computer was able to grow rapidly in the market for MS-DOS personal computers during the 1990s at the expense of the product's pioneer, IBM, largely because IBM lacked what Compaq possessed: the state-of-the-art manufacturing facilities to build low-cost computers.

Complementary assets also include marketing know-how, an adequate sales force, access to distribution systems, and an after-sales service and support network. Furthermore, the Internet is making it easier for small companies to develop a nationwide presence since it offers a low-cost way to advertise and sell products to customers. All these assets can help an innovator build brand loyalty. They also help the innovator achieve market penetration more rapidly.[7] In turn, the resulting increases in volume facilitate more rapid movement down the experience curve.

Developing such complementary assets can be very expensive, and embryonic companies often need large infusions of capital for this purpose. That is the reason first movers often lose out to late movers that are large, successful companies, often established in other industries, with the resources to develop a presence in the new industry quickly. Hewlett-Packard and 3M exemplify companies that can move quickly to capitalize on the opportunities arising when other companies open up new product markets, such as compact disks or floppy disks. For instance, Hewlett-Packard began producing personal computers that competed directly with those of Compaq, IBM, and Apple, the early movers.

Height of Barriers to Imitation

Barriers to imitation are introduced in Chapter 4, in the discussion of the durability of competitive advantage. As you may recall, **barriers to imitation** are factors that prevent rivals from imitating a company's distinctive competencies. Barriers to imitation also prevent rivals, particularly second or late movers, from imitating a company's innovation. Although ultimately any innovation can be copied, the higher the barriers, the longer it takes for rivals to imitate.

Barriers to imitation give an innovator time to establish a competitive advantage and build more enduring barriers to entry in the newly created market. Patents, for example, are among the most widely used barriers to imitation. By protecting its photocopier technology with a thicket of patents, Xerox was able to delay any significant imitation of its product for seventeen years. However, patents are often easy to "invent around." For example, one study found that this happened to 60 percent of patented innovations within four years.[8] If patent protection is weak, a company might try to slow imitation by developing new products and processes in secret. The most famous example of this approach is Coca-Cola, which has kept the formula for Coke a secret for generations. But Coca-Cola's success in this regard is an exception. A study of 100 companies has estimated that proprietary information about a company's decision to develop a major new product or process is known to its rivals within about twelve to eighteen months of the original development decision.[9]

Capable Competitors

Capable competitors are companies that can move quickly to imitate the pioneering company. Competitors' capability to imitate a pioneer's innovation depends primarily on two factors: (1) R&D skills and (2) access to complementary assets. In general, the greater the number of capable competitors with access to the R&D skills and complementary assets needed to imitate an innovation, the more rapid is imitation likely to be.

In this context, R&D skills refer to the ability of rivals to reverse-engineer an innovation in order to find out how it works and quickly develop a comparable product. As an example, consider the CAT scanner. GE bought one of the first CAT scanners produced by EMI, and its technical experts reverse-engineered it. Despite the product's technological complexity, GE developed its own version of it, which allowed GE to imitate EMI quickly and ultimately to replace EMI as the major supplier of CAT scanners.

With regard to complementary assets, the access that rivals have to marketing, sales know-how, or manufacturing capabilities is one of the key determinants of the rate of imitation. If would-be imitators lack critical complementary assets, not only do they have to imitate the innovation, but they may also have to imitate the innovator's complementary assets. This is expensive, as AT&T discovered when it tried to enter the personal computer business in 1984. AT&T lacked the marketing assets (sales force and distribution systems) necessary to support personal computer products. The lack of these assets and the time it takes to build them partly explain why four years after it originally entered the market AT&T had lost $2.5 billion and still had not emerged as a viable contender.

Three Innovation Strategies

The way in which these three factors—complementary assets, height of barriers to imitation, and the capability of competitors—influence the choice of innovation strategy is summarized in Table 7.1. The competitive strategy of *developing and marketing the innovation alone* makes most sense when (1) the innovator has the complementary assets necessary to develop the innovation, (2) the barriers to imitating a new innovation are high, and (3) the number of capable competitors is limited. Complementary assets allow rapid development and promotion of the

TABLE 7.1

Strategies for Profiting from Innovation

Strategy	*Does Innovator Have All Required Complementary Assets?*	*Likely Height of Barriers to Imitation*	*Number of Capable Competitors*
Going it alone	Yes	High	Few
Entering into alliance	No	HIgh	Limited
License innovation	No	Low	Many

innovation. High barriers to imitation buy the innovator time to establish a competitive advantage and build enduring barriers to entry through brand loyalty and/or experience-based cost advantages. The fewer the capable competitors, the less likely it is that any one of them will succeed in circumventing barriers to imitation and quickly imitating the innovation. The availability of the Internet makes this strategy more viable since a company can promote an innovation much more easily and inexpensively.

The competitive strategy of *developing and marketing the innovation jointly with other companies through a strategic alliance or joint venture* makes most sense when (1) the innovator lacks complementary assets, (2) barriers to imitation are high, and (3) there are several capable competitors. In such circumstances, it makes sense to enter into an alliance with a company that already has the complementary assets, in other words, with a capable competitor. Theoretically, such an alliance should prove to be mutually beneficial, and each partner can share in high profits that neither could earn on its own. The attempt by Body Shop International, described in Strategy in Action 7.1, to go it alone in the effort to enter the U.S. market rather than to form an alliance with U.S. partners illustrates the benefit of alliances in quickly exploiting an innovation.

The third strategy, *licensing*, makes most sense when (1) the innovating company lacks the complementary assets, (2) barriers to imitation are low, and (3) there are many capable competitors. The combination of low barriers to imitation and many capable competitors makes rapid imitation almost certain. The innovator's lack of complementary assets further suggests that an imitator will soon capture the innovator's competitive advantage. Given these factors, since rapid diffusion of the innovator's technology through imitation is inevitable, by licensing out its technology the innovator can at least share in some of the benefits of this diffusion.[11]

STRATEGY IN MATURE INDUSTRIES

As a result of fierce competition in the shakeout stage, an industry becomes consolidated, and so a mature industry is often dominated by a small number of large companies. Although a mature industry may also contain many medium-sized

7.1 **STRATEGY *in* ACTION**

The Body Shop Opens Too Late

In 1976, Anita Roddick, a former flower child and the owner of a small hotel in southern England, had an idea. Rising sentiment against the use of animals in testing cosmetics and a wave of environmentalism that focused on "natural" products gave her the idea for a range of skin creams, shampoos, and lotions made from fruit and vegetable oils rather than animal products. Her products, moreover, would not be tested on animals. Roddick began to sell her line of new products from a small shop in Brighton, a seaside town, and the results surpassed her wildest expectations. Her line of cosmetics was an instant success, and to capitalize on it, she began to franchise the right to open stores called The Body Shop to sell her products. By 1993, there were more than 700 of these stores around the world, with combined sales of more than $250 million.

In Britain and Europe, to speed the growth of the company, Roddick mainly franchised her stores through alliances with other individuals and companies. In her push to enter the U.S. market in 1988, however, she decided to own her stores and forgo the rapid expansion that franchising would have made possible. This was a costly mistake. Large U.S. cosmetic companies such as Estée Lauder and entrepreneurs such as Leslie Wexner of The Limited were quick to see the opportunities that Roddick had opened up in this rapidly growing market segment. They moved fast to imitate her product lines, which was not technically difficult to do, and began to market their own natural cosmetics. For example, Estée Lauder brought out its Origins line of cosmetics, and Wexner opened the Bath and Body Works to sell his own line of natural cosmetics. Both these ventures have been very successful and have gained a large share of the market.

Realizing the competitive threat from imitators, in 1990 Roddick began to move quickly to franchise The Body Shop in the United States, and by 1993 more than 150 stores had opened. Although the stores have been successful, the delay in opening them gave Roddick's competitors the opportunity to establish their own brand names and robbed her enterprise of the uniqueness that its products enjoy throughout Europe. Given that the United States is by far the world's biggest cosmetics market and natural cosmetics are its fastest-growing segment, this mistake cost Body Shop billions of dollars in lost revenues.

Roddick acknowledged that her strategy was a mistake; however, during the 1990s, she failed to energize her company, and in 1998 a new CEO, Patrick Gourmay, took over. He moved quickly to revive flagging sales by opening new stores at a very fast rate, by increasing the level of product innovation, and by using the Internet to raise sales. In 1999, for example, he was aiming for product innovation growth of 60 percent as opposed to the 25 percent that the company had managed earlier.[10] Gourmay has obviously learnt the lesson well: when an innovation is easy to imitate and there are many capable competitors, a company must do all it can to speed the development and sale of a new product.

companies and a host of small specialized ones, the large companies determine the nature of the industry's competition because they can influence the five competitive forces. Indeed, these are the companies that developed the most successful generic business-level strategies in the industry.

By the end of the shakeout stage, strategic groups of companies pursuing similar generic competitive strategies have emerged in the industry. As we discuss in Chapter 6, all the companies pursuing a low-cost strategy can be viewed as composing one strategic group; all those pursuing differentiation constitute another; and the focusers form a third. Companies in an industry constantly analyze each other's business-level strategies, and they know that if they move to change their strategies, their actions are likely to stimulate a competitive response from rivals in their strategic group and from companies in other groups that may be threatened by the change in strategy.

For example, a differentiator that starts to lower its prices because it has adopted a more cost-efficient technology not only threatens other differentiators in its group, but also threatens low-cost companies, which see their competitive edge being eroded. These other companies may now change their strategies in response—most likely by reducing their prices, too, as is currently happening in the personal computer industry. Thus, the way one company changes or fine-tunes its business-level strategy over time affects the way the other companies in the industry pursue theirs. Hence, by the mature stage of the industry life cycle, companies have learned just how *interdependent* their strategies are.

In fact, the main challenge facing companies in a mature industry is to adopt a competitive strategy that *simultaneously* allows each individual company to protect its competitive advantage and preserves industry profitability. No generic strategy will generate above-average profits if competitive forces in an industry are so strong that companies are at the mercy of each other, potential entrants, powerful suppliers, powerful customers, and so on. As a result, in mature industries, competitive strategy revolves around understanding how large companies try *collectively* to reduce the strength of the five forces of industry competition to preserve both company and industry profitability.

Interdependent companies can help protect their competitive advantage and profitability by adopting competitive moves and tactics to reduce the threat of each competitive force. In the next sections, we examine the various price and nonprice competitive moves and tactics that companies use—first, to deter entry into an industry, and second, to reduce the level of rivalry within an industry. We then discuss methods that companies can employ to gain more control over suppliers and buyers.

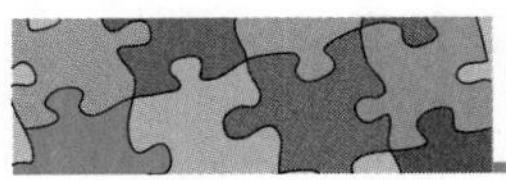

STRATEGIES TO DETER ENTRY IN MATURE INDUSTRIES

Companies can utilize three main methods to deter entry by potential rivals and hence maintain and increase industry profitability. As Figure 7.2 shows, these methods are product proliferation, price cutting, and excess capacity.

FIGURE 7.2

Strategies for Deterring Entry of Rivals

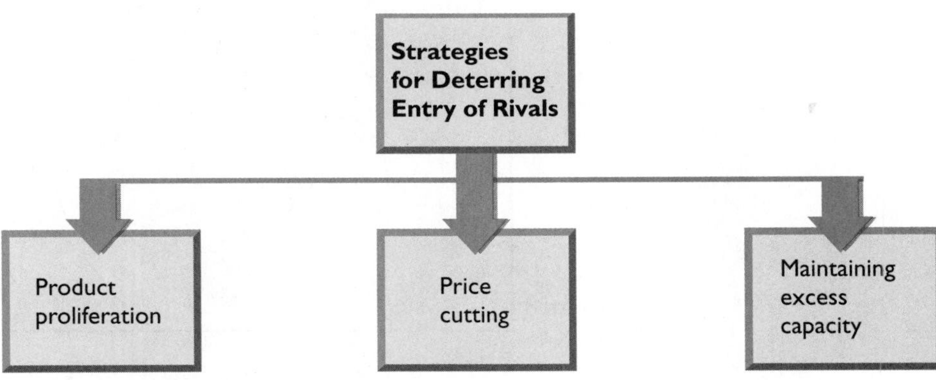

Product Proliferation

Companies seldom produce just one product. Most commonly, they produce a range of products aimed at different market segments so that they have broad product lines. Sometimes, to diminish the threat of entry, companies expand the range of products they make to fill a wide variety of niches. Such expansion creates a barrier to entry because potential competitors now find it harder to break into an industry in which all the niches are filled.[12] This strategy of pursuing a broad product line to deter entry is known as **product proliferation.**

Because the large U.S. carmakers were so slow to fill the small-car niches (they did *not* pursue a product proliferation strategy), they were vulnerable to the entry of the Japanese into these market segments in the United States. American carmakers had no excuse for this situation, for in their European operations they had a long history of small-car manufacturing. They should have seen the opening and filled it ten years earlier, but their view was that small cars meant small profits. In the breakfast-cereal industry, on the other hand, competition is based on the production of new kinds of cereal to satisfy or create new desires by consumers. Thus, the number of breakfast cereals proliferates, making it very difficult for prospective entrants to attack a new market segment.

Figure 7.3 indicates how product proliferation can deter entry. It depicts product space in the restaurant industry along two dimensions: (1) atmosphere, which ranges from fast food to candlelight dining; and (2) quality of food, which ranges from average to gourmet. The circles represent product spaces filled by restaurants located along the two dimensions. Thus, McDonald's is situated in the average quality/fast-food area. A gap in the product space gives a potential entrant or an existing

FIGURE 7.3

Product Proliferation in the Restaurant Industry

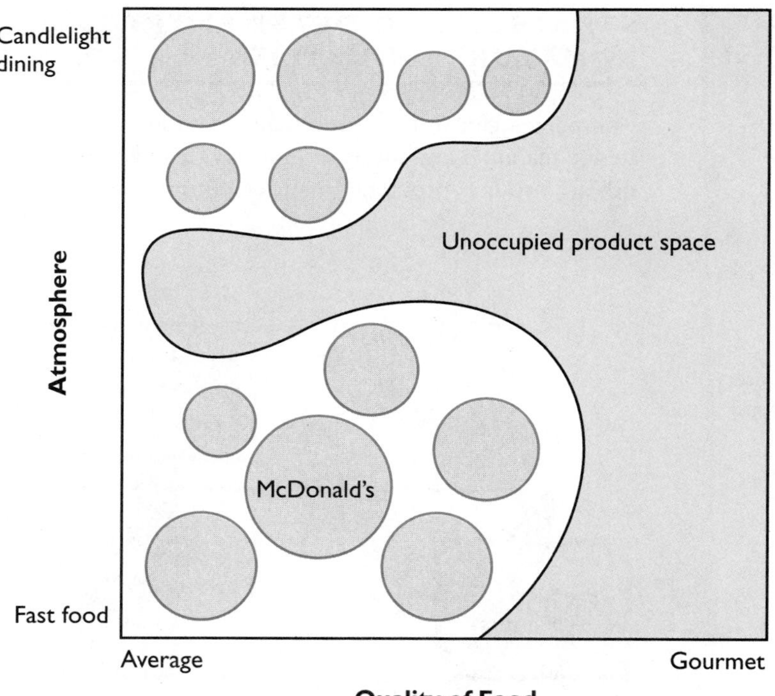

rival an opportunity to enter the market and make inroads. The shaded unoccupied product space represents areas where new restaurants can enter the market. Filling all the product spaces, however, creates a barrier to entry and makes it much more difficult for a new company to gain a foothold in the market and differentiate itself.

Price Cutting

In some situations, pricing strategies involving **price cutting** can be used to deter entry by other companies, thus protecting the profit margins of companies already in an industry. One price-cutting strategy, for example, is to charge a high price initially for a product and seize short-term profits but then to cut prices aggressively in order to build market share *and* deter potential entrants simultaneously.[13] The incumbent companies thus signal to potential entrants that if they enter the industry, the incumbents will use their competitive advantage to drive down prices to a level at which new companies will be unable to cover their costs.[14] This pricing strategy also allows a company to ride down the experience curve and obtain substantial economies of scale. Since costs fall with prices, profit margins could still be maintained.

This strategy, though, is unlikely to deter a strong potential competitor—an established company that is trying to find profitable investment opportunities in other industries. It is difficult, for example, to imagine that 3M would be afraid to enter an industry because companies there threaten to drive down prices. A company such as 3M has the resources to withstand any short-term losses. Hewlett-Packard also had few worries about entering the highly competitive personal computer industry because of its powerful set of distinctive competencies. Hence, it may be in the interest of incumbent companies to accept new entry gracefully, giving up market share gradually to the new entrants to prevent price wars from developing, and thus save their profits, if this is feasible.

Most evidence suggests that companies first skim the market and charge high prices during the growth stage, maximizing short-run profits.[15] Then they move to increase their market share and charge a lower price to expand the market rapidly; develop a reputation; and obtain economies of scale, driving down costs and barring entry. As competitors do enter, the incumbent companies reduce prices to retard entry and give up market share to create a stable industry context—one in which they can use nonprice competitive tactics, such as product differentiation, to maximize long-run profits. At that point, nonprice competition becomes the main basis of industry competition, and prices are quite likely to rise as competition stabilizes. Thus, competitive tactics such as pricing and product differentiation are linked in mature industries; competitive decisions are taken to maximize the returns from a company's generic strategy. The airline industry, discussed in Strategy in Action 7.2, offers an illustration of how and when companies use both price and nonprice competitive tactics to build barriers to entry that deter new entrants and reduce rivalry.

Maintaining Excess Capacity

The third competitive technique that allows companies to deter entry involves maintaining excess capacity, that is, producing more of a product than customers currently demand. Existing industry companies may deliberately develop some limited amount of excess capacity because it serves to warn potential entrants that if they enter the industry, existing firms can retaliate by increasing output and forcing

7.2 STRATEGY *in* ACTION

Ups and Downs in the Airline Industry

Before deregulation in 1978, competition over fares and ticket prices was not permitted in the airline industry, and the airlines had to find other ways to compete. Their response was to attract customers by offering more frequent flights and better service—a form of product differentiation. Since all airlines imitated one another, however, no airline was able to get a competitive advantage over its rivals, and each airline's costs rose dramatically because of the expense of extra flights, improved meals, and so on. To cover the higher costs, the airlines constantly applied for fare increases. As a result, customers paid higher and higher fares to compensate for the airlines' inefficiency. In an attempt to cure this problem, the U.S. Congress decided to deregulate the industry, permitting competition in ticket prices and allowing free entry into the industry. The airlines did not want deregulation. (Why should they? They were receiving a nice profit as a protected industry.) However, deregulation did take place in 1979, and the result was chaos.

Deregulation destroyed the old competitive tactics and maneuvers the airlines had long adopted. Before deregulation, the major airlines knew each other's competitive moves by heart. In the new world of price competition, entry into the industry was easy, and a host of small airlines entered to compete with the major companies. During regulation, no airline had had to develop a generic strategy. There had been no incentive to keep costs low because cost increases could be passed on to consumers. In addition, all firms had used the same means to differentiate themselves, so that no airline had a competitive advantage in being unique. With no rules to tell them how to compete and no experience of free competition, the airlines waged a price war as new, low-cost entrants such as People Express and Southwest Airlines sought to gain market share from the major players.

To survive in this environment, the major airlines have adopted new competitive tactics to protect their business-level strategies. One of these tactics is the development of hub-and-spoke networks, which have allowed them to build national route structures at low cost. These networks also make it difficult for new firms to enter the industry, because the major airlines hold most of the available gates at large airports. Through nonprice means, the major companies have tried to create new barriers to entry, thereby reducing the threat of new entrants. They have tried to develop new competitive rules of the game to stabilize competition within the industry and prevent price competition.

The use of all these price and nonprice techniques did reduce the number of new entrants, and by 1995 the industry had become profitable, after losing billions of dollars in the early 1990s. However, since 1995, there have been increasing customer complaints about lost bags, poor quality or nonexistent food, cramped seats, and higher fares as the major airlines have sought to reduce their costs and increase their profits. In addition, the wave of strategic alliances in the industry, for example, between American Airlines and British Airlines and between Continental Airlines and Northwest Airlines have led many analysts to conclude that customers may see even more price hikes and cuts in quality as the airlines enjoy their strong bargaining position.

down prices until entry would become unprofitable. However, the threat to increase output has to be *credible,* that is, companies in an industry must collectively be able to raise the level of production quickly if entry appears likely.

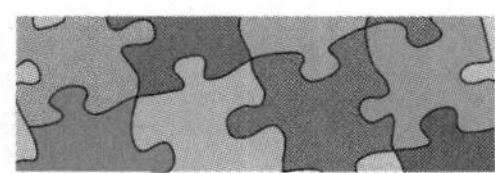

STRATEGIES TO MANAGE RIVALRY IN MATURE INDUSTRIES

Beyond seeking to deter entry, companies also wish to develop a competitive strategy to manage their competitive interdependence and decrease rivalry. As we noted earlier, unrestricted competition over prices or output reduces the level of company and industry profitability. Several competitive tactics and gambits are available to companies to manage industry relations. The most important are price signaling, price leadership, nonprice competition, and capacity control.

Price Signaling

Most industries start out fragmented, with small companies battling for market share. Then, over time, the leading players emerge, and companies start to interpret each other's competitive moves. Price signaling is the first means by which companies attempt to structure competition within an industry in order to control rivalry among competitors.[16] **Price signaling** is the process by which companies increase or decrease product prices to convey their intentions to other companies and so influence the way they price their products.[17] There are two ways in which companies use price signaling to help defend their generic competitive strategies.

First, companies may use price signaling to announce that they will respond vigorously to hostile competitive moves that threaten them. For example, companies may signal that if one company starts to cut prices aggressively, they will respond in kind—hence the term **tit-for-tat strategy** is often used to describe this kind of market signaling. The outcome of a tit-for-tat strategy is that nobody gains. Similarly, as we note in the last section, companies may signal to potential entrants that if the latter do enter the market, they will fight back by reducing prices and the new entrants may incur significant losses.

A second, and very important, use of price signaling is to allow companies indirectly to coordinate their actions and avoid costly competitive moves that lead to a breakdown in the pricing policy within an industry. One company may signal that it intends to lower prices because it wishes to attract customers who are switching to the products of another industry, not because it wishes to stimulate a price war. On the other hand, signaling can be used to improve profitability within an industry. The airline industry is a good example of the power of price signaling. In the 1980s, signals of lower prices set off price wars, but in the 1990s, the airlines have used price signaling to obtain uniform price increases. Nonrefundable tickets, too, originated as a market signal by one company that was quickly copied by all other companies in the industry. In sum, price signaling allows companies to give one another information that enables them to understand each other's competitive product/market strategy and make coordinated competitive moves.

Price Leadership

Price leadership—the taking on by one company of the responsibility for setting industry prices—is a second tactic used to enhance the profitability of companies in a mature industry.[18] Formal price leadership, or price setting by companies jointly, is illegal under antitrust laws, so the process of price leadership is often very subtle. In the auto industry, for example, auto prices are set by imitation. The price set by the weakest company—that is, the one with the highest costs—is often used as the basis for competitors' pricing. Thus, U.S. carmakers set their prices, and Japanese carmakers then set theirs with reference to the U.S. prices. The Japanese are happy to do this because they have lower costs than U.S. companies and are making higher profits than U.S. carmakers without competing with them by price. Pricing is done by market segment. The prices of different auto models in the model range indicate the customer segments that the companies are aiming for and the price range they believe the market segment can tolerate. Each manufacturer prices a model in the segment with reference to the *prices* charged by its competitors, not by reference to competitors' costs. Price leadership allows differentiators to charge a premium price and also helps low-cost companies by increasing their margins.

Although price leadership can stabilize industry relationships by preventing head-to-head competition and thus raise the level of profitability within an industry, it has its dangers. Price leadership helps companies with high costs, allowing them to survive without becoming more productive or more efficient. Thus, it may foster complacency; companies may keep extracting profits without reinvesting any to improve their productivity. In the long term, such behavior will make them vulnerable to new entrants that have lower costs because they have developed new productive techniques. That is what happened in the U.S. auto industry after the Japanese entered the market. Following years of tacit price fixing, with General Motors as the leader, the carmakers were subjected to growing low-cost Japanese competition, to which they were unable to respond. Indeed, many U.S. auto companies have survived into the 1990s only because the Japanese carmakers were foreign firms. Had the foreign firms been new U.S. entrants, the government would probably not have taken steps to protect Chrysler, Ford, or General Motors, and they would be much smaller companies today.

Nonprice Competition

A third very important aspect of product/market strategy in mature industries is the use of **nonprice competition** to manage rivalry within an industry. Using various tactics and maneuvers to try to prevent costly price cutting and price wars does not preclude competition by product differentiation. Indeed, in many industries, product differentiation is the principal competitive tactic used to prevent competitors from obtaining access to a company's customers and attacking its market share. In other words, companies rely on product differentiation to deter potential entrants and manage rivalry within their industry. Product differentiation allows industry rivals to compete for market share by offering products with different or superior features or by applying different marketing techniques. In Figure 7.4, product and market segment dimensions are used to identify four nonprice competitive strategies based on product differentiation. (Notice that this model applies to new market segments, not new markets.)[19]

FIGURE 7.4

Four Nonprice Competitive Strategies

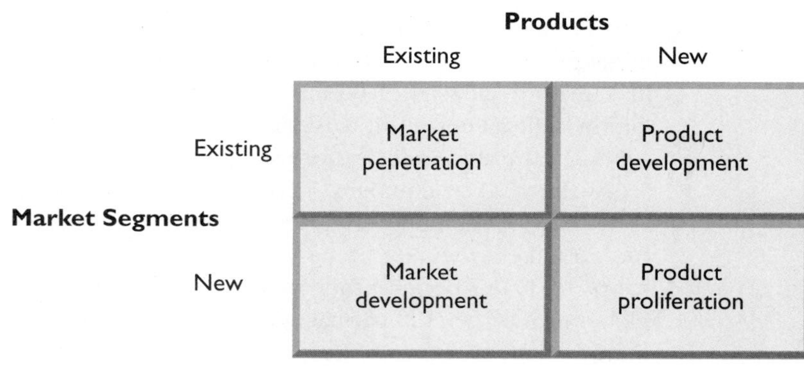

7.3 STRATEGY *in* ACTION

Warfare in Toyland

Toys 'R' Us, based in Paramus, New Jersey, grew at an astonishing 25 percent annual rate throughout the 1980s and today holds a 20 percent share of the $15 billion retail toy market, which makes it the industry leader. To reach its commanding position, the company used a strategy of market penetration based on developing a nationwide chain of retail outlets and a cost-leadership strategy. To lower costs, Toys 'R' Us developed efficient materials-management techniques for ordering and distributing toys to its stores. It also provided only a low level of customer service. Together, these moves allowed it to obtain a very low expense-to-sales ratio of 17 percent. Toys 'R' Us then used its low costs to promote a philosophy of everyday low pricing. The company deliberately set out to undercut the prices of its rivals, and it succeeded. In fact, its two largest competitors in the 1980s, Child World and Lionel, went bankrupt.[22] Pursuing a market-penetration strategy based on low cost thus brought spectacular results for Toys 'R' Us.

In the 1990s, however, the company's commanding position was threatened by a new set of rivals, which were also pursuing market-penetration strategies. Companies such as Wal-Mart, Kmart, and Target Stores rapidly expanded the number of their stores and beat Toys 'R' Us at its own game by selling toys at prices that were often below those of Toys 'R' Us. Indeed, Toys 'R' Us saw its sales fall from 25 percent in 1990 to 17 percent by 1999, and Wal-Mart is now the market leader with 18 percent.

The new competition squeezed profits for Toys 'R' Us and forced the company to turn to nonprice competition to attract customers. For example, Toys 'R' Us promoted its wide range of products as a competitive advantage; it made its stores more attractive; and it also increased the level of customer service by offering customers more personalized attention. In addition, it also went on-line and is in the process of developing a major Web presence. However, it was slow to do so and eToys, an Internet start-up, is the current leader in this market segment.[23] However, analysts feel that Toys 'R' Us, under newly appointed CEO Bob Moog, is rebuilding its brand name and that the company is poised to regain its leading position in the industry.

Market Penetration When a company concentrates on expanding market share in its existing product markets, it is engaging in a strategy of **market penetration.**[20] Market penetration involves heavy advertising to promote and build product differentiation. In a mature industry, the thrust of advertising is to influence consumers' brand choice and create a brand-name reputation for the company and its products. In this way, a company can increase its market share by attracting the customers of its rivals. Because brand-name products often command premium prices, building market share in this situation is very profitable.

In some mature industries—for example, soap and detergent, disposable diapers, and brewing—a market-penetration strategy becomes a way of life.[21] In these industries, all companies engage in intensive advertising and battle for market share. Each company fears that by not advertising it will lose market share to rivals. Consequently, in the soap and detergent industry, for instance, Procter & Gamble spends more than 20 percent of sales revenues on advertising, with the aim of maintaining and perhaps building market share. These huge advertising outlays constitute a barrier to entry for prospective entrants. As Strategy in Action 7.3 details, Toys 'R' Us rose to prominence in the retail toy market by pursuing a market-penetration strategy.

Product Development **Product development** is the creation of new or improved products to replace existing ones.[24] The wet-shaving industry is another industry that depends on product replacement to create successive waves of consumer demand, which then create new sources of revenue for companies in the industry. Gillette, for example, periodically comes out with a new and improved razor—such as the Sensor shaving system—which often gives a massive boost to its market share. Similarly, in the car industry, each major car company replaces its models every three to five years to encourage customers to trade in their old models and buy the new one.

Product development is important for maintaining product differentiation and building market share.[25] For instance, the laundry detergent Tide has gone through more than fifty different changes in formulation during the past forty years to improve its performance. The product is always advertised as Tide, but it is a different product each year. The battle over diet colas is another interesting example of competitive product differentiation by product development. Royal Crown Cola developed Diet Rite, the first diet cola. However, Coca-Cola and PepsiCo responded quickly with their versions of the diet drink, and by massive advertising, they soon took over the market. Refining and improving products is an important competitive tactic in defending a company's generic competitive strategy in a mature industry, but this kind of competition can be as vicious as a price war because it is very expensive and raises costs dramatically.

Market signaling to competitors can also be an important part of a product development strategy. One company may let the others know that it is proceeding with product innovations that will provide a competitive advantage the others will be unable to imitate effectively because their entry into the market will be too late. For example, software companies such as Microsoft often announce new operating systems years in advance. The purpose of such an announcement is to deter prospective competitors from making the huge investments needed to compete with the industry leaders and to let its customers know that the company still has the competitive edge so important to retaining customers' loyalty. However, preemptive signaling can backfire, as IBM found out when it announced that its PS/2 operating system would not be compatible with the operating systems presently standard in the industry. Other companies in the industry collectively signaled to IBM and IBM's customers that they would band together to protect the existing operation systems, thus preserving industry standards and preventing IBM from obtaining a competitive advantage from its new technology. IBM subsequently backed down. If a preemptive move is to succeed, competitors must believe that a company will act according to its signals and stick to its position. If the threat is not credible, the signaling company weakens its position.

Market Development **Market development** finds new market segments for a company's products. A company pursuing this strategy wants to capitalize on the brand name it has developed in one market segment by locating new market segments in which to compete. In this way, it can exploit the product differentiation advantages of its brand name. The Japanese auto manufacturers provide an interesting example of the use of market development. When they first entered the market, each Japanese manufacturer offered a car, such as the Toyota Corolla and the Honda Accord, aimed at the economy segment of the auto market. However, the Japanese upgraded each car over time, and now each is directed at a more expensive market segment. The Accord is a leading contender in the mid-size-car segment, while the Corolla fills the small-car segment that used to be occupied by the Celica, which is now aimed at a sportier market segment. By redefining their product offerings, Japanese manufacturers have profitably developed their market segments and successfully attacked their industry rivals, wresting market share from these companies. Although the Japanese used to compete primarily as low-cost producers, market development has allowed them to become differentiators as well. Toyota is an example of a company that has used market development to pursue simultaneously a low-cost and a differentiation strategy.

Product Proliferation **Product proliferation** can be used to manage rivalry within an industry and to deter entry. The strategy of product proliferation generally means that large companies in an industry all have a product in each market segment or niche and compete head-to-head for customers. If a new niche develops, such as sports utility vehicles, designer sunglasses, or Internet Web sites, then the leader gets a first-mover advantage, but soon all the other companies catch up, and once again competition is stabilized and rivalry within the industry is reduced. Product proliferation thus allows the development of stable industry competition based on product differentiation, not price—that is, nonprice competition based on the development of new products. The battle is over a product's perceived quality and uniqueness, *not* over its price.

Capacity Control

Although nonprice competition helps mature industries avoid the cutthroat price reductions that shrink both company and industry levels of profitability, in some industries price competition does periodically break out. This occurs most commonly when there is industry overcapacity—that is, when companies collectively produce too much output so that lowering the price is the only way to dispose of it. If one company starts to cut prices, the others quickly follow because they fear that the price cutter will be able to sell all its inventory and they will be left holding unwanted goods. **Capacity control** strategies are the last set of competitive tactics and maneuvers for managing rivalry within an industry that we discuss in this chapter.

Excess capacity may be caused by a shortfall in demand, as when a recession lowers the demand for cars and causes car companies to give customers price incentives to purchase a new car. In this situation, companies can do nothing except wait for better times. By and large, however, excess capacity results from companies within an industry simultaneously responding to favorable conditions: they all invest in new plants to be able to take advantage of the predicted upsurge in demand. Paradoxically, each individual company's effort to outperform the others means that collectively the companies create industry overcapacity, which hurts them all. Figure 7.5 illustrates this situation. Although demand is rising, the consequence of each company's decision to increase capacity is a surge in industry capacity, which drives down prices.

To prevent the accumulation of costly excess capacity, companies must devise strategies that let them control—or at least benefit from—capacity expansion programs. Before we examine these strategies, however, we need to consider in greater detail the factors that cause excess capacity.[26]

FIGURE 7.5

Changes in Industry Capacity and Demand

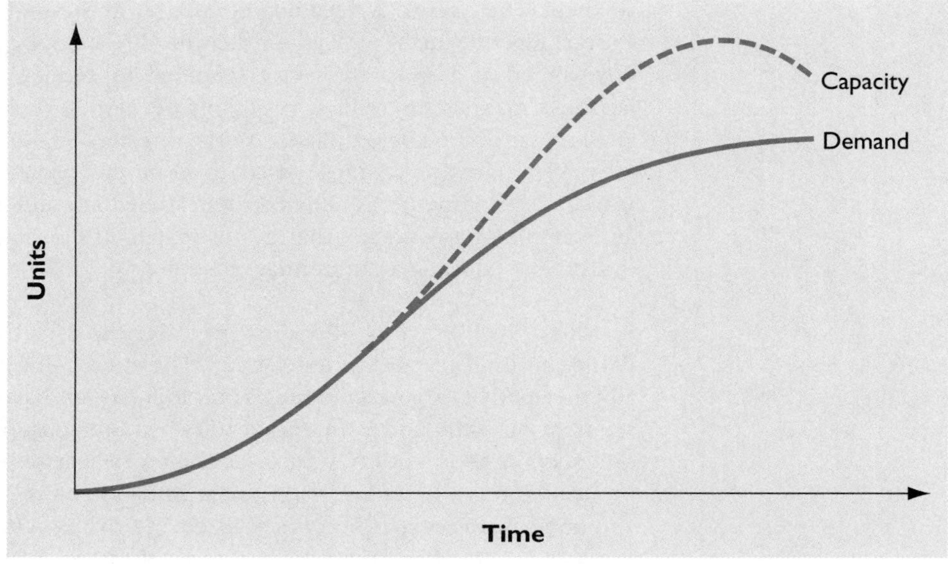

Factors Causing Excess Capacity The problem of excess capacity often derives from technological factors. Sometimes new, low-cost technology is the culprit because, to prevent being left behind, all companies introduce it simultaneously. Excess capacity occurs because the new technology can produce more than the old. In addition, new technology is often introduced in large increments, which generate overcapacity. For instance, an airline that needs more seats on a route must add another plane, thereby adding hundreds of seats even though only fifty are needed. To take another example, a new chemical process may operate efficiently only at the rate of 1,000 gallons a day, whereas the previous process was efficient at 500 gallons a day. If all companies within an industry change technologies, industry capacity may double and enormous problems can result.

Overcapacity may also be caused by competitive factors within an industry. Entry into an industry is one such factor. Japan's entry into the semiconductor industry caused massive overcapacity and price declines for microchips. Similarly, the collapse of OPEC was due to the entry of new countries able to produce oil at competitive prices. Sometimes the age of a company's plant is the source of the problem. For example, in the hotel industry, given the rapidity with which the quality of hotel furnishings declines, customers are attracted to new hotels. The building of new hotel chains alongside the old chains, however, can cause excess capacity. Often companies are making simultaneous competitive moves based on industry trends, but those moves eventually lead to head-to-head competition. Most fast-food chains, for instance, establish new outlets whenever demographic data show population increases. However, the companies seem to forget that all chains use the same data. Thus, a locality that has no fast-food outlets may suddenly see several being built at the same time. Whether they can all survive depends on the growth rate of demand relative to the growth rate of the fast-food chains.

Choosing a Capacity-Control Strategy Given the various ways in which capacity can expand, companies clearly need to find some means of controlling it. If they are always plagued by price cutting and price wars, companies will be unable to recoup the investments in their generic strategies. Low profitability within an industry caused by overcapacity forces not just the weakest companies but sometimes the major players as well to exit the industry. In general, companies have two strategic choices. Either (1) each company individually must try to preempt its rivals and seize the initiative, or (2) the companies collectively must find indirect means of coordinating with each other so that they are all aware of the mutual effects of their actions.

To *preempt* rivals, a company must foresee a large increase in demand in the product market and then move rapidly to establish large-scale operations that will be able to satisfy the predicted demand. By achieving a first-mover advantage, the company may deter other firms from entering the market since the preemptor will usually be able to move down the experience curve, reduce its costs, and therefore its prices as well, and threaten a price war if necessary.

This strategy, however, is extremely risky, for it involves investing resources in a generic strategy before the extent and profitability of the future market are clear. Wal-Mart, with its strategy of locating in small rural towns to tap an underexploited market for discount goods, preempted Sears and Kmart. Wal-Mart has been able to engage in market penetration and market expansion because of the secure base it established in its rural strongholds.

A preemptive strategy is also risky if it does not deter competitors and they decide to enter the market. If the competitors have a stronger generic strategy or more resources, such as AT&T or IBM, they can make the preemptor suffer. Thus, for the strategy to succeed, the preemptor must generally be a credible company with enough resources to withstand a possible price war.

To *coordinate* with rivals as a capacity-control strategy, caution must be exercised since collusion on the timing of new investments is illegal under antitrust law. However, tacit coordination is practiced in many industries as companies attempt to understand and forecast the competitive moves of each other. Generally, companies use market signaling and engage in a kind of tit-for-tat strategy to secure coordination. They make announcements about their future investment decisions in trade journals and newspapers. In addition, they share information about their production levels and their forecasts of demand within an industry to bring supply and demand into equilibrium. Thus, a coordination strategy reduces the risks associated with investment in the industry.

SUPPLY AND DISTRIBUTION STRATEGY IN MATURE INDUSTRIES

As you saw in Chapter 3, when an industry becomes consolidated and comprises a few large companies, it gains strength over its suppliers and customers. Suppliers become dependent on the industry for buying their inputs and on customers for obtaining the industry's outputs. By the mature stage, to protect their market share and improve product quality, many companies want to take over more of the distribution of their products and control the source of inputs crucial to the production process. When they seek ownership of supply or distribution operations, they are pursuing a strategy of *vertical integration,* which is considered in detail in Chapter 9. In this chapter, we discuss how the way a company controls its supplier and distributor relationships protects its generic strategy and helps it develop a competitive advantage.

By controlling supplier and distributor relationships, a company can safeguard its ability to dispose of its outputs or to acquire inputs in a timely, reliable manner. This in turn, can reduce costs and improve product quality. One way to analyze the issues involved in choosing a distribution/supplier strategy is to contrast the situation that exists between a company and its suppliers and distributors in Japan with the situation that exists in the United States.

In the United States, it is common for a company and its suppliers and distributors to have an anonymous relationship in which each party tries to strike the best bargain to make the most profit. Often purchasing and distribution personnel are routinely rotated to prevent kickbacks. In contrast, the relationship between a company and its suppliers and distributors in Japan is based on long-term personal relationships and trust. Suppliers in Japan are sensitive to the needs of the company, respond quickly to changes in the specification of inputs, and adjust supply to meet the requirements of a company's just-in-time inventory system. The results of this close relationship are lower costs and the ability to respond to unexpected changes in customers' demand. Developing close supplier/distributor relationships is a tactic that supports Japanese companies' generic strategies. Clearly, it pays a company to develop a long-term relationship with its suppliers and distributors, and more and more U.S. companies such as Xerox, Motorola, Kodak, McDonald's, and Wal-Mart have formed close linkages with their suppliers.

A company has many options to choose from in deciding on the appropriate way to distribute its products to gain a competitive advantage. It may distribute its products to an independent distributor, which in turn distributes them to retailers. Alternatively, a company might distribute directly to retailers or even to the final customer. More and more companies are using this option as they turn to the Internet to market and sell their products. Strategy in Action 7.4 illustrates this shift.

In general, the *complexity of a product* and the *amount of information* needed about its operation and maintenance determine the distribution strategy chosen. Car companies, for example, use franchisees rather than "car supermarkets" to control the distribution of their autos. The reason is the high level of after-sales service and support needed to satisfy customers. Carmakers are able to penalize franchisees by withholding cars from a dealership if customers' complaints rise, giving them effective control over franchisees' behavior.

On the other hand, large electronics manufacturers and producers of consumer durables such as appliances generally prefer to use a network of distributors to control distribution. To enhance market share and control the way products are sold and serviced, manufacturers choose five or six large distributors per state to control distribution. The distributors are required to carry the full line of a company's products and invest in after-sales service facilities. The result is that the manufacturer receives good feedback on how its products are selling, and the distributor becomes knowledgeable about a company's products and thus helps the company maintain and increase its control over the market. The company is able to discipline its distributors if they start to discount prices or otherwise threaten the company's reputation or generic strategy.

Large manufacturers such as Johnson & Johnson, Procter & Gamble, and General Foods typically sell directly to a retailer and avoid giving profits to a distributor or wholesaler. They do so in part because they have lower profit margins than the

7.4 **STRATEGY *in* ACTION**

Compaq and Dell Go Head-to-Head in Distribution

As new developments in technology alter the nature of competition in the personal computer industry, the distribution strategies of its major players are also changing. These changes are evident in the struggle between Dell Computer and Compaq Computer for domination of the personal computer market. Founded by a team of engineers, Compaq has from the start emphasized the engineering and research side of the PC business. For example, it was the first company to bring out a computer using Intel's new 486 chip. Its differentiation strategy was to produce high-end PCs based on the newest technology, which would command a premium price. Compaq specialized in the business market, and it developed a sophisticated, 2,000-strong dealer network to distribute, sell, and service its expensive PCs.[27]

Dell, on the other hand, focused from the beginning on the marketing and distribution end of the PC business. Its low-cost strategy was to assemble a PC and then sell it directly to consumers through mail-order outlets, cutting out the dealer in order to offer a rock-bottom price. The company was viewed by its managers primarily as a distribution or mail-order company, not as an engineering one.

As computers increasingly became commodity products and prices fell drastically, Compaq realized that its strategy of selling only through high-priced dealers would mean disaster. It changed its strategy to produce a low-cost computer, and in the 1990s began its own mail-order distribution, offering its machines directly to consumers, and more recently to businesses.

However, Compaq has not been as successful as Dell in its on-line distribution strategy, both because Dell was first to engage in such distribution and established a first-mover advantage, and because Dell has established a more customer-friendly Web site and enjoys the record for fewest customer complaints. Moreover, while each company offers next-day delivery and installation of computers, as well as extended warranties, Dell has reached ahead in providing the best on-line customer service, and indeed is making quality customer service, as well as price, a main focus of its competitive advantage.[28]

In 1999, Compaq's new CEO, Michael Capellas, announced a bold new Internet distribution and sales strategy to make Compaq the leader in on-line selling to businesses and consumers.[29] Clearly, the battle between these companies is not over.

makers of electronic equipment and consumer durables. However, this strategy also allows them to influence a retailer's behavior directly. For example, they can refuse to supply a particular product that a retailer wants unless the retailer stocks the entire range of the company's products. In addition, the companies are assured of shelf space for new products. Coca-Cola and PepsiCo are two companies that are able to influence retailers to reduce the shelf space given to competing products or even to exclude them. They can do so because soft drinks have the highest profit margins of any product sold in supermarkets. Gallo is one of the few winemakers that control the distribution and retailing of their products. This is one reason that Gallo is so consistently profitable.

In sum, devising the appropriate strategy for acquiring inputs and disposing of outputs is a crucial part of competitive strategy in mature industry environments. Companies can gain a competitive advantage through the means they choose to control their relationships with distributors and suppliers. By selecting the right strategy, they are able to control their costs, their price and nonprice strategies, their reputation, and the quality of their products. These are crucial issues in mature industries.

STRATEGIES IN DECLINING INDUSTRIES

Sooner or later many industries enter into a decline stage, in which the size of the total market starts to shrink. The railroad, tobacco, and steel industries are at this stage. Industries start declining for a number of reasons, including technological change, social trends, and demographic shifts. The railroad and steel industries began to decline when technological changes brought viable substitutes for the products these industries manufactured. The advent of the internal combustion engine drove the railroad industry into decline, and the steel industry fell into decline with the rise of plastics and composite materials. As for the tobacco industry, changing social attitudes toward smoking, which are themselves a product of growing concerns about the health effects of smoking, have caused decline.

There are four main strategies that companies can adopt to deal with decline: (1) a **leadership strategy,** by which a company seeks to become the dominant player in a declining industry; (2) a **niche strategy,** which focuses on pockets of demand that are declining more slowly than the industry as a whole; (3) a **harvest strategy,** which optimizes cash flow; and (4) a **divestment strategy,** by which a company sells off the business to others. Before examining each of these strategies in detail, it is important to note that the choice of strategy depends in part on the *intensity* of the competition.

The Severity of Decline

When the size of the total market is shrinking, competition tends to intensify in a declining industry and profit rates tend to fall. The intensity of competition in a declining industry depends on four critical factors, which are indicated in Figure 7.6. First, the intensity of competition is greater in industries in which decline is rapid as opposed to industries, such as tobacco, in which decline is slow and gradual.

Second, the intensity of competition is greater in declining industries in which exit barriers are high. As you recall from Chapter 3, high exit barriers keep compa-

FIGURE 7.6

Factors That Determine the Intensity of Competition in Declining Industries

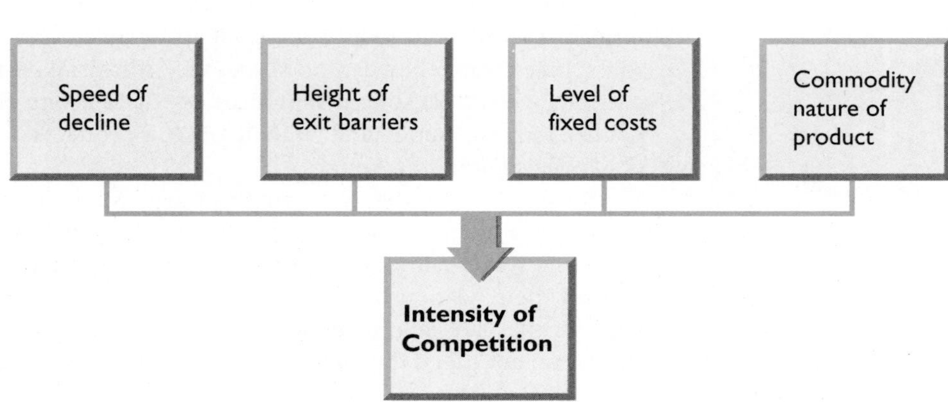

nies locked into an industry even when demand is falling. The result is the emergence of excess productive capacity, and hence an increased probability of fierce price competition.

Third, and related to the previous point, the intensity of competition is greater in declining industries in which fixed costs are high (as in the steel industry). The reason is that the need to cover fixed costs, such as the costs of maintaining productive capacity, can make companies try to utilize any excess capacity they have by slashing prices—an action that can trigger a price war.

Finally, the intensity of competition is greater in declining industries in which the product is perceived as a commodity (as it is in the steel industry) in contrast to industries in which differentiation gives rise to significant brand loyalty, as was true until very recently of the declining tobacco industry.

Not all segments of an industry typically decline at the same rate. In some segments, demand may remain reasonably strong, despite decline elsewhere. The steel industry illustrates this situation. Although bulk steel products, such as sheet steel, have suffered a general decline, demand has actually risen for specialty steels, such as those used in high-speed machine tools. Vacuum tubes provide another example. Although demand for them collapsed when transistors replaced them as a key component in many electronics products, for years afterward vacuum tubes still had some limited applications in radar equipment. Consequently, demand in this vacuum tube segment remained strong despite the general decline in the demand for vacuum tubes. The point, then, is that there may be *pockets of demand* in an industry in which demand is declining more slowly than in the industry as a whole or not declining at all. Price competition thus may be far less intense among the companies serving such pockets of demand than within the industry as a whole.

Choosing a Strategy

As already noted, four main strategies are available to companies in a declining industry: a leadership strategy, a niche strategy, a harvest strategy, and a divestment strategy. Figure 7.7 provides a simple framework for guiding strategic choice. Note that intensity of competition in the declining industry is measured on the vertical axis and that a company's strengths *relative* to remaining pockets of demand are measured on the horizontal axis.

Leadership Strategy A leadership strategy aims at growing in a declining industry by picking up the market share of companies that are leaving the industry. A leadership strategy makes most sense (1) when the company has distinctive strengths that allow it to capture market share in a declining industry and (2) when the speed of decline and the intensity of competition in the declining industry are moderate. Philip Morris has pursued such a strategy in the tobacco industry. By aggressive marketing, Philip Morris has increased its market share in a declining industry and earned enormous profits in the process.

The tactical steps companies might use to achieve a leadership position include aggressive pricing and marketing to build market share; acquiring established competitors to consolidate the industry; and raising the stakes for other competitors, for

FIGURE 7.7

Strategy Selection in a Declining Industry

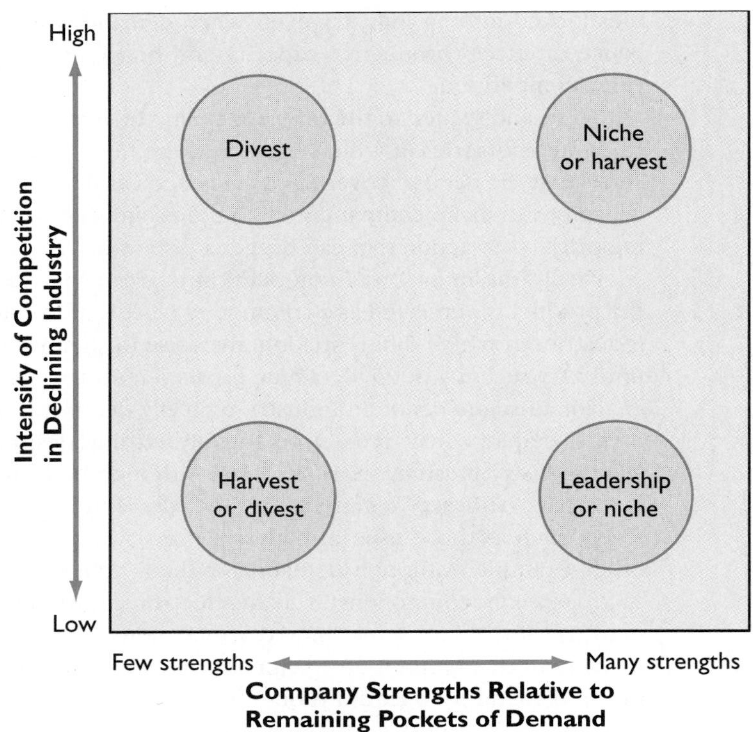

instance, by making new investments in productive capacity. Such competitive tactics signal to other competitors that the company is willing and able to stay and compete in the declining industry. These signals may persuade other companies to exit the industry, which would further enhance the competitive position of the industry leader. Strategy in Action 7.5 offers an example of a company, Richardson Electronics, that has prospered by taking a leadership position in a declining industry. It is one of the last companies in the vacuum tube business.

Niche Strategy A niche strategy focuses on those pockets of demand in the industry in which demand is stable or declining less rapidly than the industry as a whole. The strategy makes sense when the company has some unique strengths related to those niches where demand remains relatively strong. As an example, consider Naval, a company that manufactures whaling harpoons, as well as small guns to fire them, and makes money doing so. This might be considered rather odd, since whaling has been outlawed by the world community. However, Naval survived the terminal decline of the harpoon industry by focusing on the one group of people who are still allowed to hunt whales, although only in very limited numbers—North American Eskimos. Eskimos are permitted to hunt bowhead whales, provided that they do so only for food and not for commercial purposes. Naval is the sole supplier of small harpoon whaling guns to Eskimo communities, and its monopoly position allows it to earn a healthy return in this small market.[31]

7.5 **STRATEGY *in* ACTION**

How to Make Money in the Vacuum Tube Business

At its peak in the early 1950s, the vacuum tube business was a major industry in which companies such as Westinghouse, General Electric, RCA, and Western Electric had a large stake. Then along came the transistor, making most vacuum tubes obsolete, and one by one all the big companies exited the industry. Richardson Electronics, however, not only stayed in the business but also demonstrated that high returns are possible in a declining industry. Primarily a distributor (although it does have some manufacturing capabilities), Richardson bought the remains of a dozen companies in the United States and Europe as they exited the vacuum tube industry. Richardson now has a warehouse that stocks more than 10,000 different types of vacuum tubes. The company is the world's only supplier of many of them, which helps explain why its gross margin is in the 35 percent to 40 percent range.

Richardson survives and prospers because vacuum tubes are vital parts of some older electronic equipment that would be costly to replace with solid-state equipment. In addition, vacuum tubes still outperform semiconductors in some limited applications, including radar and welding machines. The U.S. government and General Motors are big Richardson customers.

Speed is the essence of Richardson's business. The company's Illinois warehouse offers overnight delivery to some 40,000 customers, processing 650 orders a day, whose average price is $550. Customers such as GM don't really care whether a vacuum tube costs $250 or $350; what they care about is the $40,000 to $50,000 downtime loss that they face when a key piece of welding equipment isn't working. By responding quickly to the demands of such customers and by being the only major supplier of many types of vacuum tubes, Richardson has placed itself in a position that many companies in growing industries would envy—a monopoly position. In 1997, however, a new company, Westrex, was formed to take advantage of the growing popularity of vacuum tubes in high-end stereo systems, and by 1999 it was competing head-to-head with Richardson in some market segments.[30] Clearly, competition can be found even in a declining industry.

Harvest Strategy As we note in Chapter 6, a harvest strategy is the best choice when a company wishes to get out of a declining industry and perhaps optimize cash flow in the process. This strategy makes the most sense when the company foresees a steep decline and intense future competition or when it lacks strengths relative to remaining pockets of demand in the industry. A harvest strategy requires the company to cut all new investments in capital equipment, advertising, R&D, and the like. As illustrated in Figure 7.8, the inevitable result is that the company will lose market share, but because it is no longer investing in this business, initially its positive cash flow will increase. Essentially, the company is taking cash flow in exchange for market share. Ultimately, however, cash flows will start to decline, and at this stage it makes sense for the company to liquidate the business. Although this strategy is very appealing in theory, it can be somewhat difficult to put into practice. Employee morale in a business that is being run down may suffer. Furthermore, if customers catch on to what the company is doing, they may defect rapidly. Then market share may decline much faster than the company expected.

Divestment Strategy A divestment strategy rests on the idea that a company can maximize its net investment recovery from a business by selling it early, before the industry has entered into a steep decline. This strategy is appropriate when the

FIGURE 7.8

A Harvest Strategy

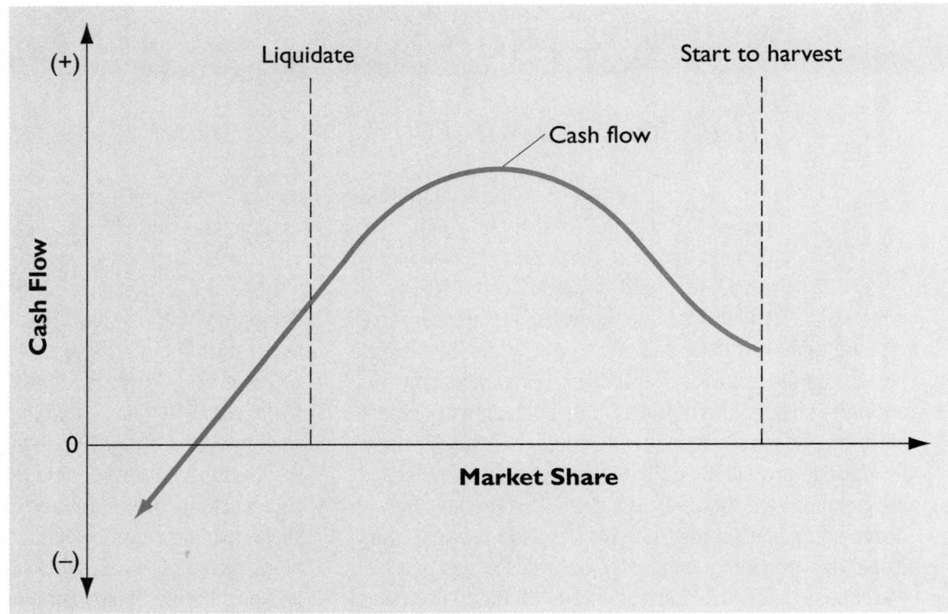

company has few strengths relative to whatever pockets of demand are likely to remain in the industry and when the competition in the declining industry is likely to be intense. The best option may be to sell out to a company that is pursuing a leadership strategy in the industry. The drawback of the divestment strategy is that it depends for its success on the ability of the company to spot accurately its industry's decline before it becomes serious and to sell out while the company's assets are still valued by others.

SUMMARY OF CHAPTER

The purpose of this chapter is to discuss the competitive strategies that companies can use in different industry environments to protect and enhance their generic business-level strategies. Developing a generic competitive strategy and an investment strategy is only the first part, albeit a crucial one, of business-level strategy. Choosing industry-appropriate competitive tactics, gambits, and maneuvers is the second part of successful strategy formulation at the business level. Companies must always be on the alert for changes in conditions within their industry and in the competitive behavior of their rivals if they are to respond to these changes in a timely manner. The chapter makes the following main points:

- ✔ In fragmented industries composed of a large number of small and medium-sized companies, the principal forms of competitive strategy are chaining, franchising, horizontal merger, and using the Internet.
- ✔ In embryonic and growth industries, developing a strategy to profit from technical innovations is a crucial aspect of competitive strategy. The three strategies a company can choose from are (1) to develop and market the technology itself, (2) to do so jointly with another company, or (3) to license the technology to existing companies.
- ✔ Mature industries are composed of a few large companies whose actions are so highly interdependent that the success of one company's strategy depends on the responses of its rivals.
- ✔ The principal competitive tactics and moves used by companies in mature industries to deter entry are product proliferation, price cutting, and maintaining excess capacity.

- The principal competitive tactics and maneuvers used by companies in mature industries to manage rivalry are price signaling, price leadership, nonprice competition, and capacity control.
- Companies in mature industries also need to develop a supply-and-distribution strategy to protect the source of their competitive advantage.
- In declining industries, in which market demand has leveled off or is falling, companies must tailor their price and nonprice strategies to the new competitive environment. They also need to manage industry capacity to prevent the emergence of capacity expansion problems.
- There are four main strategies a company can pursue when demand is falling: leadership, niche, harvest, and divestment strategies. The choice of strategy is determined by the severity of industry decline and the company's strengths relative to the remaining pockets of demand.

DISCUSSION QUESTIONS

1. Why are industries fragmented? What are the main ways in which companies can turn a fragmented industry into a consolidated one?
2. What are the key problems involved in maintaining a competitive advantage in a growth industry environment? What are the dangers associated with being the leader?
3. Discuss how companies can use (a) product differentiation and (b) capacity control to manage rivalry and increase an industry's profitability.

Practicing Strategic Management

SMALL-GROUP EXERCISE
How to Keep the Hot Sauce Hot

Break up into groups of three to five people, and discuss the following scenario:

You are the managers of a company that has pioneered a new kind of hot sauce for chicken that has taken the market by storm. The hot sauce's differentiated appeal is based on a unique combination of spices and packaging that allows you to charge a premium price. Within the last three years, your hot sauce has achieved a national reputation, and now major food companies such as Kraft and Nabisco, seeing the potential of this market segment, are beginning to introduce hot sauces of their own, imitating your product.

1. Describe the generic business-level strategy you are pursuing.
2. Describe the industry's environment in which you are competing.
3. What kinds of competitive tactics and maneuvers could you adopt to protect your generic strategy in this kind of environment?
4. What do you think is the best strategy for you to pursue in this situation?

STRATEGIC MANAGEMENT PROJECT
Module 7

This part of the project continues the analysis of your company's business-level strategy and considers how conditions in the industry's environment affect the company's competitive strategy.

1. In what kind of industry environment (for example, embryonic, mature) does your company operate? (Use the information from Strategic Management Project: Module 3 to answer this question.)
2. Discuss how your company has attempted to develop a competitive strategy to protect its business-level strategy. For example, if your company is operating in an embryonic industry, discuss the ways it has attempted to increase its competitive advantage over time. If it is operating in a mature industry, discuss how it has tried to manage the five forces of industry competition.
3. What new strategies would you advise your company to pursue to increase its competitive advantage? For example, what kinds of strategy toward buyers or suppliers should it adopt? How should it attempt to differentiate its products in the future?
4. Based on this analysis, do you think your company will be able to maintain its competitive advantage in the future? Why or why not?

ARTICLE FILE 7

Find examples of the ways in which a company or group of companies has adopted a competitive strategy to protect or enhance its business-level strategy.

EXPLORING THE WEB
Visiting Wal-Mart

Enter the Web site of retailer Wal-Mart (www.wal.mart.com/). Click on "Corporate Information," and then click on "Corporate Timeline." Study the events in Wal-Mart's timeline, and from them outline the way Wal-Mart's competitive strategy in the retailing industry has developed over time.

Search the Web for a company that has recently changed its competitive strategy in some way. What precipitated the shift in its strategy? What strategy changes did the company make?

CLOSING CASE

The Burger Wars

DURING THE 1990S, in the mature and saturated fast-food industry, competition for customers between the different hamburger chains has been intense. McDonald's, the industry leader, has been under pressure to maintain its profit margins, because, as the price of fast food has fallen, price wars have periodically broken out. Taco Bell started a major price war when it introduced its $.99 taco, for instance, which pushed McDonald's and other burger chains such as Burger King and Wendy's to find ways to lower their costs and prices. As a result of price competition, all the burger chains were forced to learn how to make a cheaper hamburger, and they have been able to lower their prices.

With most fast-food restaurants now offering comparable prices, the focus of competition between the burger chains has shifted to other aspects of their products. First, the major chains are all introducing bigger burger patties. The battle was started by Burger King, which is still waging an aggressive campaign to increase its market share at the expense of McDonald's. In 1994, Burger King added a full ounce of beef to its 1.8 ounce regular patty and followed this with an intense advertising campaign based on the slogan, "Get Your Burger's Worth," directed at McDonald's burger, which was more than 40 percent lighter. The campaign worked for Burger King, and the chain's market share rose by 18 percent in 1995. As a result, in May 1996, McDonald's announced that it would enlarge its regular patty by 25 percent to beat back the challenge from Burger King and from Wendy's, which has always offered a larger burger (and whose "Where's the Beef?" slogan helped it gain market share in the 1980s).[32]

Developing bigger burgers is only one part of competitive strategy in the fast-food industry, however. The main burger chains are constantly experimenting with new and improved kinds of burgers to appeal to customers—burgers that add cheese, bacon, different kinds of vegetables, and exotic sauces. They are also trying whole-meal offerings, such as McDonald's "value meals," to provide a competitive package to attract customers.[33]

Furthermore, recognizing the competition from other kinds of fast-food chains, such as those specializing in chicken or Mexican food, the burger chains have moved to broaden their menus. McDonald's, for example, offers chicken dishes, pizza, and salads; it also allows restaurants to customize their menus to suit the tastes of customers in the region in which they are located. Thus, McDonald's restaurants in New England have lobster on the menu, and those in Japan serve sushi. Product development is a major part of competitive strategy in the industry.

Another major competitive strategy that Burger King and McDonald's have adopted is market penetration: opening up new restaurants to attract customers. Because all the big chains have thousands of restaurants each, many analysts thought that the market was saturated, meaning that it would not be profitable to open more restaurants. However, McDonald's in particular has opened hundreds of restaurants in new locations such as gas stations and large retail stores (for example, Wal-Mart), all of which are profitable and have helped it protect its market share and maintain its margins.

Finally, a major aspect of the burger chains' competitive strategy has been to take their core competencies and apply them on an international level by building global restaurant empires. Indeed, so important have global operations become that both McDonald's and Burger King earn a significant part of their profits from their foreign operations. In the mature fast-food industry, developing new competitive strategies to fend off attacks by other companies within the industry and to protect and enhance competitive advantage is a never-ending task for strategic managers. Even McDonald's is currently experiencing many problems because of the intense competition in the industry.[34]

Case Discussion Questions

1. Describe the nature of competition and the industry environment of the fast-food industry.
2. What strategies are fast-food restaurants pursuing today to protect their competitive position?

End Notes

1. *www.ebay.com* (1999).
2. Press releases, *www.amazon.com* (1999).
3. M. Porter, *Competitive Strategy: Techniques for Analyzing Industries and Competitors* (New York: Free Press, 1980), pp. 191–200.
4. S. A. Shane, "Hybrid Organizational Arrangements and Their Implications for Firm Growth and Survival: A Study of New Franchisors," *Academy of Management Journal,* 1 (1996), 216–234.
5. Much of this section is based on C. W. L. Hill, M. Heeley, and J. Sakson, "Strategies for Profiting from Innovation," *Advances in Global High Technology Management* (Greenwich, Conn.: JAI Press, 1993), III, 79–95.
6. The importance of complementary assets was first noted by D. J. Teece. See D. J. Teece, "Profiting from Technological Innovation," in *The Competitive Challenge,* ed. D. J. Teece (New York: Harper & Row, 1986), pp. 26–54.
7. M. J. Chen and D. C. Hambrick, "Speed, Stealth, and Selective Attack: How Small Firms Differ from Large Firms in Competitive Behavior," *Academy of Management Journal,* 38 (1995), 453–482.
8. E. Mansfield, M. Schwartz, and S. Wagner, "Imitation Costs and Patents: An Empirical Study," *Economic Journal,* 91 (1981), 907–918.
9. E. Mansfield, "How Rapidly Does New Industrial Technology Leak Out?" *Journal of Industrial Economics,* 34 (1985), 217–223.
10. "Reshaping the Body Shop," *Global Cosmetic Industry,* (July 1999), 10.
11. This argument has been made in the game theory literature. See R. Caves, H. Cookell, and P. J. Killing, "The Imperfect Market for Technology Licenses," *Oxford Bulletin of Economics and Statistics,* 45 (1983), 249–267; N. T. Gallini, "Deterrence by Market Sharing: A Strategic Incentive for Licensing," *American Economic Review,* 74 (1984), 931–941; and C. Shapiro, "Patent Licensing and R&D Rivalry," *American Economic Review,* 75 (1985), 25–30.
12. J. Brander and J. Eaton, "Product Line Rivalry," *American Economic Review,* 74 (1985), 323–334.
13. P. Milgrom and J. Roberts, "Predation, Reputation, and Entry Deterrence," *Journal of Economic Theory,* 27 (1982), 280–312.
14. S. M. Oster, *Modern Competitive Analysis* (New York: Oxford University Press, 1990), pp. 262–264.
15. D. A. Hay and D. J. Morris, *Industrial Economics: Theory and Evidence* (New York: Oxford University Press, 1979), pp. 192–193.
16. Porter, *Competitive Strategy,* pp. 76–86.
17. O. Heil, and T. S. Robertson, "Towards a Theory of Competitive Market Signaling: A Research Agenda," *Strategic Management Journal,* 12 (1991), 403–418.
18. Scherer, *Industrial Market Structure and Economic Performance,* Chapter 8.
19. The model differs from Ansoff's model for this reason. See H. I. Ansoff, *Corporate Strategy* (London: Penguin Books, 1984).
20. Ibid, pp. 97–100.
21. R. D. Buzzell, B. T. Gale, and R. G. M. Sultan, "Market Share—A Key to Profitability," *Harvard Business Review* (January–February 1975), 97–103; R. Jacobson and D. A. Aaker, "Is Market Share All That It's Cracked Up to Be?" *Journal of Marketing,* 49 (1985), 11–22.
22. M. Maremont and G. Bowens, "Brawls in Toyland," *Business Week,* December 21, 1992, pp. 36–37.
23. S. Eads, "The Toys 'R' Us Empire Strikes Back, *Business Week,* June 7, 1999, pp. 55–59.
24. Ansoff, *Corporate Strategy,* pp. 98–99.
25. S.L. Brown and K. M. Eisenhardt, "Product Development: Past Research, Present Findings, and Future Directions," *Academy of Management Review,* 20 (1995), 343–378.
26. The next section draws heavily on M. B. Lieberman, "Strategies for Capacity Expansion," *Sloan Management Review,* 8 (1987), 19–27; and Porter, *Competitive Strategy,* pp. 324–338.
27. K. Pope, "Out for Blood, For Compaq and Dell Accent Is on Personal in the Computer Wars," *Wall Street Journal,* February 13, 1993, pp. A1, A6.
28. M. Stepanek, "What Does No.1 Do for an Encore," *Business Week,* November 2, 1998, pp. 44–47.
29. A. Taylor III, "Compaq Looks Inside for Salvation," *Fortune,* August 16, 1999, pp. 124–129.
30. P. Haynes, "Western Electric Redux," *Forbes,* January 26, 1998, pp. 46–47.
31. J. Willoughby, "The Last Iceman," *Forbes,* July 13, 1987, pp. 183–202.
32. R. Gibson, "Bigger Burger By McDonald's: A Two-Ouncer," *Wall Street Journal,* April 18, 1996, p. B1.
33. D. Leonhardt, "McDonald's: Can It Regain Its Golden Touch?" *Business Week,* February 28, 1998, pp. 22–27.
34. D. Leonhardt and A.T. Palmer, "Getting Off Their McButts," *Business Week,* February 22, 1999, pp. 65–66.

8 Strategy in the Global Environment

OPENING CASE

Global Strategy at General Motors

IN MANY RESPECTS, General Motors is one of the oldest multinational corporations in the world. Founded in 1908, GM established its first international operations in the 1920s. General Motors is now the world's largest industrial corporation and full-line automobile manufacturer, with annual revenues of more than $100 billion. The company sells 8 million vehicles per year, 3.2 million of which are produced and marketed outside of its North American base. In 1997, GM had a 31 percent share of the North American market and an 8.9 percent share of the market in the rest of the world.

Historically, the bulk of GM's foreign operations have been concentrated in Western Europe. Local brand names such as Opel, Vauxhall, Saab, and Holden, helped the company sell 1.7 million vehicles in 1997 and gain an 11.3 percent market share, second only to that of Ford. Although GM has long had a presence in Latin America and Asia, until recently sales there accounted for only a relatively small fraction of the company's total international business. However, GM's plans call for this to change rapidly over the next few years. Sensing that Asia, Latin America, and eastern Europe may be the automobile industry's growth markets early in the next century, GM has embarked on ambitious plans to invest $2.2 billion in four new manufacturing facilities in Argentina, Poland, China, and Thailand. One of the most significant things about this expansion is that it is going hand in hand with a sea change in GM's philosophy toward the management of its international operations.

Traditionally, GM saw the developing world as a dumping ground for obsolete technology and outdated models. Just a few years ago, for example, GM's Brazilian factories were churning out U.S.-designed Chevy Chevettes that hadn't been produced in North America for years. GM's Detroit-based executives saw this as a way of squeezing the maximum cash flow from the company's investments in aging technology. GM managers in the developing world, however, took it as an indication that the center did not view developing world operations as being of great significance. This feeling was exacerbated by the fact that most operations in the developing world were instructed to carry out manufacturing and marketing plans formulated in the company's Detroit headquarters, rather than being trusted to develop their own.

OPENING CASE *(continued)*

In contrast, GM's European operations were traditionally managed on an arm's length basis. The company's national operations were often being allowed both to design their own cars and manufacturing facilities and to formulate their own marketing strategies. This regional and national autonomy made it possible for GM's European operations to produce vehicles that were closely tailored to the needs of local customers. However, it also meant costly duplication of effort in design and manufacturing operations, as well as a failure to share valuable technology, skills, and practices across different national subsidiaries. Thus, while General Motors exerted tight control over its operations in the developing world, its control over operations in Europe was perhaps too lax. Clearly, the company's international operations lacked overall strategic coherence.

Now, in an effort to change this state of affairs, GM is switching from its Detroit-centric view of the world to a philosophy that centers of excellence may be found anywhere in the company's global operations. The company is consciously trying to tap these centers of excellence to provide its global operations with the very latest technology. The four new manufacturing plants being constructed in the developing world are an embodiment of this new approach. All four will be identical, incorporating state-of-the-art technology, and all have been designed not by Americans, but by a team of Brazilian and German engineers. By building identical plants, GM should be able to mimic Toyota, whose plants are so much alike that a change in a car in Japan can be quickly replicated around the world. The GM plants are modeled after GM's Eisenach facility in Germany, which is managed by the company's Opel subsidiary. It was at the Eisenach plant that GM figured out how to implement the lean production system pioneered by Toyota. The plant is now the most efficient auto-manufacturing operation in Europe and the best within GM, with a productivity rate at least twice that of most North American assembly operations. When completed, each of these new plants will produce state-of-the-art vehicles for local consumption.

In order to realize scale economies, GM is also trying to design and build vehicles that share a common global platform. Engineering teams located in Germany, Detroit, South America, and Australia are designing these common vehicle platforms. The idea is that local plants will be allowed to customize certain features of the vehicles to match the tastes and preferences of local customers. At the same time, adhering to a common global platform will enable the company to spread its costs of designing a car over greater volume and to realize scale economies in the manufacture of shared components—both of which should help GM lower its overall cost structure. The first fruits of this effort include the 1998 Cadillac Seville, which was designed to be sold in more than forty countries. GM's family of front-wheel-drive minivans was also designed around a common platform, which will allow the vehicles to be produced in multiple locations around the globe, as was the 1998 Opel Astra, GM's best-selling car in Europe.

Despite GM's bold moves toward greater global integration, numerous problems still loom on its horizon. Compared with Ford, Toyota, or the new Daimler/Chrysler combination, GM still suffers from high costs, low perceived quality, and a profusion of brands. Moreover, while its aggressive move into emerging markets may be based on the reasonable assumption that demand will grow strong in these areas, other automobile companies are also expanding their production facilities in the same markets, raising the specter of global excess capacity and price wars. Finally, and perhaps most significantly, there are those within GM who argue that the push toward "global cars" is misconceived. In particular, the engineering staff at Opel's Russelsheim design facility, which takes the lead on design of many key global models, has voiced concern that the distinctively European engineering features they deem essential to a car's local success may be dropped in the drive to devise what they see as blander "global" cars.[1]

OVERVIEW

This chapter examines the strategies companies adopt when they expand outside their domestic marketplace and start to compete globally. One option companies have is to sell the same basic product worldwide, that is, use a global strategy. For example, Intel sells the same basic microprocessors worldwide; it does not customize the product to take into account the tastes and preferences of consumers in different nations. By offering a standardized product worldwide, Intel can realize substantial scale economies and build a competitive advantage based on low cost. However, such a strategy often conflicts with the need to customize products to the tastes and preference of consumers in different marketplaces, primarily because customization tends to raise costs. The tension between how much to standardize and how much to customize is one of the fundamental conflicts that global companies have to resolve.

In this chapter, we explore the nature of this conflict and suggest some guidelines that companies can use to identify the best strategy, given their resources, capabilities, and the nature of the markets in which they compete. Toward this end, we consider the different strategies that companies use to compete in the global marketplace and discuss the advantages and disadvantages of each. We also scrutinize two closely related issues: (1) the decision as to which foreign markets to enter, when to enter them, and on what scale; and (2) the choice of entry mode, as well as the different means by which companies enter foreign markets, including exporting, licensing, setting up a joint venture, and setting up a wholly owned subsidiary. The chapter closes with a discussion of the benefits and costs of entering into strategic alliances with global competitors. By the time you have completed this chapter you will have a good understanding of the various strategic issues that companies face when they decide to expand their operations outside of their home country.

General Motors, which is profiled in the opening case, gives us a preview of some of the issues that we shall be dealing with in the current chapter. As described in the case, General Motor's international expansion is being driven by a belief that emerging markets offer the greatest potential for future demand growth. GM is not alone in this belief. Not only are many other automobile firms pursuing a similar expansion strategy, but so are firms from a wide range of industries. Although GM has long had operations overseas, until recently these took second place in the company's Detroit-centric view of the world. Now GM is recognizing that to compete successfully in emerging markets, it is no longer enough to transfer outdated technology and designs from Detroit. It must build a globally integrated corporation that draws on centers of excellence wherever they may be in the world to engineer global cars and state-of-the-art production systems. For all of its economic benefits, though, the trend toward greater integration of its global operations is clearly causing worry within GM's European units. They fear that an ability to respond to local market needs may be lost in the process. As we shall see in this chapter, GM's struggle with this issue is not unique. Many multinational enterprises are striving to find the right balance between global integration and local responsiveness.

PROFITING FROM GLOBAL EXPANSION

Expanding globally allows companies, large or small, to increase their profitability in ways not available to purely domestic enterprises. Companies that operate internationally can (1) earn a greater return from their distinctive competencies; (2) realize what we refer to as location economies by dispersing individual value creation activities to those locations where they can be performed most efficiently; and (3) ride down the experience curve ahead of competitors, thereby lowering the costs of value creation.

Transferring Distinctive Competencies

In Chapter 4, where the concept is first considered, **distinctive competencies** are defined as *unique strengths that allow a company to achieve superior efficiency, quality, innovation, or customer responsiveness*. Such strengths typically find their expression in product offerings that other companies find difficult to match or imitate. Thus, distinctive competencies form the bedrock of a company's competitive advantage. They enable a company to lower the costs of value creation and/or to perform value creation activities in ways that lead to differentiation and premium pricing.

Companies with valuable distinctive competencies can often realize enormous returns by applying those competencies, and the products they produce, to foreign markets where indigenous competitors lack similar competencies and products. For example, as described in Strategy in Action 8.1, McDonald's has expanded rapidly overseas in recent years to exploit its distinctive competencies in managing fast-food operations. These competencies have proved to be just as valuable in countries as diverse as France, Russia, China, Germany, and Brazil as they have been in the United States. Before McDonald's entry, none of these countries had U.S.-style fast-food chains, so McDonald's was bringing in unique skills and a unique product. The lack of indigenous competitors with similar competencies and products has greatly enhanced the profitability of this strategy for McDonald's.

In an earlier era, U.S. firms such as Kellogg, Coca-Cola, H. J. Heinz, and Procter & Gamble expanded overseas to exploit their competencies in developing and marketing branded consumer products. These competencies and the resulting products—which were developed in the U.S. market during the 1950s and 1960s—yielded enormous returns when applied to European markets, where most indigenous competitors lacked similar marketing skills and products. Their near-monopoly on consumer marketing skills allowed these U.S. firms to dominate many European consumer product markets during the 1960s and 1970s. Similarly, in the 1970s and 1980s, many Japanese firms expanded globally to exploit their skills in production, materials management, and new product development—competencies that many of their indigenous North American and European competitors seemed to lack at the time. Today, retail companies such as Wal-Mart and financial companies such as Citigroup, Merrill Lynch, and American Express are transferring the valuable competencies they developed in their core home market to other developed and emerging markets where indigenous competitors lack those competencies.

Realizing Location Economies

Location economies are the economies that arise from performing a value creation activity in the optimal location for that activity, wherever in the world that might be (transportation costs and trade barriers permitting). Locating a value creation activity in the optimal location for that activity can have one of two effects: (1) *lower the costs of value creation, helping the company achieve a low-cost position*, or (2) *enable a company to differentiate its product offering and charge a premium price*. Thus, efforts to realize location economies are consistent with the generic business-level strategies of low cost and differentiation. In theory, a company that realizes location economies by dispersing each of its value creation activities to its optimal location should have a competitive advantage over a company that bases all its value creation activities at a single location. It should be better able to differentiate its product offering and lower its cost structure than its single-location competitor. In a world where competitive pressures are increasing, such a strategy may well become an imperative for survival.

For an example of location economies, consider Swan Optical, a U.S.-based manufacturer and distributor of eyewear. With sales revenues only in the $20 million to $30 million range, Swan is hardly a giant, yet it manufacturers its eyewear in low-cost factories in Hong Kong and China that it jointly owns with a Hong Kong–based partner. Swan also has a minority stake in eyewear design houses in Japan, France, and Italy. Swan Optical, thus, is a company that has dispersed its manufacturing and design processes to different locations around the world in order to take advantage of the favorable skill base and cost structure found in other countries. Investments in Hong Kong and then China have helped Swan lower its cost structure, whereas investments in Japan, France, and Italy have helped it produce differentiated designer eyewear for which it can charge a premium price. The critical point is that by dispersing its manufacturing and design activities in this way, Swan has been able to establish a competitive advantage for itself in the global marketplace for eyewear.[3]

Boeing's strategy for manufacturing its new commercial jet aircraft, the 777, also illustrates location economies. The 777 uses 132,500 engineered parts produced around the world by 545 different suppliers. For example, eight Japanese suppliers make parts of the fuselage, doors, and wings; a supplier in Singapore makes the doors for the nose landing gear; and three suppliers in Italy manufacture wing flaps. Part of Boeing's rationale for outsourcing so much production to foreign suppliers is that these various suppliers are the best in the world at performing their particular activity when measured on the basis of cost and quality. Therefore, the result of having foreign suppliers build specific parts is a better final product and a competitive advantage for Boeing in the global marketplace.[4]

Generalizing from the Swan and Boeing examples, we can say that one result of this kind of thinking is the creation of a **global web** of value creation activities, with different stages of the value chain being dispersed to those locations around the globe where value added is maximized, or where the costs of value creation are minimized. To bring in still another example, consider the case of GM's Pontiac Le Mans cited in Robert Reich's *The Work of Nations*.[5] Marketed primarily in the United States, the car was designed in Germany; key components were manufactured in Japan, Taiwan, and Singapore; the assembly operation was performed in South Korea; and the advertising strategy was formulated in Great Britain. The car was designed in Germany because GM believed the designers in its German subsidiary had the skills most suited to the job at hand. (They were the most capable of producing a design that added value.) Components were manufactured in Japan, Taiwan, and Singapore because favorable factor conditions there—relatively low cost, skilled labor—suggested that those locations had a comparative advantage in the production of components (which helped reduce the costs of value creation). The car was assembled in South Korea because GM believed that the low labor costs there would minimize the costs of assembly (also helping to minimize the costs of value creation). Finally, the advertising strategy was formulated in Great

8.1 STRATEGY *in* ACTION

McDonald's Everywhere

Established in 1955, McDonald's faced a problem by the early 1980s. After three decades of rapid growth, the U.S. fast-food market was beginning to show signs of market saturation. McDonald's response to the slowdown was to expand abroad rapidly. In 1980, the chain opened 28 percent of its new restaurants abroad; in 1986, the figure reached 40 percent, in 1990 it was close to 60 percent, and in 1997 it surpassed 70 percent. Since the early 1980s, the firm's foreign revenues and profits have grown at the rate of 22 percent per year. By 1997, McDonald's had 10,752 restaurants in 108 countries, aside from the United States. Together, these restaurants generated $16.5 billion (53 percent) of the company's $31 billion in revenues. Moreover, McDonald's shows no signs of slowing down. Management notes that there is still only one McDonald's restaurant for every 500,000 people in the foreign countries where it currently does business. This compares with one McDonald's restaurant for every 25,000 people in the United States. The company's plans call for its foreign expansion to continue at a rapid rate. In England, France, and Germany combined, the chain opened 500 more restaurants between 1995 and 1997, for a total gain of 37 percent. In 1997, McDonald's announced that it would open 2,000 restaurants per year for the foreseeable future, the majority of them outside the United States. The plan includes major expansion in Latin America, where the company expects to invest $2 billion over the next few years.

One of the keys to McDonald's successful foreign expansion is detailed planning. When the company enters a foreign country, it does so only after some very careful preparation. In what is a fairly typical pattern, before McDonald's opened its first Polish restaurant in 1992, the company spent eighteen months establishing essential contacts and getting to know the local culture. Locations, real estate, construction, supply, personnel, legal, and government relations were all worked out in advance. In June 1992, a team of fifty employees from the United States, Russia, Germany, and Britain went to Poland to help with the opening of the first four restaurants. One of their primary objectives was to hire and train local personnel. By mid 1994, all of these employees except one had returned to their home countries. They were replaced by Polish nationals, who had been trained up to the skill level required for running a McDonald's operation.

Another key to the firm's international strategy is the export not only of its fast-food products, but also of the management skills that spurred its growth in the United States. McDonald's U.S. success was built on a formula of close relations with suppliers, nationwide marketing might, tight control over store-level operating procedures, and a franchising system that encourages entrepreneurial individual franchisees. Although this system has worked flawlessly in the United States, some modifications must be made in other countries. One of the firm's biggest chal-

Britain, because GM believed a particular advertising agency there was the most able to produce an advertising campaign that would help sell the car. (This decision was consistent with GM's desire to maximize the value added.)

Moving Down the Experience Curve

As you recall from Chapter 5, the experience curve refers to the systematic decrease in production costs that has been observed to occur over the life of a product. In Chapter 5, we point out that learning effects and economies of scale underlie the experience curve and that moving down the experience curve allows a company to lower the costs of value creation. The company that moves down the experience curve most rapidly will have a cost advantage over its competitors. Moving down the experience curve is therefore consistent with the business-level strategy of cost leadership.

lenges had been to infuse each store with the same culture and standardized operating procedures that have been the hallmark of its success in the United States. To aid in this task, in many countries McDonald's has enlisted the help of large partners through joint venture arrangements. The partners play a key role in learning and transplanting the organization's values to local employees.

Foreign partners have also played a key role in helping McDonald's adapt its marketing methods and menu to local conditions. Although U.S.-style fast food remains the staple fare on the menu, local products have been added. In Brazil, for instance, McDonald's sells a soft drink made from the guarana, an Amazonian berry. Patrons of McDonald's in Malaysia, Singapore, and Thailand savor milk shakes flavored with durian, a foul-smelling (to U.S. tastes, at least) fruit considered an aphrodisiac by the locals. In Arab countries, McDonald's restaurants maintain "Halal" menus, which signify compliance with Islamic laws on food preparation, especially beef. In 1995, McDonald's opened the first kosher restaurant in suburban Jerusalem. The restaurant does not serve dairy products. And in India, the Big Mac is made with lamb and called the "Maharaja Mac."

McDonald's greatest problem, however, has been to replicate its U.S. supply chain in other countries. U.S. suppliers are fiercely loyal to McDonald's; they must be, because their fortunes are closely linked to those of McDonald's. McDonald's maintains very rigorous specifications for all the raw ingredients it uses—the key to its consistency and quality control. Outside the United States, however, McDonald's has found suppliers far less willing to make the investments required to meet its specifications. In Great Britain, for example, McDonald's had problems getting local bakeries to produce the hamburger bun. After experiencing quality problems with two local bakeries, McDonald's built its own bakery to supply its stores there. In a more extreme case, when McDonald's decided to open a restaurant in Russia, it found that local suppliers lacked the capability to produce goods of the quality it demanded. The firm was forced to vertically integrate through the local food industry on a heroic scale, importing potato seeds and bull semen and indirectly managing dairy farms, cattle ranches, and vegetable plots. It also had to construct the world's largest food-processing plant, at a cost of $40 million. The restaurant itself cost only $4.5 million.

Now that it has a successful foreign operation, McDonald's is experiencing benefits that go beyond the immediate financial ones. Increasingly the firm is finding that its foreign franchisees are a source of valuable new ideas. The Dutch operation created a prefabricated modular store, which can be moved over a weekend and is now widely used to set up temporary restaurants at big outdoor events. The Swedes came up with an enhanced meat freezer, which is now used companywide. And satellite stores, or low-overhead mini McDonald's, which are now appearing in hospitals and sports arenas in the United States, were invented in Singapore.[2]

Many of the underlying sources of experience-based cost economies are to be found in the plant. This is true of most learning effects and of the economies of scale derived from spreading the fixed costs of building productive capacity over a large output. It follows that the key to riding down the experience curve as rapidly as possible is to increase the accumulated volume *produced by a plant* as quickly as possible. Since global markets are larger than domestic markets, companies that serve a global market *from a single location* are likely to build up accumulated volume faster than companies that focus primarily on serving their home market or on serving multiple markets from multiple production locations. Thus, serving a global market from a single location is consistent with moving down the experience curve and establishing a low-cost position.

In addition, to get down the experience curve quickly, companies need to price and market very aggressively so that demand expands rapidly. They also need to build production capacity capable of serving a global market. Another point to bear in mind is that the cost advantages of serving the world market from a single location will be all the more significant if that location is also the optimal one for performing that value creation activity—that is, if the company is *simultaneously* realizing cost economies from experience-curve effects *and* from location economies.

One company that has excelled in the pursuit of such a strategy is Matsushita. Along with Sony and Philips NV, in the 1970s Matsushita was in the race to develop a commercially viable VCR. Although Matsushita initially lagged behind both Philips and Sony, it was ultimately able to get its VHS format accepted as the world standard and to reap enormous experience-curve cost economies in the process. This cost advantage subsequently constituted a formidable barrier to new competition. Matsushita's strategy was to build global volume as rapidly as possible. To ensure that it could accommodate worldwide demand, it increased production capacity thirty-threefold, from 205,000 units in 1977 to 6.8 million units by 1984. By serving the world market from a single location in Japan, Matsushita was able to realize significant learning effects and economies of scale. These allowed it to drop its prices by 50 percent within five years of selling its first VHS-formatted VCR. As a result, by 1983 Matsushita was the world's major VCR producer, accounting for approximately 45 percent of world production and enjoying a significant cost advantage over its main competitors. The next largest company, Hitachi, accounted for only 11.1 percent of world production in 1983.[6]

Global Expansion and Business-Level Strategy

It is important to recognize that the different ways of profiting from global expansion are all linked to the generic *business-level strategies* of cost leadership and differentiation. Companies that transfer distinctive competencies to other countries are trying to realize greater gains from their low-cost or differentiation-based competitive advantage. Companies such as Swan Optical that attempt to realize location economies are trying to lower their costs and/or increase value added so that they can better differentiate themselves from their competitors. And companies that serve a global market in order to ride more quickly down the experience curve are trying to build a competitive advantage based on low cost, as Matsushita did with its VHS-formatted VCRs.

PRESSURES FOR COST REDUCTIONS AND LOCAL RESPONSIVENESS

Companies that compete in the global marketplace typically face two types of competitive pressures: *pressures for cost reductions* and *pressures to be locally responsive* (see Figure 8.1).[7] These competitive pressures place conflicting demands on a company. Responding to pressures for cost reductions requires that a company try to minimize its unit costs. To attain this goal, a company may have to base its productive activities at the most favorable low-cost location, wherever in the world that might be. It may also have to offer a standardized product to the global marketplace in order to ride down the experience curve as quickly as possible. On the other hand, responding to pressures to be locally responsive requires that a company differentiate its product offering and marketing strategy from country to country in an effort to accommodate the diverse demands arising from national differences in

FIGURE 8.1

Pressures for Cost Reduction and Local Responsiveness

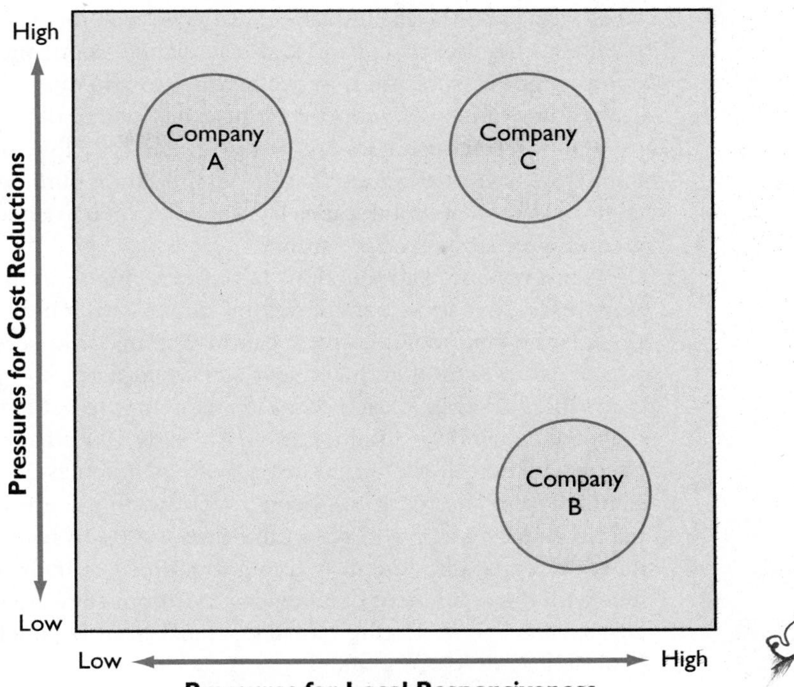

consumer tastes and preferences, business practices, distribution channels, competitive conditions, and government policies. Because differentiation across countries can involve significant duplication and a lack of product standardization, it may raise costs.

Whereas some companies, such as company A in Figure 8.1, face high pressures for cost reductions and low pressures for local responsiveness, and others, such as company B, face low pressures for cost reductions and high pressures for local responsiveness, many companies are in the position of company C. They face high pressures for *both* cost reductions and local responsiveness. Dealing with these conflicting and contradictory pressures is a difficult strategic challenge for a company, primarily because being locally responsive tends to raise costs. In the remainder of this section, we consider the sources of pressures for cost reductions and local responsiveness, and in the next section we examine the strategies that companies adopt in order to deal with these pressures.

Pressures for Cost Reductions

Increasingly, international companies must cope with pressures for cost reductions. Pressures for cost reductions can be particularly intense in industries producing commodity-type products, where meaningful differentiation on nonprice factors is difficult and price is the main competitive weapon. Products that serve universal needs tend to fall into this category. Universal needs exist when the tastes and preferences of consumers in different nations are similar, if not identical. This obviously applies to conventional commodity products such as bulk chemicals, petroleum, steel, sugar, and the like. It also tends to be true for many industrial and consumer products—for instance, hand-held calculators, semiconductor chips, and personal computers. Pressures for cost reductions are also intense in industries where major competitors are based in low-cost locations, where there is persistent excess capacity, and where consumers are powerful and face low switching costs. Many commentators have also argued that the liberalization of the world trade and investment environment in recent decades has generally increased cost pressures by facilitating greater international competition.[8]

Pressures for cost reductions have been intense in the global tire industry in recent years. Tires are a commodity product for which differentiation is difficult and price is the main competitive weapon. The major buyers of tires, automobile companies, are powerful and face low switching costs, so they have been playing tire companies off against each other in an attempt to get lower prices. And the decline in global demand for automobiles in the early 1990s has created a serious excess capacity situation in the tire industry, with as much as 25 percent of world capacity standing idle. The result has been a worldwide price war, with almost all tire companies suffering heavy losses in the early 1990s. In response to the cost pressures, most tire companies are now trying to rationalize their operations in a way consistent with the attainment of a low-cost position. They are moving production to low-cost facilities and offering globally standardized products in an attempt to realize experience-curve economies.[9]

Pressures for Local Responsiveness

Pressures for local responsiveness arise from differences in consumer tastes and preferences, differences in infrastructure and traditional practices, differences in distribution channels, and host government demands.

Differences in Consumer Tastes and Preferences Strong pressures for local responsiveness emerge when consumer tastes and preferences differ significantly between countries, as they may for historical or cultural reasons. In such cases, the product and marketing messages have to be customized to appeal to the tastes and preferences of local consumers. This typically creates pressures for the delegation of production and marketing functions to national subsidiaries.

In the automobile industry, for example, there is a strong demand among North American consumers for pickup trucks. This is particularly true in the South and West, where many families have a pickup truck as a second or third car. In contrast, in European countries pickup trucks are seen purely as utility vehicles and are purchased primarily by companies rather than individuals. Consequently, the marketing message needs to be tailored to the different nature of demand in North America and Europe.

As a counterpoint, in a now famous article Professor Theodore Levitt of the Harvard Business School argued that consumer demands for local customization are on the decline worldwide.[10] According to Levitt, modern communications and transport technologies have created the conditions for a convergence of the tastes and preferences of consumers from different nations. The result is the emergence of enormous global markets for standardized consumer products. As evidence of the increasing homogeneity of the global marketplace, Levitt cites worldwide acceptance of McDonald's hamburgers, Coca-Cola, Levi Strauss blue jeans, and Sony television sets, all of which are sold as standardized products.

Levitt's argument, however, has been characterized as extreme by many commentators. For example, Christopher Bartlett and Sumantra Ghoshal have observed that in the consumer electronics industry buyers reacted to an overdose of standardized global products by showing a renewed preference for products that are differentiated to local conditions.[11] They note that Amstrad, the fast-growing British computer and electronics company, got its start by recognizing and responding to local consumer needs. Amstrad captured a major share of the British audio player market by moving away from the standardized inexpensive music centers marketed by global companies such as Sony and Matsushita. Amstrad's product was encased in teak rather than metal cabinets, with a control panel tailor-made to appeal to British consumers' preferences. In response, Matsushita had to reverse its earlier bias toward standardized global design and place more emphasis on local customization.

Differences in Infrastructure and Traditional Practices Pressures for local responsiveness arise from differences in infrastructure and/or traditional practices among countries, creating a need to customize products accordingly. Fulfilling this need may require the delegation of manufacturing and production functions to foreign subsidiaries. For example, in North America consumer electrical systems are based on 110 volts, whereas in some European countries 240-volt systems are standard. Thus, domestic electrical appliances have to be customized to take this difference in infrastructure into account. Traditional practices also often vary across nations. For example, in Britain people drive on the left-hand side of the road, creating a demand for right-hand drive cars, whereas in France people drive on the right-hand side of the road and therefore want left-hand drive cars. Obviously, automobiles have to be customized to take this difference in traditional practices into account.

Differences in Distribution Channels A company's marketing strategies may have to be responsive to differences in distribution channels among countries. This may necessitate the delegation of marketing functions to national subsidiaries. In the pharmaceutical industry, for instance, the British and Japanese distribution system is radically different from the U.S. system. British and Japanese doctors will not accept or respond favorably to a U.S.-style high-pressure sales force. Thus, pharmaceutical companies have to adopt different marketing practices in Britain and Japan compared with the United States, switching from hard sell to soft sell.

Host Government Demands Economic and political demands imposed by host country governments may necessitate a degree of local responsiveness. For example, the politics of health care around the world requires that pharmaceutical companies manufacture in multiple locations. Pharmaceutical companies are subject to local clinical testing, registration procedures, and pricing restrictions, all of which make it necessary that the manufacturing and marketing of a drug should meet local requirements. Moreover, since governments and government agencies control a significant proportion of the health care budget in most countries, they are in a powerful position to demand a high level of local responsiveness.

More generally, threats of protectionism, economic nationalism, and local content rules (which require that a certain percentage of a product should be manufactured locally) all dictate that international businesses manufacture locally. As an example, consider Bombardier, the Canadian-based manufacturer of railcars, aircraft, jet boats, and snowmobiles. Bombardier has twelve railcar factories across Europe. Critics of the firm argue that the resulting duplication of manufacturing facilities leads to high costs and helps explain why Bombardier makes lower profit margins on its railcar operations than on its other business lines. In reply, managers at Bombardier argue that in Europe informal rules with regard to local content favor people who use local workers. To sell railcars in Germany, they claim, you must manufacture in Germany. The same goes for Belgium, Austria, and France. To try and address its cost structure in Europe, Bombardier has centralized its engineering and purchasing functions, but it has no plans to centralize manufacturing.[12]

Implications Pressures for local responsiveness imply that it may not be possible for a company to realize the full benefits from experience-curve effects and location economies. It may not be possible, for instance, to serve the global marketplace from a single low-cost location, producing a globally standardized product and marketing it worldwide to achieve experience-curve cost economies. In practice, the need to customize the product offering to local conditions may work against the implementation of such a strategy. As noted earlier, automobile companies have found that Japanese, U.S., and European consumers demand different kinds of cars, which means customizing products for local markets. In response, companies such as Honda, Ford, and Toyota are pursuing a strategy of establishing top-to-bottom design and production facilities in each of these regions so that they can better serve local demands. Although such customization brings benefits, it also limits the ability of a company to realize significant experience-curve cost economies and location economies. In addition, pressures for local responsiveness imply that it may not be possible to transfer wholesale from one nation to another the skills and products associated with a company's distinctive competencies. Concessions often have to be made to local conditions. For an example, take another look at Strategy in Action 8.1 and its description of the concessions to local conditions that McDonald's has had to make in different national markets.

STRATEGIC CHOICE

Companies use four basic strategies to enter and compete in the international environment: an international strategy, a multidomestic strategy, a global strategy, and a transnational strategy.[13] Each of these strategies has its advantages and disadvantages. The appropriateness of each varies with the extent of pressures for cost reductions and local responsiveness. Figure 8.2 illustrates when each of these strategies is most appropriate. In this section, we describe each strategy, identify when it is appropriate, and discuss its pros and cons.

FIGURE 8.2

Four Basic Strategies

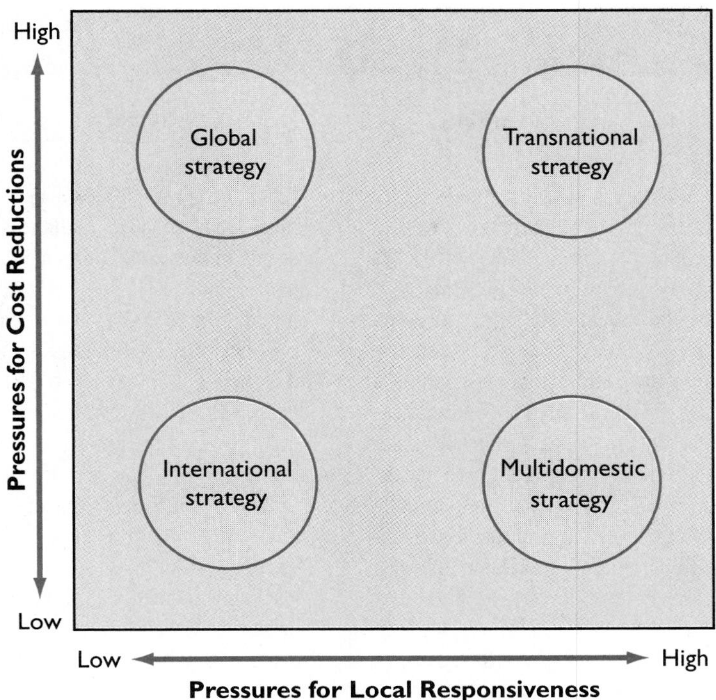

International Strategy

Companies that pursue an international strategy try to create value by transferring valuable skills and products to foreign markets where indigenous competitors lack those skills and products. Most international companies have created value by transferring differentiated product offerings developed at home to new markets overseas. Accordingly, they tend to centralize product development functions (for instance, R&D) at home. However, they also tend to establish manufacturing and marketing functions in each major country in which they do business. But although they may undertake some local customization of product offering and marketing strategy, this tends to be rather limited in scope. Ultimately, in most international companies the head office retains tight control over marketing and product strategy.

International companies include such enterprises as Toys 'R' Us, McDonald's, IBM, Kellogg, and Procter & Gamble. Indeed, the majority of U.S. companies that expanded abroad in the 1950s and 1960s fall into this category. Procter & Gamble, which is profiled in Strategy in Action 8.2, can serve as an example. Traditionally, the company has had production facilities in all its major markets outside the United States, including Britain, Germany, and Japan. These facilities, however, manufactured differentiated products that had been developed by the U.S. parent company and that were often marketed using the marketing message developed in the United States. Historically at least, while there has been some local responsiveness at P&G, it has been rather limited.

8.2 STRATEGY *in* ACTION

Procter & Gamble's International Strategy

Procter & Gamble (P&G), the large U.S. consumer products company, has a well-earned reputation as one of the world's best marketers. With more than eighty major brands, P&G generates more than $20 billion in revenues worldwide. Together with Unilever, P&G is a dominant global force in laundry detergents, cleaning products, and personal-care products. P&G expanded abroad in the post–World War II years by pursuing an international strategy: transferring brands and marketing policies developed in the United States to Western Europe, initially with considerable success. Over the next thirty years, this policy resulted in the development of a classic international firm in which new product development and marketing strategies were pioneered in the United States and only then transferred to other countries. Although some adaptation of marketing policies to accommodate country differences was pursued, by and large the adaptation was fairly minimal.

The first signs that this strategy was flawed began to emerge in the 1970s when P&G suffered a number of major setbacks in Japan. By 1985, after thirteen years in Japan, P&G was still losing $40 million a year there. After introducing disposable diapers in Japan and at one time commanding an 80 percent share of the market, by the early 1980s P&G had seen its share slip to a miserable 8 percent. In P&G's place, three major Japanese consumer products firms dominated the market. P&G's problem was that its diapers, developed in the United States, were deemed too bulky by Japanese consumers. Consequently, the Japanese consumer products firm Kao developed a line of trim-fit diapers more suited to the preferences of Japanese consumers. Kao supported the introduction of its product with a marketing blitz and was quickly rewarded with a 30 percent share of the market. As for P&G, only belatedly did it realize that it had to modify its diapers to accommodate the preferences of Japanese consumers. Once it did so, it managed to increase its share of the Japanese market to 30 percent. Moreover, in an example of global learning, P&G's trim-fit diapers, originally developed for the Japanese market, became a bestseller in the United States.

P&G's experience with disposable diapers in Japan prompted the company to rethink its new-product devel-

An international strategy makes sense if a company has a valuable distinctive competency that indigenous competitors in foreign markets lack and if the company faces relatively weak pressures for local responsiveness and cost reductions. In such circumstances, an international strategy can be very profitable. However, when pressures for local responsiveness are high, companies pursuing this strategy lose out to companies that place a greater emphasis on customizing the product offering and market strategy to local conditions. Moreover, because of the duplication of manufacturing facilities, companies that pursue an international strategy tend to incur high operating costs. Hence this strategy is often inappropriate in industries where cost pressures are high.

Multidomestic Strategy

Companies pursuing a multidomestic strategy orient themselves toward achieving maximum local responsiveness. The key distinguishing feature of multidomestic firms is that they extensively customize both their product offering and their marketing strategy to match different national conditions. Consistent with this approach, they tend to establish a complete set of value creation activities—including production, marketing, and R&D—in each major national market in which they do

opment and marketing philosophy. It had to admit that its U.S.-centered way of doing business would no longer work. Since the late 1980s, P&G has been attempting to delegate far more responsibility for new-product development and marketing strategy to its major subsidiary firms in Japan and Europe. The result has been the creation of a company that is more responsive to local differences in consumer tastes and preferences and more willing to admit that good new products can be developed outside the United States.

Despite the apparent changes at P&G, it is still not clear that it has achieved the revolution in thinking needed to alter its long-established practices. P&G's recent venture into the Polish shampoo market perhaps illustrates that the company still has some way to go. In the summer of 1991 P&G entered the Polish market with its Vidal Sasson Wash & Go, an all-in-one shampoo and conditioner that is a bestseller in the United States and Europe. The product launch was supported by a U.S.-style marketing blitz on a scale never before seen in Poland. At first, the campaign seemed to be working as P&G captured more than 30 percent of the market for shampoos in Poland, but in early 1992 sales suddenly plummeted. Then came the rumors that Wash & Go caused dandruff and hair loss—allegations P&G strenuously denied. Next came the jokes. One doing the rounds in Poland ran as follows: "I washed my car with Wash & Go and the tires went bald." And when the then President Lech Walesa proposed that he also become prime minister, critics derided the idea as a "two-in-one solution, just like Wash & Go."

Where did P&G go wrong? The most common theory is that it promoted Wash & Go too hard in a country that has little enthusiasm for brash, American-style advertising. A poll by Pentor, a private market research company in Warsaw, found that almost three times as many Poles disliked P&G's commercials as liked them. Pentor also argues that the high-profile marketing campaign backfired because years of Communist Party propaganda led Polish consumers to suspect that advertising is simply a way to shift goods that nobody wants. Some also believe that Wash & Go, which was developed for U.S. consumers who shampoo daily, was far too sophisticated for Polish consumers who are less obsessed with personal hygiene. Underlying all these criticisms seems to be the idea that P&G was once again stumbling because it had transferred a product and marketing strategy wholesale from the United States to another country without modification to accommodate the tastes and preferences of local consumers.[14]

business. As a result, they generally cannot realize value from experience-curve effects and location economies. Accordingly, many multidomestic firms have a high-cost structure. They also tend to do a poor job of leveraging core competencies within the firm. General Motors, profiled in the Opening Case, is a good example of a company that has historically functioned as a multidomestic corporation, particularly with regard to its extensive European operations, which are largely self-contained entities.

A multidomestic strategy makes most sense when there are high pressures for local responsiveness and low pressures for cost reductions. The high-cost structure associated with the duplication of production facilities makes this strategy inappropriate in industries where cost pressures are intense (which is the case in the automobile industry, a fact that explains GM's current attempts to change its strategic orientation). Another weakness of this strategy is that many multidomestic companies have developed into decentralized federations, in which each national subsidiary functions in a largely autonomous manner. Consequently, after a time they begin to lose the ability to transfer the skills and products derived from distinctive competencies to their various national subsidiaries around the world. In a famous case that illustrates the problems this can cause, the failure of Philips NV to establish its V2000 VCR format as the dominant design in the VCR industry during the late 1970s, as opposed to Matsushita's VHS format, was due to the refusal of its U.S. subsidiary company to adopt the V2000 format. Instead, the subsidiary bought VCRs produced by Matsushita and put its own label on them.

Global Strategy

Companies that pursue a global strategy focus on increasing profitability by reaping the cost reductions that come from experience-curve effects and location economies. That is, they are pursuing a low-cost strategy. The production, marketing, and R&D activities of companies pursuing a global strategy are concentrated in a few favorable locations. Global companies tend not to customize their product offering and marketing strategy to local conditions. The reason is that customization raises costs, for it involves shorter production runs and the duplication of functions. Instead, global companies prefer to market a standardized product worldwide so that they can reap the maximum benefits from the economies of scale that underlie the experience curve. They also tend to use their cost advantage to support aggressive pricing in world markets.

This strategy makes most sense in those cases where there are strong pressures for cost reductions and where demands for local responsiveness are minimal. Increasingly, these conditions prevail in many industrial goods industries. In the semiconductor industry, for example, global standards have emerged, creating enormous demands for standardized global products. Accordingly, companies such as Intel, Texas Instruments, and Motorola all pursue a global strategy. However, as noted earlier, these conditions are not found in many consumer goods markets, where demands for local responsiveness remain high (as in the markets for audio players, automobiles, and processed food products). The strategy is inappropriate when demands for local responsiveness are high.

Transnational Strategy

Christopher Bartlett and Sumantra Ghoshal argue that in today's environment, competitive conditions are so intense that in order to survive in the global marketplace companies *must exploit experience-based cost economies and location economies, transfer distinctive competencies within the company, and at the same time pay attention to pressures for local responsiveness.*[15] Moreover, they note that in the modern multinational enterprise, distinctive competencies do not reside just in the home country but can develop in any of the company's worldwide operations. Thus, they maintain that the flow of skills and product offerings should not be all one way, from home company to foreign subsidiary, as in the case of companies pursuing an international strategy. Rather, the flow should also be from foreign subsidiary to home country, and from foreign subsidiary to foreign subsidiary—a process Bartlett and Ghoshal refer to as **global learning**. They term the strategy pursued by companies that are trying to achieve all of these objectives simultaneously a **transnational strategy**.

A transnational strategy makes sense when a company faces high pressures for cost reductions and high pressures for local responsiveness. In essence, *companies that pursue a transnational strategy are trying to simultaneously achieve low-cost and differentiation advantages*. As attractive as this sounds, in practice the strategy is not an easy one to pursue. As mentioned earlier, pressures for local responsiveness and cost reductions place conflicting demands on a company. Being locally responsive raises costs, which obviously makes cost reductions difficult to achieve. How then can a company effectively pursue a transnational strategy?

Some clues can be derived from the case of Caterpillar. The need to compete with low-cost rivals such as Komatsu of Japan has forced Caterpillar to look for greater cost economies. However, variations in construction practices and government regulations across countries mean that Caterpillar also has to be responsive to local demands. Therefore, as illustrated in Figure 8.3, Caterpillar confronts significant pressures for cost reductions and for local responsiveness.

To deal with cost pressures, Caterpillar redesigned its products to use many identical components and invested in a few large-scale component manufacturing facilities, sited at favorable locations, to fill global demand and realize scale economies. At the same time, the company augments the centralized manufacturing of components with assembly plants in each of its major global markets. At these plants, Caterpillar adds local product features, tailoring the finished product to local needs. Thus, Caterpillar is able to realize many of the benefits of global manufacturing while reacting to pressures for local responsiveness by differentiating its product among national markets.[16] Caterpillar started to pursue this strategy in 1979, and by 1997 had succeeded in doubling output per employee, significantly reducing its overall cost structure in the process. Meanwhile, Komatsu and Hitachi, which are still wedded to a Japan-centric global strategy, have seen their cost advantages evaporate and have been steadily losing market share to Caterpillar. (It should be noted that General Motors is trying to pursue a similar strategy with its development of common global platforms for some of its vehicles, as detailed in the Opening Case.)

FIGURE 8.3

Cost Pressures and Pressures for Local Responsiveness Facing Caterpillar

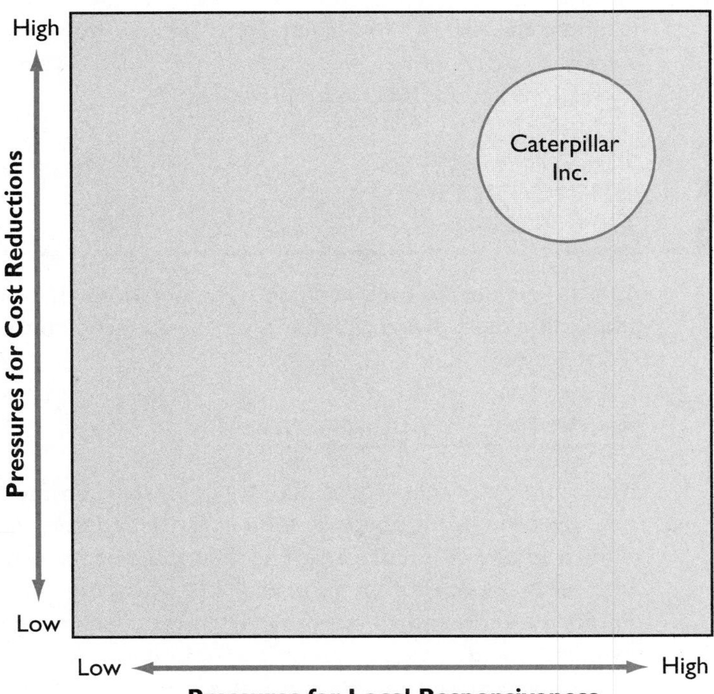

Examples such as Caterpillar and General Motors notwithstanding, Bartlett and Ghoshal admit that building an organization capable of supporting a transnational strategic posture is a complex and difficult task. The core of the problem is that simultaneously trying to achieve cost efficiencies, global learning, and local responsiveness places contradictory demands on an organization. Exactly how a company can deal with the dilemmas posed by such difficult organizational issues is a topic that we return to and discuss in more detail in Chapter 13, when we examine the structure of international business. For now, it is important to note that the organizational problems associated with pursuing what are essentially conflicting objectives constitute a major impediment to implementing a transnational strategy. Companies that attempt to pursue a transnational strategy can become bogged down in an organizational morass that only leads to inefficiencies.

It might also be noted that, by presenting it as the only viable strategy, Bartlett and Ghoshal may be overstating the case for the transnational. Although doubtless in some industries the company that can adopt a transnational strategy will have a competitive advantage, in other industries global, multidomestic, and international strategies remain viable. In the global semiconductor industry, for example, pressures for local customization are minimal and competition is purely a cost game, making a global strategy optimal. Indeed, this is the case in many industrial goods markets, where the product serves universal needs. On the other hand, the argument can be made that to compete in certain consumer goods markets, such as the consumer electronics industry, a company has to try and adopt a transnational strategy.

Summary

The advantages and disadvantages of each of the four strategies discussed above are summarized in Table 8.1. Although a transnational strategy appears to offer the most advantages, it should not be forgotten that implementing it raises difficult organizational issues. More generally, as already shown in Figure 8.2, the appropriateness of each strategy depends on the relative strength of pressures for cost reductions and for local responsiveness.

BASIC ENTRY DECISIONS

In this section, we look at three basic decisions that a firm contemplating foreign expansion must make: which markets to enter, when to enter those markets, and on what scale?

Which Foreign Markets?

There are more than 160 different nation-states in the world. They do not all hold out the same profit potential for a company contemplating foreign expansion. The choice among different foreign markets must be made on the basis of an assessment of their long-run profit potential. The attractiveness of a country as a potential market for an international business depends on balancing the benefits, costs, and risks associated with doing business in that country. The long-run economic benefits of doing business in a country are a function of factors such as the size of a market (in

TABLE 8.1

The Advantages and Disadvantages of Different Strategies for Competing Globally

Strategy	*Advantages*	*Disadvantages*
International	• Transfer of distinctive competencies to foreign markets	• Lack of local responsiveness • Inability to realize location economies • Failure to exploit experience-curve effects
Multidomestic	• Ability to customize product offerings and marketing in accordance with local responsiveness	• Inability to realize location economies • Failure to exploit experience-curve effects • Failure to transfer distinctive competencies to foreign markets
Global	• Ability to exploit experience-curve effects • Ability to exploit location economies	• Lack of local responsiveness
Transnational	• Ability to exploit experience-curve effects • Ability to exploit location economies • Ability to customize product offerings and marketing in accordance with local responsiveness • Reaping benefits of global learning	• Difficulties in implementation because of organizational problems

terms of demographics), the present wealth (purchasing power) of consumers in that market, and the likely future wealth of consumers. While some markets are very large when measured by numbers of consumers (for instance, China and India), low living standards may imply limited purchasing power and, therefore, a relatively small market when measured in economic terms. The costs and risks associated with doing business in a foreign country are typically lower in economically advanced and politically stable democratic nations, and greater in less developed and politically unstable nations.

The benefit-cost-risk calculator is complicated by the fact that the potential long-run benefits bear little relationship to a nation's current stage of economic development or political stability. Rather, they depend on likely future economic growth rates, and economic growth appears to be a function of a free market system and a country's capacity for growth (which may be greater in less developed nations). Thus, other things being equal, the benefit/cost/risk tradeoff is likely to be most favorable in politically stable developed and developing nations that have free market systems and do not have a dramatic upsurge in either inflation rates or private sector debt. It is likely to be least favorable in politically unstable developing nations that operate with a mixed or command economy, or in developing nations where speculative financial bubbles have led to excess borrowing.

By applying the type of reasoning processes indicated above, a company can come up with a ranking of countries in terms of their attractiveness and long-run profit potential.[17] Obviously, preference is then given to entering markets that rank high. The entry into foreign markets of the American financial services company

Merrill Lynch, whose situation is profiled in more detail in Strategy in Action 8.3, illustrates this approach. Merrill Lynch has recently expanded into the United Kingdom, Canada, and Japan. All three of these countries have a large pool of private savings and exhibit relatively low political and economic risks—so it makes sense that they would be attractive to Merrill Lynch. By offering its financial service products, such as mutual funds and investment advice, Merrill Lynch should be able to capture a large enough proportion of the private savings pool in each country to justify its investment in setting up business there. Of the three countries, Japan is probably the most risky given the fragile state of its financial system, which is still suffering from a serious bad debt problem. However, the large size of the Japanese market, and the fact that its government seems to be embarking on significant reform, explains why Merrill has been attracted to this nation.

One other factor of importance is the value that an international business can create in a foreign market. This depends on the suitability of its product offering to that market, and the nature of indigenous competition.[18] If the international business can offer a product that has not been widely available in that market and that satisfies an unmet need, the value of that product to consumers is likely to be much greater than if the international business simply offers the same type of product that indigenous competitors and other foreign entrants are already offering. In turn, greater value translates into an ability to charge higher prices and/or build up unit sales volume more rapidly. Again, on this count Japan is clearly very attractive to Merrill Lynch. Japanese households invest only 3 percent of their savings in individual stocks and mutual funds (much of the balance being in low-yielding bank accounts or government bonds). In comparison, over 40 percent of U.S. households invest in individual stocks and mutual funds. Moreover, Japan's own indigenous financial institutions have been very slow to offer stock-based mutual funds to retail investors, and other foreign firms have yet to establish a significant presence in the market. It follows that Merrill Lynch can create potentially enormous value by bringing Japanese consumers a range of products that they have not been offered previously, and that satisfy unmet needs for greater returns from their savings.

Timing of Entry

Once a set of attractive markets has been identified, it is important to consider the timing of entry. With regard to the **timing of entry**, we say that entry is early when an international business enters a foreign market before other foreign firms, and late when it enters after other international businesses have already established themselves in the market. Several first-mover advantages are frequently associated with entering a market early.[20] One is the ability to preempt rivals and capture demand by establishing a strong brand name. A second advantage is the ability to build up sales volume in that country and ride down the experience curve ahead of rivals. To the extent that this is possible, it gives the early entrant a cost advantage over later entrants. This cost advantage may enable the early entrant to respond to later entry by cutting prices below the (higher) cost structure of later entrants, thereby driving them out of the market. A third advantage is the ability of early entrants to create switching costs that tie customers into their products or services. Such switching costs make it difficult for later entrants to win business.

The case of Merrill Lynch in Japan, described in Strategy in Action 8.3, can be used to illustrate these concepts. By entering the private client market in Japan early, Merrill hoped to establish a brand name that later entrants would find difficult to match. Moreover, by entering early with a valuable product offering, Merrill hoped to build up its sales volume rapidly. That would enable the company to spread the fixed costs associated with setting up operations in Japan over a large volume, thereby realizing scale economies. These fixed costs include the costs of establishing a network of appropriately equipped branches in Japan. In addition, as Merrill trains its Japanese staff, their productivity should rise due to learning economies, which again translates into lower costs. Thus, Merrill should be able to ride down the experience curve, and this would give it a lower-cost structure than later entrants could have. Finally, Merrill's business philosophy is to establish close relationships between its financial advisers (that is, its stockbrokers) and private clients. These advisers are taught to find out what their clients need and so help manage their finances more effectively. People rarely change these relationships once they are established; in other words, because of switching costs, they are unlikely to shift their business to later entrants. This effect is likely to be particularly strong in a country such as Japan, where long-term relationships have traditionally been very important in business and social settings. For all of these reasons, Merrill Lynch may be able to capture first-mover advantages that will enable it to enjoy a strong competitive position in Japan for years to come.

It is important to realize that there can also be disadvantages associated with entering a foreign market before other international businesses—often referred to as **first-mover disadvantages**.[21] These disadvantages may give rise to **pioneering costs,** or costs that an early entrant has to bear but a later entrant can avoid. Pioneering costs arise when the business system in a foreign country is so different from that in a firm's home market that the enterprise has to devote considerable effort, time, and expense to learning the rules of the game. Pioneering costs include the costs of business failure if the firm, because of its ignorance of the foreign environment, makes some major mistakes. Put differently, there is a certain liability associated with being a foreigner, and this liability is greater for foreign firms that enter a national market early.[22] Recent research evidence seems to confirm that the probability of survival increases if an international business enters a national market *after* several other foreign firms have already done so.[23] The late entrant, it would appear, benefits by observing and learning from the mistakes made by early entrants.

Pioneering costs also include the costs of promoting and establishing a product offering, including the costs of educating customers. These costs can be particularly significant when the product being promoted is one that local consumers are not familiar with. In many ways, Merrill Lynch will have to bear such pioneering costs in Japan. Most Japanese are not familiar with the type of investment products and services that Merrill intends to sell, so Merrill will have to invest significant resources in customer education. In contrast, later entrants may be able to get a free ride on an early entrant's investments in learning and customer education by noting how the early entrant proceeded in the market, by avoiding costly mistakes made by the early entrant, and by exploiting the market potential created by the early entrant's investments in customer education.

Scale of Entry and Strategic Commitments

The final issue that an international business needs to consider when contemplating market entry is the scale of entry. Entering a market on a large scale involves the commitment of significant resources to that venture. While not all companies have

8.3 **STRATEGY *in* ACTION**

Merrill Lynch in Japan

Merrill Lynch, the U.S.-based financial services institution, is an investment banking titan. It is the world's largest underwriter of debt and equity and the third largest mergers and acquisitions adviser behind Morgan Stanley and Goldman Sachs. As one might expect, Merrill Lynch's investment banking operations have long had a global reach. The company has a dominant presence not only in New York, but also in London and Tokyo. However, until recently Merrill's international presence was limited to the investment banking side of its business. In contrast, its private client business—which offers banking, financial advice, and stockbrokerage services to individuals—has historically been concentrated in the United States. This is now changing rapidly. In 1995, Merrill purchased Smith New Court, the largest stockbrokerage firm in Britain. This was followed in 1997 by the acquisition of Mercury Asset Management, the United Kingdom's leading manager of mutual funds. Then, in 1998, Merrill acquired Midland Walwyn, Canada's last major independent stockbrokerage firm. The company's boldest moves, however, have probably been in Japan.

Merrill first started to establish a private client business in Japan in the 1980s but met with very limited success. At the time, it was the first foreign firm to enter Japan's private client investment market. The company found it extremely difficult to attract employee talent and customers away from Japan's big four stockbrokerage firms, which traditionally had monopolized the Japanese market. Moreover, restrictive regulations made it almost impossible for Merrill to offer its Japanese private clients the range of services it was offering clients in the United States. For example, foreign exchange regulations meant that it was very difficult for Merrill to sell non-Japanese stocks, bonds, and mutual funds to Japanese investors. In 1993, the company admitted defeat, closed its six retail branches in Kobe and Kyoto, and withdrew from the private client market in Japan.

Over the next few years, however, things started to change. In the mid 1990s, Japan embarked on a wide-ranging deregulation of its financial services industry. Among other things, this led to the removal of many of the restrictions that had made it so difficult for Merrill to do business in Japan. For example, the relaxation of foreign exchange controls meant that by 1998 it was possible for Japanese citizens to purchase foreign stocks, bonds, and mutual funds. Meanwhile, Japan's big four stockbrokerage firms continued to struggle with serious financial problems. These problems were the result of the 1991 crash of that country's stock market. Indeed, in November 1997, in what was a dramatic shock to many Japanese, one of these firms, Yamaichi Securities, declared that it was bankrupt due to $2.2 billion in accumulated "hidden losses" and would shut its doors. Recognizing that the country's financial system was strained and in need of fresh capital, know-how, and the stimulus of greater com-

the resources necessary to enter on a large scale, even some large enterprises prefer to enter foreign markets on a small scale and then build their presence slowly over time as they become more familiar with the foreign market. The original entry by Merrill Lynch into the private client market in Japan was on a small scale, involving as it did only a handful of branches. In contrast, Merrill's reentry into the Japanese market in 1997 was on a significant scale.

The consequences of entering on a significant scale are associated with the value of the resulting strategic commitments.[24] A **strategic commitment** is a decision that has a long-term impact and is difficult to reverse. Deciding to enter a foreign market on a significant scale is a major strategic commitment. Strategic commitments, such as large-scale market entry, can have an important influence on the nature of competition in a market. For example, by entering Japan's private client business on a significant scale, Merrill has signaled its commitment to the

petition, the Japanese government signaled that it would adopt a much more relaxed attitude toward foreign entry into its financial services industry. This attitude underlay Japan's wholehearted endorsement of a 1997 deal brokered by the World Trade Organization to liberalize global financial services. Among other things, the WTO deal made it much easier for foreign firms to sell financial service products to Japanese investors.

By 1997, it had become clear to Merrill Lynch that the climate in Japan had changed significantly. The big attraction of the market was still the same—the financial assets owned by Japanese households are huge, amounting to a staggering Y1,220 trillion in late 1997, only 3 percent of which were then invested in mutual funds (most are invested in low-yielding bank accounts and government bonds). However, attitudes were changing and it looked as if it would be much easier to do business in Japan. Accordingly, in mid 1997, Merrill started to consider reentering the Japanese private client market. Initially, the company considered a joint venture with Sanwa Bank to sell Merrill's mutual fund products to Japanese consumers through Sanwa's 400 retail branches. The proposed alliance had the advantage of allowing Merrill to leverage Sanwa's existing distribution system, rather than having to build a distribution system of its own from scratch. However, in the long run, such a strategy would not have given Merrill the presence on the ground that it felt it needed to build a solid financial services business in Japan. Merrill's executives reasoned that it was important for them to make a major commitment to the Japanese market in order to establish its brand name as a premier provider of investment products and financial advice to individuals. This would enable the company to entrench itself as a major player before other foreign institutions entered the market—and before Japan's own stockbrokerages rose to the challenge. At the same time, given their prior experience in Japan, Merrill's executives were hesitant to go down this road because of the huge costs and risks involved.

The problem of how best to enter the Japanese market was solved by the bankruptcy of Yamaichi Securities. Suddenly Yamaichi's nationwide network of offices and 7,000 employees were up for grabs. In late December 1997, Merrill announced that it would hire some 2,000 of Yamaichi's employees, and acquire up to fifty of Yamaichi's branch offices. The deal, which was enthusiastically endorsed by the Japanese government, significantly lowered Merrill's costs of establishing a retail network in Japan. Merrill's goal for the new subsidiary was to have $20 billion under management by 2000. The company was off to a quick start. In February 1998, Merrill launched its first mutual fund in Japan and saw the value of its assets swell to $1 billion by April. The company now has a significant head start over other foreign financial service institutions that may be contemplating building a private client network in Japan. Indeed, Merrill's hope is that by the time other foreign institutions enter it will already have a commanding presence in Japan, which will be difficult to challenge.[19]

market. This will have several effects. On the positive side, it will make it easier for Merrill to attract clients. The scale of entry gives potential clients reason to believe that Merrill will remain in the market for the long run. The scale of entry may also give other foreign institutions considering entry into Japan's market pause for thought, since now they will have to compete not only against Japan's indigenous institutions, but also against an aggressive and successful U.S. institution. On the negative side, the move may wake up Japan's financial institutions and elicit a vigorous competitive response from them. Moreover, by committing itself heavily to Japan, Merrill may have fewer resources available to support expansion in other desirable markets. In other words, Merrill's commitment to Japan limits its strategic flexibility.

As suggested by this example, significant strategic commitments are neither unambiguously good nor bad. Rather, they tend to change the competitive playing field and unleash a number of changes, some of which may be desirable and some of which will not be. It is therefore important for a firm to think through the implications of large-scale entry into a market and act accordingly. Of particular relevance is trying to identify how actual and potential competitors might react to large-scale entry into a market. It is also important to bear in mind that there is a connection between large-scale entry and first-mover advantages. Specifically, the large-scale entrant is more likely than the small-scale entrant to capture the first-mover advantages associated with demand preemption, scale economies, and switching costs.

Although it is difficult to generalize, what seems clear is that the value of the commitments flowing from large-scale entry into a foreign market must be balanced against the resulting risks and lack of flexibility associated with significant commitments. At the same time, it is worth stressing that strategic inflexibility can also have value. A famous example from military history that illustrates the value of inflexibility concerns Hernando Cortés's conquest of the Aztec Empire in Mexico. When he landed in Mexico, Cortés ordered his men to burn all but one of his ships. Cortés reasoned that by eliminating their only method of retreat, his men had no choice but to fight hard to win—and ultimately they did fight hard and win.[25]

Balanced against the value and risks of the commitments associated with large-scale entry are the benefits of small-scale entry. Small-scale entry has the advantage of allowing a firm to learn about a foreign market while simultaneously limiting the firm's exposure to that market. In this sense, small-scale entry can be seen as a way of gathering more information about a foreign market before deciding whether or not to enter on a significant scale and how best to enter that market. Thus, by giving the firm time to collect information, small-scale entry reduces the risks associated with a subsequent large-scale entry. On the other hand, the lack of commitment associated with small-scale entry may make it more difficult for the small-scale entrant to build market share and to capture first-mover or early-mover advantages. The risk-averse firm that enters a foreign market on a small scale may limit its potential losses, but it may also miss the chance to capture first-mover advantages to another international business.

Summary

It is important to realize that there are no "right" decisions, here, but just decisions that are associated with different levels of risk and reward. Entering a large developing nation such as China or India before most other international businesses in the company's industry, and entering on a large scale, will be associated with high levels of risk. In such cases, the liability of being foreign is increased by the absence of prior foreign entrants, whose experience can be a useful guide. At the same time, the potential long-term rewards associated with such a strategy are great. The early large-scale entrant into a major developing nation may be able to capture significant first-mover advantages, which will bolster its long-run position in that market. In contrast, entering developed nations such as Australia or Canada after other international businesses in the company's industry, and entering initially on a small scale in order to first learn more about those markets, will be associated with much lower levels of risk. However, the potential long-term rewards are also likely to be lower since the company is forgoing the opportunity to capture first-mover advantages and since the lack of commitment to the market signaled by small-scale entry may limit its future growth potential.

THE CHOICE OF ENTRY MODE

Considering entry into a foreign market raises the question of the best mode of such entry. There are five main choices: exporting, licensing, franchising, entering into a joint venture with a host country company, and setting up a wholly owned subsidiary in the host country. Each entry mode has its advantages and disadvantages, and managers must weigh these carefully when deciding which mode to use.[26]

Exporting

Most manufacturing companies begin their global expansion as exporters and only later switch to one of the other modes for serving a foreign market. Exporting has two distinct advantages: it avoids the costs of establishing manufacturing operations in the host country, which are often substantial, and it may be consistent with realizing experience-curve cost economies and location economies. By manufacturing the product in a centralized location and then exporting it to other national markets, the company may be able to realize substantial scale economies from its global sales volume. That is how Sony came to dominate the global television market, how Matsushita came to dominate the VCR market, and how many Japanese auto companies originally made inroads into the U.S. auto market.

On the other hand, there are a number of drawbacks to exporting. First, exporting from the company's *home* base may not be appropriate if there are lower-cost locations for manufacturing the product abroad (that is, if the company can realize location economies by moving production elsewhere). Thus, particularly in the case of a company pursuing a global or transnational strategy, it may pay to manufacture in a location where conditions are most favorable from a value creation perspective and then export from that location to the rest of the globe. This, of course, is not so much an argument against exporting as an argument against exporting from the company's *home* country. For example, many U.S. electronics companies have moved some of their manufacturing to Asia because low-cost but highly skilled labor is available there. They export from that location to the rest of the globe, including the United States.

Another drawback is that high transport costs can make exporting uneconomical, particularly in the case of bulk products. One way of getting around this problem is to manufacture bulk products on a regional basis. Such a strategy enables the company to realize some economies from large-scale production while limiting transport costs. Thus, many multinational chemical companies manufacture their products on a regional basis, serving several countries in a region from one facility.

Tariff barriers, too, can make exporting uneconomical, and the threat to impose tariff barriers by the government of a country the company is exporting to can make the strategy very risky. Indeed, the implicit threat from Congress to impose tariffs on Japanese cars imported into the United States led directly to the decision by many Japanese auto companies to set up manufacturing plants in the United States.

Finally, a common practice among companies that are just beginning to export also poses risks. A company may delegate marketing activities in each country in which it does business to a local agent, but there is no guarantee that the agent will act in the company's best interest. Often foreign agents also carry the products of competing companies and thus have divided loyalties. Consequently, they may not do as good a job as the company would do if it managed marketing itself. One way to solve this problem is to set up a wholly owned subsidiary in the host country to handle local marketing. By so doing, the company can both reap the cost advantages that arise from manufacturing the product in a single location and exercise tight control over marketing strategy in the host country.

Licensing

International licensing is an arrangement whereby a foreign licensee buys the rights to produce a company's product in the licensee's country for a negotiated fee (normally, royalty payments on the number of units sold). The licensee then puts up most of the capital necessary to get the overseas operation going.[27]

The advantage of licensing is that the company does not have to bear the development costs and risks associated with opening up a foreign market. Licensing, therefore, can be a very attractive option for companies that lack the capital to develop operations overseas. It can also be an attractive option for companies that are unwilling to commit substantial financial resources to an unfamiliar or politically volatile foreign market, where political risks are particularly high.

Licensing has three serious drawbacks, however. First, it does not give a company the tight control over manufacturing, marketing, and strategic functions in foreign countries that it needs to have in order to realize experience-curve cost economies and location economies—as companies pursuing both global and transnational strategies try to do. Typically, each licensee sets up its own manufacturing operations. Hence, the company stands little chance of realizing experience-curve cost economies and location economies by manufacturing its product in a centralized location. When these economies are likely to be important, licensing may not be the best way of expanding overseas.

Second, competing in a global marketplace may make it necessary for a company to coordinate strategic moves across countries so that the profits earned in one country can be used to support competitive attacks in another. Licensing, by its very nature, severely limits a company's ability to coordinate strategy in this way. A licensee is unlikely to let a multinational company take its profits (beyond those due in the form of royalty payments) and use them to support an entirely different licensee operating in another country.

A third problem with licensing is the risk associated with licensing technological know-how to foreign companies. For many multinational companies, technological know-how forms the basis of their competitive advantage, and they would want to maintain control over the use to which it is put. By licensing its technology, a company can quickly lose control over it. RCA, for instance, once licensed its color television technology to a number of Japanese companies. The Japanese companies quickly assimilated RCA's technology and then used it to enter the U.S. market. Now the Japanese have a bigger share of the U.S. market than the RCA brand.

There are ways of reducing this risk, however, and one of them is to enter into a cross-licensing agreement with a foreign firm. Under a **cross-licensing agreement**, a firm might license some valuable intangible property to a foreign partner, but in addition to a royalty payment, the firm might also request that the foreign partner license some of its valuable know-how to the firm. Such agreements are reckoned to reduce the risks associated with licensing technological know-how, since the licensee realizes that if it violates the spirit of a licensing contract (by using the knowledge obtained to compete directly with the licensor), the licensor can do the same to it. Put differently, cross-licensing agreements enable firms to hold each other hostage, which reduces the probability that they will behave opportunistically toward each other.[28] Such cross-licensing agreements are increasingly common in high-technology industries. For example, the U.S. biotechnology firm Amgen has licensed one of its key drugs, Nuprogene, to Kirin, the Japanese pharmaceutical company. The license gives Kirin the right to sell Nuprogene in Japan. In return, Amgen receives a royalty payment, but it also gained the right, through a licensing agreement, to sell certain of Kirin's products in the United States.

Franchising

In many respects, franchising is similar to licensing, although franchising tends to involve longer-term commitments than licensing. **Franchising** is basically a specialized form of licensing in which the franchiser not only sells intangible property (normally a trademark) to the franchisee, but also insists that the franchisee agree to abide by strict rules as to how it does business. Often, the franchiser will also assist the franchisee on an ongoing basis in running the business. As with licensing, the franchiser typically receives a royalty payment, which amounts to some percentage of the franchisee's revenues.

Whereas licensing is a strategy pursued primarily by manufacturing companies, franchising is a strategy employed chiefly by service companies. McDonald's is a good example of a firm that has grown by using a franchising strategy. McDonald's has set down strict rules as to how franchisees should operate a restaurant. These rules extend to control over the menu, cooking methods, staffing policies, and the design and location of a restaurant. McDonald's also organizes the supply chain for its franchisees and provides management training and financial assistance for them.[29]

The advantages of franchising are similar to those of licensing. Specifically, the franchiser does not have to bear the development costs and risks of opening up a foreign market on its own, for the franchisee typically assumes those costs and risks. Thus, using a franchising strategy, a service company can build up a global presence quickly and at a low cost.

The disadvantages, however, are less pronounced than in the case of licensing. Since franchising is a strategy used by service companies, a franchiser does not have to consider the need to coördinate manufacturing in order to achieve experience-curve effects and location economies. Nevertheless, franchising may inhibit a company's ability to achieve global strategic coordination.

A more significant disadvantage of franchising is the lack of quality control. The foundation of franchising arrangements is the notion that the company's brand name conveys a message to consumers about the quality of the company's product. Thus, business travelers booking into a Hilton International hotel in Hong Kong can reasonably expect the same quality of room, food, and service as they would receive in New York. The Hilton brand name is a guarantee of the consistency of product quality. However, foreign franchisees may not be as concerned about quality as they should be, and poor quality may mean not only lost sales in the foreign market, but also a decline in the company's worldwide reputation. For example, a bad experience at the Hilton in one location may cause the business traveler never go to another Hilton hotel anywhere and steer colleagues away as well. The geographic distance separating the franchiser from its foreign franchisees and the sheer number of individual franchisees—tens of thousands in the case of McDonald's—can make it difficult for the franchiser to detect poor quality. Consequently, quality problems may persist.

To obviate this drawback, a company can set up a subsidiary in each country or region in which it is expanding. The subsidiary might be wholly owned by the company or a joint venture with a foreign company. The subsidiary then assumes the rights and obligations to establish franchisees throughout that particular country or region. The combination of proximity and the limited number of independent franchisees that have to be monitored reduces the quality control problem. Besides, since the subsidiary is at least partly owned by the company, the company can place its own managers in the subsidiary to ensure the kind of quality monitoring it wants. This organizational arrangement has proved very popular in practice. It has been used by McDonald's, KFC, and Hilton Hotels to expand their international operations, to name just three examples.

Joint Ventures

Establishing a joint venture with a foreign company has long been a favored mode for entering a new market. One of the most famous long-term joint ventures, the Fuji-Xerox joint venture to produce photocopiers for the Japanese market, is discussed in Strategy in Action 8.4. The most typical form of joint venture is a 50/50 venture, in which each party takes a 50 percent ownership stake and operating control is shared by a team of managers from both parent companies (as is in the Fuji-Xerox joint venture). Some companies, however, have sought joint ventures in which they have a majority shareholding (for example, a 51/49 ownership split). This permits tighter control by the dominant partner.[30]

Joint ventures have a number of advantages. First, a company may feel that it can benefit from a local partner's knowledge of a host country's competitive conditions, culture, language, political systems, and business systems. Second, when the development costs and risks of opening up a foreign market are high, a company might gain by sharing these costs and risks with a local partner. Third, in some countries political considerations make joint ventures the only feasible entry mode.[31] For instance, historically, many U.S. companies found it much easier to get permission to set up operations in Japan if they went in with a Japanese partner than if they tried to enter on their own. Indeed, this was a prime motivation behind the establishment of the Fuji-Xerox joint venture.

Despite these advantages, joint ventures can be difficult to establish and run because of two main drawbacks. First, as in the case of licensing, a company that enters into a joint venture risks losing control over its technology to its venture partner. To minimize this risk, a company can seek a majority ownership stake in the joint venture, for as the dominant partner it would be able to exercise greater control over its technology. The trouble with this strategy is that it may be difficult to find a foreign partner willing to accept a minority ownership position.

The second disadvantage is that a joint venture does not give a company the tight control over its subsidiaries that it might need in order to realize experience-curve effects or location economies—as both global and transnational companies try to do—or to engage in coordinated global attacks against its global rivals. Consider the entry of Texas Instruments (TI) into the Japanese semiconductor market. When TI established semiconductor facilities in Japan, its sole purpose was to limit Japanese manufacturers' market share and the amount of cash available to them to invade TI's global market. In other words, TI was engaging in global strategic coordination. To implement this strategy, TI's Japanese subsidiary had to be prepared to take instructions from the TI corporate headquarters regarding competitive strategy. The strategy also required that the Japanese subsidiary be run at a loss if necessary. Clearly, a Japanese joint venture partner would have been unlikely to accept such conditions since they would have meant a negative return on investment. Thus, in order to implement this strategy, TI set up a wholly owned subsidiary in Japan instead of entering this market through a joint venture.

Wholly Owned Subsidiaries

A **wholly owned subsidiary** is one in which the parent company owns 100 percent of the subsidiary's stock. To establish a wholly owned subsidiary in a foreign market, a company can either set up a completely new operation in that country or acquire an established host country company and use it to promote its products in the host market (as Merrill Lynch did when it acquired various assets of Yamaichi Securities—see Strategy in Action 8.3).

Setting up a wholly owned subsidiary offers three advantages. First, when a company's competitive advantage is based on its control of a technological competency, a wholly owned subsidiary will normally be the preferred entry mode, since it reduces the company's risk of losing this control. Consequently, many high-tech companies prefer wholly owned subsidiaries to joint ventures or licensing arrangements. Wholly owned subsidiaries tend to be the favored entry mode in the semiconductor, electronics, and pharmaceutical industries. Second, a wholly owned subsidiary gives a company the kind of tight control over operations in different countries that it needs if it is going to engage in global strategic coordination—taking profits from one country to support competitive attacks in another. Third, a wholly owned subsidiary may be the best choice if a company wants to realize location economies and experience-curve effects. As you saw earlier, when cost pressures are intense, it may pay a company to configure its value chain in such a way that value added at each stage is maximized. Thus, a national subsidiary may specialize in manufacturing only part of the product line or certain components of the end product, exchanging parts and products with other subsidiaries in the company's

8.4 STRATEGY in ACTION

Fuji-Xerox

Originally established in 1962, Fuji-Xerox is structured as a 50/50 joint venture between the Xerox Group, the U.S. maker of photocopiers, and Fuji Photo Film, Japan's largest manufacturer of film products. With 1995 sales of more than $8 billion, Fuji-Xerox provides Xerox with more than 20 percent of its worldwide revenues. A prime motivation for the initial establishment of the joint venture was the fact that in the early 1960s the Japanese government did not allow foreign companies to set up wholly owned subsidiaries in Japan. The joint venture was originally conceived as a marketing organization to sell xerographic products that would be manufactured by Fuji Photo under license from Xerox. However, when the Japanese government refused to approve the establishment of a joint venture intended solely as a sales company, the joint venture agreement was revised to give Fuji-Xerox manufacturing rights. Day-to-day management of the venture was placed in the hand of a Japanese management team, which was given autonomy to develop its own operations and strategy, subject to oversight by a board of directors that contained representatives from both Xerox and Fuji Photo.

Initially, Fuji-Xerox followed the lead of Xerox in manufacturing and selling the large high-volume copiers developed by Xerox in the United States. These machines were sold at a premium price to the high end of the market. However, Fuji-Xerox noticed that in the Japanese market new competitors, such as Canon and Ricoh, were making significant inroads by building small low-volume copiers and focusing on the mid- and low-priced segments of the market. This led to Fuji-Xerox's development of its first "homegrown" copier, the FX2200, which at the time was billed as the world's smallest copier. Introduced in 1973, the FX200 hit the market just in time to allow Fuji-Xerox to hold its own against a blizzard of new competition in Japan, which followed the expiration of many of Xerox's key patents.

Around the same time, Fuji-Xerox also embarked on a total quality control (TQC) program. The aims of the program were to speed up the development of new products, reduce waste, improve quality, and lower manufacturing costs. Its first fruit was the FX3500. Introduced in 1977, by 1979 the FX3500 had broken the Japanese record for the number of copiers sold in one year. Partly because of the FX3500's success, in 1980 the company won Japan's prestigious Deming Prize. The success of this copier was all the more notable because at the same time Xerox was canceling a series of programs to develop low- to mid-level copiers and reaffirming instead its commitment to serving the high end of the market.

By the early 1980s, Fuji-Xerox was number two in the Japanese copier market, with a share in the 20 percent to

global system. Establishing such a global production system requires a high degree of control over the operations of national affiliates. Different national operations have to be prepared to accept centrally determined decisions as to how they should produce, how much they should produce, and how their output should be priced for transfer between operations. A wholly owned subsidiary would, of course, have to comply with these mandates, whereas licensees or joint venture partners would most likely shun such a subservient role.

On the other hand, establishing a wholly owned subsidiary is generally the most costly method of serving a foreign market. The parent company must bear all the costs and risks of setting up overseas operations—in contrast to joint ventures, where the costs and risks are shared, or licensing, where the licensee bears most of the costs and risks. But the risks of learning to do business in a new culture dimin-

22 percent range, just behind that of market leader Canon. In contrast, Xerox was running into all sorts of problems in the U.S. market. As its patents had expired, a number of companies, including Canon, Ricoh, Kodak, and IBM, had begun to take market share from Xerox. Canon and Ricoh were particularly successful by focusing on that segment of the market that Xerox had ignored—the low end. As a result, Xerox's market share in the Americas fell from 35 percent in 1975 to 25 percent in 1980, while its profitability slumped.

Seeking to recapture share, Xerox began to sell Fuji-Xerox's FX3500 copier in the United States. Not only did the FX3500 help Xerox halt the rapid decline in its share of the U.S. market, but it also opened Xerox's eyes to the benefits of Fuji-Xerox's TQC program. Xerox found that the reject rate for Fuji-Xerox parts was only a fraction of that for U.S. parts. Visits to Fuji-Xerox revealed another important truth: quality in manufacturing does not increase real costs; it lowers them by decreasing the number of defective products and reducing service costs. These developments forced Xerox to rethink the way it did business.

From being the main provider of products, technology, and management know-how to Fuji-Xerox, Xerox became in the 1980s the willing pupil of Fuji-Xerox. In 1983, Xerox introduced its Leadership Through Quality program, which was based on Fuji-Xerox's TQC program. As part of this effort, Xerox launched quality training for its suppliers and was rewarded when the number of defective parts from suppliers fell from 25,000 per million in 1983 to 300 per million by 1992.

In 1985 and 1986, Xerox began focusing on its new-product development process. One goal was to design products that, while customized to market conditions in different countries, also contained a large number of globally standardized parts. Another goal was to reduce the time it took to design new products and bring them to market. To achieve these goals, Xerox set up joint product development teams with Fuji-Xerox. Each team managed the design, component sources, manufacturing, distribution, and follow-up customer service on a worldwide basis. The use of design teams cut as much as one year from the overall product development cycle and saved millions of dollars.

The new approach to product development led to the creation of the 5100 copier—the first product designed jointly by Xerox and Fuji-Xerox for the worldwide market. Manufactured in U.S. plants, it was launched in Japan in November 1990 and in the United States the following February. The global design of the 5100 reportedly reduced overall time to market and saved the company more than $10 million in development costs.

Thanks to the skills and products acquired from Fuji-Xerox, Xerox's position improved markedly during the 1980s. The company was able to regain market share from its competitors and to boost its profits and revenues. Xerox's share of the U.S. copier market increased from a low of 10 percent in 1985 to 18 percent in 1991.[32]

ish if the company acquires an established host country enterprise. Acquisitions, though, raise a whole set of additional problems, such as trying to marry divergent corporate cultures, and these problems may more than offset the benefits. (The problems associated with acquisitions are discussed in Chapter 10).

Choosing Among Entry Modes

The advantages and disadvantages of the various entry modes are summarized in Table 8.2. Inevitably, there are tradeoffs in choosing one entry mode over another. For example, when considering entry into an unfamiliar country with a track record of nationalizing foreign-owned enterprises, a company might favor a joint venture

TABLE 8.2

The Advantages and Disadvantages of Different Entry Modes

Entry Mode	*Advantages*	*Disadvantages*
Exporting	• Ability to realize location and experience-curve economies	• High transport costs • Trade barriers • Problems with local marketing agents
Licensing	• Low development costs and risks	• Inability to realize location and experience-curve economies • Inability to engage in global strategic coordination • Lack of control over technology
Franchising	• Low development cost and risks	• Inability to engage in global strategic coordination • Lack of control over quality
Joint ventures	• Access to local partner's knowledge • Shared development costs and risks • Political dependency	• Inability to engage in global strategic coordination • Inability to realize location and experience-curve economies • Lack of control over technology
Wholly owned subsidiaries	• Protection of technology • Ability to engage in global strategic coordination • Ability to realize location and experience-curve economies	• High costs and risks

with a local enterprise. Its rationale might be that the local partner will help it establish operations in an unfamiliar environment and will speak out against nationalization should the possibility arise. But if the company's distinctive competency is based on proprietary technology, entering into a joint venture might mean risking loss of control over that technology to the joint venture partner, which would make this strategy unattractive. Despite such hazards, some generalizations can be offered about the optimal choice of entry mode.

Distinctive Competencies and Entry Mode When companies expand internationally to earn greater returns from their distinctive competencies, transferring the skills and products derived from their competencies to foreign markets where indigenous competitors lack those skills, the companies are pursuing an international strategy. The optimal entry mode for such companies depends to some degree on the nature of their distinctive competency. In particular, we need to distinguish between companies with a distinctive competency in technological know-how and those with a distinctive competency in management know-how.

If a company's competitive advantage—its distinctive competency—derives from its control of proprietary *technological know-how*, licensing and joint venture arrangements should be avoided, if possible, in order to minimize the risk of losing control of that technology. Thus, if a high-tech company is considering setting up operations in a foreign country in order to profit from a distinctive competency in technological know-how, it should probably do so through a wholly owned subsidiary.

This rule, however, should not be viewed as a hard and fast one. For instance, a licensing or joint venture arrangement might be structured in such a way as to reduce the risks of a company's technological know-how being expropriated by licensees or joint venture partners (as was the case with the Fuji-Xerox venture). We consider this kind of arrangement in more detail later in the chapter when we discuss the issue of structuring strategic alliances. To take another exception to the rule, a company may perceive its technological advantage as being only transitory and expect rapid imitation of its core technology by competitors. In such a case, the company might want to license its technology as quickly as possible to foreign companies in order to gain global acceptance of its technology before imitation occurs.[33] Such a strategy has some advantages. By licensing its technology to competitors, the company may deter them from developing their own, possibly superior, technology. It also may be able to establish its technology as the dominant design in the industry (as Matsushita did with its VHS format for VCRs), ensuring a steady stream of royalty payments. Such situations apart, however, the attractions of licensing are probably outweighed by the risks of losing control of technology, and therefore licensing should be avoided.

The competitive advantage of many service companies, such as McDonald's or Hilton Hotels, is based on *management know-how*. For such companies, the risk of losing control of their management skills to franchisees or joint venture partners is not that great. The reason is that the valuable asset of such companies is their brand name, and brand names are generally well protected by international laws pertaining to trademarks. Given this fact, many of the issues that arise in the case of technological know-how do not arise in the case of management know-how. As a result, many service companies favor a combination of franchising and subsidiaries to control franchisees within a particular country or region. The subsidiary may be wholly owned or a joint venture. In most cases, however, service companies have found that entering into a joint venture with a local partner in order to set up a controlling subsidiary in a country or region works best because a joint venture is often politically more acceptable and brings a degree of local knowledge to the subsidiary.

Pressures for Cost Reduction and Entry Mode The greater the pressures for cost reductions, the more likely it is that a company will want to pursue some combination of exporting and wholly owned subsidiaries. By manufacturing in the locations where factor conditions are optimal and then exporting to the rest of the world, a company may be able to realize substantial location economies and experience-curve effects. The company might then want to export the finished product to marketing subsidiaries based in various countries. Typically, these subsidiaries would be wholly owned and have the responsibility for overseeing distribution in a particular country. Setting up wholly owned marketing subsidiaries is preferable to a joint ventures arrangement or to using a foreign marketing agent because it gives the company the tight control over marketing that might be required to coordinate a globally dispersed value chain. In addition, tight control over a local operation enables the company to use the profits generated in one market to improve its competitive position in another market. Hence, companies pursuing global or transnational strategies prefer to establish wholly owned subsidiaries.

GLOBAL STRATEGIC ALLIANCES

Strategic alliances are cooperative agreements between companies that may also be competitors. In this section, we deal specifically with strategic alliances between companies from different countries. Strategic alliances run the range from formal joint ventures, in which two or more companies have an equity stake, to short-term contractual agreements in which two companies may agree to cooperate on a particular problem (such as developing a new product).

Advantages of Strategic Alliances

Companies enter into strategic alliances with actual or potential competitors in order to achieve a number of strategic objectives.[34] First, as noted earlier in this chapter, strategic alliances may be a way of facilitating entry into a foreign market. For example, Motorola initially found it very difficult to gain access to the Japanese cellular telephone market. In the mid 1980s, the company complained loudly about formal and informal Japanese trade barriers. The turning point for Motorola came in 1987, when it formed its alliance with Toshiba to build microprocessors. As part of the deal, Toshiba provided Motorola with marketing help—including some of its best managers. This aided Motorola in the political game of winning government approval to enter the Japanese market and obtaining allocations of radio frequencies for its mobile communications systems. Since then, Motorola has played down the importance of Japan's informal trade barriers. Although privately the company still admits they exist, with Toshiba's help Motorola has become skilled at getting around them.[35]

Second, many companies have entered into strategic alliances in order to share the fixed costs (and associated risks) that arise from the development of new products or processes. Motorola's alliance with Toshiba was partly motivated by a desire to share the high fixed costs associated with setting up an operation to manufacture microprocessors. The microprocessor business is so capital intensive—it cost Motorola and Toshiba close to $1 billion to set up their facility—that few companies can afford the costs and risks of going it alone.

Third, many alliances can be seen as a way of bringing together complementary skills and assets that neither company could easily develop on its own. For example, in 1990 AT&T struck a deal with NEC of Japan to trade technological skills. Under the agreement, AT&T transferred some of its computer-aided design technology to NEC. In return, NEC gave AT&T access to the technology underlying NEC advanced-logic computer chips. Such equitable trading of distinctive competencies seems to underlie many of the most successful strategic alliances.

Finally, it may make sense to enter into an alliance if it helps the company set technological standards for its industry and if those standards benefit the company. For example, in 1992 the Dutch electronics company Philips entered into an alliance with its global competitor, Matsushita, to manufacture and market the digital compact cassette (DDC) system pioneered by Philips. The motive for this action was that linking up with Matsushita would help Philips establish the DCC system as a new technological standard in the recording and consumer electronics industries. The issue is an important one because Sony has developed a competing minicompact disk technology, which Sony hopes to establish as a new technical standard. Since the two technologies do very similar things, there is probably room for only one new standard. The technology that becomes the new standard will be the one to succeed. The loser in this race will probably have to write off an investment worth billions of dollars. Philips sees the alliance with Matsushita as a tactic for winning the race, for it ties a potential major competitor into its standard.

Disadvantages of Strategic Alliances

The various advantages discussed above can be very significant. Nevertheless, some commentators have criticized strategic alliances on the grounds that they give competitors a low-cost route to gain new technology and market access. For example, Robert Reich and Eric Mankin have argued that strategic alliances between U.S. and Japanese companies are part of an implicit Japanese strategy to keep higher-paying, higher-value-added jobs in Japan while gaining the project-engineering and production-process skills that underlie the competitive success of many U.S. companies.[36] They have viewed Japanese success in the machine tool and semiconductor industries as largely built on U.S. technology acquired through various strategic alliances. They have also asserted that increasingly U.S. managers are aiding the Japanese in achieving their goals by entering into alliances that channel new inventions to Japan and provide a U.S. sales and distribution network for the resulting products. Although such deals may generate short-term profits, in the long run, according to Reich and Mankin, the result is to "hollow out" U.S. companies, leaving them with no competitive advantage in the global marketplace.

Reich and Mankin have a point; alliances do have risks. Unless it is careful, a company can give away more than it gets in return. On the other hand, there are so many examples of apparently successful alliances between companies, including alliances between U.S. and Japanese companies, that Reich and Mankin's position seems more than a little extreme. It is difficult to see how the Motorola-Toshiba alliance or Fuji-Xerox fits their thesis. In these cases, both partners seemed to have gained from the alliance. Since Reich and Mankin undoubtedly do have a point, the question becomes, ***why do some alliances benefit the company, whereas in others it can end up giving away technology and market access and get very little in return?*** The next section provides an answer to this question.

MAKING STRATEGIC ALLIANCES WORK

The failure rate for international strategic alliances seems to be quite high. For example, one study of forty-nine international strategic alliances found that two-thirds run into serious managerial and financial troubles within two years of their formation, and that although eventually many of these problems are solved, 33 percent are ultimately rated as failures by the parties involved.[37] Below we argue that the success of an alliance seems to be a function of three main factors: partner selection, alliance structure, and the manner in which the alliance is managed.

Partner Selection

One of the keys to making a strategic alliance work is to select the right kind of partner. A good partner has three principal characteristics. First, a good partner helps the firm achieve its strategic goals—whether they be achieving market access, sharing the costs and risks of new-product development, or gaining access to critical core competencies. In other words, the partner must have capabilities that the company lacks and that it values.

Second, a good partner shares the firm's vision for the purpose of the alliance. If two companies approach an alliance with radically different agendas, the chances are great that the relationship will not be harmonious and will end in divorce. This seems to have been the case with the alliance between GM and Daewoo, discussed in Strategy in Action 8.5. GM's agenda was to use Daewoo as a source of cheap labor to produce cars for the Korean and U.S. markets, whereas Daewoo wanted to use GM's know-how and distribution systems to grow its own business not just in Korea and the United States, but also in Europe. Different perceptions of the strategic role of the venture contributed to the dissolution of the alliance.

Third, a good partner is unlikely to try to opportunistically exploit the alliance for its own ends; that is, to expropriate the company's technological know-how while giving little in return. In this respect, firms that have a reputation for fair play and want to maintain it probably make the best partners. For example, IBM is involved in so many strategic alliances that it would not pay the company to trample roughshod over individual alliance partners. Such actions would tarnish IBM's hard-won reputation of being a good partner and would make it more difficult for IBM to attract alliance partners in the future. Similarly, their reputations lessen the likelihood that such Japanese companies as Sony, Toshiba, and Fuji, which have a history of alliances with non-Japanese firms, would opportunistically exploit an alliance partner.

To select a partner with these three characteristics, a company needs to conduct comprehensive research on potential alliance candidates. To increase the probability of selecting a good partner, the firm should collect as much pertinent, publicly available information about potential allies as possible; collect data from informed third parties, including companies that have had alliances with the potential partners, investment bankers who have had dealings with them, and some of their former employees; and get to know potential partners as well as possible before committing to an alliance. This last step should include face-to-face meetings between senior managers (and perhaps middle-level managers) to ensure that the chemistry is right.

Alliance Structure

Having selected a partner, the alliance should be structured so that the company's risk of giving too much away to the partner is reduced to an acceptable level. Figure 8.4 depicts the four safeguards against opportunism by alliance partners that we discuss here. (**Opportunism** includes the "theft" of technology and/or markets that Reich and Mankin describe.) First, alliances can be designed to make it difficult (if not impossible) to transfer technology not meant to be transferred. Specifically, the design, development, manufacture, and service of a product manufactured by an alliance can be structured so as to "wall off" sensitive technologies and thus prevent

8.5 **STRATEGY *in* ACTION**

General Motors and Daewoo

In June 1984, General Motors and Daewoo of Korea signed an agreement that called for each to invest $100 million in a Korean-based 50/50 joint venture, Daewoo Motor Company, which would manufacture a subcompact car, the Pontiac LeMans, based on GM's popular German-designed Opel Kadett. (Opel is GM's German subsidiary.) Daewoo executives would be in charge of the day-to-day management of the alliance, and a few GM executives would provide managerial and technical advice. Initially, the alliance was seen as a smart move for both companies. GM doubted that a small car could be built profitably in the United States because of high labor costs, and it saw enormous advantages in this marriage of German technology and Korean cheap labor. Roger Smith, then GM's chairman, told Korean reporters that GM's North American operation would probably end up importing 80,000 to 100,000 cars a year from Daewoo Motors. As for Daewoo, it saw itself getting access to the superior engineering skills of GM and an entrée into the world's largest car market—the United States.

Eight years of financial losses later, the joint venture collapsed in a blizzard of mutual recriminations between Daewoo and General Motors. From GM's perspective, things started to go seriously wrong in 1987, just as the first LeMans was rolling off Daewoo's production line. Korea had lurched toward democracy, and workers throughout the country demanded better wages. Daewoo was hit by a series of bitter strikes, which repeatedly halted LeMans production. To calm the labor troubles, Daewoo Motor more than doubled workers' wages, and suddenly it was cheaper to build Opels in Germany. (German wages were still higher, but German productivity was also much higher, which translated into lower labor costs.)

Equally problematic was the poor quality of the cars rolling off the Daewoo production line. Electrical systems often crashed on the LeMans, and the braking system had a tendency to fail after just a few thousand miles. The LeMans soon gained a reputation for poor quality, and U.S. sales plummeted to 37,000 vehicles in 1991, down 86 percent from their 1988 high point. Hurt by the reputation of LeMans as a lemon, Daewoo's share of the rapidly growing Korean car market also slumped from a high of 21.4 percent in 1987 to 12.3 percent in 1991.

If GM was disappointed in Daewoo, that was nothing compared with Daewoo's frustration with GM. Daewoo's chairman, Kim WooChoong, complained that GM executives were arrogant and treated him shabbily. He was angry that GM tried to prohibit him from expanding the market for Daewoo's cars. In late 1988, he negotiated a deal to sell 7,000 Daewoo Motor's cars in eastern Europe. GM executives immediately tried to kill the deal, telling Kim that Europe was the territory of GM's German subsidiary, Opel. To make matters worse, when Daewoo developed a new sedan and asked GM to sell it in the United States, GM refused. By this point, Kim's frustration at having his expansion plans for eastern Europe and the United States held back by GM was clear to all. Daewoo management also believed that poor sales of the LeMans in the United States were not due to quality problems, but to GM's poor marketing efforts.

Events came to a head in 1991 when Daewoo asked GM to agree to expand the manufacturing facilities of the joint venture. The plan called for each partner to put in another $100 million and for Daewoo to double its output. GM refused on the grounds that increasing output would not help Daewoo Motor unless the venture could first improve its product quality. The matter festered until late 1991, when GM delivered a blunt proposal to Daewoo: either GM would buy out Daewoo's stake, or Daewoo would buy out GM's stake in the joint venture. Much to GM's surprise, Daewoo agreed to buy out GM's stake. The divorce was completed in November 1992 with an agreement by Daewoo to pay GM $170 million over three years for its 50 percent stake in Daewoo Motor Company.[38]

FIGURE 8.4

Structuring Alliances to Reduce Opportunism

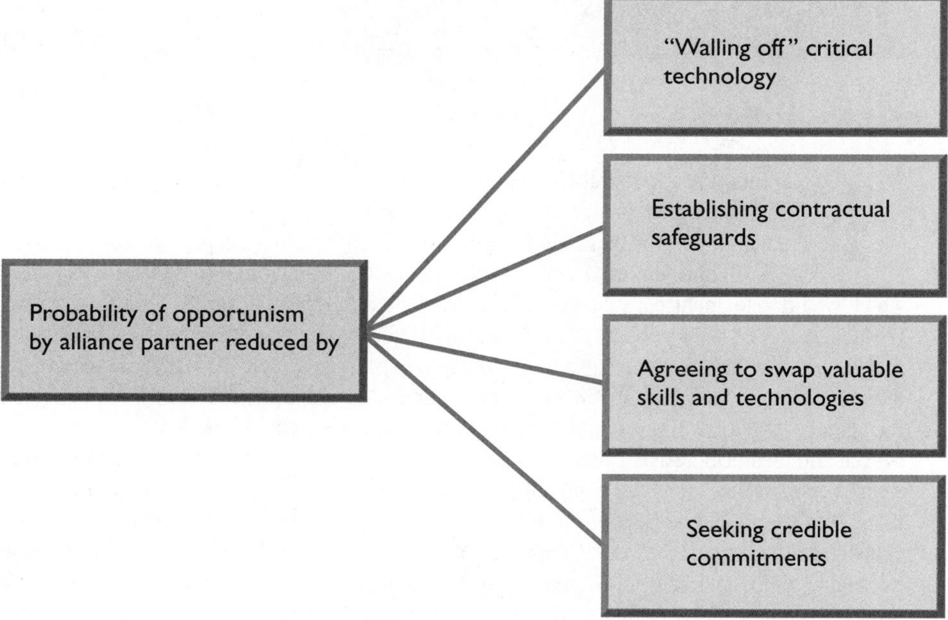

their leakage to the other participant. In the alliance between General Electric and Snecma to build commercial aircraft engines, for example, GE reduced the risk of "excess transfer" by walling off certain sections of the production process. The modularization effectively cut off the transfer of what GE regarded as key competitive technology, while permitting Snecma access to final assembly. Similarly, in the alliance between Boeing and the Japanese to build the 767, Boeing walled off research, design, and marketing functions considered central to its competitive position, while allowing the Japanese to share in production technology. Boeing also walled off new technologies not required for 767 production.[39]

Second, contractual safeguards can be written into an alliance agreement to guard against the risk of opportunism by a partner. For example, TRW has three strategic alliances with large Japanese auto component suppliers to produce seat belts, engine valves, and steering gears for sale to Japanese-owned auto assembly plants in the United States. TRW has clauses in each of its alliance contracts that bar the Japanese firms from competing with TRW to supply U.S.-owned auto companies with component parts. By means of these clauses, TRW is protecting itself against the possibility that the Japanese companies are entering into the alliances merely as a means of gaining access to the North American market to compete with TRW in its home market.

Third, both parties to an alliance can agree in advance to swap skills and technologies, thereby ensuring a chance for equitable gain. Cross-licensing agreements are one way to achieve this goal. For example, in the alliance between Motorola and Toshiba, Motorola has licensed some of its microprocessor technology to Toshiba, and in return Toshiba has licensed some of its memory chip technology to Motorola.

Fourth, the risk of opportunism by an alliance partner can be reduced if the firm extracts a significant credible commitment from its partner in advance. The long-term alliance between Xerox and Fuji to build photocopiers for the Asian market, discussed in Strategy in Action 8.4, perhaps best illustrates this approach. Rather than enter into an informal agreement or some kind of licensing arrangement (which Fuji Photo initially wanted), Xerox insisted that Fuji invest in a 50/50 joint venture to serve Japan and East Asia. This venture constituted such a significant investment in people, equipment, and facilities that Fuji Photo was committed from the outset to making the alliance work in order to earn a return on its investment. By agreeing to the joint venture, Fuji made a credible commitment to the alliance, and Xerox felt secure in transferring its photocopier technology to Fuji.[40]

Managing the Alliance

Once a partner has been selected and an appropriate alliance structure agreed on, the task facing the company is to maximize the benefits from the alliance. One important ingredient of success appears to be a sensitivity to cultural differences. Differences in management style can often be attributed to cultural differences. Managers need to make allowances for such differences when dealing with their partner. In addition, managing an alliance successfully means building interpersonal relationships among managers from the different companies—a lesson that can be drawn from the successful strategic alliance between Ford and Mazda to jointly develop cars for the global auto industry. This partnership has resulted in the development of such best-selling cars as the Ford Explorer and the Mazda Navajo. Ford and Mazda have set up a framework of meetings within which managers from Ford and Mazda not only discuss matters pertaining to the alliance but also have sufficient nonwork time to allow them to get to know each other better. The resulting personal friendships can help build trust and facilitate harmonious relations between the two companies. Moreover, personal relationships can create an informal management network between the companies, and this network can then be used to help solve problems that arise in more formal contexts, such as joint committee meetings between personnel from both firms.

A major factor determining how much a company gains from an alliance is its ability to learn from alliance partners. Gary Hamel, Yves Doz, and C. K. Prahalad reached this conclusion after a five-year study of fifteen strategic alliances between major multinationals. They focused on a number of alliances between Japanese companies and western (European or American) partners. In every case in which a Japanese company emerged from an alliance stronger than its western partner, the Japanese company had made a greater effort to learn. Indeed, few western companies seemed to want to learn from their Japanese partners. They tended to regard the alliance purely as a cost-sharing or risk-sharing device, rather than as an opportunity to learn how a potential competitor does business.[41] As a counterpoint, however, it is worth noting that Xerox clearly used the Fuji-Xerox joint venture to learn about "Japanese" manufacturing practices, such as total quality control and design for manufacturing (see Strategy in Action 8.4).

On the other hand, the joint effort of General Motors and Toyota to build the Chevrolet Nova exemplifies an alliance that reveals a clear learning asymmetry. Structured as a formal joint venture, called New United Motor Manufacturing, this alliance gives both parties a 50 percent equity stake. The venture owns an auto plant in Fremont, California. According to one of the Japanese managers, Toyota achieved most of its objectives from the alliance: "We learned about U.S. supply and transportation. And we got the confidence to manage U.S. workers." All that knowledge was then quickly transferred to Georgetown, Kentucky, where Toyota opened a plant of its own in 1988. By contrast, although General Motors got a new product, the Chevrolet Nova, some GM managers complained that their new knowledge was never put to good use inside GM. They say that they should have been kept together as a team to educate GM's engineers and workers about the Japanese system. Instead they were dispersed to different GM subsidiaries.[42]

When entering an alliance, a company must take some measures to ensure that it learns from its alliance partner and then puts that knowledge to good use within its own organization. One suggested approach is to educate all operating employees about the partner's strengths and weaknesses and make clear to them how acquiring particular skills will bolster their company's competitive position. For such learning to be of value, the knowledge acquired from an alliance has to be diffused throughout the organization—as did not happen at GM. To spread this knowledge, the managers involved in an alliance should be used as a resource in familiarizing others within the company about the skills of an alliance partner.

SUMMARY OF CHAPTER

This chapter examines the various ways in which companies can profit from global expansion and reviews the strategies that companies engaged in global competition can adopt. It also discusses the optimal choice of entry mode to serve a foreign market and explores the issue of strategic alliances. The chapter makes the following main points:

- ✔ For some companies, international expansion represents a way of earning greater returns by transferring the skills and product offerings derived from their distinctive competencies to markets where indigenous competitors lack those skills.
- ✔ Because of national differences, it pays a company to base each value creation activity it performs at the location where factor conditions are most conducive to the performance of that activity. We refer to this strategy as focusing on the attainment of location economies.
- ✔ By building sales volume more rapidly, international expansion can assist a company in the process of moving down the experience curve.
- ✔ The best strategy for a company to pursue may depend on the kind of pressures it must cope with: pressures for cost reductions or for local responsiveness. Pressures for cost reductions are greatest in industries producing commodity-type products, where price is the main competitive weapon. Pressures for local responsiveness arise from differences in consumer tastes and preferences, as well as from national infrastructure and traditional practices, distribution channels, and host government demands.
- ✔ Companies pursuing an international strategy transfer the skills and products derived from distinctive competencies to foreign markets, while undertaking some limited local customization.
- ✔ Companies pursuing a multidomestic strategy customize their product offering, marketing strategy, and business strategy to national conditions.
- ✔ Companies pursuing a global strategy focus on reaping the cost reductions that come from experience-curve effects and location economies.
- ✔ Many industries are now so competitive that companies must adopt a transnational strategy. This involves a simultaneous focus on reducing costs, transferring skills and products, and local responsiveness. Implementing such a strategy, however, may not be easy.
- ✔ The most attractive foreign markets tend to be found in politically stable developed and developing nations with free market systems, but without a dramatic upsurge in either inflation rates or private sector debt.
- ✔ Entering a national market early, before other international businesses have established themselves, brings several advantages, but these advantages must be balanced against the pioneer-

ing costs that early entrants often have to bear, including the greater risk of business failure.

- Large-scale entry into a national market constitutes a major strategic commitment, which is likely to change the nature of competition in that market and limit the entrant's future strategic flexibility. The firm needs to think through the implications of such commitments before embarking on a large-scale entry. Although making major strategic commitments can yield many benefits, there are also risks associated with such a strategy.
- The five different ways of entering a foreign market are exporting, licensing, franchising, entering into a joint venture, and setting up a wholly owned subsidiary. The optimal choice of entry mode depends on the company's strategy.
- Strategic alliances are cooperative agreements between actual or potential competitors. The advantages of alliances are that they facilitate entry into foreign markets, enable partners to share the fixed costs and risks associated with new products and processes, facilitate the transfer of complementary skills between companies, and help companies establish technical standards.
- The drawbacks of a strategic alliance are that the company risks giving away technological know-how and market access to its alliance partner while getting very little in return.
- The disadvantages associated with alliances can be reduced if the company selects partners carefully, paying close attention to reputation, and if it structures the alliance so as to avoid unintended transfers of know-how.

DISCUSSION QUESTIONS

1. Plot the position of the following companies on Figure 8.1: Procter & Gamble, IBM, Coca-Cola, Dow Chemical, AOL, and McDonald's. In each case, justify your answer.
2. Are the following global industries or multidomestic industries: bulk chemicals, pharmaceuticals, branded food products, moviemaking, television manufacture, personal computers, airline travel, and Internet on-line services such as AOL and MSN?
3. Discuss how the need for control over foreign operations varies with the strategy and distinctive competencies of a company. What are the implications of this relationship for the choice of entry mode?
4. Licensing proprietary technology to foreign competitors is the best way to give up a company's competitive advantage. Discuss.
5. What kind of companies stand to gain the most from entering into strategic alliances with potential competitors? Why?

Practicing Strategic Management

SMALL-GROUP EXERCISE
Developing a Global Strategy

Break up into a group of three to five people and discuss the following scenario:

You work for a company in the soft-drink industry that has developed a line of carbonated fruit-based drinks. You have already establishing a significant presence in your home market, and now you are planning the global strategy development of the company in the soft-drink industry. You need to decide the following:

1. What overall strategy to pursue—a global strategy, multidomestic strategy, international strategy, or transnational strategy?
2. Which markets to enter first?
3. What entry strategy to pursue (for instance, franchising, joint venture, wholly owned subsidiary)?

What information do you need in order to make these kinds of decision? Based on what you do know, what strategies would you recommend?

STRATEGIC MANAGEMENT PROJECT
Module 8

This module requires you to identify how your company might profit from global expansion, the strategy that your company should pursue globally, and the entry mode that it might favor. With the information you have at your disposal, answer the questions regarding the following two situations:

ARTICLE FILE 8

Find an example of a multinational company that has switched its strategy in recent years from a multidomestic, international, or global strategy to a transnational strategy. Identify why the company made the switch and any problems that the company may be encountering while it tries to change its strategic orientation.

Your Company Is Already Doing Business in Other Countries

1. Is your company creating value or lowering the costs of value creation by realizing location economies, transferring distinctive competencies abroad, or realizing cost economies from the experience curve? If not, does it have the potential to do so?
2. How responsive is your company to differences between nations? Does it vary its product and marketing message from country to country? Should it?
3. What are the cost pressures and pressures for local responsiveness in the industry in which your company is based?
4. What strategy is your company pursuing to compete globally? In your opinion, is this the correct strategy, given cost pressures and pressures for local responsiveness?
5. What major foreign market does your company serve and what mode has it used to enter this market? Why is your company active in these markets, and not others? What are the advantages and disadvantages of using this mode? Might another mode be preferable?

Your Company Is Not Yet Doing Business in Other Countries

1. What potential does your company have to add value to its products or lower the costs of value creation by expanding internationally?
2. On the international level, what are the cost pressures and pressures for local responsiveness in the industry in which your company is based? What implications do these pressures have for the strategy that your company might pursue if it chose to expand globally?
3. What foreign market might your company enter and what entry mode should it use to enter this market? Justify your answer.

EXPLORING THE WEB
Visting IBM

IBM is the acronym of International Business Machines. Using the significant resources located at IBM's corporate Web site, including annual reports and company history, explain what "International" means in IBM. Specifically, how many countries is IBM active in? How does it create value by expanding into foreign markets? What entry mode does it adopt in most markets? Can you find any exceptions to this? How would you characterize IBM's strategy for competing in the global marketplace? Is the company pursuing a transnational, global, international, or multidomestic strategy?

General Task Search the Web for a company site where there is a good description of that company's international operations. On the basis of this information, try to establish how the company enters foreign markets and what overall strategy it is pursuing (global, international, multidomestic, transnational).

CLOSING CASE

IKEA

ESTABLISHED IN THE 1940S IN SWEDEN BY INGVAR KAMPRAD, IKEA has grown rapidly in recent years to become one of the world's largest retailers of home furnishings. In its initial push to expand globally, IKEA largely ignored the retailing rule that international success requires tailoring product lines closely to national tastes and preferences. Instead, IKEA stuck with the vision, articulated by Kamprad, that wherever it ventures in the world the company should sell a basic product range that is "typically Swedish." The company also remained primarily production oriented; that is, the Swedish management and design group decided what it was going to sell and then presented it to the worldwide public, often with very little research as to what the public actually wanted. Moreover, the company emphasized its Swedish roots in its international advertising, even going as far as to insist on a "Swedish" blue and yellow color scheme for its stores.

Despite breaking some key rules of international retailing, the formula of selling Swedish-designed products in the same way everywhere seemed to work. Between 1974 and 1994, IKEA expanded from a company with 10 stores, only one of which was outside Scandinavia, and annual revenues of $210 million, to a group with 125 stores in twenty-six countries and sales of nearly $5 billion. In 1994, only 11 percent of its sales were generated in Sweden. Of the balance, 29.6 percent came from Germany, 42.5 percent from the rest of western Europe, and 14.2 percent from North America. IKEA's expansion in North America has been its most recent international venture.

The source of IKEA's success has been its ability to offer consumers good value for money. IKEA's approach starts with a global network of suppliers, which comprises 2,700 firms in sixty-seven countries. An IKEA supplier gains long-term contracts, technical advice, and leased equipment from the company. In return, IKEA demands an exclusive contract and low prices. IKEA's designers work closely with suppliers to build savings into the products from the outset by designing products that can be produced at a low cost. IKEA displays its enormous range of more than 10,000 products in cheap out-of-town stores. It sells most of its furniture as knocked-down kits for customers to take home and assemble themselves. The firm reaps huge economies of scale from the size of each store and the big production runs made possible by selling the same products all over the world. This strategy allows IKEA to match its rivals on quality, while undercutting them by up to 30 percent on price and still maintaining a healthy after-tax return on sales of around 7 percent.

This strategy has consistently worked well for IKEA until 1985, when the company decided to enter the North American market. Between 1985 and 1990 IKEA opened six stores in North America—but unlike the company's stores across Europe, the new stores did not quickly become profitable. Instead, by 1990 it was clear that IKEA's North American operations were in trouble. IKEA's unapologetically Swedish products, which had sold so well across Europe, jarred with U.S. tastes and sometimes with physiques as well. Swedish beds were narrow and measured in centimeters. IKEA did not sell the matching bedroom suites that U.S. consumers liked. Its kitchen cupboards were too narrow for the large dinner plates needed for pizza. Its glasses were too small for a nation

CLOSING CASE *(continued)*

that adds ice to everything. And the drawers in IKEA's bedroom chests were too shallow for American consumers, who tend to store sweaters in them.

In 1990, the company's top management came to the realization that if IKEA was to succeed in North America, it would have to customize its product offerings to North American tastes. The company set about redesigning its product range. The drawers on bedroom chests were made two inches deeper—and sales immediately increased by 30 to 40 percent. IKEA now sells U.S.-style king- and queen-size beds, measured in inches, and it sells them as part of complete bedroom suites. Currently, it is redesigning its entire range of kitchen furniture and kitchenware to better appeal to U.S. tastes. The company had also boosted the amount of products being sourced locally from 15 percent in 1990 to 45 percent in 1994, a move that has made it far less vulnerable to adverse movements in exchange rates.

This break with its traditional strategy has paid off for IKEA. Between 1990 and 1994, its North American sales tripled to $480 million, and the company claims that it has been making a profit in North America since early 1993, although it admits that profit margins are still lower in North America than in Europe. By 1995, the company had also expanded the number of North American stores to fifteen.[43]

Case Discussion Questions

1. How would you characterize IKEA's original strategy for profiting from foreign markets?
2. Why did the strategy work so well in Europe but break down in the United States?
3. How would you chacterize IKEA's post-1990 strategy? How successful has this strategy been? (Hint: Use the Web to collect details about IKEA's recent financial results. www.ikea.com)

End Notes

1. R. Blumenstein, "GM Is Building Plants in Developing Nations to Woo New Markets," *Wall Street Journal*, August 4, 1997, p. A1; H. Simonian, "GM Hopes to Turn Corner with New Astra," *Financial Times*, November 29, 1997, p. 15; D. Howes, "GM, Ford Play for Keeps Abroad," *The Detroit News*, March 8, 1998, p. D1.
2. K. Deveny et al., "McWorld?" *Business Week*, October 13, 1986, pp. 78–86; "Slow Food," *Economist*, February 3, 1990, p. 64; H. S. Byrne, "Welcome to McWorld," *Barron's*, August 29, 1994, pp. 25–28; A. E. Serwer, "McDonald's Conquers the World," *Fortune*, October 17, 1994, pp. 103–116.
3. C. S. Tranger, "Enter the Mini-Multinational," *Northeast International Business* (March 1989), 13–14.
4. I. Metthee, "Playing a Large Part," *Seattle-Post Intelligence*, April 9, 1994, p. 13.
5. R. B. Reich, *The Work of Nations* (New York: Knopf, 1991).
6. "Matsushita Electrical Industrial in 1987," in *Transnational Management*, ed. C. A. Bartlett and S. Ghoshal (Homewood, Ill.: Irwin, 1992).
7. C. K. Prahalad and Y. L. Doz, *The Multinational Mission: Balancing Local Demands and Global Vision* (New York: Free Press, 1987); also see J. Birkinshaw, A. Morrison, and J. Hulland, "Structural and Competitive Determinants of a Global Integration Strategy," *Strategic Management Journal*, 16 (1995), 637–655.
8. Prahalad and Doz, *The Multinational Mission*.
9. "The Tire Industry's Costly Obsession with Size," *Economist*, June 8, 1993, p. 65–66.
10. T. Levitt, "The Globalization of Markets," *Harvard Business Review*, (May–June 1983), 92–102.
11. C. A. Bartlett and S. Ghoshal, *The Transnational Solution: Managing Across Borders*, (Boston: Harvard Business School Press, 1989).
12. C. J. Chipello, "Local Presence Is Key to European Deals," *Wall Street Journal*, June 30, 1998, p. A15.
13. Bartlett and Ghoshal, *Managing Across Borders*.
14. G. de Jonquieres and C. Bobinski, "Wash and Get into a Lather in Poland," *Financial Times*, May 28, 1989, p. 2; "Perestroika in Soapland," *Economist*, June 10, 1989, pp. 69–71; "After Early Stumbles P&G Is Making Inroads Overseas," *Wall Street Journal*, February 6, 1989, p. B1; Bartlett and Ghoshal, *Managing Across Borders*; G. Das, "Local Memoirs of a Global Business Manager," *Harvard Business Review* (March 1993), 38–48.
15. Bartlett and Ghoshal, *Managing Across Borders.*
16. T. Hout, M. E. Porter, and E. Rudden, "How Global Companies Win Out," *Harvard Business Review*, (September–October, 1982), 98–108.
17. See C. W. L. Hill, *International Business: Competing in the Global Marketplace* (Burr Ridge, Ill.: 2000).
18. This can be reconceptualized as the resource base of the entrant, relative to indigenous competitors. For work that focuses on this issue, see W. C. Bogenr, H. Thomas, and J. McGee, "A Longitudinal Study of the Competitive Positions and Entry Paths of European Firms in the U.S. Pharmaceutical Market," *Strategic Management Journal*, 17 (1996), 85–107; D. Collis, "A Resource-Based Analysis of Global Competition," *Strategic Management Journal,* 12 (1991) 49–68; and S. Tallman, "Strategic Management Models and Resource-Based Strategies Among MNE's in a Host Market," *Strategic Management Journal*, 12 (1991), 69–82.
19. "Japan's Big Bang. Enter Merrill," *Economist,* January 3, 1998, p. 72; J. P. Donlon, "Merrill Cinch," *Chief Executive* (March 1998), p. 28–32; D. Holley, "Merrill Lynch to Open 31 Offices Throughout Japan," *Los Angeles Times*, February 13, 1998, p. D1; A. Rowley, "Merrill Thunders into Japan," *Banker* (March 1998), 6.
20. For a discussion of first-mover advantages, see M. Liberman and D. Montgomery, "First Mover Advantages," *Strategic Management Journal*, 9 (Special Issue on Strategy Content, Summer 1988), 41–58.
21. J. M. Shaver, W. Mitchell, and B. Yeung, "The Effect of Own Firm and Other Firm Experience on Foreign Direct Investment Survival in the United States 1987–92," *Strategic Management Journal*, 18 (1997), 811–824.
22. S. Zaheer and E. Mosakowski, "The Dynamics of the Liability of Foreignness: a Global Study of Survival in the Financial Services Industry," *Strategic Management Journal*, 18 (1997), 439–464.
23. Shaver, Mitchell, and Yeung, "The Effect of Own Firm and Other Firm Experience."
24. P. Ghemawat, *Commitment: The Dynamics of Strategy* (New York: Free Press, 1991).
25. R. Luecke, *Scuttle Your Ships Before Advancing* (Oxford: Oxford University Press, 1994).
26. This section draws on several studies including C. W. L. Hill, P. Hwang, and W. C. Kim, "An Eclectic Theory of the Choice of International Entry Mode," *Strategic Management Journal,* 11 (1990), 117–28; C. W. L. Hill and W. C. Kim, "Searching for a Dynamic Theory of the Multinational Enterprise: A Transaction Cost Model," *Strategic Management Journal*, 9 (Special Issue on Strategy Content, 1988), 93–104; E. Anderson and H. Gatignon, "Modes of Foreign Entry: A Transaction Cost Analysis and Propositions," *Journal of International Business Studies* 17 (1986), 1–26; F. R. Root, *Entry Strategies for International Markets* (Lexington, Mass.: D. C. Heath, 1980); A. Madhok, "Cost, Value and Foreign Market Entry: The Transaction and the Firm," *Strategic Management Journal*, 18 (1997), 39–61.
27. F. J. Contractor, "The Role of Licensing in International Strategy," *Columbia Journal of World Business* (Winter 1982), 73–83.
28. O. E. Williamson, *The Economic Institutions of Capitalism* (New York: Free Press, 1985).
29. A. E. Serwer, "McDonald's Conquers the World."
30. B. Kogut, "Joint Ventures: Theoretical and Empirical Perspectives," *Strategic Management Journal*, 9 (1988), 319–332.
31. D. G. Bradley, "Managing Against Expropriation," *Harvard Business Review* (July–August 1977), 78–90.

32. R. Howard, "The CEO as Organizational Architect," *Harvard Business Review* (September–October 1992), 106–123; D. Kearns, "Leadership Through Quality," *Academy of Management Executive*, 4 (1990), 86–89; K. McQuade and B. Gomes-Casseres, "Xerox and Fuji-Xerox," *Harvard Business School* Case No. 9-391-156; E. Terazono and C. Lorenz, "An Angry Young Warrior," *Financial Times*, September 19, 1994, p. 11.
33. C. W. L. Hill, "Strategies for Exploiting Technological Innovations," *Organization Science*, 3 (1992), 428–441.
34. See K. Ohmae, "The Global Logic of Strategic Alliances," *Harvard Business Review* (March–April 1989), 143–154; G. Hamel, Y. L. Doz, and C. K. Prahalad, "Collaborate with Your Competitors and Win!" *Harvard Business Review* (January–February 1988), 133–139; W. Burgers, C. W. L. Hill, and W. C. Kim, "Alliances in the Global Auto Industry," *Strategic Management Journal*, 14 (1993), 419–432.
35. "Asia Beckons," *Economist*, May 30, 1992, pp. 63–64.
36. R. B. Reich and E. D. Mankin, "Joint Ventures with Japan Give Away Our Future," *Harvard Business Review*, (March–April 1986), 78–90.
37. J. Bleeke and D. Ernst, "The Way to Win in Cross-Border Alliances," *Harvard Business Review* (November–December 1991), 127–135.
38. D. Darlin, "Daewoo Will Pay GM $170 Million for Venture Stake," *Wall Street Journal*, November 11, 1992, p. A6; D. Darlin and J. B. White, "Failed Marriage," *Wall Street Journal*, January 16, 1992, p. A1.
39. W. Roehl and J. F. Truitt, "Stormy Open Marriages Are Better," *Columbia Journal of World Business* (Summer 1987), 87–95.
40. K. McQuade and B. Gomes-Casseres, "Xerox and Fuji-Xerox."
41. Hamel, Doz, and Prahalad, "Collaborate with Your Competitors and Win!"
42. B. Wysocki, "Cross Border Alliances Become Favorite Way to Crack New Markets," *Wall Street Journal*, March 4, 1990, p. A1.
43. "Furnishing the World," *Economist*, November 19, 1994, pp. 79–80; H. Carnegy, "Struggle to Save the Soul of IKEA," *Financial Times*, March 27, 1995, p. 12.

9 Corporate Strategy: Vertical Integration, Diversification, and Strategic Alliances

OPENING CASE

Bombardier

BOMBARDIER is one of the great business success stories to come out of Canada in the second half of the twentieth century. A manufacturer of transportation equipment, including snowmobiles, railcars, and jet aircraft of seventy seats or less, the company has grown from sales of $10 million in the mid 1960s to around $7 billion in 1999, and it has posted consistent year-on-year growth in revenues and earnings. The key to this growth has been successful diversification.

Established in 1942 as a manufacturer of snowgoing equipment (tracked vehicles for crossing snow, such as snow cats), Bombardier expanded into the closely related market of snowmobiles in the 1960s. As oil prices surged in the early 1970s because of action by the Organization of Petroleum Exporting Countries (OPEC), demand for snowmobiles plummeted. Bombardier's response was to diversify into the manufacture of railcars. Laurent Beaudoin, the company's CEO for a thirty-three-year period that ended in 1999, reasoned that Bombardier's engineering skills and manufacturing capacity could be quickly converted from the manufacture of snowmobiles to the manufacture of railcars.

In a make-or-break gamble, he purchased a French license for a subway car design and boldly bid on, and won, a huge contract to build cars for the Montreal subway system. This contract was followed by a 1982 deal to build 825 cars for the New York subway system. Today, Bombardier builds cars for mass-transit systems on four continents, ranking number two in the world railcar market. It also produces freight cars and locomotives. The railcar and locomotive business now accounts for around one-quarter of the company's business.

The next diversification move came in 1986, when Bombardier purchased Canadair from the Canadian government for what many viewed as a bargain basement price. A struggling manufacturer of small regional aircraft, Canadair had been saved from total collapse when it was bought by the Canadian government. The key asset that interested Bombardier was the design and manufacturing

OPENING CASE *(continued)*

technology behind Canadair's small corporate jet, the Challenger. Shortly after the acquisition, Bombardier invested an amount equivalent to half the market capitalization of the company to develop a fifty-seat regional jet that just about everyone else thought the industry did not need. At the time, propeller-driven aircraft dominated the regional aircraft market. Just about everybody was wrong. The jet, and it successor aircraft, including a seventy-seat plane, have sold well. The Canadair acquisition was followed by several other purchases of troubled manufacturers of small aircraft, including Short Brother in Northern Ireland, de Havilland in Canada, and Learjet in the United States. In each case, Bombardier was able to purchase these companies for a relatively low price because of their financial troubles.

By imposing good management and tight financial discipline, and by developing a well-thought-out range of smaller jet aircraft in the twenty- to ninety-seat range, Bombardier has managed to weld this grab bag of companies into a coherent and significant force in the global aerospace market. Now the third largest civilian aerospace company in the world, behind Boeing and Airbus, Bombardier has thrived by focusing on a niche where Boeing and Airbus do not compete. In 1998, it received a record 200 orders for its small regional jet aircraft. In total, the units now account for more than half of Bombardier's revenues and profits.

Bombardier's management attributes much of the company's success with diversification to a number of factors. It has entered only those niches where it thought it had a good chance of being the number one or two player in the world, and it has acquired valuable technology at a relatively low cost. Furthermore, it has managed its different businesses within a decentralized organizational structure, which gives the managers of business units the freedom to pursue what they think are the appropriate competitive and operations strategies, subject of course to a detailed review from the top. The company has deliberately taken big risks in its diversification moves. According to the current CEO, Bob Brown, Bombardier's key values are boldness and energy. "When you take action," he says, "take bold action. And when you decide to do something, do it 150 percent."[1]

OVERVIEW

The principal concern of corporate strategy is identifying the business areas in which a company should participate in order to maximize its long-run profitability. When choosing business areas to compete in, a company has several options. It can focus on just one business; it can diversify into a number of different business areas as Bombardier, discussed in the Opening Case, has done; or it can vertically integrate, either upstream to produce its own inputs or downstream to dispose of its own outputs. This chapter explores the various options in depth and examines their pros and cons. It also considers strategic alliances as alternatives to vertical integration and diversification.

As described in the Opening Case, Bombardier made diversification its corporate strategy. From the manufacture of snowgoing equipment such as snow cats, it diversified first into that of snowmobiles (and later skidoos, or water scooters), then into railcar and locomotive manufacture, and finally into the manufacture of small (less than 100-seat) commercial aircraft. The diversification into making snowmobiles was a successful attempt to apply the company's engineering skills in developing and producing snowgoing equipment for the recreational market. By diversifying into railcar manufacture, the company strove to reduce its dependence on the volatile snowmobile business, as well as utilize its excess capacity in manufacturing and engineering talent. The move into aerospace was a bold effort to take advantage of an unexploited opportunity in the market for small jet aircraft. In each case, Bombardier was able to create value. In snowmobiles, it created value by using its existing skill base to manufacture a revolutionary new recreational product. In railcars and locomotives, it initially created value by using diversification to profitably exploit its excess capacity in engineering talent and manufacturing capacity. In aerospace, it created value by consolidating a fragmented market and developing a successful family of innovative small jet aircraft aimed at the regional commuter market.

In this chapter, we repeatedly stress that to succeed, corporate-level strategies should *create value*. To understand what this means, we have to go back to the concept of value creation and the value chain, introduced in Chapter 4: *To create value, a corporate strategy should enable a company, or one or more of its business units, to perform one or more of the value creation functions at a lower cost, or perform one or more of the value creation functions in a way that allows for differentiation and a premium price*. Thus, a company's *corporate* strategy should help in the process of establishing a distinctive competency and competitive advantage *at the business level*. There is, therefore, a very important link between corporate-level strategy and competitive advantage at the business level.

CONCENTRATION ON A SINGLE BUSINESS

For many companies, the appropriate corporate-level strategy does not involve vertical integration or diversification. Instead, corporate strategy entails concentrating on competing successfully within the confines of a single business (that is, focusing on a single industry or market). Examples of companies that currently pursue such a strategy include McDonald's with its focus on the fast-food restaurant business; Coca-Cola, with its focus on the soft drink business; and Sears with its focus on department store retailing. Interestingly enough, both Coca-Cola and Sears at one time pursued diversification strategies. Coca-Cola once owned Columbia Pictures and a wine-producing business; Sears owned Allstate Insurance, Caldwell Banker (a real estate operation), and Dean Witter (a financial services enterprise). However, both companies found that diversification dissipated rather than created value and so they divested their businesses, refocusing on a single operation. They made the change because there are clear advantages to concentrating on just one business area.

One advantage is that the company can focus its total managerial, financial, technological, and physical resources and capabilities on competing successfully in a single area. This strategy can be important in fast-growing industries, where demands on the company's resources and capabilities are likely to be substantial, but where the long-term profits that flow from establishing a competitive advantage are also likely to be very significant. For example, it would make little sense for a company such as America Online to pursue a diversification strategy while the on-line industry still has many years of rapid growth ahead of it and while competing successfully in that marketplace is placing significant demands on the managerial, financial, and technological resources and capabilities of America Online. If it did diversify, America Online would probably run the risk of starving its fast-growing core business of necessary resources, which could quickly result in the decline of that operation.

Nor do just fast-growing companies benefit from focusing an organization's resources and capabilities on one business activity. Some diversified companies active in more mature businesses have also stretched scarce resources too thinly over too many activities, and their performance has declined as a consequence. Sears, for example, found that its diversification into financial services and real estate diverted top management's attention away from its core retailing business, which contributed to a decline in the profitability of that activity. Similarly, Coca-Cola's decision to divest Columbia Pictures was in part driven by a realization that running an entertainment business was diverting valuable top management attention from its core soft drink operation.

Another advantage of concentrating on a single businesses is that the company thereby "sticks to its knitting."[2] What this means is that the company sticks to doing what it knows best, and does not make the mistake of diversifying into areas that it knows little about and where its existing resources and capabilities add little value. Companies undertaking such diversification are likely to discover after the event that they are involved in a business they do not understand and that their uninformed decision making may have a serious and perhaps detrimental effect. For example, in 1991 the Japanese consumer electronics concern Matsushita acquired the U.S. movie and music group MCA. The senior executives at Matsushita, however, soon realized that they knew very little about either the music or the movie businesses. Matsushita's hamfisted attempts to give strategic guidance to top managers at MCA alienated those managers, several of whom left the organization; others engaged in what amounted to an open rebellion, ignoring attempts by Japanese executives to intervene in the running of MCA. At one time it was rumored in the financial press that as many as 100 top MCA managers were considering defecting from the organization. This proved to be very damaging in a business where one of the prime assets is people. Matsushita soon found itself trying to fix managerial problems in a business it did not understand. In 1995, it divested MCA, admitting at the time that it had made an expensive mistake. (Matsushita reportedly lost $2 billion on the deal.)[3]

Concentrating on just one business area, however, also has disadvantages. As the next section shows, a certain amount of vertical integration may be necessary to create value and establish a competitive advantage within a company's core business. Moreover, companies that concentrate on just one business may be missing out on opportunities to create value and make greater profits by leveraging their resources and capabilities to other activities. As Bombadier's success, described in the Opening Case indicates, diversification can help create value by allowing a company to leverage valuable resources and capabilities across businesses.

VERTICAL INTEGRATION

A strategy of **vertical integration** means that a company is producing its own inputs (backward, or upstream, integration) or is disposing of its own outputs (forward, or downstream, integration). A steel company that supplies its iron ore needs from company-owned iron ore mines exemplifies backward (upstream) integration. An automaker that sells its cars through company-owned distribution outlets illustrates forward (downstream) integration. Figure 9.1 shows the four *main* stages in a typical raw-material-to-consumer production chain. For a company based in the assembly stage, backward integration means moving into intermediate manufacturing

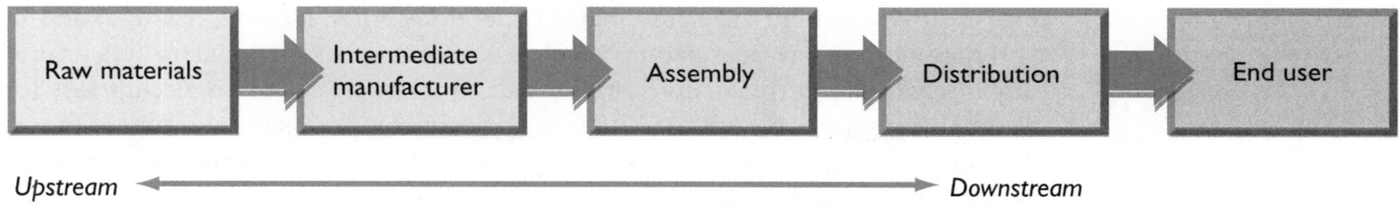

FIGURE 9.1

Stages in the Raw-Material-to-Consumer Value Chain

and raw-material production. Forward integration means moves into distribution. At each stage in the chain, *value is added* to the product. What this means is that a company at that stage takes the product produced in the previous stage and transforms it in some way so that it is worth more to a company at the next stage in the chain and, ultimately, to the end user.

As an example of the value-added concept, consider the production chain in the personal computer industry, illustrated in Figure 9.2. In this industry, the raw materials companies include the manufacturers of specialty ceramics, chemicals, and metals such as Kyocera of Japan, which makes the ceramic substrate for semiconductors. These companies sell their output to the manufacturers of intermediate products. The intermediate manufacturers, which include Intel, Seagate, and Micron Technology, transform the ceramics, chemicals, and metals they purchase into computer components such as microprocessors, memory chips, and disk drives. In doing so they *add value* to the raw materials they purchase. These components are then sold to assembly companies such as Apple, Dell, and Compaq, which take these components and transform them into personal computers—that is, *add value* to the components they purchase. Many of the completed personal computers are then sold to distributors such as Office Max and Computer World, or value-added resellers, which in turn sell them to final customers. The distributors also *add value* to the product by making it accessible to customers and by providing service and support. Thus, value is added by companies at each stage in the raw-materials-to-consumer chain.

Viewed this way, vertical integration presents companies with a choice about which value-added stages of the raw-material-to-consumer chain to compete in. In the personal computer industry, most companies have not integrated into adjacent

FIGURE 9.2

The Raw-Material-to-Consumer Value Chain in the Personal Computer Industry

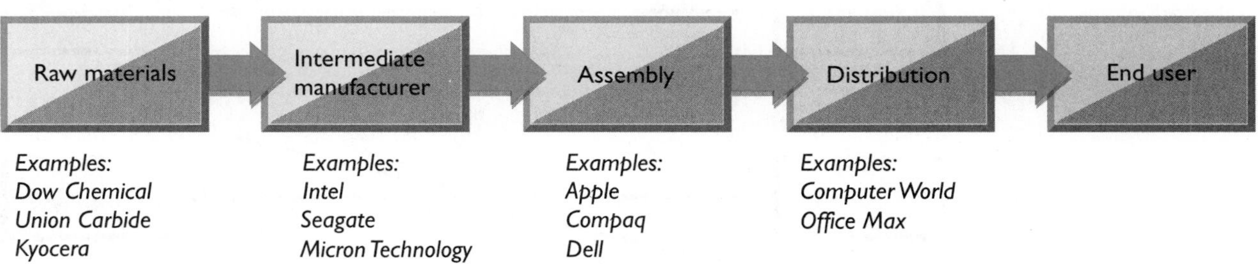

stages. However, there are some major exceptions. Intel, for one, has operated in both the intermediate manufacturer and assembly stage of the industry. It is a vertically integrated enterprise, not only producing microprocessors and chip sets for personal computers, but also assembling personal computers for computer companies under an Original Equipment Manufacturer (OEM) arrangement, which lets the downstream company put its brand label on an Intel PC.

Besides forward and backward integration, it is also possible to distinguish between **full integration** and **taper integration** (see Figure 9.3).[4] A company achieves full integration when it produces all of a particular input needed for its processes or when it disposes of all its output through its own operations. Taper integration occurs when a company buys from independent suppliers in addition to company-owned suppliers, or when it disposes of its output through independent outlets in addition to company-owned outlets. The advantages of taper integration over full integration are discussed later in the chapter.

Creating Value Through Vertical Integration

A company pursuing vertical integration is normally motivated by a desire to strengthen the competitive position of its original, or core, business.[5] There are four main arguments for pursuing a vertical integration strategy. Vertical integration (1) enables the company to build barriers to new competition, (2) facilitates investments in efficiency-enhancing specialized assets, (3) protects product quality, and (4) results in improved scheduling.

Building Barriers to Entry By vertically integrating backward to gain control over the source of critical inputs or vertically integrating forward to gain control over distribution channels, a company can build barriers to new entry into its industry. To the extent that this strategy is effective, it limits competition in the company's industry, thereby enabling the company to charge a higher price and make greater profits than it could otherwise.[6] To grasp this argument, consider a famous example of this strategy from the 1930s.

At that time, commercial smelting of aluminum was pioneered by companies such as Alcoa and Alcan. Aluminum is derived from smelting bauxite. Although bauxite is a common mineral, the percentage of aluminum in bauxite is usually so low that it is not economical to mine and smelt. During the 1930s, only one large-

FIGURE 9.3

Full and Taper Integration

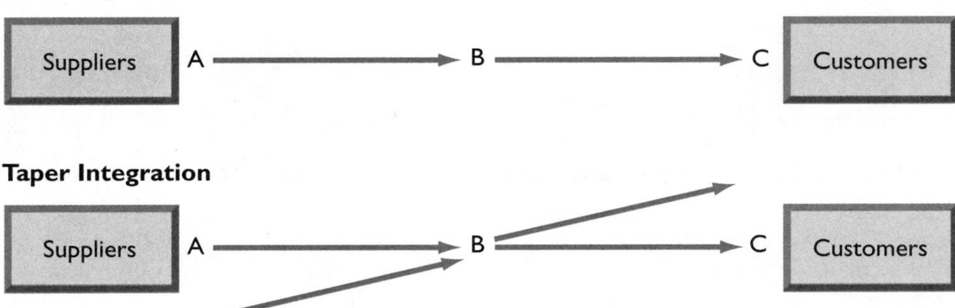

scale deposit of bauxite had been discovered where the percentage of aluminum in the mineral made smelting economical. This deposit was on the Caribbean island of Jamaica. Alcoa and Alcan vertically integrated backward and acquired ownership over this deposit. This action created a barrier to entry into the aluminum industry. Potential competitors were deterred from entry because they could not get access to high-grade bauxite; it was all owned by Alcoa and Alcan. Because they had to use lower-grade bauxite, those that did enter the industry found themselves at a cost disadvantage. This situation persisted until the 1950s, when new high-grade deposits were discovered in Australia and Indonesia.

During the 1970s and 1980s, a similar strategy was pursued by vertically integrated companies in the computer industry such as IBM and Digital Equipment. These companies manufactured the main components of computers such as microprocessors and memory chips, designed and assembled the computers, produced the software that ran the computers, and sold the final product directly to end users. The original rationale behind this strategy was that many of the key components and software used in computers contained proprietary elements. These companies reasoned that by producing the proprietary technology in-house they could limit rivals' access to it, thereby building barriers to entry. Thus, when IBM introduced its PS/2 personal computer system in the mid 1980s, it announced that certain component parts incorporating proprietary technology would be manufactured in-house by IBM.

While this strategy worked well from the 1960s until the early 1980s, it has been failing since then, particularly in the personal computer and server segments of the industry. In the early 1990s, the worst performers in the computer industry were precisely the companies that pursued the vertical integration strategy: IBM and Digital Equipment. What seems to have happened is that the shift to open standards in computer hardware and software has nullified the advantages for computer companies of being extensively vertically integrated. In addition, new personal computer companies such as Dell and Compaq found that they could quickly reverse-engineer and duplicate the proprietary components that companies such as IBM placed in their personal computers, effectively circumventing this barrier to entry.

Facilitating Investments in Specialized Assets A specialized asset is an asset that is designed to perform a specific task and whose value is significantly reduced in its next best use.[7] A specialized asset may be a piece of equipment that has very specialized uses, or it may be the know-how or skills that an individual or company has acquired through training and experience. Companies (and individuals) invest in specialized assets because these assets allow them to lower the costs of value creation and/or to better differentiate their product offering from that of competitors, thereby facilitating premium pricing. A company might invest in specialized equipment because that enables it to lower its manufacturing costs and increase its quality, or it might invest in developing highly specialized technological knowledge because doing so lets it develop better products than its rivals. Thus, specialization can be the basis for achieving a competitive advantage at the business level.

A company, however, may find it very difficult to persuade other companies in *adjacent* stages in the raw-material-to-consumer production chain to undertake investments in specialized assets. To realize the economic gains associated with such investments, the company may have to integrate vertically into the adjacent stages and make the investments itself. Imagine, for instance, that Ford has developed a new, high-performance, high-quality, and uniquely designed carburetor. The carburetor will increase fuel efficiency, which in turn will help differentiate Ford's cars from those of its rivals—that is, it will give Ford a competitive advantage. Ford has to decide whether to make the carburetor in-house (vertical integration) or contract out manufacturing to an independent supplier (outsourcing). Manufacturing these carburetors requires substantial investments in equipment that can be used only for this purpose. Because of its unique design, the equipment cannot be used to manufacture any other type of carburetor for Ford or any other auto firm. Thus, the investment in this equipment constitutes an investment in specialized assets.

An independent supplier that has been asked by Ford to make this investment might reason that once it has done so it will become dependent on Ford for business *since Ford is the only possible customer for the output of this equipment*. The supplier perceives the situation as putting Ford in a strong bargaining position and worries that Ford might use the position to squeeze down prices for the carburetors. Given this risk, the supplier declines to make the investment in specialized equipment.

Ford, too, might fear excessive dependence. It might reason that by contracting out production of these carburetors to an independent supplier it might have to rely on that supplier for a vital input. Because of the specialized equipment needed to produce the carburetors, Ford would not be able to switch its orders easily to other suppliers, since they would lack that equipment. Ford perceives the situation as increasing the bargaining power of the supplier and worries that the supplier might use its bargaining strength to demand higher prices.

The condition of ***mutual dependence*** that would be created by the investment in specialized assets makes Ford hesitant to contract out and makes any potential suppliers hesitant to undertake such investments. The real problem here is a lack of trust. Neither Ford nor the supplier completely trusts the other to play fair in this situation. The lack of trust arises from the **risk of holdup**, that is, of being taken advantage of by a trading partner after the investment in specialized assets has been made.[8] Because of this risk, Ford might reason that the only safe way to get the new carburetors is to manufacture them itself.

To generalize from this example, when achieving a competitive advantage requires one company to make investments in specialized assets in order to trade with another, the risk of holdup may serve as a deterrent, and the investment may not take place. In those circumstances, the potential for competitive gains from specialization would be lost. To prevent such loss, companies vertically integrate into adjacent stages in the value chain. This consideration has driven automobile companies to vertically integrate backward into the production of component parts, steel companies to vertically integrate backward into the production of iron, computer companies to vertically integrate backward into chip production, and aluminum companies to vertically integrate backward into bauxite mining. The rationale underlying vertical integration in the aluminum industry is explored in greater detail in Strategy in Action 9.1.

Protecting Product Quality By protecting product quality, vertical integration enables a company to become a differentiated player in its core business. The banana industry illustrates this situation. Historically, a problem facing food companies that import bananas was the variable quality of delivered bananas, which often arrived on the shelves of American stores either too ripe or not ripe enough. To correct this problem, major U.S. food companies such as General Foods have integrated

9.1 STRATEGY *in* ACTION

Specialized Assets and Vertical Integration in the Aluminum Industry

Aluminum refineries are designed to refine bauxite ore and produce aluminum. The metal content and chemical composition of bauxite ore vary from deposit to deposit. Each type of ore requires a specialized refinery—that is, the refinery must be designed for a particular type of ore. Running one type of bauxite through a refinery designed for another type reportedly increases production costs by 20 percent to 100 percent.[9] Thus, the value of an investment in a specialized aluminum refinery and the cost of the output produced by that refinery depend on its receiving the right kind of bauxite ore.

Let us assume that an aluminum company has to decide whether to invest in an aluminum refinery designed to refine a certain type of ore and that this ore is produced only by a bauxite company at a single bauxite mine. Using a different type of ore would raise production costs by 50 percent. The value of the aluminum company's investment depends on the price it must pay the bauxite company for this bauxite. But once the aluminum company has made the investment in a new refinery, what is to stop the bauxite company from raising bauxite prices? The answer is nothing; once it has made the investment the aluminum company is locked into its relationship with its bauxite supplier. The bauxite company can increase bauxite prices secure in the knowledge that as long as the resulting increase in the total production costs of the aluminum company is less than 50 percent, the aluminum company will continue to buy from it. Consequently, once the aluminum company has made the investment, the bauxite company can hold up the aluminum company.

How can the aluminum company reduce the risk of hold up? The answer is by purchasing the bauxite company. If the aluminum company can purchase the bauxite company, or that company's bauxite mine, it need no longer fear that bauxite prices will be increased after the investment in an aluminum refinery has been made. In other words, it makes economic sense for the aluminum company contemplating the investment to engage in vertical integration. By eliminating the risk of holdup, vertical integration makes the specialized investment worthwhile. In practice, it has been argued, these kinds of considerations have driven aluminum companies to pursue vertical integration to such an extent that, according to one study, 91 percent of the total volume of bauxite is transferred within vertically integrated aluminum companies.[10]

backward to gain control over supply sources. Consequently, they have been able to distribute bananas of a standard quality at the optimal time for consumption. Knowing they can rely on the quality of these brands, consumers are willing to pay more for them. Thus, by vertically integrating backward into plantation ownership, the banana companies have built consumer confidence, which enables them to charge a premium price for their product. Similarly, when McDonald's decided to open its first restaurant in Moscow, it found, much to its initial dismay, that in order to serve food and drink indistinguishable from that served in McDonald's restaurants elsewhere, it had to vertically integrate backward and supply its own needs. The quality of Russian-grown potatoes and meat was simply too poor. Thus, to protect the quality of its product, McDonald's set up its own dairy farms, cattle ranches, vegetable plots, and food-processing plant within Russia.

The same kind of considerations can result in forward integration. Ownership of distribution outlets may be necessary if the required standards of after-sales service for complex products are to be maintained. For example, in the 1920s Kodak owned retail outlets for distributing photographic equipment. The company felt that few established retail outlets had the skills necessary to sell and service its photographic equipment. By the 1930s, however, Kodak decided that it no longer needed to own its retail outlets because other retailers had begun to provide satisfactory distribution and service for Kodak products. The company then withdrew from retailing.

Improved Scheduling It is sometimes argued that strategic advantages arise from the easier planning, coordination, and scheduling of adjacent processes made possible in vertically integrated organizations.[11] Such advantages can be particularly important to companies trying to realize the benefits of just-in-time inventory systems, discussed in detail in Chapter 5. For example, in the 1920s Ford profited from the tight coordination and scheduling that is possible with backward vertical integration. Ford integrated backward into steel foundries, iron ore shipping, and iron ore mining. Deliveries at Ford were coordinated to such an extent that iron ore unloaded at Ford's steel foundries on the Great Lakes was turned into engine blocks within twenty-four hours. Thus, Ford substantially lowered its cost structure by eliminating the need to hold excessive inventories.

The enhanced scheduling that vertical integration makes feasible may also enable a company to respond better to sudden changes in demand, or to get its product into the marketplace faster. A situation in the microprocessor industry of the early 1990s illustrates this point. Demand for microprocessors was running at an all-time high, and most microprocessor manufacturing plants were operating at full capacity. At that time, several microprocessor companies that specialized in chip design but contracted out manufacturing found themselves at a strategic disadvantage. For example, in 1991 Chips & Technologies succeeded in designing a clone of Intel's 386 microprocessor. Chips & Technologies sent its clone design to Texas Instruments (TI) to be manufactured, only to find that it had to wait fourteen weeks until TI could schedule time to manufacture that item. In that short span of time, the price for a 386 microprocessor fell from $112 to $50. By the time TI produced the 386 clone for Chips & Technologies, the company had missed the best part of the market. Had Chips & Technologies been vertically integrated into manufacturing, this loss would not have occurred.[12]

Arguments Against Vertical Integration

Vertical integration has its disadvantages. Most important among them are (1) cost disadvantages, (2) disadvantages that arise when technology is changing fast, and (3) disadvantages that arise when demand is unpredictable. These disadvantages imply that the benefits of vertical integration are not always as substantial as they might seem initially.

Cost Disadvantages Although often undertaken to gain a production cost advantage, vertical integration can raise costs if a company becomes committed to purchasing inputs from company-owned suppliers when low-cost external sources of supply exist. For example, during the early 1990s General Motors made 68 percent of the component parts for its vehicles in-house, more than any other major automaker (at Chrysler the figure was 30 percent, and at Toyota 28 percent). That vertical integration caused GM to be the highest-cost producer among the world's major car companies. In 1992, GM was paying $34.60 an hour in United Auto Workers wages and benefits to its employees at company-owned suppliers for work that rivals could get done by independent nonunionized suppliers at half these rates.[13] Thus, vertical integration can be a disadvantage when a company's own sources of supply have higher operating costs than those of independent suppliers.

Company-owned suppliers might have high operating costs compared with independent suppliers because company-owned suppliers know that they can always sell their output to other parts of the company. Not having to compete for orders lessens the incentive to minimize operating costs. Indeed, the managers of the supply operation may be tempted to pass on any cost increases to other parts of the company in the form of higher transfer prices, rather than looking for ways to lower those costs. Thus, the lack of incentive to reduce costs can raise operating costs. The problem may be less serious, however, when the company pursues taper, rather than full, integration, since the need to compete with independent suppliers can produce a downward pressure on the cost structure of company-owned suppliers.

Technological Change When technology is changing fast, vertical integration poses the hazard of tying a company to an obsolescent technology.[14] Consider a radio manufacturer that in the 1950s integrated backward and acquired a manufacturer of vacuum tubes. When in the 1960s transistors replaced vacuum tubes as a major component in radios, this company found itself tied to a technologically obsolescent business. Switching to transistors would have meant writing off its investment in vacuum tubes. Therefore, the company was reluctant to change and instead continued to use vacuum tubes in its radios while its nonintegrated competitors were rapidly switching to the new technology. Since it kept making an outdated product, the company rapidly lost market share. Thus, vertical integration can inhibit a company's ability to change its suppliers or its distribution systems to match the requirements of changing technology.

Demand Uncertainty Vertical integration can also be risky in unstable or unpredictable demand conditions. When demand is stable, higher degrees of vertical integration might be managed with relative ease. Stable demand allows better scheduling and coordination of production flows among different activities. When demand conditions are unstable or unpredictable, achieving close coordination among vertically integrated activities may be difficult.

The problem is to balance capacity among different stages of a process. For example, an auto manufacturer might vertically integrate backward to acquire a supplier of carburetors that has a capacity exactly matching the auto manufacturer's needs. However, if demand for autos subsequently falls, the automaker will find itself locked into a business that is running below capacity. Clearly, this would be uneconomical. The auto manufacturer could avoid this situation by continuing to buy carburetors on the open market rather than making them itself. If demand conditions are unpredictable, taper integration might be somewhat less risky than full integration. When a company obtains only part of its total input requirements from company-owned suppliers, in times of low demand it can keep its in-house suppliers running at full capacity by ordering exclusively from them.

Bureaucratic Costs and the Limits of Vertical Integration

As already noted, although vertical integration can create value, it may also result in substantial costs caused by a lack of incentive on the part of company-owned suppliers to reduce their operating costs, by a possible lack of strategic flexibility in times of changing technology, or by uncertain demand. Together, these costs form a major component of what we refer to as the **bureaucratic costs** of vertical integration. Bureaucratic costs are simply the costs of running an organization. They include the costs that stem from bureaucratic inefficiencies, such as those we have just discussed. Bureaucratic costs place a limit on the amount of vertical integration that can be profitably pursued; it makes sense for a company to vertically integrate only if the value created by such a strategy exceeds the bureaucratic costs associated with expanding the boundaries of the organization to incorporate additional upstream or downstream activities.

Commonsense reasoning suggests that not all vertical integration opportunities have the same potential for value creation. Although vertical integration may initially have a favorable impact, the value created by additional integration into areas more distant from a company's core business is likely to become increasingly marginal. The more marginal the value created by a vertical integration move, the more likely it is that the bureaucratic costs associated with expanding the boundaries of the organization into new activities will outweigh the value created. Once this occurs, a limit to profitable vertical integration has been reached.[15]

It is worth bearing in mind, however, that the pursuit of taper rather than full integration may decrease the bureaucratic costs of vertical integration. The reason is that taper integration creates an incentive for in-house suppliers to reduce their operating costs and increases the company's ability to respond to changing demand conditions. Hence it reduces some of the organizational inefficiencies that raise bureaucratic costs.

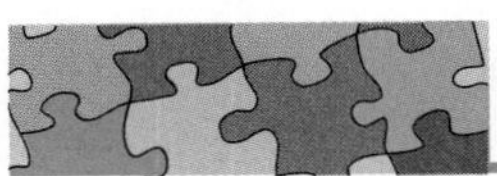

ALTERNATIVES TO VERTICAL INTEGRATION: COOPERATIVE RELATIONSHIPS AND STRATEGIC OUTSOURCING

The disadvantages associated with vertical integration raise the question whether it is possible to reap the benefits of vertical integration without having to bear the associated bureaucratic costs. Can the benefits associated with vertical integration be captured through outsourcing activities to other companies? The answer seems to be a qualified yes. Under certain circumstances, companies can realize the gains linked with vertical integration, without having to bear the bureaucratic costs, if they enter into long-term cooperative relationships with their trading partners. Such long-term relationships are typically referred to as strategic alliances. However, companies will generally be unable to realize the gains associated with vertical integration if they enter into short-term contracts with their trading partners. To see why this is so, we first discuss the problems associated with short-term contracts. Then we look at strategic alliances and long-term contracts as an alternative to vertical integration and discuss how companies can build enduring, long-term relationships with their trading partners.

Short-Term Contracts and Competitive Bidding

A short-term contract is one that lasts for a year or less. Many companies use short-term contracts to structure the purchasing of their inputs or the sale of their outputs. A classic example is the automobile company that uses a **competitive bidding strategy** to negotiate the price for a particular part produced by component suppliers. General Motors for example, often solicits bids from a number of different suppliers for producing a component part and awards a one-year contract to the supplier submitting the lowest bid. At the end of the year, the contract is put out for competitive bid again. Thus, there is no guarantee that the company that won the contract one year will hold on to it the following year.

The benefit of this strategy is that it forces suppliers to keep down their prices. But GM's lack of long-term commitment to individual suppliers may make them very hesitant to undertake the type of investments in specialized assets that may be needed to improve the design or quality of component parts or to improve scheduling between GM and its suppliers. Indeed, with no guarantee that it would remain a GM supplier the following year, the supplier may refuse to undertake investments in specialized assets. GM then may have to vertically integrate backward in order to realize the gains associated with specialization.

In other words, the strategy of short-term contracting and competitive bidding, *because it signals a lack of long-term commitment to its suppliers on the part of a company*, will make it very difficult for that company to realize the gains associated with vertical integration. This is not a problem when there is minimal need for close cooperation between the company and its suppliers to facilitate investments in specialized assets, improve scheduling, or improve product quality. In such cases competitive bidding may be optimal. However, when this need is significant, a competitive bidding strategy can be a serious drawback.

Interestingly enough, there are indications that in the past GM, by adopting a competitive bidding stance with regard to its suppliers, placed itself at a competitive disadvantage. In 1992, the company instructed its part suppliers to cut their prices by 10 percent, regardless of prior pricing agreements. In effect, GM tore up existing contracts and tried to force through its policy by threatening to weed out suppliers that did not agree to the price reduction. Although such action may yield short-term benefits for companies, there is a long-term cost to be borne: the loss of trust and the hostility created between the company and its suppliers. According to press reports, several suppliers claimed that they cut back on research for future GM parts. They also indicated that they would first impart new ideas to Chrysler (now DaimlerChrysler) or Ford, both of which took a more cooperative approach to forging long-term relationships with suppliers.[16]

Strategic Alliances and Long-Term Contracting

Long-term contracts are long-term cooperative relationships between two companies. Such agreements are often referred to in the popular press as **strategic alliances**. Typically in these arrangements, one company agrees to supply the other, and the other company agrees to continue purchasing from that supplier; both make a commitment to jointly seek ways of lowering the costs or raising the quality of inputs into the downstream company's value creation process. If it is achieved, such a stable long-term relationship lets the participating companies share the value that might be created by vertical integration while avoiding many of the bureaucratic costs linked to ownership of an adjacent stage in the raw-material-to-consumer production chain. Thus, long-term contracts can substitute for vertical integration.

The cooperative relationships that many Japanese auto companies have with their component-parts suppliers (the *keiretsu* system) exemplify successful long-term contracting. These relationships often go back decades. Together, the auto companies and their suppliers work out ways to increase value added—for instance, by implementing just-in-time inventory systems or by cooperating on component-part designs to improve quality and lower assembly costs. As part of this process, the suppliers make substantial investments in specialized assets in order to better serve the needs of the auto companies. Thus, the Japanese automakers have been able to capture many of the benefits of vertical integration without having to bear the associated bureaucratic costs. The component-parts suppliers also benefit from these relationships, for they grow with the company they supply and share in its success.[17]

In contrast to their Japanese counterparts, U.S. auto companies historically tended to pursue formal vertical integration.[18] According to several studies, the increased bureaucratic costs of managing extensive vertical integration helped place GM and Ford at a disadvantage relative to their Japanese competition.[19] Moreover, when U.S. auto companies decided not to integrate vertically, they did not necessarily enter into cooperative long-term relationships with independent component suppliers. Instead, they tended to use their powerful position to pursue an aggressive competitive bidding strategy, playing off component suppliers against each other.[20] This mindset seems to be changing. Strategy in Action 9.2 details how DaimlerChrysler has tried to build long-term cooperative relationships with suppliers.

Building Long-Term Cooperative Relationships

Given the lack of trust and the fear of holdup that arises when one company has to invest in specialized asset in order to trade with another, how can companies achieve stable long-term strategic alliances with each other? How have companies such as Toyota managed to develop enduring relationships with their suppliers?

Companies can take some specific steps to ensure that a long-term cooperative relationship will work and to lessen the chances of a partner reneging on an agreement. One of those steps is for the company making investments in specialized assets to demand a hostage from its partner. Another is to establish a credible commitment on both sides to build a trusting long-term relationship.[22]

Hostage Taking Hostage taking is a means of guaranteeing that a partner will keep its side of the bargain. The cooperative relationship between Boeing and Northrop illustrates this type of situation. Northrop is a major subcontractor for Boeing's commercial airline division, providing many component parts for the 747 and 767 aircraft. To serve Boeing's special needs, Northrop has had to make substantial investments in specialized assets. In theory, because of the sunk costs associated with such investments, Northrop is dependent on Boeing, and Boeing is in a position to renege on previous agreements and use the threat to switch orders to other suppliers as a way of driving down prices. However, in practice Boeing is unlikely to do so since the company is also a major supplier to Northrop's defense division, providing many parts for the Stealth bomber. Boeing has had to make substantial investments in specialized assets in order to serve Northrop's needs. Thus, the companies are *mutually dependent*. Boeing, therefore, is unlikely to renege on any pricing agreements with Northrop, since it knows that Northrop could respond in kind. Each company holds a hostage that can be used as insurance against the other company's unilateral reneging on prior pricing agreements.

Credible Commitments A credible commitment is a believable commitment to support the development of a long-term relationship between companies. To understand the concept of credibility in this context, consider the following relation-

9.2 STRATEGY *in* ACTION

DaimlerChrysler's U.S. Keiretsu

Like many long established companies, Chrysler (now DaimlerChrysler) for most of its history managed suppliers through a competitive bidding process, in which suppliers were selected on the basis of their ability to supply components at the lowest possible cost to Chrysler. A supplier's track record on performance and quality was relatively unimportant in this process. Contracts were renegotiated every two years with little or no commitment from Chrysler to continue to do business with a particular supplier. As a result, the typical relationship between Chrysler and its suppliers was characterized by mutual distrust, suspicion, and the suppliers' reluctance to invest too much in that relationship.

Since the early 1990s, however, Chrysler has systematically reorganized its dealings with suppliers in an attempt to build stable long-term relationships. The aim of this new approach has been to try and get suppliers to help Chrysler develop new products and improve its production processes. To encourage suppliers to cooperate and make investments that are specific to Chrysler's needs, the company has moved sharply away from its old adversarial approach. The average contract with suppliers has been lengthened from two years to over four and a half years. Furthermore, Chrysler has given 90 percent of its suppliers oral commitments that business will be extended for at least the life of a model, if not beyond that. The company has also committed itself to share with suppliers the benefits of any process improvements they might suggest. The basic thinking behind offering suppliers such credible commitments is to align incentives between Chrysler and its suppliers—to create a sense of shared destiny, which would encourage mutual cooperation to increase the size of the financial pie available to both.

The fruits of this new approach are beginning to appear. By involving suppliers early on in product development and giving them greater responsibility for design and manufacturing, DaimlerChrysler has substantially compressed its product development cycle and also taken a lot of cost out of the product development effort. DaimlerChrysler's U.S. operation has reduced the time it takes to develop a new vehicle from 234 weeks during the mid 1980s to about 160 weeks today. The total cost of developing a new vehicle has also fallen by 20 percent to 40 percent, depending on the model. With development costs in the automobile industry running between $1 and $2 billion, that translates into huge financial savings—often the direct result of engineering improvements suggested by suppliers, or of improved coordination between the company and suppliers in the design process. To facilitate this process, the number of resident engineers from suppliers who work side by side with DaimlerChrysler engineers in cross-company design teams increased from 30 in 1989 to more than 300 by 1996.

Beginning in 1990, Chrysler also implemented a program known internally as the Supplier Cost Reduction Effort (or SCORE). SCORE focuses on cooperation between DaimlerChrysler and suppliers to identify opportunities for process improvements. In its first two years of operation, SCORE generated 875 ideas from suppliers, which were worth $170.8 million in annual savings to suppliers. In 1994, suppliers submitted 3,786 ideas, which produced $504 million in annual savings. By December 1995, Chrysler had implemented a total of 5,300 ideas that have generated more than $1.7 billion in annual savings. One supplier alone, Magna International, had submitted 214 proposals by December 1995; Chrysler adopted 129 of them, for a total cost saving of $75.5 million. Many of the ideas have a relatively small financial impact in themselves—for example, a Magna suggestion to change the type of decorative wood grain used on minivans saved $0.5 million per year. But the cumulative impact of thousands of such ideas has been very significant on DaimlerChrysler's bottom line.[21]

ship between General Electric and IBM. GE is one of the major suppliers of advanced semiconductor chips to IBM, and many of the chips are customized to IBM's own requirements. To meet IBM's specific needs, GE has had to make substantial investments in specialized assets that have little other value. As a consequence, GE is dependent on IBM and faces the risk that IBM will take advantage of this dependence to demand lower prices. Theoretically, IBM could back up its demand with the threat to switch to another supplier. However, GE reduced this risk by having IBM enter into a contractual agreement that committed IBM to purchase chips from GE for a ten-year period. In addition, IBM agreed to share in the costs of developing the customized chips, thereby reducing GE's investments in specialized assets. Thus, by publicly committing itself to a long-term contract and by putting some money into the development of the customized chips, IBM has essentially made a *credible commitment* to continue purchasing those chips from GE.

Maintaining Market Discipline A company that has entered into a long-term relationship can become too dependent on an inefficient partner. Since it does not have to compete with other organizations in the marketplace for the company's business, the partner may lack the incentive to be cost efficient. Consequently, a company entering into a cooperative long-term relationship must be able to apply some kind of market discipline to its partner.

The company holds two strong cards. First, even long-term contracts are periodically renegotiated, generally every four to five years. Thus, a partner knows that if it fails to live up to its commitments, the company may refuse to renew the contract. Second, some companies engaged in long-term relationships with suppliers use a **parallel sourcing policy**—that is, they enter into a long-term contract with two suppliers for the same part (as is the practice at Toyota, for example).[23] This arrangement gives the company a hedge against a defiant partner, for each supplier knows that if it fails to comply with the agreement, the company can switch all its business to the other. This threat is rarely made explicit, since that would be against the spirit of building a cooperative long-term relationship. But the mere awareness of parallel sourcing serves to inject an element of market discipline into the relationship, signaling to suppliers that if the need arises, they can be replaced at short notice.

Summary By establishing credible commitments or by taking hostages, companies may be able to use long-term contracts to realize much of the value associated with vertical integration, yet not have to bear the bureaucratic costs of formal vertical integration. As a general point, note that the growing importance of just-in-time inventory systems as a way of reducing costs and enhancing quality is increasing the pressure on companies to enter into long-term agreements in a wide range of industries. These agreements thus might become much more popular in the future. However, when such agreements cannot be reached, formal vertical integration may be called for.

Strategic Outsourcing and the Virtual Corporation

The opposite of vertical integration is **outsourcing** value creation activities to subcontractors. In recent years, there has been a clear move among many enterprises to outsource noncore activities.[24] This process typically begins with a company identifying those value creation activities that form the basis of its competitive advantage (its distinctive or core competencies). The idea is to keep performing these core value creation activities within the company. The remaining activities are then reviewed to see whether they can be performed more effectively and efficiently by independent suppliers. If they can, these activities are outsourced to those suppliers. The relationships between the company and the suppliers are then often structured as long-term contractual relationships, although in some instances it may make sense to manage relationships on the basis of competitive bidding. The term **virtual corporation** has been coined to describe companies that have pursued extensive strategic outsourcing.[25]

In recent years, Xerox has been relying heavily on strategic outsourcing. The company has determined that its distinctive competencies lie in the design and manufacture of photocopying systems. To reduce the cost of performing noncore value creation activities, Xerox has outsourced the responsibility for performing many of them to other companies. For example, Xerox has a $3.2 billion contract with Electronic Data Systems (EDS) under which EDS runs all Xerox's internal computer and telecommunications networks. As part of this relationship, 1,700 Xerox employees have been transferred to EDS. Since the relationship involves substantial investments in specialized assets on the part of EDS, Xerox has structured it as a long-term cooperative alliance.[26]

To use another example, NIKE, the world's largest manufacturer of athletic shoes, has outsourced all its manufacturing operations to Asian partners, while keeping its core product design and marketing capabilities in-house.

Strategic outsourcing offers several advantages.[27] First, by outsourcing a noncore activity to a supplier that is more efficient at performing that particular activity, the company may be able to reduce its own cost structure. Second, by outsourcing a noncore value creation activity to a supplier that has a distinctive competency in that particular activity, the company may also be able to better differentiate its final product. For example, Cincinnati Bell has developed a distinctive competency in the customer care function (customer care includes activating accounts, billing customers, and dealing with customer inquiries). Accordingly, several other telephone companies, including AT&T Wireless and MCI Long Distance, outsource their customer care function to Cincinnati Bell. Both companies believe that Cincinnati Bell can provide a better customer care service than they can. Thus, outsourcing helps AT&T Wireless and MCI Long Distance to better differentiate their service offering. A third advantage of strategic outsourcing is that it enables the company to concentrate scarce human, financial, and physical resources on further strengthening its core or distinctive competencies. Thus, AT&T Wireless can devote all its energies to building wireless networks, secure in the knowledge that Cincinnati Bell can look after the customer care functions. Finally, it has been argued that strategic outsourcing enables a company to be more flexible and responsive to changing market conditions. The belief is that, unencumbered by commitments to internal suppliers, a company can switch more easily between providers of noncore value creation activities in response to changing market conditions than can a comparable company that undertakes those activities itself.

The disadvantages of strategic outsourcing need to be recognized as well. By outsourcing an activity, a company loses both the ability to learn from that activity and the opportunity to transform it into a distinctive competency. Thus, although outsourcing customer care activities to Cincinnati Bell may make sense right now for AT&T Wireless, one potential problem with this strategy is that AT&T Wireless will fail to build a valuable internal competency in customer care. Ultimately, there is a risk that this lack may place AT&T Wireless at a competitive disadvantage, in regard to wireless providers that have such a competency, particularly if customer care becomes an important feature of competition in the marketplace. A further drawback of outsourcing is that the company may become too dependent on a particular supplier. In the long run, this may hurt the company if the performance of that supplier starts to deteriorate, or if the supplier starts to use its power to demand higher prices from the company. Another concern is that in its enthusiasm for strategic outsourcing, a company might go too far and outsource value creation activities that are central to the maintenance of its competitive advantage. By doing so, the company might well lose control over the future development of a competency, and as a result its performance might ultimately decline. None of this is meant to imply that strategic outsourcing should not be pursued, but it does indicate that managers should carefully weigh the pros and cons of the strategy before pursuing it.

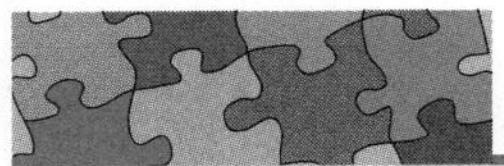

DIVERSIFICATION

The third major option for a company when it is choosing business areas to compete in is diversification. There are two main types of diversification: related diversification and unrelated diversification. **Related diversification** is diversification into a new business activity that is linked to a company's existing business activity, or activities, by commonality between one or more components of each activity's value chain. Normally, these linkages are based on manufacturing, marketing, or technological commonalities. The diversification of Philip Morris into the brewing industry with the acquisition of Miller Brewing is an example of related diversification because there are marketing commonalities between the brewing and tobacco business (both are consumer product businesses in which competitive success depends on brand-positioning skills). **Unrelated diversification** is diversification into a new business area, which has no obvious connection with any of the company's existing areas.

In this section, we first consider how diversification can create value for a company, and then we examine some reasons why so much diversification apparently dissipates rather than creates value. We also take into account the bureaucratic costs of diversification. Finally, we discuss some of the factors that determine the choice between the strategies of related and unrelated diversification.

Creating Value Through Diversification

Most companies first consider diversification when they are generating financial resources *in excess* of those necessary to maintain a competitive advantage in their original, or core, business.[28] The question they must tackle is how to invest the excess resources in order to create value. The diversified company can create value in three main ways: (1) through superior internal governance, (2) by transferring competencies among businesses, and (3) by realizing economies of scope.

Superior Internal Governance The term ***internal governance*** refers to the manner in which the top executives of a company manage (or "govern") subunits and individuals within the organization. In the context of a diversified company, governance has to do with the effectiveness of senior managers in managing businesses. Diversification can create value when the senior executives of a company manage the different business units within the organization so well that they perform better than they would if they were independent companies.[29] That is not easy to accomplish. However, certain senior executives seem to have developed a skill for managing businesses and pushing the heads of those business units to achieve superior performance. Jack Welch at General Electric, Bill Gates and Steve Balmer at Microsoft, and Dennis Kozlowski at Tyco International stand out as examples. (See Strategy in Action 9.3 for details of Kozlowski at Tyco.)

An examination of companies that succeed at creating value through superior internal governance reveals a number of shared features. First, the company's different business units tend to be placed into self-contained divisions. For example, Tyco has different divisions for its disposable medical products, security systems, and electronic components businesses. Second, these divisions tend to be managed by senior executives in a very decentralized fashion. The executives do not get involved in the day-to-day operations of such divisions; instead, they set challenging financial goals for each division, probe the general managers of each division about their strategy for attaining these goals, monitor divisional performance, and hold the general managers accountable for that performance. Third, these internal monitoring and control mechanisms are linked with progressive incentive pay systems, which reward divisional personnel for attaining or surpassing performance goals. Although this strategy sounds like a relatively easy one to pursue, in practice it seems to require very good senior executives to carry it through.

A variant of this approach might be characterized as an **acquisition and restructuring** strategy, which is based on the presumption that a company with superior internal governance systems can create value by acquiring inefficient and poorly managed enterprises and improving their efficiency. This strategy can be considered diversification because the acquired company does not have to be in the same industry as the acquiring company.

The efficiency of the acquired company can be improved by various means. First of all, the acquiring company usually replaces the top management team of the acquired company with a more aggressive top management team. Then, the new top management team is prompted to sell off any unproductive assets, such as executive jets and elaborate corporate headquarters, and to reduce staffing levels. It is also encouraged to intervene in the running of the acquired businesses to seek out ways of improving their efficiency, quality, innovativeness, and customer responsiveness. Furthermore, to motivate the new top management team and other employees of the acquired unit to undertake such actions, increases in their pay may be linked to improvement in the unit's performance. In addition, the acquiring company often establishes performance goals for the acquired company that cannot be met without significant improvements in operating efficiency. It also makes the new top management aware that failure to achieve performance improvements consistent with these goals within a given amount of time will probably result in their losing their jobs. This system of rewards and punishments established by the acquiring company gives the new managers of the acquired enterprise every incentive to look for ways of improving the efficiency of the unit under their charge. Tyco International, discussed in Strategy in Action 9.3, exemplifies this approach.

Transferring Competencies Companies that base their diversification strategy on transferring competencies seek out new businesses related to their existing

9.3 STRATEGY *in* ACTION

Tyco International

Tyco International is a diversified U.S. conglomerate with operations in a broad range of industries, including medical supplies, electronic security and electrical components, flow control products, fire suppression and detection equipment, and environmental services. Between 1992 and 1998, Tyco's revenues grew at an annual rate of 26 percent, increasing from $3.6 billion to $12.3 billion. During that period, the company's profits grew even faster, expanding by an average of 52 percent every year—from $95.3 million to $1.2 billion. The key to Tyco's revenue growth has been a series of major acquisitions, including those of U.S. Surgical, a medical supplies company, and AMP, the global leader in electronic connectors. The key to the company's profit growth has been the management of the existing and acquired businesses in a way that improves their profitability beyond what they would generate as independent companies. The man who deserves most of the credit for this performance is Dennis Kozlowski, the company's CEO, whom many supporters compare with General Electric's legendary CEO, Jack Welch.

Kozlowski has a very clear methodology for managing existing and acquired businesses. He keeps Tyco very decentralized. Headquarters consists of fewer than seventy employees, most of whom are engaged in companywide functions such as taxation, legal services and investor relations. Each operating division is a self-contained and operationally autonomous entity. The heads of Tyco's divisions are to be found where the operations are located. Perks for senior managers, such as first-class air travel, country club memberships, extensive severance packages, and the like, are an anathema. Reporting requirements are minimal and limited to regular reporting of key financial and strategic indicators. Most of the conversations between Kozlowski and the general managers of operating divisions are unstructured one-on-one debates about the strategy that the division is pursuing. Kozlowski's goal in these debates is to test the thinking of the managers—and to push them to think through strategic decisions in a thorough manner.

Kozlowski has married this decentralized structure with a very performance-oriented set of incentive systems. No bonuses are paid out to anyone at Tyco unless annual net income growth exceeds 15 percent. However, bonus payouts ramp up quickly for each increment above that minimum and are unlimited for general managers. Other managers can also receive bonuses that are multiples of their salary. Supervisors down at the plant level get cash or stock option grants that can be worth as much as 40 percent of their salary. Even hourly factory workers share in the bonus system, receiving two to three weeks of extra pay a year in bonuses if their unit exceeds performance targets. To make sure that people don't engage in game playing to hit or exceed their performance targets, Kozlowski does check profit contribution against cash flow to ascertain that managers are not fiddling with accounting concepts such as asset write-downs, inventories, or receivables to make their numbers look better.

In Kozlowski's view, combining decentralization with progressive incentives and strategic probing on the part of top management makes for a very liberating and transforming system which has enabled Tyco to unlock much of the value in its acquisitions. The system encourages employees to control costs and look for ways to grow revenues. As a result, operating margins have soared at many newly acquired enterprises. At the security company ADT, for example, which Tyco acquired in 1996, operating margins increased from 12 percent to 22 percent in just two years under the Tyco banner. At AMP, acquired in 1998, the goal is to increase operating margins from 9 percent to 18 percent in just two years.[30]

business by one or more value creation functions—for example, manufacturing, marketing, materials management, and research and development. They may want to create value by drawing on distinctive skills in one or more of their existing value creation functions in order to improve the competitive position of the new business. Alternatively, they may acquire a company in a different business area in the belief that some of the skills of the acquired company can improve the efficiency of their existing value creation activities. If successful, such competency transfers can lower the costs of value creation in one or more of a company's diversified businesses or enable one or more of these businesses to perform their value creation functions in a way that leads to differentiation and a premium price. The transfer of marketing skills by Philip Morris to Miller Brewing, discussed earlier, is perhaps one of the classic examples of how value *can* be created by competency transfers. Drawing on its marketing and brand-positioning skills, Philip Morris pioneered the introduction of Miller Lite, the product that redefined the brewing industry and moved Miller from number six to number two in the market.

For such a strategy to work, the competencies being transferred must involve activities that are important for establishing a competitive advantage. All too often companies assume that any commonality is sufficient for creating value. The acquisition of Hughes Aircraft by General Motors, made simply because autos and auto manufacturing were going electronic and Hughes was an electronics concern, demonstrates the folly of overestimating the commonalities among businesses. To date, the acquisition has failed to realize any of the anticipated gains for GM, whose competitive position has not improved.

In the technology arena, there is a group of companies that have made leveraging competencies a way of life. They include 3M, Hewlett-Packard, Canon, and Thermo Electron (which is profiled in the Closing Case). Each of these companies has developed certain skill sets (competencies), which they then have leveraged to produce new products in diversified areas. For example, Canon began as a manufacturer of cameras. To succeed in this market, Canon had to develop skills in precision mechanics, optics, and microelectronics. Subsequently, Canon has drawn on these skill sets to produce a wide range of products that address diverse markets, including fax machines, laser jet printers, scanners, and copiers. The value here arises from applying skills developed to support one business opportunity and applying them to another opportunity.[31]

Economies of Scope The sharing of resources such as manufacturing facilities, distribution channels, advertising campaigns, and R&D costs by two or more business units gives rise to **economies of scope**. Each business unit that shares resources has to invest less in the shared functions.[32] For example, the costs of General Electric's advertising, sales, and service activities in major appliances are low because they are spread over a wide range of products. Similarly, one of the motives behind the 1998 merger of Citicorp and Travelers to form Citigroup was that the merger would let Travelers sell its insurance products and financial services through Citicorp's retail banking network. Put differently, the merger allows the expanded group to better utilize an existing asset—its retail banking network.

It is important to understand that economies of scope are related to economies of scale. For example, by producing the components for the assembly operations of two distinct businesses, a component-manufacturing plant may be able to operate at greater capacity, thereby realizing *economies of scale* in addition to economies of scope. Thus, a diversification strategy based on economies of scope can help a company attain a low-cost position in each of the businesses in which it operates. Diversification to realize economies of scope can therefore be a valid way of supporting the generic business-level strategy of cost leadership.

However, like competency transfers, diversification to realize economies of scope is possible only when there are significant commonalities between one or more of the value creation functions of a company's existing and new activities.

Moreover, managers need to be aware that the bureaucratic costs of coordination necessary to achieve economies of scope within a company often outweigh the value that can be created by such a strategy.[33] Consequently, the strategy should be pursued only when sharing is likely to generate a *significant* competitive advantage in one or more of a company's business units.

Procter & Gamble's disposable diaper and paper towel businesses offer one of the best examples of the successful realization of economies of scope. These businesses share the costs of procuring certain raw materials (such as paper) and developing the technology for new products and processes. In addition, a joint sales force sells both products to supermarket buyers, and both products are shipped by means of the same distribution system. This resource sharing has given both business units a cost advantage that has enabled them to undercut their less diversified competitors.[34]

Bureaucratic Costs and the Limits of Diversification

While diversification can create value for a company, it often ends up doing just the opposite. For example, in a study that looked at the diversification of thirty-three major U.S. corporations over a thirty-five-year time period, Michael Porter observed that the track record of corporate diversification has been dismal.[35] Porter found that most of the companies had divested many more diversified acquisitions than they had kept. He concluded that the corporate diversification strategies of most companies have dissipated value instead of creating it. More generally, a large number of academic studies support the conclusion that *extensive* diversification tends to depress rather than improve company profitability.[36]

One reason for the failure of diversification to achieve its aims is that all too often the *bureaucratic costs* of diversification exceed the value created by the strategy. The level of bureaucratic costs in a diversified organization is a function of two factors: (1) the number of businesses in a company's portfolio and (2) the extent of coordination required between the different businesses of the company in order to realize value from a diversification strategy.

Number of Businesses The greater the number of businesses in a company's portfolio, the more difficult it is for corporate management to remain informed about the complexities of each business. Management simply does not have the time to process all the information needed to assess the strategic plan of each business unit objectively. This problem began to occur at General Electric in the 1970s. As the then CEO Reg Jones commented,

> I tried to review each plan in great detail. This effort took untold hours and placed a tremendous burden on the corporate executive office. After a while I began to realize that no matter how hard we would work, we could not achieve the necessary in-depth understanding of the 40-odd business unit plans.[37]

The information overload in extensively diversified companies may lead corporate-level management to base important resource allocation decisions on only the most superficial analysis of each business unit's competitive position. Thus, for example, a promising business unit may be starved of investment funds, while other business units receive far more cash than they can profitably reinvest in their operations. Furthermore, the lack of familiarity with operating affairs on the part of corporate-level management increases the chances that business-level managers might deceive corporate-level managers. For instance, business-unit managers might blame poor performance on difficult competitive conditions, even when it is the consequence of poor management. Thus, information overload can result in substantial inefficiencies within extensively diversified companies that cancel out the value created by diversification. These inefficiencies include the suboptimal allocation of cash resources within the company and a failure by corporate management to successfully encourage and reward aggressive profit-seeking behavior by business-unit managers.

The inefficiencies arising from information overload can be viewed as one component of the bureaucratic costs of extensive diversification. Of course, these costs can be reduced to manageable proportions if a company limits the scope of its diversification. Indeed, a desire to decrease these costs lay behind the 1990s and 1980s divestments and strategic concentration strategies of highly diversified conglomerates created in the 1960s and 1970s, such as Esmark, General Electric, ITT, Textron, Tenneco, and United Technologies. For example, under the leadership of Jack Welch, GE switched its emphasis from forty main business units to sixteen contained within three clearly defined sectors.

Coordination Among Businesses The coordination required to realize value from a diversification strategy based on competency transfers or economies of scope can also be a source of bureaucratic costs. Both the transfer of distinctive competencies and the achievement of economies of scope demand close coordination among business units. The bureaucratic mechanisms needed for this coordination give rise to bureaucratic costs.

A more serious matter, however, is that substantial bureaucratic costs can result from a firm's inability to identify the unique profit contribution of a business unit that is sharing resources with another unit in an attempt to realize economies of scope. Consider a company that has two business units—one producing household products (such as liquid soap and laundry detergent) and another producing packaged food products. The products of both units are sold through supermarkets. In order to lower the costs of value creation, the parent company decides to pool the marketing and sales functions of each business unit. Pooling allows the business units to share the costs of a sales force (one sales force can sell the products of both divisions) and gain cost economies from using the same physical distribution system. The organizational structure required to achieve this might be similar to that illustrated in Figure 9.4. The company is organized into three divisions: a household products division, a food products division, and a marketing division.

Although such an arrangement may create value, it can also give rise to substantial control problems and hence bureaucratic costs. For example, if the performance of the household products business begins to slip, identifying who is to be held accountable—the management of the household products division or the management of the marketing division—may prove difficult. Indeed, each may blame the other for poor performance: The management of the household products division might blame the marketing policies of the marketing division, and the management of the marketing division might blame the poor quality and high costs of products produced by the household products division. Although this kind of problem can be resolved if corporate management directly audits the affairs of both divisions, doing so is costly in terms of both the time and the effort that corporate management must expend.

FIGURE 9.4

Structure of a Company Sharing Marketing Between Two Business Units

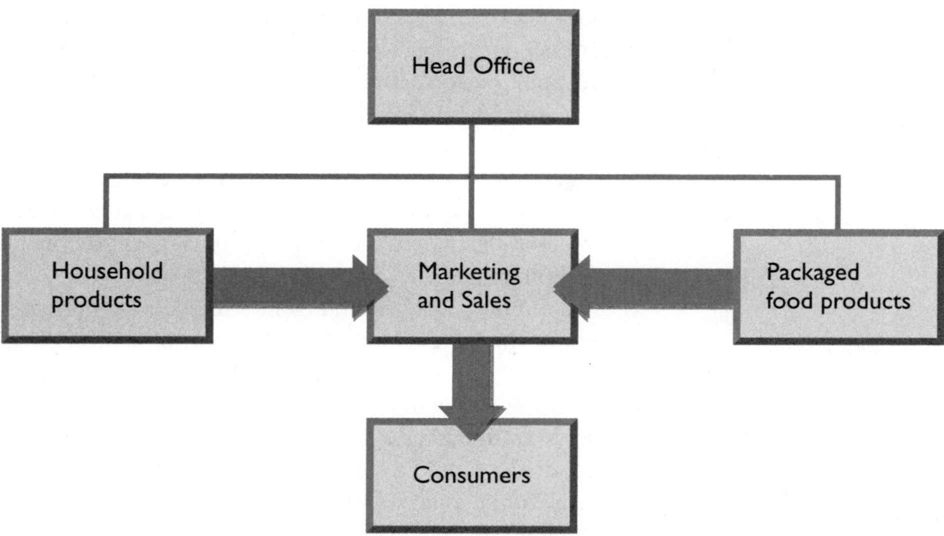

Now imagine the situation within a company that is trying to create value by sharing marketing, manufacturing, and R&D resources across ten businesses rather than just two. Clearly, the accountability problem could become far more severe in such a company. Indeed, the problem might become so acute that the effort involved in trying to tie down accountability might create a serious information overload for corporate management. When this occurs, corporate management effectively loses control of the company. If accountability cannot be sorted out, the consequences may include poor resource allocation decisions, a generally high level of organizational slack, and an inability by corporate management to encourage and reward aggressive profit-seeking behavior by business-unit managers. All these inefficiencies can be considered part of the bureaucratic costs of diversification to realize economies of scope.

Limits of Diversification Thus, although diversification can create value for a company, it inevitably involves bureaucratic costs. As in the case of vertical integration, the existence of bureaucratic costs places a limit on the amount of diversification that can be profitably pursued. It makes sense for a company to diversify only as long as the value created by such a strategy exceeds the bureaucratic costs associated with expanding the boundaries of the organization to incorporate additional business activities.

It bears repeating that the greater the number of business units within a company and the greater the need for coordination among those business units, the larger the bureaucratic costs are likely to be. Hence a company that has twenty businesses, all of which are trying to share resources, incurs much larger bureaucratic costs than a company that has ten businesses, none of which is trying to share resources. The implications of this relationship are quite straightforward. Specifically, the greater the number of businesses already in a company's portfolio and the greater the need for coordination among those businesses, the more probable it is that the value created by a diversification move will be outweighed by the resulting increase in bureaucratic costs. Once this occurs, a profitable limit to the diversified scope of the enterprise will be reached. However, many companies continue to diversify past this limit, and their performance declines. To solve this problem, a company must reduce the scope of the enterprise through divestments. Strategy in Action 9.4 discusses a company—ICI—that overdiversified and subsequently had to divest itself of previously acquired businesses. In Chapter 10, we look at a number of other companies that have made the same mistake.

9.4 **STRATEGY in ACTION**

Diversification and Divestments at ICI

Formed in 1926 by the merger of a number of chemical concerns, Britain's Imperial Chemical Industries (ICI) has always been a diverse company, but in the 1980s ICI embarked on a new wave of diversified acquisitions aimed at expanding its presence in a broad range of high-value-added specialty chemicals operations. By the early 1980s, ICI was already involved in such markets as bulk chemicals, explosives, fertilizers, paints, commodity plastics, and pharmaceuticals. In 1985, it added to this portfolio the advanced plastics materials operations of the U.S. firm Beatrice Company, purchased for $750 million. In 1986, it bought Glidden, another American company, for $580 million. This acquisition made ICI the world's biggest paint manufacturer, and it was followed in 1987 by the acquisition of American Stauffer Chemical for $1.7 billion. ICI retained American Stauffer's specialty agrochemical business but sold off the rest. By the end of the 1980s, ICI was Britain's largest manufacturing enterprise and the world's fourth largest chemical company.

However, expanding the scope of ICI's business activities did little for the company's bottom line. In 1990, ICI saw its pretax profits drop by 36 percent to $1.7 billion on sales of $23 billion. Meanwhile, ICI's specialty chemicals operations did not do as well as the company had hoped. Paints and other specialty products had a profit margin of only 2.8 percent that year, compared with a margin of 5.7 percent in the company's more traditional bulk chemical operations.

In May 1991, these financial problems attracted the attention of Hanson PLC, one of Britain's best known corporate raiders. Hanson has thrived by purchasing conglomerates such as ICI and then breaking them up and selling the parts off to other companies, typically for a substantial profit. Hanson purchased a 4.1 percent stake in ICI and threatened to make a full takeover bid. Although the full bid never materialized, and Hanson subsequently sold off its stake for a handsome profit, the threatened takeover started a debate in ICI as to the rationale behind its diversification strategy.

After much consideration, ICI's top management came to two main conclusions. First, although many of ICI's businesses were linked in some way to the chemical industry, there were far fewer synergies between its operations than management had initially thought. In the final analysis, ICI's top management concluded that there was little commonality between bulk chemicals and pharmaceuticals, between plastics and paint, and between explosives and advanced materials. Second, the company had become so diverse that top management found itself spread too thinly over too many different businesses. The company was simply unable to give the kind of top management attention and financial resources that many of its businesses required. In other words, the value created by the strategy of diversification was questionable, while the bureaucratic costs of managing a large and complex diversified entity were substantial. Thus, diversification at ICI dissipated rather than created value.

In 1992, ICI's top management decided to break the company into its constituent parts. The first stage in this process was completed in March 1993, when ICI was split into two parts. One part, which kept the name ICI, consists of industrial chemicals, paints, and explosives. According to the company, bits of this operation will probably be sold off in the future. The other part, which is now called Zeneca, has taken ICI's drugs, pesticides, seeds, and specialty chemicals businesses. ICI believes that the two companies will do better on their own than they did as part of a larger enterprise.[38]

Diversification That Dissipates Value

The failue of so much diversification to create value is also due to the fact that many companies diversify for the wrong reasons. This is particularly true of diversification to pool risks or to achieve greater growth, both of which are often given by company managers as reasons for diversification.

In the case of risk pooling, the benefits are said to come from merging imperfectly correlated income streams to create a more stable income stream. An example of risk pooling might be USX's diversification into the oil and gas industry in an effort to offset the adverse effects of cyclical downturns in the steel industry. According to advocates of risk pooling, the more stable income stream reduces the risk of bankruptcy and is in the best interests of the company's stockholders.

However, this simple argument ignores two facts. First, stockholders can easily eliminate the risks inherent in holding an individual stock by diversifying their own portfolios, and they can do so at a much lower cost than the company can. Thus, far from being in the best interests of stockholders, attempts to pool risks through diversification represent an unproductive use of resources. Second, research on this topic suggests that corporate diversification is not a very effective way to pool risks.[39] The business cycles of different industries are not easy to predict and in any case tend to be less important in terms of their impact on profits than a general economic downturn, which hits all industries simultaneously.

As for diversification to achieve greater growth, it is not a coherent strategy because growth on its own does not create value. Growth should be the *by-product*, not the objective, of a diversification strategy. However, companies sometimes diversify for reasons of growth alone, rather than to gain any well-thought-out strategic advantage. ITT under the leadership of Harold Geneen took this path. Geneen turned ITT from an international telecommunications company into a broadly based conglomerate comprising more than 100 separate businesses, with interests in such diverse areas as baking, car rental, defense electronics, fire hydrants, insurance, hotels, paper products, and telecommunications. The strategy had more to do with Geneen's desire to build an empire than with maximizing the company's value. After Geneen's departure in 1979, ITT's management divested many of the businesses acquired under his leadership in order to concentrate on insurance and financial services. This process reached its logical conclusion in 1996, when the remaining three businesses of ITT were spun off as independent entities.

Related Versus Unrelated Diversification

One issue a company must resolve is whether to diversify into totally new businesses or businesses related to its existing business by value-chain commonalities. The distinction is between related diversification and unrelated diversification. By definition, a related company can create value by resource sharing and by transferring competencies between businesses. It can also carry out some restructuring. In contrast, since there are no commonalities between the value chains of unrelated businesses, an unrelated company cannot create value by sharing resources or transferring competencies. Unrelated diversifiers can create value only by pursuing an acquisition and restructuring strategy.

Since related diversification can create value in more ways than unrelated diversification, one might think that related diversification should be the preferred strategy. In addition, related diversification is normally perceived as involving fewer risks because the company is moving into business areas about which top management has some knowledge. Probably because of those considerations, most diversified companies display a preference for related diversification.[40] However, research suggests that the average related company is, at best, only marginally more profitable than the average unrelated company.[41] How can this be, if related diversification is associated with more benefits than unrelated diversification?

The answer is quite simple. Bureaucratic costs arise from (1) the number of businesses in a company's portfolio and (2) the extent of coordination required among the different businesses in order to realize value from a diversification strategy. An unrelated company does not have to achieve coordination between business units and so it has to cope only with the bureaucratic costs that arise from the number of businesses in its portfolio. In contrast, a related diversified company has to achieve coordination between business units if it is to realize the value that comes from skill transfers and resource sharing. Consequently, it has to cope with the bureaucratic costs that arise ***both*** from the number of business units in its portfolio ***and*** from coordination among business units. Thus, although it is true that related diversified companies can create value in more ways than unrelated companies, they have to bear higher bureaucratic costs in order to do so. These higher costs may cancel out the higher benefits, making the strategy no more profitable than one of unrelated diversification. Table 9.1 lists the sources of value and costs for each strategy.

How then is a company to choose between these strategies? The choice depends on a comparison of the relative value added and the bureaucratic costs associated with each strategy. In making this comparison, it should be noted that the opportunities for creating value from related diversification are a function of the extent of commonalities between the skills required to compete in the company's core business and the skills required to compete in other industrial and commercial areas. Some companies' skills are so specialized that they have few applications outside the core businesses. For example, since the commonalities between steel making and other industrial or commercial operations are few, most steel companies have diversified into unrelated industries (LTV into defense contracting, USX into oil and gas). When companies have less specialized skills, they can find many more related diversification opportunities outside the core business. Examples include chemical companies (such as Dow Chemical and Du Pont) and electrical engineering companies (such as General Electric). Consequently, the opportunities available to them to create value from related diversification are much greater.

TABLE 9.1

Comparing Related and Unrelated Diversification

Strategy	*Ways of Creating Value*	*Source of Bureaucratic Costs*
Related diversification	• Restructuring • Transferring skills	• Number of businesses • Coordination among businesses • Economies of scope
Unrelated diversification	• Restructuring	• Number of businesses

Thus, it pays a firm to concentrate on related diversification when (1) the company's core skills are applicable to a wide variety of industrial and commercial situations and (2) the bureaucratic costs of implementation do not exceed the value that can be created through resource sharing or skill transfers. The second condition is likely to hold only for companies that are moderately diversified. At high levels of related diversification, the bureaucratic costs of additional diversification are likely to outweigh the value created by that diversification, and the strategy may become unprofitable.

By the same logic, it may pay a company to concentrate on unrelated diversification when (1) the company's core functional skills are highly specialized and have few applications outside the company's core business; (2) the company's top management is skilled at acquiring and turning around poorly run businesses (and many are not); and (3) the bureaucratic costs of implementation do not exceed the value that can be created by pursuing a restructuring strategy. However, the third condition is *unlikely* to hold for companies that are highly diversified. Thus, no matter whether a company pursues a related or an unrelated diversification strategy, the existence of bureaucratic costs suggests that there are very real limits to the profitable diversification of the company.

STRATEGIC ALLIANCES AS AN ALTERNATIVE TO DIVERSIFICATION

Diversification can be unprofitable because of the bureaucratic costs associated with implementing the strategy. One way of trying to realize the value associated with diversification, without having to bear the same level of bureaucratic costs is to enter into a strategic alliance with another company to start a new business venture.

In this context, strategic alliances are essentially agreements between two or more companies to share the costs, risks, and benefits associated with developing new business opportunities. Many strategic alliances are constituted as formal joint ventures, in which each party has an equity stake. Other alliances take the form of a long-term contract between companies in which they agree to undertake some joint activity that benefits both. Agreements to work together on joint R&D projects often take this form.

Strategic alliances seem to be a particularly viable option when a company wishes to create value from transferring competencies or sharing resources between diversified businesses in order to realize economies of scope. Alliances offer companies a framework within which to share the resources required to establish a new business. Alternatively, alliances enable companies to swap complementary skills to produce a new range of products. For example, consider the alliance between United Technologies and Dow Chemical to build plastic-based composite parts for the aerospace industry. United Technologies was already involved in the aerospace industry (it built Sikorsky helicopters), and Dow Chemical had skills in the development and manufacture of plastic-based composites. The alliance called for United Technologies to contribute its advanced aerospace skills and for Dow to contribute its skills in developing and manufacturing plastic-based composites to a joint venture in which each company would have a 50 percent equity stake. The joint venture was to undertake the task of developing, manufacturing, and marketing a new line of plastic-based composite parts for the aerospace industry. Through the alliance, both companies would become involved in new activities. They would, in short, be able to realize some of the benefits associated with related diversification without having to merge activities formally or bear the costs and risks of developing the new products on their own.

Bureaucratic costs have been reduced because neither Dow nor United Technologies actually expanded its own organization, nor did either company have to coordinate internal skill transfers. Rather, since incorporation, the joint venture has been operating as an independent company, and both Dow and United Technologies receive payment in the form of dividends.

Of course, there is a downside to such alliances. For one thing, profits must be split with an alliance partner, whereas with full diversification a company gets to keep all the profits. Another problem is that when a company enters into an alliance, it always runs the risk that it might give away critical know-how to its alliance partner, which might then use that know-how to compete directly with the company in the future. For example, having gained access to Dow's expertise in plastic-based composites, United Technologies might dissolve the alliance and produce these materials on its own. However, such risk can be minimized if Dow gets a *credible commitment* from United Technologies. By entering into a formal joint venture, rather than a more loosely structured alliance, United Technologies has given such a commitment because it has had to invest substantial amounts of capital. Thus, if United Technologies tried to produce plastic-based composites on its own, it would essentially be competing against itself.

SUMMARY OF CHAPTER

The purpose of this chapter is to examine the different corporate-level strategies that companies pursue in order to maximize their value. The chapter makes the following main points:

- Corporate strategies should *add value* to a corporation, enabling it, or one or more of its business units, to perform one or more of the value creation functions at a lower cost or in a way that allows differentiation and brings a premium price.
- Concentrating on a single business lets a company focus its total managerial, financial, technological, and physical resources and capabilities on competing successfully in just one area. It also ensures that the company sticks to doing what it knows best.
- The company that concentrates on a single business may be missing out on the opportunity to create value through vertical integration and/or diversification.
- Vertical integration can enable a company to achieve a competitive advantage by helping build barriers to entry, facilitating investments in specialized assets, protecting product quality, and helping improve scheduling between adjacent stages in the value chain.
- The disadvantages of vertical integration include cost disadvantages if a company's internal source of supply is a high-cost one, and lack of flexibility when technology is changing fast or when demand is uncertain.
- Entering into a long-term contract can enable a company to realize many of the benefits associated with vertical integration without having to bear the same level of bureaucratic costs. However, to avoid the risks associated with becoming too dependent on its partner, a company entering into a long-term contract needs to seek a credible commitment from its partner or establish a mutual hostage-taking situation.
- The strategic outsourcing of noncore value creation activities may allow a company to lower its costs, better differentiate its product offering, and make better use of scarce resources, while also enabling it to respond rapidly to changing market

conditions. However, strategic outsourcing may have a detrimental effect if the company outsources important value creation activities, or if it becomes too dependent on key suppliers of those activities.

- ✔ Diversification can create value through the pursuit of a restructuring strategy, competency transfers, and the realization of economies of scope.
- ✔ The bureaucratic costs of diversification are a function of the number of independent business units within the company and the extent of coordination between those business units.
- ✔ Diversification motivated by a desire to pool risks or achieve greater growth is often associated with the dissipation of value.
- ✔ Related diversification is preferred to unrelated diversification because it enables a company to engage in more value creation activities and is less risky. If a company's skills are not transferable, the company may have no choice but to pursue unrelated diversification.
- ✔ Strategic alliances can enable companies to realize many of the benefits of related diversification without having to bear the same level of bureaucratic costs. However, when entering into an alliance, a company does run the risk of giving away key technology to its partner. This risk can be minimized if a company gets a credible commitment from its partner.

DISCUSSION QUESTIONS

1. Why was it profitable for General Motors and Ford to integrate backward into component-parts manufacturing in the past, and why are both companies now trying to buy more of their parts from outside?
2. Under what conditions might concentration on a single business be inconsistent with the goal of maximizing stockholder wealth? Why?
3. General Motors integrated vertically in the 1920s, diversified in the 1930s, and expanded overseas in the 1950s. Explain these developments with reference to the profitability of pursuing each strategy. Why, do you think, vertical integration is normally the first strategy to be pursued after concentration on a single business?
4. What value creation activities should a company outsource to independent suppliers? What are the risks involved in outsourcing these activities?
5. When is a company likely to choose related diversification and when is it likely to choose unrelated diversification? Discuss with reference to an electronics manufacturer and an ocean shipping company.

Practicing Strategic Management

SMALL-GROUP EXERCISE
Comparing Vertical Integration Strategies

Break up into a group of three to five people. Then read the following description of the activities of Quantum Corporation and Seagate Technologies, both of which manufacture computer disk drives. On the basis of this description, outline the pros and cons of a vertical integration strategy. Which strategy do you think makes most sense in the context of the computer disk drive industry?

Quantum Corporation and Seagate Technologies are both major producers of disk drives for personal computers and workstations. The disk drive industry is characterized by sharp fluctuations in the level of demand, intense price competition, rapid technological change, and product life cycles of no more than twelve to eighteen months. In recent years, Quantum and Seagate have pursued very different vertical integration strategies. Seagate is a vertically integrated manufacturer of disk drives, both designing and manufacturing the bulk of its own disk drives. Quantum specializes in design, while outsourcing most of its manufacturing to a number of independent suppliers, including, most importantly, Matsushita Kotobuki Electronics (MKE) of Japan. Quantum makes only its newest and most expensive products in-house. Once a new drive is perfected and ready for large-scale manufacturing, Quantum turns over manufacturing to MKE. MKE and Quantum have cemented their partnership over eight years. At each stage in designing a new product, Quantum's engineers send the newest drawings to a production team at MKE. MKE examines the drawings and is constantly proposing changes that make new disk drives easier to manufacture. When the product is ready for manufacture, eight to ten Quantum engineers travel to MKE's plant in Japan for at least a month to work on production ramp-up.

STRATEGIC MANAGEMENT
Project Module 9

This module requires you to assess the vertical integration and diversification strategy being pursued by your company. With the information you have at your disposal, answer the questions:

1. How vertically integrated is your company? If your company does have vertically integrated operations, is it pursuing a strategy of taper or full integration?
2. How diversified is your company? If your company is already diversified, is it pursuing a related diversification strategy, an unrelated diversification strategy, or some mix of the two?
3. Assess the potential for your company to create value through vertical integration. In reaching your assessment, also consider the bureaucratic costs of managing vertical integration.
4. On the basis of your assessment in question 3, do you think your company should (a) outsource some operations that are currently performed in-house or (b) bring some operations in-house that are currently outsourced? Justify your recommendations.
5. Is your company currently involved in any long-term cooperative relationships with suppliers or buyers? If so, how are these relationships structured? Do you think that these relationships add value to the company? Why?
6. Is there any potential for your company to enter into (additional) long-term cooperative relationships with suppliers or buyers? If so, how might these relationships be structured?
7. Assess the potential for your company to create value through diversification. In reaching your assessment, also consider the bureaucratic costs of managing diversification.
8. On the basis of your assessment in question 7, do you think your company should (a) sell off some diversified operations or (b) pursue additional diversification? Justify your recommendations.
9. Is your company currently trying to transfer skills or realize economies of scope by entering into strategic alliances with other companies? If so, how are these relationships structured? Do you think that these relationships add value to the company? Why?

10. Is there any potential for your company to transfer skills or realize economies of scope by entering into (additional) strategic alliances with other companies? If so, how might these relationships be structured?

ARTICLE FILE 9

Find an example of a company whose vertical integration or diversification strategy appears to have dissipated rather than created value. Identify why this has happened and what the company should do to rectify the situation.

EXPLORING THE WEB
Visiting Motorola

Visit the Web site of Motorola (http://www.motorola.com) and review the various business activities of the company. Using this information, answer the following questions:

1. To what extent is Motorola vertically integrated?
2. Does vertical integration help Motorola establish a competitive advantage, or does it put the company at a competitive disadvantage?
3. How diversified is Motorola? What diversification strategy is Motorola pursuing—related or unrelated diversification?
4. How, if at all, does Motorola's diversification strategy create value for the company's stockholders?

General Task Search the Web for an example of a company that has pursued a diversification strategy. Describe that strategy and assess whether the strategy creates or dissipates value for the company.

CLOSING CASE

Thermo Electron

IN 1983, George Hatsopoulos, the founder and CEO of Thermo Electron, was puzzling over the future of the company. At the time, Thermo Electron was a $200-million-a-year manufacturer of energy and environmental equipment. Hatsopoulos noted that most new technology enterprises were not started by big companies. Rather, they were started by independent entrepreneurs working on their own. Yet most of these start-ups failed, crippled either by an inability to raise capital or by the high cost of capital they did raise. Hatsopoulos wondered whether there might be a way to combine the best of big and small companies.

The solution he came up with has been the diversification engine of Thermo Electron ever since. Thermo's strategy has been to draw on its R&D know-how to develop radically new products for discrete market niches not already addressed by the company or its subsidiaries. These products are then spun off as the core of stand-alone companies, in which Thermo holds a majority equity stake. Between 1983 and 1998, Thermo Electron produced twenty-three such spinoffs, all but three of which were publicly traded. In the process, Thermo diversified into a wide range of businesses, including power plants, artificial hearts, and laser hair removers, and grew its sales to more than $3.6 billion.

Although Thermo kept a majority stake in each spinoff, it would give the new companies far more freedom than a conventional subsidiary might have done. Day-to-day control of operations, along with aggressive stock option contracts, were typically handed over to each subsidiary. Each subsidiary also kept the capital that it raised through an initial public offering, using it in the way that made most sense for that particular business. To encourage the senior executives of spinoffs to couple their strategy with that of the entire family of companies, the stock options were split so that 40 percent were linked to the performance of the particular spinoff, 40 percent of them to that of the parent company, Thermo Electron, and 20 percent to that of its sibling.

Validating the strategy, the company's financial record of accomplishment during the 1983–1997 period was very strong, with the compound return to shareholders averaging 28 percent annually. However, the company has had its critics. Its multiplication of subsidiaries has given rise to a corporate structure that looks more like an intertwined strand of DNA than a typical chain of command. Such complexity can have a damping effect on share price. Some investors have complained that the corporate structure is to complicated. Having twenty-three public subsidiaries means producing twenty-three annual reports, and filing ninety-two quarterly earnings statements a year, a not inexpensive endeavor. The ongoing process of spinning off companies can spread scarce management and engineering talent too thinly over too many disparate businesses. In addition, bad performance by one subsidiary can cast a shadow over the whole company and adversely affect both revenues and share price. In July 1998, a Thermo subsidiary warned of lower-than-expected revenues, which would make just a small dent in the parent company's third-quarter profits—but Thermo's share price fell 17 percent. In addition, control by the parent can complicate any business that the spinoff may try to do with competitors of the parent or other subsidiaries.

In 1998 and 1999, the company's critics had a field day as Thermo Electron's performance began to slump. In the wake of a series of disappointed financial results, George Hatsopoulos admitted that the spinoff strategy may have been pushed too far and that the company had spun off business that did not meet its own criteria for growth and management depth. He also acknowledged that in striving to boost their stock prices and realize stock option gains, some subsidiaries may have rushed to market products that were not adequately engineered or tested. The results have included slow sales and product recalls, which have reflected poorly on the entire corporation. In June 1999, Hatsopoulos stepped down as CEO. His replacement announced that the company would refocus its effort on a smaller number of subsidiaries—eleven—with the remainder being closed, sold, or consolidated into the larger entity. [42]

Case Discussion Questions

1. Historically, how has Thermo Electron's unusual diversification strategy created value for the company and its shareholders?
2. What are the significant drawbacks of this strategy?
3. Do the problems Thermo Electron experienced in 1998 and 1999 invalidate the strategy?

End Notes

1. W. H. Miller, "After 33 Years, New Leader," *Industry Week*, July 5, 1999, p. 41; "Subway to the Sky," *Economist*, August 23, 1997, p. 52; A. dePalma, "The Transportation Giant Up North," *New York Times*, December 25, 1988, p. 1.
2. T. J. Peters and R. H. Waterman, *In Search of Excellence* (New York: Harper & Row, 1982).
3. D. P. Hamilton, "Red-Faced Matsushita Gets Back to Basics," *Wall Street Journal*, April 10, 1995, p. A14.
4. K. R. Harrian, "Formulating Vertical Integration Strategies," *Academy of Management Review*, 9 (1984), 638–652.
5. This is the essence of the argument made by A. D. Chandler, *Strategy and Structure* (Cambridge, Mass.: MIT Press, 1962); the same argument is also made by Jeffrey Pfeffer and Gerald R. Salancik, *The External Control of Organizations*, (New York: Harper & Row, 1978). See also K. R. Harrigan, *Strategic Flexibility* (Lexington, Mass.: Lexington Books, 1985); K. R. Harrigan, "Vertical Integration and Corporate Strategy," *Academy of Management Journal*, 28 (1985), 397–425; and F. M. Scherer, *Industrial Market Structure and Economic Performance* (Chicago: Rand McNally, 1981).
6. This section is based on the transaction cost approach popularized by O. E. Williamson, *The Economic Institutions of Capitalism* (New York: Free Press, 1985).
7. Williamson, *Economic Institutions*. For recent empirical work that uses this framework, see L. Poppo and T. Zenger, "Testing Alternative Theories of the Firm: Transaction Cost, Knowledge-Based, and Measurement Explanations for Make or Buy Decisions in Information Services," *Strategic Management Journal*, 19 (1998), 853–878.
8. Williamson, *Economic Institutions*.
9. J. F. Hennart, "Upstream Vertical Integration in the Aluminum and Tin Industries," *Journal of Economic Behavior and Organization*, 9 (1988), 281–299.
10. Ibid.
11. A. D. Chandler, *The Visible Hand* (Cambridge, Mass.: Harvard University Press, 1977).
12. Julia Pitta, "Score One for Vertical Integration," *Forbes*, January 18, 1993, pp. 88–89.
13. J. White and N. Templin, "Harsh Regimen: A Swollen GM Finds It Hard to Stick with Its Crash Diet," *Wall Street Journal*, September 9, 1992, p. A1.
14. Harrigan, *Strategic Flexibility*, pp. 67–87.
15. For a detailed theoretical rationale for this argument see G. R. Jones and C. W. L. Hill, "A Transaction Cost Analysis of Strategy-Structure Choice," *Strategic Management Journal*, 9 (1988), 159–172.
16. K. Kelly, Z. Schiller, and J. Treece, "Cut Costs or Else," *Business Week*, March 22, 1993, pp. 28–29.
17. X. Martin, W. Mitchell, and A. Swaminathan, "Recreating and Extending Japanese Automobile Buyer-Supplier Links in North America," *Strategic Management Journal*, 16 (1995), 589–619; C. W. L. Hill, "National Institutional Structures, Transaction Cost Economizing, and Competitive Advantage," *Organization Science*, 6 (1995), 119–131.
18. Standard & Poor's "Autos—Auto Parts," *Industry Surveys*, June 24, 1993.
19. See J. Womack, D. Jones, and D. Roos, *The Machine That Changed the World* (New York: Rawson Associates, 1990); and J. Richardson, "Parallel Sourcing and Supplier Performance in the Japanese Automobile Industry," *Strategic Management Journal*, 14 (1993), 339–350.
20. R. Mudambi and S. Helper, "The Close but Adversarial Model of Supplier Relations in the U.S. Auto Industry," *Strategic Management Journal*, 19 (1998), 775–792.
21. J. H. Dyer, "How Chrysler Created an American Keiretsu," *Harvard Business Review* (July–August 1996), 42–56.
22. Williamson, *Economic Institutions*; see also J. H. Dyer, "Effective Inter-Firm Collaboration: How Firms Minimize Transaction Costs and Maximize Transaction Value," *Strategic Management Journal*, 18 (1997), 535–556.
23. Richardson, "Parallel Sourcing."
24. W. H. Davidow and M. S. Malone, *The Virtual Corporation* (New York: Harper & Row, 1992).
25. Ibid.
26. "The Outing of Outsourcing," November 25, 1995, pp. 57–58.
27. Davidow and Malone, *Virtual Corporation*; H. W. Chesbrough and D.J. Teece, "When is Virtual Virtuous? Organizing for Innovation," *Harvard Business Review* (January–February, 1996), 65–74.
28. This resource-based view of diversification can be traced to E. Penrose's seminal book, *The Theory of the Growth of the Firm* (Oxford: Oxford University Press, 1959).
29. See, for example, Jones and Hill, "A Transaction Cost Analysis"; and O. E. Williamson, *Markets and Hierarchies*, (New York: Free Press, 19), pp. 132–175.
30. J. R. Lang, "Tyco's Titan," *Barron's*, April 12, 1999, 27–32; M. Quan, "Connector Maker Eyes Expansion Under New Owner Tyco," *Electronic Engineering Times*, July 26, 1999; Web site (www.tycoint.com).
31. G. Hamel and C. K. Prahalad, *Competing for the Future* (Boston: Harvard Business School Press, 1994).
32. D. J. Teece, "Economies of Scope and the Scope of the Enterprise," *Journal of Economic Behavior and Organization*, 3 (1980), 223–247. For recent empirical work on this topic, see C. H. St. John and J. S. Harrison, "Manufacturing Based Relatedness, Synergy and Coordination," *Strategic Management Journal*, 20 (1999), 129–145.
33. For a detailed discussion, see C. W. L. Hill and R. E. Hoskisson, "Strategy and Structure in the Multiproduct Firm," *Academy of Management Review*, 12 (1987), pp. 331–341.
34. M. E. Porter, *Competitive Advantage: Creating and Sustaining Superior Performance* (New York: Free Press, 1985), p. 326.
35. M. E. Porter, "From Competitive Advantage to Corporate Strategy," *Harvard Business Review* (May–June 1987), 43–59.

36. For reviews of the evidence, see V. Ramanujam and P. Varadarajan, "Research on Corporate Diversification: A Synthesis," *Strategic Management Journal*, 10 (1989), 523–551; and G. Dess, J. F. Hennart, C. W. L. Hill, and A. Gupta, "Research Issues in Strategic Management," *Journal of Management*, 21 (1995), 357–392.
37. C. R. Christensen et al., *Business Policy Text and Cases* (Homewood, Ill.: Irwin, 1987), p. 778.
38. S. McMurray, "ICI Changes Tack and Splits Itself into Two Businesses," *Wall Street Journal*, March 5, sec. B, p. 3; "Hanson Likes the Look of ICI," *Economist*, May 18, 1991, pp. 69–70.
39. For evidence, see C. W. L. Hill, "Conglomerate Performance over the Economic Cycle," *Journal of Industrial Economics*, 32 (1983), 197–212; and D. T. C. Mueller, "The Effects of Conglomerate Mergers," *Journal of Banking and Finance*, 1 (1977), 315–347.
40. For example, see C. W. L. Hill, "Diversified Growth and Competition," *Applied Economics*, 17 (1985), 827–847; and R. P. Rumelt, *Strategy, Structure and Economic Performance* (Boston: Harvard Business School Press, 1974). See also Jones and Hill, "A Transaction Cost Analysis."
41. See H. K. Christensen and C. A. Montgomery, "Corporate Economic Performance: Diversification Strategy Versus Market Structure," *Strategic Management Journal*, 2 (1981), 327–343; and Jones and Hill, "A Transaction Cost Analysis"; G. Dess et al. "Research Issues"; C. W. L. Hill, "The Role of Headquarters in the Multidivisional Firm," in ed. R. Rumelt, D. J. Teece, and D. Schendel, *Fundamental Issues in Strategy Research* (Cambridge, Mass: Harvard Business School Press, 1994), pp. 297–321.
42. "Spinning It Out at Thermo Electron," *Economist*, April 12, 1997, pp. 57–58; B. Knestout, "Thermo Electron and All Its Children," *Kiplinger's Personal Finance Magazine*, 52 (October 1998), 36; R. Kerber, "Thermo Electron Announces Further Restructuring Moves; Will Take $450M Pretax Charge, Sell Units, Cut Jobs," *The Boston Globe*, May 25, 1999, p. D1.

10 Corporate Development: Building and Restructuring the Corporation

OPENING CASE

Changing the Focus at Hewlett-Packard

HEWLETT-PACKARD (HP) is a corporate legend. The company was established in 1938 by two Stanford University professors, William Hewlett and David Packard, who built their first product, an audio oscillator used to test sound, in a Palo Alto garage. Subsequently, the company grew to become the world's largest manufacturer of test and measurement equipment before diversifying into medical equipment in the early 1960s, and computers and peripherals in the mid 1960s. Along the way, former HP employees "seeded" numerous small start-ups, helping to create Silicon Valley.

By 1998, the company was generating revenues of $47 billion in a wide range of related businesses that spanned the test and measurement, medical equipment, and computer industries. However, the company had a problem: its growth rate had fallen below that of more focused computer industry rivals, such as Sun Microsystems and IBM. The perception in the industry was that HP was letting an opportunity pass it by to seize a leadership position in the fast-growing Internet arena. An internal business review undertaken by CEO Lewis Platt and his senior colleagues in late 1998 and early 1999 came to a similar conclusion. Over the previous two years, HP had tried to boost its profitability by a combination of job cuts and new-product introductions, such as a printer-copier hybrid, but to no avail. Platt and his colleagues decided that the key problem lay in a lack of corporate focus. The company had become too big and too diversified to respond effectively to new challenges, such as the challenge presented by the rapid emergence of the Internet. Moreover, because of problems in Asia and cutbacks in medical spending, the test and measurement and medical equipment businesses had performed quite poorly in recent years. Declining sales in these areas had dragged down the performance of the entire company and masked the respectable (although less than excellent) performance of the computer-related businesses. Moreover, senior managers found that they had to devote much of their time and energy to fixing problems in the non-computer businesses, to the detriment of the computer operation.

Platt decided that the time had come for bold action and a reconfiguration of the corporate portfolio. On March 3, 1999, the company announced that it would spin off its test and measurement and medical equipment businesses into an as yet unnamed independent company with revenues of around $7.6 billion. Once the spinoff is completed, HP will become a more focused manufacturer of printers, personal computers, and servers, a set of operations that have far more in common with each other than with those the company decided to spin off. The company reportedly also considered spinning off its printer business but decided against doing so because of the complex technology licensing arrangements that would be required between the computer and printer operations. At the same time, Platt announced that he would be stepping down as CEO and initiated a search for his successor.

This announcement was followed by another, in May 1999, that the core computer business would henceforth pursue a broad-based Internet-centric strategy, dubbed E-services. This strategy has two components. First, HP is developing software that will let companies search the Web for almost any service—for example, a database that will provide the best price on a microprocessor or the cheapest place to rent computing power to support a big on-line promotion. To gain the technology required for this strategy, HP has acquired a number of small Internet-based companies and invested more than $100 million in a dozen other Internet-related companies. Second, HP will move aggressively into the computer outsourcing market, renting out space and software on HP servers located at huge server farms, and providing technical support and consulting services. HP has calculated that many companies will prefer this approach, rather than invest millions of dollars to buy dedicated hardware and hire technical support staff. HP also plans to works closely with major software vendors, such as SAP and Oracle, and communications companies such as Qwest. For example, a partnership between HP, Qwest Communications, and SAP will charge mid-sized companies a few hundred dollars a month so that they can run SAP software on HP machines over Qwest's high-speed fiber optic communications network.

The final piece in the restructuring puzzle fell into place in July 1999, when HP announced that Carly Fiorina would become HPs new CEO. Prior to her appointment, Fiorina ran the global services division of Lucent. At forty-four, she is not only one of the youngest people to head one of the twenty largest public corporations in America, she is also the first woman to do so and the first outsider to head HP. Many viewed Fiorina's appointment as a clear indication that HP intended to break with its past and go full bore after opportunities in the Internet arena.[1]

OVERVIEW

Chapter 9 discusses the corporate-level strategies that companies pursue in order to become multibusiness enterprises. This chapter builds on Chapter 9 by addressing central issues of corporate development. **Corporate development** is concerned with identifying *which* business opportunities a company should pursue, *how* it should pursue those opportunities, and *how* it should exit from businesses that do not fit the company's strategic vision. The Opening Case touched on some of these issues. Historically, Hewlett-Packard's strategy has been to diversify into related areas through internal new ventures. This strategy took HP from test and measurement into medical equipment, then into computers, and finally into computer peripherals. More recently, senior executives at HP decided that they should pursue opportunities in the fast-developing Internet arena. They decided to pursue these opportunities through a combination of vehicles, including new-product offerings, acquisitions, and alliances, such as the alliance between HP, SAP, and Qwest Communications, described in the Opening Case. At the same time, they decided to restructure to company and spin off any business that could not be tied into the core computer and Internet operations and did not fit the new vision. The result was the spinoff of HP's test and measurement and medical equipment businesses.

In this chapter, we start by looking at approaches that companies can take to reviewing their portfolio of businesses. The objectives of such a review are to help determine which of its existing businesses a company should continue to participate in, which it should exit from, and whether the company should consider entering any new business areas. Then, we turn our attention to the different *vehicles*, or means, that companies use to enter and develop new business areas. The choice here is among acquisitions, internal new ventures, and joint ventures. **Acquisitions** involve buying an existing business; **internal new ventures** start a new business from scratch; and **joint ventures** typically establish a new business with the assistance of a partner.

The chapter closes with a look at restructuring and exit strategy. For reasons that we first touched on in Chapter 9 and discuss further in this chapter, during the 1970s and 1980s many companies became too diversified or too vertically integrated. In recent years, there has been a notable shift away from these strategies, with companies selling off many of their diversified activities and refocusing on their core businesses.

REVIEWING THE CORPORATE PORTFOLIO

A central concern of corporate development is identifying which business opportunities a company should pursue. A common starting point is to review a company's existing portfolio of businesses activities. As stated earlier, the purpose of such a review is to help determine which of its existing businesses a company should continue to participate in, which it should exit from, and whether the company should consider entering any new business areas. In this section, we discuss two different approaches to undertaking such a review.

The first approach utilizes a set of techniques known as "portfolio planning matrices."[2] Developed primarily by management consultants, these techniques are meant to compare the competitive position of the different businesses in a company's portfolio against each other on the basis of common criteria. Below, we argue that these techniques contain some flaws and that their application has produced some bad decisions.

The second approach we consider has been championed by Gary Hamel and C.K. Prahalad. This approach reconceptualizes a company as a portfolio of core competencies, as opposed to a portfolio of businesses.[3] Corporate development is oriented toward maintaining existing competencies, building new competencies, and leveraging competencies by applying them to new business opportunities. For example, according to Hamel and Prahalad, the success of a company such as 3M in creating new business has come from its ability to apply its core competency in adhesives to a wide range of businesses opportunities, from Scotch Tape to Post-it Notes.

Portfolio Planning

One of the most famous portfolio planning matrices is referred to as the growth-share matrix. This was developed by the Boston Consulting Group (BCG), principally to help senior managers identify the cash flow requirements of different businesses in their portfolio and to help determine whether they need to change the mix of businesses in the portfolio. We review the growth-share matrix in order to illustrate both the value and the limitations of portfolio planning tools. The growth-share matrix has three main steps: (1) dividing a company into strategic business units (SBUs); (2) assessing the prospects of each SBU and comparing them against each other by means of a matrix; and (3) developing strategic objectives for each SBU.

Identifying SBUs According to the BCG, a company must create an SBU for each economically distinct business area that it competes in. Normally, a company defines its SBUs in terms of the product markets they are competing in. For example, Ciba Geigy, Switzerland's largest chemical and pharmaceutical company and an active user of portfolio planning techniques, has identified thirty-three strategic business units in areas such as proprietary pharmaceuticals, generic pharmaceuticals, seed treatments, reactive dyes, detergents, resins, paper chemicals, diagnostics, and composite materials (see Strategy in Action 10.1).

Assessing and Comparing SBUs Having defined SBUs, top managers then assess each according to two criteria: (1) the SBU's relative market share and (2) the growth rate of the SBU's industry. **Relative market share** is the ratio of an SBU's market share to the market share held by the largest rival company in its industry. If SBU X has a market share of 10 percent and its largest rival has a market share of 30 percent, SBU X's relative market share is 10/30, or 0.3. Only if an SBU is a market leader in its industry will it have a relative market share greater than 1.0. For example, if SBU Y has a market share of 40 percent and its largest rival has a market share of 10 percent, then SBU Y's relative market share is 40/10, or 4.0. According to the BCG, market share gives a company cost advantages from economies of scale and learning effects. An SBU with a relative market share greater than 1.0 is assumed to be farther down the experience curve and therefore to have a significant cost advantage over its rivals. By similar logic, an SBU with a relative market share smaller than 1.0 is assumed to lack the scale economies and low-cost position of the market leader.

The growth rate of an SBU's industry is assessed according to whether it is faster or slower than the growth rate of the economy as a whole. BCG's position is that high-growth industries offer a more favorable competitive environment and better long-term prospects than slow-growth industries.

Given the relative market share and industry growth rate for each SBU, management compares SBUs against each other by way of a matrix similar to that illustrated in Figure 10.1. The horizontal dimension of this matrix measures relative market share; the vertical dimension measures industry growth rate. The center of each circle corresponds to the position of an SBU on the two dimensions of the matrix. The size of each circle is proportional to the sales revenue generated by each business in the company's portfolio. The bigger the circle, the larger is the SBU's revenue relative to total corporate revenues.

10.1 STRATEGY in ACTION

Portfolio Planning at Ciba-Geigy

Ciba-Geigy is a large Swiss-based company with interests in chemicals and pharmaceuticals and annual revenues in excess of $25 billion. Since 1984, the company has been using portfolio planning techniques as a tool to assist corporate management in the process of strategic planning, resource allocation, and performance assessment. Although the company looked closely at the growth-share matrix devised by the Boston Consulting Group, it decided to develop a customized portfolio planning tool that would better suit its needs.

Ciba had divided the company into thirty-three separate strategic business units, such as proprietary pharmaceuticals, generic pharmaceuticals, seed treatments, reactive dyes, detergents, resins, paper chemicals, diagnostics, and composite materials. At Ciba, each SBU is assessed according to two main criteria: the likely future growth rate of its industry, and the competitive position of the SBU relative to its rivals. In deriving a measure of competitive position, Ciba looks at relative market share, but unlike the original BCG growth-share matrix, the company also considers a range of other competitive factors, such as cost structure, product quality, core competencies, and relative profitability.

Using these data, Ciba classifies its SBUs into one of five categories: development, growth, pillar, niche, and core. Development businesses are in the early stage of their life cycle and usually require substantial R&D investments. Growth businesses are competitive SBUs based in large and/or growing markets. Ciba will commit substantial funds in order to build the competitive position of such a business. Pillar businesses are market leaders that are based in attractive industries, such as Ciba's pharmaceutical businesses. They typically receive a high priority in R&D funding and resource allocation in order to maintain their pillar status. Niche businesses are market leaders that are constrained because they serve a relatively small market (Ciba's animal health business, for example, was defined as a niche business). Core businesses are large SBUs that compete in mature industries (Ciba's dyes, polymers, and pigments SBUs are all classified as core). Core businesses are seen as generating excess cash that can be used to fund investments elsewhere within the company.

What is interesting about Ciba's approach is that these classifications are not taken as gospel. The company is quite willing to violate the investment rules associated with the different categories if that seems appropriate. For example, in 1994 Ciba committed itself to major new investments in its pigments SBU to upgrade its U.S. production facilities, even though its portfolio planning categories suggest that this was a mature low-growth core business that should be used to generate funds for investment elsewhere within the company. Ciba's view appears to be that the utility of portfolio planning lies not so much in its role as a guide to resource allocation, as it does in helping top managers set reasonable strategic expectations and objectives for the different SBUs within the company. Thus, Ciba's corporate managers will assign very different strategic and financial objectives to SBUs classified as growth businesses compared with those classified as pillars. Pillars would be expected to earn a higher return on assets, generate greater cash flow, and contribute more of their earnings to the corporate bottom line than a growth business. By the same token, however, growth businesses would be expected to grow their revenues and earnings at a faster rate than pillars. The performance of managers running these SBUs is then compared against these different expectations.[4]

The matrix is divided into four cells. SBUs in cell 1 are defined as **stars**, in cell 2 as **question marks**, in cell 3 as **cash cows**, and in cell 4 as **dogs**. BCG argues that these different types of SBUs have different long-term prospects and different implications for cash flows.

- *Stars*. The leading SBUs in a company's portfolio are the stars. Stars have a high relative market share and are based in high-growth industries. Accordingly, they offer attractive long-term profit and growth opportunities.

FIGURE 10.1

The BCG Matrix

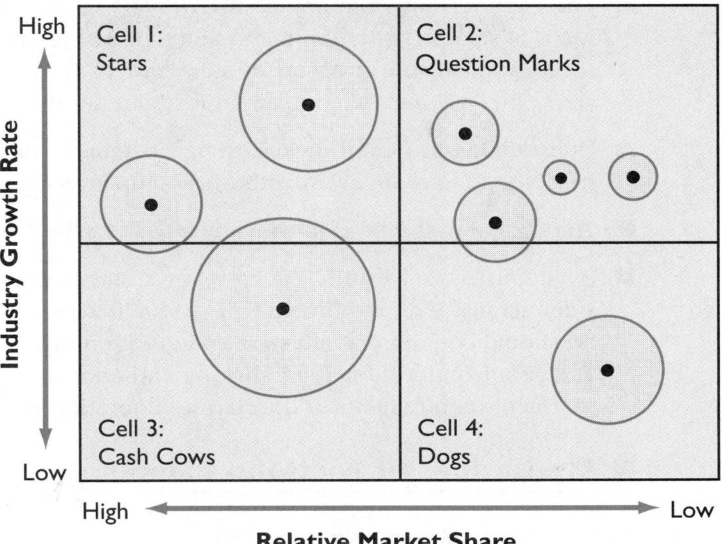

Source: Perspectives, No. 66, "The Product Portfolio." Adapted by permission from The Boston Consulting Group, Inc., 1970.

- *Question marks*. Question marks are SBUs that are relatively weak in competitive terms (they have low relative market shares) but are based in high-growth industries and thus may offer opportunities for long-term profit and growth. A question mark can become a star if nurtured properly. To become a market leader, a question mark requires substantial net injections of cash; it is cash hungry. The corporate head office has to decide whether a particular question mark has the potential to become a star and is therefore worth the capital investment necessary to achieve stardom.
- *Cash cows.* SBUs that have a high market share in low-growth industries and a strong competitive position in mature industries are cash cows. Their competitive strength comes from being farthest down the experience curve. They are the cost leaders in their industries. BCG argues that this position enables such SBUs to remain very profitable. However, low growth implies a lack of opportunities for future expansion. As a consequence, BCG argues that the capital investment requirements of cash cows are not substantial, and thus they are depicted as generating a strong positive cash flow.
- *Dogs.* SBUs that are in low-growth industries but have a low market share are dogs. They have a weak competitive position in unattractive industries and thus are viewed as offering few benefits to a company. BCG suggests that such SBUs are unlikely to generate much in the way of a positive cash flow and indeed may become cash hogs. Though offering few prospects for future growth in returns, dogs may require substantial capital investments just to maintain their low market share.

Strategic Implications The objective of the BCG portfolio matrix is to identify how corporate cash resources can best be used to maximize a company's future growth and profitability. BCG recommendations include the following:

- The cash surplus from any cash cows should be used to support the development of selected question marks and to nurture stars. The long-term objective is to consolidate the position of stars and to turn favored question marks into stars, thus making the company's portfolio more attractive.
- Question marks with the weakest or most uncertain long-term prospects should be divested to reduce demands on a company's cash resources.
- The company should exit from any industry where the SBU is a dog.
- If a company lacks sufficient cash cows, stars, or question marks, it should consider acquisitions and divestments to build a more balanced portfolio. A portfolio should contain enough stars and question marks to ensure a healthy growth and profit outlook for the company and enough cash cows to support the investment requirements of the stars and question marks.

Limitations of Portfolio Planning

Though portfolio planning techniques may sound reasonable, if we take the BCG matrix as an example, there at least four main flaws. First, the model is simplistic. An assessment of an SBU in terms of just two dimensions, market share and industry growth, is bound to be misleading, for a host of other relevant factors should be taken into account. Although market share is undoubtedly an important determinant of an SBU's competitive position, companies can also establish a strong competitive position by differentiating their product to serve the needs of a particular segment of the market. A business having a low market share can be very profitable and have a strong competitive position in certain segments of a market. The auto manufacturer BMW is in this position, yet the BCG matrix would classify BMW as a dog because it is a low-market-share business in a low-growth industry. Similarly, industry growth is not the only factor determining industry attractiveness. Many factors besides growth determine competitive intensity in an industry and thus its attractiveness.

Second, the connection between relative market share and cost savings is not as straightforward as BCG suggests. High market share does not always give a company a cost advantage. In some industries—for example, the U.S. steel industry—low-market-share companies using a low-share technology (minimills) can have lower production costs than high-market-share companies using high-share technologies (integrated mills). The BCG matrix would classify minimill operations as the dogs of the U.S. steel industry, whereas in fact their performance over the last decade has characterized them as star businesses.

Third, a high market share in a low-growth industry does not necessarily result in the large positive cash flow characteristic of cash cow businesses. The BCG matrix would classify General Motors' auto operations as a cash cow. However, the capital investments needed to remain competitive are so substantial in the auto industry that the reverse is more likely to be true. Low-growth industries can be very competitive, and staying ahead in such an environment can require substantial cash investments.

To be fair, several companies and management consulting enterprises have recognized the limitations of the BCG approach and developed alternative approaches that address the weaknesses noted above. For example, Ciba-Geigy, whose use of portfolio planning techniques is reviewed in Strategy in Action 10.1, has devised a planning approach that recognizes a wider range of competitive factors needed to be taken into consideration when assessing an SBU's position. Similarly, the management consultants McKinsey and Company developed a portfolio matrix that uses a much wider range of factors to assess the attractiveness of an industry in which an SBU competes, as well as the competitive position of an SBU (see Figure 10.2). Included in the assessment of industry attractiveness are factors such as industry size, growth, cyclicality, competitive intensity, and technological dynamism. The assessment of competitive position relies on factors such as market share and an SBU's relative position with regard to production costs, product quality, price competitiveness, distribution, and innovation.

Although there is no doubt that the approaches adopted by Ciba and McKinsey represent a distinct improvement over the original BCG model, in general all portfolio planning techniques suffer from significant flaws. Most important, they fail to pay attention to the source of value creation from diversification. They treat business units as independent, whereas in fact they may be linked by the need to transfer skills and competencies or to realize economies of scope. Moreover, portfolio planning approaches tend to trivialize the process of managing a large diversified company. They suggest that success is simply a matter of putting together the right portfolio of businesses, whereas in reality it comes from managing a diversified portfolio to *create value*, whether by leveraging distinctive competencies across business units, by sharing resources to realize economies of scope, or by achieving

FIGURE 10.2

The McKinsey Matrix

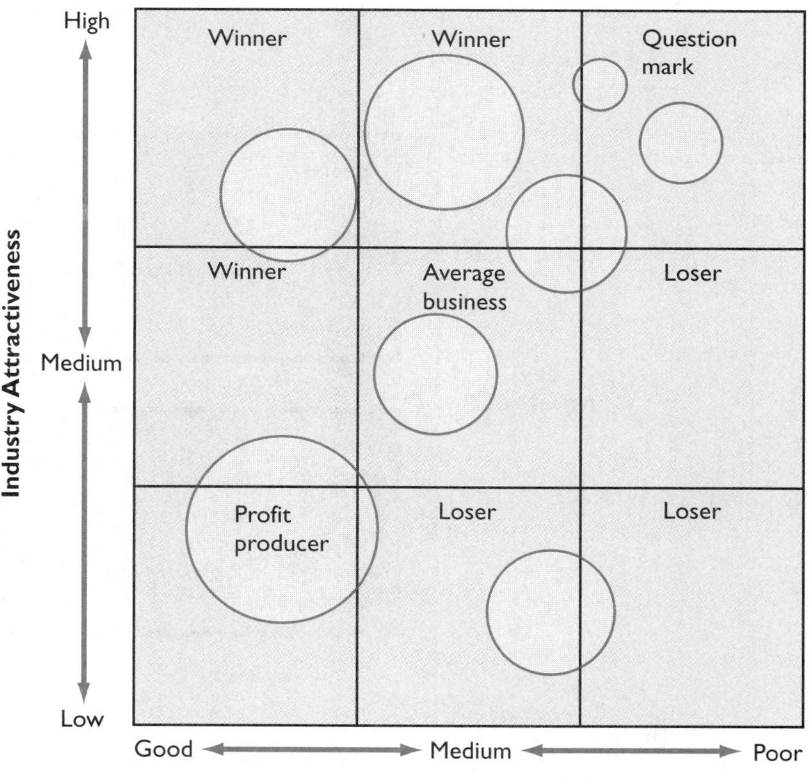

superior governance. In diverting top management's attention away from these vital tasks and legitimizing underinvestment in core business areas designated as cash cows, portfolio management techniques may have done a great disservice to the corporations that adopted them.

The Corporation as a Portfolio of Core Competencies

According to Gary Hamel and C.K. Prahalad, a more fruitful approach toward identifying the different business opportunities open to a company is to reconceptualize the company as a portfolio of core competencies—as opposed to a portfolio of businesses—and then consider how those competencies might be developed to sustain existing businesses and leveraged to create new business opportunities.[5] As you may recall, we introduce the concept of a *competency* in Chapter 4, when we discuss how distinctive competencies can form the bedrock of a company's competitive advantage. According to Hamel and Prahalad, **a core competency** is a central *value-creating* capability of an organization—a core skill. They argue, for example, that Canon, the Japanese concern best known for its cameras and photocopiers, has core competencies in precision mechanics, fine optics, microelectronics, and electronic imaging.

Hamel and Prahalad maintain that identifying *current* core competencies is the first step to take for a company engaged in the process of deciding which business opportunities to pursue. Once a company has identified its core competencies, Hamel and Prahalad advocate using a matrix similar to that shown in Figure 10.3 to establish an agenda for building and leveraging core competencies to create new business opportunities. This matrix distinguishes between existing and new compe-

FIGURE 10.3

Establishing a Core Competency Agenda

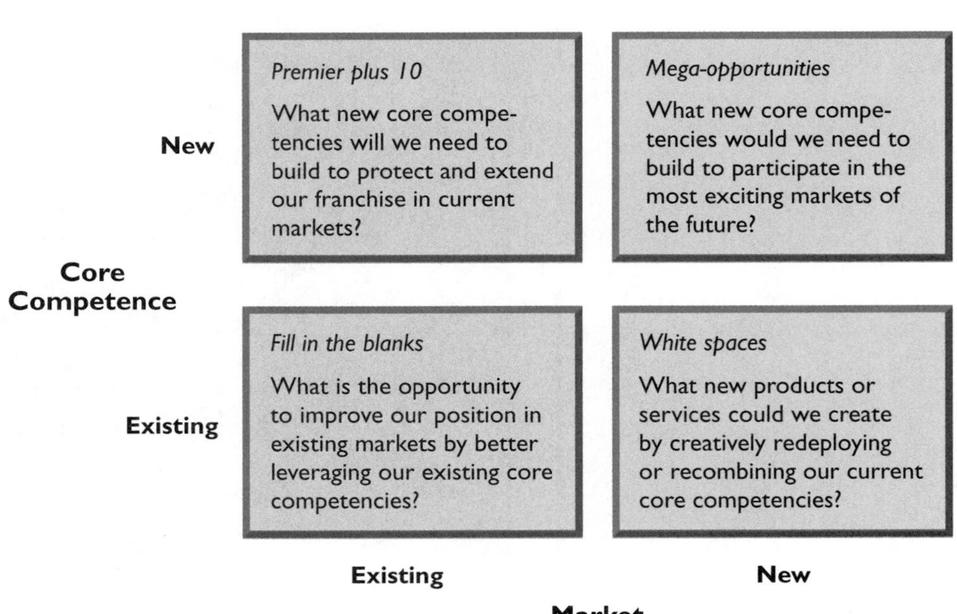

Source: G. Hamel and C. K. Prahalad, *Competing for the Future* (Cambridge, Mass.: Harvard Business School Press, 1994), p. 227.

tencies, and between existing and new-product markets. Each quadrant in the matrix has a title, the strategic implications of which are discussed in the following paragraphs.

Fill in the Blanks The lower left quadrant represents the company's existing portfolio of competencies and products. Ten years ago, for example, Canon had competencies in precision mechanics, fine optics, and microelectronics and was active in two basic businesses—producing cameras and photocopiers. The competencies in precision mechanics and fine optics were used in the production of basic mechanical cameras. These two competencies plus an additional competence in microelectronics were required to produce plain-paper copiers. The phrase *fill in the blanks* refers to the opportunity to improve the company's competitive position in existing markets by leveraging existing core competencies. So, for example, Canon was able to improve the position of its camera business by leveraging microelectronics skills from its copier business to support the development of cameras with electronic features, such as autofocus capabilities.

Premier Plus 10 The upper left quadrant is referred to as premier plus 10. The term is meant to suggest another important question: What new core competencies must be built today to ensure that the company remains a *premier* provider of its existing products in *ten* years' time? Canon, for example, decided that in order to maintain a competitive edge in its copier business, it was going to have to build a new competency in electronic imaging (which refers to the ability to capture and store images in a digital format, as opposed to using more traditional, chemical-based photographic processes). In turn, this new competency has subsequently helped Canon to extend its product range to include laser copiers, color copiers, and digital cameras.

White Spaces The lower right quadrant is referred to as white spaces. The question to be addressed here is how best to fill the white space by creatively redeploying or recombining current core competencies. In Canon's case, the company has been able to recombine its established core competencies in precision mechanics and fine optics and its recently acquired competency in electronic imaging to enter the market for fax machines and bubble jet printers.

Mega-Opportunities Opportunities represented by the upper right quadrant of Figure 10.3 do not overlap with the company's current market position, or its current competency endowment. Nevertheless, a company may choose to pursue such opportunities if they are seen to be particularly attractive, significant, or relevant to the company's existing business opportunities. For example, back in 1979 Monsanto was primarily a manufacturer of chemicals, including fertilizers. However, the company saw that there were enormous opportunities in the emerging field of biotechnology. Specifically, senior research scientists at Monsanto felt that it might be possible to produce genetically engineered crop seeds that would produce their own "organic" pesticides. That year, the company began a massive investment, which ultimately amounted to several hundred of millions of dollars, to build a world-class competency in biotechnology. This investment was funded by cash flows generated by Monsanto's core chemical operations. The investment started to bear fruit in the mid 1990s, when Monsanto introduced a series of genetically engineered crop seeds, including Bollgard, a cotton seed that is resistant to many common pests, including the bollworm, and Roundup resistant soybean seeds (Round up is a herbicide produced by Monsanto).[6]

Like more traditional tools for reviewing the corporate portfolio, such as the portfolio planning matrices discussed earlier, the framework advocated by Hamel and Prahalad helps to identify business opportunities and has clear implications for allocating resources (as exemplified by the Monsanto case just discussed). However, the great advantage of Hamel and Prahalad's framework is that it focuses explicitly on how a company can *create value* by building new competencies or by recombining existing competencies to enter new business areas (as Canon did with fax machines and bubble jet printers). Whereas traditional portfolio tools treat businesses as independent, Hamel and Prahald's framework recognizes the interdependencies between businesses and focuses on the opportunities for creating value by building and leveraging competencies. In this sense, their framework is far more "strategic" than the frameworks once advocated by the Boston Consulting Group and others like them.

Entry Strategy

Having reviewed the different businesses in the company's portfolio, corporate management might decide to enter a new business area, as Monsanto did when it decided in 1979 to enter the biotechnology field. There are three vehicles that companies use to enter new business areas: internal ventures, acquisition, and joint ventures. In the next three sections, we review the benefits and risks associated with each entry mode and consider how those risks can be minimized. Then we discuss the factors that influence the choice among these three modes in a given situation.

INTERNAL NEW VENTURING

Attractions of Internal New Venturing

Internal new venturing is typically employed as an entry strategy when a company possesses a set of valuable competencies (resources and capabilities) in its existing businesses that can be leveraged or recombined to enter the new business area. As a rule, science-based companies that use their technology to create market opportunities in related areas tend to favor internal new venturing as an entry strategy. Du Pont, for example, has created whole new markets with products such as cellophane, nylon, Freon, and Teflon—all internally generated innovations. Another company, 3M, has a near-legendary knack for shaping new markets from internally generated ideas. Hewlett-Packard moved into computers and peripherals by creating internal new ventures. Intel offers yet another example of a company that has leveraged its core competencies to enter new markets. Intel started off as a manufacturer of memory devices (DRAMs), but it subsequently built on its core competencies in semiconductor design and fabrication to enter the microprocessor business, and then the flash memory business. Interestingly enough, Intel exited the DRAM business in the late 1980s, but it remains the world's largest producer of microprocessors and flash memories.

Even if it lacks the competencies required to compete in a new business area, a company may pursue an internal venturing strategy when it is entering a newly emerging or embryonic industry in which there are no established players that possess the competencies required to compete in that industry. In such a case, the option of acquiring an established enterprise possessing those competencies is ruled out and the company may have no choice but to enter through an internal new venture. That was the position Monsanto found itself in when, in 1979, it contemplated entering the biotechnology field to produce herbicides and pest-resistant crop seeds. The biotechnology field was young at that time, and there were no incumbent companies focused on applying biotechnology to agricultural products. Accordingly, Monsanto established an internal new venture to enter the field, even though at the time it lacked the required competencies. Indeed, Monsanto's whole venturing strategy was developed around the notion that it needed to build competencies ahead of other potential competitors, thereby gaining a strong competitive lead in this newly emerging field.

Pitfalls of Internal New Venturing

Despite the popularity of the internal new venture strategy, its failure is reportedly very high. The evidence on the failure rate of new products indicates the scope of the problem, since most internal new ventures are associated with new product offerings. According to the evidence, somewhere between 33 and 60 percent of all new products that reach the marketplace fail to generate an adequate economic return.[7] Three reasons are often given to explain the relatively high failure rate of internal new ventures: (1) market entry on too small a scale, (2) poor commercialization of the new venture product, and (3) poor corporate management of the venture process.[8]

Scale of Entry Research suggests that *on average* large-scale entry into a new business is often a critical precondition of new-venture success. Although in the short run, large-scale entry means significant development costs and substantial losses, in the long run (which can be as long as five to twelve years, depending on the industry) it brings greater returns than small-scale entry.[9] The reasons for this include the ability of large-scale entrants to more rapidly realize scale economies, build brand loyalty, and gain access to distribution channels, all of which increase the probability that a new venture will succeed. In contrast, small-scale entrants may find themselves handicapped both by high costs, due to a lack of scale economies, and by a lack of market presence, which limits their ability to build brand loyalties and gain access to distribution channels. These scale effects are probably particularly significant when a company is entering an established industry, where incumbent companies have scale economies, brand loyalties, and access to distribution channels, and the new entrant often has to match these in order to succeed.

Figure 10.4 plots the relationships among scale of entry, profitability, and cash flow over time for successful small-scale and large-scale ventures. The figure shows that successful small-scale entry incurs lower initial losses, but in the long run large-scale entry generates greater returns. However, perhaps because of the costs of large-scale entry and the potential losses if the venture fails, many companies prefer a small-scale entry strategy. Acting on this preference can be a mistake, for the company fails to build up the market share necessary for long-term success.

FIGURE 10.4

Scale of Entry, Profitability, and Cash Flow

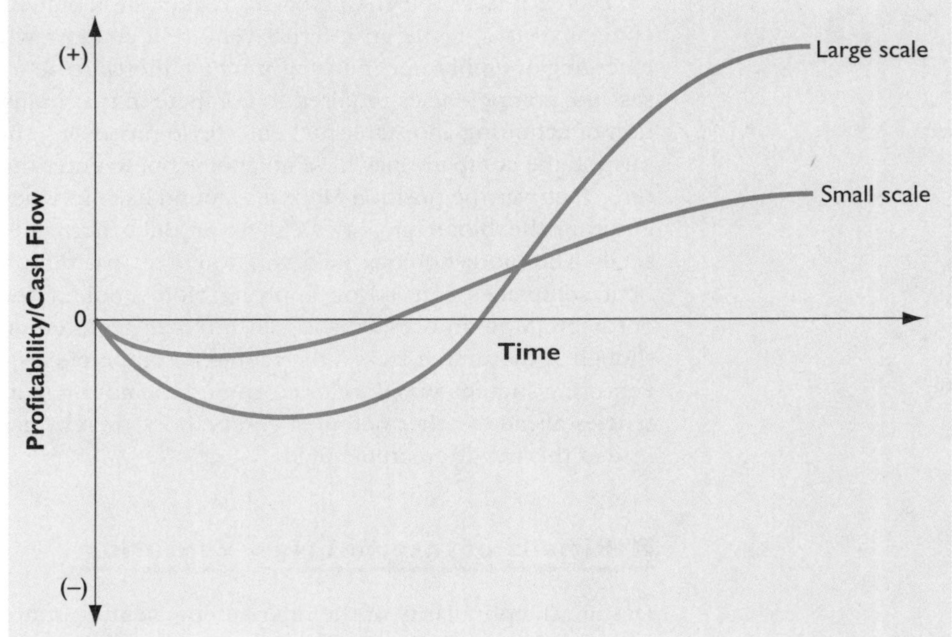

Commercialization Many internal new ventures are high-technology operations. To be commercially successful, science-based innovations must be developed with market requirements in mind. Many internal new ventures fail when a company ignores the basic needs of the market. A company can become blinded by the technological possibilities of a new product and fail to analyze market opportunities properly. Thus, a new venture may fail because of a lack of commercialization or because it is marketing a technology for which there is no demand. One of the most dramatic new venture failures in recent years, that of the Iridium satellite communications system developed by Motorola, is discussed in Strategy in Action 10.2. As you will see, Iridium failed because, even though the technology was impressive, the market demand did not materialize and may never have been there in the first place.

The desktop computer marketed by NeXT, the company started by the founder of Apple, Steven Jobs, is another example of a new venture that miscarried. The NeXT system failed to gain market share because the computer incorporated an array of expensive technologies that consumers simply did not want—such as optical disk drives and hi-fi sound. The optical disk drives, in particular, turned customers off because they made it difficult to switch work from a PC with a floppy drive to a NeXT machine with an optical drive. In other words, NeXT failed because its founder was so dazzled by leading-edge technology that he ignored customer needs.

Poor Implementation Managing the new-venture process raises difficult organizational issues.[11] Although we deal with the specifics of implementation in later chapters, we must note some of the most common mistakes here.[12] The shotgun approach of supporting many different internal new-venture projects can be a major error, for it places great demands on a company's cash flow and can result in the best ventures being starved of the cash they need for success.

10.2 STRATEGY *in* ACTION

Iridium Falls to Earth

The Iridium project was dreamed up by Motorola engineers back in the 1980s. The project was breathtaking in its scope. It called for sixty-six communications satellites to be placed in an orbital network. In theory, this network of flying telecommunications switches would enable anyone with an Iridium satellite phone to place and receive calls, no matter where the individual was on the planet—deep in the urban canyons of New York, at the bottom of the Grand Canyon, or in the most remote parts of the Amazon jungle. Motorola's CEO, Christopher Galvin, called the project the eighth wonder of the world. Five billion dollars later, Iridium went live on November 1, 1998. Motorola had spun the company off a few years earlier but still held 18 percent of the equity and several lucrative supply contracts with Iridium. Nine months later, Iridium declared bankruptcy after defaulting on scheduled debt service payments. Although Iridium had received 1.5 million inquiries from people interested in the service, only 20,000 subscribers had signed on, compared with a first-year target of 500,000. With so few customers, Iridium could not generate the income required to service its debt payments.

To its critics, the Iridium project was a classic case of a company being so blinded by the promise of a technology that it ignored market realities. The project had several serious shortcomings that limited its market acceptance. First, the phones themselves were large and heavy by current cell phone standards, weighing more than a pound. They were difficult to use and came with all sorts of attachments that perplexed many customers. Call clarity was poor and despite the "can be used anywhere" marketing theme, the phones could not be used inside cars or buildings—the favorite hangouts of the busy globetrotting executives at whom the service was aimed. Second, the service was expensive. The phones themselves cost $3,000 each, and airtime ranged from $4 to $9 per minute—placing the service way out of the reach of a mass market. Third, Iridium had a very poor sales and distribution system. Someone wishing to purchase a phone and sign up for the service would have had a hard time finding a distributor. And finally, the wide acceptance of a much cheaper and more convenient substitute, the conventional cell phone, limited the need for the Iridium Satellite phone. True, because of incompatible standards and limited coverage, cell phones cannot be used everywhere but nowadays an executive visiting a foreign country can easily rent a cell phone at the airport, and it will suffice for most, if not all, of his or her needs. Given this, who would pay $3,000 for the privilege of owning a phone the size and weight of a brick that would not work in places where cell phones do work—such as buildings and cars?[10]

Another common mistake is failure by corporate management to set the strategic context within which new-venture projects should be developed. Simply allowing a team of research scientists to do research in their favorite field may produce novel results, but these results may have little strategic or commercial value. It is necessary to be very clear about the strategic objectives of the venture and to understand how the venture will seek to establish a competitive advantage.

Failure to anticipate the time and costs involved in the venture process constitutes a further mistake. Many companies have unrealistic expectations regarding the time frame required. Reportedly, some companies operate with a philosophy of killing new businesses if they do not turn a profit by the end of the third year—clearly an unrealistic view, given the evidence that it can take five to twelve years before a venture generates substantial profits.

Guidelines for Successful Internal New Venturing

To avoid the pitfalls just discussed, a company should adopt a structured approach to managing internal new venturing. New venturing typically begins with R&D. To make effective use of its R&D capacity, a company must first spell out its strategic objectives and then communicate them to its scientists and engineers. Research, after all, makes sense only when it is undertaken in areas relevant to strategic goals.[13]

To increase the probability of commercial success, a company should foster close links between R&D and marketing personnel, for this is the best way to ensure that research projects address the needs of the market. The company should also foster close links between R&D and manufacturing personnel, to ensure that the company has the capability to manufacture any proposed new products.

Many companies successfully integrate different functions by setting up project teams. Such teams comprise representatives of the various functional areas; their task is to oversee the development of new products. For example, Compaq's success in introducing new products in the personal computer industry has been linked to its use of project teams, which oversee the development of a new product from its inception to its market introduction.

Another advantage of such teams is that they can significantly reduce the time it takes to develop a new product. Thus, while R&D personnel are working on the design, manufacturing personnel can be setting up facilities, and marketing personnel can be developing its plans. Because of such integration, Compaq needed only six months to take the first portable personal computer from an idea on the drawing board to a marketable product.

To use resources most effectively, a company must also devise a selection process for choosing only the ventures that demonstrate the greatest probability of commercial success. Picking future winners is a tricky business, since by definition new ventures have an uncertain future. One study found the uncertainty surrounding new ventures to be so great that it usually took a company four to five years after launching the venture to reasonably estimate the venture's future profitability.[14] Nevertheless, a selection process is necessary if a company is to avoid spreading its resources too thinly over too many projects.

Once a project has been selected, management needs to monitor the progress of the venture closely. Evidence suggests that the most important criterion for evaluating a venture during its first four to five years is market share growth rather than cash flow or profitability. In the long run, the most successful ventures are those that increase their market share. A company should have clearly defined market share objectives for an internal new venture and decide to retain or kill it in its early years on the basis of its ability to achieve market share goals. Only in the medium term should profitability and cash flow begin to take on greater importance.

Finally, the association of large-scale entry with greater long-term profitability suggests that a company can increase the probability of success for an internal new venture by thinking big. Thinking big means the construction of efficient-scale manufacturing facilities ahead of demand, large marketing expenditures to build a market presence and brand loyalty, and a commitment by corporate management to accept initial losses as long as market share is expanding.

ACQUISITIONS AS AN ENTRY STRATEGY

Attractions of Acquisitions

Companies often use acquisition to enter a business area that is new to them when they lack important competencies (resources and capabilities) required to compete in that area, but when they can purchase an incumbent company that has those competencies and do so at a reasonable price. Companies also have a preference for acquisitions as an entry mode when they feel the need to move fast. As discussed earlier, building a new business through internal venturing can be a relatively slow process. In contrast, acquisition is a much quicker way to establish a significant market presence and generate profitability. A company can purchase a market leader in a strong cash position overnight, rather than spend years building up a market-leadership position through internal development. Thus, when speed is important, acquisition is the favored entry mode.

Acquisitions are also often perceived to be somewhat less risky that internal new ventures, primarily because they involve less uncertainty. Because of the nature of internal new ventures, large uncertainties are associated with projecting future profitability, revenues, and cash flows. In contrast, when a company makes an acquisition, it is acquiring known profitability, known revenues, and known market share; thus it reduces uncertainty. An acquisition allows a company to buy an established business with a track record, and for this reason many companies favor acquisitions.

Finally, acquisitions may be the preferred entry mode when the industry to be entered is well established and incumbent enterprises enjoy significant protection from barriers to entry. As you may recall from Chapter 3, barriers to entry arise from factors associated with product differentiation (brand loyalty), absolute cost advantages, and economies of scale. When such barriers are substantial, a company finds entering an industry through internal new venturing difficult. To enter, a company may have to construct an efficient-scale manufacturing plant, undertake massive advertising to break down established brand loyalties, and quickly build up distribution outlets—all goals that are hard to achieve and likely to involve substantial expenditures. In contrast, by acquiring an established enterprise, a company can circumvent most entry barriers. It can purchase a market leader, which already benefits from substantial scale economies and brand loyalty. Thus, the greater the barriers to entry, the more likely it is that acquisitions will be the favored entry mode. (We should note, however, that the attractiveness of an acquisition is predicated on the assumption that an incumbent company can be acquired for less than it would cost to enter the same industry by way of an internal new venture. As we shall see in the next section, the validity of this assumption is often questionable.)

Pitfalls of Acquisitions

For the reasons just noted, acquisitions have long been a popular vehicle for expanding the scope of an organization into new business areas. Despite their popularity, however, there is ample evidence that many acquisitions fail to add value for the acquiring company and, indeed, often end up dissipating value. For example, a study by Mercer Management Consulting looked at 150 acquisitions, worth more than $500 million each, that were undertaken between January 1990 and July 1995.[15] The Mercer study concluded that 50 percent of these acquisitions ended up eroding, or substantially eroding, shareholder value, while another 33 percent created only marginal returns. Just 17 percent of the acquisitions were judged to be successful.

More generally, there is a wealth of evidence from academic research suggesting that many acquisitions fail to realize their anticipated benefits.[16] In a major study of the postacquisition performance of acquired companies, David Ravenscraft and Mike Scherer concluded that many good companies were acquired and, on average, their profits and market shares declined following acquisition.[17] They also noted that a smaller but substantial subset of those good companies experienced traumatic difficulties, which ultimately led to their being sold off by the acquiring company. In other words, Ravenscraft and Scherer's evidence, like that presented by McKinsey and Company, suggests that many acquisitions destroy rather than create value.

Why do so many acquisitions apparently fail to create value? There appear to be four major reasons: (1) companies often experience difficulties when trying to integrate divergent corporate cultures; (2) companies overestimate the potential economic benefits from an acquisition; (3) acquisitions tend to be very expensive; and (4) companies often do not adequately screen their acquisition targets.

Postacquisition Integration Having made an acquisition, the acquiring company has to integrate the acquired business into its own organizational structure. Integration can entail the adoption of common management and financial control systems, the joining together of operations from the acquired and the acquiring company, or the establishment of linkages to share information and personnel. When integration is attempted, many unexpected problems can occur. Often they stem from differences in corporate cultures. After an acquisition, many acquired companies experience high management turnover, possibly because their employees do not like the acquiring company's way of doing things.[18] Research evidence suggests that the loss of management talent and expertise, to say nothing of the damage from constant tension between the businesses, can materially harm the performance of the acquired unit.[19] For an example of what can occur, see Strategy in Action 10.3, which examines the high management turnover at The Boston Company, after it was acquired by Mellon Bank in 1993.

Overestimating Economic Benefits Even when companies achieve integration, they often overestimate the potential for creating value by joining together different businesses. They overestimate the strategic advantages that can be derived from the acquisition and thus pay more for the target company than it is probably worth. Richard Roll has attributed this tendency to hubris on the part of top management. According to Roll, top managers typically overestimate their ability to create value from an acquisition, primarily because rising to the top of a corporation has given them an exaggerated sense of their own capabilities.[21]

Coca-Cola's 1975 acquisition of a number of medium-sized winemaking companies illustrates the situation in which a company overestimates the economic benefits from an acquisition. Reasoning that a beverage is a beverage, Coca-Cola wanted to use its distinctive competency in marketing to dominate the U.S. wine industry. But after buying three wine companies and enduring seven years of marginal prof-

10.3 STRATEGY *in* ACTION

Postacquisition Problems at Mellon Bank

In the early 1990s, Frank Cahouet, the CEO of Philadelphia-based Mellon Bank, conceived of a corporate strategy that would reduce the vulnerability of Mellon's earnings to changes in interest rates. Cahouet's solution was to diversify into financial services in order to gain access to a steady flow of fee-based income from money management operations. As part of this strategy, in 1993 Mellon acquired The Boston Company for $1.45 billion. Boston is a high-profile money management company that manages investments for major institutional clients, such as state and corporate pension funds. In 1994, Mellon followed up its Boston acquisition with the acquisition of Dreyfus, a mutual fund provider, for $1.7 billion. As a result, by 1995 almost half of Mellon's income was generated from fee-based financial services.

However, in 1995 Mellon hit some serious bumps on the road in its attempt to become a money market powerhouse. Problems at Boston began to surface soon after the Mellon acquisition. From the start, there was a clear clash of cultures. At Mellon, many managers arrive at their mundane offices by 7 A.M. and put in twelve-hour days for pay that is modest by banking industry standards. They are also accustomed to a firm management hierarchy, carefully controlled by Frank Cahouet, whose management style emphasizes cost containment and frugality. Boston managers also put in twelve-hour days, but they expect considerable autonomy, flexible work schedules, high pay, ample perks, and large performance bonuses. In most years, the top twenty executives at Boston earn between $750,000 and $1 million each. Mellon executives who visited the Boston unit were dumbstruck by the country club atmosphere and opulence they saw. In its move to streamline Boston, Mellon insisted that Boston cut expenses and introduced new regulations for restricting travel, entertainment, and perks.

Things started to go wrong in October 1993, when the Wisconsin state pension fund complained to Mellon of lower returns on a portfolio run by Boston. In November, Mellon liquidated the portfolio, taking a $130 million charge against earnings. Mellon also fired the responsible portfolio manager, who, it claimed, was making "unathorized trades." At Boston, however, many managers saw Mellon's action as violating guarantees of operating autonomy that Mellon had given Boston at the time of the acquisition. They blamed Mellon for prematurely liquidating a portfolio whose strategy, they claimed, Mellon executives had approved—a portfolio, moreover, that could still prove a winner if interest rates fell (which they subsequently did).

Infuriated by Mellon's interference in the running of Boston, in March seven managers at Boston's asset management unit, including the unit's CEO, Desmond Heathwood, proposed a management buyout to Mellon. This unit was one of the gems in Boston's crown, with over $26 billion in assets under management. Heathwood had been openly disdainful of Mellon's bankers, believing that they were out of their league in the investment business. In April, Mellon rejected the buyout proposal, and Heathwood promptly left to start his own investment management company. A few days later Mellon asked employees at Boston to sign employment contracts that limited their ability to leave and work for Heathwood's competing business. Another thirteen senior employees refused to sign and quit to join Heathwood's new money management operation.

The defection of Heathwood and his colleges was followed by a series of high-profile client defections. The Arizona state retirement system, for example, pulled $1 billion out of Mellon and transferred it to Heathwood's firm, and the Fresno Country retirement system transferred $400 million in assets over to Heathwood. As one client stated, "We have a relationship with The Boston Co. that goes back over 30 years, and the people who worked on the account are the people who left—so we left too."

Reflecting on the episode, Frank Cahouet noted that "we've clearly been hurt. . . . But this episode is very manageable. We are not going to lose our momentum." Others weren't so sure. In this incident, they saw yet another example of how difficult it can be to merge two divergent corporate cultures, and how the management turnover that results from such attempts can deal a serious blow to any attempt to create value out of an acquisition.[20]

its, Coca-Cola finally conceded that wine and soft drinks are very different products, with different kinds of appeal, pricing systems, and distribution networks. In 1983, it sold the wine operations to Joseph E. Seagram & Sons for $210 million—the price Coca-Cola had paid and a substantial loss when adjusted for inflation.[22]

The Expense of Acquisitions Acquisitions of companies whose stock is publicly traded tend to be very expensive. When a company bids to acquire the stock of another enterprise, the stock price frequently gets bid up in the acquisition process. This is particularly likely to occur in the case of contested bids, where two or more companies simultaneously bid for control of a single target company. Thus, the acquiring company must often pay a premium over the current market value of the target. In the early 1980s, acquiring companies paid an average premium of 40 to 50 percent over current stock prices for an acquisition. Between 1985 and 1988, when takeover activity was at its peak, premiums of 80 percent were not uncommon. Indeed, in the giant contested takeover bid for RJR Nabisco during late 1988, the stock price of RJR was bid up from $45 per share prior to the takeover attempt to $110 per share by the time RJR was sold—a premium of over 200 percent! By the first half of the 1990s, the takeover premium was once more in the 40 to 50 percent range.

The debt taken on to finance such expensive acquisitions can later become a noose around the acquiring company's neck, particularly if interest rates rise. Moreover, if the market value of the target company prior to an acquisition was a true reflection of that company's worth under its management at that time, a premium of 50 over this value means that the acquiring company has to improve the performance of the acquired unit by just as much if it is to reap a positive return on its investment. Such performance gains, however, can be very difficult to achieve.

Inadequate Preacquisition Screening After researching acquisitions made by twenty different companies, a study by Philippe Haspeslagh and David Jemison concluded that one reason for the failure of acquisitions is management's inadequate attention to preacquisition screening.[23] It found that many companies decide to acquire other firms without thoroughly analyzing the potential benefits and costs. Then, after the acquisition has been completed, the companies discover that instead of a well-run business, they have bought a troubled organization. That was Xerox's experience when it purchased the Crum and Forster insurance business in the early 1980s. Only after completing the acquisition did Xerox learn that Crum and Forster was a high-cost and inefficient provider of insurance. Xerox subsequently divested the business at a significant financial loss.

Guidelines for Successful Acquisition

To avoid pitfalls and make successful acquisitions, companies need to take a structured approach with three main components: (1) target identification and preacquisition screening, (2) bidding strategy, and (3) integration.[24]

Screening Thorough preacquisition screening increases a company's knowledge about potential takeover targets, leads to a more realistic assessment of the problems involved in executing an acquisition and integrating the new business into the company's organizational structure, and lessens the risk of purchasing a potential problem business. The screening should begin with a detailed assessment of the strategic rationale for making the acquisition and identification of the kind of enterprise that would make an ideal acquisition candidate.

Next, the company should scan a target population of potential acquisition candidates, and evaluate each according to a detailed set of criteria, focusing on (1) financial position, (2) product market position, (3) competitive environment, (4) management capabilities, and (5) corporate culture. Such an evaluation should enable the company to identify the strengths and weaknesses of each candidate, the extent of potential economies of scope between the acquiring and the acquired companies, the compatibility of the two corporate cultures, and potential integration problems.

The company should then reduce the list of candidates to the most favored ones and evaluate them further. At this stage, it should sound out third parties, such as investment bankers, whose opinions may be important and who may be able to give valuable insights about the efficiency of target companies. The company that leads the list after this process should be the acquisition target.

Bidding Strategy The objective of bidding strategy is to reduce the price that a company must pay for an acquisition candidate. The essential element of a good bidding strategy is timing. For example, Hanson PLC, one of the most successful takeover machines of the 1980s, always looked for essentially sound businesses that were suffering from short-term problems due to cyclical industry factors or from problems localized in one division. Such companies are typically undervalued by the stock market and thus can be picked up without payment of the standard 40 or 50 percent premium over current stock prices. With good timing, a company can make a bargain purchase.

Integration Despite good screening and bidding, an acquisition will fail unless positive steps are taken to integrate the acquired company into the organizational structure of the acquiring one. Integration should center on the source of the potential strategic advantages of the acquisition—for instance, opportunities to share marketing, manufacturing, procurement, R&D, financial, or management resources. Integration should also be accompanied by steps to eliminate any duplication of facilities or functions. In addition, any unwanted activities of the acquired company should be sold. Finally, if the different business activities are closely related, they will require a high degree of integration. In the case of a company like Hanson PLC, the level of integration can be minimal, for the company's strategy is one of unrelated diversification. But a company such as Philip Morris requires greater integration because its strategy is one of related diversification.

JOINT VENTURES AS AN ENTRY STRATEGY

Attractions of Joint Ventures

A company may prefer internal new venturing to acquisition as an entry strategy into new business areas, yet hesitate to commit itself to an internal new venture because of the risks and costs of building a new operation from the ground up. Such a situation is most likely to occur when a company sees the possibility of establishing a new business in an embryonic or growth industry but the risks and costs associated with the project are more than it is willing to assume on its own. In these circumstances, the company may decide to enter into a joint venture with another company and use the joint venture as a vehicle for entering the new business area. Such an arrangement enables the company to share the substantial risks and costs involved in a new project.

To illustrate, in 1990 IBM and Motorola set up a joint venture with the aim of providing a service that allowed computer users to communicate over radio waves. Customers buying the service can use hand-held computers, made by Motorola, to communicate by means of a private network of radio towers that IBM has built across the United States. The venture targets the potentially enormous market of people who could benefit from using computers in the field—for instance, people who repair equipment in offices and insurance claims adjusters. Analysts estimate that the market for such a service is currently in the tens of millions of dollars but could reach billions over the next decade.[25]

Because of the embryonic nature of the industry, the venture faces substantial risks. A number of competing technologies are on the horizon. For example, laptop computers are being fitted with modems that can communicate with host computers through cellular telephone networks. Although cellular networks are more crowded and less reliable than radio networks, that state of affairs could change. Given this uncertainty, it makes sense for IBM and Motorola to combine in a joint venture and share the risks associated with building up this business.

In addition, a joint venture makes sense when a company can increase the probability of successfully establishing a new business by joining forces with another company. For a company that has some of the skills and assets necessary to establish a successful new venture, teaming up with another company that has complementary skills and assets may increase the probability of success.

Again, the venture between IBM and Motorola provides an example. Motorola dominates the market for mobile radios and already manufactures hand-held computers, but it lacks a nationwide radio network through which users of hand-held computers might communicate with each other. IBM lacks radio technology, but it does have a private network of radio towers (originally built for communicating with 20,000-plus IBM service people in the field), which covers more than 90 percent of the country. Combining Motorola's skills in radio technology with IBM's radio network in a single joint venture increases significantly the probability of establishing a successful new business.

Drawbacks of Joint Ventures

There are three main drawbacks to joint venture arrangements. First, a joint venture allows a company to share the risks and costs of developing a new business, but it also requires the sharing of profits if the new business succeeds. Second, a company that enters into a joint venture always runs the risk of giving critical know-how away to its joint venture partner, which might use that know-how to compete directly with the company in the future. As we point out in discussing global strategic alliances in Chapter 8, however, joint ventures can be structured to minimize this risk. Third, the venture partners must share control. If the partners have different business philosophies, time horizons, or investment preferences, substantial problems can arise. Conflicts over how to run the joint venture can tear it apart and result in business failure.

In sum, although joint ventures often have a distinct advantage over internal new venturing as a means of establishing a new business operation, they also have certain drawbacks. When deciding whether to go it alone or cooperate with another company in a joint venture, strategic managers need to assess carefully the pros and cons of the alternatives.

RESTRUCTURING

So far we have focused on strategies for expanding the scope of a company into new business areas. We turn now to their opposite: strategies for reducing the scope of the company by *exiting* business areas. In recent years, reducing the scope of a company through restructuring has become an increasingly popular strategy, particularly among the companies that diversified their activities during the 1960s, 1970s, and 1980s. In most cases, companies that are engaged in restructuring are divesting themselves of diversified activities in order to concentrate on their core businesses.[26] They include General Electric, which began restructuring when Jack Welch became its CEO, and Sears, which sold off Allstate Insurance, Coldwell Banker Real Estate, and the brokerage Dean Witter Reynolds, in order to focus more on its core retailing operations. (For details of restructuring at Sears, see Strategy in Action 10.4.)

The first question that must be asked is, why are so many companies restructuring at this particular time? After answering it, we examine the different strategies that companies adopt for exiting from business areas. Then we discuss the various turnaround strategies that companies employ to revitalize their core business area.

Why Restructure?

One reason for so much restructuring in recent years is overdiversification. There is plenty of evidence that in the heyday of the corporate diversification movement, which began in the 1960s and lasted until the early 1980s, many companies overdiversified.[27] More precisely, the bureaucratic inefficiencies created by expanding the scope of the organization outweighed the additional value that could be created, and company performance declined. As performance declined, the stock price of many of these diversified companies fell, and they found themselves vulnerable to hostile takeover bids. Indeed, a number of diversified companies were acquired in the 1980s and subsequently broken up. This is what happened to U.S. Industries and SCM, two diversified conglomerates that were acquired and then broken up by Hanson PLC. Similarly, after the diversified consumer products business RJR Nabisco was acquired by Kohlberg, Kravis & Roberts in a 1988 leveraged buyout, RJR sold off many of its diversified businesses to independent investors or to other companies.

A second factor driving the current restructuring trend is that in the 1980s and 1990s many diversified companies found their core business areas under attack from new competition. For example, due to deregulation AT&T now faces a much

10.4 STRATEGY *in* ACTION

The Restructuring of Sears

In 1981, Sears, which was then the largest retailer in the United States, announced in a single week that it would acquire Dean Witter Reynolds, the country's fifth largest stockbrokerage, and Coldwell Banker, the nation's biggest real estate broker, for a total of $800 million. The idea was to team those two financial service operations with Allstate Insurance, which Sears had acquired in 1934 and which was then the world's second largest personal property and casualty insurer. At the heart of this strategy was the desire on the part of Sears to leverage its fabled "bond of trust" with the consumer into the fast-growing financial services industry—a strategy its CEO, Edward Brennan, often referred to as "socks to stocks." Sears felt that its retail customers would be strongly attracted to financial services providers that were owned by Sears. Indeed, the company planned to locate offices for its financial services operations in Sears department stores, and to use its catalog mailing list as a channel for selling financial services.

However, the 1980s and early 1990s were not kind to Sears. While the financial services operations of the company did well, its core retailing operation ran into serious problems. During most of the 1980s, the earnings of the Sears retail group fell at an annual rate of 7 to 8 percent and its market share slumped. The share of department store merchandise accounted for by Sears fell from 9 percent in 1982 to 6 percent in 1992. More significantly, Sears did little to keep up with the growth of discount and niche retailers such as Wal-Mart, Costco, Home Depot, and Toys 'R' Us, all of which ate into Sears's blue-collar clientele. Critics charged that senior executives at Sears seemed more interested in new ventures and the potential for synergy than in the basic business of running the Sears stores. As a result, Sears was slow to respond to new competition and its sales stagnated.

The problems in the retail operations at Sears attracted the scorn of Wall Street and at least one abortive takeover attempt in early 1988, when rumors of a $50.2 billion takeover bid by Revlon's Chairman Ronald O. Perelman were making the rounds on Wall Street. Sears responded by announcing a decision to sell off its Chicago headquarters and introducing an "everyday low pricing" strategy at its stores. Both moves failed. After a year, Sears abandoned attempts to sell the Sears Tower. Furthermore, it never could convince consumers that it had the lowest prices in town—probably because it didn't.

Meanwhile, the stock continued to slump. To make matters worse, in 1992 Sears's fabled "bond of trust" with consumers was blown apart when it was revealed that its automobile services operation had been systematically overcharging consumers for repair services. At the same time, Moody's Investors Service, noting Sears's growing burden of debt, lowered the company's bond rating. The stock slumped further, and investors pushed the company to take drastic action. In September 1992, Sears announced plans to sell Dean Witter Reynolds and Coldwell Banker and to spin off 20 percent of Allstate to independent investors. In effect, Sears was turning its back on thirteen years of diversification and an investment of billions of dollars so that top management could devote more time to revitalizing its troubled retailing arm. This shift was a humiliating admission by top management, and particularly CEO Brennan, that they had mishandled the company's strategy.[28]

more competitive environment in its core long-distance business, which helped to drive its decision to exit from noncore activities. Similarly, Sears still faces profound competitive challenges in the retailing industry, where demand is shifting from department stores such as Sears to low-cost discounters such as Costco, or niche stores like The Gap (see Strategy in Action 10.4). The top management of these companies found that in order to devote the necessary attention to their troubled core business it had to shed its diversified activities, which had become an unwelcome distraction.

A final factor of some importance is that innovations in management processes and strategy have diminished the advantages of vertical integration or diversification. In response, companies have reduced the scope of their activities through restructuring and divestments. For example, ten years ago there was little understanding of how long-term cooperative relationships between a company and its suppliers could be a viable alternative to vertical integration. Most companies considered only two alternatives for managing the supply chain: vertical integration or competitive bidding. As we note in Chapter 9, however, if the conditions are right, a third alternative for managing the supply chain, *long-term contracting*, can be a strategy that is superior to both vertical integration and competitive bidding. Like vertical integration, long-term contracting facilitates investments in specialization. But unlike vertical integration, it does not involve high bureaucratic costs, nor does it dispense with market discipline. As this strategic innovation has spread throughout the business world, the relative advantages of vertical integration have declined.

Exit Strategies

Companies can choose from three main strategies for exiting business areas: divestment, harvest, and liquidation. You have already encountered all three in Chapter 7, where we discuss strategies for competing in declining industries. We review them briefly here.

Divestment Of the three main strategies, divestment is usually favored. It represents the best way for a company to recoup as much of its initial investment in a business unit as possible. The idea is to sell the business unit to the highest bidder. Three types of buyers are independent investors, other companies, and the management of the unit to be divested. Selling off a business unit to independent investors is normally referred to as a **spinoff**. A spinoff makes good sense when the unit to be sold is profitable and when the stock market has an appetite for new stock issues (which is normal during market upswings, but *not* during market downswings). Thus, for example, in 1992 the timber products company Weyerhaeuser successfully spun off its Paragon Trade Brands to independent investors. Investors snapped up the stock of the new issue, which makes "own label" disposable diapers for supermarket chains and is highly profitable. However, spinoffs do not work if the unit to be spun off is unprofitable and unattractive to independent investors or if the stock market is slumping and unresponsive to new issues.

Selling off a unit to another company is a strategy frequently pursued when a unit can be sold to a company in the same line of business as the unit. In such cases, the purchaser is often prepared to pay a considerable amount of money for the opportunity to substantially increase the size of its business virtually overnight. For example, in 1987 Hanson PLC sold off its Glidden paint subsidiary, which it acquired six months earlier in the takeover of SCM, to Imperial Chemicals Industry (ICI). Glidden was the largest paint company in the United States, and ICI was the largest manufacturer of paint outside the United States, so the match made a good deal of sense from ICI's perspective, while Hanson was able to get a substantial price for the sale.

Selling off a unit to its management is normally referred to as a **management buyout (MBO)**. MBOs are very similar to leveraged buyouts (LBOs), discussed in

Chapter 2. In an MBO, the unit is sold to its management, which often finances the purchase through the sale of high-yield bonds to investors. The bond issue is normally arranged by a buyout specialist, such as Kohlberg, Kravis & Roberts, which, along with management, will typically hold a sizable proportion of the shares in the MBO. MBOs often take place when financially troubled units have only two other options: a harvest strategy or liquidation.

An MBO can be very risky for the management team involved, since its members may have to sign personal guarantees to back up the bond issue and may lose everything if the MBO ultimately fails. On the other hand, if the management team succeeds in turning around the troubled unit, its reward can be a significant increase in personal wealth. Thus, an MBO strategy can be characterized as a ***high risk–high return*** strategy for the management team involved. Faced with the possible liquidation of their business unit, many management teams are willing to take the risk. However, the viability of this option depends not only on a willing management team, but also on there being enough buyers of high yield–high risk bonds—so-called junk bonds—to be able to finance the MBO. In recent years, the general slump in the junk bond market has made the MBO strategy a more difficult one for companies to follow.

Harvest and Liquidation Since the pros and cons of harvest and liquidation strategies are discussed in detail in Chapter 6, we note just a few points here. First, a harvest or liquidation strategy is generally considered inferior to a divestment strategy since the company can probably best recoup its investment in a business unit by divestment. Second, a harvest strategy means halting investment in a unit in order to maximize short- to medium-term cash flow from that unit before liquidating it. Although this strategy seems fine in theory, it is often a poor one to apply in practice. Once it becomes apparent that the unit is pursuing a harvest strategy, the morale of the unit's employees, as well as the confidence of the unit's customers and suppliers in its continuing operation, can sink very quickly. If this occurs, as it often does, then the rapid decline in the unit's revenues can make the strategy untenable. Finally, a liquidation strategy is the least attractive of all to pursue since it requires the company to write off its investment in a business unit, often at a considerable cost. However, in the case of a poorly performing business unit for which a selloff or spinoff is unlikely and an MBO cannot be arranged, liquidation may be the only viable alternative.

TURNAROUND STRATEGY

Many companies restructure their operations, divesting themselves of their diversified activities, because they wish to focus more on their core business area. As in the case of Sears, this often occurs because the core business area is itself in trouble and needs top management attention. An integral part of restructuring, therefore, is the development of a strategy for turning around the company's core or remaining business areas. In this section, we review in some detail the various steps that companies take to turn around troubled business areas. We first look at the causes of corporate decline and then discuss the main elements of successful turnaround strategies.

The Causes of Corporate Decline

Seven main causes stand out in most cases of corporate decline: poor management, overexpansion, inadequate financial controls, high costs, the emergence of powerful new competition, unforeseen shifts in demand, and organizational inertia.[29] Normally, several, if not all, of these factors are present in a decline. For example, IBM's decline in the early 1990s was brought on by a high-cost structure, powerful new low-cost competition from personal computer makers, a shift in demand away from mainframe computers (IBM's main business), and IBM's slow response to these factors due to organizational inertia.

Poor Management Poor management covers a multitude of sins, ranging from sheer incompetence to neglect of core businesses and an insufficient number of good managers. Although not necessarily a bad thing, one-person rule often seems to be at the root of poor management. One study found that the presence of a dominant and autocratic chief executive with a passion for empire-building strategies often characterizes failing companies.[30] Another study of eighty-one turnaround situations found that in thirty-six cases troubled companies suffered from an autocratic manager who tried to do it all, but, in the face of complexity and change, could not.[31] In a review of the empirical studies of turnaround situations, Richard Hoffman identified a number of other management defects commonly found in declining companies.[32] These included a lack of balanced expertise at the top (for example, too many engineers), a lack of strong middle management, a failure to provide for orderly management succession by a departing CEO (which may result in an internal succession battle), and a failure by the board of directors to monitor adequately management's strategic decisions.

Overexpansion The empire-building strategies of autocratic CEOs often involve rapid expansion and extensive diversification. Much of this diversification tends to be poorly conceived and adds little value to the company. As already noted in this chapter and Chapter 9, the consequences of too much diversification include loss of control and an inability to cope with recessionary conditions. Moreover, companies that expand rapidly tend to do so by taking on large amounts of debt financing. Adverse economic conditions can limit a company's ability to meet its debt requirements and thus precipitate a financial crisis.

Inadequate Financial Controls The most common aspect of inadequate financial controls is the failure to assign profit responsibility to key decision makers within the organization. The lack of accountability for the financial consequences of their actions can encourage middle-level managers to employ excess staff and spend resources beyond what is necessary for maximum efficiency. In such cases, bureaucracy may balloon and costs spiral out of control. This is precisely what happened at Chrysler during the 1970s. As Lee Iacocca later noted, Jerry Greenwald, whom Iacocca brought in to head the finance function in 1980, "had a hell of a time finding anybody who could be identified as having specific responsibility for anything. They would tell him, 'Well, everyone is responsible for controlling costs.' Jerry knew very well what that meant—in the final analysis nobody was."[33]

High Costs Inadequate financial controls can lead to high costs. Beyond this, the most common cause of a high-cost structure is low labor productivity. It may stem from union-imposed restrictive working practices (as in the case of the auto and steel industries), management's failure to invest in new labor-saving technologies, or, more often, a combination of both. Other common causes include high wage rates (a particularly important factor for companies competing on costs in the global marketplace) and a failure to realize economies of scale because of low market share.

New Competition Competition in capitalist economies is a process characterized by the continual emergence of new companies championing new ways of doing business. In recent years few industries and few established companies have been spared the competitive challenge of powerful new competition. Indeed, many established businesses have failed or run into serious trouble because they did not respond quickly enough to such threats. Powerful new competition is a central cause of corporate decline. IBM has been hammered by powerful new competition from personal computer makers and Sears has been hard hit by powerful new competition from discount and niche stores (see Strategy in Action 10.4). In both these cases, the established company failed to appreciate the strength of new competitors until it was in serious trouble.

Unforeseen Demand Shifts Unforeseen, and often unforeseeable, shifts in demand can be brought about by major changes in technology, economic or political conditions, and social and cultural norms. Although such changes can open up market opportunities for new products, they also threaten the existence of many established enterprises, necessitating restructuring. A recent example is the rapid rise of the Internet and the World Wide Web, which, among other things, blind-sided Microsoft, the dominant software company in the personal computer market. Although Microsoft has since responded to the rise of the Internet, doing so required the company to remake its strategy.

Organizational Inertia On their own, the emergence of powerful new competition and unforeseen shifts in demand might not be enough to cause corporate decline. What is also required is an organization that is slow to respond to such environmental changes. As you saw in Chapter 4, where we first touched on the issue of corporate decline, organizational inertia stands out as a major reason why companies are often so slow to respond to new competitive conditions.

The Main Steps of Turnaround

There is no standard model of how a company should respond to a decline. Indeed, there can be no such model because every situation is unique. However, in most successful turnaround situations, a number of common features are present. They include changing the leadership, redefining the company's strategic focus, divesting or closing unwanted assets, taking steps to improve the profitability of remaining operations, and, occasionally, making acquisitions to rebuild core operations.

Changing the Leadership Since the old leadership bears the stigma of failure, new leadership is an essential element of most retrenchment and turnaround situations. For example, as the first step in implementing a turnaround, IBM replaced CEO John Akers with an outsider, Lou Gerstner. To resolve a crisis, the new leader should be someone who is able to make difficult decisions, motivate lower-level managers, listen to the views of others, and delegate power when appropriate.

Redefining Strategic Focus For a single-business enterprise, redefining strategic focus involves a reevaluation of the company's business-level strategy. A failed cost leader, for example, may reorient toward a more focused or differentiated strategy. For a diversified company, redefining strategic focus means identifying the businesses in the portfolio that have the best long-term profit and growth prospects and concentrating investment there.

Asset Sales and Closures Having redefined its strategic focus, a company should divest as many unwanted assets as it can find buyers for and liquidate whatever remains. It is important not to confuse unwanted assets with unprofitable assets. Assets that no longer fit in with the redefined strategic focus of the company may be very profitable. Their sale can bring the company much-needed cash, which it can invest in improving the operations that remain.

Improving Profitability Improving the profitability of the operations that remain after asset sales and closures requires a number of steps to improve efficiency, quality, innovation, and customer responsiveness. We discuss in Chapter 5 many of the functional-level strategies that companies can pursue to achieve these ends, so you may want to review that chapter for details. Note, though, that improving profitability typically involves one or more of the following: (1) laying off white- and blue-collar employees; (2) investing in labor-saving equipment; (3) assigning profit responsibility to individuals and subunits within the company, by a change of organizational structure if necessary; (4) tightening financial controls; (5) cutting back on marginal products; (6) reengineering business processes to cut costs and boost productivity; and (7) introducing total quality management processes.

Acquisitions A somewhat surprising but quite common turnaround strategy is to make acquisitions, primarily to strengthen the competitive position of a company's remaining core operations. For example, Champion International used to be a very diversified company, manufacturing a wide range of paper and wood products. After years of declining performance, in the mid 1980s Champion decided to focus on its profitable newsprint and magazine paper business. The company divested many of its other paper and wood products businesses, but at the same time it paid $1.8 billion for St. Regis, one of the country's largest manufacturers of newsprint and magazine paper.

SUMMARY OF CHAPTER

This chapter builds on the material in Chapter 9 by addressing central issues of corporate development. **Corporate development** is concerned with identifying *which* business opportunities a company should pursue, *how* it should pursue those opportunities, and *how* it should exit from businesses that do not fit the company's strategic vision. The chapter makes the following points:

- A common way for starting to identify which business opportunities to pursue is to review a company's existing portfolio of business activities. One approach to undertaking such a review utilizes a set of techniques known as portfolio planning matrices. The purpose of these techniques is to compare the competitive position of the different businesses in a company's portfolio on the basis of common criteria.

- ✔ A second approach to the corporate development process, championed by Gary Hamel and C.K. Prahalad, reconceptualizes a company as a portfolio of core competencies—as opposed to a portfolio of businesses. In this approach, corporate development is oriented toward maintaining existing competencies, building new competencies, and leveraging competencies by applying them to new business opportunities.
- ✔ The advantage of Hamel and Prahalad's framework is that it focuses explicitly on how a company can *create value* by building new competencies, or by recombining existing competencies to enter new business areas. While traditional portfolio planning matrices treat businesses as independent, Hamel and Prahald's framework recognizes the interdependencies between businesses and focuses on the opportunities for creating value by building and leveraging competencies.
- ✔ There are three vehicles that companies use to enter new business areas: internal ventures, acquisitions, and joint ventures.
- ✔ Internal new venturing is typically employed as an entry strategy when a company possesses a set of valuable competencies in its existing businesses that can be leveraged or recombined to enter the new business area.
- ✔ Many internal ventures fail because of entry on too small a scale, poor commercialization, and poor corporate management of the internal venture process. Guarding against failure involves a structured approach toward project selection and management, integration of R&D and marketing to improve commercialization of a venture idea, and entry on a significant scale.
- ✔ Acquisitions are often favored as an entry strategy when the company lacks important competencies (resources and capabilities) required to compete in an area, but when it can purchase an incumbent company that has those competencies and do so at a reasonable price. Acquisitions also tend to be favored when the barriers to entry into the target industry are high, and when the company is unwilling to accept the time frame, development costs, and risks of internal new venturing.
- ✔ Many acquisitions fail because of poor postacquisition integration, overestimation of the value that can be created from an acquisition, the high cost of acquisition, and poor preacquisition screening. Guarding against acquisition failure requires structured screening, good bidding strategies, and positive attempts to integrate the acquired company into the organization of the acquiring one.
- ✔ Joint ventures may be the preferred entry strategy when (1) the risks and costs associated with setting up a new business unit are more than the company is willing to assume on its own and (2) the company can increase the probability of successfully establishing a new business by teaming up with another company that has skills and assets complementing its own.
- ✔ The current popularity of restructuring is due to (1) overdiversification by many companies in the 1970s and 1980s, (2) the rise of competitive challenges to the core business units of many diversified enterprises, and (3) innovations in the management process that have reduced the advantages of vertical integration and diversification.
- ✔ Exit strategies include divestment, harvest, and liquidation. The choice of exit strategy is governed by the characteristics of the relevant business unit.
- ✔ The causes of corporate decline include poor management, overexpansion, inadequate financial controls, high costs, the emergence of powerful new competition, unforeseen shifts in demand, and organizational inertia.
- ✔ Responses to corporate decline include changing the leadership, redefining the company's strategic focus, divestment or closure of unwanted assets, taking steps to improve the profitability of the operations that remain, and occasionally, acquisitions to rebuild core operations.

DISCUSSION QUESTIONS

1. Under what circumstances might it be best to enter a new business area by acquisition, and under what

circumstances might internal new venturing be the preferred entry mode?

2. IBM has decided to diversify into the cellular telecommunication business. What entry strategy would you recommend that the company pursue? Why?

3. Review the change in the composition of GE's portfolio of businesses under the leadership of Jack Welch (1981 to the present). How has GE's portfolio been reorganized? From a value creation perspective, what is the logic underlying this reorganization?

Practicing Strategic Management

SMALL-GROUP EXERCISE
Dun & Bradstreet

Break up into groups of three to five people. Then read the following news release from Dun & Bradstreet. On the basis of this information, identify the strategic rationale for the split and evaluate how the split might affect the performance of three successor companies. If you were a stockholder in the old Dun & Bradstreet, would you approve of this split? Why?

D&B TRANSFORMED INTO THREE INDEPENDENT PUBLIC COMPANIES

WILTON, CONN., Jan. 9, 1996—Dun & Bradstreet CEO Robert E. Weissman today announced a sweeping strategy that will transform the 155-year-old business information giant into three publicly traded, global corporations.

"This important action is designed to increase shareholder value by unlocking D&B's substantial underlying franchise strengths," said Weissman.

Building on preeminent Dun & Bradstreet businesses, the reorganization establishes three independent companies focused on high-growth information markets; financial information services; and consumer-product market research.

"Since the 1800s, D&B has grown by effectively managing a portfolio of businesses and gaining economies of scale," stated Weissman. "But the velocity of change in information markets has dramatically altered the rules of business survival. Today, market focus and speed are the primary drivers of competitive advantage. This plan is our blueprint for success in the 21st century," said Weissman.

The plan, approved today at a special meeting of D&B's board of directors, calls for D&B to create three separate companies by spinning off two of its businesses to shareholders. "D&B is the leader in business information," said Weissman. "By freeing our companies to tightly focus on our core vertical markets, we can more rapidly leverage this leadership position into emerging growth areas."

The three new companies are:

- Cognizant Corporation, a new high-growth company, which includes IMS International, the leading global supplier of marketing information to the pharmaceutical and health care industries; Nielsen Media Research, the leader in audience measurement for electronic media; and Gartner Group, the premier provider of advisory services to high-tech users, vendors and suppliers, in which Cognizant will hold a majority interest.
- The Dun & Bradstreet Corporation, consisting of Dun & Bradstreet Information Services, the world's largest source of business-to-business marketing and commercial-credit information; Moody's Investors Service, a global leader in rating debt; and Reuben H. Donnelley, a premier provider of Yellow Pages marketing and publishing.
- A. C. Nielsen, the global leader in marketing information for the fast-moving consumer packaged goods industry.

"These three separate companies will tailor their strategies to the unique demands of their markets, determining investments, capital structures and policies that will strengthen their respective global capabilities. This plan also clarifies D&B from an investor's perspective by grouping the businesses into three logical investment categories, each with distinct risk/reward profiles," said Weissman.

The Dun & Bradstreet Corporation is the world's largest marketer of information, software and services for business decision making, with worldwide revenue of \$4.9 billion in 1994.

STRATEGIC MANAGEMENT PROJECT
Module 10

This module requires you to assess your company's use of acquisitions, internal new ventures, and joint ventures as strategies for entering a new business area and/or as attempts to restructure its portfolio of businesses.

ARTICLE FILE 10

Find an example of a company that has made an acquisition that apparently failed to create any value. Identify and critically evaluate the rationale used by top management to justify the acquisition at the time it was made. Explain why the acquisition subsequently failed.

A. If Your Company Has Entered a New Business Area During the Last Decade

1. Pick one new business area that your company has entered during the last ten years.
2. Identify the rationale for entering this business area.
3. Identify the strategy used to enter this business area.
4. Evaluate the rationale for using this particular entry strategy. Do you think that this was the best entry strategy to use? Justify your answer.
5. Do you think that the addition of this business area to the company has added or dissipated value? Again, justify your answer.

B. If Your Company Has Restructured Its Business During the Last Decade

1. Identify the rationale for pursuing a restructuring strategy.
2. Pick one business area that your company has exited from during the last ten years.
3. Identify the strategy used to exit from this particular business area. Do you think that this was the best exit strategy to use? Justify your answer.
4. In general, do you think that exiting from this business area has been in the company's best interest?

EXPLORING THE WEB
Visiting General Electric

Visit the Web site of General Electric (http://www.ge.com). Using the information contained within that Web site, answer the following questions:

1. Review GE's portfolio of major businesses. Does this portfolio make sense from a value creation perspective? Why?
2. What (if any) changes would you make to GE's portfolio of businesses? Why would you make these changes?
3. What (if any) core competencies do you think are held in common by one or more of GE's major business units? Is there any evidence that GE creates new businesses by leveraging its core competencies?

General Task By searching through information sources on the Web, find an example of a company that has recently restructured its portfolio of businesses. Identify and evaluate the strategic rationale behind this restructuring. Does it make sense?

CLOSING CASE

Breaking Up AT&T

On September 20, 1995, AT&T, the world's largest telecommunications company, with annual revenues of $75 billion, announced that it would split itself into three independent companies. The largest of these, which was to retain the AT&T name, would manage the company's long-distance, international, and wireless telecommunications businesses. The new AT&T would retain its position as the largest provider of telecommunications service in the world, with 1995 revenues in excess of $50 billion. Second in size of the new companies was to be the network equipment business. Renamed Lucent Technologies, this business generated 1995 revenues of $21 billion and ranked as the third largest provider of telecommunication network equipment in the world after Germany's Alcatel and Motorola of the United States. The smallest of the new companies was AT&T's Global Information Solutions business, a manufacturer of computer systems, with annual revenues of $9 billion. Global Information Solutions was built around NCR, a computer company that AT&T acquired in 1991 for $7.5 billion.

The decision to break up AT&T into three parts was the result of a number of factors that came to a head in the mid 1990s. First was the impending deregulation of the U.S. telecommunications industry. After deregulation, local and long-distance telephone companies would be free to enter each other's markets. AT&T would face more competition in its core long-distance business as the Regional Bell Operating Companies (RBOCs) tried to enter this market. At the same time, AT&T would be able to en-

CLOSING CASE *(continued)*

ter the local phone businesses and compete directly against the RBOCs. The second factor was the privatization of state-owned telephone companies around the world and the deregulation of many foreign telephone markets. These developments created enormous opportunities for AT&T, which for the first time saw the possibility of building a truly global telephone network by forming alliances with newly privatized telephone companies and by entering foreign markets. The third factor was rapid change in the telecommunications business as new technologies, such as wireless communications and the Internet, created significant opportunities and threats for AT&T. Faced with such changes in its operating environment, AT&T's management realized that it needed to focus all its energies and resources on the company's core telecommunications business, unencumbered by the distractions presented by the network equipment and computer businesses.

AT&T's management was also aware that the performance of the computer and network equipment businesses had suffered as a result of their association with AT&T. The equipment business was trying to sell products to companies that competed directly against AT&T, such as MCI and Sprint, or would compete against AT&T after deregulation, such as the RBOCs. These potential customers were increasingly reluctant to purchase equipment from a supplier that was also a competitor. For example, just before the breakup was announced, Motorola beat AT&T to a $800 million order for wireless telecommunications equipment from GTE. GTE had long been one of AT&Ts largest equipment customers, but now it faced the threat of competing against AT&T in the local phone business. Freed from its association with AT&T, the network equipment business would have a greater chance of capturing business from other telephone service providers.

As for the computer business, this was forecast to lose around $1 billion in 1995. Although AT&T had always had some significant computer skills—after all, many network equipment products, such as digital switches, are essentially specialized computers—it had never been able to establish a profitable computer operation. During the 1980s, AT&T lost billions of dollars trying to establish a presence in the personal computer market through an internal new venture. Moreover, its 1991 acquisition of NCR—which was an attempt to strengthen this venture—turned out to be a disaster, partly because the computer market shifted away from the kind of customized equipment provided by NCR, and partly because there was a clash between the management cultures of the two companies, which led to high management turnover in the acquired unit. Many now felt that AT&T's deep pockets had kept the computer operation in markets that it should have exited years ago—such as the personal computer market. They believed that an independent computer operation might be more responsive to market demands and would not be burdened by the clashing cultural heritage of AT&T and NCR.[34]

Case Discussion Questions

1. What changes in AT&T's operating environment triggered its 1995 decision to break up the company into three entities?
2. How has the breakup created value for shareholders?
3. Does the 1995 breakup imply that AT&T's pre-1995 strategic vision was seriously flawed?

End Notes

1. "HP: No Longer Lost in Cyberspace?" *Business Week*, May 31, 1999, p. 124; I. J. Dugan, "Hewlett to Become 2 Companies," *Washington Post*, March 3, 1999, p. E1; D. P. Hamilton and S. Thurm, "HP to Spin Off Its Measurement Operations," *Wall Street Journal,* March 3, 1999, p. A3; D. P. Hamilton and R. Blumenstein, "HP Names Carly Fiorina, a Lucent Star, to Be CEO," *Wall Street Journal,* July 20, 1999, p. B1.
2. C. W. Hofer and D. Schendel, *Strategy Formulation: Analytical Concepts* (St. Paul, Minn.: West, 1979); R. A. Bettis and W. K. Hall, "Strategic Portfolio Management in the Multibusiness Firm," *California Management Review*, 24 (1981), 23–28.
3. G. Hamel and C. K. Prahalad, *Competing for the Future* (Cambridge, Mass: Harvard Business School Press, 1994).
4. D. J. Collis, "Portfolio Planning at Ciba Geigy and the Newport Investment Proposal," *Harvard Business School Case* No. 795-040, 1995; Ciba-Geigy's World Wide Web page (http://www.cina.com).
5. G. Hamel and C. K. Prahalad, *Competing for the Future*.
6. D. L. Barton and G. Pisano, "Monsanto's March into Biotechnology," *Harvard Business School Case* No. 690-009 (1990). See Monsanto's home page for details of its genetically engineered seed products (http://www.monsanto .com).
7. See Booz, Allen, & Hamilton, *New Products Management for the 1980's*, privately published research report, 1982; A. L. Page, *PDMA's New Product Development Practices Survey: Performance and Best Practices,* PDMA 15th Annual International Conference, Boston, October 16, 1991; and E. Mansfield, "How Economists See R&D," *Harvard Business Review* (November–December 1981), 98–106.
8. See R. Biggadike, "The Risky Business of Diversification," *Harvard Business Review* (May–June 1979), 103–111; R. A. Burgelman, "A Process Model of Internal Corporate Venturing in the Diversified Major Firm," *Administrative Science Quarterly,* 28 (1983), 223–244; and Z. Block and I. C. Macmillan, *Corporate Venturing* (Cambridge, Mass: Harvard Business School Press, 1993).
9. R. Biggadike, "The Risky Business of Diversification"; Block and Macmillan, *Corporate Venturing.*
10. R. O. Crockett and C. Yang, "Why Motorola Should Hang Up on Iridium," *Business Week*, August 30, 1999, p. 46; L. Cauley, "Iridium's Downfall: The Marketing Took a Back Seat to the Science," *Wall Street Journal,* August 18, 1999, p. A1; J. N. Seth and R. Sisodia, "Why Cell Phones Succeeded Where Iridium Failed," *Wall Street Journal*, August 23, 1999, p. A14.
11. I. C. MacMillan and R. George, "Corporate Venturing: Challenges for Senior Managers," *Journal of Business Strategy*, 5 (1985), 34–43.
12. See R. A. Burgelman, M. M. Maidique, and S. C. Wheelwright, *Strategic Management of Technology and Innovation* (Chicago: Irwin, 1996), pp. 493–507.
13. See Z. Block and I. C. Macmillan, *Corporate Venturing,* (Cambridge, Mass.: Harvard Business School Press, 1993); Burgelman, Maidique, and Wheelwright, *Strategic Management of Technology and Innovation.*
14. G. Beardsley and E. Mansfield, "A Note on the Accuracy of Industrial Forecasts of the Profitability of New Products and Processes," *Journal of Business,* 23 (1978), 127–130.
15. J. Warner, J. Templeman, and R. Horn, "The Case Against Mergers," *Business Week*, October 30, 1995, 122–134.
16. For evidence on acquisitions and performance, see R. E. Caves, "Mergers, Takeovers, and Economic Efficiency," *International Journal of Industrial Organization*, 7 (1989), 151–174; M. C. Jensen and R. S. Ruback, "The Market for Corporate Control: The Scientific Evidence," *Journal of Financial Economics*, 11 (1983), 5–50; R. Roll; "Empirical Evidence on Takeover Activity and Shareholder Wealth," in *Knights, Raiders and Targets*, ed. J. C. Coffee, L. Lowenstein, and S. Rose (Oxford: Oxford University Press, 1989); Schleifer and Vishny, "Takeovers in the 60s and 80s" and T. H. Brush, "Predicted Changes in Operational Synergy and Post Acquisition Performance of Acquired Businesses," *Strategic Management Journal,* 17 (1996), 1–24.
17. D. J. Ravenscraft and F. M. Scherer, *Mergers, Selloffs, and Economic Efficiency* (Washington, D.C.: Brookings Institution, 1987).
18. See J. P. Walsh, "Top Management Turnover Following Mergers and Acquisitions," *Strategic Management Journal,* 9 (1988), 173–183.
19. See A. A. Cannella and D. C. Hambrick, "Executive Departure and Acquisition Performance," *Strategic Management Journal,* 14 (1993), 137–152.
20. M. Murray and J. Rebello, "Mellon Bank Corp: One Big Unhappy Family," *Wall Street Journal,* April 28, 1995, pp. B1, B4; K. Holland, "A Bank Eat Bank World—With Indigeston," *Business Week*, October 30, 1995, p. 130.
21. R. Roll, "The Hubris Hypothesis of Corporate Takeovers," *Journal of Business,* 59 (1986), 197–216.
22. "Coca-Cola: A Sobering Lesson from Its Journey into Wine," *Business Week*, June 3, 1985, pp. 96–98.
23. P. Haspeslagh and D. Jemison, *Managing Acquisitions*. (New York: Free Press, 1991).
24. For views on this issue, see L. L Fray, D. H. Gaylin, and J. W. Down, "Successful Acquisition Planning," *Journal of Business Strategy*, 5 (1984), 46–55; C. W. L. Hill, "Profile of a Conglomerate Takeover: BTR and Thomas Tilling," *Journal of General Management,* 10 (1984), 34–50; D. R. Willensky, "Making It Happen: How to Execute an Acquisition," *Business Horizons* (March–April 1985), 38–45; Haspeslagh and Jemison, *Managing Acquisitions;* P. L. Anslinger and T. E. Copeland, "Growth Through Acquisition: A Fresh Look," *Harvard Business Review* (January–February 1996), 126–135.
25. P. B. Carroll, "IBM, Motorola Plan Radio Link for Computers," *Wall Street Journal*, January 29, 1990, pp. B1, B5.
26. For a recent review of the evidence, and some contrary empirical evidence, see D. E. Hatfield, J. P. Liebskind, and T. C.

Opler, "The Effects of Corporate Restructuring on Aggregate Industry Specialization," *Strategic Management Journal*, 17 (1996), 55–72.

27. For example, see A. Schleifer and R. W. Vishny, "Takeovers in the 60s and 80s: Evidence and Implications," *Strategic Management Journal*, 12 (Special Issue, Winter 1991), 51–60.
28. See G. A. Patterson, and F. Schwadel, "Back in Time," *Wall Street Journal*, September 30, 1992, p. 1; J. Flynn, "Smaller but Wiser," *Business Week*, October 12, 1992, pp. 28–29; B. Bremner, "The Big Store's Trauma," *Business Week*, July 10, 1989, pp. 50–55.
29. See J. Argenti, *Corporate Collapse: Causes and Symptoms* (New York: McGraw-Hill, 1976); R. C. Hoffman, "Strategies for Corporate Turnarounds: What Do We Know About Them?" *Journal of General Management*, 14 (1984), 46–66; D. Schendel, G. R. Patton, and J. Riggs, "Corporate Turnaround Strategies: A Study of Profit Decline and Recovery," *Journal of General Management*, 2 (1976), 1–22; and S. Siafter, *Corporate Recovery: Successful Turnaround Strategies and Their Implementation* (Hammondsworth, England: Penguin Books, 1984), pp. 25–60.
30. D. B. Bibeault, *Corporate Turnaround* (New York: McGraw-Hill, 1982).
31. Hoffman, "Strategies for Corporate Turnarounds."
32. Ibid.
33. Lee Iacocca, *Iacocca: An Autobiography* (New York: Bantam Books, 1984), p. 254.
34. T. Jackson, "Giant Bows to Colossal Pressure," *Financial Times*, September 22, 1995, p. 13; "AT&T's Three Way Split," *The Economist*, September 23, 1995, pp. 51–52; "Fatal Attraction," *Economist*, March 23, 1996, pp. 73–74; A. Ramirez, "Opportunity and New Risk for a Spinoff," *New York Times*, September 22, 1995, pp. C1, C4.

PART FOUR

Implementing Strategy

11. Designing Organizational Structure
12. Designing Strategic Control Systems
13. Matching Structure and Control to Strategy
14. Implementing Strategic Change

11 Designing Organizational Structure

OPENING CASE

Microsoft's New E-Structure

IN THE 1990s, Microsoft emerged as the dominant global company in the computer software industry. However, as it has grown it has run into management problems, many of them stemming from the growth of the Internet and e-commerce and their effect on Microsoft's main business, desktop computer software. So serious are these problems that in 1999 Microsoft moved to radically change its organizational structure.

Over time, Microsoft had developed a structure with five levels in the hierarchy. Given that it had only 30,000 employees, its structure was quite flat, and flat structures help speed decision making. However, the problem at Microsoft was that Bill Gates, Microsoft's CEO, and Steve Ballmer, its president had, over time, begun to increasingly involve themselves in all important organizational decision making and had developed a very centralized approach to management. As the challenges of keeping up with the Internet increased, managers lower down the hierarchy felt themselves under increasing scrutiny and complained that Microsoft was becoming excessively bureaucratic. What is more, Gates and Ballmer's close involvement in decision making had seriously slowed down the decision-making process, and since the Internet business changes frequently and in unpredictable ways. The slow response to these changes threatened Microsoft's future.

To increase Microsoft's ability to respond to these changes Ballmer and Gates knew they had to alter its structure. Previously, the company had two main product divisions: the operating systems division responsible for developing Windows, and a product development division responsible for developing applied uses as varied as Microsoft Word and Internet Explorer. Within each division, employees were organized into product teams, in which they worked together on specific projects. In the new structure, the product development division is divided up into six different groups based on the needs of different kinds of customers. The six groups target corporate customers, knowledge workers, home PC users, computer game buyers, Web surfers, and cyber shoppers. In this new market structure, each group is responsible for interfacing with its customer group, researching customers' needs, and then developing state-of-the-art software applications to meet those needs.[1]

Recognizing that this change in structure would pay off only if they changed their management style, Gates and Ballmer also resolved to change their management style. Henceforth, they decided, they would not intervene in each division's strategy; they would decentralize control to the heads of the six market divisions and to the team leaders in each division.[2] In this way, they hoped to transfer authority down the line, and speed the decision-making process, something vital in a fast-changing environment.

So far, the effect of these changes is unknown. Some analysts think that Gates and Ballmer will have a difficult time stepping back from decision making and that at the first sign of danger they will rush in to take up the reins. However, analysts also agree that Microsoft had to take some action if it did not want to experience the same problems of inertia and bureaucracy that plagued other giants, such as IBM and GM.

OVERVIEW

As the Opening Case suggests, in this chapter we consider how a company should organize its activities to create the most value. In Chapter 1, we define *strategy implementation* as the way in which a company creates the organizational arrangements that allow it to pursue its strategy most effectively. Strategy is implemented through organizational design. **Organizational design** means selecting the combination of organizational structure and control systems that lets a company pursue its strategy most effectively—that lets it *create and sustain a competitive advantage.*

The primary role of organizational structure and control is twofold: (1) to *coordinate* the activities of employees so that they work together most effectively to implement a strategy that increases competitive advantage and (2) to *motivate* employees and provide them with the incentives to achieve superior efficiency, quality, innovation, or customer responsiveness. Microsoft's strategy, for example, was to speed decision making and new-product development by moving to a new decentralized organizational structure. This structure allowed lower-level managers and teams to make decisions and respond quickly to the ever changing nature of competition in the Internet industry.

Organizational structure and control shape the way people behave and determine how they will act in the organizational setting. If a new CEO wants to know why it takes a long time for people to make decisions in a company, why there is a lack of cooperation between sales and manufacturing, or why product innovations are few and far between, he or she needs to look at the design of the organizational structure and control system and analyze how it coordinates and motivates employees' behavior. An analysis of how structure and control work makes it possible to change them to improve both coordination and motivation. Good organizational design allows an organization to improve its ability to create value and obtain a competitive advantage.

In this chapter, we examine the organizational structures available to strategic managers to coordinate and motivate employees. In Chapter 12, we consider the strategic control systems that managers use in conjunction with their organizational structures to monitor, motivate, and reward corporate, divisional, and functional performance. In Chapter 13, we trace the ways in which different strategy choices lead to the use of different kinds of structure and control systems. After reading these three chapters, you will be able to understand the principles behind Microsoft's redesign of its organizational structure and control system and you will be able to choose the right organizational design for implementing a company's strategy.

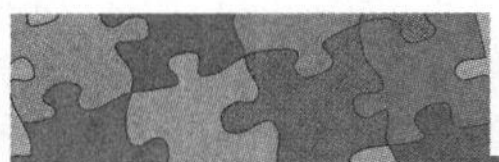

THE ROLE OF ORGANIZATIONAL STRUCTURE

After formulating a company's strategy, management must make designing organizational structure its next priority, for strategy is implemented through organizational structure. The value creation activities of organizational members are meaningless unless some type of structure is used to assign people to tasks and connect the activities of different people and functions.[3] As we discuss in Chapter 4, each organizational function needs to develop a distinctive competency in a value creation activity in order to increase efficiency, quality, innovation, or customer responsiveness. Thus, each function needs a structure designed to allow it to develop its skills and become more specialized and productive. As functions become increasingly specialized, however, they often begin to pursue their own goals exclusively and lose sight of the need to communicate and coordinate with other functions. The goals of R&D, for example, center on innovation and product design, whereas the goals of manufacturing often revolve around increasing efficiency. Left to themselves, the functions may have little to say to one another, and value creation opportunities will be lost.

The role of organizational structure is to provide the vehicle through which managers can coordinate the activities of the various functions or divisions to exploit fully their skills and capabilities. To pursue a cost-leadership strategy, for example, a company must design a structure that facilitates close coordination between the activities of manufacturing and R&D to ensure that innovative products can be produced both reliably and cost effectively. To achieve gains from synergy between divisions, managers must design mechanisms that allow divisions to communicate and share their skills and knowledge. In pursuing a global or multidomestic strategy, managers must create the right kind of organizational structure for managing the flow of resources and capabilities between domestic and foreign divisions. In Chapter 13, we examine in detail how managers match their strategies to different kinds of structure and control systems. Our goal now is to examine the basic building blocks of organizational structure to understand how it shapes the behavior of people, functions, and divisions.

Building Blocks of Organizational Structure

The basic building blocks of organizational structure are differentiation and integration. **Differentiation** is the way in which a company allocates people and resources to organizational tasks in order to create value.[4] Generally, the greater the number of different functions or divisions in an organization and the more skilled and specialized they are, the higher is the level of differentiation. For example, a company such as General Motors, with more than 300 different divisions and a multitude of different sales, research and development, and design departments, has a much greater level of differentiation than a local manufacturing company or restaurant. In deciding how to differentiate the organization to create value, strategic managers face two choices.

First, strategic managers must choose how to distribute *decision-making authority* in the organization to control value creation activities best; these are **vertical differentiation** choices.[5] For example, corporate managers must decide how much authority to delegate to managers at the divisional or functional level. Second, corporate managers must choose how to divide people and tasks into functions and divisions to increase their ability to create value; these are **horizontal differentiation** choices. Should there be separate sales and marketing departments, for example, or should the two be combined? What is the best way to divide the sales force to maximize its ability to serve customers' needs—by type of customer or by region in which customers are located?

Integration is the means by which a company seeks to coordinate people and functions to accomplish organizational tasks.[6] As just noted, when separate and distinct value creation functions exist, they tend to pursue their own goals and objectives. An organization has to create an organizational structure that lets the different functions and divisions coordinate their activities to pursue a strategy effectively. An organization uses integrating mechanisms, as well as the various types of control systems discussed in the next chapter, to promote coordination and cooperation between functions and divisions. In the case of Microsoft, for instance, to speed innovation and product development, the company established teams so that employees could work together to effectively exchange information and ideas. Similarly, establishing organizational norms, values, and a common culture that supports innovation promotes integration.

In short, differentiation refers to the way in which a company divides itself into parts (functions and divisions), and integration refers to the way in which the parts are then combined. Together, the two processes determine how an organizational structure will operate and how successfully strategic managers will be able to create value through their chosen strategies.

Differentiation, Integration, and Bureaucratic Costs

Implementing a structure to coordinate and motivate task activities is very expensive. The costs of operating an organizational structure and control system are called **bureaucratic costs**. The more complex the structure—that is, the higher the level of differentiation and integration—the higher are the bureaucratic costs of managing it. The more differentiated the company, for example, the more managers there are in specialized roles and the more resources each manager requires to perform that role effectively. Managers are expensive, and the more managers a company employs, the higher are its bureaucratic costs.

Similarly, the more integrated the company, the more managerial time is spent in face-to-face meetings to coordinate task activities. Managerial time also costs money, and thus the higher the level of integration, the more costly it is to operate the structure. A large company such as IBM or GM spends billions of dollars a year to operate its structures: that is, to pay its managers and employees and to provide them with the resources—offices, computers, equipment, laboratories, and so forth—they need to create value.

The high bureaucratic costs associated with strategy implementation can reduce a company's profits as fast or faster than poor strategy formulation, and thus they directly affect bottom-line organizational performance. This is why good organizational design is so important. You will recall from Chapter 4 that profit is the difference between revenues and costs. Bureaucratic costs are a large component of the cost side of the equation. Thus, a poor organizational design (for instance, one that has too many levels in the hierarchy or a badly thought-out pattern of work relationships) results in high costs, which reduce profits. By contrast, good organizational design, which economizes on bureaucratic costs, can give a company a low-cost advantage, which raises profits.

Organizational design also affects the revenue side of the equation. If strategic managers choose the right structure to coordinate value creation activities, they enhance the company's ability to create value, charge a premium price, and thus increase revenues. Bill Gates hopes that Microsoft's new structure will increase its ability to create value and a stream of new Internet software products for the different customer groups. Thus, good design affects both the revenue and the cost side of the profit equation, as Figure 11.1 illustrates. This is why strategy implementation is such a vital issue. In today's competitive environment, more and more companies are restructuring or reengineering their organizations to improve bottom-line performance through good organizational design. Consequently, it is necessary to understand the principles behind organizational design. We start by looking at differentiation.

FIGURE 11.1

How Organizational Design Increases Profitability

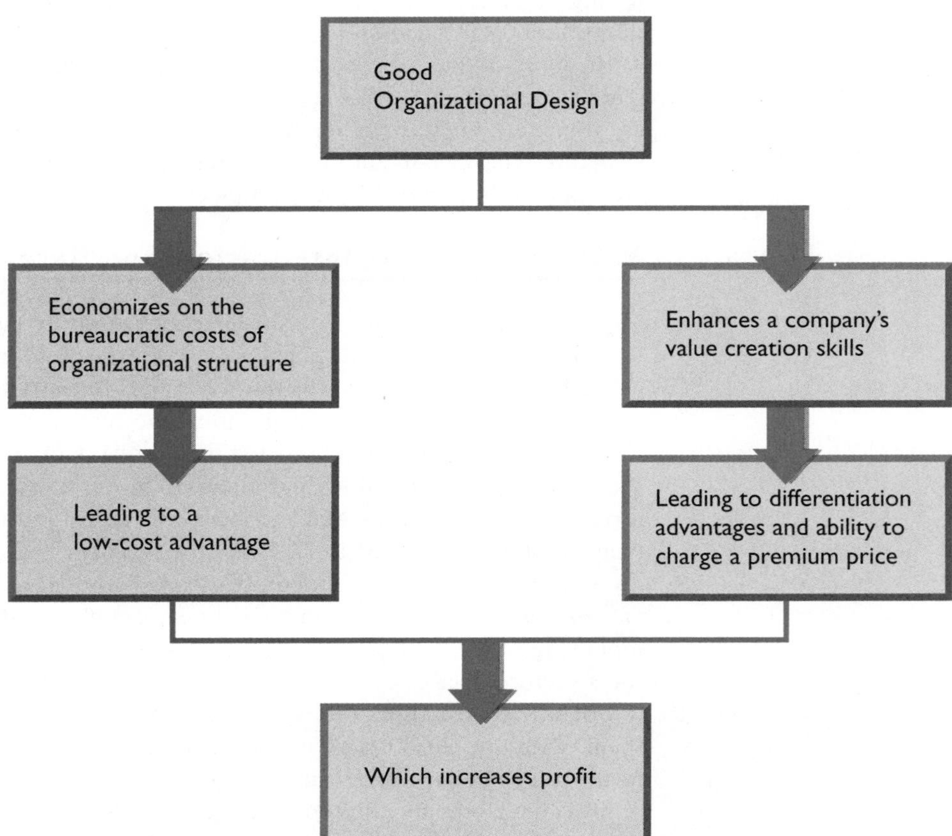

VERTICAL DIFFERENTIATION

The aim of vertical differentiation is to specify the reporting relationships that link people, tasks, and functions at all levels of a company. Fundamentally, this means that management chooses the appropriate number of hierarchical levels and the correct span of control for implementing a company's strategy most effectively.

The organizational hierarchy establishes the authority structure from the top to the bottom of the organization. The **span of control** is defined as the number of subordinates a manager directly manages.[7] The basic choice is whether to aim for a **flat structure**, with few hierarchical levels and thus a relatively wide span of control, or a **tall structure**, with many levels and thus a relatively narrow span of control (see Figure 11.2). Tall structures have many hierarchical levels relative to size; flat structures have few levels relative to size.[8] For example, research suggests that the average number of hierarchical levels for a company employing 3,000 persons is seven. Thus, an organization having nine levels would be called tall, and one having four would be called flat. With its 30,000 employees and five hierarchical levels, Microsoft, for instance, had a relatively flat structure.

Companies choose the number of levels they need on the basis of their strategy and the functional tasks necessary to achieve this strategy.[9] High-tech companies, for example, often pursue a strategy of differentiation based on service and quality. Consequently, these companies usually have flat structures, giving employees wide discretion to meet customers' demands without having to refer constantly to supervisors.[10] (We discuss this subject further in Chapter 12.) The crux of the matter is that the allocation of authority and responsibility in the organization must match the needs of corporate-, business-, and functional-level strategies.[11]

FIGURE 11.2

Tall and Flat Structures

Tall Structure
(8 levels)

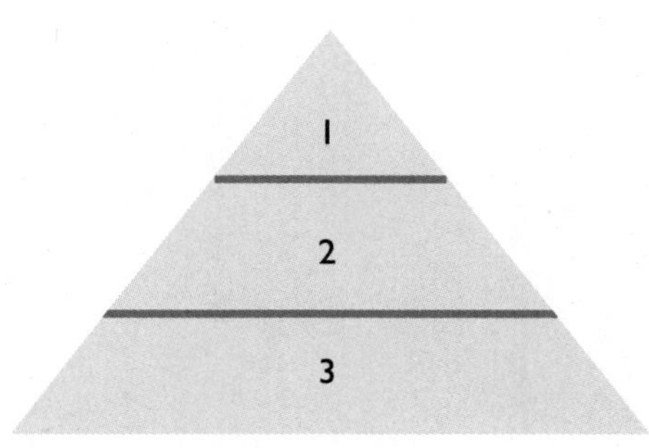

Flat Structure
(3 levels)

Problems with Tall Structures

As a company grows and diversifies, the number of levels in its hierarchy of authority increases to allow it to efficiently monitor and coordinate employee activities. Research shows that the number of hierarchical levels relative to company size is predictable as the size increases (see Figure 11.3).[12]

Companies with approximately 1,000 employees usually have four levels in the hierarchy: chief executive officer, departmental vice presidents, first-line supervisors, and shop-floor employees. Those with 3,000 employees have increased their level of vertical differentiation by raising the number of levels to eight. Something interesting happens to those with more than 3,000 employees, however. Even when companies grow to 10,000 employees or more, the number of hierarchical levels rarely increases beyond nine or ten. As organizations grow, managers apparently try to limit the number of hierarchical levels.

Managers try to keep the organization as flat as possible and follow what is known as the **principle of the minimum chain of command,** which states that an organization should choose a hierarchy with the minimum number of levels of authority necessary to achieve its strategy. Managers try to keep the hierarchy as flat as possible because when companies become too tall, problems occur, making strategy more difficult to implement and raising the level of bureaucratic costs.[13] Several factors that raise bureaucratic costs are illustrated in Figure 11.4 and discussed in the following paragraphs.

Coordination Problems Too many hierarchical levels impede communication and coordination between employees and functions and raise bureaucratic costs. Communication between the top and the bottom of the hierarchy takes much longer as the chain of command lengthens. This leads to inflexibility, and valuable

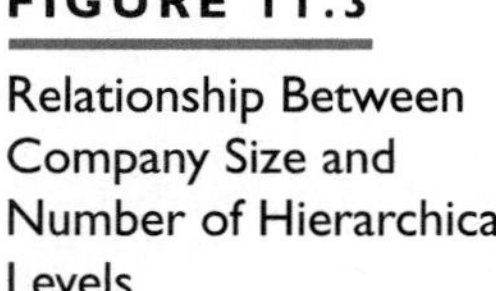

FIGURE 11.3

Relationship Between Company Size and Number of Hierarchical Levels

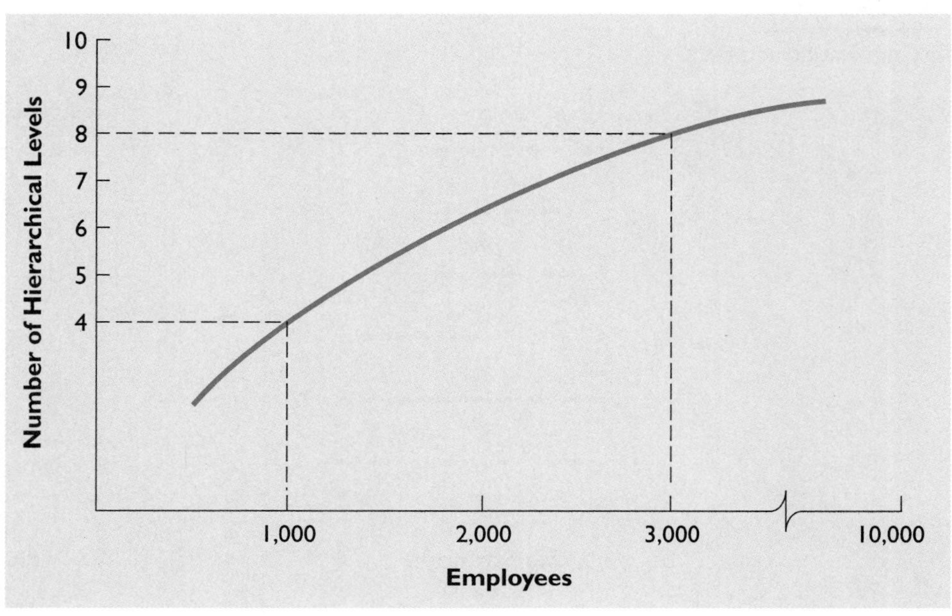

FIGURE 11.4

Sources of Bureaucratic Costs

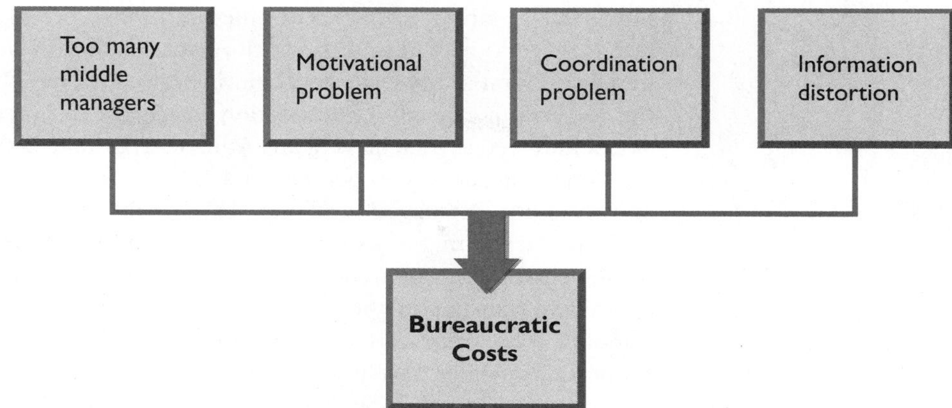

time is lost in bringing a new product to market or in keeping up with technological developments.[14] For Federal Express, communication and coordination are vital. Therefore, to avoid problems with them, the company allows a maximum of only five layers of management between the employee and the CEO.[15] In contrast, Procter & Gamble had a tall hierarchy, with the result that the company needed twice as much time as its competitors to introduce new products. To improve coordination and reduce costs, the company moved to streamline its structure and reduce its number of hierarchical levels.[16] Other companies have also taken measures to flatten their structures in order to speed communication and decision making. Strategy in Action 11.1 describes the changes made at General Electric and Alcoa.

Information Distortion More subtle, but just as important, are the problems of information distortion that occur as the hierarchy of authority lengthens. Going

11.1 STRATEGY *in* ACTION

How to Flatten Structure

Tall hierarchies cause such severe coordination and communications problems that many companies have been striving to shrink their hierarchies. For example, General Electric CEO Jack Welch has flattened the hierarchy from nine levels to four to bring him closer to his divisional managers and shorten the time it takes them to make decisions. At Alcoa, planning and decision making at the divisional level once were scrutinized by five levels of corporate management before divisional managers were allowed to proceed with their plans. Chairman Paul O'Neill wiped out these layers so that divisional managers would report directly to him. At both companies, these changes have brought top management closer to customers and provided divisional managers with the autonomy to be innovative and responsive to customers' needs. Moreover, flattening the hierarchy has saved these companies billions of dollars in managerial salaries and significantly reduced bureaucratic costs. Flattening their structures has clearly paid off for them.

down the hierarchy, managers at different levels (for example, divisional or corporate managers) may misinterpret information, either through accidental garbling of messages or on purpose, to suit their own interests. In either case, information from the top may not reach its destination intact. For instance, a request to share divisional knowledge to achieve gains from synergy may be overlooked or ignored by divisional managers who perceive it as a threat to their autonomy and power. This attitude among managers was one of the problems that led Lee Iacocca to reorganize Chrysler so that cost-cutting measures could be coordinated across divisions.

Information transmitted upward in the hierarchy may also be distorted. Subordinates may transmit to their superiors only information that improves their own standing in the organization. The greater the number of hierarchical levels, the more scope subordinates have to distort facts, so that the bureaucratic costs of managing the hierarchy increase. Similarly, bureaucratic costs increase if managers start to compete with each other. When they are free of close corporate supervision, they may hoard information to promote their own interests at the expense of the organization's. This also reduces coordination.

Motivational Problems As the number of levels in the hierarchy increases, the amount of authority possessed by managers at each hierarchical level falls. For example, consider the situation of two identically sized organizations, one of which has three levels in its hierarchy and the other seven. Managers in the flat structure have much more authority, and greater authority increases their motivation to perform effectively and take responsibility for the organization's performance. Besides, when there are fewer managers, their performance is more visible and they can expect greater rewards when the business does well.

By contrast, the ability of managers in a tall structure to exercise authority is limited, and their decisions are constantly scrutinized by their superiors. As a result, managers tend to pass the buck and refuse to take the risks that are often necessary when new strategies are pursued. This increases the bureaucratic costs of managing the organization because more managerial time is spent coordinating task activities. Thus, the shape of the organization's structure strongly affects the motivation of people within it and the way in which strategy is implemented.[17]

Too Many Middle Managers Another drawback of tall structures is that having many hierarchical levels implies having many middle managers, and employing managers is expensive. As noted earlier, managerial salaries, benefits, offices, and secretaries are a huge expense for an organization. If the average middle manager costs a company a total of $200,000 a year, then employing 100 surplus managers costs $20 million a year. Most large U.S. companies have recognized this fact, and in the 1990s companies such as IBM, GM, Compaq, and Procter & Gamble have moved to downsize their hierarchies, terminating thousands of managers. When these companies made billions of dollars in profits, they had little incentive to control the number of levels in the hierarchy and the number of managers. Once they grew aware of the cost of these managers, however, the companies ruthlessly purged the hierarchy, reducing the number of levels and thus the number of managers in order to lower bureaucratic costs and restore profitability.

To offer another example, when companies grow and are successful, they often hire personnel and create new positions without much regard for the effect of these actions on the organizational hierarchy. Later, when managers review that structure, it is quite common to see the number of levels reduced because of the disadvantages just discussed. Deregulation, too, prompts a reduction in levels and personnel. In a deregulated environment, companies must respond to increased competition. Since deregulation of the banking industry and the development of nationwide banks, banks like Bank of America and Chase Manhattan have reduced costs and streamlined their structures so that they could respond more rapidly to opportunities and threats brought about by increased competition. For example, Bank of America has laid off 20 percent of its work force.[18]

In sum, many problems arise when companies become too tall and the chain of command becomes too long. Strategic managers tend to lose control over the hierarchy, which means that they lose control over their strategies. Disaster often follows because a tall organizational structure decreases, rather than promotes, motivation and coordination between employees and functions and, as a result, bureaucratic costs escalate. One way to overcome such problems, at least partially, and to lessen bureaucratic costs is to decentralize authority—that is, vest authority in the hierarchy's lower levels as well as at the top. Because this is one of the most important implementation decisions a company can make, we discuss it next in more detail.

Centralization or Decentralization?

Authority is centralized when managers at the upper levels of the organizational hierarchy retain the authority to make the most important decisions. When authority is decentralized, it is delegated to divisions, functions, and managers and workers at lower levels in the organization. By delegating authority in this fashion, managers can economize on bureaucratic costs and avoid communication and coordination problems because information does not have to be constantly sent to the top of the organization for decisions to be made. There are three advantages to decentralization.

First, when strategic managers delegate operational decision-making responsibility to middle and first-level managers, they reduce information overload, enabling strategic managers to spend more time on strategic decision making. Consequently, they can make more effective decisions.

Second, when managers in the bottom layers of the organization become responsible for adapting the organization to suit local conditions, their motivation and accountability increase. The result is that decentralization promotes organizational flexibility and reduces bureaucratic costs because lower-level managers are authorized to make on-the-spot decisions. As AT&T has demonstrated, this can be an enormous advantage for business strategy. AT&T has a tall structure, but it is well known for the amount of authority it delegates to lower-level employees. Operational personnel can respond quickly to customers' needs and so ensure superior service, which is a major source of AT&T's competitive advantage. Similarly, to revitalize its product strategy, Westinghouse has massively decentralized its operations to give divisions more autonomy and encourage risk taking and a quick response to customers' needs.[19] Union Pacific also took that route, as detailed in Strategy in Action 11.2.

The third advantage of decentralization is that when lower-level employees are given the right to make important decisions, fewer managers are needed to oversee their activities and tell them what to do. Fewer managers mean lower bureaucratic costs.

If decentralization is so effective, why do not all companies decentralize decision making and avoid the problems of tall hierarchies? The answer is that centralization also has advantages. Centralized decision making allows easier coordination

11.2 STRATEGY *in* ACTION

Union Pacific Decentralizes to Increase Customer Responsiveness

In 1998, Union Pacific, one of the biggest rail freight carriers in the United States, was experiencing a crisis. The U.S. economic boom was causing a record increase in the amount of freight that the railroad had to transport, but the railroad was experiencing record delays in moving the freight. Union Pacific's customers were irate, complaining bitterly about the problem. Besides, the delays were costing the company a tremendous amount in penalty payments—$150 million.[20]

Why was there a problem? In its effort to cut costs, Union Pacific had developed a very centralized management approach. All the scheduling and route planning were handled centrally at its headquarters in the attempt to promote operating efficiency. The job of regional managers was largely to ensure the smooth flow of freight through their regions. Recognizing that efficiency had to be balanced by responsiveness to customers, Union Pacific's CEO, Dick Davidson, announced a sweeping reorganization to the company's customers. Henceforth, regional managers were to have the authority to make operational decisions at the level at which it was most important—field operations. Regional managers would be able to alter scheduling and routing to accommodate customers' requests even if this raised costs, for the goal of the organization now was to "return to excellent performance by simplifying our processes and becoming easier to deal with."[21] In making this decision, the company was following the lead of its competitors, most of which had already moved to decentralize their operations, recognizing the many advantages of doing so.

of the organizational activities needed to pursue a company's strategy. If managers at all levels can make their own decisions, overall planning becomes extremely difficult, and the company may lose control of its decision making.

Centralization also means that decisions fit broad organization objectives. When its branch operations were getting out of hand, for example, Merrill Lynch increased centralization by installing more information systems to give corporate managers greater control over branch activities. Similarly, Hewlett-Packard centralized research and development responsibility at the corporate level to provide a more directed corporate strategy. Furthermore, in times of crisis, centralization of authority permits strong leadership because authority is focused on one person or group. This focus allows for speedy decision making and a concerted response by the whole organization.

Perhaps Lee Iacocca personifies the meaning of centralization in times of crisis. Iacocca provided the centralized control and vision needed for Chrysler's managers to respond creatively to the company's problems and move to the product-team structure, which has helped restore the company's profitability. On the other hand, Honda's experience with recentralizing authority, described in Strategy in Action 11.3, warns against going too far.

Summary

Managing the strategy-structure relationship when the number of hierarchical levels becomes too great is difficult and expensive. Depending on a company's situation, the bureaucratic costs of tall hierarchies can be reduced by decentralization. As company size increases, however, decentralization may become less effective. How then, as firms grow and diversify, can they economize on bureaucratic costs without

11.3 STRATEGY *in* ACTION

Honda's Change of Heart

In the early 1990s, Honda, like many other Japanese firms, found itself facing increased competition in a depressed global marketplace. It realized that its strategy of relying on product innovation to increase its sales growth had caused it to neglect the cost and efficiency side of the equation. As a result, its profit margins were eroding. Under its founder, Shoichiro Honda, the company had pioneered the concept of the Honda Way, based on a decentralized, participative, consensus approach to management. Teams led the decision-making process, and authority was decentralized throughout the company.

However, Honda's new president, Nobuhiko Kawamoto, concluded that this process had gone too far. He decided to recentralize authority in order to provide the control and direction needed to slash costs and increase efficiency. He began to give Honda's top managers more and more authority for corporatewide strategy and made them responsible for overseeing both the company's domestic and global strategy. The effect of this move was unexpected: Many of his top executives found it physically impossible to assume the extra responsibility that this new policy of centralization required. One key executive, Shoichiro Irimajiri, who was assigned responsibility for overseeing both Honda's global R&D *and* manufacturing operations, was forced to resign abruptly after his doctors told him that his extra workload had pushed him to the brink of a heart attack. As Kawamoto commented, maybe he had given Irimajiri too much responsibility.[22]

Since the new policy of centralization was not working, Kawamoto had to find another solution to the centralization-decentralization dilemma. He decided to delegate more authority down the hierarchy on a global basis. Managers in Honda's North American, European, and Japanese divisions would take over responsibility for managing strategy for their divisions. The role of Honda's corporate executives in Japan would be to provide coordination among divisions and facilitate the sharing of skills and resources to reduce costs. In this way, Honda hoped to strike a new balance between centralization and decentralization, so that the company could remain innovative and responsive to customers' needs in order to encourage sales growth but, at the same time, become more efficient in order to reduce costs.

Kawamoto's idea for a new structure for Honda has proved very successful. The new policy of decentralization has allowed divisional managers to form closer ties with Honda's suppliers and with its dealers, as well as make decisions faster. Suppliers are providing Honda with significantly lower cost inputs, and its close ties with dealers have allowed it to tailor its product line to better match customer needs.[23] The result has been that Honda's costs have fallen and its sales have risen dramatically, and by 1998 Honda was making record profits.[24] The company has returned to the Honda Way it pioneered.

becoming too tall or too decentralized? How can a firm such as Exxon control 300,000 employees without becoming too bureaucratic and inflexible? There must be alternative ways of creating organizational arrangements to achieve corporate objectives. The first of these ways is to choose the appropriate form of horizontal differentiation, that is, to decide how best to group organizational activities and tasks in order to create value.

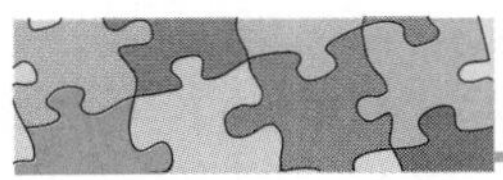

HORIZONTAL DIFFERENTIATION

Whereas vertical differentiation concerns the division of authority, horizontal differentiation focuses on the division and grouping of tasks to meet the objectives of the business.[25] Because, to a large degree, an organization's tasks are a function of its strategy, the dominant view is that companies choose a form of horizontal differentiation or structure to match their organizational strategy. Perhaps the first person to address this issue formally was the Harvard business historian Alfred D. Chandler.[26] After studying the organizational problems experienced in large U.S. corporations such as Du Pont and General Motors as they grew and diversified in the early decades of this century, Chandler reached two conclusions: (1) that in principle organizational structure follows the growth strategy of a company, or, in other words, the range and variety of tasks it chooses to pursue and (2) that U.S. companies' structures change as their strategy changes in a predictable way over time.[27] The kinds of structure that companies adopt are discussed in this section.

Simple Structure

The simple structure is normally used by the small, entrepreneurial company producing a single product or a few related ones for a specific market segment. Often in this situation, one person, the entrepreneur, takes on most of the managerial tasks. No formal arrangements regarding organization exist, and horizontal differentiation is low because employees perform multiple duties.

A classic example of this structure is Apple Computer in its earliest stage, as a venture between two persons. Steven Jobs and Steven Wozniak worked together in a garage to perform all the necessary tasks to market their personal computer. They bought the component parts, assembled the first machines, and shipped them to customers. The success of their product, however, made this simple structure outdated almost as soon as it was adopted. To grow and perform all the tasks required by a rapidly expanding company, Apple needed a more complex form of horizontal differentiation. It needed to invest resources in creating an infrastructure to develop and enhance its distinctive competencies. Although developing a more complex structure raises bureaucratic costs, this is acceptable as long as the structure increases the amount of value a company can create.

Functional Structure

As companies grow, two things happen. First, the range of tasks that must be performed expands. For example, it suddenly becomes apparent that the services of a professional accountant or a production manager or a marketing expert are needed to take control of specialized tasks. Second, no one person can successfully perform more than one organizational task without becoming overloaded. The founder, for instance, can no longer simultaneously make and sell the product. The question that arises is what grouping of activities, or what form of horizontal differentiation, can most efficiently handle the needs of the growing company at least cost? The answer for most companies is a functional structure.

Functional structures group people on the basis of their common expertise and experience or because they use the same resources.[28] For example, engineers are grouped in a function because they perform the same tasks and use the same skills or equipment. Figure 11.5 shows a typical functional structure. Each of the rectangles represents a different functional specialization—research and development, sales and marketing, manufacturing, and so on—and each function concentrates on its own specialized task.

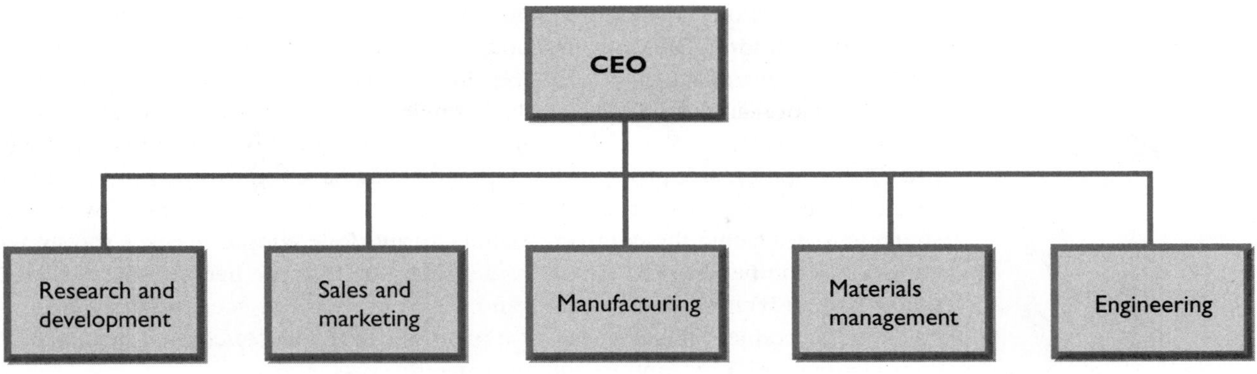

FIGURE 11.5

Functional Structure

Advantages of a Functional Structure

Functional structures have several advantages. First, if people who perform similar tasks are grouped together, they can learn from one another and become better—more specialized and productive—at what they do.

Second, they can monitor each other to make sure that all are performing their tasks effectively and not shirking their responsibilities. As a result, the work process becomes more efficient, reducing manufacturing costs and increasing operational flexibility.

A third important advantage of functional structures is that they give managers greater control of organizational activities. As already noted, many difficulties arise when the number of levels in the hierarchy increases. If people are grouped into different functions, however, each with their own managers, then *several different hierarchies are created*, and the company can avoid becoming too tall. There will be one hierarchy in manufacturing, for example, and another in accounting and finance. Managing the business is much easier when different groups specialize in different organizational tasks and are managed separately.

Disadvantages of a Functional Structure

In adopting a functional structure, a company increases its level of horizontal differentiation to handle more complex tasks. The structure allows it to keep control of its activities as it grows. This structure serves the company well until it starts to grow and diversify. If the company becomes geographically diverse and begins operating in many locations or if it starts producing a wide range of products, control and coordination problems arise that lower a company's ability to coordinate its activities and increase bureaucratic costs.[29]

Communications Problems As separate functional hierarchies evolve, functions grow more remote from one another. As a result, it becomes increasingly difficult to communicate across functions and to coordinate their activities. This communication problem stems from **functional orientations**.[30] With greater differentiation, the various functions develop different orientations to the problems and issues facing the organization. Different functions have different time or goal orientations. Some, such as manufacturing, see things in a short time frame and concentrate on achieving short-run goals, such as reducing manufacturing costs. Others, such as research and development, see things from a long-term point of view, and their goals (that is, innovation and product development) may have a time horizon of several years. These factors may cause each function to develop a different view of the strategic issues facing the company. Manufacturing, for example, may see the strategic issue as the need to reduce costs, sales may see it as the need to increase customer responsiveness, and research and development may see it as the need to create new products. In such cases, the functions have trouble communicating and coordinating with one another, and bureaucratic costs increase.

Measurement Problems As the number of its products proliferates, a company may find it difficult to gauge the contribution of a product or a group of products to its overall profitability. Consequently, the company may turn out some unprofitable products without realizing it and may also make poor decisions about resource allocation. This means that the company's measurement systems are not complex enough to serve its needs. Dell Computer's explosive growth in the early 1990s, for example, caused it to lose control of its inventory management systems; hence, it could not accurately project supply and demand for the components that go into its personal computers. Problems with its organizational structure plagued Dell, reducing efficiency and quality. As one manager commented, designing its structure to keep pace with its growth was like "building a high performance car while going around the race track."[31] However, Dell succeeded and today enjoys a 10 percent cost advantage over competitors such as Compaq in part because of its innovative organizational design.

Location Problems Location factors may also hamper coordination and control. If a company is producing or selling in many different regional areas, then the centralized system of control provided by the functional structure no longer suits it because managers in the various regions must be flexible enough to respond to the needs of these regions. Thus, the functional structure is not complex enough to handle regional diversity.

Strategic Problems Sometimes the combined effect of all these factors is that long-term strategic considerations are ignored because management is preoccupied with solving communication and coordination problems. As a result, a company may lose direction and fail to take advantage of new opportunities while bureaucratic costs escalate.

Experiencing these problems is a sign that the company does not have an appropriate level of differentiation to achieve its objectives. A company must change its mix of vertical and horizontal differentiation if it is to perform effectively the organizational tasks that will enhance its competitive advantage. Essentially, these problems indicate that the company has outgrown its structure. It needs to invest more resources in developing a more complex structure, one that can meet the needs of its competitive strategy. Once again, this is expensive, but as long as the value a company can create is greater than the bureaucratic costs of operating the structure, it makes sense to adopt a more complex structure. Many companies choose a multidivisional structure.

Multidivisional Structure

The multidivisional structure possesses two main innovations over a functional structure, innovations that let a company grow and diversify yet overcome problems that stem from loss of control. First, each distinct product line or business unit is placed in its own *self-contained unit or division*, with all support functions. For example, PepsiCo has two major divisions—soft drinks and snack foods—and each has its own functions, such as marketing and research and development. The result is a higher level of horizontal differentiation.

Second, the office of *corporate headquarters staff* is created to monitor divisional activities and to exercise financial control over each of the divisions.[32] This staff contains corporate managers who oversee the activities of divisional and functional managers, and it constitutes an additional level in the organizational hierarchy. Hence, there is a higher level of vertical differentiation in a multidivisional structure than in a functional structure.

Figure 11.6 presents a typical multidivisional structure found in a large chemical company such as Du Pont. Although this company might easily have seventy operating divisions, only three—the oil, pharmaceuticals, and plastics divisions—are represented here. As a self-contained business unit, each division possesses a full array of

FIGURE 11.6

Multidivisional Structure

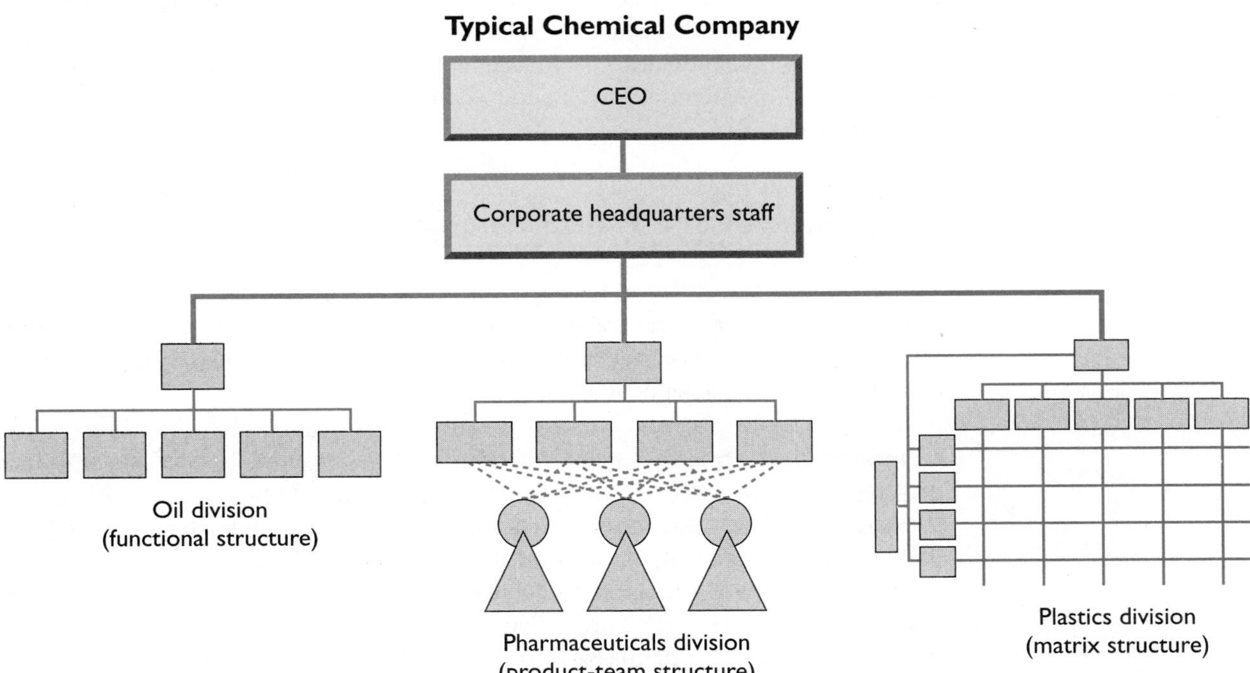

support services. For example, each has self-contained accounting, sales, and personnel departments. Each division functions as a profit center, making it much easier for corporate headquarters staff to monitor and evaluate each division's activities.[33]

The bureaucratic costs of operating a multidivisional structure are very high compared with those at a functional structure. The size of the corporate staff is a major expense, and companies such as GM and IBM have thousands of managers on their corporate staffs even after their massive downsizing. Similarly, the use of product divisions, each with its own specialist support functions such as research and development and marketing, is a major expense. However, once again, if higher bureaucratic costs are offset by a higher level of value creation, it makes sense to move to a more complex structure.

Each division is also able to adopt the structure that best suits its needs. Figure 11.6 shows that the oil division has a functional structure because its activities are standardized; the pharmaceuticals division has a product-team structure; and the plastics division has a matrix structure. (The latter two structures are discussed in detail later in this chapter.) Similarly, General Motors operates the whole corporation through a multidivisional structure, but each auto division organizes itself into different product groups, based on the type of auto made.

In the multidivisional structure, day-to-day operations of a division are the responsibility of divisional management; that is, divisional management has **operating responsibility**. Corporate headquarters staff, however, which includes members of the board of directors as well as top executives, is responsible for overseeing long-term plans and providing the guidance for interdivisional projects. This staff has **strategic responsibility**. Such a combination of self-contained divisions with a centralized corporate management represents a higher level of both vertical and horizontal differentiation, as noted earlier. These two innovations provide the extra control necessary to coordinate growth and diversification. Because this structure, despite its high bureaucratic costs, has now been adopted by more than 90 percent of all large U.S. corporations, we need to consider its advantages and disadvantages in more detail.

Advantages of a Multidivisional Structure

When managed effectively at both the corporate and the divisional levels, a multidivisional structure offers several advantages. Together, they can raise corporate profitability to a new peak because they allow the organization to operate more complex kinds of corporate-level strategy.

Enhanced Corporate Financial Control The profitability of different business divisions is clearly visible in the multidivisional structure.[34] Because each division is its own profit center, financial controls can be applied to each business on the basis of profit criteria. Typically, these controls cover establishing targets, monitoring performance on a regular basis, and selectively intervening when problems arise. Corporate headquarters is also in a better position to allocate corporate financial resources among competing divisions. The visibility of divisional performance means that corporate headquarters can identify the divisions in which investment of funds will yield the greatest long-term returns. In a sense, the corporate office is in a position to act as the investor or banker in an internal capital market, channeling funds to high-yield uses.

Enhanced Strategic Control The multidivisional structure frees corporate staff from operating responsibilities. The staff thus gains time for contemplating wider strategic issues and for developing responses to environmental changes. The multidivisional structure also enables corporate headquarters to obtain the proper information to perform strategic planning functions. For example, separating individual businesses is a necessary prerequisite for portfolio planning.

Growth The multidivisional structure lets the company overcome an organizational limit to its growth. By reducing information overload at the center, corporate managers can handle a greater number of businesses. They can consider opportunities for further growth and diversification. Communication problems are reduced because the same set of standardized accounting and financial control techniques can be used for all divisions. Also, corporate managers are able to implement a policy of management by exception, which means that they intervene only when problems arise.

Stronger Pursuit of Internal Efficiency Within a functional structure, the interdependence of functional departments means that the *individual* performance of each function inside a company cannot be measured by objective criteria. For example, the profitability of the finance function, marketing function, or manufacturing function cannot be assessed in isolation because they are only part of the whole. This often means that within the functional structure considerable degrees of organizational slack—that is, functional resources that are used unproductively—can go undetected. For example, the head of the finance function might employ a larger staff than required for efficiency to reduce work pressures inside the department and to bring the manager higher status.

In a multidivisional structure, however, the individual efficiency of each autonomous division can be directly observed and measured in terms of the profit it generates. Thus, autonomy makes divisional managers accountable for their own performance; they can have no alibis for poor performance. The corporate office is thus in a better position to identify inefficiencies.

Disadvantages of a Multidivisional Structure

Probably because a multidivisional structure has a number of powerful advantages, it seems to be the preferred choice of most large diversified enterprises today. Indeed, research suggests that large companies that adopt this structure outperform those that retain the functional structure.[35] A multidivisional structure has its disadvantages as well, however. Good management can eliminate some of them, but others are inherent in the way the structure operates and require constant managerial attention. These disadvantages are discussed next.

Establishing the Divisional-Corporate Authority Relationship The authority relationship between corporate headquarters and the divisions must be correctly established. The multidivisional structure introduces a new level in the hierarchy—the corporate level. The problem lies in deciding how much authority and control to assign to the operating divisions and how much authority to retain at corporate headquarters.

This problem was first noted by Alfred Sloan, the founder of General Motors. He introduced the multidivisional structure at General Motors, which became the first company to adopt it, and created General Motors' familiar five-automobile divisions: Chevrolet, Pontiac, Oldsmobile, Buick, and Cadillac.[36] What Sloan found, however, was that when headquarters retained too much power and authority, the operating divisions lacked sufficient autonomy to develop the business strategy that might best meet the needs of the division. On the other hand, when too much power was delegated to the divisions, they pursued divisional objectives, with little heed to the needs of the whole corporation. As a result, for example, not all of the potential gains from synergy discussed earlier could be achieved.

Thus, the central issue in managing the multidivisional structure is how much authority should be *centralized* at corporate headquarters and how much should be *decentralized* to the divisions. This issue must be decided by each company in reference to the nature of its business- and corporate-level strategies. There are no easy answers, and over time, as the environment changes or the company alters its strategies, the balance between corporate and divisional control will also change. Strategy in Action 11.4 illustrates this problem. It highlights the changes that Amoco, one of the largest U.S. oil companies, has made in its divisional structure.

Distortion of Information If corporate headquarters puts too much emphasis on divisional return on investment—for instance, by setting very high and stringent return-on-investment targets—divisional managers may choose to distort the information they supply top management and paint a rosy picture of the present situation at the expense of future profits. That is, divisions may maximize short-run profits, perhaps by cutting product development or new investments or marketing expenditures. This may cost the company dearly in the future. The problem stems from too tight financial control. General Motors has suffered from this problem in recent years, as declining performance has prompted divisional managers to try to make their divisions look good to corporate headquarters. Managing the corporate-divisional interface requires coping with subtle power issues.

Competition for Resources The third problem of managing a multidivisional structure is that the divisions themselves may compete for resources, and this rivalry prevents synergy gains or economies of scope from emerging. For example, the amount of money that corporate personnel has to distribute to the divisions is fixed. Generally, the divisions that can demonstrate the highest return on investment will get the lion's share of the money. Because that large share strengthens them in the next time period, the strong divisions grow stronger. Consequently, divisions may actively compete for resources and, by doing so, reduce interdivisional coordination.

Transfer Pricing Divisional competition may also lead to battles over **transfer pricing**. As we discuss in Chapter 9, one of the problems with vertical integration or related diversification is setting transfer prices between divisions. Rivalry among divisions increases the problem of setting fair prices. Each supplying division tries to set the highest price for its outputs to maximize its own return on investment. Such competition can completely undermine the corporate culture and make a

11.4 **STRATEGY *in* ACTION**

Amoco's New Approach

As with most other global oil companies, Amoco is engaged in three major activities: oil exploration, refining, and chemicals manufacturing. To manage these activities, Amoco used a three-legged structure and created three independent operating subsidiaries to manage each of its three main activities. Each subsidiary had its own set of managers, who were responsible for overseeing all the many different business divisions inside each subsidiary. The managers of all three subsidiaries then reported to Amoco's corporate-level managers, who oversaw their activities and made the final decision on what each subsidiary should be doing. Thus, all important decision making at Amoco took place at the top of the organization. As a result, it often took a long time to make decisions because of the many managerial layers between Amoco's corporate managers and its divisional managers. Since divisional managers were responsible for developing an effective business-level strategy, the slow decision-making process hampered their attempts to build a competitive advantage.[37]

In the 1990s, however, Amoco, like other global oil companies such as Exxon, British Petroleum, and Mobil, experienced intense pressure to reduce costs because of flat gas prices. To try to boost profits, Amoco laid off more than one-quarter of its work force, but this did not have the desired effect. Therefore, Amoco's managers took a close look at the company's structure to see whether there was a way to increase its performance.

Amoco's chairman and CEO, H. Laurance Fuller, concluded that a massive reorganization of Amoco's structure was necessary. Fuller decided to eliminate Amoco's three-legged structure completely and to remove all the managers at the subsidiary level. The three subsidiaries were divided into seventeen independent business divisions, and Amoco changed to a multidivisional structure. Henceforth, decision-making authority was decentralized to the managers of each division, who could choose their own strategy for the division. Each division was to be evaluated on the basis of its ability to reach certain growth targets set by corporate managers, but the way the divisions achieved those targets would be determined by their own managers.

By 1996, it was clear that Fuller's idea for a new, flatter, decentralized product-division structure had worked. Managers were acting more entrepreneurially and the company was operating more efficiently. In 1998, in another attempt to increase efficiency, Fuller agreed to merge Amoco with British Petroleum (BP). The companies are still in the process of deciding how to combine the activities of their various divisions, many of whose activities overlap and duplicate one another, so that the company can compete effectively in the new century.[38]

company a battleground. Many companies have a history of competition among divisions. Some, of course, may encourage competition, if managers believe that it leads to maximum performance.

Short-Term Research and Development Focus If extremely high ROI targets are set by corporate headquarters, there is a danger that the divisions will cut back on research and development expenditures to improve the financial performance of the division. Although this inflates divisional performance in the short term, it reduces a division's ability to develop new products and leads to a fall in the stream of long-term profits. Hence, corporate headquarters personnel must carefully control their interactions with the divisions to ensure that both the short- and long-term goals of the business are being achieved.

Bureaucratic Costs As noted earlier, because each division possesses its own specialized functions, such as finance or research and development, multidivisional structures are expensive to run and manage. Research and development is especially costly, and so some companies centralize such functions at the corporate level to serve all divisions. The duplication of specialist services is not a problem if the gains from having separate specialist functions outweigh the costs. Again, strategic managers must decide whether duplication is financially justified. Activities are often centralized in times of downturn or recession, particularly advisory services and planning functions; divisions, however, are retained as profit centers.

The advantages of divisional structures must be balanced against their disadvantages, but, as we already noted, the disadvantages can be managed by an observant, professional management team that is aware of the issues involved. The multidivisional structure is the dominant one today, which clearly suggests its usefulness as the means of managing the multibusiness corporation.

Matrix Structure

A matrix structure differs from the structures discussed so far in that it is based on two forms of horizontal differentiation rather than on one, as in the functional structure.[39] In the matrix design, activities on the vertical axis are grouped by *function,* so that there is a familiar differentiation of tasks into functions such as engineering, sales and marketing, and research and development. In addition, superimposed on this vertical pattern is a horizontal pattern based on differentiation by *product or project.* The result is a complex network of reporting relationships among projects and functions, as depicted in Figure 11.7.

This structure also employs an unusual kind of vertical differentiation. Although matrix structures are flat, with few hierarchical levels, employees inside the matrix have two bosses: a **functional boss**, who is the head of a function, and a **project boss**, who is responsible for managing the individual projects. Employees work on a project team with specialists from other functions and report to the project boss on project matters and the functional boss on matters relating to functional issues. All employees who work in a project team are called **two-boss employees** and are responsible for managing coordination and communication among the functions and projects.

Matrix structures were first developed by companies that are in high-technology industries such as aerospace and electronics—for example, TRW and Hughes Aircraft. These companies were developing radically new products in uncertain, competitive environments, and speed of product development was the crucial consideration. They needed a structure that could respond to this need, but the functional structure was too inflexible to allow the complex role and task interactions necessary to meet new-product development requirements. Moreover, employees in these companies tend to be highly qualified and professional and perform best in autonomous, flexible working conditions. The matrix structure provides such conditions.

For example, this structure requires a minimum of direct hierarchical control by supervisors. Team members control their own behavior, and participation in project teams allows them to monitor other team members and learn from each other. Furthermore, as the project goes through its different phases, different specialists from various functions are required. Thus, for example, at the first stage, the services of research and development specialists may be called for; then at the next stage, engi-

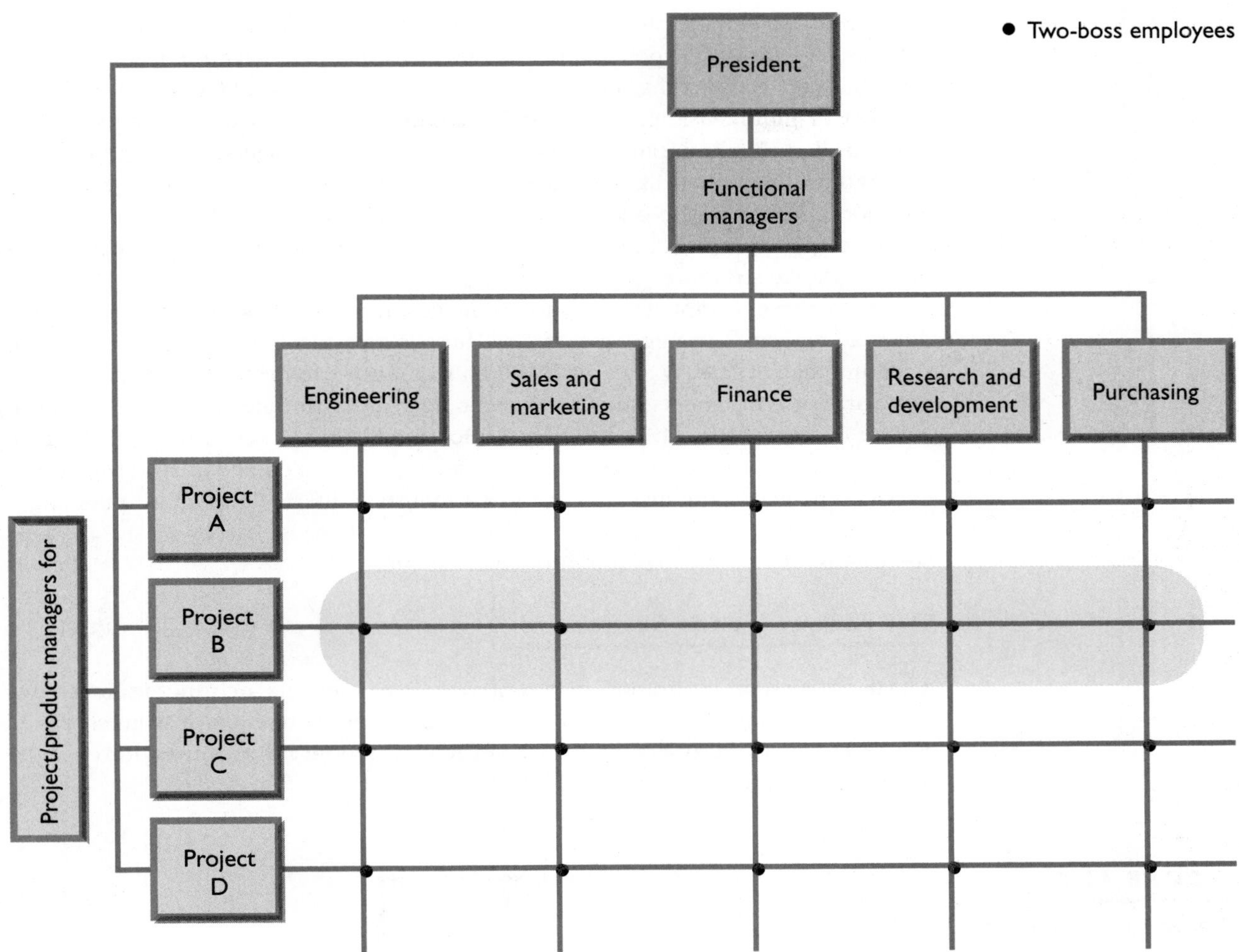

FIGURE 11.7

Matrix Structure

neers and marketing specialists may be needed to make cost and marketing projections. As the demand for the type of specialist changes, team members can be moved to other projects that require their services. The matrix structure, therefore, can make maximum use of employees' skills as existing projects are completed and new ones come into existence.

Finally, the freedom given by the matrix not only provides the autonomy to motivate employees, but also leaves top management free to concentrate on strategic issues, since they do not have to become involved in operating matters. On all these counts, the matrix is an excellent tool for creating the flexibility necessary for quick reactions to competitive conditions.

The matrix structure does have disadvantages, however.[40] First, the bureaucratic costs of operating this structure are very high compared with those of operating a functional structure. Because employees tend to be highly skilled, both salaries and overhead are high. Second, the constant movement of employees around the matrix means that time and money are spent establishing new team relationships and getting the project off the ground. Third, the two-boss employee's role, balancing as it does the interests of the project with those of the function, is difficult to manage, and care must be taken to avoid conflict between functions and projects over resources. Over time, it is possible that project managers will take the leading role in planning and goal setting, in which case the structure would work more like a product or multidivisional structure. If function and project relationships are left uncontrolled, they can lead to power struggles among managers, resulting in stagnation and decline rather than increased flexibility. Finally, the larger the organization, the more difficult it is to operate a matrix structure, because task and role relationships become complex. In such situations, the only option may be to change to a multidivisional structure.

Given these advantages and disadvantages, the matrix is generally used only when a company's strategy warrants it. There is no point in using a more complex structure than necessary because it will only cost more to manage. In dynamic product/market environments, such as biotechnology and computers, the benefits of the matrix in terms of flexibility and innovation are likely to exceed the high bureaucratic costs of using it, and so it becomes an appropriate choice of structure. However, companies in the mature stage of an industry's life cycle or those pursuing a low-cost strategy would rarely choose this structure because it is expensive to operate. We discuss matrix structure further in Chapter 13.

Product-Team Structure

A major structural innovation in recent years has been the **product-team structure**. Its advantages are similar to those of a matrix structure, but it is much easier and far less costly to operate because of the way people are organized into permanent cross-functional teams, as Figure 11.8 illustrates.

FIGURE 11.8

Product-Team Structure

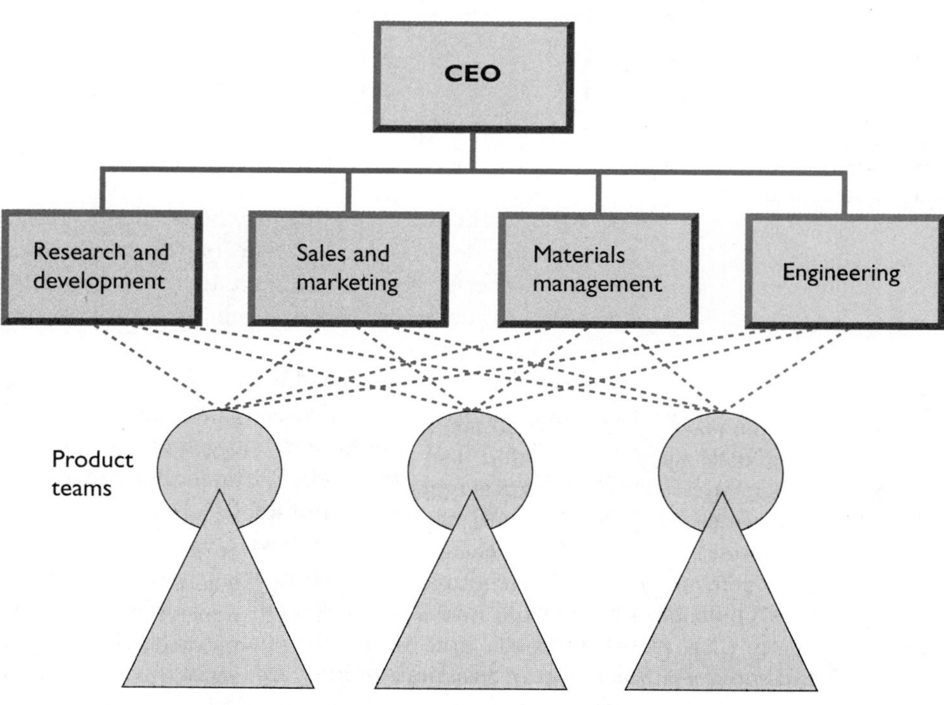

In the product-team structure, as in the matrix structure, tasks are divided along product or project lines to reduce bureaucratic costs and to increase management's ability to monitor and control the manufacturing process. However, instead of being assigned only *temporarily* to different projects, as in the matrix structure, functional specialists are placed in *permanent* cross-functional teams. As a result, the costs associated with coordinating their activities are much lower than in a matrix structure, in which tasks and reporting relationships change rapidly.

Cross-functional teams are formed right at the beginning of the product-development process so that any difficulties that arise can be ironed out early, before they lead to major redesign problems. When all functions have direct input from the beginning, design costs and subsequent manufacturing costs can be kept low. Moreover, the use of cross-functional teams speeds innovation and customer responsiveness because when authority is decentralized to the team, decisions can be made more quickly. Strategy in Action 11.5 profiles Lexmark, which shifted to a product-team structure to reduce costs and speed product development.

11.5 STRATEGY *in* ACTION

Restructuring at Lexmark

Lexmark, a printer and typewriter manufacturer, was a division of IBM until it was sold to a New York investment firm in 1992. As an IBM division, it had performed badly, and IBM sold it after years of losses brought on by high operating costs and an inability to produce new products that could compete with Hewlett-Packard and Japanese printer makers such as Epson. Its new top-management team, led by Marvin Mann, an ex-IBM executive, had the task of reengineering its structure to turn the company around.

Mann first destroyed the organizational structure that the company had developed under its former IBM management. Like the rest of IBM, the division had a tall, centralized structure, where all important decisions were made high in the organization by top managers. This slowed decision making and made it very difficult to communicate across functions because so many managers at different levels and in different functions had to approve new plans.

Moving quickly to change this system, Mann streamlined the company's hierarchy, which meant terminating 50 percent of its managers and eliminating all staff managers—that is, those with no direct-line responsibility. This action cut out three levels in the hierarchy. He then decentralized authority to the product managers of the company's four product groups and told them to develop their own plans and goals. In addition, to continue the process of decentralization, product managers were instructed to develop cross-functional teams comprising employees from all functions, with the goal of finding new and improved ways of organizing task activities to reduce costs. The teams were to use competitive benchmarking and evaluate their competitors' products in order to establish new performance standards to guide their activities. Finally, as an incentive for employees to work hard at increasing efficiency, innovation, and quality, Mann established a company stock ownership scheme to reward employees for their efforts.

The reengineering of the organizational structure to a product-team structure has been very successful for Lexmark. The cost of launching new products has gone down by 50 percent and it has speeded up its new-product development cycle by 30 percent. The company's net income was \$149 million in 1997 and increased to \$243 million in 1998.[41] Since its share price has jumped from \$20 a share in 1993 to more than \$100 in 1999, its employees have shared in its success too.

Geographic Structure

When a company operates as a geographic structure, geographic regions become the basis for the grouping of organizational activities. For example, a company may divide its manufacturing operations and establish manufacturing plants in different regions of the country. This allows it to be responsive to the needs of regional customers and reduces transportation costs. Similarly, service organizations such as store chains or banks may organize their sales and marketing activities on a regional, rather than on a national, level to get closer to their customers.

A geographic structure provides more control than a functional structure because there are several regional hierarchies carrying out the work previously performed by a single centralized hierarchy. A company such as Federal Express clearly needs to operate a geographic structure to fulfill its corporate goal: next-day delivery. Large merchandising organizations, such as Neiman Marcus, Dillard Department Stores, and Wal-Mart, also moved to a geographic structure soon after they started building stores across the country. With this type of structure, different regional clothing needs (for example, sun wear in the Southwest, down coats in the East) can be handled as required. At the same time, because the purchasing function remains centralized, one central organization can buy for all regions. Thus, in using a geographic structure a company can both achieve economies of scale in buying and distribution and reduce coordination and communication problems.

Neiman Marcus developed a geographic structure similar to the one shown in Figure 11.9 to manage its nationwide chain of stores. In each region, it established a team of regional buyers to respond to the needs of customers in each geographic area—for example, the western, central, eastern, and southern regions. The regional

FIGURE 11.9

Geographic Structure

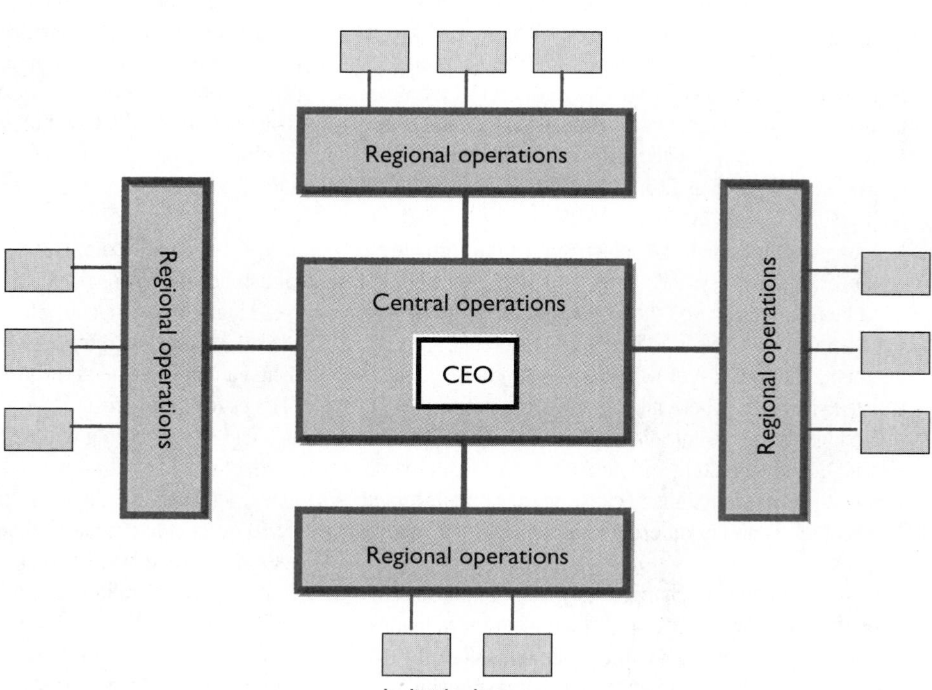

buyers then fed their information to the central buyers at corporate headquarters, who coordinated their demands to obtain purchasing economies and to ensure that Neiman Marcus's high-quality standards, on which its differentiation advantage depends, were maintained nationally.

The usefulness of the matrix, product-team, or geographic structure depends, however, on the size of the company and its range of products and regions. If a company starts to diversify into unrelated products or to integrate vertically into new industries, these structures cannot handle the increased diversity, and a company must move to a multidivisional structure. Only the multidivisional structure is complex enough to deal with the needs of the large, multibusiness company.

INTEGRATION AND INTEGRATING MECHANISMS

As just discussed, an organization must choose the appropriate form of differentiation to match its strategy. Greater diversification, for example, requires that a company move from a functional structure to a multidivisional structure. Differentiation, however, is only the first organizational design decision to be made. The second decision concerns the level of integration necessary to make an organizational structure work effectively. As noted earlier, *integration* refers to the extent to which an organization seeks to coordinate its value creation activities and make them interdependent. The design issue can be summed up simply: the higher a company's level of differentiation, the higher is the level of integration needed to make organizational structure work effectively.[42] Thus, if a company adopts a more complex form of differentiation, it requires a more complex form of integration to accomplish its goals. Federal Express, for example, needs an enormous amount of integration and coordination to allow it to fulfill its promise of next-day package delivery. It is renowned for its innovative use of integrating mechanisms, such as customer-liaison personnel, to manage its transactions quickly and efficiently.

Forms of Integrating Mechanisms

There is a series of integrating mechanisms a company can use to increase its level of integration as its level of differentiation increases.[43] These mechanisms—on a continuum from simple to complex—are listed in Table 11.1, together with examples of the individuals or groups that might perform these integrating roles. As is the case when increasing the level of differentiation, however, increasing the level of integration is expensive. There are high bureaucratic costs associated with using managers to coordinate value creation activities. Hence, a company only uses more complex integrating mechanisms to coordinate its activities to the extent necessary to implement its strategy effectively.

Direct Contact The aim behind establishing direct contact among managers is to set up a context within which managers from different divisions or functions can work together to solve mutual problems. Managers from different functions have different goals and interests but equal authority, and so they may tend to compete rather than cooperate when conflicts arise. In a typical functional structure, for example, the heads of each of the functions have equal authority; the nearest common

TABLE 11.1

Types and Examples of Integrating Mechanisms

Direct contact	Sales and production managers
Liason roles	Assistant sales and plant managers
Task forces	Representatives from sales, production, and research and development
Teams	Organizational executive committee
Integrating roles	Assistant vice president for strategic planning or vice president without portfolio
Matrix	All roles are integrating roles

point of authority is the CEO. Consequently, if disputes arise, no mechanism exists to resolve the conflicts apart from the authority of the boss.

In fact, one sign of conflict in organizations is the number of problems sent up the hierarchy for upper-level managers to solve. This wastes management time and effort, slows down strategic decision making, and makes it difficult to create a cooperative culture in the company. For this reason, companies generally choose more complex integrating mechanisms to coordinate interfunctional and divisional activities.

Interdepartmental Liaison Roles A company can improve its interfunctional coordination through the interdepartmental liaison role. When the volume of contacts between two departments or functions increases, one of the ways of improving coordination is to give one manager in *each* division or function the responsibility for coordinating with the other. These managers may meet daily, weekly, monthly, or as needed. Figure 11.10a depicts the nature of the liaison role, the small dot representing the manager inside the functional department who has responsibility for coordinating with the other function. The responsibility for coordination is part of a manager's full-time job, but through these roles a permanent relationship forms between the managers involved, greatly easing strains between departments. Furthermore, liaison roles offer a way of transferring information across the organization, which is important in large, anonymous organizations, whose employees may know no one outside their immediate department.

Temporary Task Forces When more than two functions or divisions share common problems, direct contact and liaison roles are of limited value because they do not provide enough coordination. The solution is to adopt a more complex form of integrating mechanism called a task force. The nature of the task force is represented diagrammatically in Figure 11.10b. One member of each function or division is assigned to a task force created to solve a specific problem. Essentially, task forces are *ad hoc committees,* and members are responsible for reporting back to their departments on the issues addressed and solutions recommended. Task forces are temporary because, once the problem has been solved, members return to their normal roles in their own departments or are assigned to other task forces. Task force members also perform many of their normal duties while serving on the task force.

FIGURE 11.10

Forms of Integrating Mechanisms

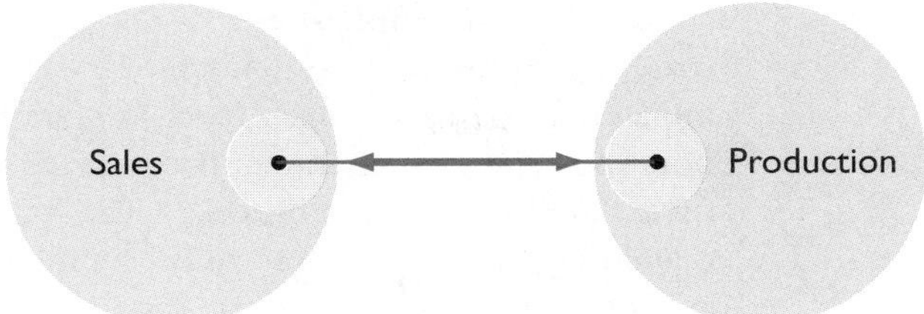

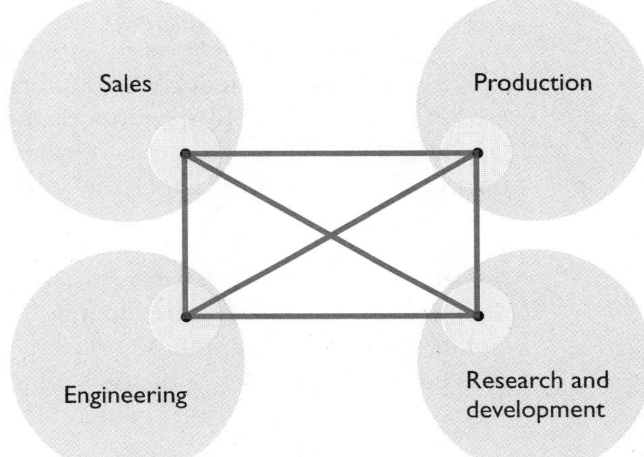

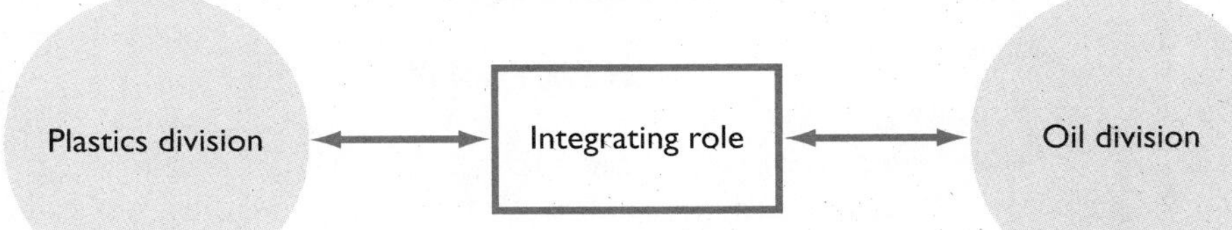

• Indicates manager with responsibility for integration

Permanent Teams In many cases, the issues addressed by a task force recur. To deal with these issues effectively, an organization must establish a permanent integrating mechanism, such as a permanent team. An example of a permanent team is a new-product development committee, which is responsible for the choice, design, and marketing of new products. Such an activity obviously requires a great deal of integration among functions if new products are to be successfully introduced, and establishing a permanent integrating mechanism accomplishes this. Intel, for instance, emphasizes teamwork. It formed a council system based on approximately ninety cross-functional groups, which meet regularly to set functional strategy in areas such as engineering and marketing and to develop business-level strategy.

The importance of teams in the management of the organizational structure cannot be overemphasized. Essentially, permanent teams are the organization's *standing committees,* and much of the strategic direction of the organization is formulated in their meetings. Henry Mintzberg, in a study of how the managers of corporations spend their time, discovered that they spend more than 60 percent of their time in these committees.[44] The reason is not bureaucracy but rather the fact that integration is possible only in intensive, face-to-face sessions, in which managers can understand others' viewpoints and develop a cohesive organizational strategy. The more complex the company, the more important these teams become. Westinghouse, for example, has established a whole new task force and team system to promote integration among divisions and improve corporate performance.

As discussed earlier, the product-team structure is based on the use of cross-functional teams to speed products to market. These teams assume the responsibility for all aspects of product development. The way in which AT&T made use of cross-functional teams to speed product development in its race to compete with Japanese manufacturers (described in Strategy in Action 11.6) illustrates how these teams can increase coordination and integration among functions.

Integrating Roles The only function of the integrating role is to prompt integration among divisions or departments; it is a full-time job. As Figure 11.10c indicates, the role is independent of the subunits or divisions being integrated. It is staffed by an independent expert, who is normally a senior manager with a great deal of experience in the joint needs of the two departments. The job is to coordinate the deci-

11.6 STRATEGY *in* ACTION

Teamwork at AT&T

Like other large companies, AT&T had developed a very tall, centralized structure to manage its activities. While the telephone industry was regulated, AT&T cared little about the way its massive bureaucracy slowed down decision making. However, after deregulation a major problem facing the company was how to speed the development of new telephones and answering machines that could compete with those of Japanese companies such as Panasonic and Sony. These companies led the market in terms of both the features and the low price of telephone products, and AT&T was a poor third in the competitive marketplace.

AT&T's answer was to bypass the bureaucracy by creating cross-functional teams. Previously, AT&T had employed the usual functional approach to managing product development. The product started in engineering and then went to manufacturing, which in turn handed the product over to marketing. This was a slow and time-consuming process. In the new approach, John Hanley, the AT&T vice president of product development, decided to form teams of six to twelve people from all these functions to handle all aspects of the development process. Each team was given a deadline for the various project phases and then left to get on with the job. The results were astonishing. Product development time was reduced by 50 percent (for example, AT&T's new 4200 phone was produced in one year, not the usual two), costs went down, and quality went up. Today, AT&T's answering machines and cordless phones are the market leaders, and AT&T has extended the use of cross-functional teams throughout its business.

sion process among departments or divisions so that synergetic gains from cooperation can be obtained. One study found that Du Pont had created 160 integrating roles to provide coordination among the different divisions of the company and improve corporate performance.[45] Once again, the more differentiated the company, the more common are these roles. Often people in these roles take the responsibility for chairing task forces and teams, and this provides additional integration.

Integrating Departments Sometimes the number of integrating roles becomes so high that a permanent integrating department is established at corporate headquarters. Normally, this occurs only in large, diversified corporations that see the need for integration among divisions. This department consists mainly of strategic planners and may indeed be called the strategic planning department. Corporate headquarters staff in a divisional structure can also be viewed as an integrating department from the divisional perspective.

Matrix Structure Finally, when differentiation is very high and the company must be able to respond quickly to the environment, a matrix structure becomes the appropriate integrating device. The matrix contains many of the integrating mechanisms already discussed. The subproject managers integrate among functions and projects, and the matrix is built on the basis of temporary task forces.

Integration and Control

Clearly, firms have a large number of options open to them when they increase their level of differentiation as a result of increased growth or diversification. The implementation issue is for managers to match differentiation with the level of integration to meet organizational objectives. Note that while too much differentiation and not enough integration leads to a failure of implementation, the converse is also true. That is, the combination of low differentiation and high integration leads to an overcontrolled, bureaucratized organization, in which flexibility and speed of response are reduced rather than enhanced by the level of integration. Besides, too much integration is expensive for the company because it raises bureaucratic costs. For these reasons, the goal is to decide on the optimum amount of integration necessary for meeting organizational goals and objectives. A company needs to operate the simplest structure consistent with implementing its strategy effectively. In practice, integrating mechanisms are only the first means through which a company seeks to increase its ability to control and coordinate its activities; modern information systems are a second.

Information Systems and Organizational Structure

As we discuss throughout this book, advances in software information systems and Internet technology are having important effects on managers and organizations. By improving the ability of managers to coordinate and control the activities of the organization, and by helping managers make more effective decisions, modern computer-based information systems have become a central component of any organization's structure. Evidence is growing, too, that information systems can be a source of competitive advantage; organizations that do not adopt leading-edge information systems are likely to be at a competitive disadvantage. In this section, we examine how the rapid growth of computerized information systems is affecting organizational structure and competitive advantage.

Until the development of modern computer-based information systems, there was no viable alternative to the organizational hierarchy, despite the information problems associated with it discussed earlier. The rapid rise of computer-based information systems has been associated with a "delayering" (flattening) of the organizational hierarchy and a move toward greater decentralization and horizontal information flows within organizations.[46] By electronically providing managers with high-quality, timely, and relatively complete information, modern information systems have reduced the need for tall management hierarchies. Modern information systems have reduced the need for a hierarchy to function as a means of controlling the activities of the organization. In addition, they have reduced the need for a management hierarchy to coordinate organizational activities.

E-mail systems, the development of software programs for sharing documents electronically, and the development of the Internet has all increased horizontal information flows within organizations. The development of organizationwide computer networks is breaking down the barriers that have traditionally separated departments, and the result has been improved performance and superior efficiency, quality, innovation, and customer responsiveness.[47] One reason for an increase in efficiency is that the use of advanced information systems can reduce the number of employees required to perform organizational activities. At one time, for example, thirteen layers of management separated Eastman Kodak's general manager of manufacturing and factory workers. Now, with the help of information systems, the number of layers has been reduced to four. Similarly, Intel has found that by increasing the sophistication of its information systems it has been able to cut the number of hierarchical layers in the organization from ten to five.[48]

Moreover, by increasing horizontal information flows and helping to break down the barriers that separate departments, computer networks are allowing managers to boost quality, innovation, and responsiveness to customers. The experience of Lotus Development, the company that developed Lotus Notes, illustrates how information systems can speed product development. Using their own Notes technology, Lotus managers found that software writers in Asia and Europe can work almost in parallel with their U.S. counterparts, sharing documentation and messages among themselves on a real-time basis. As a result, a Japanese version of a new product can be introduced within three or four weeks of its English-language release, instead of the three or four months that were necessary before the adoption of Notes.[49]

Thus, state-of-the-art information technology can improve the competitiveness of an organization. Indeed, the search for competitive advantage is driving much of the rapid development and adoption of such systems. By improving the decision-making capability of managers, modern information systems help an organization enhance its competitive position. To facilitate the use of information software systems and to make organizational structure work, however, a company must create a control and incentive structure to motivate people and subunits to raise organizational performance. In the next chapter, we discuss the various kinds of strategic control systems that organizations can use to make their organizational structures work effectively.

SUMMARY OF CHAPTER

This chapter discusses the issues involved in designing a structure to meet the needs of a company's strategy. Companies can adopt a large number of structures to match changes in their size and strategy over time. The structure a company selects is the one whose logic of grouping activities (that is, whose form of horizontal differentiation) best meets the needs of its business or businesses. The company must match its form of horizontal differentiation to vertical differentiation. That is, it must choose a structure and then make choices about levels in the hierarchy and the degree of centralization or decentralization. It is the combination of both kinds of differentiation that produces internal organizational arrangements.

Once a company has divided itself into parts, however, it then must integrate itself. A company must choose the appropriate level of integration to match its level of differentiation if it is to coordinate its value creation activities successfully. Since differentiation and integration are expensive, a company's goal is to economize on bureaucratic costs by adopting the simplest structure consistent with achieving its strategy. We stress the following points:

- Implementing a strategy successfully depends on selecting the right organizational structure and control system to match a company's strategy.
- The basic tool of strategy implementation is organizational design. Good organizational design increases profits in two ways. First, it economizes on bureaucratic costs and lowers the costs of value creation activities. Second, it enhances the ability of a company's value creation functions to achieve superior efficiency, quality, innovation, and customer responsiveness and to obtain a differentiation advantage.
- Differentiation and integration are the two design concepts that govern how a structure will work. The higher the level of differentiation and integration, the higher are bureaucratic costs.
- Differentiation has two aspects: (1) vertical differentiation, which refers to how a company chooses to allocate its decision-making authority, and (2) horizontal differentiation, which refers to the way a company groups organizational activities into functions, departments, or divisions.
- The basic choice in vertical differentiation is whether to have a flat or a tall structure. Tall hierarchies have a number of disadvantages, such as problems with communication and information transfer, motivation, and cost. Decentralization, or delegation of authority, however, can solve some of these problems.
- As a company grows and diversifies, it adopts a multidivisional structure. Although a multidivisional structure has higher bureaucratic costs than a functional structure, it overcomes the control problems associated with a functional structure and gives a company the capability to handle its value creation activities effectively.
- Other specialized kinds of structures include the matrix, product-team, and geographic structures. Each has a specialized use and, to be chosen, must match the needs of the organization.
- The more complex the company and the higher its level of differentiation, the higher is the level of integration needed to manage its structure.
- The kinds of integrating mechanisms available to a company range from direct contact to matrix structure. The more complex the mechanism, the greater are the costs of using it. A company should take care to match these mechanisms to its strategic needs.

DISCUSSION QUESTIONS

1. What is the difference between vertical and horizontal differentiation? Rank the various structures discussed in this chapter along these two dimensions.
2. What kind of structure best describes the way your (a) business school and (b) university operate? Why is the structure appropriate? Would another structure fit better?
3. When would a company decide to change from a functional to a multidivisional structure?
4. When would a company choose a matrix structure? What are the problems associated with managing this structure, and why might a product-team structure be preferable?

Practicing Strategic Management

SMALL-GROUP EXERCISE
Speeding Up Product Development

Break up into groups of three to five people, and discuss the following scenario:

You are the top functional managers of a small greeting card company whose new lines of humorous cards for every occasion are selling out as fast as they are reaching the stores. Currently, your employees are organized into different functions such as card designers, artists, and joke writers, as well as functions such as marketing and manufacturing. Each function works on a wide range of different kinds of cards—birthday, Christmas, Hanukkah, Thanksgiving, and so on. Sometimes the design department comes up with the initial idea for a new card and sends the idea to the artists, who draw and color the picture. Then the card is sent to the joke writers who write the joke to suit the card. At other times, the process starts with writing the joke, which is sent to the design department to find the best use for the idea.

The problem you are experiencing is that your current functional structure does not allowing you to produce new cards fast enough to satisfy customers' demands. It typically takes a new card one year to reach the market, and you want to shorten this time by half to protect and expand your market niche.

1. Discuss ways in which you can improve the operation of your current functional structure to speed the product-development process.
2. Discuss the pros and cons of moving to a (a) multidivisional, (b) matrix, and (c) product-team structure to reduce card development time.
3. Which of these structures, do you think, is most appropriate and why?

STRATEGIC MANAGEMENT PROJECT
Module 11

This module asks you to identify the type of organizational structure used by your organization and to explain why your company has selected this form of differentiation and integration. If you are studying a company in your area, you will probably have more information about the company's structure than if you are studying a company using published sources. However, you can make many inferences about the company's structure from the nature of its activities, and if you write to the company, it may provide you with an organizational chart and other information.

1. How large is the company as measured by the number of its employees? How many levels in the hierarchy does it have from the top to the bottom?
2. Based on these two measures and any other information you may have, would you say your company operates with a relatively tall or flat structure? What effect does this have on people's behavior?
3. Does your company have a centralized or a decentralized approach to decision making? How do you know?
4. In what ways do the company's vertical differentiation choices affect the behavior of people and subunits? Do you think the company's choice of vertical differentiation is appropriate for its activities? Why or why not?
5. What changes (if any) would you make in the way the company operates in a vertical direction?
6. Draw an organizational chart showing the main way in which your company groups its activities. Based on this chart, what kind of structure (functional or divisional) does your company operate with?
7. Why did your company choose this structure? In what ways is it appropriate for its business? In what ways is it not?
8. What changes (if any) would you make in the way your company operates in a horizontal direction?
9. Given this analysis, does your company have a low or a high level of differentiation?
10. What kind of integration or integration mechanisms does your company use? Why? Does its level of integration match its level of differentiation?
11. Based on the analysis of your company's level of differentiation and integration, would you say your company is coordinating and motivating its people and subunits effectively? Why or why not?

12. What changes would you make in the company's structure to increase the firm's effectiveness? What changes has the company itself made to improve effectiveness? Why?

ARTICLE FILE 11

Find an example (or examples) of a company that has recently changed its organizational structure. What changes did it make? Why did it make these changes? What effect did these changes have on the behavior of people and subunits?

EXPLORING THE WEB
What Kind of Organizational Structure?

Explore the Web to find a Web site that displays a company's organizational chart or that talks about a company's method of managing its structure. (For example, does it use a centralized or decentralized approach?) What kind of structure does the company use to manage its activities?

CLOSING CASE

Chrysler's Cross-Functional Product Teams

AFTER MANY YEARS of poor performance and mounting losses, Chrysler, the number three U.S. carmaker, has been experiencing a turnaround in the 1990s. Its new car models such as the Dodge Viper, the Stratus, and the cab-forward LH cars have been attracting many customers back to the company and away from Japanese imports. The company's profits and stock price have surged upward as a result. How has Chrysler achieved this turnaround? Chrysler's top management attributes its success to its new product-team structure, which uses cross-functional teams.

Like other U.S. car companies, Chrysler used to have a functional approach to designing and producing its cars. In the functional approach, the responsibility for the design of a new car was allocated to many different design departments, each of which was responsible for the design of one component, such as the engine or the body. Managers further up the hierarchy were responsible for coordinating the activities of the different design departments in order to ensure that the components were compatible with one another. Top managers were also responsible for coordinating the activities of support functions, such as purchasing, marketing, and accounting, with the design process as their contributions were needed. When the design process was finished, the new car was then turned over to the manufacturing department, which decided how best to produce it.

Chrysler's functional approach slowed down the product-development process and made cross-functional communication difficult and slow. Each function pursued its activities in isolation from other functions, and it was left to top management to provide the integration necessary to coordinate functional activities. As a result, it took Chrysler an average of five years to bring a new car to market, a figure that was well behind the record of the Japanese, who took two to three years. Chrysler's structure was raising its costs, slowing innovation, and making the company less responsive to the needs of its customers. The company's top managers began to search for a new way of organizing its value creation activities to turn the company around. To begin this process, top management looked at the way Japanese companies were organized, particularly at the way Honda structured its value creation activities. Chrysler sent fourteen of its managers to study Honda's system and report back on its operation.[50]

Honda had pioneered the Honda Way concept of organizing its activities. It created small teams, comprising members from various functions, and gave them the responsibility and authority to manage a project from its conception through all design activities to final manufacture and sale. Honda had found that when it used these cross-functional teams, product development time dropped dramatically because functional communication and coordination were much easier in teams. Moreover, design costs were much lower when different functions worked together to solve problems as they emerged, because to change a design later (for example, to add a second air bag) could cost millions of dollars. Honda had also found that its policy of decentralizing authority to the team kept the organization flexible, innovative, and able to take advantage of emerging technical opportunities.

CLOSING CASE *(continued)*

Chrysler decided to imitate Honda's structure and took the opportunity to do so when it chose to build an expensive luxury car called the Viper. To manage the development of this new car, Chrysler created a cross-functional product team consisting of eighty-five people.[51] It established the team in a huge new research and development center it had built in Auburn Hills, Michigan, and gave it the authority and responsibility to bring the car to market. The outcome was dramatic. Within one year, top management could see that the team had achieved what would have taken three years under Chrysler's old system. In fact, the team brought the car to market in just thirty-six months at a development cost of $75 million, results that compared favorably with those obtained by Japanese companies.

With this success in hand, Chrysler's top management moved to restructure the whole company according to the product-team concept. Top management divided up functional personnel and assigned them to work in product teams charged with developing new cars, such as those with the cab-forward design. The number of levels in Chrysler's hierarchy decreased since authority was decentralized to managers in the product teams, who were responsible for all aspects of new-car development. Instead of having to integrate the activities of different functions, top managers could concentrate on allocating resources among projects, deciding future product developments, and continually challenging the teams to improve their efforts. Chrysler's efforts brought the reward of a dramatic drop in costs and an increase in quality and customer responsiveness. The price of the firm's shares soared during the 1990s as customers rushed to buy its cars.

Case Discussion Questions

1. What are the main differences between a functional and a product-team structure?
2. What are the advantages of Chrysler's new team structure, and what are some potential problems associated with it?

End Notes

1. Press release, www.microsoft.com (1999).
2. M. Moeller, S. Hamm, and T. J. Mullaney, "Remaking Microsoft: Why America's Most Successful Company Needed an Overhaul," *Business Week*, May 17, 1999, pp. 52–56.
3. J. R. Galbraith, *Designing Complex Organizations* (Reading, Mass.: Addison-Wesley, 1973).
4. J. Child, *Organization: A Guide for Managers and Administrators* (New York: Harper & Row, 1977), pp. 50–72.
5. R. H. Miles, *Macro Organizational Behavior* (Santa Monica, Calif.: Goodyear, 1980), pp. 19–20.
6. Galbraith, *Designing Complex Organizations*.
7. V. A. Graicunas, "Relationship in Organization," in *Papers on the Science of Administration,* eds. L. Gulick and L. Urwick (New York: Institute of Public Administration, 1937), pp. 181–185; J. C. Worthy, "Organizational Structure and Company Morale," *American Sociological Review*, 15 (1950), 169–179.
8. Child, *Organization*, pp. 50–52.
9. G. R. Jones, "Organization-Client Transactions and Organizational Governance Structures," *Academy of Management Journal*, 30 (1987), 197–218.
10. H. Mintzberg, *The Structuring of Organizations* (Englewood Cliffs, N.J.: Prentice-Hall, 1979), p. 435.
11. B. Woolridge and S. W. Floyd, "The Strategy Process, Middle Management Involvement, and Organizational Performance," *Strategic Management Journal*, 11 (1990), 231–241.
12. Child, *Organization*, p. 51.
13. R. Carzo Jr. and J. N. Yanousas, "Effects of Flat and Tall Organization Structure," *Administrative Science Quarterly*, 14 (1969), 178–191.
14. A. Gupta and V. Govindardan, "Business Unit Strategy, Managerial Characteristics, and Business Unit Effectiveness at Strategy Implementation," *Academy of Management Journal*, 27 (1984), 25–41; R. T. Lenz, "Determinants of Organizational Performance: An Interdisciplinary Review," *Strategic Management Journal*, 2 (1981), 131–154.
15. W. H. Wagel, "Keeping the Organization Lean at Federal Express," *Personnel* (March 1984), 4.
16. J. Koter, "For P&G Rivals, the New Game Is to Beat the Leader, Not Copy It," *Wall Street Journal*, May 6, 1985, p. 35.
17. G. R. Jones, "Task Visibility, Free Riding and Shirking: Explaining the Effect of Organization Structure on Employee Behavior," *Academy of Management Review*, 4 (1984), 684–695.
18. Press release, www.BankofAmerica.com (September, 1999).
19. "Operation Turnaround—How Westinghouse's New Chairman Plans to Fire Up an Old Line Company," *Business Week*, December 14, 1983, pp. 124–133.
20. "Union Pacific to Reorganize," cnnfn.com (August 20, 1998), p. 20.
21. Press release, www.unionpacific.com (1998).
22. C. Chandler and J. B. White, "Honda's Middle Managers Will Regain Authority in New Overhaul of Company," *Wall Street Journal*, May 16, 1992, p. A2.
23. J. H. Sheridan, "Best of Everything," *Industry Week*, January 19, 1998, pp. 13–14.
24. T. Clark, "How Honda Thrives," *Industry Week*, October 5, 1998, pp. 50–54.
25. R. L. Daft, *Organizational Theory and Design*, 3rd ed. (St. Paul, Minn.: West, 1986), p. 215.
26. Alfred D. Chandler, *Strategy and Structure* (Cambridge, Mass.: MIT Press, 1962).
27. This discussion draws heavily on Chandler, *Strategy and Structure*; and B. R. Scott, *Stages of Corporate Development* (Cambridge, Mass.: Intercollegiate Clearing House, Harvard Business School, 1971).
28. J. R. Galbraith and R. K. Kazanjian, *Strategy Implementation: Structure System and Process*, 2nd ed. (St. Paul, Minn.: West, 1986); Child, *Organization;* R. Duncan, "What Is the Right Organizational Structure?" *Organizational Dynamics* (Winter 1979), 59–80.
29. O. E. Williamson, *Markets and Hierarchies: Analysis and Antitrust Implications* (New York: Free Press, 1975).
30. P. R. Lawrence and J. Lorsch, *Organization and Environment* (Boston: Division of Research, Harvard Business School, 1967).
31. K. Pope, "Dell Refocuses on Groundwork to Cope with Rocketing Sales," *Wall Street Journal*, June 18, 1993, p. B5.
32. Chandler, *Strategy and Structure*; Williamson, *Markets and Hierarchies*; L. Wrigley, "Divisional Autonomy and Diversification" (Ph.D. diss., Harvard Business School, 1970).
33. R. P. Rumelt, *Strategy, Structure, and Economic Performance* (Boston: Division of Research, Harvard Business School, 1974); Scott, *Stages of Corporate Development*; Williamson, *Markets and Hierarchies*.
34. The discussion draws on each of the sources cited in endnotes 20–27 and on G. R. Jones and C. W. L. Hill, "Transaction Cost Analysis of Strategy-Structure Choice," *Strategic Management Journal,* 9 (1988), 159–172.
35. H. O. Armour and D. J. Teece, "Organizational Structure and Economic Performance: A Test of the Multidivisional Hypothesis," *Bell Journal of Economics*, 9 (1978), 106–122.
36. Alfred Sloan, *My Years at General Motors* (New York: Doubleday, 1983), Chapter 3.
37. C. Soloman, "Amoco to Cut More Jobs and Radically Alter Its Structure" *Wall Street Journal*, July 22, 1995, p. B4.
38. "Shell Reorganizes for Speed and Profit," *Oil & Gas Journal*, December 21, 1998, p. 31.
39. S. M. Davis and R. R. Lawrence, *Matrix* (Reading, Mass.: Addison-Wesley, 1977); J. R. Galbraith, "Matrix Organization Designs: How to Combine Functional and Project Forms," *Business Horizons*, 14 (1971), 29–40.
40. Duncan, "What Is the Right Organizational Structure?"; Davis and Lawrence, *Matrix*.

41. K. M. Kroll, "Making 4 Minus 3 Equal 2," *Industry Week*, March 1, 1999, pp.46–51.
42. P. R. Lawrence and J. Lorsch, *Organization and Environment*, pp. 50–55.
43. Galbraith, *Designing Complex Organizations,* Chapter 1; Galbraith and Kazanjian, *Strategy Implementation,* Chapter 7.
44. H. Mintzberg, *The Nature of Managerial Work* (Englewood Cliffs, N.J.: Prentice-Hall, 1973), Chapter 10.
45. Lawrence and Lorsch, *Organization and Environment*, p. 55.
46. Davidow and Malone, *The Virtual Corporation* (Homewood, Ill: Irwin, 1996).
47. Ibid.
48. Ibid., p. 168.
49. Stewart, "Managing in a Wired Company," *Business Week*, September 16, 1998, pp. 40–44.
50. D. Woodruff and E. Lesly, "Surge at Chrysler," *Fortune*, November 9, 1992, pp. 88–96.
51. "Chrysler Reengineers Product Development Process," *Information Week*, September 7, 1992, p. 20.

12 Designing Strategic Control Systems

OPENING CASE

Oracle's New Approach to Control

ORACLE is the second largest independent software company after Microsoft. Like Bill Gates, Microsoft's chairman, Oracle's founder and chairman, Larry Ellison, recognized that his company had a major problem in 1999. Ellison woke up to the fact that his own company was not using the latest Internet software—software it had developed itself—to control its activities even though its customers were using it. As a result, Oracle was having a difficult time understanding its customers' needs; and, internally Oracle was not experiencing the cost savings that result from implementing its own database and financial control software. Ellison moved quickly to change Oracle's control systems so that they were Internet based.

One of the main advantages of Internet-based control software is that it permits the centralized management of a company's widespread operations. A company's corporate managers can easily compare and contrast in real time the performance of different divisions spread throughout the globe; as a result, they can quickly identify problems and take corrective action. However, to his embarrassment, Ellison discovered that Oracle's financial and human resource information was located on more than seventy different computing systems across the world. Tracking such basics as the size of the company's work force and the sales of its leading products required a lot of time and effort. Consequently, corrective action was unduly delayed, and many opportunities were being missed.

Recognizing the absurdity of the situation, Ellison ordered his managers to totally change the way the company controlled—that is, monitored and evaluated—its activities and to implement its new Internet-based control systems as quickly as possible. His goal was to have all of the company's sales, cost, profit, and human resource information systems consolidated in two, rather than forty locations, and to make this information available to managers throughout the company instantaneously with one click of a mouse. In addition, he instructed managers to investigate which kinds of activities were being monitored and controlled by people, and wherever possible to substitute Internet-based control. For example, previously Oracle had more than 300 people responsible for monitoring and managing such tasks as paper-based travel-planning and expense report systems. These tasks were automated into software systems and put on-line; and employees were then made responsible for filing their own. The 300 people displaced by this new approach were transferred into sales and consulting positions.[1] The savings for the company totaled more than $1 billion a year.

By using control systems based on Internet software, Oracle's managers are also able to get closer to their customers. In 1999, Oracle gave all its salespeople new customer-relationship management software and in-

OPENING CASE *(continued)*

structed them to enter into the system detailed information about the customers' purchases, future plans, web orders, and service requests. As a result, headquarters managers can track sales orders easily. If they see problems such as lost sales or multiple service requests, they can quickly contact customers to solve these difficulties and thus build better customer relations.

So amazed has Ellison been at the result of implementing Internet software systems that he has radically rethought Oracle's management control systems. He now believes that, because of the advances of modern computer information systems, Oracle's employees should be doing only one of three things: building its products, servicing its products, or selling its products. All other activities should be automated by developing new information control systems, and it should be the job of the managers to use control only to facilitate one of these three frontline activities.

OVERVIEW

As we note in Chapter 11, strategy implementation requires selecting the right combination of structure and control for achieving a company's strategy. An organizational structure assigns people to tasks and roles (differentiation) and specifies how these are to be coordinated (integration). Nevertheless, organizational structure does not of itself provide or contain the mechanism through which people can be *motivated* to make it work. Hence the need for control. The purpose of strategic control is to provide managers with (1) a means of motivating employees to work toward organizational goals and (2) specific feedback on how well an organization and its members are performing. Structure provides an organization with a skeleton, but control gives it the muscles, sinews, nerves, and sensations that allow managers to regulate and govern its activities.

In this chapter, we first look in detail at the nature of strategic control and describe the main steps in the control process. We then discuss the main types of strategic control systems available to managers to shape and influence employees—financial controls, output controls, behavior controls, and control through the values and norms of an organization's culture. Finally, we discuss how the design of reward systems becomes an important part of the strategic control process. By the end of this chapter, you will appreciate the rich variety of different control systems available to managers and understand why developing an appropriate control system is vital to maximizing the performance of an organization and its members.

WHAT IS STRATEGIC CONTROL?

Strategic control is the process by which managers monitor the ongoing activities of an organization and its members to evaluate whether activities are being performed efficiently and effectively and to take corrective action to improve performance if they are not. First, strategic managers choose the organizational strategy and structure they hope will allow the organization to use its resources most effectively to create value for its customers. Second, strategic managers create control systems to monitor and evaluate whether, in fact, their organization's strategy and structure are working as the managers intended, how they could be improved, and how they should be changed if they are not working.

Strategic control does not just mean reacting to events *after* they have occurred; it also means keeping an organization on track, anticipating events that might occur, and responding swiftly to new opportunities that present themselves. As you will recall from Chapter 1, *strategic intent* refers to the obsession strategic managers have for building organizational resources and capabilities in order to dominate their environments, but it also involves "focusing the organization's attention on the essence of winning; motivating people by communicating the value of the target; leaving room for individual and team contributions; sustaining enthusiasm ... and using intent consistently to guide resource allocation."[2] Behind the concept of strategic intent is a vision of strategic control as a system that sets ambitious goals and targets for all managers and employees and then develops performance measures that stretch and encourage the mangers and employees to excel in their quest to raise performance.

Thus, strategic control is not just about monitoring how well an organization and its members are achieving current goals or about how well the firm is utilizing its existing resources. It is also about keeping employees motivated, focused on the important problems confronting an organization now and in the future, and working together to find solutions that can help an organization perform better over time.[3]

The Importance of Strategic Control

To understand the vital importance of strategic control, consider how it helps managers to obtain superior efficiency, quality, innovation, and responsiveness to customers, the four basic building blocks of competitive advantage.

Control and Efficiency To determine how *efficiently* they are using organizational resources, managers must be able to measure accurately how many units of inputs (raw materials, human resources, and so on) are being used to produce a unit of output. They must also be able to measure the number of units of outputs (goods and services) they produce. A control system contains the measures or yardsticks that allow managers to assess how efficiently they are producing goods and services. Moreover, if managers experiment with changing the way they produce goods and services to find a more efficient way of producing them, these measures tell managers how successful they have been.

Thus, for example, when managers at Chrysler decided to change to a product-team structure to design, engineer, and manufacture their new cars (See Closing Case, Chapter 11), they used such measures as time taken to design a new car and cost savings per car produced to evaluate how well this new structure worked. When they used these measures to compare the performance of the new structure with that of the old structure, they found that the new structure performed better. Without a control system in place, managers have no idea how well their organization is performing and how they can make it perform better, and such knowledge is becoming increasingly important in today's highly competitive environment.[4]

Control and Quality Today, much of the competition between organizations revolves around increasing the *quality* of goods and services. In the car industry, for example, within each price range, cars compete against one another in terms of their features, design, and reliability over time. So whether a customer buys a Ford Taurus, a GM Cavalier, a Chrysler Intrepid, a Toyota Camry, or a Honda Accord depends significantly on the quality of each company's product. Organizational control is important in determining the quality of goods and services because it gives managers feedback on product quality. If managers of an organization such as Chrysler consistently measure the number of customers' complaints and the number of new cars returned for repairs, they have a good indication of how much quality they have built into their product. That is, do they have a car that does not break down?

Strategic managers create a control system that consistently monitors the quality of goods and services so that they can make continuous improvements to quality over time—which gives them a competitive advantage. Total quality management, an organizationwide control system that focuses on improving quality and reducing costs, is discussed at length in Chapter 5.

Control and Innovation Strategic control can also help to raise the level of *innovation* in an organization. Successful innovation takes place when managers create an organizational setting in which employees feel empowered to be creative and in which authority is decentralized to employees so that they feel free to experiment and take risks. Deciding on the appropriate control systems to encourage risk taking is a major management challenge, and, as discussed later in the chapter, an organization's culture becomes important in this regard. At Chrysler, for example, to encourage each product team to perform, top managers monitor the performance of each team separately (for instance, by examining how each team reduced costs or increased quality) and then pay each team on a bonus system related to its performance. The product team manager then evaluates each team member's individual performance, and the most innovative employees receive promotions and rewards based on their performance level.

Control and Responsiveness to Customers Finally, strategic managers can help make their organizations more *responsive to customers* if they develop a control system that allows them to evaluate how well employees with customer contact are performing their jobs. Monitoring employees' behavior can help managers find ways to help increase employees' performance level, perhaps by revealing areas in which skill training can help employees or by finding new procedures that allow employees to perform their jobs better. When employees know their behaviors are being monitored, they may have more incentive to be helpful and consistent in the way they act toward customers. To help improve customer service, for example, Chrysler regularly surveys customers about their experiences with particular Chrysler dealers. If a dealership receives too many complaints from customers, Chrysler's managers investigate the dealership to uncover the sources of the problems and suggest solutions. If necessary, they can threaten to reduce the number of cars a dealership receives to force it to improve the quality of customer service.

A Balanced Scorecard Approach to Strategic Control

As just discussed, strategic control entails developing performance measures that allow managers both to evaluate how well they have utilized organizational resources to create value *and* to sense new opportunities for creating value in the future. One increasingly influential model that guides managers through the process of creating the right kind of strategic control systems to enhance organizational performance is the balanced scorecard model.[5]

According to the **balanced scorecard model**, strategic managers have traditionally relied on financial measures of performance such as profit and return on investment to evaluate organizational performance. But financial information, though important, is not enough by itself. If strategic managers are to obtain a true picture of organizational performance, financial information must be supplemented with performance measures that indicate how well an organization has been achieving the four building blocks of competitive advantage—efficiency, quality, innovation, and responsiveness to customers. This is so because financial results simply inform strategic managers about the results of decisions they have *already taken*; the other measures balance this picture of performance by informing managers about how accurately the organization has in place the building blocks that drive *future performance*.[6]

One version of the way the balanced scorecard operates is presented in Figure 12.1. Based on an organization's mission and goals, strategic managers develop a set of strategies to build competitive advantage to achieve these goals. They then establish an organizational structure to use resources to obtain a competitive advantage.[7] To evaluate how well the strategy and structure are working, managers develop specific performance measures that assess how well the four building blocks of competitive advantage are being achieved.

- *Efficiency* can be measured by the level of production costs, the number of hours needed to produce a product, and the cost of raw materials.
- *Quality* can be measured by the number of rejects, the number of defective products returned from customers, and the level of product reliability over time.

FIGURE 12.1

A Balance Scorecard Approach

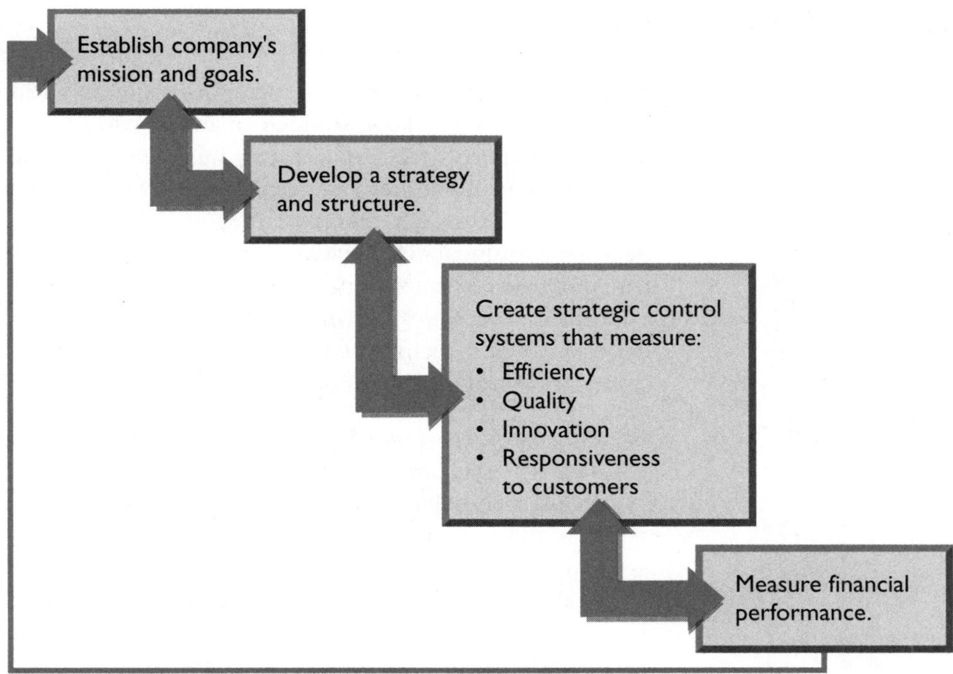

- *Innovation* can be measured by the number of new products introduced, the time taken to develop the next generation of new products in comparison with the competition, and the expense or cost of product development.
- *Responsiveness to customers* can be measured by the number of repeat customers, the level of on-time delivery to customers, and the level of customer service.

As R. S. Kaplan and D. P. Norton, the developers of this approach suggest,

> Think of the balanced scorecard as the dials and indicators in an airplane cockpit. For the complex task of navigating and flying an airplane, pilots need detailed information about many aspects of the flight. They need information on fuel, air speed, altitude, learning, destination, and other indicators that summarize the current and predicted environment. Reliance on one instrument can be fatal. Similarly, the complexity of managing an organization today requires that managers be able to view performance in several areas simultaneously.[8]

The way in which strategic managers' ability to build a competitive advantage translates into organizational performance is then measured using financial measures such as cash flow, quarterly sales growth, increase in market share, and return on investment or equity. Based on an evaluation of the complete set of measures in the balanced scorecard, strategic managers are in a good position to reevaluate the company's mission and goals. They can also take action to rectify problems or to exploit new opportunities by changing the organization's strategy and structure—which is the purpose of strategic control.

STRATEGIC CONTROL SYSTEMS

Strategic control systems are the formal target-setting, measurement, and feedback systems that allow strategic managers to evaluate whether a company is achieving superior efficiency, quality, innovation, and customer responsiveness and implementing its strategy successfully. An effective control system should have three characteristics. It should be *flexible* enough to allow managers to respond as necessary to unexpected events; it should provide *accurate information,* giving a true picture of organizational performance; and it should supply managers with the information in a *timely manner* because making decisions on the basis of outdated information is a recipe for failure.[9] As Figure 12.2 shows, designing an effective strategic control system requires four steps.

1. *Establish the standards and targets against which performance is to be evaluated.* The standards and targets managers select are the ways in which a company chooses to evaluate its performance. General performance standards often derive from the goal of achieving superior efficiency, quality, innovation, or customer responsiveness. Specific performance targets are derived from the strategy pursued by the company. For example, if a company is pursuing a low-cost strategy, then reducing costs by 7 percent a year might be a target. If the company is a service organization such as Wal-Mart or McDonald's, its standards might include time targets for serving customers or guidelines for food quality.

FIGURE 12.2

Steps in Designing an Effective Control System

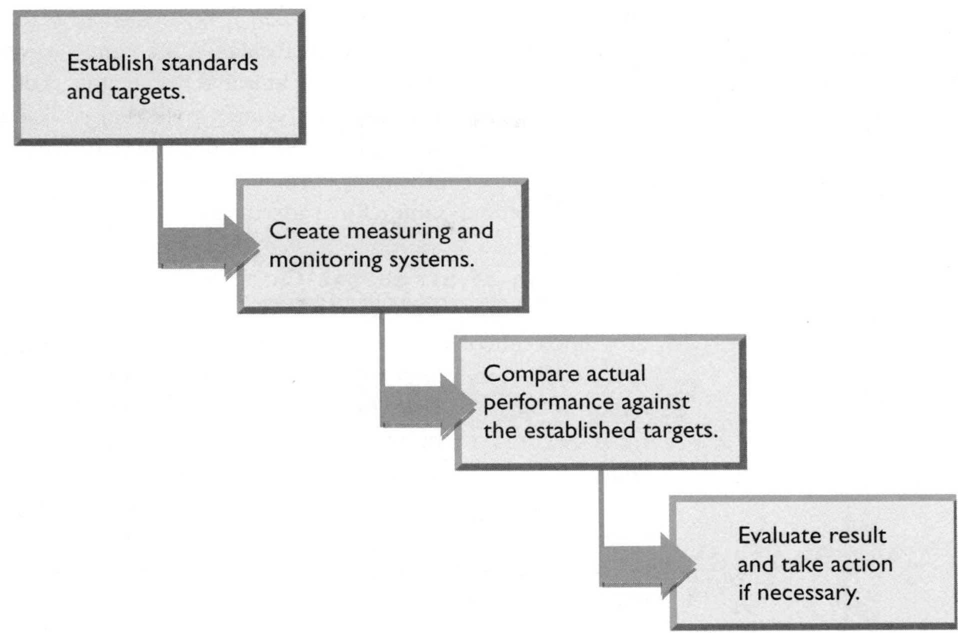

2. *Create the measuring and monitoring systems that indicate whether the standards and targets are being reached.* The company establishes procedures for assessing whether work goals at all levels in the organization are being achieved. In some cases, measuring performance is fairly straightforward. For example, managers can measure quite easily how many customers their employees serve by counting the number of receipts from the cash register. In many cases, however, measuring performance is a difficult task because the organization is engaged in many complex activities. How can managers judge how well their research and development department is doing when it may take five years for products to be developed? How can they measure the company's performance when the company is entering new markets and serving new customers? How can they evaluate how well divisions are integrating? The answer is that managers need to use various types of control systems, which we discuss later in this chapter.

3. *Compare actual performance against the established targets.* Managers evaluate whether and to what extent performance deviates from the standards and targets developed in step 1. If performance is higher, management may decide that it has set the standards too low and may raise them for the next time period. The Japanese are renowned for the way they use targets on the production line to control costs. They are constantly trying to raise performance, and they raise the standards to provide a goal for managers to work toward. On the other hand, if performance is too low, managers must decide whether to take remedial action. This decision is easy when the reasons for poor performance can be identified—for instance, high labor costs. More often, however, the reasons for poor performance are hard to uncover. They may stem from involved external factors, such as a recession, or from internal ones. For instance, the research and development laboratory may have underestimated the problems it would encounter or the extra costs of doing unforeseen research. For any form of action, however, step 4 is necessary.

4. *Initiate corrective action when it is decided that the standards and targets are not being achieved.* The final stage in the control process is to take the corrective action that will allow the organization to meet its goals. Such corrective action may mean changing any aspect of strategy or structure discussed in this book. For example, managers may invest more resources in improving R&D, or diversify, or even decide to change their organizational structure. The goal is to enhance continually an organization's competitive advantage.

Levels of Strategic Control

Strategic control systems are developed to measure performance at four levels in an organization: the corporate, divisional, functional, and individual levels. Managers at all levels must develop the most appropriate set of measures to evaluate corporate-, business-, and functional-level performance. As the balanced scorecard approach suggests, these measures should be tied as closely as possibly to the goals of achieving superior efficiency, quality, innovativeness, and responsiveness to customers. Care must be taken, however, to ensure that the standards used at each level do not cause problems at the other levels—for example, that the attempts of divisions to improve their performance do not conflict with corporate performance. Furthermore, controls at each level should provide the basis on which managers at the levels below can select their control systems. Figure 12.3 illustrates these links.

FIGURE 12.3

Levels of Organizational Control

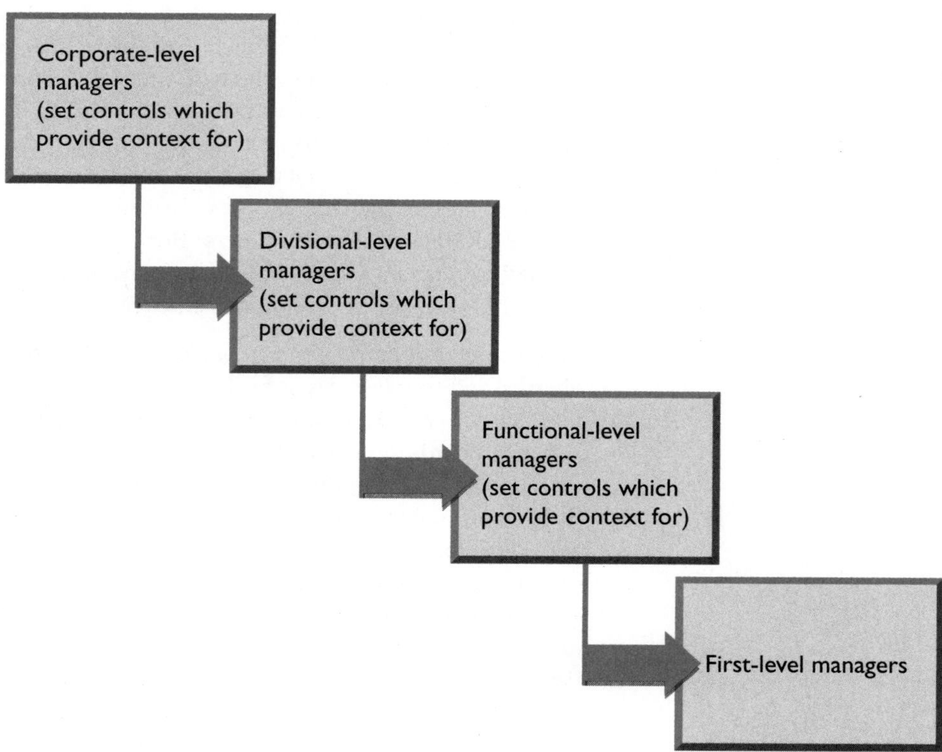

TABLE 12.1

Types of Control Systems

Financial Controls	*Output Controls*	*Behavior Controls*	*Organizational Culture*
Stock price	Divisional goals	Budgets	Values
ROI	Functional goals	Standardization	Norms
	Individual goals	Rules and procedures	Socialization

Table 12.1 shows the various types of strategic control systems managers can use to monitor and coordinate organizational activities. Each of these types of control and its use at various organizational levels—corporate, divisional, functional, and individual—is discussed in the next sections.

Financial Controls

As noted earlier, the most common measures managers and other stakeholders use to monitor and evaluate a company's performance are financial controls. Typically, strategic managers select financial goals they wish their company to achieve, such as growth, profitability, and return to shareholders, and then they measure whether or not these goals have been achieved. One reason for the popularity of financial performance measures is that they are objective. The performance of one company can be compared with that of another in terms of its stock market price, return on investment, market share, or even cash flow so that strategic managers and other stakeholders, particularly shareholders, have some way of judging their company's performance relative to that of other companies.

Stock price, for example, is a useful measure of a company's performance primarily because the price of the stock is determined competitively by the number of buyers and sellers in the market. The stock's value is an indication of the market's *expectations* for the firm's future performance. Thus, movements in the price of a stock provide shareholders with feedback on a company's and its managers' performance. Stock market price acts as an important measure of performance because top managers watch it closely and are sensitive to its rise and fall, particularly its fall. When, Ford Motor's stock price failed to increase in 1996, for example, CEO Alex Trotman took heed of the shareholders' complaint that Ford's product development costs and car prices were too high. In response, he took steps to reduce costs and boost the company's ROI and stock price. Finally, because stock price reflects the long-term future return from the stock, it can be regarded as an indicator of the company's long-run potential.

Return on investment (ROI), determined by dividing net income by invested capital, is another popular kind of financial control. At the corporate level, the performance of the whole company can be evaluated *against* that of other companies to gauge its relative performance. Top managers, for example, can assess how well their strategies have worked by comparing their company's performance with that of similar companies. In the personal computer industry, companies such as Dell, Compaq, and Apple use ROI to gauge their performance relative to that of their competitors. A declining ROI signals a potential problem with a company's strategy or structure. Apple's ROI, for example, has been falling in relation to Dell's and Compaq's. The reason, according to analysts, is that Apple has been rather slow both in product innovation and in reacting to the price-cutting moves of its rivals.

ROI can also be used inside the company at the divisional level to judge the performance of an operating division by comparing it with that of a similar freestanding business or other internal division. Indeed, one reason for selecting a multidivisional structure is that each division can be evaluated as a self-contained profit center. Consequently, management can directly measure the performance of one division against another. General Motors moved to a divisional structure partly because it could use this standard. It gave GM's corporate managers information about the relative costs of the various divisions, allowing them to base capital allocations on relative performance.

Similarly, manufacturing companies often establish production facilities at different locations, domestically and globally, so that they can measure the relative performance of one against the other. For example, Xerox was able to identify the relative inefficiency of its U.S. division by comparing its profitability with that of its Japanese counterpart. ROI is a powerful form of control at the divisional level, especially if divisional managers are rewarded on the basis of their performance vis-à-vis other divisions. The most successful divisional managers are promoted to become the next generation of corporate executives.

Failure to meet stock price or ROI targets also indicates that corrective action is necessary. It signals the need for corporate reorganization in order to meet corporate objectives, and such reorganization can involve a change in structure or liquidation and divestiture of businesses. It can also indicate the need for new strategic leadership. In recent years, the CEOs of American Express, Digital Equipment, Westinghouse, and GM have all been ousted by disgruntled boards of directors, dismayed at the declining performance of their companies relative to that of the competition.

Output Controls

While financial goals and controls are an important part of the balanced scorecard approach, it is also necessary to develop goals and controls that tell managers how well their strategies are creating a competitive advantage and building distinctive competencies and capabilities that will lead to future success. When strategic managers implement the balanced scorecard approach and establish goals and measures to evaluate efficiency, quality, innovation, and responsiveness to customers, they are using output control. **Output control** is a system of control in which strategic managers estimate or forecast appropriate performance goals for each division, department, and employee and then measure actual performance relative to these goals. Often a company's reward system is linked to performance on these goals, so that output control also provides an incentive structure for motivating employees at all levels in the organization.

Divisional Goals Divisional goals state corporate managers' expectations for each division concerning performance on such dimensions as efficiency, quality, innovation, and responsiveness to customers. Generally, corporate managers set challenging divisional goals to encourage divisional managers to create more effective strategies and structures in the future. At General Electric, for example, CEO Jack Welch has set clear performance goals for GE's more than 150 divisions. He expects each division to be number one or two in its industry in terms of market share. Divisional managers are given considerable autonomy to formulate a strategy to meet this goal (to find ways to increase efficiency, innovation, and so on), and the divisions that fail are divested.

Functional and Individual Goals Output control at the functional and individual levels is a continuation of control at the divisional level. Divisional managers set goals for functional managers that will allow the division to achieve its goals. As at the divisional level, functional goals are established to encourage development of competencies that provide the company with a competitive advantage. The same four building blocks of competitive advantage (efficiency, quality, innovation, and customer responsiveness) act as the goals against which functional performance is evaluated. In the sales function, for example, goals related to efficiency (such as cost of sales), quality (such as number of returns), and customer responsiveness (such as the time needed to respond to customer needs) can be established for the whole function.

Finally, functional managers establish goals that individual employees are expected to achieve to allow the function to achieve its goals. Sales personnel, for example, can be given specific goals (related to functional goals), which they in turn are required to achieve. Functions and individuals are then evaluated on the basis of achieving or not achieving their goals, and in sales compensation is commonly pegged to achievement. The achievement of these goals is a sign that the company's strategy is working and meeting organizational objectives. Strategy in Action 12.1 describes how Cypress Semiconductor's CEO, T. J. Rodgers, uses his company's information systems and intranet as a form of output control.

Management by Objectives

To use output control most effectively, many organizations implement management by objectives. **Management by objectives (MBO)** is a system of evaluating managers by their ability to achieve specific organizational goals or performance standards and to meet their operating budgets.[12] A management by objectives system requires these steps:

1. *Establishing specific goals and objectives at each level of the organization.* Management by objectives starts when corporate managers establish overall organizational objectives, such as specific financial performance goals already discussed. Then the objective setting cascades down the organization as managers at the divisional and functional levels set their objectives so as to achieve corporate objectives.[13]

2. *Making goal setting a participatory process.* An important part of a management by objectives system is that, at every level, managers sit down with their subordinate managers to determine jointly appropriate and feasible objectives and to decide on the budget that will be needed to achieve them. Thus, subordinates participate in the objective-setting process, which is a way of getting their commitment to achieve those goals and meet their budgets.[14]

12.1 STRATEGY *in* ACTION

Control at Cypress Semiconductor

In the fast-moving semiconductor business, a premium is placed on organizational adaptability. At Cypress Semiconductor, CEO T. J. Rodgers was facing a problem. How could he control his growing, 1,500-employee organization without developing a bureaucratic management hierarchy? Rodgers believed that a tall hierarchy hinders the ability of an organization to adapt to changing conditions. He was committed to maintaining a flat and decentralized organizational structure with a minimum of management layers. At the same time, he needed to control his employees to ensure that they perform in a manner that is consistent with the goals of the company. How could he achieve this without resorting to direct supervision and the management hierarchy that it implies?

The solution that Rodgers adopted was to implement a computer-based information system through which he can manage what every employee and team is doing in his fast-moving and decentralized organization.[10] Each employee maintains a list of ten to fifteen goals, such as "Meet with marketing for new product launch" or "Make sure to check with customer X." Noted next to each goal is when it was agreed upon, when it is due to be finished, and whether it has been finished. All of this information is stored on a central computer. Rodgers claims that he can review the goals of all 1,500 employees in about four hours, and he does so each week.[11] How is this possible? He manages by exception and looks only for employees who are falling behind. He then calls them, not to scold but to ask whether there is anything he can do to help them get the job done. It takes only about half an hour each week for employees to review and update their lists. This system allows Rodgers to exercise control over his organization without resorting to the expensive layers of a management hierarchy.

3. *Periodic review of progress toward meeting goals.* Once specific objectives have been agreed upon for managers at each level, managers become accountable for meeting them. Periodically, they sit down with their subordinates and evaluate their progress. Normally, salary raises and promotions are linked to the goal-setting process, and managers who have achieved their goals receive the most rewards. The issue of how to design reward systems to motivate managers and other organizational employees is detailed later in the chapter.

One company that has spent considerable time developing an effective MBO system is Zytec, a leading manufacturer of power supplies for computers and other electronic equipment. All Zytec's managers and workers are involved in its goal-setting process. Top managers first set up six cross-functional teams to create a five-year plan for the company and to set broad goals for each function.[15] This plan is then reviewed by employees from all areas of the company, who evaluate its feasibility and make suggestions as to how it could be modified or improved. Each function then uses the broad goals in the plan to set more specific goals for each manager within each function, which are reviewed with top managers. At Zytec, the MBO system is organizationwide and fully participatory; performance is reviewed both from an annual and a five-year perspective in keeping with the company's five-year plan. So successful has Zytec's MBO system been that not only have its costs dropped dramatically but it also won the Baldrige Award for quality.

12.2 STRATEGY *in* ACTION

How Not to Use Output Control to Get Ahead

William J. Fife masterminded the turnaround of Giddings and Lewis, a manufacturer of automated factory equipment for companies such as GM, Boeing, AMR, and Ford. In 1988, the company was losing money and had a declining customer base. By 1993, Fife had made it the largest company in the industry, with sales that for every quarter exceeded year-earlier results and a stock price that had quadrupled since Fife sold its stock on the open market in 1989. Nevertheless, in April 1993, the board of directors decided that Fife was no longer a suitable leader and asked him to resign because, as the board saw it, his use of output controls was damaging the future of the company.

Fife's turnaround strategy relied on broadening the company's product base by innovating products to suit new kinds of customers, for example, airlines and consumer manufacturing companies. Then his goal was to increase sales by promoting customer responsiveness. As an example to his managers and employees, Fife would fly anywhere in the United States to solve customer problems personally. To promote his strategy of increasing sales through innovation and customer responsiveness, Fife made extensive use of output controls as the main way of evaluating the performance of his product and financial managers. Periodically, he would sit down with his executives to review the financial, sales, and cost figures for a product or product range.

However, when the figures failed to please him, he would verbally attack and abuse the executive concerned in front of his or her peers, who sat through the assault in embarrassed silence. Any attempts to fight back would merely prolong the attack, and top managers began to complain to board members that Fife was destroying working relationships. Moreover, top mangers claimed that Fife's preoccupation with the short-term bottom line was causing problems for the organization because his focus on sales and cost targets was forcing them to cut back on research and development or customer service to meet the stringent targets that he set. Eventually, they pointed out, this practice would hurt customer relations. Thus, Fife's managers claimed that his exclusive focus on output control goal setting was reducing flexibility and integration and threatening the company's future performance.

Whatever the truth in these claims, the board of directors (which Fife had appointed) listened to the disgruntled managers and decided that for the good of the organization they should ask Fife to resign. As Clyde Folley, the acting chairman put it, the board wanted, "nice, quiet, level leadership" and the reestablishment of good working relationships between managers at all levels. However, the stock market reacted differently to the news of Fife's departure, and the company's stock price plunged by more than 20 percent on the announcement. Clearly, shareholders liked the effect of Fife's output controls on the company's performance, even if his mangers did not.

While Zytec illustrates the advantages of MBO, the story of Giddings and Lewis, highlighted in Strategy in Action 12.2, illustrates some of the problems that can arise if it is used inappropriately.

The inappropriate use of output control can also promote conflict among divisions. In general, setting across-the-board output targets, such as ROI targets, for divisions can lead to destructive results if divisions single-mindedly try to maximize divisional profits at the expense of corporate objectives. Moreover, to reach output targets, divisions may start to distort the numbers and engage in strategic manipulation of the figures to make their divisions look good.[16]

In sum, strategic managers need to use the balanced scorecard approach to design the set of output controls that will best promote long-run profitability. In practice, output controls must be used in conjunction with behavior controls and organizational culture if the right strategic behaviors are to be encouraged.

Behavior Controls

The first step in strategy implementation is for managers to design the right kind of organizational structure. To make the structure work, however, employees must learn the kinds of behaviors they are expected to perform. Using managers to tell employees what to do lengthens the organizational hierarchy, is expensive, and raises bureaucratic costs; consequently, strategic managers rely on behavior controls. **Behavior control** is control through the establishment of a comprehensive system of rules and procedures to direct the actions or behavior of divisions, functions, and individuals.[17]

In using behavior controls, the intention is not to specify the goals, but to standardize the way of reaching them. Rules standardize behavior and make outcomes predictable. If employees follow the rules, then actions are performed and decisions handled the same way time and time again. The result is predictability and accuracy, the aim of all control systems. The main types of behavior controls are operating budgets and standardization.

Operating Budgets

Once managers at each level have been given a goal to achieve, operating budgets that regulate how managers and workers are to attain those goals are established. An **operating budget** is a blueprint that states how managers intend to use organizational resources to achieve organizational goals most efficiently. Most commonly, managers at one level allocate to managers at a lower level a specific amount of resources to use to produce goods and services.

Once they have been given a budget, managers must decide how they will allocate certain amounts of money for different organizational activities. These lower-level managers are then evaluated on the basis of their ability to stay within the budget and make the best use of it. Thus, for example, managers at GE's washing machine division might have a budget of $50 million to develop and sell a new line of washing machines, and they have to decide how much money to allocate to R&D, engineering, sales, and other areas so that the division generates the most revenue and hence makes the biggest profit.

Most commonly, large organizations treat each division as a stand-alone profit center, and corporate managers evaluate each division's performance by its relative contribution to corporate profitability. Strategy in Action 12.3 describes how Japanese companies have been using operating budgets and setting challenging goals to increase efficiency.

Standardization

Standardization refers to the degree to which a company specifies how decisions are to be made so that employees' behavior becomes predictable.[19] In practice, there are three things an organization can standardize: *inputs, conversion activities,* and *outputs.*

12.3 STRATEGY *in* ACTION

Japan Focuses on Budgets

In the 1990s, Japanese companies have been facing increasing problems in competing in the global marketplace because the rising value of the yen has made their products so expensive abroad. In addition, the Japanese have experienced difficulties because their global competitors have lowered their costs by imitating many of the cost-saving innovations in manufacturing that Japanese companies pioneered, such as total quality management. With their competitive advantage eroding because their foreign competitors' costs are as low or lower than theirs, Japanese companies have been seeking new ways to cut costs to increase their efficiency.

At the top of their list of ways to reduce costs is making ingenious use of budgets to increase efficiency, but to do so in a way that does not destroy innovation. One of the techniques is to decentralize the responsibility for meeting budgets targets right down to the level of the first-line supervisor and worker. At Kirin's brewery in Kyoto, for example, managers at all levels compete against one another to report the biggest profits, and information about costs is posted on the wall for all employees to see how their day-to-day performance affects progress toward meeting goals and budget targets.[18] Some companies have divided up their work force into small teams and even split into many divisions so that employees are more aware of how the level of their performance affects costs and profits. The high-tech Kyocera company, for example, divided itself up into more than 800 small units (nicknamed amoebas) that trade with each other and try to get the most value for what they do.

Furthermore, recognizing that a large proportion of their costs are payments for inputs such as components parts, Japanese companies work with their suppliers to help them reduce costs and raise product quality. Members of their research and development, engineering, and manufacturing functions become part of cross-company teams established to find new ways to reduce costs, not the least of which is to teach their suppliers how to use budgets and goals to lower their costs. This new focus on budgets as a control system has paid off, and companies such as Toyota and Honda have enjoyed enormous cost savings by developing in-depth relationships with non-Japanese suppliers that have led to record profits despite the high value of the yen.

1. *Standardization of inputs.* One way in which an organization can control the behavior of both people and resources is to standardize the inputs into the organization. This means that managers screen inputs according to preestablished criteria or standards and then decide which inputs to allow into the organization. If employees are the input in question, for example, then one way of standardizing them is to specify which qualities and skills they must possess and then to select only those applicants who possess them. Arthur Andersen, the accounting firm, is a very selective recruiter, as are most prestigious organizations.

   If the inputs in question are raw materials or component parts, then the same considerations apply. The Japanese are renowned for the high quality and precise tolerances they demand from component parts to minimize problems with the product at the manufacturing stage. Just-in-time inventory systems also help standardize the flow of inputs.

2. *Standardization of conversion activities.* The aim of standardizing conversion activities is to program work activities so that they are done the same way time and time again. The goal is predictability. Behavior controls, such as rules and procedures, are

among the chief means by which companies can standardize throughputs. Fast-food restaurants such as McDonald's and Burger King, for example, standardize all aspects of their restaurant operations; the result is standardized fast food.

3. *Standardization of outputs.* The goal of standardizing outputs is to specify what the performance characteristics of the final product or service should be—what dimensions or tolerances the product should conform to, for example. To ensure that their products are standardized, companies apply quality control and use various criteria to measure this standardization. One criterion might be the number of goods returned from customers or the number of customers' complaints. On production lines, periodic sampling of products can indicate whether they are meeting performance characteristics.

   Given the intensity of foreign competition, companies are devoting extra resources to standardizing outputs, not just to reduce costs but to retain customers. If the product's performance satisfies customers, they will continue buying from that company. For example, if a consumer purchases a Japanese car and has no problems with its performance, which car is he or she most likely to buy next time? That is why companies such as U.S. carmakers have been emphasizing the quality dimension of their products. They know how important standardizing outputs is in a competitive market.

Rules and Procedures As with other kinds of controls, the use of behavior control is accompanied by potential pitfalls that must be managed if the organization is to avoid strategic problems. Top management must be careful to monitor and evaluate the usefulness of behavior controls over time. Rules constrain people and lead to standardized, predictable behavior. However, rules are always easier to establish than to get rid of, and over time the number of rules an organization uses tends to increase. As new developments lead to additional rules, often the old rules are not discarded, and the company becomes overly bureaucratized. Consequently, the organization and the people in it become inflexible and are slow to react to changing or unusual circumstances. Such inflexibility can reduce a company's competitive advantage by lowering the pace of innovation and by reducing customer responsiveness.

Inside the organization, too, integration and coordination may fall apart as rules impede communication between functions. Managers must therefore be continually on the alert for opportunities to reduce the number of rules and procedures necessary to manage the business and should always prefer to discard a rule rather than add a new one. Hence, reducing the number of rules and procedures to the essential minimum is important. Strategic managers frequently neglect this task, however, and often only a change in strategic leadership brings the company back on course.

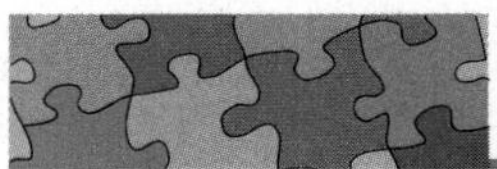

ORGANIZATIONAL CULTURE

The first function of strategic control is to shape the behavior of organizational members to ensure they are working toward organizational goals and to take corrective action if those goals are not being met. The second function, however, is to keep organizational members focused on thinking about what is best for their organization in the future and to keep them looking for new opportunities to use organizational resources and competencies to create value. One important kind of strategic control system that serves this dual function is organizational culture.

What Is Organizational Culture?

Organizational culture is the specific collection of values and norms that are shared by people and groups in an organization and that control the way they interact with each other and with stakeholders outside the organization.[20] **Organizational values** are beliefs and ideas about what kinds of goals members of an organization should pursue and about the appropriate kinds or standards of behavior organizational members should use to achieve these goals. Jack Welch of General Electric is a CEO who is famous for the set of organizational values that he emphasizes, which include entrepreneurship, ownership, honesty, frankness, and open communication. By stressing entrepreneurship and ownership, Welch has been trying to get GE to behave less like a big bureaucracy and more like a collection of smaller and very adaptive companies. He has emphasized giving lower-level managers considerable decision-making autonomy and encouraged them to take risks—that is, to be more like entrepreneurs and less like corporate bureaucrats. The stress Welch places on values such as honesty, frankness, and open communication is a reflection of his belief that an open internal dialogue is necessary for successful operations at General Electric.[21]

From organizational values develop **organizational norms**, guidelines or expectations that *prescribe* appropriate kinds of behavior by employees in particular situations and control the behavior of organizational members toward one another. The norms of behavior for software programmers at Microsoft, the world's largest manufacturer of computer software, include working long hours and weekends, wearing whatever clothing is comfortable (but never a suit and tie), consuming junk food, and communicating with other employees via electronic mail and the company's state-of-the-art intranet.

Organizational culture functions as a type of control in that strategic managers can influence the kind of values and norms that develop in an organization—values and norms that specify appropriate and inappropriate behaviors and that shape and influence the way its members behave.[22] Strategic managers such as Jack Welch, for example, deliberately cultivate values that tell their subordinates they should perform their roles in innovative, creative ways. They establish and support norms dictating that, to be innovative and entrepreneurial, employees should feel free to experiment and go out on a limb even if there is a significant chance of failure. Top managers at organizations such as Intel, Microsoft, and Sun Microsystems also encourage their employees to adopt such values to support their commitment to innovation as a source of their competitive advantage.

Other managers, however, might cultivate values that say employees should always be conservative and cautious in their dealings with others, consult with their superiors before they make important decisions, and record their actions in writing so they can be held accountable for what happens. Managers of organizations such as chemical and oil companies, financial institutions, and insurance companies—any organization in which caution is needed—may encourage a conservative, wary approach to making decisions.[23] In a bank or mutual fund, for example, the risk of losing all of the investors' money makes a cautious approach to investing highly appropriate. Thus, we might expect that managers of different kinds of organizations will deliberately try to cultivate and develop the organizational values and norms best suited to their strategy and structure.

Organizational socialization is the term used to describe how people learn organizational culture. Through socialization, people internalize and learn the norms and values of the culture so that they *become* organizational members.[24] Control through culture is so powerful because, once these values have been internalized, they become a part of the individual's values, and the individual follows organizational values without thinking about them.[25] Very often the values and norms of an organization's culture are transmitted to its members through the stories, myths, and language that people in the organization use, as well as by other means (see Figure 12.4). This chapter's Closing Case, for example, mentions some of the stories that Wal-Mart's associates use to remind themselves about the values of the company. In addition, there are many stories about Sam Walton and about how frugal he was (for example, that he used to drive a thirty-year-old pickup truck and lived in a very modest home) to reinforce Wal-Mart's low-cost strategy and frugal approach. Some of the rites and ceremonies that Wal-Mart uses are the Wal-Mart cheer that happens every morning at the store and a huge extravaganza every year at the company's headquarters to which all high-performing associates are invited.

Culture and Strategic Leadership

Since both an organization's structure (the design of its task and reporting relationships) and its culture shape employees' behavior, it is crucial to match organizational structure and culture to implement strategy successfully. The ways that organizations design and create their structures are discussed in Chapter 11. The question that remains is, how do they design and create their cultures? In general, organizational culture is the product of strategic leadership.

The Influence of the Founder First, organizational culture is created by the strategic leadership provided by an organization's founder and top managers. The organization's founder is particularly important in determining culture because the

FIGURE 12.4

Ways of Transmitting Organizational Culture

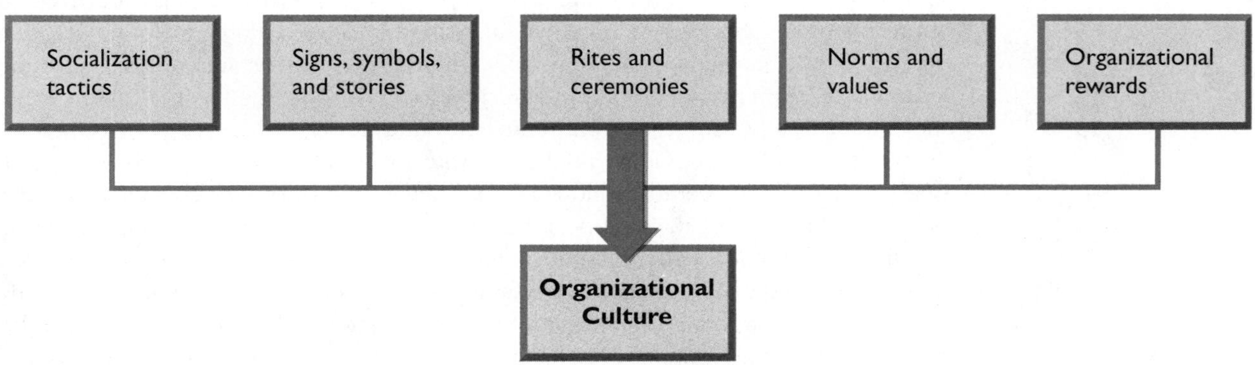

founder imprints his or her values and management style on the organization. For instance, Walt Disney's conservative influence on the company he established continued until well after his death. Managers were afraid to experiment with new forms of entertainment because they were afraid Walt Disney wouldn't like it. It took the installation of a new management team under Michael Eisner to turn around the company's fortunes and allow it to deal with the realities of the new entertainment industry.

As another example, consider Hewlett-Packard (HP), a recognized leader in the electronic instrumentation industry. The company was established in the 1940s, and its culture is an outgrowth of the strong personal beliefs of its founders, Bill Hewlett and Dave Packard. Bill and Dave, as they were known within the company, created HP's culture in a formal statement of HP's basic values: to serve everyone who had a stake in the company with integrity and fairness, including customers, suppliers, employees, stockholders, and society in general. Bill and Dave helped establish these values and build HP's culture by hiring like-minded people and by letting these values guide their own actions as managers. One outgrowth of their commitment to employees was a policy that HP would not be a "hire and fire company." This principle was severely tested on a couple of occasions in the 1970s, when declines in business forced the company to adopt the policy of a nine-day fortnight, under which all staff took a 10 percent pay cut and worked 10 percent fewer hours. While other companies laid off workers, HP kept its full complement of staff, thereby emphasizing the company's commitment to its employees.[26]

Thus, the values developed by HP's founders helped guide managerial action at HP and led directly to the policy of no layoffs. In turn, the commitment to employees that this action signaled has helped foster a productive work force at HP that is willing to go to great lengths to help the company succeed. The result has been superior company performance over time.

The leadership style established by the founder is transmitted to the company's managers, and as the company grows, it typically attracts new managers and employees who share the same values. Moreover, members of the organization typically recruit and select only those who do share their values. Thus, a company's culture becomes more and more distinct as its members become more similar. The virtue of these shared values and common culture is that it *increases integration and improves coordination among organizational members.* For example, the common language that typically emerges in an organization because people share the same beliefs and values facilitates cooperation among managers. Similarly, rules and procedures and direct supervision are less important when shared norms and values control behavior and motivate employees. When organizational members buy into cultural norms and values, this bonds them to the organization and increases their commitment to find new ways to help it succeed. That is, employees are more likely to commit themselves to organizational goals and work actively to develop new skills and competencies to help achieve those goals. Strategy in Action 12.4 details how Ray Kroc built a strong culture at McDonald's.

Organizational Structure Strategic leadership also affects organizational culture through the way managers design organizational structure—that is, the way managers delegate authority and divide up task relationships. Michael Dell, chairman of Dell Computer, for example, has always tried to keep his company as flat as possible

12.4 STRATEGY *in* ACTION

How Ray Kroc Established McDonald's Culture

In the restaurant business, maintaining product quality is a major problem because the quality of the food, the service, and the restaurant premises varies with the chefs and waiters. If a customer gets a bad meal, poor service, or dirty silverware, the restaurant may lose not only that customer, but other potential customers, too, as negative comments travel by word of mouth. In this context, consider the problem Ray Kroc, the man who pioneered McDonald's growth, faced when McDonald's franchises began to open by the thousands throughout the United States. How could he maintain product quality to protect the company's reputation as it grew? Moreover, how could he try to build a corporate culture that made the organization responsive to the needs of customers to promote its competitive advantage? Kroc's answer was to develop a sophisticated control system, which specified every detail of how each McDonald's restaurant was to be operated and managed, in order to create an organizational culture.

First, Kroc developed a comprehensive system of rules and procedures for both franchise owners and employees to follow in running each restaurant. The most effective way to perform such tasks as cooking burgers, making fries, greeting customers, and cleaning tables was worked out in advance, written down in rule books, and then taught to each McDonald's manager and employee through a formal training process. Prospective franchise owners had to attend "Hamburger University," the company's training center in Chicago, where in an intensive, month-long program they learned all aspects of a McDonald's operation. In turn, they were expected to train their work force and make sure that employees understood operating procedures thoroughly. Kroc's goal in establishing this system of rules and procedures was to build a common culture so that whatever franchise customers walked into, they would always find the same level of quality in food and service. If customers always get what they expect from a restaurant, the restaurant has developed superior customer responsiveness.

However, Kroc's attempt to build culture went well beyond written rules and procedures specifying the performance of various tasks. He also developed McDonald's franchise system to help the company control its structure as it grew. Kroc believed that a manager who is also a franchise owner (and who receives a large share of the profits) is more motivated to buy into a company's culture than a manager paid a straight salary. Thus, McDonald's reward and incentive system allowed it to keep control over its operating structure as it expanded. Moreover, McDonald's was very selective in selling its franchises; the franchisees had to be people with the skills and capabilities that Kroc believed McDonald's managers should have.

Within each restaurant, franchise owners were also instructed that they should pay particular attention to training their employees and instilling in them the norms and values of quality service. Having learned about McDonald's core cultural values at their training sessions, franchise owners were expected to transmit McDonald's concepts of efficiency, quality, and customer service to their employees. The development of shared norms, values, and an organizational culture also helped McDonald's standardize employees' behavior so that customers would know how they would be treated in a McDonald's restaurant. Moreover, McDonald's tried to include customers in its culture. It had customers bus their own tables, but it also showed concern for customers' needs by building playgrounds, offering Happy Meals, and organizing birthday parties for customers' children. In creating its family-oriented culture, McDonald's was ensuring future customer loyalty because satisfied children are likely to remain loyal customers as adults.

and has decentralized authority to lower-level managers and employees, who are charged with striving to get "as close to the customer" as they can. As a result, he has created a customer-service culture at Dell in which employees go out of their way to provide high-quality customer service. By contrast, Henry Ford I designed his company to give him absolute control over decision making. He even scrutinized the actions of his top-management team, and his successor, Henry Ford II, continued to manage the company in a highly centralized way. The result for Ford Motor Car Company was an organizational culture in which managers became conservative and afraid to take risks, and the company was known for its slow pace of change and innovation. Thus, the way an organization designs its structure affects the cultural norms and values that develop within the organization. Managers need to be aware of this fact when implementing their strategies.

Adaptive and Inert Cultures

Few environments are stable for a prolonged period of time. Thus, if an organization is to survive, managers must take actions that enable an organization to adapt to environmental changes. If they do not take such action, they may find themselves faced with declining demand for their products. In the last section, we suggest that strategic managers can build an organizational culture that encourages employees to find new ways of developing organizational competencies to exploit new opportunities in the environment. Research evidence has largely confirmed this. In a study of 207 companies, John Kotter and James Heskett distinguished between adaptive cultures and inert cultures.[27] **Adaptive cultures** are those that are innovative and encourage and reward initiative by middle and lower-level managers. **Inert cultures** are those that are cautious and conservative, do not value initiative on the part of middle and lower-level managers, and may even actively discourage such behavior.

According to Kotter and Heskett, managers in organizations with adaptive cultures are able to introduce changes in the way the organization operates, including changes in its strategy and structure, that allow the organization to adapt to changes occurring in the external environment. This does not occur at organizations with inert cultures. As a result, organizations with adaptive cultures are more likely to survive in a changing environment and indeed should have higher performance than organizations with inert cultures. This, in fact, is exactly what Kotter and Heskett found among the 207 companies they examined.

When an organization has an inert culture, strategic problems can result. If, for example, top managers all accept the same set of norms and values, the danger arises that they will be unable to steer the organization in a new strategic direction should the environment change and new competitors or technology demand that the company change. Furthermore, having designed their structures, managers become used to the way they operate, and they rarely recognize the important effect structure has on cultural norms and values. Thus, organizational culture can promote inertia. At IBM, for instance, managers were unable to see, until it was too late, that the development of powerful personal computers and interactive, networking software would have long-term implications for IBM's cash cow, mainframe computers. Their blindness resulted from the tenets of IBM's culture that mainframes would always be the dominant product design and personal computers would only be appendages to mainframes. Moreover, IBM's tall, centralized structure slowed decision making and encouraged the development of conservative norms and values, making managers averse to risk and reluctant to challenge the status quo.

As Chapter 1 points out, cognitive biases can distort the decision-making process. Over time, the norms and values of an organization's culture can bias decision making and cause managers to misperceive the reality of the situation facing their company. To prevent these strategic leadership problems from arising, great care needs to be taken in composing the top-management team.

The Composition of the Top-Management Team

The composition of the top-management team helps determine the company's strategic direction, and the personalities and vision of the team's members establish the values and norms that lower-level managers will follow. Researchers have found that when a company has a diverse top-management team, with managers drawn from different functional backgrounds or from different organizations or national cultures, the threat of inertia and of faulty decision making is reduced and the culture becomes adaptive. One of the reasons for IBM's failure to change was that almost all its top managers came from inside IBM and from the mainframe computer division. They had all been exposed to the same set of learning experiences and had developed similar norms and values. When Coca-Cola concluded that its top-management team was becoming too inbred and homogeneous, it deliberately recruited a new top-management team, including the CEO, composed of several foreign nationals, to manage its global strategy. Like Coca-Cola, many organizations are paying increasing attention to planning for executive succession in the top-management team so that they can manage their cultures over time.

Traits of Strong and Adaptive Corporate Cultures

Several scholars in the field have tried to uncover the common traits that strong and adaptive corporate cultures share and to find out whether there is a particular set of values that dominates adaptive cultures but is missing from weak or inert ones. An early but still influential attempt is T. J. Peters and R. H. Waterman's account of the values and norms characterizing successful organizations and their cultures.[28] They argue that adaptive organizations show three common value sets.

First, successful companies have values promoting a *bias for action.* The emphasis is on autonomy and entrepreneurship, and employees are encouraged to take risks—for example, to create new products, even though there is no assurance that these products will be winners. Managers are closely involved in the day-to-day operations of the company and do not simply make strategic decisions while isolated in some ivory tower, and employees have a "hands-on, value-driven approach."

The second set of values stems from the *nature of the organization's mission.* The company must stick with what it does best and maintain control over its core activities. A company can easily get sidetracked into pursuing activities outside its area of expertise just because they seem to promise a quick return. Management should cultivate values so that a company sticks to its knitting, which means staying with the businesses it knows best. A company must also establish close relationships with customers as a way of improving its competitive position. After all, who knows more about a company's performance than those who use its products or services? By emphasizing customer-oriented values, organizations are able to learn customers' needs and improve their ability to develop the products and services that customers desire. All these management values are strongly represented in companies such as Microsoft, Hewlett-Packard, and Toyota, which are sure of their mission and take constant steps to maintain it.

The third set of values bears on *how to operate the organization.* A company should try to establish an organizational design that will motivate employees to do their best. Inherent in this set of values is the belief that productivity is obtained through people and that respect for the individual is the primary means by which a company can create the right atmosphere for productive behavior. As William Ouchi has noted, a similar philosophy pervades the culture of Japanese companies.[29] Many U.S. companies—for instance, Eastman Kodak, Procter & Gamble, and Levi Strauss—pay this kind of attention to their employees. An emphasis on entrepreneurship and respect for the employee leads to the establishment of a structure that gives employees the latitude to make decisions and motivates them to succeed. Because a simple structure and a lean staff best fit this situation, the organization should be designed with only the number of managers and hierarchical levels that are necessary to get the job done. The organization should also be sufficiently decentralized to permit employees' participation, but centralized enough for management to make sure that the company pursues its strategic mission and that cultural values are followed.

These three main sets of values are at the heart of an organization's culture, and management transmits and maintains them through strategic leadership. Strategic managers need to establish the values and norms that will help them bring their organizations into the future. When this is accomplished, only those people who fit the values are recruited into the organization, and, through training, they become a part of the organization's culture. Thus, the types of control systems chosen should reinforce and build on one another in a cohesive way. However, organizational culture cannot by itself make structure work. It must be backed by output and behavior controls and matched to a reward system so that employees will in fact cultivate organizational norms and values and pursue organizational goals.

STRATEGIC REWARD SYSTEMS

Organizations also strive to control employees' behavior by linking reward systems to their control systems.[30] Based on a company's strategy (low cost or differentiation, for example), strategic managers must decide which behaviors to reward. They then create a control system to measure these behaviors and link the reward structure to them. Determining how to relate rewards to performance is a crucial strategic decision because it determines the incentive structure that affects the way managers and employees at all levels in the organization behave. You learned earlier how structure and control shape employees' behavior. The design of the organization's incentive system is a vital element in the control process because it motivates and reinforces desired behaviors.

As Chapter 2 points out, top managers can be encouraged to work in the shareholders' interests by being rewarded with stock options linked to the company's long-term performance. Furthermore, companies such as Kodak and GM require managers to buy company stock. When managers are made shareholders, they are more motivated to pursue long-term rather than short-term goals. Similarly, in designing a pay system for salespeople, the choice is whether to motivate salespeople through straight salary or salary plus a bonus based on how much is sold. Neiman Marcus, the luxury retailer, pays employees a straight salary because it wants to encourage high-quality service but to discourage a hard-sell approach. Thus, there are no incentives based on quantity sold. On the other hand, the pay system for rewarding car salespeople encourages high-pressure selling; it typically contains a large bonus for the number and price of cars sold.

Since the design of a company's reward system affects the way managers and employees behave, the reward system also affects the ***kinds of norms, values, and culture that develop in an organization.*** Thus, top-management teams rewarded solely by salary and those rewarded by stock options linked to performance are likely to have different norms and values. Specifically, top-management teams rewarded with stock options may be more entrepreneurial and more concerned with increasing quality and innovation than those that lack this reward. Companies such as Sears, GM, Kodak, and Westinghouse, which previously made little attempt to link performance to rewards, had slow-moving, bureaucratic cultures. All these companies now require managers to own company stock.

We now take a closer look at the types of reward systems available to strategic managers.[31] Generally, reward systems are found at the individual and group or total organizational levels. Often these systems are used in combination; for example, merit raises at the individual level may be accompanied by a bonus based on divisional or corporate performance. Within each type, several forms of reward systems are available.

Individual Reward Systems

Piecework Plans Piecework plans are used when outputs can be objectively measured. Essentially, employees are paid on the basis of some set amount for each unit of output produced. Piecework plans are most commonly used for employees on production lines, where individuals work alone and their performance can be directly measured. Because this system encourages quantity rather than quality, the company normally applies stringent quality controls to ensure that the quality is acceptable.

Commission Systems Commission systems resemble piecework systems, except that they are normally tied not to what is produced, but to how much is sold. Thus, they are most commonly found in sales situations. Often the salaries of salespeople are based principally on commission to encourage superior performance. First-rate salespeople can earn more than $1 million per year in many industries.

Bonus Plans Bonus plans at the individual level generally reward the performance of a company's key individuals, such as the CEO and senior vice presidents.[32] The performance of these people is visible to the organization as a whole and to stakeholders such as shareholders. Consequently, there is a strong rationale for paying these individuals according to some measure of functional or divisional performance. A company must proceed carefully, however, if it is to avoid problems such as emphasis on short-run rather than long-term objectives. For example, paying bonuses based on quarterly or yearly ROI rather than on five-year growth can have a markedly different effect on the way strategic managers behave. Insisting that members of a top-management team own stock in the company motivates managers and ties their interests to those of the shareholders.

Promotion Last, but not least, promotion is an important source of reward for individuals at all organizational levels. Managers compete for promotion to the next level in the hierarchy; the highest-performing functional managers become the next generation of divisional managers, and the highest-performing divisional managers become the next generation of corporate managers. Promotion is so important because salary and bonuses rise sharply as managers ascend the hierarchy. The CEO often earns in salary alone 50 percent more than the person next in the chain of command. In 1996, for example, the average CEO in the top *Fortune* 200 companies earned nearly $4.7 million dollars, almost double the $2.4 million earned by the next highest-ranking executive.[33] The rewards from promotion are enormous, and this is why organizational career ladders are closely watched by aspiring managers. Some organizations deliberately encourage promotion tournaments, contests between managers for promotion, to motivate high performance.

Group and Organizational Reward Systems

Group and organizational reward systems provide additional ways in which companies can relate pay to performance. The increasing use of product-team structures and cross-functional teams has led many organizations to develop some form of group-based rewards system to encourage high team performance. The most common reward systems at these levels are group bonuses, profit sharing, employee stock options, and organization bonuses.

Group-Based Bonus Systems Sometimes a company can establish project teams, or work groups, that perform all the operations needed to turn out a product or provide a service. This arrangement makes it possible to measure group performance and offer rewards on the basis of group productivity. The system can be highly motivating because employees are allowed to develop the best work procedures for doing the job and are responsible for improving their own productivity. For example, Wal-Mart supports a group bonus plan based on controlling shrinkage (that is, employee theft).

Profit Sharing Systems Profit sharing plans are designed to reward employees on the basis of the profit a company earns in any one time period. Such plans encourage employees to take a broad view of their activities and feel connected to the company as a whole. Wal-Mart uses this method as well to develop its organizational culture.

Employee Stock Option Plans Rather than reward employees on the basis of short-term profits, a company sometimes establishes an employee stock ownership plan (ESOP) and allows employees to buy its shares at below-market prices, heightening employees' motivation. As shareholders, the employees focus not only on short-term profits but also on long-term capital appreciation, for they are now the company's owners. Over time, if enough employees participate, they can control a substantial stock holding, as do the employees of United Airlines, and thus become vitally interested in the company's performance. ESOPs can be very important in developing an adaptive corporate culture because employees share in the profits that result.

Organization Bonus Systems Profit is not the only basis on which a company can reward organizationwide performance. Rewards are also commonly based on cost savings, quality increases, and production increases obtained in the most recent time period. Because these systems usually require that outputs be measured accurately, they are most common in assembly-line organizations or in service companies, where it is possible to cost out the price of the services of personnel. The systems are mainly a backup to other forms of pay systems. In rare situations, however, they become the principal means of control. That is the case at Lincoln Electric, a company renowned for the success of its cost-savings group plan.

Control through organizational reward systems complements all the other forms of control we discuss in this chapter. Rewards act as the oil that makes a control system function effectively. To ensure that the right strategic behaviors are being rewarded, rewards should be closely linked to an organization's strategy. Moreover, they should be so designed that they do not lead to conflicts among divisions, functions, or individuals. Since organizational structure and organizational control and reward systems are not independent dimensions of organizational design but are highly interrelated, they must be compatible if an organization is to implement its strategy successfully. Matching structure and control to strategy is the issue we focus on in Chapter 13.

SUMMARY OF CHAPTER

Choosing a control system to match the firm's strategy and structure offers management a number of important challenges. Management must select controls that provide a framework to monitor, measure, and evaluate accurately whether or not it has achieved its goals and strategic objectives. Financial and output controls must be backed up with behavior controls and organizational culture to ensure that the firm is achieving its goals in the most efficient way possible. In general, these controls should reinforce one another, and care must be taken to ensure that they do not result in unforeseen consequences, such as competition among functions, divisions, and individuals. Many top managers point to the difficulty of changing organizational culture when they talk about reengineering their organization so that it can pursue new strategic goals. This difficulty arises because culture is the product of the complex interaction of many factors, such as top management, organizational structure, and the organization's reward and incentive systems. The chapter makes the following main points:

- ✔ Organizational structure does not operate effectively unless the appropriate control and incentive systems are in place to shape and motivate employees' behavior.
- ✔ Strategic control is the process of setting targets and monitoring, evaluating, and rewarding organizational performance. The balanced scorecard approach to strategic control suggests that managers should develop strategic control systems that measure all important aspects of their organization's performance.
- ✔ Control takes place at all levels in the organization—corporate, divisional, functional, and individual.
- ✔ Effective control systems are flexible, accurate, and able to provide quick feedback to strategic planners.
- ✔ Many kinds of performance standards are available to implement a company's strategy. The kinds of measures managers choose affect the way a company operates.
- ✔ Control systems range from those directed at measuring outputs to those measuring behaviors or actions.
- ✔ The two main forms of financial control are stock market price and return on investment (ROI).
- ✔ Output controls establish goals for divisions, functions, and individuals. They can be used only when outputs can be objectively measured and are often linked to a management by objectives system.
- ✔ Behavior controls are achieved through budgets, standardization, and rules and procedures.
- ✔ Organizational culture is the collection of norms and values that govern the way in which people act and behave inside the organization.

- An organization's culture is the product of a founder's or top-management team's values and attitudes, of the way managers choose to design the organization's structure, and of the strategic reward systems managers use to shape and motivate employees' behavior.
- An organization's reward systems constitute the final form of control. A company designs its reward systems to provide employees with the incentives to make its structure work effectively and to align their interests with organizational goals and objectives.
- Organizations use all these forms of control simultaneously. Management must select and combine those that are consistent with each other and with the strategy and structure of the organization.

DISCUSSION QUESTIONS

1. What are the relationships among differentiation, integration, and strategic control systems? Why are these relationships important?
2. For each of the structures we discuss in Chapter 11, outline the most suitable control systems.
3. What kind of control and reward systems would you be likely to find in (a) a small manufacturing company, (b) a chain store, (c) a high-tech company, and (d) a Big Five accounting firm?

Practicing Strategic Management

SMALL-GROUP EXERCISE
Creating a Strategic Control System

Break up into groups of three to five people, and discuss the following scenario:

You are managers in charge of project teams of design engineers, each of which is working on a different aspect of the design for a new generation of luxury sports sedans. You are meeting to design a control system that will be used to motivate and reward all the teams. Your objective is to create a control system that will help to increase the performance of each team separately and facilitate cooperation between the teams, something that is necessary since the various projects are interlinked and affect one another (the different parts of the car must fit together). Since competition in the luxury-car market is intense, it is imperative that the car be of the highest quality possible and incorporate all state-of-the-art technology.

1. Using the balanced scorecard approach, discuss what kind of output controls are most important for measuring the teams' performance.
2. Discuss what kinds of behavior controls you should establish to facilitate interactions both within the teams and between the teams.
3. Discuss how you might go about developing a culture to help promote high team performance.

STRATEGIC MANAGEMENT PROJECT
Module 12

For this part of your project, you need to obtain information about your company's control and incentive systems, which may be difficult to do unless your project pertains to a real company and you can interview managers directly. Some forms of information, such as compensation for top management, are available in the company's annual reports or 10-K. If your company is well known, magazines such as *Fortune* or *Business Week* frequently report on corporate culture or control issues. Nevertheless, you may be forced to make some bold assumptions to complete this part of the project.

1. What are the major kinds of control problems facing your company? How do these control problems relate to your organization's structure, which you identified in the last chapter?
2. With the information at your disposal, list the main kinds of control systems used by your organization to solve these problems. Specifically, what use does your company make of (a) financial controls, (b) output controls, (c) behavior controls, and (d) organizational culture?
3. What kinds of behaviors is the organization trying to (a) shape and (b) motivate through the use of these control systems?
4. What role does the top-management team play in creating the culture of your organization? Can you identify the characteristic norms and values that describe the way people behave in your organization? How does the design of the organization's structure affect its culture?
5. Collect the salary and compensation data for your company's top management from its annual reports. How does the organization use rewards to shape and motivate its managers? For example, how much of top managers' total compensation is based on bonuses and stock options, and how much is based on straight salary?
6. Does the organization offer other kinds of employees any incentives based on performance? What kinds of incentives? For example, is there an employee stock ownership plan in operation?
7. Based on this analysis, do you think that your organization's control system is functioning effectively? For example, is your organization collecting the right kinds of information? Is it measuring the right kinds of behavior? How could the control system be improved?
8. To what degree is there a match between your company's structure and its control and incentive systems? That is, are its control systems allowing it to operate its structure effectively? How could they be improved?

ARTICLE FILE 12

Find an example of a company that has recently changed one or more of its control and incentive systems. Which of its control systems did it change (for instance, output control or culture)? Why did it make the change? What does it hope to achieve by the change? How will changing the control system affect the way its structure operates?

EXPLORING THE WEB
What Kind of Control?

Search the Web for an example of a company that uses one or more of the types of control systems discussed in the chapter. What control system is it? Why does the company use it?

CLOSING CASE

Sam Walton's Approach to Control

WAL-MART, HEADQUARTERED IN BENTONVILLE, Arkansas, is the largest retailer in the world, with sales of almost $100 billion in 1996. Its success rests on the nature of the strategic control systems that its founder, the late Sam Walton, established for the company. Walton wanted all his managers and workers to have a hands-on approach to their jobs and to be fully committed to Wal-Mart's main goal, which he defined as total customer satisfaction. To motivate his employees, Walton created a strategic control system that gave employees at all levels continuous feedback about their and the company's performance.

First, Walton developed a financial control system that provided managers with day-to-day feedback about the performance of all aspects of the business. Through a sophisticated companywide satellite system, corporate managers at the Bentonville headquarters can evaluate the performance of each store, and even of each department in each store. Information about store profits and the rate of turnover of goods is provided to store managers on a daily basis, and store managers in turn communicate this information to Wal-Mart's 625,000 employees (who are called associates). By sharing such information, Walton's method encourages all associates to learn the fundamentals of the retailing business so they can work to improve it.[34]

If any store seems to be underperforming, managers and associates meet to probe the reasons and to find solutions to help raise performance. Wal-Mart's top managers routinely visit stores having problems to lend their expertise, and each month top managers use the company's aircraft to fly to various Wal-Mart's stores so they can keep their fingers on the pulse of the business. In addition, it is customary for Wal-Mart's top managers to spend their Saturdays meeting together to discuss the week's financial results and their implications for the future.[35]

Walton also insisted on linking performance to rewards. Each manager's individual performance, measured by his or her ability to meet specific goals or output targets, is reflected in pay raises and chances for promotion (promotion both to bigger stores in the company's 2,000-store empire and even to corporate headquarters, since Wal-Mart routinely promotes from within the company rather than hiring managers from other companies). While top managers receive large stock options linked to the company's performance targets and stock price, even ordinary associates receive stock in the company. An associate who started with Walton in the 1970s would by now have accumulated more than $250,000 in stock because of the appreciation of Wal-Mart's stock over time.

Walton also instituted an elaborate system of controls, such as rules and budgets, to shape employees' behavior. Each store performs the same activities in the same way, and all employees receive the same kind of training so they know how to behave toward customers. In this way, Wal-Mart is able to standardize its operations, which leads to major cost savings and allows managers to make storewide changes easily when they need to.

Finally, Walton was not content just to use output and behavior controls and monetary rewards to motivate his associates. To involve his associates in the business and encourage them to develop work behaviors focused on providing quality customer service, he established strong cultural values and norms for his company. Some norms that associates are expected to follow include the *ten-foot attitude*, which developed when Walton, during his visits

CLOSING CASE *(continued)*

to the stores, encouraged associates to "promise that whenever you come within 10 feet of a customer you will look him in the eye, greet him, and ask him if you can help him"; the *sundown rule,* which states that employees should strive to answer customers' requests by sundown on the day they receive them; and the *Wal-Mart cheer* ("Give me a *W*, give me an *A*," and so on), which is used in all its stores.

The strong customer-oriented values that Walton created are exemplified in the stories its members tell one another about the company's concern for its customers. They include stories such as the one about Sheila, who risked her own safety when she jumped in front of a car to prevent a little boy from being struck; about Phyllis, who administered CPR to a customer who had suffered a heart attack in her store; and about Annette, who gave up the Power Ranger she had on layaway for her own son so a customer's son could have his birthday wish.[36] The strong Wal-Mart culture helps control and motivate its employees, spurring the associates to achieve the stringent output and financial targets the company has set for itself.[37]

Case Discussion Questions

1. What were the main elements of the control system created by Sam Walton?
2. In what ways will this control system facilitate Wal-Mart's present strategy of global expansion?

End Notes

1. M. Moeller, "Oracle: Practising What it Preaches," *Business Week*, August 16, 1999, pp. 1–5.
2. G. Hamel and C. K. Prahalad, "Strategic Intent," *Harvard Business Review* (May–June 1989), 64.
3. R. Simmons, "Strategic Orientation and Top Management Attention to Control Systems," *Strategic Management Journal*, 12 (1991), 49–62.
4. R. Simmons, "How New Top Managers Use Control Systems as Levers of Strategic Renewal," *Strategic Management Journal*, 15 (1994), 169–189.
5. R. S. Kaplan and D. P. Norton, "The Balanced Scorecard—Measures That Drive Performance," *Harvard Business Review* (January–February 1992), 71–79.
6. R. S. Kaplan and D. P. Norton, "Using the Balanced Scorecard as a Strategic Management System," *Harvard Business Review* (January–February 1996), 75–85.
7. R. S. Kaplan and D. P. Norton, "Putting the Balanced Scorecard to Work," *Harvard Business Review* (September–October 1993), 134–147.
8. Kaplan and Norton, "The Balanced Scorecard," p. 72.
9. W. G. Ouchi, "The Transmission of Control Through Organizational Hierarchy," *Academy of Management Journal*, 21 (1978), 173–192; W. H. Newman, *Constructive Control* (Englewood Cliffs, N.J.: Prentice-Hall, 1975).
10. Press release, www.cypress.com (1998).
11. B. Dumaine, "The Bureaucracy Busters," *Fortune*, June 17, 1991, 46.
12. P. F. Drucker, *The Practise of Management* (New York: Harper & Row, 1954).
13. S. J. Carroll and H. L. Tosi, *Management by Objectives: Applications and Research* (New York: Macmillan, 1973).
14. R. Rodgers and J. E. Hunter, "Impact of Management by Objectives on Organizational Productivity," *Journal of Applied Psychology*, 76 (1991), 322–326.
15. Bureau of Business Practice, *Profiles of Malcolm Baldrige Award Winners* (Boston: Allyn & Bacon, 1992).
16. E. Flamholtz, "Organizational Control Systems as a Managerial Tool," *California Management Review* (Winter 1979), 50–58.
17. O. E. Williamson, *Markets and Hierarchies* (New York: Free Press, 1975); W. G. Ouchi, "Markets, Bureaucracies, and Clans," *Administrative Science Quarterly*, 25 (1980), 129–141.
18. "In Praise of the Blue Suit," *Economist*, January 13, 1996, p. 59.
19. H. Mintzberg, *The Structuring of Organizations* (Englewood Cliffs, N.J.: Prentice-Hall, 1979), pp. 5–9.
20. L. Smircich, "Concepts of Culture and Organizational Analysis," *Administrative Science Quarterly*, 28 (1983), 339–358.
21. "General Electric," *Harvard Business School Case* No. 9-385-315, 1984.
22. Ouchi, "Markets, Bureaucracies, and Clans," p. 130.
23. G. R. Jones, *Organizational Theory* (Reading, Mass.: Addison-Wesley, 1997).
24. J. Van Maanen and E. H. Schein, "Towards a Theory of Organizational Socialization," in *Research in Organizational Behavior*, ed. B. M. Staw (Greenwich, Conn.: JAI Press, 1979), pp. 1, 209–264.
25. G. R. Jones, "Socialization Tactics, Self-Efficacy, and Newcomers' Adjustments to Organizations," *Academy of Management Journal*, 29 (1986), 262–279.
26. For details of The HP Way, see J. P. Kotter and J. L. Heskett, *Corporate Culture and Performance* (New York: Free Press, 1992), Chapter 5.
27. Kotter and Heskett, *Corporate Culture*.
28. T. J. Peters and R. H. Waterman, *In Search of Excellence: Lessons from America's Best-Run Companies* (New York: Harper & Row, 1982).
29. W. G. Ouchi, *Theory Z: How American Business Can Meet the Japanese Challenge* (Reading, Mass.: Addison-Wesley, 1981).
30. E. E. Lawler III, *Motivation in Work Organizations* (Monterey, Calif.: Brooks/Cole, 1973); J. Galbraith and R. Kazanjian, *Strategy Implementation* (St. Paul, Minn.: West, 1992), Chapter 6.
31. E. E. Lawler III, "The Design of Effective Reward Systems," in *Handbook of Organizational Behavior*, ed. J. W. Lorsch (Englewood Cliffs, N.J.: Prentice-Hall, 1987), 386–422; R. Mathis and J. Jackson, *Personnel*, 2nd ed. (St. Paul, Minn.: West, 1979), p. 456.
32. H. L. Tosi Jr. and L. R. Gomez-Mejia, "CEO Compensation and Firm Performance," *Academy of Management Journal*, 37 (1994), 1002–1016.
33. T. Y. Hausman, "Second Behind," *Wall Street Journal*, April 11, 1996, p. A4.
34. J. Pettet, "Wal-Mart Yesterday and Today," *Discount Merchandiser* (December 1995), 66–67.
35. M. Reid, "Stores of Value," *Economist*, March 4, 1995 pp. ss5–ss7.
36. www.walmart.com, 1999.
37. M. Troy, "The Culture Remains the Constant," *Discount Store News*, June 8, 1998, pp. 95–98.

13 Matching Structure and Control to Strategy

OPENING CASE

Compaq's New Internet Strategy

IN A BOOMING ENVIRONMENT, where computer firms such as Dell and IBM are reporting record profits, Compaq reported losses in 1999.[1] Why? Its new CEO, Michael Capellas, attributes its problems to three factors: (1) the difficulties associated with integrating Digital Equipment's operations into Compaq's after the takeover of Digital Equipment in 1998; (2) Compaq's slowness in developing an Internet strategy and reaching out to customers, both corporate and individual, on-line; and (3) its failure to control inventory costs at a time when rivals such as Dell and Gateway are perfecting ways to streamline their operations and gain a low-cost advantage. To solve these problems, Capellas and his top-management team implemented a new strategy and structure for Compaq in 1999.

As it had grown through the 1990s, Compaq had implemented a matrix structure to control its diverse businesses. Over time, however, the matrix structure resulted in increasingly slow decision making because geography—especially after the Digital acquisition—rather than product considerations drove strategy making.[2] The needs of the whole corporation were being ignored as the needs of each geographic business or division took precedence.

Consequently, Capellas decided to scrap the decentralized matrix structure. He replaced it with a multidivisional one, based on product line—for example, personal computers or high-end corporate workstations. At the same time, he made each business a profit center and gave each division's managers clear sales and profit objectives and the responsibility to achieve those objectives.[3]

Capellas then announced a new strategy for the company: henceforth, Compaq would pursue an Internet strategy, both to increase its direct sales to customers and to streamline and integrate its own operations in order to reduce costs and speed decision making. Capellas charged a team of corporate managers with establishing a series of Internet teams to speed the development of Internet-based software systems to facilitate direct sales to all types of customers—for example, commercial, individual, and education. Moreover, he demanded that these systems be standardized across business divisions. His aim was both to integrate the divisions' activities and to allow them to work together to provide large customers with a complete computer package consisting of mainframes and servers, as well as desktop and portable computers.

Recognizing that Compaq had been slow to use the Internet to facilitate the management of its value chain, Capellas also instructed managers to take Compaq's functional operations on-line. For example, Compaq was not closely connected to its suppliers on-line whereas Dell, its major competitor, was. Dell had achieved a 10 percent cost advantage over Compaq as a result of its ability to reduce inventory and warehousing costs by using a state-of-the-art Internet information system. Furthermore, Dell has also been leading the way in direct selling to customers over the Internet. Capellas recognized that Compaq must match Dell in this regard if it is to regain its competitive position. His goal is to raise direct sales from 15 percent of total sales to 25 percent by the end of 1999, and to increase this figure in the years ahead.

Although the effects of Compaq's new strategy and structure on its bottom-line performance are still unknown, analysts feel that Capellas has made many of the right moves. They worry, however, that Compaq waited too long to reinvent itself. With such strong and agile competitors in the market as Dell, IBM, and Sun Microsystems, it is not clear that Compaq will be able to recover its preeminent position in the marketplace.

OVERVIEW

At Compaq, Michael Capellas and his top-management team moved to implement the right mix of structure and control systems so that the company could pursue a new strategy to manage the competitive environment. In this chapter, we discuss how the nature of a company's corporate-, business-, and functional-level strategy affects the choice of structure and control systems—in other words, how strategic managers should match different forms of structure and control to strategy. As we emphasized in Chapter 1, the issue facing strategic managers is to match strategy formulation with strategy implementation. All the tools of strategy formulation and implementation are discussed in previous chapters. In this chapter, we put the two sides of the equation together and examine how strategic managers match strategy and structure to build competitive advantage.

First, we consider how functional-level strategy and the attempt to achieve superior efficiency, quality, innovation, and customer responsiveness affect structure and control. Second, we examine how a company's choice of generic business-level strategy influences the choice of structure and control for implementing the strategy. Third, we focus on the implementation of a global strategy and discuss how to match different global strategies with different global structures. Finally, we take up the special problems that different kinds of corporate-level strategy pose for strategic managers in designing a structure and note how changes in corporate-level strategy over time affect the form of structure and control systems adopted by a company. By the end of this chapter, you will understand how to match strategy to structure to create a high-performing organization.

STRUCTURE AND CONTROL AT THE FUNCTIONAL LEVEL

Chapter 5, on functional-level strategy, discusses how a company's functions can help it achieve superior efficiency, quality, innovation, and customer responsiveness—the four building blocks of competitive advantage. It also discusses how strategic managers can help each function to develop a distinctive competency. We now examine the way in which strategic managers can create a structure and control system to encourage the development of various distinctive functional competencies, or skills.

Decisions at the functional level fall into two categories: choices about the level of vertical differentiation and choices about monitoring and evaluation systems. (Choices about horizontal differentiation are *not* relevant here because we are considering each function individually.) The choices depend on the distinctive competency a company is pursuing.

Manufacturing

In manufacturing, functional strategy usually centers on improving efficiency, quality, and responsiveness to customers. A company must create an organizational setting in which managers can learn from experience-curve effects how to economize on costs. Traditionally, to move down the experience curve quickly, companies have exercised tight control over work activities and employees and developed tall, centralized hierarchies to squeeze out costs wherever possible. As part of their attempt to increase efficiency, companies have also made great use of behavior and output controls to reduce costs. Activities are standardized. For example, human inputs are standardized through the recruitment and training of skilled personnel, the work process is standardized or programmed to reduce costs, and quality control is used to make sure that outputs are being produced correctly. In addition, managers use output controls such as operating budgets to monitor and contain costs continuously.

Following the lead of Japanese companies such as Toyota and Sony, which operate total quality management (TQM) and flexible manufacturing systems, many U.S. companies have moved to change the way they design the manufacturing setting. As detailed in Chapter 5, successful TQM requires a different approach to organizational design. With TQM, the inputs and involvement of all employees in the decision-making process are necessary to improve production efficiency and quality. Thus, authority has to be decentralized in order to motivate employees to improve the production process. In TQM, work teams are created and workers are given the responsibility and authority to discover and implement improved work procedures. Quality control circles are formed to exchange information and suggestions about problems and work procedures. Frequently, a bonus system or employee stock ownership plan (ESOP) is established to motivate workers and allow them to share in the increased value that TQM often produces.

No longer are managers employed purely to supervise workers and make sure they are doing the job. Managers assume the role of coach and facilitator, and team members jointly take on the supervisory burden, reducing bureaucratic costs. Work teams are often given the responsibility of controlling and disciplining their members; they may even have to decide who should work in their team. Frequently, work teams develop strong norms and values, and work-group culture becomes an important means of control. This type of control matches the new decentralized team approach.

Although workers are given more freedom to control their activities, the extensive use of output controls and the continuous measurement of efficiency and quality ensure that the work team's activities meet the goals set for the function by management. Efficiency and quality increase as new and improved work rules and procedures are developed to raise the level of standardization. The aim is to find the right match between structure and control and a TQM approach, so that manufacturing develops the distinctive competency leading to superior efficiency and quality.

Research and Development

The functional strategy for a research and development department is to develop a distinctive competency in innovation and to develop technology that results in products that fit customers' needs. Consequently, the R&D department's structure and control systems should be designed to provide the coordination necessary for scientists and engineers to bring products quickly to market. Moreover, these systems should motivate R&D scientists to develop innovative products or processes.

In practice, R&D departments typically have flat, decentralized structures that group scientists into teams. Flat structures give research and development personnel the freedom and autonomy to be innovative. Furthermore, because the performance of scientists and engineers can typically be judged only over the long term (because it may take several years for a project to be completed), adding layers of hierarchy would simply raise bureaucratic costs and waste resources.[4]

By using teams, strategic managers can take advantage of scientists' ability to work jointly in solving problems and to enhance each other's performance. In small teams, too, the professional values and norms that highly trained employees bring to the situation promote coordination. A culture for innovation frequently emerges to control employees' behavior, as has occurred at Motorola and Intel, where the race to be first energizes the R&D teams. Strategy in Action 13.1 describes Intel's use of R&D teams to innovate and improve computer chips.

To spur teams to work effectively, the reward system should be linked to the performance of the team. If scientists, individually or in a team, do not share in the profits a company obtains from its new products or processes, they may have little motivation to contribute wholeheartedly to the team. To prevent the departure of their key employees and to encourage high motivation, companies such as Merck, Intel, and Microsoft give their researchers stock options and rewards tied to their individual performance, their team performance, and the company's performance. As a result, many of these scientists and engineers have become multimillionaires.

Sales

Like research and development, the sales function usually has a flat structure. Most commonly, three hierarchical levels—sales director, regional or product sales managers, and individual salespeople—can accommodate even large sales forces. Flat structures are possible because the organization does not depend on direct supervision for control. Salespeople's activities are often complex; moreover, because they are dispersed in the field, these employees are difficult to monitor. Rather than depend on the hierarchy, the sales function usually employs output and behavior controls.

Output controls, such as specific sales goals or goals for increasing responsiveness to customers, can be easily established and monitored by supervisors. Then output controls can be linked to a bonus reward system to motivate salespeople. Behavior controls—for instance, detailed reports that salespeople file describing their

13.1 STRATEGY *in* ACTION

Intel's R&D Department

Intel is the world leader in the development of chips, the microprocessors that are the heart of all computers. Intel is very profitable, and throughout the 1990s it earned record profits because it had a monopoly on the production of the Pentium chip, which is still the industry standard. In the race to produce new and improved chips, Intel is constantly under attack from companies such as Motorola, IBM, and Japan's NEC and has to protect its competitive advantage. Consequently, the need to develop new chips or improved versions of existing ones (such as the Pentium Pro) forms the basis of Intel's differentiation strategy.

To speed product development, Intel has implemented a team structure in its R&D department. To try to ensure that it will always have the leading-edge technology, the company has six different teams working on the next generation of chips; each team's innovations can then be put together to create the final state-of-the-art product. However, it also has six teams working simultaneously on the subsequent generation of chips, and six teams working on the generation of chips to follow that one. In other words, to sustain its leading-edge technology and maintain its monopoly, the company has created a team structure in which its scientists and engineers work on the frontiers of chip research so that they can control the technology of tomorrow.[5] This approach has certainly paid off for Intel. The company's stock price has increased more than 600 percent in the 1990s. Indeed, Intel is expected to outperform the market for as long as its teams succeed in making the company the innovation leader in the chip industry.

interactions with customers—can also be used to standardize salespeople's behavior and make it easier for supervisors to review their performance.[6]

Similar design considerations apply to the other functions, such as accounting, finance, engineering, and human resource management. Managers must select the right combination of structure and control mechanisms to allow each function to contribute to achieving superior efficiency, quality, innovation, and responsiveness to customers. When, as now, reducing costs is often required for survival, more and more companies are flattening their functional hierarchies and decentralizing control to reduce bureaucratic costs. Strategic managers must develop control and incentive systems that align employees' interests with those of the organization and that motivate employees.

STRUCTURE AND CONTROL AT THE BUSINESS LEVEL

Building competitive advantage through organizational design starts at the functional level. However, the key to successful strategy implementation is a structure that *links and combines* the skills and competencies of a company's value creation functions, allowing it to pursue a business-level strategy successfully. In this section, we consider the organizational design issues for a company seeking to implement one of the generic competitive business-level strategies to build and sustain its competitive advantage.

Generic Business-Level Strategies

Designing the right mix of structure and control at the business level is a continuation of designing a company's functions. Having implemented the right structure and control system for each individual function, the company must then implement the organizational arrangements so that all the functions can be managed together to achieve business-level strategy objectives. Because the focus is on managing *cross-functional relationships*, the choice of horizontal differentiation (the grouping of organizational activities) and integration for achieving business-level strategies becomes very important.[7] Control systems must also be selected with the monitoring and evaluating of cross-functional activities in mind. Table 13.1 summarizes the appropriate organizational structure and control systems that companies can use when following a low-cost, differentiation, or focus strategy.

Cost-Leadership Strategy and Structure

The aim of the cost-leadership strategy is to make the company pursuing it the lowest-cost producer in the market.[8] At the business level, this means reducing costs not just in production, but across *all* functions in the organization, including research and development and sales and marketing.

If a company is pursuing a cost-leadership strategy, its research and development efforts probably focus on product and process development rather than on the more expensive product innovation, which carries no guarantee of success. In other words, the company stresses research that improves product characteristics

TABLE 13.1

Generic Strategy, Structure, and Control

	Strategy		
	Cost Leadership	***Differentiation***	***Focus***
Appropriate Structure	Functional	Product team or matrix	Functional
Integrating Mechanisms	Center on manufacturing	Center on R&D or marketing	Center on product or customer
Output Controls	Great use (e.g., cost control)	Some use (e.g., quality goals)	Some use (e.g., cost and quality)
Behavior Controls	Some use (e.g., budgets, standardization)	Great use (e.g., rules, budgets)	Some use (e.g., budgets)
Organizational Culture	Little use (e.g., quality control circles)	Great use (e.g., norms and values)	Great use (e.g., norms and values)

or lowers the cost of making existing products. Similarly, the company tries to decrease the cost of sales and marketing by offering a standard product to a mass market rather than by offering different products aimed at different market segments, which is also more expensive.[9]

To implement a cost-leadership strategy, the company chooses a structure and control system that has a low level of bureaucratic costs. As we discuss in earlier chapters, bureaucratic costs are those of managing a company's strategy through structure and control. Structure and control are expensive, and the more complex the structure—that is, the higher its level of differentiation and integration—the higher are bureaucratic costs. To economize on bureaucratic costs, a cost leader will, therefore, choose the simplest or least expensive structure compatible with the needs of the low-cost strategy.

In practice, the structure chosen is normally a functional structure. This structure is relatively inexpensive to operate because it is based on a low level of differentiation and integration. Even in a functional structure, cross-functional teams can be organized around the manufacturing function. For example, a TQM program implemented through task forces and teams can be developed to integrate the activities of manufacturing and the other functions. This allows for continuous improvements in the rules and procedures for standardizing task activities, which is a major source of cost saving.[10]

A cost-leadership company also tries to keep its structure as flat as possible to reduce bureaucratic costs, and functional structures are relatively flat. The cost leader constantly evaluates whether it needs that extra level in the hierarchy and whether it can decentralize authority (perhaps to the work group) to keep costs low. Seagate Technology, a producer of hard disks, exemplifies a cost leader that continually streamlines its structure to maintain a competitive advantage. It periodically reduces levels in the hierarchy and institutes strict production controls to minimize costs. This process has kept it ahead of its Japanese competitors. Similarly, John Reed, the chairman of Citicorp, flattened his organization's structure, wiping out two levels of management and terminating dozens of executives to reduce costs. His cost-cutting efforts helped turn a loss of $457 million in 1991 into record profits throughout the 1990s, and Citicorp's share price has soared as a result.[11]

To further reduce costs, cost-leadership companies try to use the cheapest and easiest forms of control available—output controls. For each function, a company adopts output controls that allow it to monitor and evaluate functional performance closely. In the manufacturing function, for instance, the company imposes tight controls and stresses meeting budgets based on production, cost, or quality targets.[12] In research and development, too, the emphasis falls on the bottom line. R&D personnel, eager to demonstrate their contribution to cost savings, may focus their efforts on improving process technology, where actual savings are calculable.

H. J. Heinz clearly illustrates such efforts. In following a cost-leadership strategy, it places enormous emphasis on production improvements that can reduce the cost of a can of beans. Like manufacturing and research and development, the sales function is closely monitored, and sales targets are usually challenging. Cost-leadership companies, however, are likely to reward employees through generous incentive and bonus plans to encourage high performance. Often their culture is based on values that emphasize the bottom line. Lincoln Electric and PepsiCo are other examples of such companies.

In short, pursuing a successful cost-leadership strategy requires close attention to the design of structure and control to limit bureaucratic costs. Managers, rules, and organizational control mechanisms cost money, and low-cost companies must try to economize when implementing their structures. When a company's competitive advantage depends on building and sustaining a low-cost advantage, adopting the right organizational arrangements is vital.

Differentiation Strategy and Structure

To pursue a differentiation strategy, a company must develop a distinctive competency in a function such as research and development or marketing and sales. As we have already discussed, doing so usually means that a company produces a wider range of products, serves more market niches, and generally has to customize its products to the needs of different customers. These factors make it difficult to standardize activities; they also increase the demands made on functional managers. Hence, the differentiated company usually employs a more complex structure—that is, a structure with a higher level of differentiation and integration—than the cost leader. The bureaucratic costs of a differentiator are higher than those of a cost leader, but these costs are recouped through the higher value it adds to its differentiated products.

To make its product unique in the eyes of the customer, for example, a differentiated company must design its structure and control system around the *particular source* of its competitive advantage.[13] Suppose that the differentiator's strength lies in technological competency; the company has the cutting-edge technology. In this case, the company's structure and control systems should be designed around the research and development function. Implementing a *matrix structure*, as Texas Instruments and TRW Systems have done, promotes innovation and speeds product development, for this type of structure permits intensive cross-functional integration. Integrating mechanisms, such as task forces and teams, help transfer knowledge among functions and are designed around the research and development function. Sales, marketing, and production targets are geared to research and development goals; marketing devises advertising programs that focus on technological possibilities, and salespeople are evaluated on their understanding of new-product characteristics and their ability to inform potential customers about them. Stringent sales targets are unlikely to be set in this situation because the goal is quality of service.

As detailed in Chapter 11, however, there are many problems associated with a matrix structure. The changing composition of product teams, the ambiguity arising from having two bosses, the use of more complex integration mechanisms, and the greater difficulty of monitoring and evaluating the work of teams greatly increase the bureaucratic costs necessary to coordinate and control task activities. Nevertheless, companies are willing to incur the higher bureaucratic costs of a matrix structure when it allows them to create more value from their differentiation strategy.

Sometimes the advantages of a differentiation strategy can be obtained from a less expensive structure. For example, when the source of the differentiator's competitive advantage is superior quality or responsiveness to customers, companies design a structure around their products, and a *product-team* or *geographic* structure may fit best. In a product-team structure, each product group can focus on the needs of a particular product market. Support functions such as research and development or sales are organized by product, and task forces and teams have a product, not a research, orientation.

If a company's differentiation strategy is based on serving the needs of a number of different market segments, a geographic structure becomes appropriate. Thus, if it focuses on types of customers, a differentiated company may use a geographic structure designed according to a regional logic or even according to different types of customers, such as businesses, individual consumers, or the government. Both Compaq and Rockwell International have reorganized their structures to concentrate on the needs of specific customers or regions. The new geographic structure allows them to become more responsive to the needs of specific groups of customers and to serve those needs better. For example, information about changes in customers' preferences can be quickly fed back to R&D and product design so that a company can protect its competitive advantage.

The control systems used to match the structure can also be geared to the company's distinctive competency. For the differentiator, it is important that the various functions do not pull in different directions; indeed, cooperation among the functions is vital for cross-functional integration. However, when functions work together, output controls become much harder to use. In general, it is much more difficult to measure the performance of people in different functions when they are engaged in cooperative efforts. Consequently, a company must rely more on behavior controls and shared norms and values when pursuing a strategy of differentiation.

That is why companies pursuing a differentiation strategy often have a markedly different kind of culture from those pursuing a low-cost strategy. Because human resources—good scientists, designers, or marketing people—are often the source of differentiation, these organizations have a culture based on professionalism or collegiality, a culture that emphasizes the distinctiveness of the human resource rather than the high pressure of the bottom line.[14] Hewlett-Packard, Motorola, and Coca-Cola, all of which emphasize some kind of distinctive competency, exemplify companies with professional cultures.

The bureaucratic costs of operating the structure and control system of the differentiator are higher than the cost leader's, but the benefits are also greater if companies can reap the rewards of a premium price. Companies are willing to accept a higher level of bureaucratic costs provided their structure and control systems lead to superior efficiency, quality, innovation, or responsiveness to customers.

Implementing a Combined Differentiation and Cost-Leadership Strategy

As we point out in Chapter 6, pursuing a combined differentiation and low-cost strategy is the most difficult challenge facing a company at the business level. On the one hand, the company has to coordinate its activities around manufacturing and materials management to implement a cost-reduction strategy. On the other, it must also coordinate its activities around the source of its differentiation advantage, such as R&D or marketing, to protect its competency in innovation or responsiveness to customers. For many companies in this situation, the answer has been the product-team structure, discussed in Chapter 11. It is far less costly to operate than a matrix structure but provides a much higher level of cross-functional integration than the functional structure.

As you recall from Chapter 11, a product-team structure groups tasks by product, and each product line is managed by a cross-functional team, which provides all the support services necessary to bring the product to market. The role of the product team is to protect and enhance a company's differentiation advantage and at the same time coordinate with manufacturing to lower costs. DaimlerChrysler, Hallmark

Cards, and Xerox are among the companies that have reorganized from a functional to a product-team structure so that they can simultaneously speed product development and control their operating costs.

John Fluke Manufacturing, a leader in electronic testing tools, is a good example of a company that has made use of product teams to speed product development. The company assembles "Phoenix teams," which are cross-functional groups that are given 100 days and $100,000 to identify a market need and a new product to fill it.[15] So far, these teams have led to the development of two successful new products. As Strategy in Action 13.2 shows, 3M also uses cross-functional teams to promote a culture of innovation.

13.2 **STRATEGY *in* ACTION**

How 3M Uses Teams to Build Culture

A company well known for product innovation, 3M aims to achieve at least 25 percent of its growth each year through new products developed within the last five years. To promote product development, 3M has always taken care to design its structure and culture so that employees are provided with the freedom and motivation to experiment and take risks. For example, 3M has an informal norm that researchers should use 15 percent of their time to develop projects of their own choosing. It was this norm that brought about the development of new products such as Post-it Notes. In addition, 3M has been careful to establish career ladders for its scientists in order to gain their long-term commitment, and it rewards successful product innovators with substantial bonuses. All these practices have gained the loyalty and support of its scientists and helped create a culture of innovation.

The company has also recognized the increasing importance of linking and coordinating the efforts of people in different functions to speed product development. As noted earlier, people in different functions tend to develop different subunit orientations and to focus their efforts on their own tasks to the exclusion of the needs of other functions. The danger of such tendencies is that each function will develop norms and values that suit its own needs but do little to promote organizational coordination and integration.

To avoid this problem, 3M has established a system of cross-functional teams composed of members of product development, process development, marketing, manufacturing, packaging, and other functions to create organizationwide norms and values of innovation. So that all groups have a common focus, the teams work closely with customers; customers' needs become the platform on which the different functions can then apply their skills and capabilities.[16] For example, one of 3M's cross-functional teams worked closely with disposable diaper manufacturers to develop the right kind of sticky tape for their needs.

To promote integration in the team and foster cooperative norms and values, each team is headed by a "product champion," who takes the responsibility for building cohesive team relationships and developing a team culture. In addition, one of 3M's top managers becomes a "management sponsor," whose job is to help the team get resources and to provide support when the going gets tough. After all, product development is a very risky process, and many projects do not succeed. Finally, 3M established the Golden Step Program, which gives employees substantial monetary bonuses to honor and reward cross-functional teams, to create a culture in which innovation is a valued activity, and to develop norms and values that support and reward the sharing of information among scientists and among people in different functions. Clearly, all this attention to creating a culture of innovation has paid off for 3M.

Focus Strategy and Structure

In Chapter 6, we define *focus strategy* as a strategy directed at a particular market or customer segment. A company focuses on a product or range of products aimed at one sort of customer or region. This strategy tends to have higher production costs than the other two strategies because output levels are lower, making it harder to obtain substantial economies of scale. As a result, a company using a focus strategy must exercise cost control. On the other hand, because some attribute of its product—possibly its ability to provide customers with high-quality, personalized service—usually gives such a company its unique advantage, a company using a focus strategy has to develop a unique competency. For both these reasons, the structure and control system adopted by a company following a focus strategy has to be inexpensive to operate but flexible enough to allow a distinctive competency to emerge.

A company using a focus strategy normally adopts a functional structure to meet these needs. This structure is appropriate because it is complex enough to manage the activities necessary to serve the needs of the market segment or produce a narrow range of products. At the same time, the bureaucratic costs of operating a functional structure are relatively low, and there is less need for complex, expensive integrating mechanisms. This structure permits more personal control and flexibility than the other two, and so it reduces bureaucratic costs while fostering the development of a distinctive competency.[17] Given its small size, a company using a focus strategy can rely less on output and behavior controls and more on culture, which is vital to the development of a service competency. Although output controls need to be used in production and sales, this form of control is inexpensive in a small organization.

The combination of functional structure and low cost of control helps offset the higher costs of production and at the same time allows the firm to develop unique strengths. It is little wonder, therefore, that there are so many companies using a focus strategy. Additionally, because such a company's competitive advantage is often based on personalized service, the flexibility of this kind of structure lets the company respond quickly to customers' needs and change its products in response to customers' requests. The structure then backs up the strategy and helps the firm develop and maintain its distinctive competency. The way in which Wang Laboratories reorganized itself, highlighted in Strategy in Action 13.3, shows how a company pursuing a focus strategy can achieve a strategy-structure fit.

Summary

Companies pursuing a generic business-level strategy must adopt the appropriate form of structure and control if they are to use their resources effectively to develop superior efficiency, quality, innovation, and responsiveness to customers. Companies are willing to bear the bureaucratic costs of operating organizational structure and control systems if these systems increase their ability to create value from lowering their costs or charging a premium price for their products. Hence, over time, companies must manage and change their structures to allow them to create value. However, many companies do *not* use the right forms of structure over time and fail to manage their strategies. These companies are not as successful and do not survive as long as those that do match their strategy, structure, and control systems.[20]

13.3 STRATEGY *in* ACTION

Wang's New Focused Strategy

In the 1980s, Wang Laboratories was one of the biggest and most successful computer companies in the world. But in the early 1990s, it almost went bankrupt because it could not compete against giants such as IBM and EDS. The company exists today only because a new CEO, Joseph Tucci, reorganized it, switched to a focus strategy, and radically altered Wang's structure so that the strategy could be pursued cost effectively.

Rather than compete head-to-head with IBM and EDS in providing software consulting services, Wang specializes in installing easy to use software systems based on Microsoft's Windows NT system. It has built up many contracts with small and large businesses to provide them with the support they need when they install new or improved computer systems. To operate this new focus strategy Tucci was forced to wield the knife. He slashed Wang's work force from 20,000 to 5,300 and cut out four levels of management, reducing the number of hierarchical levels from seven to three.[18] He also decentralized authority to lower-level managers so that they could handle customer requests responsively and held them accountable and rewarded them based on quarterly reviews.

This combination of a focused software services strategy and a new streamlined structure has worked well. Wang is now the fourth largest services company in the United States, and by 1998, it once again employed more than 20,000 people.[19]

DESIGNING A GLOBAL STRUCTURE

In Chapter 8, we note that the strategies of most large companies have a global dimension if the firms produce and sell their products in international markets. Procter & Gamble and food companies such as H. J. Heinz, Kellogg, and Nestlé Enterprises, for example, have production operations throughout the world, as do the large automakers and computer makers. In this section, we examine how each of the four principal global strategies affects a company's choice of structure and control.

As you'll recall from Chapter 8, (1) a *multidomestic strategy* is oriented toward local responsiveness, and a company establishes semiautonomous national units in each country in which it operates to produce and customize products to local markets; (2) an *international strategy* is based on R&D and marketing being centralized at home and all the other value creation functions being decentralized to national units; (3) a *global strategy* is oriented toward cost reduction, with all the principal value creation functions centralized at the optimal global location; and (4) a *transnational strategy* is focused so that it can achieve local responsiveness as well as global integration, and therefore some functions are centralized at the optimal global location while others are decentralized, both to achieve local responsiveness and to facilitate global learning.

If a company is to operate each strategy successfully, the need to coordinate and integrate global tasks increases as the company moves from a multidomestic to an international to a global and then to a transnational strategy. The bureaucratic costs of managing a transnational strategy are much higher than those of managing a multidomestic strategy. To implement a transnational strategy, a company transfers its distinctive competencies to the global location where they can create the most value, and then it establishes a global network to coordinate its foreign and domestic divisions. This coordination involves managing global resource transfers to facilitate global learning. Compared with the other strategies, more managerial time has to be spent coordinating organizational resources and capabilities to achieve the global synergies that justify pursuing a transnational strategy.

By contrast, pursuing a multidomestic strategy does not require coordination of activities on a global level because value creation activities are handled locally, by country or world region. The international and global strategies fit between the other two strategies. Although products have to be sold and marketed globally, and hence global product transfers must be managed, there is less need to coordinate resource transfers than in the case of a transnational strategy.

The implication is that as companies change from a multidomestic to an international, global, or transnational strategy, they require a more complex structure and control system to coordinate the value creation activities associated with that strategy. Therefore, the bureaucratic costs increase at each stage. For a multidomestic strategy, they are low; for an international strategy, medium; for a global strategy, high; and for a transnational strategy, very high (see Table 13.2). In general, the choice of structure and control systems for managing a global business is a function of three factors:

1. The decision how to distribute and allocate responsibility and authority between domestic and foreign managers so that effective control over a company's foreign operations is maintained
2. The selection of a level of horizontal differentiation that groups foreign operations with domestic operations in a way that allows the best use of resources and serves the needs of foreign customers most effectively

TABLE 13.2

Global Strategy/Structure Relationships

	Multidomestic Strategy	*International Strategy*	*Global Strategy*	*Transnational Strategy*
	Low ←	*Need for Coordination*	→	*High*
	Low ←	*Bureaucratic Costs*	→	*High*
Centralization of Authority	Decentralized to national unit	Core competencies centralized, others decentralized to national units	Centralized at optimal global location	Simultaneously centralized and decentralized
Horizontal Differentiation	Global-area structure	International-division structure	Global product-group structure	Global-matrix structure, matrix in the mind
Need for Complex Integrating Mechanisms	Low	Medium	High	Very High
Organizational Culture	Not important	Quite important	Important	Very important

FIGURE 13.1

Global-Area Structure

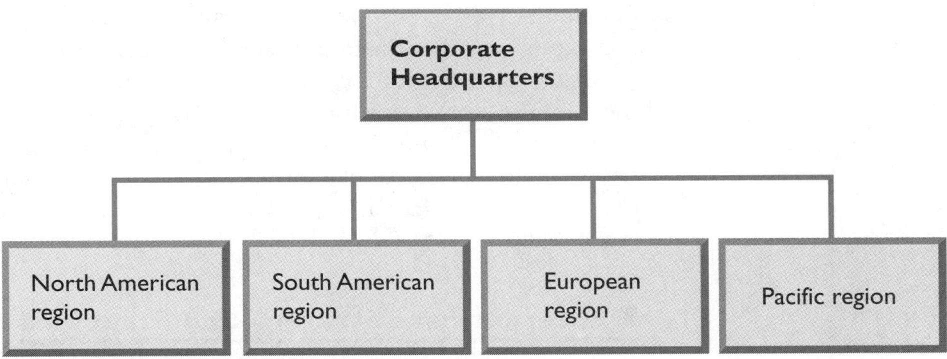

3. The selection of the right kinds of integration mechanism and organizational culture to make the structure function effectively

Table 13.2 summarizes the appropriate design choices for companies pursuing each of these strategies.

Multidomestic Strategy and Structure

When a company pursues a multidomestic strategy, it generally operates with a global-area structure (see Figure 13.1). When using this structure, a company duplicates all value creation activities and establishes a foreign division in every country or world area in which it operates. Authority is then decentralized to managers in each foreign division, and they devise the appropriate strategy for responding to the needs of the local environment. Because corporate headquarters managers are so far away from the scene of operations, it makes sense to decentralize control and grant decision-making authority to managers in the foreign operations. Managers at global headquarters use market and output controls, such as rate of return, growth in market share, and operation costs, to evaluate the performance of foreign divisions. On the basis of such global comparisons, they can make decisions about capital allocation and orchestrate the transfer of new knowledge among divisions.

A company that makes and sells the same products in many different markets often groups its foreign subsidiaries into world regions to simplify the coordination of products across countries. Europe might be one region, the Pacific Rim another, and the Middle East a third. Such grouping allows the same set of market and behavior controls to be applied across all divisions inside a region. Thus, companies can obtain synergies from dealing with broadly similar cultures because information can be transmitted more easily. For example, consumers' preferences regarding product design and marketing are likely to be more similar among countries in one world region than among countries in different world regions.

Because the foreign divisions themselves have little or no contact with each other, no integrating mechanisms are needed. Nor does a global organizational culture develop, since there are no transfers of personnel or informal contacts among managers from the various world regions. Car companies such as Chrysler, General Motors, and Ford all used to employ global-area structures to manage their foreign operations. Ford of Europe, for example, had little or no contact with its U.S. parent, and capital was the principal resource exchanged.

One problem with a global-area structure and a multidomestic strategy is that the duplication of specialist activities raises costs. Moreover, the company is not taking advantage of opportunities to trade information and knowledge on a global basis or of low-cost manufacturing opportunities. Multidomestic companies have chosen to keep behavior costs low; however, they lose the many benefits of operating globally.

International Strategy and Structure

A company pursuing an international strategy adopts a different route to global expansion. Normally, the company shifts to this strategy when it begins selling its domestically made products in foreign markets. Until recently, companies such as Mercedes-Benz and Jaguar made no attempt to produce in a foreign market; instead, they distributed and sold their domestically produced cars internationally. Such companies usually just add a **foreign operations department** to their existing structure and continue to use the same control system. If a company is using a functional structure, this department has to coordinate manufacturing, sales, and research and development activities with the needs of the foreign market. Efforts at customization are minimal, however.

In the foreign country, the company usually establishes a subsidiary to handle sales and distribution. For example, the Mercedes-Benz foreign subsidiaries allocate dealerships, organize supplies of spare parts, and, of course, sell cars. A system of behavior controls is then established to keep the home office informed of changes in sales, spare parts requirements, and so on.

A company with many different products or businesses operating from a multidivisional structure has the challenging problem of coordinating the flow of different products across different countries. To manage these transfers, many companies create an international division, which they add to their existing divisional structure[21] (see Figure 13.2).

International operations are managed as a separate divisional business, whose managers are given the authority and responsibility for coordinating domestic product divisions and foreign markets. The international division also controls the foreign subsidiaries that market the products and decides how much authority to delegate to foreign management. This arrangement permits the company to engage in more complex foreign operations at relatively low bureaucratic cost. However, managers in the foreign countries are essentially under the control of managers in the international division, and if the domestic and foreign managers compete for control of operations in the foreign country, conflict and lack of cooperation can result.

Global Strategy and Structure

A company embarks on a global strategy when it starts to locate manufacturing and all the other value creation activities in the lowest-cost global location to increase efficiency, quality, and innovation. In seeking to obtain the gains from global learning, a company must cope with greater coordination and integration problems. It has to find a structure that can coordinate resource transfers between corporate

FIGURE 13.2

International-Division Structure

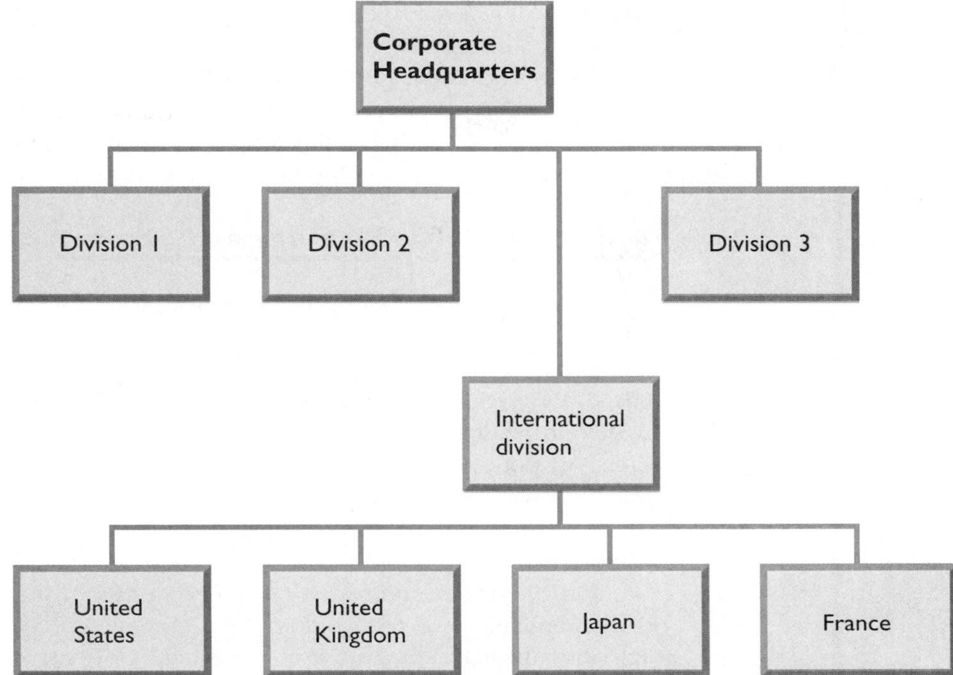

headquarters and foreign divisions and at the same time provide the centralized control that a global strategy requires. The answer for many companies is a **global product group structure** (see Figure 13.3).

In this structure, a product-group headquarters (similar to an SBU headquarters) is created to coordinate the activities of the domestic and foreign divisions within the product group. Product-group managers in the home country are responsible for organizing all aspects of value creation on a global basis. The product-group

FIGURE 13.3

Global Product-Group Structure

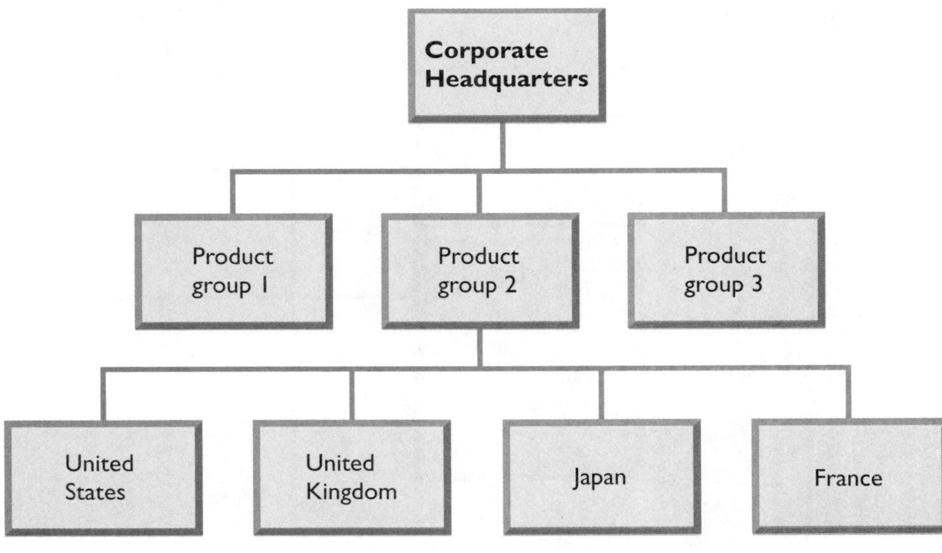

structure allows managers to decide how best to pursue a global strategy—for example, to decide which value creation activities, such as manufacturing or product design, should be performed in which country to increase efficiency. Increasingly, U.S. and Japanese companies are moving manufacturing to low-cost countries such as China but establishing product-design centers in Europe or the United States to take advantage of foreign skills and capabilities.

Transnational Strategy and Structure

The main failing of the global product-group structure is that while it allows a company to achieve superior efficiency and quality, it is weak when it comes to responsiveness to customers because the focus is still on centralized control to reduce costs. Moreover, this structure makes it difficult for the different product groups to trade information and knowledge and to obtain the benefits of cooperation. Sometimes the potential gains from sharing product, marketing, or research and development knowledge between product groups are very high, but because a company lacks a structure that can coordinate the groups' activities, these gains cannot be achieved.

More and more, companies are adopting **global matrix structures**, which let them simultaneously reduce costs by increasing efficiency *and* differentiate their activities through superior innovation and responsiveness to customers. Figure 13.4 shows such a structure, adopted by a large chemical company such as Du Pont or Amoco.

On the vertical axis, instead of functions, there are the company's *product groups,* which provide specialist services such as R&D, product design, and marketing information to the foreign divisions, or SBUs. For example, these might be the petroleum, plastics, pharmaceuticals, or fertilizer product groups. On the horizontal axis are the company's *foreign divisions, or SBUs,* in the various countries or world

FIGURE 13.4

Global-Matrix Structure

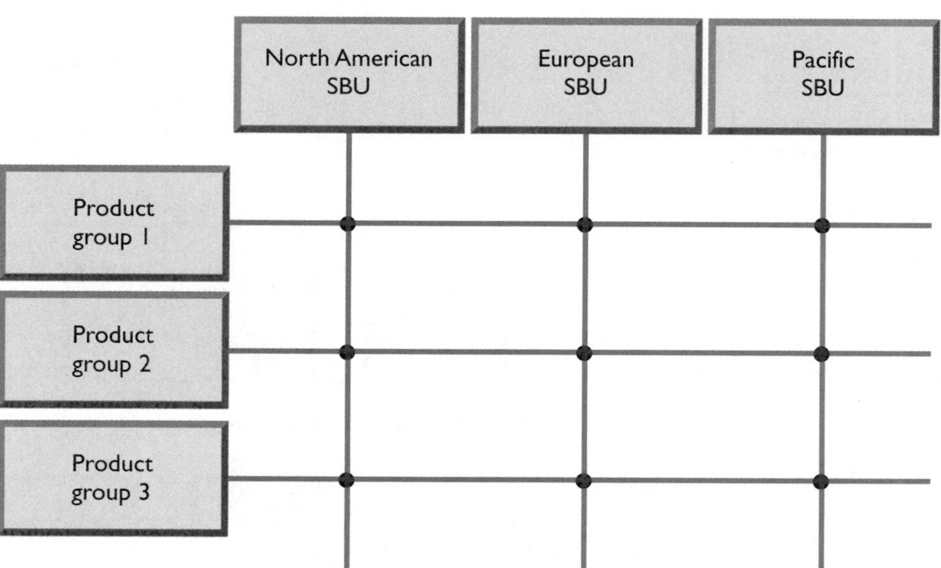

regions in which it operates. Managers in the foreign subsidiary control foreign operations and through a system of behavior controls report to divisional personnel back in the United States. They are also responsible, together with U.S. divisional personnel, for developing control and reward systems that promote the sharing of marketing or research and development information to achieve gains from synergies.

This structure both provides a great deal of local flexibility and gives divisional personnel in the United States considerable access to information about local affairs. The matrix structure also allows knowledge and experience to be transferred among geographic regions and among divisions and regions. Since it offers many opportunities for face-to-face contact between domestic and foreign managers, the matrix facilitates the transmission of a company's norms and values and, hence, the development of a global corporate culture. This is especially important for an international company, for which lines of communication are longer and information is subject to distortion. Club Med, for instance, fully exploits these synergies in the way it manages its holiday resorts.

The matrix also lets each home division balance production so that, for example, a lack of demand in one region of the world can be compensated by increased demand in another. For example, Philip Morris balances cigarette production so that slumping demand in the United States is countered by expanding demand in other regions of the world. Similarly, Japanese car manufacturers plan their international strategy to compensate for import restrictions or currency changes in the world market.

To make these matrix structures work, many companies strive to develop a strong international organizational culture to facilitate communication and coordination among managers. For example, companies are increasingly transferring managers between foreign and domestic operations so that they can develop a global view. Furthermore, to improve integration, companies are trying to form global networks of managers so that they can turn to each other for help. The idea is to create a **matrix in the mind**—an information network that lets a company capitalize globally on the skills and capabilities of its personnel.[22]

To foster the development of the matrix-in-the-mind concept and promote cooperation, companies are also using electronic integrating devices such as on-line teleconferencing, E-mail, and global intranets between different parts of their operations, both globally and domestically. For example, Hitachi coordinates its nineteen Japanese laboratories by means of an on-line teleconferencing system, and both Microsoft and Hewlett-Packard make extensive use of electronic computer systems to integrate their activities.

These integration mechanisms provide the extra coordination that helps the global-matrix structure work effectively. It is a very complex structure to operate and carries a high level of bureaucratic costs. However, the potential gains for a company in terms of superior efficiency, quality, innovation, and responsiveness to customers make these costs worthwhile. In the complicated game of international competition, companies must increasingly adopt many of these elements of a global matrix to survive. Nestlé found itself in this situation, as Strategy in Action 13.4 details.

Summary

Most large companies have an international component in their organizational structures. The issue for international companies, as for all others, is to adopt the structure and control system that best fits their strategy. The need to implement

13.4 STRATEGY in ACTION

Reengineering Nestlé's Global Structure

Nestlé, based in Vevey, Switzerland, is the world's biggest food company. In 1996, its global sales passed $50 billion a year, a figure it wants to double by the year 2001. To achieve this goal, the company has been pursuing an ambitious program of global expansion by acquiring many famous companies—for instance, Perrier, the French mineral water producer, and Rowntree Mackintosh, the British candy maker. In the United States, Nestlé bought the giant Carnation Company in 1985, and it also purchased Stouffer Foods and Contadina, among other large food companies.

Traditionally, Nestlé pursued a multidomestic strategy and managed its operating companies through a global area structure. In each country, each individual company (such as Carnation) was responsible for managing all aspects of its business-level strategy: in other words, companies were free to control their own product development and marketing and to manage all local operations. Acquisitions, expansions, and corporate resource decisions, such as capital investment, were made at the Vevey headquarters by Nestlé's corporate executives. Because all important decisions were made centrally, the size of the corporate staff increased dramatically. In the early 1990s, Nestlé's chairman, Helmut Maucher, realized that the company had major problems.

Corporate managers had become very remote from the difficulties experienced by the operating companies, and the centralized operating structure slowed down decision making. Nestlé had trouble responding quickly to the changing environment. Moreover, the company was forfeiting all the gains from global learning and possible synergies from resource sharing between operating companies and world regions because each company was operated separately and corporate executives made no attempt to integrate across companies around the world. Maucher realized that the company could not increase its sales and profits through its existing operating structure. To create more value, it had to find a new way of organizing its activities.

Maucher started the reengineering of Nestlé's structure from the top down. He massively reduced the power of corporate management by decentralizing authority to the managers of seven product groups, which he created to oversee the company's major product lines (for example, coffee, milk, and candy) on a global level. The role of each product group was to integrate the activities of operating companies in its area in order to obtain synergies and the gains from global learning. After the change, managers in the candy product group, for instance, began orchestrating the marketing and sale of Rowntree candy products, such as After Eight Mints and Smarties, throughout Europe, and sales climbed by 60 percent.

Maucher then turned his attention to the way the operating companies worked in each country or world region. He grouped all the operating companies within a country or region into one SBU and then created a team of SBU managers to link and coordinate the activities of the various companies in that country. When the different companies or divisions started to share joint purchasing, marketing, and sales activities, major cost savings resulted. In the United States, the SBU management team, headed by Timm Krull, reduced the number of sales officers nationwide from 115 to 22 and decreased the number of suppliers of packaging from 43 to 3.

Finally, Maucher decided to use a matrix structure to integrate the activities of the seven global product groups with the operations of Nestlé's country- or region-based SBUs. The goal of this matrix structure is to have the company pursue a transnational strategy, allowing it to obtain the gains from global learning and cost reduction. For example, Timm Krull now spends one week every month in Vevey with product-group executives, discussing ways of exploiting and sharing the resources of the company on a global basis. Moreover, managers are also looking to strategic alliances as a way of obtaining cost savings from shared distribution networks.[23]

So far, this new decentralized matrix structure has speeded decision making and product development and has enabled the company to integrate the activities of its many new acquisitions. Maucher hopes that it will help Nestlé reach its ambitious sales goal by the year 2001.

international strategy successfully has put increasing pressures on corporate managers to design the company's structure and controls so that the firm can respond to the challenges of the world market.

STRUCTURE AND CONTROL AT THE CORPORATE LEVEL

At the corporate level, strategic managers need to choose the organizational structure that will allow them to operate a number of different businesses efficiently. The structure normally chosen at the corporate level is the multidivisional structure. The larger and more diverse the businesses in the corporate portfolio, the more likely the company is to have a multidivisional structure. The reason is that each division requires its own set of specialist support functions to operate efficiently, and a headquarters corporate staff is needed to oversee and evaluate divisional operations to ensure that corporate goals are being achieved. Once strategic managers select a multidivisional structure, they must then make choices about what kind of integrating mechanisms and control systems to use to make the structure work efficiently. Later in this chapter, we discuss how the corporate-level strategies of unrelated diversification, vertical integration, and related diversification affect the choice of structure and control systems.

As discussed in Chapter 9, the main reason a company pursues vertical integration is to achieve *economies of integration* among divisions.[24] For example, a company can coordinate resource-scheduling decisions among divisions to reduce costs and improve quality. This might mean locating a rolling mill next to a steel furnace to save the costs of reheating steel ingots and make it easier to control the quality of the final product. Similarly, the chief gains from related diversification come from obtaining synergies or *economies of scope* among divisions. Divisions benefit by transferring of core competencies such as R&D or by sharing distribution and sales networks. With both these strategies, the benefits to the company come from some *transfer of resources* among divisions, and so the company must coordinate activities among divisions to secure these benefits. Consequently, structure and control must be designed to handle the transfer of resources among divisions.

In the case of unrelated diversification, however, the benefits to the company come from restructuring and establishing of an *internal capital market,* which allows corporate personnel to make better allocations of capital than would be possible in an external capital market. With this strategy, there are no transactions or exchanges among divisions, each operates separately. Structure and control must therefore be designed to allow each division to operate independently.

A company's choice of structure and control mechanisms depends on the degree to which a company must control the interactions among divisions. The more interdependent the divisions—that is, the more they depend on each other for resources—the more complex are the control and integration mechanisms required to integrate their activities and make the strategy work.[25] Consequently, as the need for integration increases, so, too, does the level of bureaucratic costs, but a company is willing to bear the increased bureaucratic costs stemming from a more complex strategy if the strategy creates more value.[26] This is illustrated in Table 13.3, which also indicates what forms of structure and control companies should adopt to manage the three corporate strategies. We examine them in detail in the next sections.

TABLE 13.3

Corporate Strategy and Structure and Control

			Type of Control		
Corporate Strategy	*Appropriate Structure*	*Need for Integration*	*Financial Control*	*Behavior Control*	*Organizational Culture*
Unrelated diversification	Multidivisional	Low (no exchanges between divisions)	Great use (e.g., ROI)	Some use (e.g., budgets)	Little use
Vertical integration	Multidivisional	Medium (scheduling resource transfers)	Great use (e.g., ROI, transfer pricing)	Great use (e.g., standardization, budgets)	Some use (e.g., shared norms and values)
Related diversification	Multidivisional	High (acheiving synergies between divisions by integrating roles)	Little use	Great use (e.g., rules, budgets)	Great use (e.g., norms, values, common language)

Unrelated Diversification

Because there are *no linkages* among divisions, unrelated diversification is the easiest and cheapest strategy to manage; it is associated with the lowest level of bureaucratic costs. The main requirement of the structure and control system is that it allow corporate managers to evaluate divisional performance easily and accurately. Thus, companies use a multidivisional structure, and each division is evaluated by financial controls such as return on investment. A company also applies sophisticated accounting controls to obtain information quickly from the divisions so that corporate managers can readily compare divisions on several dimensions. Textron and Dover are good examples of companies that manage their structures by using sophisticated computer networks and accounting controls, which allow them almost daily access to divisional performance.

Divisions normally have considerable autonomy, unless they fail to reach their ROI objectives. Generally, corporate headquarters is not interested in the types of business-level strategy pursued by each division unless there are problems. If problems arise, corporate headquarters may step in to take corrective action, perhaps replacing managers or providing additional financial resources, depending on the reason for the problem. If corporate personnel see no possibility of a turnaround, however, they may just as easily decide to divest the division. The multidivisional structure allows the unrelated company to operate its businesses as a portfolio of investments, which can be bought and sold as business conditions change. Usually, managers in the various divisions do not know one another, and they may not know what companies are in the corporate portfolio.

The use of financial controls to manage a company means that no integration among divisions is necessary. This is why the bureaucratic costs of managing an unrelated company are low. The biggest problem facing corporate personnel is determining capital allocations to the various divisions so that the overall profitability of the portfolio is maximized. They also have to oversee divisional managers and make sure that divisions are achieving ROI targets. Alco Standard's way of managing its businesses, described in Strategy in Action 13.5, demonstrates how to operate a strategy of unrelated diversification.

Vertical Integration

Vertical integration is a more expensive strategy to manage than unrelated diversification because *sequential resource flows* from one division to the next must be coordinated. The multidivisional structure effects such coordination. This structure provides the centralized control necessary for the vertically integrated company to achieve benefits from the control of resource transfers. Corporate personnel assume the responsibility for devising financial and behavior controls to promote the efficient transfer of resources among divisions. Complex rules and procedures are

13.5 STRATEGY *in* ACTION

Alco Standard Gets It Right

Alco Standard, based in Valley Forge, Pennsylvania, is one of the largest office supply companies in the United States, distributing office and paper supplies and materials through a nationwide network of wholly owned distribution companies. It pursues a highly successful strategy of unrelated diversification. Since 1965, the company has bought and sold more than 300 different companies. It used to be involved in more than 50 different industries, but now it operates 50 businesses in only two main areas: office products and paper distribution. However, the corporate office makes no attempt to intervene in the activities of the different divisions.

The policy of Alco's top management is that authority and control should be completely decentralized to the managers in each of the company's businesses. Each business is left alone to make its own manufacturing or purchasing decisions even though some potential synergies, in the form of corporationwide purchasing or marketing, are being lost. Top management pursues this nonintervention policy because it believes that the gains from allowing its managers to act as independent entrepreneurs exceed any potential economies of scope that might result from coordinating interdivisional activities. It believes that a decentralized operating system allows a big company to act in a way that is similar to a small company, avoiding the problem of growing bureaucracy and organizational inertia.

At Alco, top management interprets its role as relieving the divisions of administrative chores, such as bookkeeping and accounting, and collecting market information on competitive pricing and products, which allows divisional managers to improve their business-level strategy. Centralizing these information activities reduces each division's bureaucratic costs and provides the standardization that lets top management make better decisions about resource allocation. Alco's division heads are regarded as partners in the corporate enterprise and are rewarded through stock options linked to the performance of their divisions. So far, Alco has been very successful with its decentralized operating structure and has achieved a compound growth rate of 19 percent a year.

instituted to manage interdivisional relationships and specify how exchanges are to be made; consequently, bureaucratic costs rise. As previously noted, complex resource exchanges can lead to conflict among divisions, and corporate managers must try to minimize divisional conflicts.

Centralizing authority at corporate headquarters must be done with care in vertically related companies. It carries the risk of involving corporate managers in operating issues at the business level to the point at which the divisions lose their autonomy and motivation. As we point out in Chapter 11, the company must strike the right balance of centralized control at corporate headquarters and decentralized control at the divisional level if it is to implement this strategy successfully.

Because their interests are at stake, divisions need to have input into scheduling and decisions regarding resource transfer. For example, the plastics division in a chemical company has a vital interest in the activities of the oil division, for the quality of the products it gets from the oil division determines the quality of its own products. Divisional integrating mechanisms can bring about direct coordination and information transfers among divisions.[27] To handle communication among divisions, a company sets up task forces or teams for the purpose; it can also establish liaison roles. In high-tech and chemical companies, for example, integrating roles among divisions is common. These integrating mechanisms also increase bureaucratic costs.

Thus, a strategy of vertical integration is managed through a combination of corporate and divisional controls. Although the organizational structure and control systems used for managing this strategy have higher bureaucratic costs than those used for unrelated diversification, the benefits derived from vertical integration often outweigh its extra costs.

Related Diversification

In the case of related diversification, divisions share research and development knowledge, information, customer bases, and goodwill to obtain gains from synergies. The process is difficult to manage, and so a multidivisional structure is used to facilitate the transfer of resources to obtain synergies. Even with this structure, however, high levels of resource sharing and joint production by divisions make it hard for corporate managers to measure the performance of each individual division.[28] If a related company is to obtain gains from synergy, it has to adopt more complicated forms of integration and control at the divisional level to make the structure work efficiently.

First, financial control is difficult to use because divisions share resources, so it is not easy to measure the performance of an individual division. Therefore, a company needs to develop a corporate culture that stresses cooperation among divisions and corporate, rather than purely divisional, goals. Second, corporate managers must establish sophisticated integrating devices to ensure coordination among divisions. Integrating roles and teams are crucial because they provide the context in which managers from different divisions can meet and develop a common vision of corporate goals. Hewlett-Packard, for instance, created three new high-level integrating teams to ensure that the new products developed by its technology group made their way quickly to its product divisions. All this extra integration is very expensive, however, and must be carefully managed.

An organization with a multidivisional structure must have the right mix of incentives and rewards for cooperation if it is to achieve gains from sharing skills and resources among divisions.[29] With unrelated diversification, divisions operate autonomously, and the company can quite easily reward managers on their division's individual performance. With related diversification, however, rewarding divisions is more difficult because they are engaged in joint production, and strategic managers must be sensitive and alert to achieving equity in rewards among divisions. The aim always is to design the structure so that it can maximize the benefits from the strategy at the lowest bureaucratic cost.

Managing a strategy of related diversification also raises the issue of how much authority to centralize and how much to decentralize. Corporate managers need to take a close look at how their controls affect divisional performance and autonomy. If corporate managers get too involved in the day-to-day operations of the divisions, they can endanger divisional autonomy and undercut divisional managers' decision making.[30] Corporate managers, after all, see everything from a corporate, rather than a divisional, perspective. For instance, in the Heinz example mentioned earlier, management tried to develop one form of competitive advantage, a low-cost advantage, in every division.[31] Although this approach may work well for Heinz, it may be markedly inappropriate for a company that is operating a totally diverse set of businesses, each of which needs to develop its own unique competency. Too much corporate control can put divisional managers in a straitjacket. When too many managers become involved in managing the business, performance suffers and bureaucratic costs escalate. Companies such as IBM and General Motors experienced this problem; their corporate staffs became top-heavy, slowing decision making and draining the company's profits.

SPECIAL ISSUES IN STRATEGY-STRUCTURE CHOICE

As noted in Chapter 10, today many organizations are changing their corporate-level strategies and restructuring their organizations to find new ways to use their resources and capabilities to create value. In this section we focus on three strategy-structure issues that arise during the rebuilding or restructuring process: the management of mergers and acquisitions, the management of new ventures, and the management of outsourcing through the development of a network structure.

Mergers, Acquisitions, and Structure

In Chapter 10, we point out that mergers and acquisitions are the principal vehicles by which companies enter new product markets and expand the size of their operations.[32] Earlier we discuss the strategic advantages and disadvantages of mergers. We now consider how to design structure and control systems to manage new acquisitions. This issue is important because many acquisitions are unsuccessful, and one of the main reasons is that many companies do a very poor job of integrating the new divisions into their corporate structure, as happened at Compaq, profiled in the Opening Case.[33]

The first factor that makes managing new acquisitions difficult is the nature of the businesses a company acquires. If a company acquires businesses related to its existing businesses, it should find it fairly easy to integrate them into its corporate structure. The controls already being used in the related company can be adapted to the new divisions. To achieve gains from synergies, the company can expand its task forces or increase the number of integrating roles, so that the new divisions are drawn into the existing divisional structure.

If managers do not understand how to develop connections among divisions to permit gains from economies of scope, the new businesses will perform poorly.[34] Some authors have argued that this is why the quality of management is so important. A company must employ managers who have the ability to recognize synergies among apparently different businesses and so derive benefits from acquisitions and mergers.[35] For instance, Porter cites the example of Philip Morris, the cigarette producer, which took over Miller Brewing.[36] On the surface, these seem to be very different businesses. However, when their products are viewed as consumer products that are often bought and consumed together, the possibility of sales, distribution, and marketing synergies becomes clearer, and this merger was a great success. On the other hand, if companies acquire unrelated businesses only to operate them as a portfolio of investments, they should have no trouble managing the acquisitions.

Implementation problems are likely to arise only when corporate managers try to interfere in businesses they know little about or when they use inappropriate structure and controls to manage the new business and attempt to achieve the wrong kind of benefits from the acquisition. For example, if managers try to integrate unrelated companies with related ones, apply the wrong kinds of controls at the divisional level, or interfere in business-level strategy, corporate performance suffers as bureaucratic costs skyrocket. These mistakes explain why related acquisitions are sometimes more successful than unrelated ones.[37]

Therefore, strategic managers need to be very sensitive to the problems involved in taking over new businesses through mergers and acquisitions. Like other managers, they rarely appreciate the real issues inherent in managing the new business and the level of bureaucratic costs involved in managing a strategy until they have to deal with these issues personally. Even when acquiring closely related businesses, new managers must realize that each business has a unique culture, or way of doing things. Such idiosyncrasies must be understood in order to manage the new organization properly. Over time new management can change the culture and alter the internal workings of the company, but this is a difficult implementation task. Besides, the bureaucratic costs of changing a culture are often enormous because the top-management team and the organizational structure have to be changed in order to change the way people behave. We discuss this in detail in Chapter 14, which considers organizational politics and strategic change.

Internal New Ventures and Structure

The main alternative to growth through acquisition and merger is for a company to develop new businesses internally. In Chapter 10, we call this strategy internal *new venturing* and discuss its advantages for growth and diversification. Now we consider the design of the appropriate internal arrangements for encouraging the development of new ventures.

At the heart of new-venture design must be the realization by corporate managers that internal new venturing is a form of entrepreneurship. The design should encourage creativity and give new-venture managers the opportunity and resources to develop new products or markets. Hewlett-Packard, for example, gives managers a great deal of latitude in this respect. To encourage innovation, it allows them to work on informal projects while they carry out their assigned tasks.[38] More generally, management must choose the appropriate structure and controls for operating new ventures.[39]

One of the main design choices is the creation of **new-venture divisions**. To provide new-venture managers with the autonomy to experiment and take risks, the company sets up a new-venture division separate from other divisions and makes it a center for new product or project development. Away from the day-to-day scrutiny of top management, divisional personnel pursue the creation of new business as though they were external entrepreneurs. The division is operated by controls that reinforce the entrepreneurial spirit. Thus, market and output controls are inappropriate because they can inhibit risk taking. Instead, the company develops a culture for entrepreneurship in this division to provide a climate for innovation. Care must be taken, however, to institute bureaucratic controls that put some limits on freedom of action. Otherwise, costly mistakes may be made, and resources wasted on frivolous ideas.

In managing the new-venture division, it is important to use integrating mechanisms such as task forces and teams to screen new ideas. Managers from research and development, sales and marketing, and product development are heavily involved in this screening process. Generally, the champions of new products must defend their projects before a formal evaluation committee, consisting of proven entrepreneurs and experienced managers from the other divisions, to secure the resources for developing them. Companies such as 3M, IBM, and Texas Instruments are examples of successful companies that use this method for creating opportunities internally.

Care must be taken to preserve the autonomy of the new-venture division. As mentioned earlier, the costs of research and development are high, and the rewards uncertain. After spending millions of dollars, corporate managers often become concerned about the division's performance and introduce tight output controls or strong budgets to increase accountability. These measures hurt the entrepreneurial culture.

Sometimes, however, after creating a new invention, the new venture division wants to reap the benefits by producing and marketing it. If this happens, the division becomes an ordinary operating division and entrepreneurship declines.[40] Strategic managers must take steps to provide a structure that can sustain the entrepreneurial spirit.[41]

Hewlett-Packard has a novel way of dealing with new venturing. In the operating divisions, as soon as a new, self-supporting product is developed, a new division is formed to produce and market the product. By spinning off the product in this fashion, the company keeps all its divisions small and entrepreneurial. The arrangement also provides a good climate for innovation. However, Hewlett-Packard also found that having many new venture divisions was too expensive and so has merged some of them.

Internal new venturing is an important means by which large, established companies can maintain their momentum and grow from within.[42] The alternative is to acquire small businesses that have already developed some technological competency and to pump resources into them, which has been Microsoft's favored strategy in recent years as it enters the many different niches of the Internet software market. This approach can also succeed, and it obviously lessens management's burden if the company operates the new business as an independent entity.

By and large, companies are likely to operate in both ways, acquiring some new businesses and developing others internally. As increasing competition from abroad has threatened their dominance in existing businesses, companies have been forced to evaluate opportunities for maximizing long-term growth in new businesses, and many of them have made acquisitions.

Network Structure and the Virtual Organization

You will recall from Chapters 9 and 10 that the use of outsourcing is increasing rapidly as organizations recognize the many opportunities it offers to reduce costs and increase their flexibility. U.S. companies spent $100 billion on outsourcing in 1996, and this outlay reached $500 billion by 2000. Companies such as EDS, which manages the information systems of large organizations such as Xerox and Kodak, are major beneficiaries of this new organizing approach. On a global level, the development of a global network of strategic alliances between companies is an alternative to the use of the complex global-matrix structure.[43]

In order to implement outsourcing effectively, strategic managers must decide what organizational arrangements to adopt. Increasingly, a **network structure**—the set of strategic alliances that an organization creates with suppliers, manufacturers, and distributors to produce and market a product—is becoming the structure of choice to implement outsourcing. An example of a network structure is the series of strategic alliances that Japanese car companies—for instance, Toyota and Honda—formed with their suppliers of inputs such as car axles, gearboxes, and air conditioning systems. Members of the network work together on a long-term basis to find new ways to reduce costs and increase the quality of their products. Moreover, developing a network structure allows an organization to avoid the high costs of operating a complex organizational structure (the costs of employing many managers, for example).

Finally, a network structure allows a company to form strategic alliances with foreign suppliers, which gives managers access to low-cost foreign sources of inputs, keeping costs low. Strategy in Action 13.6 describes the network structure that NIKE uses to produce and market its sports shoes.

Some small companies that use a focus strategy go even further than NIKE and create a network structure to perform almost all their functional activities. Topsy Tail, a small Texas company that sells hair-styling gadgets such as false ponytails, has created strategic alliances with other companies that not only manufacture and distribute its products but also design, market, and package them. Apart from its CEO, Tomima Edmark, who orchestrates these alliances and is at the hub of the network, the company has almost no permanent employees—only outside companies and people who contract with Edmark to perform certain services, in return for which they receive a set fee.[46]

The ability of managers to develop a network structure to produce or provide the goods and services their customers want, rather than create a complex organizational structure to do so, has led many researchers and consultants to popularize the idea of the "virtual organization." The virtual organization is composed of people

13.6 STRATEGY *in* ACTION

NIKE's Network Structure

NIKE, located in Beaverton, Oregon, is the largest and most profitable sports shoe manufacturer in the world. The key to NIKE's success is the network structure that Philip Knight, NIKE's founder and CEO, created to allow his company to produce and market shoes. As discussed earlier, the most successful companies today simultaneously pursue a low-cost and a differentiation strategy. Knight realized this early on, and he created an organizational structure to allow his company to achieve this goal.

By far the largest function at NIKE's headquarters in Beaverton is the design function, staffed by talented designers who pioneer innovations in sports shoe design such as the air pump and Air Jordans that NIKE introduced so successfully. Designers use computer-aided design (CAD) to design their shoes, and all new-product information, including manufacturing instructions, is stored electronically. When the designers have done their work, they relay all the blueprints for the new products electronically to a network of suppliers and manufacturers throughout Southeast Asia with whom NIKE has formed strategic alliances.[44] Instructions for the design of a new sole, for example, may be sent to a supplier in Taiwan, and instructions for the leather uppers to a supplier in Malaysia. These suppliers produce the shoe parts, which are then sent for final assembly to a manufacturer in China with whom NIKE has established an alliance. From China these shoes are shipped to distributors throughout the world. Of the 99 million pairs of shoes NIKE makes each year, 99 percent are made in Southeast Asia.

There are two main advantages to this network structure for NIKE. First, NIKE's costs are very low because wages in Southeast Asia are a fraction of what they are in the United States and this gives NIKE a low-cost advantage. Second, NIKE is able to respond to changes in sports shoe fashion very quickly. Using its global computer system, NIKE can, literally overnight, change the instructions it gives to each of its suppliers so that within a few weeks new kinds of shoes are being produced by its foreign manufacturers.[45] If any of its alliance partners fail to perform up to NIKE's standards, they are simply replaced with new partners, so NIKE has great control over its network structure. In fact, the company works closely with its suppliers to take advantage of any new developments in technology that can help it reduce costs and increase quality.

The ability of NIKE to outsource all its manufacturing abroad allows Knight to keep NIKE's U.S. structure small and flexible. NIKE is able to use a functional structure to organize its activities, and Knight decentralizes control of the design process to teams that are assigned to develop each of the new kinds of sports shoes for which NIKE is known.

who are linked by computers, faxes, computer-aided design systems, and video teleconferencing and who may rarely if ever see one another face to face. People come and go as and when their services are needed, much as in a matrix structure, but they are not formal members of an organization, just functional experts who form an alliance with an organization, fulfill their contractual obligations, and then move on to the next project.

Andersen Consulting, the global management consulting company, is becoming just such a virtual organization. CEO George Shaheen says the company's headquarters are wherever he happens to be at the time. (He spends 80 percent of his time traveling.)[47] The company's 40,000 consultants often work from their homes, traveling to meet the company's clients throughout the world and only rarely stopping in at one of Andersen's branch offices to meet their superiors and colleagues. The consultants all pool their knowledge in a massive internal database they can easily access through computer and the company's intranet.

SUMMARY OF CHAPTER

This chapter brings together strategy formulation and strategy implementation and examines how a company's choice of strategy affects the form of its structure and control systems. The reason that many companies such as IBM and General Motors experience problems with their structure should now be clear: they have lost control over their structure, and their bureaucratic costs are escalating. The challenge for a company is to manage its structure and control systems so that it can economize on bureaucratic costs and ensure that they match the potential gains from its strategy. The following are the main points of the chapter:

- ✔ Implementing strategy through organizational structure and control is expensive, and companies need to constantly monitor and oversee their structures in order to economize on bureaucratic costs.
- ✔ At the functional level, each function requires a different kind of structure and control system to achieve its functional objectives.
- ✔ At the business level, the structure and control system must be designed to achieve business-level objectives, which means managing the relationships among all the functions to permit the company to develop a distinctive competency.
- ✔ Cost-leadership and differentiation strategies each require a structure and control system that matches the source of the company's competitive advantage. Implementing a simultaneous cost-leadership and differentiation strategy is the problem facing many companies today.
- ✔ As a company moves from a multidomestic to an international, global, and transnational strategy, it needs to switch to a more complex structure that allows it to coordinate increasingly complex resource transfers. Similarly, it needs to adopt a more complex integration and control system that facilitates global learning. When there are gains to be derived from synergy, companies frequently adopt a global-matrix structure to share knowledge and expertise.
- ✔ At the corporate level, a company must choose the structure and control system that will allow it to operate a collection of businesses efficiently.
- ✔ Unrelated diversification, vertical integration, and related diversification require different forms of structure and control if the benefits of pursuing the strategy are to be realized.
- ✔ As companies change their corporate strategies over time, they must change their structure because different strategies are managed in different ways.
- ✔ The profitability of mergers and acquisitions depends on the structure and control systems that companies adopt to manage them and the way a company integrates them into its existing businesses.
- ✔ To encourage internal new venturing, companies must design a structure that gives the new-venture division the autonomy it needs in order to develop new products and protect it from excessive interference by corporate managers.
- ✔ Increasingly, the growth of outsourcing has led companies to develop network structures. The virtual corporation is becoming a reality as computer information systems become more sophisticated.

DISCUSSION QUESTIONS

1. How should (a) a high-tech company, (b) a fast-food franchise, and (c) a small manufacturing company design their functional structures and control systems to implement a generic strategy?
2. If a related company begins to buy unrelated businesses, in what ways should it change its structure or control mechanisms to manage the acquisitions?
3. How would you design a structure and control system to encourage entrepreneurship in a large, established corporation?

Practicing Strategic Management

SMALL-GROUP EXERCISE
Deciding on an Organizational Structure

Break up into groups of three to five people, and discuss the following scenario:

You are a group of managers of a major soft drinks company that is going head-to-head with Coca-Cola to increase market share. Your strategy is to increase your product range and offer a soft drink in every segment of the market to attract customers. Currently, you have a functional structure. What you are trying to work out now is how best to implement your strategy in order to launch your new products. Should you move to a more complex kind of product structure, and, if so, which one? Alternatively, should you establish new-venture divisions and spin off each kind of new soft drink into its own company so that each company can focus its resources on its market niche? There is also a global dimension to your strategy, because it is your intention to compete with Coca-Cola for market share worldwide, and you must consider what is the best structure globally as well as domestically.

1. Debate the pros and cons of the different possible organizational structures, and decide which structure you are going to implement.
2. Debate the pros and cons of the different types of global structures, and decide which is most appropriate and which will best fit in with your domestic structure.

STRATEGIC MANAGEMENT PROJECT
Module 13

This part of the Strategic Management Project requires you to take the information you have collected in the last two chapters on organizational structure and controls and link it to the strategy pursued by your company, which you identified in earlier chapters.

1. What are the sources of your company's distinctive competencies? Which functions are most important to it? How does your company design its structure at the *functional level* to enhance its (a) efficiency, (b) quality, (c) innovation, (d) and responsiveness to customers?
2. What is your company's business-level strategy? How does it design its structure and control systems to enhance and support its business-level strategy? For example, what steps does it take to further cross-functional integration? Does it have a functional, product, or matrix structure?
3. How does your company's culture support its strategy? Can you determine any ways in which its top-management team influences its culture?
4. What kind of international strategy does your company pursue? How does it control its global activities? What kind of structure does it use? Why?
5. At the corporate level, does your company use a multidivisional structure? Why or why not? What crucial implementation problems must your company manage in order to implement its strategy effectively? For example, what kind of integration mechanisms does it employ?
6. Based on this analysis, does your company have high or low bureaucratic costs? Is this level of bureaucratic costs justified by the value it can create through its strategy?
7. Can you suggest ways of altering the company's structure to reduce the level of bureaucratic costs?
8. Can you suggest ways of altering the company's structure or control systems to allow it to create more value? Would this change increase or decrease bureaucratic costs?
9. In sum, do you think your company has achieved a good fit between its strategy and structure?

ARTICLE FILE 13

Find an example(s) of a company that has changed its structure and control systems to manage its strategy better. What were the problems with its old structure? What changes did it make to its structure and control systems? What effects does it expect these changes to have on performance?

EXPLORING THE WEB
Matching Strategy and Structure

Search the Web for a company that is in the process of modifying or changing its organizational structure (domestic or global) to manage its new strategy. What structure is it moving toward? Why is this structure more appropriate than the old one?

CLOSING CASE

Hughes Aircraft Reengineers Its Structure

HUGHES AIRCRAFT is one of the large U.S. defense companies that has been battered by the end of the cold war and the decline in the defense budget. Hughes had been accustomed to a protected environment in which lavish government revenues allowed it to develop advanced technology for military uses, such as missiles, satellites, and radar systems. However, by 1990 Hughes was confronted with a major strategic problem. How could it compete in the new environment in which government revenues were scarce? To survive, Hughes had to find a new strategy based on the development of new technology for nonmilitary uses—and find it fast.

As a first step in changing the company's direction, C. Michael Armstrong, an ex-IBM top manager, was appointed CEO of Hughes in 1991. In IBM's European division, Armstrong had developed a reputation as someone who could turn around a company and redeploy its resources quickly and effectively; investors hoped he could do so at Hughes.

Armstrong began his task by analyzing the company's strategy and structure. What he found was a firm pursuing a differentiated strategy based on developing advanced technological products. To pursue its differentiated strategy, Hughes had developed a divisional structure to lead its development efforts. It had created seven separate technology divisions, each responsible for a different kind of product—missiles, radar, and so forth. Over time, the organization had become very tall and centralized, as each technology division developed its own empire to support its efforts. The primary coordination between divisions took place at the top of the organization, where top divisional managers met regularly with corporate managers to report on and plan future product developments.

Armstrong recognized that this fit between strategy and structure might be appropriate for a company operating in a protected environment, in which money was not a problem. However, it was not appropriate for a company facing intense pressure to lower costs and develop products for nonmilitary applications, such as consumer electronics and home satellites. The divisional structure duplicated expensive R&D activities, and no mechanism was in place to promote the sharing of knowledge and expertise among the different divisions. Moreover, there were few incentives for managers to cut costs because scarce resources had not been a problem, and managers had been rewarded mainly for the success of their product development efforts. Armstrong realized that to make the company more competitive and improve the way it utilized its skills and resources, he had to find a new operating strategy and structure.

Armstrong began the process of change by focusing the company's strategy on customers and markets, not on technology and products. Henceforth, the needs of customers, not the needs of technology, would be the logic behind the organization of the company's activities. He changed the structure from a divisional one based on technology to one based on the needs of customers. The seven technology divisions were reengineered into five market groups according to the kinds of customers' needs they satisfied. Thus, consumer electronics became one market group, and industrial and commercial applications became another. Then technological expertise was reorganized to serve the needs of each kind of customer.

Continuing his reengineering program, Armstrong slashed the number of levels in the managerial hierarchy, eliminating two levels in order to bring managers closer to the customer. He continued this reengineering effort by decentralizing authority and pushing decision making down into the divisions, so that lower-level managers could better respond to customers' needs. In addition, he reorganized the company's international operations by transferring managers from the United States to foreign countries so that they would be closer to their customers.

To make this new customer-oriented structure work effectively, Armstrong also changed the organization's control systems. He created a system of output controls based on benchmarking competitors' costs to provide managers with standards against which to evaluate their performance and to force them to pay attention to costs and quality. He then set up new incentive programs for managers and workers at all levels, linking the programs to achievement of the new targets for efficiency, quality, and responsiveness to customers. Finally, he worked hard with his top management team to establish and promote the norms and values of a customer-oriented organizational culture across the new market divisions. Henceforth, at Hughes technology would be made to fit the customer, not vice versa.

Armstrong's efforts to engineer a new fit between strategy and structure at Hughes have been spectacularly successful. His top management team has fully bought into the new corporate culture, and divisional managers are adopting new entrepreneurial values based on meeting customers' needs. Some of the company's early successes include the launch of its RCA minidish satellite television system and the development of one of the largest private space-based satellite systems in the world.[48] Its stock price has soared as Hughes has used its leading-edge technology to provide customers with quality products at competitive prices. With its new simultaneous differentiation/low-cost strategy, Hughes is performing well in the new competitive environment.

Case Discussion Questions

1. What problems did Armstrong discover regarding strategy and structure with Hughes?
2. What steps did he take to reengineer the company?

End Notes

1. Press release, www.compaq.com, (September 1999).
2. M. Hays, "Compaq Maps Future," *Informationweek*, June 17, 1998, p. 14.
3. A. Taylor III, "Compaq Looks Inside for Salvation," *Fortune*, August 16, 1999, pp. 124–128.
4. W. G. Ouchi, "The Relationship Between Organizational Structure and Organizational Control," *Administrative Science Quarterly*, 22 (1977), 95–113.
5. R. Bunderi, "Intel Researchers Aim to Think Big While Staying Close to Development," *Research-Technology Management* (March/April 1998), 3–4.
6. K. M. Eisenhardt, "Control: Organizational and Economic Approaches," *Management Science*, 16 (1985), 134–148.
7. J. R. Galbraith, *Designing Complex Organizations* (Reading, Mass.: Addison-Wesley, 1973); P. R. Lawrence and J. W. Lorsch, *Organization and Environment* (Cambridge, Mass.: Harvard University Press, 1967); D. Miller, "Strategy Making and Structure: Analysis and Implications for Performance," *Academy of Management Journal*, 30 (1987), 7–32.
8. M. E. Porter, *Competitive Strategy: Techniques for Analyzing Industries and Competitors* (New York: Free Press, 1980); D. Miller, "Configurations of Strategy and Structure," *Strategic Management Journal*, 7 (1986), 233–249.
9. D. Miller and P. H. Freisen, *Organizations: A Quantum View* (Englewood Cliffs, N.J.: Prentice-Hall, 1984).
10. J. Woodward, *Industrial Organization: Theory and Practice* (London: Oxford University Press, 1965); Lawrence and Lorsch, *Organization and Environment.*
11. C. J. Loomis, "The Reed That Citicorp Leans On," *Fortune*, July 12, 1993, pp. 90–93.
12. R. E. White, "Generic Business Strategies, Organizational Context and Performance: An Empirical Investigation," *Strategic Management Journal*, 7 (1986), 217–231.
13. Porter, *Competitive Strategy;* Miller, "Configurations of Strategy and Structure."
14. E. Deal and A. A. Kennedy, *Corporate Cultures* (Reading, Mass.: Addison-Wesley, 1985); "Corporate Culture," *Business Week*, October 27, 1980, pp. 148–160.
15. B. Saporito, "How to Revive a Fading Firm," *Fortune*, March 22, 1993, p. 80.
16. G. Imperato, "3M Expert Tells How to Run Meetings that Really Work," *Fast Company*, May 23, 1999, p. 18.
17. D. Miller, "Configurations of Strategy and Structure," in R. E. Miles and C. C. Snow, *Organizational Strategy, Structure, and Process* (New York: McGraw-Hill, 1978).
18. E. Nee, "Reboot," *Forbes*, May 4, 1998, pp. 23–25.
19. Annual Report, www.wang.com, (1999).
20. Lawrence and Lorsch, *Organization and Environment.*
21. J. Stopford and L. Wells, *Managing the Multinational Enterprise* (London: Longman, 1972).
22. C. A. Bartlett and S. Ghoshal, *Managing Across Borders: The Transnational Solution* (Cambridge, Mass.: Harvard Business School, 1991).
23. A. Edgecliffe-Johnson, "Nestle and Pillsbury Forge Ice Cream Alliance in U.S.," *Financial Times*, August 20, 1999, p. 15.
24. G. R. Jones and C. W. L. Hill, "Transaction Cost Analysis of Strategy-Structure Choice," *Strategic Management Journal*, 9 (1988), 159–172.
25. Ibid.
26. R. A. D'Aveni and D. J. Ravenscraft, "Economies of Integration Versus Bureaucracy Costs: Does Vertical Integration Improve Performance?" *Academy of Management Journal*, 5 (1994), 1167–1206.
27. Lawrence and Lorsch, *Organization and Environment;* Galbraith, *Designing Complex Organizations;* M. E. Porter, *Competitive Advantage: Creating and Sustaining Superior Performance* (New York: Free Press, 1985).
28. P. R. Nayyar, "Performance Effects of Information Asymmetry and Economies of Scope in Diversified Service Firm," *Academy of Management Journal*, 36 (1993), 28–57.
29. L. R. Gomez-Mejia, "Structure and Process of Diversification, Compensation Strategy, and Performance," *Strategic Management Journal*, 13 (1992), 381–397.
30. C. C. Markides, and P. J. Williamson, "Related Diversification, Core Competencies, and Corporate Performance," *Strategic Management Journal*, 15 (Special Issue, 1994), 149–165.
31. Porter, *Competitive Strategy.*
32. M. S. Salter and W. A. Weinhold, *Diversification Through Acquisition* (New York: Free Press, 1979).
33. F. T. Paine and D. J. Power, "Merger Strategy: An Examination of Drucker's Five Rules for Successful Acquisitions," *Strategic Management Journal*, 5 (1984), 99–110.
34. G. D. Bruton, B. M. Oviatt, and M. A. White, "Performance of Acquisitions of Distressed Firms," *Academy of Management Journal*, 4 (1994), 972–989.
35. C. K. Prahalad and R. A. Bettis, "The Dominant Logic: A New Linkage Between Diversity and Performance," *Strategic Management Journal*, 7 (1986), 485–501; Porter, *Competitive Strategy.*
36. Porter, *Competitive Strategy.*
37. H. Singh and C. A. Montgomery, "Corporate Acquisitions and Economic Performance," unpublished manuscript, 1984.
38. N. D. Fast, "The Future of Industrial New Venture Departments," *Industrial Marketing Management*, 8 (1979), 264–279.
39. R. A. Burgelman, "Managing the New Venture Division: Research Findings and the Implications for Strategic Management," *Strategic Management Journal*, 6 (1985), 39–54.
40. Fast, "The Future of Industrial New Venture Departments."
41. Burgelman, "Managing the New Venture Division."

42. R. A. Burgelman, "Corporate Entrepreneurship and Strategic Management: Insights from a Process Study," *Management Science,* 29 (1983), 1349–1364.
43. B. Kogut, "Joint Ventures: Theoretical and Empirical Perspectives," *Strategic Management Journal*, 9 (1988), 319–332.
44. G. S. Capowski, "Designing a Corporate Identity," *Management Review* (June 1993), 37–38.
45. J. Marcia, "Just Doing It," *Distribution* (January 1995), 36–40.
46. "The Outing of Outsourcing," *Economist*, November 25, 1995, p. 36.
47. "Andersen's Androids," *Economist*, May 4, 1996, p. 72.
48. J. Cole, "New CEO at Hughes Studied Its Managers, Got Them on His Side," *Wall Street Journal,* March 30, 1993, pp. A1, A8.

14 Implementing Strategic Change

OPENING CASE

From Reengineering to E-Engineering at Bank of America

By 1999, Bank of America had grown to become the largest financial institution in the United States as a result of a series of mergers, most noticeably the merger with NationsBank in 1998.[1] As it has grown, Bank of America has been constantly changing its structure and control systems to help it operate more effectively. In the process it has made particular use of two change techniques: reengineering and E-engineering.

Reengineering is a change technique that helps an organization make better use of its resources; it involves changing task relationships and organizational structure. At Bank of America, for example, before the use of reengineering, it was quite common for customers to get passed around among four or five different bank employees for even routine banking matters. This was time consuming and tedious and often left customers feeling frustrated. Bank of America used reengineering to change and improve the customer-employee relationship.

Rather than having different employees be responsible for different aspects of the customer service encounter, it trained each customer service employee in all the multiple jobs needed to satisfy a customer's needs. In the process of doing so, it pushed down responsibility to each employee, which flattened the hierarchy of authority. Bank of America also created teams of specialized customer service employees to handle the needs of specific groups of customers, such as commercial customers, so that employees could learn from one another and work together. As a result of this process, fewer employees were needed to serve customers and customer and employee satisfaction increased.

Since then, Bank of America has utilized another technique to improve its customer service operations: E-engineering. Change in E-engineering is brought about through the use of new information technologies to smooth and enhance customer service. As we have seen in previous chapters, it often involves the use of the Internet. Bank of America has taken advantage of the Internet to start on-line banking. Customers are able to access their accounts and analyze their transactions; when problems arise, they can communicate with customer service employees through E-mail and soon will also be able to use instant messaging. In addition, Bank of America is establishing systems that allow customers to pay their bills on-line and make deposits on-line so that in the future there are likely to be far fewer customer visits to banks. This frees up employees' time to pamper current customers and pursue new ones, such as college students entering the work force and people who have recently relocated to a new city. In a banking environment that is becoming dominated by a few large banks, finding new customers is very important.

Moreover, Bank of America is using E-engineering to streamline its internal operations. All employees now record the details and results of customer service operations on-line so that managers have instant access to daily operations. Managers also have access to immediate information from branches around the United States. In an environment where banks can now provide other financial services—for instance, stockbroking, investment banking, and insurance—such information systems make it easier to tailor the bank's services to the needs of individual customers.[2] Finally, Bank of America is expanding globally because many of its large corporate clients, such as Alamo Rent-A-Car and Delta, have global operations, and a global Internet-based information system makes it easy to handle financial services on a worldwide scale.

In all these ways, E-engineering is allowing Bank of America to change its structure so that it can better pursue its strategy of differentiation in today's competitive banking environment.

OVERVIEW

In today's global environment, change rather than stability is the order of the day. Rapid changes in technology, competition, and customers' demands have increased the rate at which companies need to alter their strategies and structures to survive in the marketplace. As we discuss in Chapter 4, however, one of the principal reasons companies fail is their inability to change themselves and adapt to a new competitive environment because of *organizational inertia*.[3] Once an organization has been created and task and role relationships are defined, a set of forces is put into operation that makes an organization resistant to change. In considering *The Icarus Paradox* in Chapter 4, for example, we note the tendency of organizations to continue to rely on the skills and capabilities that made them successful even when those capabilities do not match the new competitive environment.[4] We also point out that there is another cause of organizational inertia: the conflict and power struggles that occur at the top of an organization as managers strive to influence decision making to protect and enhance their own positions.

In this chapter, we look at the issue strategic managers must deal with as they seek to overcome organizational inertia and change an organization's strategy and structure—the issue of how to implement strategic change. Until now in our study of strategic management, we have treated strategy formulation and implementation from an impersonal, rational perspective, one from which decisions are made coldly and logically. In reality, this picture of how strategic managers decide on and change strategy and structure is incomplete; it ignores the way power and political processes influence the decision-making process and the selection of organizational objectives.

This chapter discusses why it is difficult to change organizations and outlines the issues and problems that managers must address and solve if they are to succeed in changing a company's strategy and structure so that it matches new competitive environments. By the end of this chapter, you will understand the forces at play when strategic managers try to change their organizations and the role of power and politics in helping to implement change successfully.

STRATEGIC CHANGE

Strategic change is the movement of a company away from its present state toward some desired future state to increase its competitive advantage. In the last decade, most large *Fortune* 500 companies have gone through some kind of strategic change as their managers have tried to strengthen their existing core competencies and build new ones to compete more effectively.[5] Most of these companies have been pursuing one of three major kinds of strategic change: reengineering and E-engineering; restructuring; and innovation (see Figure 14.1).

Reengineering and E-Engineering

Often, because of drastic unexpected changes in the environment, such as the emergence of aggressive new competitors or technological breakthroughs, strategic managers need to develop a new strategy and structure to raise the level of their business's performance. One way of changing a company to allow it to operate more effectively is by reengineering. **Reengineering** is the "fundamental rethinking and radical redesign of business processes to achieve dramatic improvements in critical, contemporary measures of performance such as cost, quality, service, and speed."[6] As this definition suggests, strategic managers who use reengineering must completely rethink how their organization goes about its business. Instead of concentrating on a company's *functions*, strategic managers make *business processes* the focus of attention.

A **business process** is any activity (such as order processing, inventory control, or product design) that is vital to delivering goods and services to customers quickly or that promotes high quality or low costs. Business processes are not the

FIGURE 14.1

Three Major Types of Strategic Change

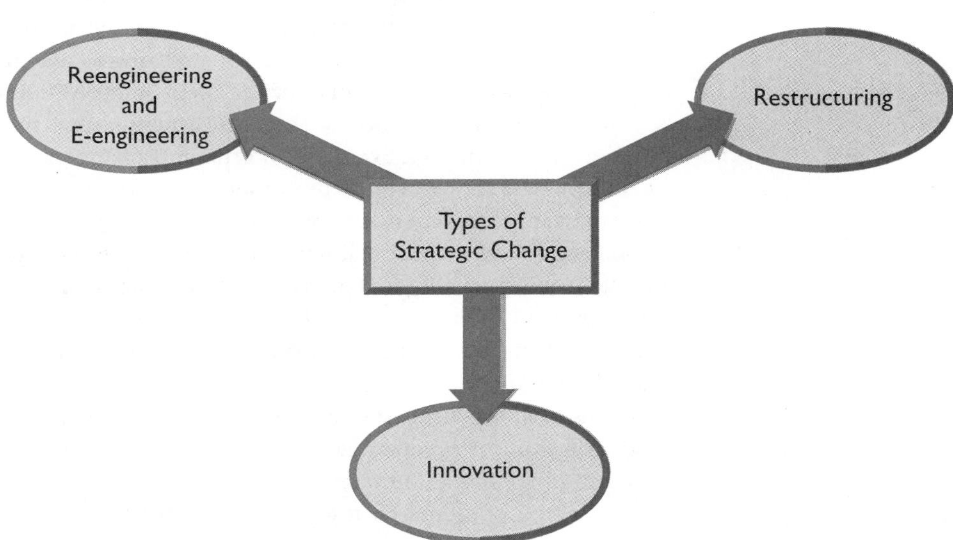

responsibility of any one function but *cut across functions*. Hallmark Cards, for example, reengineered its card-design process with great success. Before the reengineering effort, artists, writers, and editors worked in different functions to produce all kinds of cards. After reengineering, these same artists, writers, and editors were put in cross-functional teams, each of which now works on a specific type of card, such as birthday, Christmas, or Mother's Day. As a result, the time it took to bring a new card to market dropped from years to months, and Hallmark's performance increased dramatically.

Because reengineering focuses on business processes and not on functions, an organization that reengineers always has to adopt a different approach to organizing its activities. Organizations that take up reengineering ignore deliberately the existing arrangement of tasks, roles, and work activities. They start the reengineering process with the customer (not the product or service) and ask, How can we reorganize the way we do our work, our business processes, to provide the best quality and the lowest-cost goods and services to the customer?

Frequently, when companies ask this question, they realize that there are more effective ways to organize their activities. For example, a business process that currently involves members of ten different functions working sequentially to provide goods and services might be performed by one person or a few people at a fraction of the cost after reengineering. Often, individual jobs become increasingly complex, and people are grouped into cross-functional teams as business processes are reengineered to reduce costs and increase quality. This occurred at Eastman Chemicals as it reengineered itself to raise quality and responsiveness to customers.

Reengineering and total quality management (TQM), discussed in Chapter 5, are highly interrelated and complementary. After reengineering has taken place and the question, What is the best way to provide customers with the goods or service they require? has been answered, TQM takes over, focusing on the next question: How can we now continue to improve and refine the new process and find better ways of managing task and role relationships? Successful organizations examine both questions simultaneously and continuously attempt to identify new and better processes for meeting the goals of increased efficiency, quality, and customer responsiveness. Thus, they are always seeking to improve their visions of their desired future state. Another example of reengineering is the change program that took place at IBM Credit which is described in Strategy in Action 14.1.

As this example shows, the introduction of a new computer-based information system was an important aspect of change at IBM. So important has the development of new information systems been for a company's internal operations and for the way that it manages the external environment that the term E-engineering been coined to refer to change efforts centered on the introduction of new software systems. We have seen in previous chapters how the use of Internet-based systems can change the way a company's structure and control systems operate. For example, we saw how at Cypress Semiconductor the CEO uses the company's on-line management information system to monitor his managers' activities and help him keep the organizational hierarchy flat. We saw, too, how Oracle and Compaq are using Internet-based systems to streamline their operations and forge better links with their customers. E-engineering is likely to keep gaining in importance as it alters the way a company organizes its value creation functions and links them together to improve its performance.

14.1 **STRATEGY *in* ACTION**

A New Approach at IBM Credit

IBM Credit, a wholly owned division of IBM, manages the financing and leasing of IBM computers, particularly mainframes, to IBM's customers. Before the company's reengineering, when a financing request arrived at the division's headquarters in Old Greenwich, Connecticut, it went through a five-step approval process, involving the activities of five different functions. First, the IBM salesperson called up the credit department, which logged the request and recorded details about the potential customer. Second, this information was brought to the credit-checking department, where a credit check on the potential customer was made. Third, when the credit check was complete, the request was taken to the contracts department, which wrote the contract. Fourth, from there the request went to the pricing department, which determined the actual financial details of the loan, such as the interest rate and the term of the loan. Finally, the whole package of information was assembled by the dispatching department and was delivered to the sales representative, who gave it to the customer.

This series of cross-functional activities took an average of seven days to complete, and sales representatives constantly complained that this delay resulted in a low level of customer responsiveness, which reduced customer satisfaction. Also, potential customers were tempted to shop around for financing and even to look at competitors' machines. The delay in closing the deal caused uncertainty for all concerned.

The change process began when two senior IBM credit managers reviewed the whole finance-approval process. They found that the time spent by different specialists in the different functions actually processing a loan application was only ninety minutes. The approval process took seven days because of the delay in transmitting information and requests between departments. The managers also came to realize that the activities taking place in each department were not complex; each department had its own computer system containing its own work procedures, but the work done in each department was pretty routine.

Armed with this information, IBM managers concluded that the approval process could, in fact, be reengineered into one overarching process handled by one person with a computer system containing all the necessary information and work procedures to perform the five loan-processing activities. If the application proved to be very complex, a team of experts stood ready to help process it, but IBM found that after the reengineering a typical application could be finished in four hours rather than the previous seven days. A sales representative could go back to the customer the same day to close the deal, and all the uncertainty surrounding the transaction was removed. As reengineering consultants M. Hammer and J. Champy note, this *dramatic* performance increase was brought about by a *radical* change to the *process* as a whole.[7] Change through reengineering requires managers to go back to the basics and analyze each step in the work process to identify a better way of coordinating and integrating the activities necessary to provide customers with goods and services.

Restructuring

Strategic managers also turn to restructuring as a means of implementing strategic change aimed at improving performance. **Restructuring** has two basic steps. First, an organization reduces its level of differentiation and integration by eliminating divisions, departments, or levels in the hierarchy. Second, an organization *downsizes* by reducing the number of its employees to decrease operating costs. When Jack Smith took over as the head of General Motors, for example, GM had more than twenty-two levels in the hierarchy and more than 20,000 corporate managers. Describing his organization as a top-heavy bureaucracy, Smith quickly moved to slash costs and restructure the company. Today, while still tall, GM has only twelve levels in the hierarchy and half as many corporate managers.

Changes in the relationships between divisions or functions are common in restructuring programs. IBM, in an effort to cut development costs and speed cooperation among engineers, created a new division to take control of the production of microprocessors and memory systems. This restructuring move took engineers from IBM's thirteen divisions and grouped them in a brand-new headquarters in Austin, Texas, to increase their effectiveness.

There are many reasons why restructuring becomes necessary and why an organization may need to downsize its operations.[8] Sometimes an unforeseen change occurs in the business environment: perhaps a shift in technology makes a company's products obsolete, or a worldwide recession reduces the demand for its products. An organization may also find itself with excess capacity because customers no longer want the goods and services it provides, viewing them as outdated or of poor value for the money. Sometimes, too, organizations downsize because they have grown excessively tall and bureaucratic, and operating costs have skyrocketed. Even companies that hold a strong position may choose to restructure, simply to build and improve their competitive advantage and stay on top. Strategy in Action 14.2 illustrates the effort of a strong company, Quaker Oats, to improve its performance through restructuring.

All too often, however, companies must downsize and lay off employees because they have failed to continually monitor the operation of their basic business processes and have not made the incremental changes in strategies and structures that would help them contain costs and adjust to changing conditions. Paradoxically, because they have not paid attention to the need to reengineer themselves, they are forced into a position in which restructuring becomes the only way they can survive in an increasingly competitive environment.

14.2 STRATEGY *in* ACTION

Quaker Oats Wields the Ax

In six years, James F. Doyle, the head of the Gatorade division at Quaker Oats, had made the division the most profitable in the company. Each year sales and profits had increased despite the fact that the company as a whole was having a rough time because of its disastrous acquisition of the Snapple company, which it sold off in 1997 at a $1.4 billion loss. It was this fiasco that had led to the appointment of a new CEO, Robert S. Morrison, in 1998.

Imagine Doyle's surprise when, with no warning at all, Morrison told Doyle that he believed Quaker Oats had an unnecessarily complex structure and that he was eliminating the entire level of top management at Quaker Oats—the level that included Doyle. Morrison then promoted ten lower-level executives to head each of the company's food lines, such as Rice-a-Roni, Life Cereal, and Gatorade, and indicated that in the future they would report directly to him.[9] Morrison believes this move will allow him to better monitor and manage the performance of each business line and save Quaker Oats millions of dollars a year.

Innovation

As already noted, restructuring often may be necessary because changes in technology make an organization's technology, or the goods and services it produces, obsolete. For example, changes in technology have made computers both much cheaper to manufacture and more powerful and have affected what customers want. If organizations are to avoid being left behind in the competitive race to produce new goods and services, they must take steps to introduce new products or develop new technologies to produce those products reliably and at low cost.

You will recall from earlier discussions that **innovation** is the process by which organizations use their skills and resources to create new technologies or goods and services in order to change and respond better to the needs of their customers.[10] Innovation can bring a company spectacular success. Apple Computer, for instance, changed the face of the computer industry when it introduced its personal computer. Honda changed the face of the small motorbike market when it introduced 50-cc motorcycles, and Mary Kay cosmetics changed the way cosmetics were sold to customers when it introduced its at-home cosmetics parties and its personalized style of selling.

Along with change generated by innovation, however, comes a high level of risk because the outcomes of research and development activities are often uncertain.[11] Thus, while innovation can lead to the kind of change organizations want—the introduction of profitable new technologies and products—it can also usher in undesirable change—technologies that are inefficient and products customers don't want. In 1998, Informix, a software maker, almost went bankrupt when demand for its main database software plummeted because of competition from Oracle. It survived by developing Internet software for niche markets and by 1999 was profitable again.[12]

Innovation is one of the most difficult change processes to manage. As we discuss in previous chapters, when organizations rely on innovation as the source of their competitive advantage, they need to adopt flexible structures such as matrix or cross-functional team structures, which give people the freedom to experiment and be creative.[13] Functions need to coordinate their activities and work together if innovation is to be successful, and companies that rely on innovation have to facilitate the change effort and support the efforts of their members to be creative. For example, the term *skunkworks* was coined at Lockheed when that company set up a specialized unit, separate from its regular functional organization, to pioneer the development of a new spy plane, the U2. Creating a separate unit allowed managers to act more flexibly and autonomously. To try to increase the success rate of innovation and new-product development, many high-tech organizations have developed the role of "product champion" and appointed an expert manager to head a new team and lead a new project from its beginning to commercialization.[14] Of all the kinds of change programs that strategic managers can implement, innovation has the prospects for the greatest long-term success but also the greatest risks.

In order to understand the issues involved in implementing these kinds of strategic change, it is useful to focus on the series of distinct steps that strategic managers must follow if the change process is to succeed.[15] These steps are listed in Figure 14.2 and discussed in the rest of this chapter.

FIGURE 14.2

Stages in the Change Process

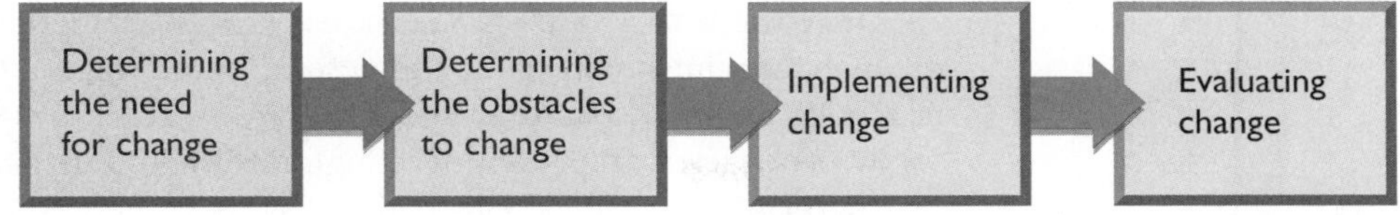

DETERMINING THE NEED FOR CHANGE

The first step in the change process is for strategic managers to recognize the need for change. Sometimes this need is obvious, as when divisions are fighting or when competitors introduce a product that is clearly superior to anything that the company has in production. More often, however, managers have trouble determining that something is going wrong in the organization. Problems may develop gradually, and organizational performance may slip for a number of years before it becomes obvious. At GM and IBM for example, profitability fell, but because these were reputable companies, the fall caused little stir. After a lapse of time, however, investors realized that these companies' stock was overvalued, and its price plunged when investors saw that managers were not taking the steps necessary to restructure the companies and turn around their performance quickly.

Thus, the first step in the change process occurs when a company's strategic managers or others in a position to take action recognize that there is a *gap between desired company performance and actual performance*.[16] Using measures such as a decline in profitability, ROI, stock price, or market share as indicators that change is needed, managers can start looking for the source of the problem. To discover it, they conduct a SWOT analysis.

Strategic managers examine the company's *strengths* and *weaknesses*. For example, management conducts a strategic audit of all functions and divisions and looks at their contribution to profitability over time. Perhaps some divisions have become relatively unprofitable as innovation has slowed without management's realizing it. Perhaps sales and marketing have failed to keep pace with changes occurring in the competitive environment. Perhaps the company's product is simply outdated. Strategic managers also analyze the company's level of differentiation and integration to make sure that it is appropriate for its strategy. Perhaps a company does not have the integrating mechanisms in place to achieve gains from synergy, or perhaps the structure has become tall and inflexible so that bureaucratic costs have escalated. Perhaps it is necessary to quickly implement a product-team structure to speed the process of product development.

Strategic managers then examine environmental *opportunities* and *threats* that might explain the problem, using all the concepts developed in Chapter 3 of this book. For instance, intense competition may have arisen unexpectedly from substitute products, or a shift in consumers' tastes or technology may have caught the company unawares. Perhaps the strategic group structure in the industry has changed and new kinds of competitors have emerged, such as one or more companies pursuing a simultaneous low-cost/differentiation strategy.

Once the source of the problem has been identified using SWOT analysis, strategic managers must determine the desired future state of the company—that is, how it should change its strategy and structure to achieve the new goals they have set for it. As occurred at IBM and Westinghouse, managers may decide to lower costs by restructuring operations. Alternatively, as happened at Merck and General Motors, the company may increase its research and development budget or diversify into new products to increase the rate of product innovation. Essentially, strategic managers apply the conceptual tools this book has described to work out the best strategy and structure for maximizing profitability. The choices they make are specific to each individual company, and, as noted earlier, there is no way that managers can determine their correctness in advance.

In sum, the first step in the change process involves determining the need for change, analyzing the organization's current position, and determining how to achieve the desired future state that strategic managers would like it to attain—by implementing a reengineering, restructuring, or innovation program, for example.

DETERMINING THE OBSTACLES TO CHANGE

Restructuring, reengineering, innovation, and other forms of strategic change are often resisted by people and groups inside an organization. Often, for example, the decision to restructure and downsize an organization requires the establishment of a new set of task and role relationships among organizational employees. Because this change may threaten the jobs of some employees, they resist the changes taking place, as happened at Eastman Chemicals profiled in the Closing Case. Many efforts at change, restructuring included, take a long time and often fail because of the strong resistance to change at all levels in the organization. Thus, the second step in implementing strategic change is to determine the obstacles or resistance to change that exists in a company.[17]

Types of Obstacles to Change

Strategic managers must analyze the factors that are causing organizational inertia and preventing the company from reaching its ideal future state. Obstacles to change can be found at four levels in the organization: corporate, divisional, functional, and individual.

Corporate Obstacles At the corporate level, several potential obstacles must be considered. Changing strategy or structure, even in seemingly trivial ways, may significantly affect a company's behavior. For example, suppose that to reduce costs a company decides to centralize all divisional purchasing and sales activities at the corporate level. Such consolidation could severely damage each division's ability to develop a unique strategy for its own individual markets. Alternatively, suppose that, in response to low-cost foreign competition, a company decides to pursue a policy of differentiation. This action would change the balance of power among functions and lead to problems as functions start fighting to retain their status in the organization. A *company's present structure and strategy* may constitute powerful obstacles to change. They produce a massive amount of inertia, which has to be overcome before change can take place. This is why strategic change is usually a slow process.[18]

The *type of structure* a company uses can be another impediment to change. For example, it is much easier to change strategy if a company is using a matrix rather than a functional structure, or if it is decentralized rather than centralized, or if it has a high rather than a low level of integration. Decentralized, matrix structures are more flexible than highly controlled functional structures, and thus there is less potential for conflict between functions or divisions because people are used to cooperative cross-functional relationships.

Although some are easier to change than others, *corporate cultures* can present still another obstacle to change. For example, change is notoriously difficult in the military because obedience and the following of orders are deemed sacred. Some cultures, however, such as Hewlett-Packard's, thrive on flexibility or even change itself; they adapt much more easily when change becomes necessary.

Divisional Obstacles Similar factors operate at the divisional level. Change at that level is difficult if divisions are *highly interrelated and trade resources,* because a shift in one division's operations affects other divisions. Consequently, it is harder to manage change if a company is pursuing a strategy of related, rather than unrelated, diversification. Furthermore, changes in strategy affect different divisions in different ways, because change generally favors the interests of some divisions over those of others. Managers in the different divisions may thus have *different attitudes to change*, and some will be less supportive than others. For example, existing divisions may resist the establishing of new product divisions because they will lose resources, and their status in the organization will diminish.

Functional Obstacles The same obstacles to change exist at the functional level. Like divisions, different functions have *different strategic orientations and goals* and react differently to the changes management proposes. For example, manufacturing generally has a short-term, cost-directed efficiency orientation; research and development is oriented toward long-term, technical goals; and sales is oriented toward satisfying customers' needs. Thus, production may see the solution to a problem as one of reducing costs, sales as one of increasing demand, and research and development as product innovation. Differences in functional orientation make it hard to formulate and implement a new strategy; they slow a company's response to changes in the competitive environment.

Individual Obstacles At the individual level, too, people are notoriously *resistant to change* because change implies uncertainty, which breeds insecurity and fear of the unknown.[19] Because managers are people, this individual resistance reinforces the tendency of each function and division to oppose changes that may have uncertain effects on them. Restructuring and reengineering efforts can be particularly stressful for managers at all levels of the organization. During the 1990s, for example, AT&T announced the layoff of thousands of its managers every few years. Successive waves of layoffs spawn fear and anxiety about the future among the remaining employees, lessening their commitment to the organization and lowering their morale.

All these obstacles make it difficult to change organizational strategy or structure quickly. That is why U.S. car manufacturers took so long to respond to the Japanese challenge and why companies such as IBM and Digital Equipment were so slow to respond to the threat of powerful workstations and personal computers from companies such as Sun Microsystems and Dell Computer. These companies were accustomed to a situation of complete dominance in their industries and had developed inflexible, centralized structures, which inhibited risk taking and quick reaction.

Paradoxically, companies that experience the greatest uncertainty may become best able to respond to it. When companies have been forced to change frequently, strategic managers often develop the ability to handle change easily.[20] Strategic managers must understand potential obstacles to change as they design a new strategy and structure. Obstacles must be recognized, and the strategic plan must take them into account. The larger and more complex the organization, the harder it is to implement change because inertia is likely to be more pervasive. Strategy in Action 14.3, which tells how Michael Walsh overcame inertia at Tenneco, illustrates a way of overcoming obstacles to change in a large, complex organization.

Organizational Conflict: An Important Obstacle to Change

The obstacles to change just discussed can also dramatically reduce a company's ability to change when they spawn organizational conflict between functions and between divisions. **Organizational conflict** is the struggle that arises when the goal-directed behavior of one organizational group blocks the goal-directed behavior of another.[21] Different functions and divisions have different orientations, so if organizational change favors one division over another, organizational conflict can erupt, resulting in a failure to move quickly to exploit new strategic opportunities. A model developed by Lou R. Pondy helps show how conflict emerges in organizations and how it can become a powerful obstacle to change in its own right.[22]

The five stages in Pondy's model of the conflict process are summarized in Figure 14.3. The first stage in the conflict process is *latent conflict,* potential conflict that can flare up when the right conditions arise. All the obstacles to change just discussed are potential sources of conflict. For example, latent conflicts are frequently activated by changes in an organization's strategy or structure that affect the relationship among functions or divisions. Suppose a company has been producing one major product type but then decides to diversify and produce different kinds of products. To overcome problems of coordinating a range of specialist services over many products, the company moves from a functional to a divisional structure. The new structure changes task relationships among divisional managers, and this in turn changes the relative status and areas of authority of the different functional and product managers. Conflict between functional and product managers or among product managers is likely to ensue.

Because every change in a company's strategy and structure alters the organizational context, conflict can easily arise unless the situation is carefully managed to avoid it. Good strategic planning allows managers to anticipate problems that may emerge later so that they can move early to prevent them.[23] For example, when managers change a company's strategy, they should also consider the effect of these changes on future group relationships. Similarly, when changing organizational

14.3 STRATEGY *in* ACTION

The Shakeout at Tenneco

A sprawling conglomerate, Tenneco operates in such businesses as natural gas, shipbuilding, auto parts, chemicals, and farm equipment. In 1991, the company, which is based in Houston, Texas, was ranked twenty-seventh in the *Fortune* 500, with sales at more than $14 billion. Nevertheless, when Michael H. Walsh became president of Tenneco in 1991, he entered a company that had experienced falling earnings for years and was expected to post a net loss of $732 million in 1991. His mission was to turn Tenneco around and restructure its assets.

Walsh was used to the challenge of changing a large company. He had successfully turned around Union Pacific, a large railroad company, and it was on the basis of his reputation as a change agent that Tenneco's board of directors had hired him. When Walsh took over the restructuring effort, his first step was to analyze Tenneco's problems in order to find their causes. He uncovered serious flaws in the company's structure and culture, which had led to poor performance in the various operating divisions. For example, Case, the company's agricultural equipment maker, was in very poor financial shape and was a major contributor to poor corporate performance. To keep Case afloat, top management had continually siphoned off the profits of the chemicals and auto parts divisions, which were doing well. As a result, managers in these divisions had little incentive to improve divisional performance or to cooperate with one another and share resources or capabilities.

Over the years, top management had failed to institute a rigorous system of financial and output controls to monitor and control divisional performance. Divisional managers had been allowed to run their operations with little corporate oversight. Consequently, they had made investments that supported their own interests, not those of the corporation. With few checks on their activities, the divisions had become top-heavy and noncompetitive. Furthermore, as already mentioned, they lacked any incentive to cooperate and improve corporate performance together.

Walsh recognized that the way Tenneco's structure and culture were working had become a powerful obstacle to change. He realized that to change divisional managers' behavior and overcome the inertia, which had brought the company continual losses, he would have to restructure the corporate-divisional relationship. He started from the top by changing managers' attitudes and behavior. First, he instituted a set of output controls and made it clear that these goals would be monitored and enforced. Second, he created a system of teams in which the managers from the different divisions met together to critique each other's performance. Third, he flattened the corporate hierarchy, wiping out three layers of corporate managers to bring him closer to the divisions and to let the heads of the divisions function as the company's top-management team. (Previously, divisional managers had met one-on-one with the CEO; now they operated as a corporate team.)

After this restructuring, Walsh decentralized more control to divisional managers. At the same time, he made them more accountable for their actions, since each manager's performance was now more visible to the CEO and to other top managers. As a result, top managers had more incentive to improve corporate performance. These changes effectively destroyed the inertia permeating Tenneco's old organizational structure and led to the evolution of a new culture, in which corporate, not divisional, goals and values guided divisional behavior.

Walsh continued these change efforts at all levels of the company. To change attitudes and behavior at the functional level, he instituted a system of quality teams in every division of the company. In these cross-functional teams, employees are expected to search for solutions to improve quality and reduce costs, and Walsh regularly videotapes messages to Tenneco's employees to exhort them to find new ways of improving performance. He also set an example by wiping out top management's perks such as private dining rooms, luxury yachts, jets, and cars.

Throughout the company, Walsh destroyed the old culture of apathy, which had made managers and other employees content to maintain the status quo and avoid confronting the company's problems. Walsh's efforts to change the company were spectacularly successful. Tenneco made record profits in the 1990s because of Walsh's restructuring efforts. Overcoming obstacles to change in a company may be a very difficult process, but as Tenneco's experience suggests, managers, employees, and shareholders can reap big dividends from it.

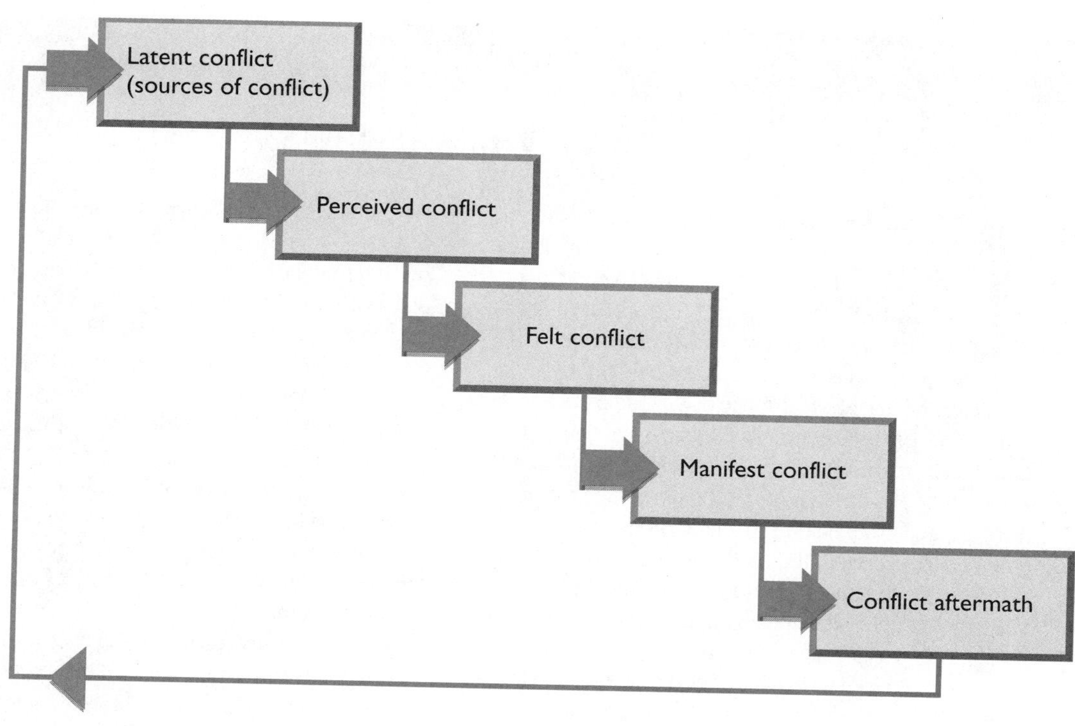

FIGURE 14.3

Stages in the Conflict Process

structure, strategic managers should anticipate the effects of the changes on functional and divisional relationships. However, because avoidance is not always possible, latent conflict may quickly lead to *perceived conflict*, the second stage.

Perceived conflict occurs when managers become aware of the clashes. After a change in strategy and structure, managers discover that the actions of another function or group obstruct the operations of their group. Managers start to react to the situation, and from the perceived stage they go quickly to the third stage, *felt conflict*. It is at this point that managers start to personalize the conflict. Opinions polarize as one function or division starts to blame the others for causing the conflict. Production might blame the inefficiency of sales for a fall in orders, while sales might blame production for a fall in product quality. Typically, there is a marked lack of cooperation at this stage, and integration among functions or divisions breaks down as the groups start to develop an us-versus-them mentality. If not managed, this stage in the conflict process leads quickly to the fourth stage, *manifest conflict*.

At this point, the conflict among functions or divisions comes into the open, and each group strives to thwart the goals of the other. Groups compete to protect their own interests and block the interests of other groups. Naturally, this blocks change and prevents an organization from adapting to its environment. Manifest conflict can take many forms. The most obvious is fighting or a lack of cooperation among top managers as they start to blame the managers of other functions or divisions for causing the problem. Other forms of manifest conflict are transfer pricing battles between divisions and knowledge hoarding. If divisional managers refuse to share resources or information, a company cannot develop synergy between divisions, and all the benefits of changing to a strategy of related diversification will be lost.

At the functional level, the effects of conflict can be equally devastating. A company in trouble cannot change and pursue a low-cost strategy if its functions are competing. For example, if sales makes no attempt to keep manufacturing informed about customers' demands, manufacturing cannot maximize the length of production runs. Similarly, a struggling company trying to change and regain its differentiated appeal cannot do so if marketing does not inform research and development about changes in consumers' preferences or if product engineering and research and development are competing over product specifications. Most companies have experienced each of these conflicts at one time or another and suffered a loss in performance and competitive advantage when conflict has blocked their ability to change and adapt quickly to a changing environment.

Manifest conflict is also common in top-management circles. There managers fight for promotion to high office or for resources to enhance their status and prestige in the organization. But if top managers are all fighting, how can a company reengineer or restructure itself successfully?

The long-term effects of manifest conflict emerge in the last stage of the conflict process, the *conflict aftermath.* Suppose that in one company a change in strategy led to conflict among division managers over transfer prices. Then divisional managers, with the help of corporate personnel, resolved the problem to everyone's satisfaction and reestablished good working relationships. In another company, however, the conflict between divisions over transfer prices was settled only by the intervention of corporate managers, who *imposed* a solution on divisional managers. A year later, a change in the environment occurred that made the transfer pricing system in both companies inequitable, and prices had to be renegotiated. How would the two companies react to the need to change again? The managers in the company in which the conflict was settled amicably would likely approach this new round of negotiations with a cooperative, not an adversarial, attitude, and necessary changes could be achieved rapidly. However, in the company in which divisions never really established an agreement, a new round of intense clashes would be likely and change would be difficult to achieve.

Conflict aftermath sets the scene for the next round of conflict, which will certainly occur because the environment is constantly changing and so must companies. The reason some companies have a long history of bad relationships among functions or divisions is that their conflict has never been managed successfully. In companies in which strategic managers have resolved the conflict, a cohesive organizational culture develops. In these companies, managers adopt a cooperative, not a competitive, attitude when conflict occurs because of change. The question that needs to be tackled, then, is how best to manage conflict strategically to avoid its bad effects and to make changes in strategy and structure as smooth as possible. There are several tactics and techniques that strategic managers can use to overcome conflict and implement strategic change effectively. Perhaps the most important of these is the way they use power and political tactics to manage strategic change.

IMPLEMENTING STRATEGIC CHANGE AND THE ROLE OF ORGANIZATIONAL POLITICS

Decisions about strategy and structure and how to change strategy and structure are not made just by following a calculated, rational plan in which only shareholders' interests are considered. In reality, strategic decision making is quite different.

When evaluating alternative courses of action and choosing a new strategic direction, managers often make decisions that will further their personal, functional, or divisional interests. **Organizational politics** are tactics that strategic managers engage in to obtain and use power to influence organizational goals and change strategy and structure to further their own interests.[24] Top-level managers constantly come into conflict over what the correct policy decisions should be, and power struggles and coalition building are a major part of strategic decision making. In this political view of decision making, obstacles to change are overcome and conflicts over goals are settled by compromise, bargaining, and negotiation between managers and coalitions of managers and by the outright use of power.[25]

In this section, we examine the relationship between strategic change and organizational politics and the process of political decision making. First, we consider the sources of politics and why politics is a necessary part of managing the strategic change process. Second, we look at how managers or divisions can increase their power so that they can influence the company's strategic direction. Third, we explore the ways in which a company can manage politics to overcome inertia and implement strategic change.

Sources of Organizational Politics

To understand why politics is an integral part of strategic change, it is useful to contrast the rational view of organizational decision making with the political view of how strategic decisions get made (see Figure 14.4). The rational view assumes that

FIGURE 14.4

Rational and Political Views of Decision Making

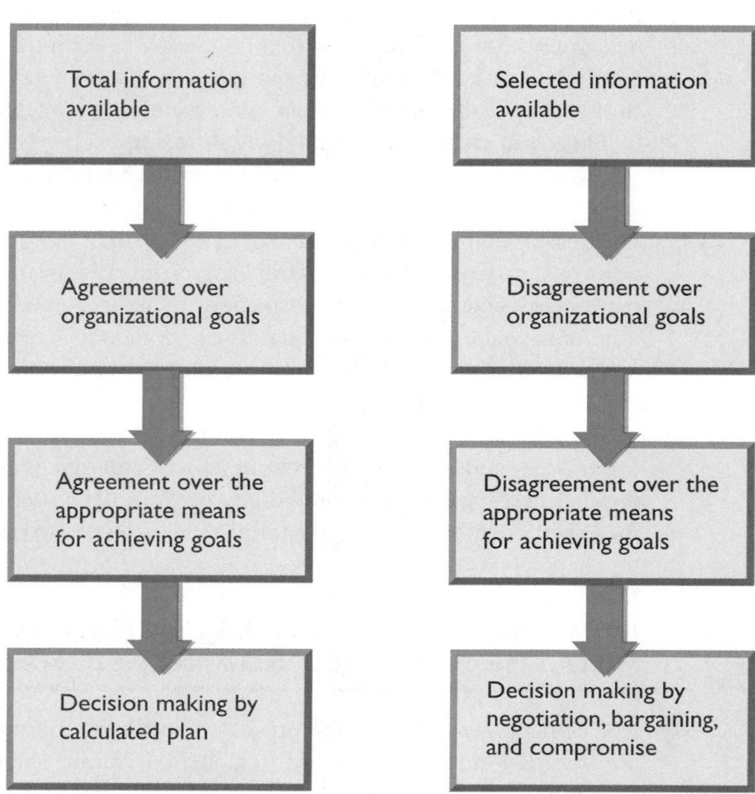

complete *information* is available and no uncertainty exists about outcomes, but the political view suggests that strategic managers can never be sure that they are making the best decisions. From a political perspective, decision making always takes place in uncertainty, in which the outcomes of strategic change are difficult to predict. According to the rational view, moreover, managers always agree about appropriate organizational *goals* and the appropriate *means,* or strategies, for achieving these goals. According to the political view, on the other hand, the choice of goals and means is linked to each individual's, function's, or division's pursuit of self-interest. Disagreement over the best course of action is inevitable in the political view because strategic change necessarily favors some individuals or divisions over others. For example, if managers decide to invest in resources to promote and develop one product, other products will not be created. Some managers win; others lose.

Given the political point of view, strategy choices are never right or wrong; they are simply better or worse. As a result, managers have to promote their ideas and lobby for support from other managers so that they can build up backing for a course of future action. Thus, coalition building is a vital part of managing strategic change.[26] Managers join coalitions to lobby for their interests because in doing so they increase their political muscle in relation to their organizational opponents.

Managers also engage in politics for personal reasons. Because organizations are shaped like pyramids, individual managers realize that the higher they rise, the more difficult it is to climb to the next position.[27] If their views prevail and the organization follows their lead, however, *and* if their decisions bear results, they reap rewards and promotions. Thus, by being successful at politics and claiming responsibility for successful change, they increase their visibility in the organization and make themselves contenders for higher organizational office.

The assumption that personal, rather than shareholder or organizational, interest governs strategic choice is what gives the word *politics* bad connotations in many people's minds. However, because no one knows for certain what will happen as a result of strategic change, letting people pursue their own interest may in the long run mean that the organization's interests are being followed. This is because competition among managers stemming from self-interest may lead to better strategic decision making and lead to an improved change plan, with successful managers moving to the top of the organization over time. If a company can maintain checks and balances in its top-management circles (by preventing any particular manager or coalition from becoming too powerful), politics can be a healthy influence, for it can prevent managers from becoming complacent about the status quo, promote strategic change, and thus avert organizational decline.

If politics grows rampant, however, and if powerful managers gain such dominance that they can suppress the views of managers who oppose their interests, major problems may arise. Checks and balances fade, organizational inertia increases, and performance suffers. For example, at Gulf & Western, as soon as its founder died, the company sold off fifty businesses that the new top management considered his pet projects and not suited to the company's portfolio. Ultimately, companies that let politics get so out of hand that shareholders' interests suffer are taken over by aggressive new management teams, which engage in major restructuring activities—often involving the layoff of thousands of employees—to turn around a company.

Figure 14.5 illustrates the effect of organizational politics on performance. The figure shows that up to point A, politics can increase organizational performance because it can *overcome inertia and induce needed organizational change*. After

FIGURE 14.5

Effect of Organizational Politics on Performance

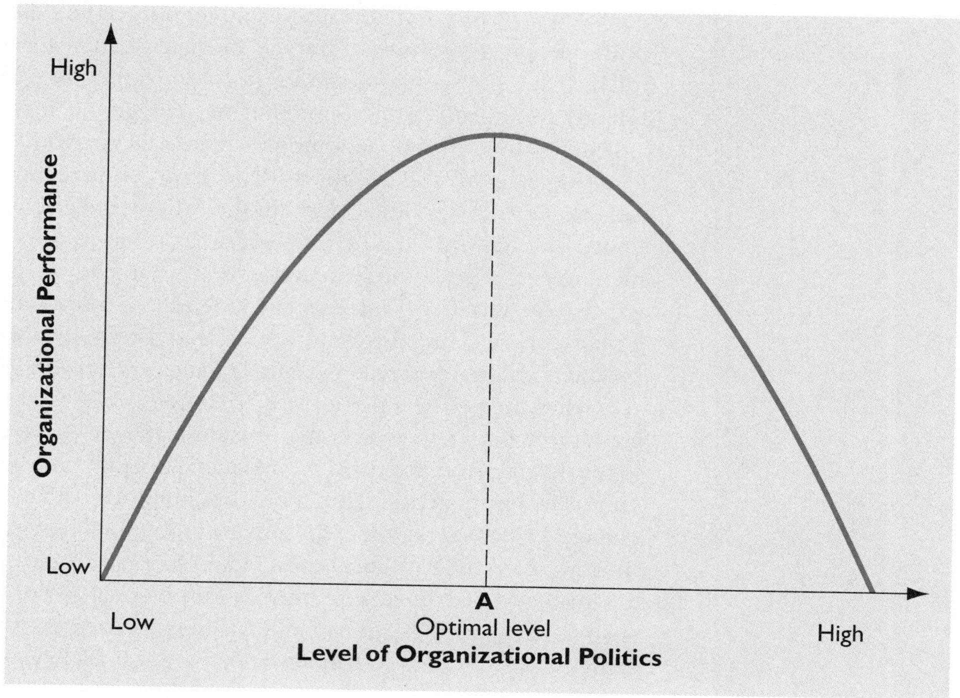

point A, however, an increase in the level of organizational politics can lead to a decline in performance, for politics gets out of control and the organization fragments into competing interest groups. Therefore, astute managers seek to keep the level of political behavior from passing the optimum point. If kept in check, politics can be a useful management tool for overcoming inertia and bringing about strategic change. The best CEOs recognize this fact and create a strategic context in which managers can fight for their ideas and reap the rewards from successfully promoting change in organizational strategy and structure. For example, 3M is well known for its top-management committee structure, in which divisional managers who request new funds and new-venture managers who champion new products must present their projects to the entire top-management team and lobby for support for their ideas. All top managers in 3M experienced this learning process, and presumably the ones in the top-management team are those who succeeded best at mobilizing support and commitment for their concepts.

Legitimate Power and Politics

To play politics and bring about the strategic change that they support, managers must have power. **Power** can be defined as the ability of one individual, function, or division to cause another individual, function, or division to do something that it would not otherwise have done.[28] Perhaps the simplest way to understand power is to look at its sources: legitimate power and informal power.

Legitimate power is the authority a manager possesses by virtue of holding a formal position in the hierarchy. This is why the CEO is so powerful. As the top manager of a company, he or she decides whom to delegate power to and how much to give. Authority also gives a manager the power to resolve conflicts and decide what needs to be done. This is the power that *gives a manager the ability to overcome obstacles to change*. For example, as discussed earlier, conflict often occurs between functions and divisions because they have different goals and interests. Because functional managers have equal authority, they cannot control each other, so when functional managers cannot solve their problems, these problems are often passed on to corporate managers or the CEO, who has the authority to impose a solution on the parties. The story of the way managers at BankAmerica took full control over another bank after a merger demonstrates the potency of legitimate power in bringing about strategic change, it helps reveal the steps that it took to become the biggest bank in the U.S. (See Opening Case.) Details are given in Strategy in Action 14.4.

Informal Sources of Power and Politics

While a considerable amount of a strategic manager's power derives from his or her level in the hierarchy, many other informal sources of power are crucial in determining what kinds of changes will be made in strategy and structure and thus in a company's future direction. To a large degree, how much informal power the managers of the different functions and divisions possess derives from a company's corporate- and business-level strategies. Different strategies make some functions or divisions, *and thus their managers*, more important than others in achieving the corporate mission and consequently confer a greater ability to implement strategic change. Figure 14.6 lists the informal sources of power that we discuss next.

Ability to Cope with Uncertainty A function or division gains power if it can reduce uncertainty for another function or division.[29] Suppose that a company is pursuing a strategy of vertical integration. A division that controls the supply and quality of inputs to another division has power over it because it controls the uncertainty facing the second division. At the business level, in a company pursuing a low-cost strategy, sales has power over production because sales provides information about customers' needs that is necessary to minimize production costs. In a company pursuing a differentiation strategy, research and development has power over marketing at the early stages in a product's life cycle because it controls product innovations. However, once innovation problems have been solved, marketing is likely to be the most powerful function because it supplies research and development with information on customers' needs. Thus, a function's power depends on the degree to which other functions rely on it.

Centrality Power also derives from the centrality of a division or function.[30] **Centrality** refers to the extent to which a division or function is at the center of resource transfers among divisions. For example, in a chemical company, the division supplying specialized chemicals is likely to be central because its activities are critical to both the petroleum division, which supplies its inputs, and the end-using divisions such as plastics or pharmaceuticals, which depend on its outputs. Its activities are central to the production process of all the company's businesses. Therefore, it can exert pressure on corporate headquarters to pursue policies in its own interest.

14.4 STRATEGY *in* ACTION

Who Has Power in a Merger?

When BankAmerica merged with Security Pacific in 1991, the merger was supposed to be a merger of equals, with the top management of both banks jointly running the new company. Richard Rosenberg, the chairman of BankAmerica, agreed to form an office of the chairman with Security Pacific's chairman, Robert Smith; it was also agreed that Smith would succeed Rosenberg as the chairman of the new bank when Rosenberg retired. Similarly, there was supposed to be a 50/50 board split between the directors of both companies, and BankAmerica agreed to name four of Security Pacific's top managers to the new top-management team.

After the merger, however, things did not work out as had been expected. BankAmerica had planned the merger hurriedly, without investigating the details of Security Pacific's financial condition thoroughly. After the merger, BankAmerica's managers began to find major flaws in the way Security Pacific's managers made loans, which had resulted in more than $300 million of write-offs for the company, with equally large sums to follow. BankAmerica's top-management team came to despise and ridicule the way Security Pacific's managers did business. They blamed a large part of the problem on Security Pacific's culture, which was decentralized and freewheeling and allowed top managers to loan large sums of money to clients on the basis of personal ties. By contrast, BankAmerica had developed a conservative, centralized decision-making style and curbed the autonomy of lower-level managers; loans were made according to company-wide criteria scrutinized by top management.

Believing that their culture was the one that had to be developed in the new organization, BankAmerica's managers began to use their legitimate power as the dominant party in the merger (Rosenberg as chairman of the bigger company had more legitimate power than Smith) to strip authority from Security Pacific's managers and to take control of the reins of the new organization. Less than two weeks after the merger, Smith found himself relieved of all important decision-making authority, which was transferred to Rosenberg and his top-management team. Similarly, whenever BankAmerica's top managers were negotiating with Security Pacific's managers over future task and authority relationships, they used their power to cut the authority of Security Pacific's managers and to drive them from the organization. After a few months, almost all of Security Pacific's top managers had left the new organization, followed by thousands of middle-level managers, who, BankAmerica managers felt, could not be trusted to maintain the company's new cultural standards and way of doing business.

At the functional level, the function that has the most centrality, and therefore power, is the one that provides the distinctive competency on which a company's business-level strategy is based.[31] Thus, at Apple Computer, the function with the greatest centrality is research and development because the company's competitive advantage rests on a technical competency. On the other hand, at Wal-Mart the purchasing and distribution function is the most central because Wal-Mart's competitive advantage depends on its ability to provide a low-cost product.

Control over Information Functions and divisions are also central if they are at the heart of the information flow—that is, if they can control the flow of information to other functions or divisions (or both).[32] Information is a power resource because, by giving or withholding information, one function or division can cause others to behave in certain ways. Sales, for instance, can control the way production operates. If sales manipulates information to satisfy its own goals—for example, responsiveness to customers—production costs will rise, but production may be un-

FIGURE 14.6

Informal Sources of Power

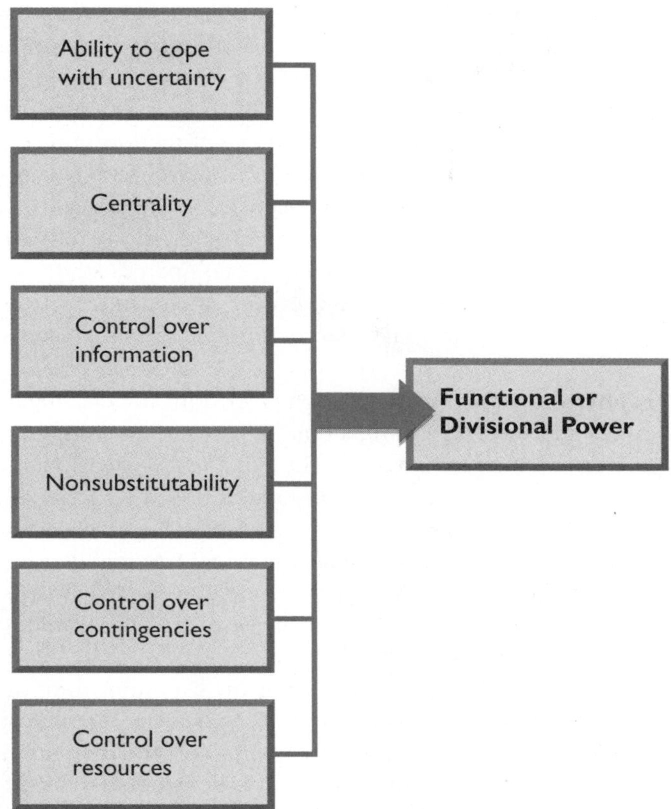

aware that costs could be lowered with a different sales strategy. Similarly, research and development can shape managers' attitudes to the competitive prospects of different kinds of products by supplying favorable information about the products it prefers and downplaying others.

In a very real sense, managers in organizations are engaging in a subtle information game when they form policies, set objectives, and influence the change process. We discuss in Chapter 11 how divisions can disguise their performance by providing only positive information to corporate managers. The more powerful a division, the more easily it can do this. In both strategy formulation and implementation, by using information to develop a power base, divisions and functions can strongly influence policy changes that favor their own interests.

Nonsubstitutability A function or division can accrue power proportionately to the degree to which its activities are **nonsubstitutable**—that is, cannot be duplicated. For example, if a company is vertically integrated, supplying divisions are nonsubstitutable to the extent that the company cannot buy in the marketplace what they produce. Thus, the petroleum products division is not very powerful if large quantities of oil are available from other suppliers. In an oil crisis, the opposite is true. On the other hand, the activities of a new-venture division—a division in which new products are developed—are nonsubstitutable to the extent that a company cannot buy another company that possesses similar knowledge or expertise. If knowledge or information can be bought, the division is substitutable.

The same holds true at the functional level. A function and the managers within it are powerful to the extent that no other function can perform their task. As in the case of centrality, which function is nonsubstitutable depends on the nature of a company's business-level strategy. If the company is pursuing a low-cost strategy, then production is likely to be the key function, and research and development or marketing has less power. However, if the company is pursuing a strategy of differentiation, then the opposite is likely to be the case.

Thus, the power that a function or division gains by virtue of its centrality or nonsubstitutability derives from the company's strategy. Eventually, as a company's strategy changes, the relative power of the functions and divisions also changes. This is the next informal source of power that we discuss.

Control over Contingencies Over time, the contingencies—that is, the opportunities and threats—facing a company from the competitive environment change as the environment changes.[33] The functions or divisions that can deal with the problems confronting the company and allow it to achieve its objectives gain power. Conversely, the functions that can no longer manage the contingency lose power. For example, consider which functional executives rose to top management positions during the last fifty years. Generally, the executives who reached the highest posts did so from functions or divisions that were able to deal with the opportunities and threats facing the company.[34]

In the 1950s, for instance, the main contingency problem a company had to cope with was to produce goods and services. Pent-up demand from the years of World War II led to a huge increase in consumer spending for automobiles, homes, and durable goods. Goods needed to be produced quickly and cheaply to meet demand, and during this period the managers who rose to the top were from the *manufacturing* function or *consumer products* divisions.

In the 1960s, the problem changed. Most companies had increased their productive capacity, and the market was saturated. Producing goods was not as difficult as selling them. Hence, *marketing and sales* functions rose to prominence. The rise of executives in companies reflected this critical contingency, for greater numbers of them emerged from the sales function and from *marketing-oriented* divisions than from any other groups.

In the 1970s, companies began to realize that competitive conditions were permanent. They had to streamline their strategies and structures to survive in an increasingly hostile environment. As a result, *accounting and finance* became the function that supplied most of the additions to the top-management team. Today, a company's business- and corporate-level strategy determines which group gains preeminence.

Control over Resources The final informal source of power examined here is the ability to control and allocate scarce resources.[35] This source gives corporate-level managers their clout. Obviously, the power of corporate managers depends to a large extent on their ability to allocate capital to the operating divisions and to allot cash to or take it from a division on the basis of their expectations of its future success.

However, the power of resources is not a function merely of the ability to allocate resources immediately; it also comes from the ability to *generate resources in the future.* Thus, individual divisions that can generate resources will have power in the corporation. For example, divisions that can generate high revenues from sales to consumers have great power. At the functional level, the same kinds of considerations apply. The ability of sales and marketing to increase customers' demand and generate revenues explains their power in the organization. In general, the function that can generate the most resources has the most power.

Summary

The most powerful division or function in a company, then, is the one that can reduce uncertainty for others, is most central and nonsubstitutable, has control over resources and can generate them, and is able to deal with the critical external strategic contingency facing the company. In practice, each function or division in a company has power from one or more of these sources, and so there is a distribution of power among functions and divisions.

At the level of individual managers, too, there are various informal ways to increase personal power. First, managers can try to make themselves *irreplaceable*.[36] For example, they may develop specialized skills—such as a knowledge of computers or special relationships with key customers—that allow them to solve problems or limit uncertainty for other managers in the organization. Second, they may specialize in an area of increasing concern to the organization so that they eventually control a crucial *contingency* facing the organization. Third, managers can also try to make themselves more *central* in an organization by deliberately accepting responsibilities that bring them into contact with many functions or managers. Finally, another tactic to obtain power is to be associated with powerful managers who are clearly on their way to the top. By supporting a powerful manager and being indispensable to him or her, it is possible to rise up the organizational ladder with that manager. Political managers cultivate both people and information, and they are able to build up a personal network of contacts in the organization that they can then use to pursue personal goals such as promotion.

Effects of Power and Politics on Strategic Change

Power and politics strongly influence a company's choice of strategy and structure, for a company has to maintain an organizational context that is responsive both to the aspirations of the various divisions, functions, and managers and to changes in the external environment.[37] The problem companies face is that the internal structure of power always lags behind changes in the environment because, in general, the environment changes faster than companies can respond. Those in power never voluntarily give up engaging in politics, but excessive politicking and power struggles reduce a company's flexibility, cause inertia, and erode competitive advantage.

To use politics to promote effective change, a company must devise organizational arrangements that create a **power balance** among the various divisions or functions so that no single one dominates the whole enterprise. If no power balance exists, power struggles proceed unchecked and change becomes impossible as divisions start to compete and to hoard information or knowledge to maximize their own returns. In such situations, exchanging resources among divisions becomes expensive, and gains from synergy are difficult to obtain. These factors in turn lower a company's profitability and reduce organizational growth.

In the divisional structure, the corporate headquarters staff plays the balancing role because they can exert power even over strong divisions and force them to share resources for the good of the whole corporation. In a single-business company, a strong chief executive officer is important because he or she must replace the corporate center and balance the power of the strong functions against the weak. The forceful CEO takes the responsibility for giving weak functions an opportunity to air their concerns and interests and tries to avoid being railroaded into decisions by the strong function pursuing its own interests. Thus, the CEO of a large corporation has great potential for exercising power to bring about change. The CEO also plays another important role, however: that of arbiter of acceptable political decision making.

Politics pervades all companies, but the CEO and top-level managers can shape its character. In some organizations, power plays are the norm because the CEOs themselves garnered power in that way. However, other companies—especially those founded by entrepreneurs who believed in democracy or in decentralized decision making—may not tolerate power struggles, and a different kind of political behavior becomes acceptable. It is based on a function or division manager's competency or expertise rather than on her or his ability to form powerful coalitions.

At PepsiCo, politics is of the cutthroat power play variety, and there is a rapid turnover of managers who fail to meet organizational aspirations. At Coca-Cola, however, ideas and expertise are much more important in politics than power plays directed at maximizing functional or divisional self-interest. Similarly, Intel does not tolerate politicking or lobbying for personal gain; instead, it rewards risk taking and makes promotion contingent on performance, not seniority.

To design an organizational structure that creates a power balance facilitating change, strategic managers can use the tools of implementation discussed in Chapters 11 and 12. First, they must create the right mix of integrating mechanisms so that functions or divisions can share information and ideas. A multidivisional structure offers one means of balancing power among divisions, and the matrix or product-team structure offers another among functions. A company can then develop norms, values, and a common culture that emphasize corporate, rather than divisional, interests and that stress the company's mission. In companies such as Microsoft or 3M, for instance, culture serves to harmonize divisional interests with the achievement of corporate goals.

Finally, as we note earlier, strong hierarchical control by a gifted chief executive officer can also create the organizational context in which politics can facilitate the change process. When CEOs use their expert knowledge as their power, they provide the strategic leadership that allows a company to overcome inertia and change its strategy and structure. Indeed, it should be part of the strategic manager's job to learn how to manage politics and power to further corporate interests, because politics is an essential part of the process of strategic change.

MANAGING AND EVALUATING CHANGE

Even with the political situation under control, implementing change—that is, managing and evaluating change—raises several questions. For instance, who should actually carry out the change: internal managers or external consultants?

Although internal managers may have the most experience or knowledge about a company's operations, they may lack perspective because they are too much a part of the organization's culture. They also run the risk of appearing to be politically motivated and of having a personal stake in the changes they recommend. Companies, therefore, often turn to external consultants, who can view a situation more objectively. Outside consultants, however, must spend a lot of time learning about the company and its problems before they can propose a plan of action. It is for both these reasons that many companies such as Quaker Oats, Tenneco, and IBM have brought in new CEOs from outside the company to spearhead their change efforts. In this way, companies can get the benefits of both inside information and external perspective.

Generally, a company can take two main approaches to managing change: top-down change or bottom-up change. With **top-down change**, a strong CEO such as a Morrison or Walsh or a top-management team analyzes how to alter strategy and structure, recommends a course of action, and then moves quickly to restructure and implement change in the organization. The emphasis is on speed of response and management of problems as they occur. **Bottom-up change** is much more gradual. Top management consults with managers at all levels in the organization. Then, over time, it develops a detailed plan for change, with a timetable of events and stages that the company will go through. The emphasis in bottom-up change is on participation and on keeping people informed about the situation, so that uncertainty is minimized.

The advantage of bottom-up change is that it removes some of the obstacles to change by including them in the strategic plan. Furthermore, the purpose of consulting with managers at all levels is to reveal potential problems. The disadvantage of bottom-up change is its slowness.

On the other hand, in the case of the much speedier top-down change, the problems may emerge later and may be difficult to resolve. Lumbering giants such as Tenneco and IBM often need top-down change because managers are so unaccustomed to and threatened by change that only a radical restructuring effort provides the momentum to overcome organizational inertia.

Managers at McDonnell Douglas learned this lesson when they sought ways to turn around their company's performance in the 1990s, after the huge cutbacks in defense spending brought about by the end of the cold war. To improve performance, managers started a program of bottom-up change and tried to involve employees in finding ways to cut costs and raise the level of innovation. After several months, they realized that nothing was changing, and so on a day that has gone down in McDonnell Douglas history as "The Monday Massacre" top managers instituted a radical program of top-down change.

They eliminated the positions of all 5,000 of McDonnell Douglas's managers and supervisors and restructured the company from seven layers in the hierarchy to five, so that in the future only 2,800 managers would be required. They then let the 5,000 managers and supervisors compete for the 2,800 new positions.[38] The placing of new managers in all-new positions totally destroyed the company's old culture and ways of operating and allowed top management to bring about needed changes in the organization quickly. The result for McDonnell Douglas was a complete turnaround of its business and, eventually, a higher rate of new-product innovation. However, for about a year after the change, the company was in upheaval as managers essentially had to create a new organizational structure to operate their business. The moral of the story is that organizations that change the most find change easiest because inertia has not yet built up and those such as McDonnell Douglas that do not change find change the most difficult.

The last step in the change process is to evaluate the effects of the changes in strategy and structure on organizational performance. A company must compare the way it operates after implementing change with the way it operated before. Managers use indexes such as changes in stock market price or market share to assess the effects of change in strategy. It is much more difficult, however, to assess the effects of changes in structure on a company's performance because they are so much harder to measure. Whereas companies can easily measure the increased revenue from increased product differentiation, they do not have any sure means of evaluating how a shift from a product to a divisional structure has affected performance. Managers can be surveyed, however, and over time it may become obvious that organizational flexibility and the company's ability to manage its strategy have increased. Managers can also assess whether the change has decreased the level of politicking and conflict and strengthened cooperation among the divisions and functions.

SUMMARY OF CHAPTER

Organizational change is a complex and difficult process for companies to manage successfully. The first hurdle is getting managers to realize that change is necessary and to admit that there is a problem. Once the need for change has been recognized, managers can go about the process of recommending a course of action and analyze potential obstacles to change. Strategic managers need to appreciate, however, that companies are not just rational decision-making systems in which managers coldly calculate the potential returns from their investments. Organizations are arenas of power, in which individuals and groups fight for prestige and possession of scarce resources. In the pursuit of their interests, managers compete and come into conflict. The very nature of the organization makes this inevitable. Managers have to deal with politics and conflict creatively to implement strategic change successfully and enhance or restore a company's competitive advantage. The most successful companies are those in which change is regarded as the norm and managers are constantly seeking to improve organizational strengths and eliminate weaknesses so that they can maximize future profitability. This chapter makes the following main points:

- Strategic change is the movement of a company away from its present state to some desired future state to increase its competitive advantage. Three main types of strategic change are reengineering and E-engineering; restructuring; and innovation.
- Strategic change is implemented through a series of steps that strategic managers must follow if the change process is to succeed.
- The first step in the change process is determining the need for change. Strategic managers must recognize a gap between actual performance and desired performance, use a SWOT analysis to define the company's present state, and then determine its desired future state.
- The second step in the change process is identifying the obstacles to change that may prevent a company from reaching its desired future state. Obstacles to change are found at the corporate, divisional, functional, and individual levels. Important obstacles include the inertia produced by an organization's present strategy, structure, culture and differences in divisional and functional goals and interests.
- Organizational conflict results from fights between divisions, functions, and individual managers pursuing different goals and interests. Conflict is also a major obstacle to change, and managers must seek ways to resolve conflict to implement strategic change successfully.
- Strategic managers play organizational politics to overcome obstacles to change, resolve conflicts,

and bring about strategic change. Organizational politics are the tactics that strategic managers engage in to use power and to influence goals and change strategy and structure to further their own interests.

- ✔ To play politics, managers must have power. Power is the ability of one party to cause another party to act in a way that it would not otherwise have done.
- ✔ Power available to strategic managers includes legitimate power and power from informal sources, such as coping with uncertainty, centrality, control over information, nonsubstitutability, and control over contingencies and resources.
- ✔ Power and politics influence a company's choice of strategy and structure and the nature of the strategic changes that are implemented.
- ✔ Strategic managers need to evaluate the results of each change process and use this analysis to define the organization's present condition so that they can start the next change process. Well-run companies are constantly aware of the need to monitor their performance, and strategic managers institutionalize change so that they can continually realign their strategy and structure to suit the competitive environment.

DISCUSSION QUESTIONS

1. What is the difference between reengineering, E-engineering, and restructuring?
2. What are the main obstacles to change that a company pursuing a differentiation strategy would face if it should be forced to pursue a cost-leadership strategy?
3. Discuss how you would set up a plan for change for an unrelated company that is starting to pursue a strategy of related diversification. What problems will the company encounter? How should it deal with them?
4. How can using politics to overcome obstacles to change and to resolve conflict help to implement strategic change?

Practicing Strategic Management

SMALL-GROUP EXERCISE
Handling Change

Break up into groups of three to five people, and discuss the following scenario:

You are a group of top-level strategic managers of a large, well-established computer company that has traditionally pursued a strategy of differentiation based on research and development. Now, because of intense competition, your company is being forced to pursue a combined low-cost/differentiation strategy. You have been charged with preparing a plan to change the company's structure and strategy, and you have decided on two main changes. First, you plan to reengineer the company and move from a multidivisional structure to one in which cross-functional product teams become responsible for developing each new computer model. Second, to decentralize decision making and reduce costs, you propose to restructure the company and severely cut the number of corporate and top divisional managers.

1. Discuss the nature of the obstacles to change at the organizational, functional, and individual level that you, as internal change agents, will encounter in implementing this new strategy and structure. Which do you think will be the most important obstacles to change?
2. Discuss some ways by which you can overcome obstacles to change to help your organization move to its desired future state.

STRATEGIC MANAGEMENT PROJECT
Module 14

For the final part of the Strategic Management Project, your task is to examine how your organization has managed the process of strategic change.

1. Find some examples of recent changes in your company's strategy or structure. What kinds of change did your company implement? Why did your company make these changes?
2. What, do you think, are the major obstacles to change in your organization?
3. Given the nature of your organization's strategy and structure, is conflict a likely obstacle to change in your organization? Can you find any examples of conflicts that have occurred in your organization?
4. Is there any evidence of political contests or struggles between top managers or between divisions or functions in your organization? What can you find out about the power of the CEO and the top-management team?
5. Using the informal sources of power discussed in the chapter (for example, centrality, control over resources), draw a map of the power relationships between the various managers, divisions, or functions inside your organization. On the basis of this analysis, which are the most powerful managers or subunits? Why? How do managers in the powerful subunits use power to influence decision making?
6. How well do you think strategic managers have managed the change process? What other changes do you think your company should make in its strategy or structure?

ARTICLE FILE 14

Find an example of a company that has been implementing a major change in its strategy and/or structure. Why did managers think that change was necessary? What kind of change was implemented, and what were its effects?

EXPLORING THE WEB
Managing Change

Search the Web to find a company that has recently been involved in some major kind of change process. What was the nature of the change? Why did the change take place? What problems did the company experience during the change process?

CLOSING CASE

Raising Quality at Eastman Chemicals

EASTMAN CHEMICALS, a former division of Eastman Kodak, is one of the success stories of the 1990s. It has totally restructured and reengineered its operations to make product quality and responsiveness to customers its major goals. So successful has it been in its quest to increase quality that it won the prestigious Malcolm Baldrige National Quality Award.[39] How did Eastman's managers bring about this change?

First, top management decided to change from its old, centralized, product-oriented divisional structure to one that was based more on the needs of its customers. Prior to the restructuring, the managers at Eastman Chemicals viewed their job as creating new kinds of chemicals and worrying about who to sell them to later. After the change, the needs of customers became their paramount concern, and they saw their business as discovering what customers wanted and then marshaling organizational resources to create new products that satisfied those wants.

Second, with their new customer-oriented structure in place, top management sat down to reengineer the product-innovation process. Under Eastman's old product-oriented division structure, all divisions operated separately and there was little communication between them. Moreover, each division was organized on functional lines and made a separate and distinct contribution to product development. The result was that product development typically took a long time, and, as mentioned earlier, the product, not the customer, was the focus. Top managers decided to change totally the way their organization worked. Cooperation between divisions and functions to speed product development and to raise product quality and customer responsiveness became the goal. Therefore, management reengineered the organization on horizontal, not vertical, lines.

Third, inside each division the old functional structure was scrapped and new cross-functional product teams, composed of people from all relevant functions, were charged with the responsibility for bringing a new product to market. To understand customers' needs better, Eastman Chemicals contacted its major customers and asked them to appoint one of their managers to work with each team. Essentially, each team was empowered to take responsibility for all aspects of the management of the project, and decision-making responsibility in the company was forced down to the team level. Fourth, top managers decided to change the reward system and introduce an employee stock ownership plan. The result of these changes, Eastman Chemicals top managers found, was an increase in motivation, faster communication and coordination, and, what they wanted most, an increase in quality and the rate of new-product innovation.

Fifth, top managers also reengineered the relationships between divisions to promote innovation, and new interdivisional teams composed of managers from each division were created. The level of cooperation and the number of new interdivisional projects started between divisions are now monitored closely by top managers, who measure performance on both a divisional and an interdivisional level. Indeed, with the new decentralized approach to decision making, corporate managers see one of their major roles as fostering integration between divisions, just as divisional managers see one of their major roles as acting as facilitators between the cross-functional teams in their respective divisions.

This dramatic change in strategy and structure at Eastman Chemicals has not been easily achieved. Many divisional managers were very skeptical of top management's efforts at change, as were managers inside each division. There was considerable resistance at all levels; managers who saw their jobs and their responsibilities shifting were afraid of the effects the changes might have on them. Nevertheless, top managers forced through the changes, and over time, as the positive effects were seen—in an increase in the number of satisfied customers, in higher profits, and in higher salaries and stock appreciation—the whole organization bought into the new philosophy. The performance of Eastman Chemicals has soared throughout the 1990s.

Questions for Discussion

1. What were the main steps in the change process?
2. What lessons can be learned by other companies from Eastman Chemicals' experiences?

End Notes

1. www.BankAmerica.com (1999).
2. B. Garrity, "BankAmerica Syndication Group's Biggest Challenge Comes from Within: How Do You Meld Philosophies of Five Different Locations?" *Investment Dealers Digest*, November 2, 1998, pp.5–6.
3. M. T. Hannan and J. Freeman, "Structural Inertia and Organizational Change," *American Sociological Review*, 49 (1984), 149–164.
4. D. Miller, *The Icarus Paradox* (New York: Harper Business, 1990).
5. J. Thackray, "Restructuring in the Name of the Hurricane," *Euromoney* (February 1987), 106–108.
6. M. Hammer and J. Champy, *Reengineering the Corporation* (New York: HarperCollins, 1993).
7. Ibid., p. 39.
8. G. D. Bruton, J. K. Keels, and C. L. Shook, "Downsizing the Firm: Answering the Strategic Questions," *Academy of Management Executive* (May 1996), 38–45.
9. D. Leonhardt, "Stirring Things Up at Quaker Oats," *Business Week*, March 30, 1998, p.42.
10. G. R. Jones, *Organizational Theory;* R. A. Burgelman and M. A. Maidique, *Strategic Management of Technology and Innovation* (Homewood, Ill.: Irwin, 1988).
11. G. R. Jones and J. E. Butler, "Managing Internal Corporate Entrepreneurship: An Agency Theory Perspective," *Journal of Management*, 18 (1992), 733–749.
12. D. Callaghan, "Aint No Mountain High Enough," *Marketing Intelligence*, June 1999, pp.72–78.
13. R. A. Burgelman, "Designs for Corporate Entrepreneurship in Established Firms," *California Management Review*, 26 (1984), 154–166.
14. D. Frey, "Learning the Ropes: My Life as a Product Champion," *Harvard Business Review* (September–October 1991), 46–56.
15. R. Beckhard, *Organizational Development* (Reading, Mass.: Addison-Wesley, 1969); W. L. French and C. H. Bell Jr., *Organizational Development*, 2nd ed. (Englewood Cliffs, NJ.: Prentice-Hall, 1978).
16. Beckhard, *Organizational Development*.
17. L. C. Coch and R. P. French Jr., "Overcoming Resistance to Change," *Human Relations* (August 1948), 512–532; P. R. Lawrence, "How to Deal with Resistance to Change," *Harvard Business Review* (January–February 1969), 4–12.
18. J. O. Huff, A. S. Huff, and H. Thomas, "Strategic Renewal and the Interaction of Cumulative Stress and Inertia," *Strategic Management Journal*, 13 (Special Issue, 1992), 55–75.
19. P. Kotter and L. A. Schlesinger, "Choosing Strategies for Change," *Harvard Business Review* (March–April 1979), 106–114.
20. J. R. Galbraith, "Designing the Innovative Organization," *Organizational Dynamics* (Winter 1982), 5–25.
21. J. A. Litterer, "Conflict in Organizations: A Reexamination," *Academy of Management Journal*, 9 (1966), 178–186; S. M. Schmidt and T. A. Kochan, "Conflict: Towards Conceptual Clarity," *Administrative Science Quarterly*, 13 (1972), 359–370.
22. L. R. Pondy, "Organizational Conflict: Concepts and Models," *Administrative Science Quarterly*, 2 (1967), 296–320.
23. A. C. Amason, "Distinguishing the Effects of Functional and Dysfunctional Conflict on Strategic Decision Making: Resolving a Paradox for Top Management Teams," *Academy of Management Journal*, 1 (1996), 123–148.
24. R. H. Miles, *Macro Organizational Behavior* (Santa Monica, Calif.: Goodyear, 1980).
25. A. M. Pettigrew, *The Politics of Organizational Decision Making* (London: Tavistock, 1973).
26. J. G. March, "The Business Firm as a Coalition," *Journal of Politics*, 24 (1962), 662–678; D. J. Vredenburgh and J. G. Maurer, "A Process Framework of Organizational Politics," *Human Relations*, 37 (1984), 47–66.
27. T. Burns, "Micropolitics: Mechanisms of Institutional Change," *Administrative Science Quarterly*, 6 (1961), 257–281.
28. R. A. Dahl, "The Concept of Power," *Behavioral Science*, 2 (1957), 201–215; G. A. Astley and P. S. Sachdeva, "Structural Sources of Intraorganizational Power," *Academy of Management Review*, 9 (1984), 104–113.
29. This section draws heavily on D. J. Hickson, C. R. Hinings, C. A. Lee, R. E. Schneck, and D. J. Pennings, "A Strategic Contingencies Theory of Intraorganizational Power," *Administrative Science Quarterly* 16, (1971), 216–227; and C. R. Hinings, D. J. Hickson, J. M. Pennings, and R. E. Schneck, "Structural Conditions of Intraorganizational Power," *Administrative Science Quarterly*, 19 (1974), 22–44.
30. Hickson et al., "A Strategic Contingencies Theory."
31. H. Ibarra, "Network Centrality, Power, and Innovation Involvement: Determinants of Technical and Administrative Roles," *Academy of Management Journal*, 36 (1993), 471–501.
32. Pettigrew, *The Politics of Organizational Decision Making*.
33. Hickson et al., "A Strategic Contingencies Theory."
34. H. A. Landsberger, "The Horizontal Dimension in Bureaucracy," *Administrative Science Quarterly*, 6 (1961), 299–322.
35. G. R. Salancik and J. Pfeffer, "The Bases and Use of Power in Organizational Decision Making: The Case of a University," *Administrative Science Quarterly*, 19 (1974), 453–473.
36. Hickson et al., "A Strategic Contingencies Theory."
37. J. Pfeffer, *Managing with Power* (Boston: Harvard Business School Press, 1992).
38. J. F. McDonnell, "Learning to Think in Different Terms: TQM & Restructuring at McDonnell Douglas," *Executive Speeches* (June–July 1994), 25–28.
39. E. A. Deavenport Jr., "Winning the Balridge Award," *Management* (June 1994), 36–38.

APPENDIX

Analyzing a Case Study and Writing a Case Study Analysis

WHAT IS CASE STUDY ANALYSIS?

Case study analysis is an integral part of a course in strategic management. The purpose of a case study is to provide students with experience of the strategic management problems faced by actual organizations. A case study presents an account of what happened to a business or industry over a number of years. It chronicles the events that managers had to deal with, such as changes in the competitive environment, and charts the managers' response, which usually involved changing the business- or corporate-level strategy. The cases in Part V of this book cover a wide range of issues and problems that managers have had to confront. Some cases are about finding the right business-level strategy to compete in changing conditions. Some are about companies that grew by acquisition, with little concern for the rationale behind their growth, and how growth by acquisition affected their future profitability. Each case is different because each organization is different. The underlying thread in all the cases, however, is the use of strategic management techniques to solve business problems.

Cases prove valuable in a strategic management course for several reasons. First, cases provide you, the student, with experience of organizational problems that you probably have not had the opportunity to experience firsthand. In a relatively short period of time, you will have the chance to appreciate and analyze the problems faced by many different companies and to understand how managers tried to deal with them.

Second, cases illustrate the theory and content of strategic management—that is, all the information presented to you in the previous chapters of this book. This information has been collected, discovered, and distilled from the observations, research, and experience of managers and academicians. The meaning and implications of this information are made clearer when they are applied to case studies. The theory and concepts help reveal what is going on in the companies studied and allow you to evaluate the solutions that specific companies adopted to deal with their problems. Consequently, when you analyze cases, you will be like a detective who, with a set of conceptual tools, probes what happened and what or who was responsible and then marshals the evidence that provides the solution. Top managers enjoy the thrill of testing their problem-solving abilities in the real world. It is important to remember, after all, that no one knows what the right answer is. All that managers can do is to make the best guess. In fact, managers say repeatedly that they are happy if they are right only half the time in solving strategic problems. Strategic management is an uncertain game, and using cases to see how theory can be put into practice is one way of improving your skills of diagnostic investigation.

Third, case studies provide you with the opportunity to participate in class and to gain experience in presenting your ideas to others. Instructors may sometimes call on students as a group to identify what is going on in a case, and through classroom discussion the issues in and solutions to the case problem will reveal themselves. In such a situation, you will have to organize your views and conclusions so that you can present them to the class. Your classmates may have analyzed the issues differently from you, and they will want you to argue your points before they will accept your conclusions; so be prepared for debate. This mode of discussion is an example of the dialectical approach to decision making that you may recall from Chapter 1. This is how decisions are made in the actual business world.

Instructors also may assign an individual, but more commonly a group, to analyze the case before the whole class. The individual or group probably will be responsible for a thirty- to forty-minute presentation of the case to the class. That presentation must cover the issues involved, the problems facing the company, and a series of recommendations for resolving the problems. The discussion then will be thrown open to the class, and you will have to defend your ideas. Through such discussions and presentations, you will experience how to convey your ideas effectively to others. Remember that a great deal of managers' time is spent in these kinds of situations, presenting their ideas and engaging in discussion with other managers, who have their own views about what is going on. Thus, you will experience in the classroom the actual process of strategic management, and this will serve you well in your future career.

If you work in groups to analyze case studies, you also will learn about the group process involved in working as a team. When people work in groups, it is often difficult to schedule time and allocate responsibility for the case analysis. There are always group members who shirk their responsibilities and group members who are so sure of their own ideas that they try to dominate the group's analysis. Most of the strategic management takes place in groups, however, and it is best if you learn about these problems now.

ANALYZING A CASE STUDY

As just mentioned, the purpose of the case study is to let you apply the concepts of strategic management when you analyze the issues facing a specific company. To analyze a case study, therefore, you must examine closely the issues with which the company is confronted. Most often you will need to read the case several times—once to grasp the overall picture of what is happening to the company and then several times more to discover and grasp the specific problems.

Generally, detailed analysis of a case study should include eight areas:

1. The history, development, and growth of the company over time
2. The identification of the company's internal strengths and weaknesses
3. The nature of the external environment surrounding the company
4. A SWOT analysis
5. The kind of corporate-level strategy pursued by the company
6. The nature of the company's business-level strategy

7. The company's structure and control systems and how they match its strategy
8. Recommendations

To analyze a case, you need to apply the concepts taught in this course to each of these areas. Where to look for a review of the concepts you need to use is obvious from the chapter titles. For example, to analyze the company's environment, you would use Chapter 3, on environmental analysis.

To help you further, we next offer a summary of some of the steps you can take to analyze the case material for each of the eight points we have just noted.

1. *Analyze the company's history, development, and growth.* A convenient way to investigate how a company's past strategy and structure affect it in the present is to chart the critical incidents in its history—that is, the events that were the most unusual or the most essential for its development into the company it is today. Some of the events have to do with its founding, its initial products, how it made new-product market decisions, and how it developed and chose functional competencies to pursue. Its entry into new businesses and shifts in its main lines of business are also important milestones to consider.
2. *Identify the company's internal strengths and weaknesses.* Once the historical profile is completed, you can begin the SWOT analysis. Use all the incidents you have charted to develop an account of the company's strengths and weaknesses as they have emerged historically. Examine each of the value creation functions of the company, and identify the functions in which the company is currently strong and currently weak. Some companies might be weak in marketing; some might be strong in research and development. Make lists of these strengths and weaknesses. The table on page C14 gives examples of what might go in these lists.
3. *Analyze the external environment.* The next step is to identify environmental opportunities and threats. Here you should apply all the concepts from Chapter 3, on industry and macroenvironments, to analyze the environment the company is confronting. Of particular importance at the industry level is Porter's five forces model and the stage of the life cycle model. Which factors in the macroenvironment will appear salient depends on the specific company being analyzed. However, use each concept in turn (for instance, demographic factors) to see whether it is relevant for the company in question.

Having done this analysis, you will have generated both an analysis of the company's environment and a list of opportunities and threats. The table on page C14 also lists some common environmental opportunities and threats that you might look for, but the list you generate will be specific to your company.

4. *Evaluate the SWOT analysis.* Having identified the company's external opportunities and threats as well as its internal strengths and weaknesses, you need to consider what your findings mean. That is, you need to balance strengths and weaknesses against opportunities and threats. Is the company in an overall strong competitive position? Can it continue to pursue its current business- or corporate-level strategy profitably? What can the company do to turn weaknesses into strengths and threats into opportunities? Can it develop new functional, business, or corporate strategies to accomplish this change? *Never merely generate the SWOT*

analysis and then put it aside. Because it provides a succinct summary of the company's condition, a good SWOT analysis is the key to all the analyses that follow.

5. *Analyze corporate-level strategy.* To analyze a company's corporate-level strategy, you first need to define the company's mission and goals. Sometimes the mission and goals are stated explicitly in the case; at other times you will have to infer them from available information. The information you need to collect to find out the company's corporate strategy includes such factors as its line(s) of business and the nature of its subsidiaries and acquisitions. It is important to analyze the relationship among the company's businesses. Do they trade or exchange resources? Are there gains to be achieved from synergy? Alternatively, is the company just running a portfolio of investments? This analysis should enable you to define the corporate strategy that the company is pursuing (for example, related or unrelated diversification, or a combination of both) and to conclude whether the company operates in just one core business. Then, using your SWOT analysis, debate the merits of this strategy. Is it appropriate, given the environment the company is in? Could a change in corporate strategy provide the company with new opportunities or transform a weakness into a strength? For example, should the company diversify from its core business into new businesses?

Other issues should be considered as well. How and why has the company's strategy changed over time? What is the claimed rationale for any changes? Often it is a good idea to analyze the company's businesses or products to assess its situation and identify which divisions contribute the most to or detract from its competitive advantage. It is also useful to explore how the company has built its portfolio over time. Did it acquire new businesses, or did it internally venture its own? All these factors provide clues about the company and indicate ways of improving its future performance.

6. *Analyze business-level strategy.* Once you know the company's corporate-level strategy and have done the SWOT analysis, the next step is to identify the company's business-level strategy. If the company is a single-business company, its business-level strategy is identical to its corporate-level strategy. If the company is in many businesses, each business will have its own business-level strategy. You will need to identify the company's generic competitive strategy—differentiation, low cost, or focus—and its investment strategy, given the company's relative competitive position and the stage of the life cycle. The company also may market different products using different business-level strategies. For example, it may offer a low-cost product range and a line of differentiated products. Be sure to give a full account of a company's business-level strategy to show how it competes.

Identifying the functional strategies that a company pursues to build competitive advantage through superior efficiency, quality, innovation, and customer responsiveness and to achieve its business-level strategy is very important. The SWOT analysis will have provided you with information on the company's functional competencies. You should further investigate its production, marketing, or research and development strategy to gain a picture of where the company is going. For example, pursuing a low-cost or a differentiation strategy successfully requires a very different set of competencies. Has the company developed the right ones? If it has, how can it exploit them further? Can it pursue both a low-cost and a differentiation strategy simultaneously?

The SWOT analysis is especially important at this point if the industry analysis, particularly Porter's model, has revealed the threats to the company from the environment. Can the company deal with these threats? How should it change its business-level strategy to counter them? To evaluate the potential of a company's business-level strategy, you must first perform a thorough SWOT analysis that captures the essence of its problems.

Once you complete this analysis, you will have a full picture of the way the company is operating and be in a position to evaluate the potential of its strategy. Thus, you will be able to make recommendations concerning the pattern of its future actions. However, first you need to consider strategy implementation, or the way the company tries to achieve its strategy.

7. *Analyze structure and control systems.* The aim of this analysis is to identify what structure and control systems the company is using to implement its strategy and to evaluate whether that structure is the appropriate one for the company. As we discuss in Chapter 13, different corporate and business strategies require different structures. Chapter 13 provides you with the conceptual tools to determine *the degree of fit between the company's strategy and structure.* For example, does the company have the right level of vertical differentiation (for instance, does it have the appropriate number of levels in the hierarchy or decentralized control?) or horizontal differentiation (does it use a functional structure when it should be using a product structure?)? Similarly, is the company using the right integration or control systems to manage its operations? Are managers being appropriately rewarded? Are the right rewards in place for encouraging cooperation among divisions? These are all issues that should be considered.

In some cases there will be little information on these issues, whereas in others there will be a lot. Obviously, in writing each case you should gear the analysis toward its most salient issues. For example, organizational conflict, power, and politics will be important issues for some companies. Try to analyze why problems in these areas are occurring. Do they occur because of bad strategy formulation or because of bad strategy implementation?

Organizational change is an issue in most of the cases because the companies are attempting to alter their strategies or structures to solve strategic problems. Thus, as a part of the analysis, you might suggest an action plan that the company in question could use to achieve its goals. For example, you might list in a logical sequence the steps the company would need to follow to alter its business-level strategy from differentiation to focus.

8. *Make recommendations.* The last part of the case analysis process involves making recommendations based on your analysis. Obviously, the quality of your recommendations is a direct result of the thoroughness with which you prepared the case analysis. The work you put into the case analysis will be obvious to the professor from the nature of your recommendations. Recommendations are directed at solving whatever strategic problem the company is facing and at increasing its future profitability. Your recommendations should be in line with your analysis; that is, they should follow logically from the previous discussion. For example, your recommendations generally will center on the specific ways of changing functional, business, and corporate strategy and organizational structure and control to improve business performance. The set of recommendations will be specific to each case, and so it is difficult to discuss these recommendations here. Such recommendations

might include an increase in spending on specific research and development projects, the divesting of certain businesses, a change from a strategy of unrelated to related diversification, an increase in the level of integration among divisions by using task forces and teams, or a move to a different kind of structure to implement a new business-level strategy. Again, make sure your recommendations are mutually consistent and are written in the form of an action plan. The plan might contain a timetable that sequences the actions for changing the company's strategy and a description of how changes at the corporate level will necessitate changes at the business level and subsequently at the functional level.

After following all these stages, you will have performed a thorough analysis of the case and will be in a position to join in class discussion or present your ideas to the class, depending on the format used by your professor. Remember that you must tailor your analysis to suit the specific issue discussed in your case. In some cases, you might completely omit one of the steps in the analysis because it is not relevant to the situation you are considering. You must be sensitive to the needs of the case and not apply the framework we have discussed in this section blindly. The framework is meant only as a guide and not as an outline that you must use to do a successful analysis.

WRITING A CASE STUDY ANALYSIS

Often, as part of your course requirements, you will need to present your instructor with a written case analysis. This may be an individual or a group report. Whatever the situation, there are certain guidelines to follow in writing a case analysis that will improve the evaluation your work will receive from your instructor. Before we discuss these guidelines and before you use them, make sure that they do not conflict with any directions your instructor has given you.

The structure of your written report is critical. Generally, if you follow the steps for analysis discussed in the previous section, *you already will have a good structure for your written discussion.* all reports begin with an *introduction* to the case. In it you outline briefly what the company does, how it developed historically, what problems it is experiencing, and how you are going to approach the issues in the case write-up. Do this sequentially by writing, for example, "First, we discuss the environment of Company X. . . . Third, we discuss Company X's business-level strategy. . . . Last, we provide recommendations for turning around Company X's business."

In the second part of the case write-up, the strategic-analysis section, do the SWOT analysis, analyze and discuss the nature and problems of the company's business-level and corporate strategy, and then analyze its structure and control systems. Make sure you use plenty of headings and subheadings to structure your analysis. For example, have separate sections on any important conceptual tool you use. Thus, you might have a section on Porter's five forces model as part of your analysis of the environment. You might offer a separate section on portfolio techniques when analyzing a company's corporate strategy. Tailor the sections and subsections to the specific issues of importance in the case.

In the third part of the case write-up, present your solutions and recommendations. Be comprehensive, and make sure they are in line with the previous analysis so that the recommendations fit together and move logically from one to the next.

The recommendations section is very revealing because, as mentioned earlier, your instructor will have a good idea of how much work you put into the case from the quality of your recommendations.

Following this framework will provide a good structure for most written reports, though obviously it must be shaped to fit the individual case being considered. Some cases are about excellent companies experiencing no problems. In such instances, it is hard to write recommendations. Instead, you can focus on analyzing why the company is doing so well, using that analysis to structure the discussion. Following are some minor suggestions that can help make a good analysis even better.

1. Do not repeat in summary form large pieces of factual information from the case. The instructor has read the case and knows what is going on. Rather, use the information in the case to illustrate your statements, to defend your arguments, or to make salient points. Beyond the brief introduction to the company, you must avoid being *descriptive;* instead, you must be *analytical.*

2. Make sure the sections and subsections of your discussion flow logically and smoothly from one to the next. That is, try to build on what has gone before so that the analysis of the case study moves toward a climax. This is particularly important for group analysis, because there is a tendency for people in a group to split up the work and say, "I'll do the beginning, you take the middle, and I'll do the end." The result is a choppy, stilted analysis because the parts do not flow from one to the next, and it is obvious to the instructor that no real group work has been done.

3. Avoid grammatical and spelling errors. They make the paper sloppy.

4. Some cases dealing with well-known companies end in 1993 or 1994 because no later information was available when the case was written. If possible, do a library search for more information on what has happened to the company in subsequent years. Following are sources of information for performing this search:

   The Internet with its World Wide Web is the place to start your research. Very often you can download copies of a company's annual report from its Web site, and many companies also keep lists of press releases and articles that have been written about them. Thoroughly search the company's Web site for information such as the company's history and performance, and download all relevant information at the beginning of your project. Yahoo is a particularly good search engine to use to discover the address of your company's Web site, although others work as well.

   Compact disk sources such as Lotus One Source and InfoTrac provide an amazing amount of good information, including summaries of recent articles written on specific companies that you can then access in the library.

   F&S Predicasts provide a listing on a yearly basis of all the articles written about a particular company. Simply reading the titles gives an indication of what has been happening in the company.

   Annual reports on a Form 10-K often provide an organization chart.

   Companies themselves provide information if you write and ask for it.

   Fortune, BusinessWeek, and *Forbes* have many articles on companies featured in the cases in this book.

Standard & Poor's industry reports provide detailed information about the competitive conditions facing the company's industry. Be sure to look at this journal.

5. Sometimes instructors hand out questions for each case to help you in your analysis. Use these as a guide for writing the case analysis. They often illuminate the important issues that have to be covered in the discussion.

If you follow the guidelines in this section, you should be able to write a thorough and effective evaluation.

GUIDELINES FOR THE STRATEGIC MANAGEMENT PROJECT

The case study guidelines just discussed also can be followed to help you conduct research for the Strategic Management Project Modules that are at the end of every chapter in this book. In order to answer the questions contained in each module, for example, it is necessary to locate and access articles on your chosen company in the same way that you will update the information on companies highlighted in the case studies. Obviously, however, you need to collect more information on your chosen company because it is *your case.*

The guidelines also can be used to help you to write your Strategic Management Project. The experience you develop from analyzing one or more of the companies in the case studies and writing the resulting report should help you improve the analytical skills needed for the Strategic Management Project. Essentially, in your Strategic Management Project, you are writing about and analyzing a company at the same time to show how that company creates value through its strategy and structure.

THE ROLE OF FINANCIAL ANALYSIS IN CASE STUDY ANALYSIS

Another important aspect of analyzing a case study and writing a case study analysis is the role and use of financial information. A careful analysis of the company's financial condition immensely improves a case write-up. After all, financial data represent the concrete results of the company's strategy and structure. Although analyzing financial statements can be quite complex, a general idea of a company's financial position can be determined through the use of ratio analysis. Financial performance ratios can be calculated from the balance sheet and income statement. These ratios can be classified into five different subgroups: profit ratios, liquidity ratios, activity ratios, leverage ratios, and shareholder-return ratios. These ratios should be compared with the industry average or the company's prior years of performance. It should be noted, however, that deviation from the average is not necessarily bad; it simply warrants further investigation. For example, young companies will have purchased assets at a different price and will likely have a different capital structure than older companies. In addition to ratio analysis, a company's cash flow position is of critical importance and should be assessed. Cash flow shows how much actual cash a company possesses.

Profit Ratios

Profit ratios measure the efficiency with which the company uses its resources. The more efficient the company, the greater is its profitability. It is useful to compare a company's profitability against that of its major competitors in its industry. Such a comparison tells whether the company is operating more or less efficiently than its rivals. In addition, the change in a company's profit ratios over time tells whether its performance is improving or declining.

A number of different profit ratios can be used, and each of them measures a different aspect of a company's performance. The most commonly used profit ratios are as follows:

1. *Gross profit margin.* The gross profit margin simply gives the percentage of sales available to cover general and administrative expenses and other operating costs. It is defined as follows:

$$\text{Gross Profit Margin} = \frac{\text{Sales Revenue} - \text{Cost of Goods Sold}}{\text{Sales Revenue}}$$

2. *Net profit margin.* Net profit margin is the percentage of profit earned on sales. This ratio is important because businesses need to make a profit to survive in the long run. It is defined as follows:

$$\text{Net Profit Margin} = \frac{\text{Net Income}}{\text{Sales Revenue}}$$

3. *Return on total assets.* This ratio measures the profit earned on the employment of assets. It is defined as follows:

$$\text{Return on Total Assets} = \frac{\text{Net Income Available to Common Stockholders}}{\text{Total Assets}}$$

   Net income is the profit after preferred dividends (those set by contract) have been paid. Total assets include both current and noncurrent assets.

4. *Return on stockholders' equity.* This ratio measures the percentage of profit earned on common stockholders' investment in the company. In theory, a company attempting to maximize the wealth of its stockholders should be trying to maximize this ratio. It is defined as follows:

$$\text{Return on Stockholders' Equity} = \frac{\text{Net Income Available to Common Stockholders}}{\text{Stockholders' Equity}}$$

Liquidity Ratios

A company's liquidity is a measure of its ability to meet short-term obligations. An asset is deemed liquid if it can be readily converted into cash. Liquid assets are current assets such as cash, marketable securities, accounts receivable, and so on. Two commonly used liquidity ratios are as follows:

1. *Current ratio.* The current ratio measures the extent to which the claims of short-term creditors are covered by assets that can be quickly converted into cash. Most companies should have a ratio of at least 1, because failure to meet these commitments can lead to bankruptcy. The ratio is defined as follows:

$$\text{Current Ratio} = \frac{\text{Current Assets}}{\text{Current Liabilities}}$$

2. *Quick ratio.* The quick ratio measures a company's ability to pay off the claims of short-term creditors without relying on the sale of its inventories. This is a valuable measure since in practice the sale of inventories is often difficult. It is defined as follows:

$$\text{Quick Ratio} = \frac{\text{Current Assets} - \text{Inventory}}{\text{Current Liabilities}}$$

Activity Ratios

Activity ratios indicate how effectively a company is managing its assets. The following two ratios are particularly useful.

1. *Inventory turnover.* This measures the number of times inventory is turned over. It is useful in determining whether a firm is carrying excess stock in inventory. It is defined as follows:

$$\text{Inventory Turnover} = \frac{\text{Cost of Goods Sold}}{\text{Inventory}}$$

   Cost of goods sold is a better measure of turnover than sales, since it is the cost of the inventory items. Inventory is taken at the balance sheet date. Some companies choose to compute an average inventory, beginning inventory, plus ending inventory, but for simplicity use the inventory at the balance sheet date.

2. *Days sales outstanding (DSO), or average collection period.* This ratio is the average time a company has to wait to receive its cash after making a sale. It measures how effective the company's credit, billing, and collection procedures are. It is defined as follows:

$$\text{DSO} = \frac{\text{Accounts Receivable}}{\text{Total Sales}/360}$$

   Accounts receivable is divided by average daily sales. The use of 360 is the standard number of days for most financial analysis.

Leverage Ratios

A company is said to be highly leveraged if it uses more debt than equity, including stock and retained earnings. The balance between debt and equity is called the *capital structure.* The optimal capital structure is determined by the individual company. Debt has a lower cost because creditors take less risk; they know they will get their interest and principal. However, debt can be risky to the firm because if enough profit is not made to cover the interest and principal payments, bankruptcy can occur.

Three commonly used leverage ratios are as follows:

1. *Debt-to-assets ratio.* The debt-to-asset ratio is the most direct measure of the extent to which borrowed funds have been used to finance a company's investments. It is defined as follows:

$$\text{Debt-to-Assets Ratio} = \frac{\text{Total Debt}}{\text{Total Assets}}$$

   Total debt is the sum of a company's current liabilities and its long-term debt, and total assets are the sum of fixed assets and current assets.

2. *Debt-to-equity ratio.* The debt-to-equity ratio indicates the balance between debt and equity in a company's capital structure. This is perhaps the most widely used measure of a company's leverage. It is defined as follows:

$$\text{Debt-to-Equity Ratio} = \frac{\text{Total Debt}}{\text{Total Equity}}$$

3. *Times-covered ratio.* The times-covered ratio measures the extent to which a company's gross profit covers its annual interest payments. If the times-covered ratio declines to less than 1, then the company is unable to meet its interest costs and is technically insolvent. The ratio is defined as follows:

$$\text{Times-Covered Ratio} = \frac{\text{Profit Before Interest and Tax}}{\text{Total Interest Charges}}$$

Shareholder-Return Ratios

Shareholder-return ratios measure the return earned by shareholders from holding stock in the company. Given the goal of maximizing stockholders' wealth, providing shareholders with an adequate rate of return is a primary objective of most companies. As with profit ratios, it can be helpful to compare a company's shareholders returns against those of similar companies. This provides a yardstick for determining how well the company is satisfying the demands of this particularly important group of organizational constituents. Four commonly used ratios are as follows:

1. *Total shareholder returns.* Total shareholder returns measure the returns earned by time $t + 1$ on an investment in a company's stock made at time t. (Time t is the time at which the initial investment is made.) Total shareholder returns include both dividend payments and appreciation in the value of the stock (adjusted for stock splits) and are defined as follows:

$$\text{Total Shareholder Returns} = \frac{\text{Stock Price } (t+1)\text{-Stock Price } (t) + \text{Sum of Annual Dividends per Share}}{\text{Stock Price } (t)}$$

   Thus, if a shareholder invests \$2 at time t, and at time $t+1$ the share is worth \$3, while the sum of annual dividends for the period t to $t + 1$ has amounted to \$0.2, total shareholder returns are equal to $(3 - 2 + 0.2)/2 = 0.6$, which is a 60 percent return on an initial investment of \$2 made at time t.

2. *Price-earnings ratio.* The price-earnings ratio measures the amount investors are willing to pay per dollar of profit. It is defined as follows:

$$\text{Price-Earnings Ratio} = \frac{\text{Market Price per Share}}{\text{Earnings per Share}}$$

3. *Market to book value.* Another useful ratio is market to book value. This measures a company's expected future growth prospects. It is defined as follows:

$$\text{Market to Book Value} = \frac{\text{Market Price per Share}}{\text{Earnings per Share}}$$

4. *Dividend yield.* The dividend yield measures the return to shareholders received in the form of dividends. It is defined as follows:

$$\text{Dividend Yield} = \frac{\text{Dividend per Share}}{\text{Market Price per Share}}$$

Market price per share can be calculated for the first of the year, in which case the dividend yield refers to the return on an investment made at the beginning of the year. Alternatively, the average share price over the year may be used. A company must decide how much of its profits to pay to stockholders and how much to reinvest in the company. Companies with strong growth prospects should have a lower dividend payout ratio than mature companies. The rationale is that shareholders can invest the money elsewhere if the company is not growing. The optimal ratio depends on the individual firm, but the key decider is whether the company can produce better returns than the investor can earn elsewhere.

Cash Flow

Cash flow position is simply cash received minus cash distributed. The net cash flow can be taken from a company's statement of cash flows. Cash flow is important for what it tells us about a company's financing needs. A strong positive cash flow enables a company to fund future investments without having to borrow money from bankers or investors. This is desirable because the company avoids the need to pay out interest or dividends. A weak or negative cash flow means that a company has to turn to external sources to fund future investments. Generally, companies in strong-growth industries often find themselves in a poor cash flow position (because their investment needs are substantial), whereas successful companies based in mature industries generally find themselves in a strong cash flow position.

A company's internally generated cash flow is calculated by adding back its depreciation provision to profits after interest, taxes, and dividend payments. If this figure is insufficient to cover proposed new-investment expenditures, the company has little choice but to borrow funds to make up the shortfall or to curtail investments. If this figure exceeds proposed new investments, the company can use the excess to build up its liquidity (that is, through investments in financial assets) or to repay existing loans ahead of schedule.

CONCLUSION

When evaluating a case, it is important to be *systematic*. Analyze the case in a logical fashion, beginning with the identification of operating and financial strengths and weaknesses and environmental opportunities and threats. Move on to assess the value of a company's current strategies only when you are fully conversant with the SWOT analysis of the company. Ask yourself whether the company's current strategies make sense, given its SWOT analysis. If they do not, what changes need to be made? What are your recommendations? Above all, link any strategic recommendations you may make to the SWOT analysis. State explicitly how the strategies you identify take advantage of the company's strengths to exploit environmental opportunities, how they rectify the company's weaknesses, and how they counter environmental threats. Also, do not forget to outline what needs to be done to implement your recommendations.

TABLE 1

A SWOT Checklist

Potential internal strengths	Potential internal weaknesses
Many product lines?	Obsolete, narrow product lines?
Broad market coverage?	Rising manufacturing costs?
Manufacturing competence?	Decline in R&D innovations?
Good marketing skills?	Poor marketing plan?
Good materials management systems?	Poor material management systems?
R&D skills and leadership?	Loss of customer good will?
Information system competencies?	Inadequate human resources?
Human resource competencies?	Inadequate information systems?
Brand name reputation?	Loss of brand name capital?
Portfolio management skills?	Growth without direction?
Cost of differentiation advantage?	Bad portfolio management?
New-venture management expertise?	Loss of corporate direction?
Appropriate management style?	Infighting among divisions?
Appropriate organizational structure?	Loss of corporate control?
Appropriate control systems?	Inappropriate organizational structure and control systems?
Ability to manage strategic change?	High conflict and politics?
Well-developed corporate strategy?	Poor financial management?
Good financial management?	Others?
Others?	
Potential environmental opportunities	**Potential environmental threats**
Expand core business(es)?	Attacks on core business(es)?
Exploit new market segments?	Increases in domestic competition?
Widen product range?	Increase in foreign competition?
Extend cost or differentiation advantage?	Change in consumer tastes?
Diversify into new growth businesses?	Fall in barriers to entry?
Expand into foreign markets?	Rise in new or substitute products?
Apply R&D skills in new areas?	Increase in industry rivalry?
Enter new related businesses?	New forms of industry competition?
Vertically integrate forward?	Potential for takeover?
Vertically integrate backward?	Existence of corporate raiders?
Enlarge corporate portfolio?	Increase in regional competition?
Overcome barriers to entry?	Changes in demographic factors?
Reduce rivalry among competitors?	Changes in economic factors?
Make profitable new acquisitions?	Downturn in economy?
Apply brand name capital in new areas?	Rising labor costs?
Seek fast market growth?	Slower market growth?
Others?	Others?

INDEX